THE INTERNATIONAL DIRECTORY OF

MILITARY AIRCRAFT

1996/97

Gerard Frawley and Jim Thorn

CONTENTS

Published by Aerospace Publications Pty Ltd (ACN: 001 570 458) PO Box 3105, Weston Creek, ACT 2611,
Australia. Phone (06) 288 1900 Fax (06) 288 2021 – Publishers of monthly *Australian Aviation* magazine.

ISBN 1 875671 20 X

Proudly Printed in Australia by Pirie Printers Pty Ltd, 140 Gladstone St, Fyshwick, ACT 2609.
Distributed throughout Australia by Network Distribution Company, 54 Park St, Sydney, 2000. Fax (02) 264 3278
Distribution in North America by Motorbooks International, 729 Prospect Ave, Osceola, Wisconsin, 54020, USA.
Fax (715) 294 4448. Co-produced and distributed throughout Europe and the UK by Airlife Publishing Ltd,
101 Longden Rd, Shrewsbury SY3 9EB, Shropshire, UK. Fax (743) 232944.

Front cover: (top left) F-4C Phantoms of the Missouri Air National Guard (now retired); (top right) Dassault's Mirage 2000-5
demonstrator; (bottom left) a Bell UH-1H of 3 Squadron Royal New Zealand Air Force; (bottom right) a British C-130K
Hercules fitted with an Allison AE 2100 turboprop for trials. Back cover: (clockwise from top left) A USAF F-15E Eagle; a
RAF Phantom FGR.2 (now retired); Lockheed SR-71; SEPECAT Jaguar; Australian F-111C; and Russian Air Force Tu-95.

INTRODUCTION

Welcome to the first ever edition of the all new, all colour *International Directory of Military Aircraft*.

This book aims to provide the aviation industry and aviation enthusiasts with the first ever updated reference work on military aircraft at an affordable price. While in itself that statement does not sound shattering, what makes this book different is that it includes aircraft still in service rather than those merely currently in production. Thus we have entries on such famous and long lived types as the MiG-15, Hawker Hunter, Douglas C-47/Dakota, Alizé, Sioux and hundreds of others alongside the very latest exemplified by the Eurofighter, F-22, Su-35 and F/A-18E Super Hornet.

The International Directory of Military Aircraft will be produced every two years. It will include the latest types under development and updated entries on the more established types. The present pace of aircraft development does not warrant an annual edition and a biennial production is a more economic and efficient answer to the problem of providing you with as much data as possible on a wide range of differing types. Consequently, this inaugural *Military Directory* will be replaced by an updated edition in early 1998.

As some readers would be aware, this book is a sister to our already successful *International Directory of Civil Aircraft*, the first edition of which was released early in 1995 and like the edition you hold before you, will itself be superseded by a new and updated edition every two years (in this case early 1997). Consequently, each year we will be producing a Directory, odd years will be Civil and even years will be Military. Together, these all colour volumes are to our knowledge the only source of data on all the aircraft of the world that are not just in production but are still in everyday use. We hope that they are of use to you and prove to be valuable reference works in *your* aviation library.

To be eligible for coverage an aircraft must still be in operational service or currently under development. There are a very small number of 'military' aircraft currently in service that are not covered in this volume – mainly light aircraft such as the Piper Navajo/Chieftain and Cessna 150/152, details of which can be found in the *International Directory of Civil Aircraft*. Other aircraft that are only in initial stages of development such as the Euroflag FLA and America's JAST/JSF are likely to appear in subsequent *Military Directory* editions when the designs of these aircraft firm.

While preparing this edition over the past three years we have sadly seen many famous types retired from service, such as the Buccaneer, Etendard IV and Shackleton. The great plethora of post WW2 and 1950s designs that held sway for so many decades have all but gone while the welcome demise of the Cold War has quickly seen many still competitive types disappear as air arms throughout the world consolidate their inventories and learn to live with greatly reduced national defence budgets.

For ease of reference aircraft are listed alphabetically by manufacturer. Where aircraft manufacturers have changed name, through mergers or acquisitions, aircraft currently in production are listed under their current manufacturer (ie Lockheed Martin F-16, rather than General Dynamics), while aircraft out of production are listed under the manufacturer name they are most commonly known by (ie Hawker Hunter).

Where a type has a long and distinguished history with numerous improved and much changed variants (the Hercules, Mirage and Phantom come to mind) we have split some of the more important models into single entries to give them fair and proper coverage. We feel this greatly enhances the overall value of this publication and makes gathering data on specific types easier for you. The format of the book is largely self explanatory (an asterix in the operators column and in the World Air Power Guide denotes on order or currently in the delivery phase) and hopefully user friendly.

In this volume both metric and imperial measures are used. While most of the world has now adopted metric as its official system of measure, aviation will continue to record its figures in knots, nautical miles and feet.

A special vote of thanks again goes to all who inspired the authors in completing this daunting project to schedule via their suggestions and encouragement. In particular thanks to Stewart Wilson, Maria Davey, Brian Pickering of Military Aircraft Photographs, Alex Radetski, Paul Merritt, Bradley Perrett and Christine Pratt. Our thanks also to the score of foreign embassies and consulates which supported us in gaining sufficient data to compile the World Airpower Guide portion of this book. Without their help it would have been impossible to consider providing this valuable service.

Finally, thanks also to Airlife (UK) and Motorbooks (USA) for having the faith in us to order this book in quantity for their respective markets. Thank you.

Gerard Frawley & Jim Thorn
Canberra, January 1996.

MILITARY AVIATION IN REVIEW

They say that money makes the world go around, and nowhere is this more true than the world of military aviation.

The twin effects of dwindling post Cold War defence budgets and spiralling new aircraft development costs ensures that few new military aircraft programs will survive cost cutting, and those aircraft currently in service will be upgraded to extend their service lives as long as economically possible. Furthermore modern radars, avionics, smart weapons and sometimes new engines fitted to old airframes can provide a substantial increase in capability without anything like the expense of acquiring a fleet of shiny new fighters or bombers.

Diminished defence budgets and ever more expensive development costs has also meant fewer aircraft programs to go around, which is forcing the world's military aircraft manufacturers to rationalise and diversify. The end result? Upgraded aircraft remaining in service for two, three and even four decades, whereas not so long ago 10 years was considered the norm. Fewer aircraft manufacturers designing and building fewer, more expensive aircraft. And rationalised air force inventories, with fewer aircraft types and less aircraft on strength.

From this perspective the future of military aviation looks set, with only small numbers of all new aircraft types likely to grace the pages of subsequent editions of the *International Directory of Military Aircraft*. Those projects that do remain have assumed an increasing importance to their manufacturers and their end users, and, because of their expense, will result in some of the most capable and exciting aircraft to take to the skies yet.

Topping the price and capability scales by a massive margin is the Northrop Grumman B-2 Spirit. At $US1bn a copy, the B-2 is by far the most expensive military aircraft yet built and represents the apex of strategic bomber development. The bulk of development funds for this stealth bomber was provided during the free spending years of the Reagan administration during the height of the Cold

War, however this big bomber rolled out in time to see the Iron Curtain fall, leaving production to be funded when military purse strings were being tightened at a rate not seen since the end of the Vietnam War. Not even the world's richest nation could afford to procure the USAF's planned fleet of 133 B-2s, and instead just 20 have been funded.

During 1995 furious debate raged within the USA on whether or not to raise this total. Proponents of the B-2 point to the fact that because it is nearly invisible to radar and has superb payload range characteristics, one or two B-2s can fly a single mission that would otherwise require dozens of conventional aircraft (comprising bombers, escorting fighters, SEAD aircraft and tankers). Opponents point to its cost. Regardless, the B-2 entered USAF service with the Whiteman AFB Missouri based 509th Bomb Wing in December 1993. The last of 20 currently funded is due to be completed in 1998.

America's next big thing is the JAST or JSF (Joint Strike Fighter), a cure all program to replace USAF F-16s, USN F/A-18s and USMC AV-8Bs. It will be built in carrier, land based and STOVL forms and could be in service by around 2008. Pictured is a Boeing JSF concept.

Less contentious has been the F-22 program. The project to develop a replacement for the F-15 Eagle is by no means cheap, although its future seems assured given the likely proliferation of Su-27s and MiG-29s to third world countries (aircraft which in some areas are the equal of the superb F-15) and Russia's development of a planned Su-27 replacement, the MiG 1.42.

Budgetary constraints have reduced the original requirement for 750 F-22s to the current 442, a figure which may be further cut before the first production F-22As are delivered from 2000. In the last few years the F-22 has gained an air-to-ground role with two JDAMs (Joint Direct Attack Munitions), passed a Critical Design Review and the first EMD aircraft have entered production. The first of these aircraft is due to fly during the course of this Directory, some time in 1997.

The most important forthcoming US military aircraft program is the Joint Strike Fighter (JSF). The JSF (until late 1995 JAST) is a joint service cure all program to replace the USAF's F-16s, the US Navy's F/A-18A/Cs and the US Marines' AV-8B Harriers. In the revised JSF timetable first

The good old days! Late model F-4E Phantoms on the McDonnell Douglas St Louis production line. During the height of the Vietnam War, Phantom production peaked at an incredible 72 aircraft a month. Today even the most optimistic manufacturer would be exceedingly happy to have orders to build that number of aircraft over two years! (MDC)

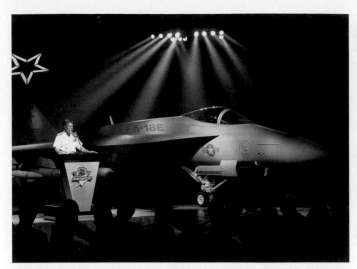

Admiral Jeremy Brown, the US Navy's Chief of Naval Operations, addresses the audience at the official rollout of the McDonnell Douglas F/A-18E Super Hornet. The F/A-18E came in under cost and ahead of time, a far cry from the ultra expensive Japanese FS-X F-16 development, Eurofighter 2000 and Dassault Rafale, all of which ironically are considerably more expensive than the more versatile and capable Super Hornet. The Super Hornet is already being proposed as an EA-6B Prowler replacement and will ultimately succeed the F-14 Tomcat, largely thanks to the demise of the long range supersonic maritime bomber threat. (MDC)

flight would be in 2004, with IOC (initial operating capability) attained possibly as early as 2008.

The JAST program began life in 1993 as a replacement for several cancelled USAF and USN programs (including A/F-X, ATA, JSSA and JAF). In 1994 the USN's Common Affordable Lightweight Fighter (CALF) was merged with JAST. CALF aimed to find a replacement for the F/A-18 and AV-8B, and would have been built in carrier launched and STOVL versions. The UK is also involved with JSF and the aircraft could replace Sea Harrier F/A.2s, Harrier GR.7s and Tornado GR.1/GR.4s.

The reorganised JSF will be built in conventional land based, carrier capable and STOVL versions (for the Marines and Royal Navy), with extra internal fuel replacing the vertical lift system in the USAF and USN aircraft. The JSF will be designed from the outset to be stealthy and agile. Primary power will be from a single Pratt & Whitney F119 (as powers the F-22). Empty weight will be in the nine to 11 tonnes (20 to 25,000lb) class, with max takeoff weight as high as 25 tonnes (55,000lb), similar to the F/A-18A/C.

During 1996 two of the three competing JSF designs will be selected for further development. Each of the two selected manufacturers will fly two prototypes, one of which will be in STOVL configuration, for a competitive evaluation. The three JSF design teams are Boeing, Lockheed Martin and McDonnell Douglas/Northrop Grumman/ BAe.

Elsewhere in the US industry the DoD finally selected the winning JPATS (Joint Primary Aircraft Training System), the Pilatus PC-9 based Raytheon Beech Mk II being the surprise winner. The Beech Mk II (presumably it will be given a 'T' designation and a more evocative name) was announced as the JPATS choice on June 22 1995. However, production aircraft will not roll off the Wichita production line until 1998, IOC with the USAF will not be until 1999 and the last Beech Mk II delivery will be in 2015, an incredible two decades hence and more than 30 years since the PC-9 first flew (not to mention the basic PT6 engine, which first appeared in the late 1950s!).

Another aircraft that has had its critics is the McDonnell

Douglas C-17 Globemaster III, which is easily the most expensive transport aircraft in the world. While the C-17 design program has had its problems, the aircraft has now matured into a very capable airlifter. However the C-17 was designed to operate into short airstrips close to the battlefront, and it was this demanding specification that added greatly to its cost and has been so heavily criticised.

Which commander is likely to risk flying such an expensive aircraft into a short field near the forward edge of the battlefield (FEBA) and expose the aircraft to the very substantial threat of man portable SAMs? The same unrealistic thinking helped derail Lockheed and the C-5A Galaxy in the mid 1960s.

Current C-17 production is capped at 40 of a requirement for 140. In late 1995 the Pentagon announced its preference for acquiring the additional 80 aircraft in favour of a fleet of Boeing C-33s (militarised 747-400F freighters). However this choice had yet to be confirmed by Congress and C-33s may yet be ordered. McDonnell Douglas is also looking at a stretched C-17 as a possible replacement for existing USAF C-5 Galaxies.

Other significant US military aircraft programs include the RAH-66 Comanche, V-22 Osprey and the F/A-18E Hornet (which rolled out in September 1995 and was due to make its first flight that December).

While the above may sound like a healthy number of projects, fewer new aircraft programs than at any time since WW2 and less aircraft being built is forcing the US aerospace industry to rationalize. Unlike Europe, US companies have attacked rationalization with gusto as firms contract and become leaner and better placed to bid for new work.

Foremost of the US consolidation has been the merger of Lockheed and Martin Marietta, producing the US Department of Defense's biggest contractor (overtaking McDonnell Douglas – a company formed by the merger of McDonnell and Douglas in the late 1960s). The merger was first announced in November 1994 and officially completed in March 1995. Earlier in 1992 Lockheed acquired the Fort Worth division of General Dynamics (a company which had hung the 'for sale' sign on a number of its divisions in the face of reduced Government spending).

A C-130H Hercules goes active with its infrared flare decoy system. This system is designed to lure away inbound heat seeking missiles, a major cause of concern for tactical transports and helicopters. Many transports are being fitted with a countermeasures suite to afford them some protection on often hazardous United Nations peacekeeping operations. (RAAF)

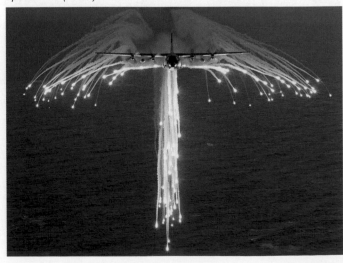

Fort Worth is the home of the F-16, and Lockheed Martin continues to aggressively market the 'Electric Jet' to the USAF (to meet F-16 attrition replacement requirements pending the delivery of the JSF) and other nations. Several modified versions of the F-16 have been offered to meet a number of international aircraft requirements, such as the diamond wing F-16U offered to (but reportedly rejected by) the UAE, and the F-16ES with dorsal conformal tanks.

The Lockheed Martin merger was preceded by the marriage of Northrop and Grumman in early 1994. In August that year the newly merged company also acquired another famous company, Vought.

Mergers have also been foreshadowed in the US helicopter industry, as manufacturers vie for dwindling military contracts. Indeed, at the turn of the century the only US military rotary wing production program will be the Bell Boeing V-22 Osprey. During 1995 reports surfaced that Bell and Boeing were discussing merging their respective military helicopter interests, while McDonnell Douglas Helicopters and Sikorsky have been identified as ideal partners, given their complimentary product ranges.

Across the Atlantic the themes of lower defence budgets and higher development costs are no less familiar. However this mix is further complicated by the fact that most of Europe's major military aircraft programs are multinational ventures, where national interest and indecision can leave already highly technologically complex programs hamstrung, increasing costs by billions and delaying service entry dates by years.

A classic example of this is the Eurofighter or EFA. The EFA started as a logical attempt for several European nations to pool their resources and build a common multirole tactical fighter. However France soon withdrew when the other partners refused Dassault program leadership and instead went ahead to independently develop the slightly smaller Rafale, a sad and unnecessary example of wasteful duplicity. The EFA/Eurofighter has also always had to contend with and reconcile the different partner nation's requirements, none moreso when in 1992 Germany called

The incredibly expensive Eurofighter EF 2000 (pictured in two seat form). By the time this aircraft finally enters service around 2001 it will have consumed a development budget over $US15bn, making it so expensive that the number its European owners can afford has almost been halved. Massive cost overruns have plagued almost all modern day combat aircraft programs, making the end product so expensive that ultimately few will be able to be placed into service. This situation must change if military aviation is to endure as an economically viable and technologically efficient entity during the first decades of the next century. (BAe)

a halt to the program and instead studied various 'cheaper' developments of EFA, including single engine and cranked delta variants.

Not surprisingly only two of the seven EFA variants worked out cheaper than the original standard EFA, and these two were adjudged inferior to improved developments of the Sukhoi Su-27 and Mikoyan MiG-29, which EFA was designed to defeat in the first place. Instead the restyled Eurofighter 2000 was relaunched in December 1992, Germany deciding to push back its first deliveries to 2002 (over two decades after the Eurofighter was first conceived) and to build its aircraft to a lower equipment specification.

The next hurdle Eurofighter faces is when the partner nations commit funding to production aircraft and production workshare is split between the partner companies. Germany has a 33% share of Eurofighter development and originally required 250 aircraft and would have had a production share equal to that purchase. However Germany is only likely to fund 120 to 140, but German industry does not want to relinquish any workshare.

Regardless when the first production Eurofighters are delivered to the UK and Italy in 2000 (and the RAF won't get its first squadron operational until 2005) these air forces will finally get an advanced and very capable multirole fighter no doubt well suited to the types of regional conflicts and UN peacekeeping/making operations (such as Bosnia) likely to be fought in the coming decades. However, whether the fighter is significantly better than existing multirole fighters (particularly the F/A-18), and whether this improvement justifies the 20 year wait and billions of pounds/marks/lire/pesetas spent on Eurofighter development is another question.

Another multinational program that looked like heading down the same tortured path of never ending pre definition and definition studies and workshare wrangling was the Euroflag FLA (Future Large Aircraft), an unimaginatively titled program to find a replacement for western Europe's C-130 Hercules and Transall C-160s.

Thankfully development of the FLA has been handed to the newly created Airbus Industrie division, the Airbus Military Company. Airbus will develop and build the FLA as a commercial project, placing production where it is economically most efficient, and not along national lines, which is probably enough to scuttle Government interest overnight. First flight could be in 2000 and the FLA is a

Following the demise of the Cold War, most air arms are downphasing and retiring older generation aircraft prematurely as a cost control measure. This has had a severe impact on the world's military aircraft industry, including the engine and systems manufacturers. Here a Rolls-Royce Pegasus turbofan is removed for maintenance from a Spanish Navy TAV-8S Harrier. Rolls-Royce has experienced a considerable decrease in spares activity (the bread and butter of every engine manufacturer) following the effects of a reduction in annual flying hours and the retirements of RR powered military aircraft. (Rolls-Royce)

The FLA (Future Large Airlifter) is Europe's next major collaborative military aircraft program. Fortunately development has been entrusted to the newly created military division of Airbus, so the FLA should hopefully be able to avoid the endless committees and studies and workshare wrangles which have marred other European programs.

likely candidate for inclusion in the next edition of this Directory.

European politics also muddied the waters of three important British acquisition programs, the C-130K replacement, new support helicopters and a new attack helicopter for the British Army. In all three cases the battle was cast (by politicians and European and British aerospace companies, not the British military) as one between the American and European aircraft industries, rather than a fair battle among competing aircraft, from which the most capable and cost effective would be selected.

French and German politicians were particularly loud in their criticism of the British Army's decision to buy the American AH-64D Apache (although built in the UK by Westland and with Rolls-Royce Turboméca RTM322 engines) in preference to the Eurocopter Tiger, unfairly calling into question Britain's commitment to Europe.

In the case of the support helicopter program, the RAF's preference for additional CH-47D Chinooks was partially overruled and instead it was forced to order a mixed fleet of CH-47Ds and EH 101s, helping keep Westland and the UK in the helicopter construction business and its workers employed.

The battle to replace half of the RAF's fleet of 60 C-130Ks was fought between the modernised C-130J Hercules 2 and the Euroflag FLA. In this case the RAF had little choice but to order the improved Hercules, as the

The Gripen multirole fighter was developed based on the concept that a small, single engined aircraft can use modern weapons to increase its overall capability. This has resulted in a cost effective and affordable fighter bomber, although the Gripen will have to fight hard for international sales against rebuilt surplus US F-16s and F/A-18s. (Saab)

FLA remains firmly on the drawing board. Even if it the FLA had been immediately available the Hercules could well have been a more cost effective option, given its lower costs. Any improvements that the all new FLA can offer over the modernised C-130J would have to come at a significant cost premium, given the slow and enormously expensive nature of new aircraft programs these days.

Further east in Europe, the aerospace industries of Poland and the Czech Republic are battling hard to eke out a niche in the post Cold War export marketplace. Both countries offer trainers (Poland the Orlik and Iryda, Czech Republic the Albatros), the most congested military aircraft market sector (as it is one of the easiest to get into). Forced to compete against entrenched western companies, they have met with little success thus far, but they could do well if they can prove their abilities to provide after sales support.

However, the problems of the United States and Europe pale in comparison to those facing Russia and the CIS where protected state companies had built thousands of fighters, bombers, transports and helicopters for a Soviet

A post Cold War phenomenon is the presence of large Russian contingent at major international airshows. Here a USAF B-1B Lancer frames a Russian Tu-95 and Il-78 tanker plus a USAF B-52. To have envisaged this scene a decade ago would have been pure fantasy, but today the Russians will even sell you commercial flight time in their latest fighters just to earn some much needed foreign currency. (Paul Merritt)

war machine that is now rapidly downscaling and can hardly afford to operate the aircraft it currently has on strength, yet alone take on new aircraft and fund development of replacement types.

With the collapse of the home market, Russian aircraft factories and designers are peddling their most advanced wares for export, although again with limited results thus far. Russian companies with little concept of western marketing, quality control and after sales support have had to compete against aggressive western companies (themselves with dwindling domestic markets) for orders, and in most cases have come off second best (Malaysia's MiG-29 buy an obvious exception).

Slowly Russia's aerospace industry is responding, and designers and factories have begun to model themselves along western lines. The foremost example of this is the 1995 merger of the Moscow Aircraft Production Company (MAPO) with the Mikoyan design bureau to form MAPO MiG, a company able to market, manufacture and support its own aircraft. Other mergers and rationalizations along these lines are likely.

While Russia's domestic order base has all but collapsed, the Russian military remains committed to a number of new aircraft programs to replace ageing and obsolete aircraft. Foremost of these programs in importance is the Mikoyan 1.42, an F-22 rivalling successor to

the Sukhoi Su-27. The 1.42, believed to be a 30 tonne canard delta monster, was due to make its much delayed first flight in 1995, but a lack of funding kept it firmly stuck in the hangar. If Russia was struggling to find funds for the 1.42's first flight, it seems unlikely that it will be able to fund 1.42 production.

Sukhoi meanwhile is believed to be working on a new advanced strike bomber, the T-60S, to replace Tu-16s, Tu-22s and Su-24s, although details remain sketchy.

At the lower end of the performance scale Mikoyan and Yakovlev are battling to have their respective designs selected to meet the Russian Air Force's requirement for a new jet trainer to replace the L-29 Delfin and L-39 Albatros. Both the MiG-AT and Yakovlev Yak-130 were unveiled in 1995 and the winning contender should be known during the life of this Directory. Regardless of the outcome both are being targeted for export.

Meanwhile Mil's Mi-28 is battling for orders against the Kamov Ka-50 to meet a Russian Army need for a new attack helicopter, one of the few current military helicopter programs in Russia. A definitive decision on this important program may still be some years away yet. Both Mil and Kamov are also working on new designs which could be the subjects of new entries in future Directories, should they make it off the drawing boards.

In comparison to Europe, the US or Russia, Asia is almost a hotbed of fighter development. In Japan, the Mitsubishi FS-X finally made its first flight in October 1995. Sadly this hugely expensive program to modify the F-16 looks set to yield a fighter only marginally more capable but two or three times as expensive as the Fighting Falcon. India meanwhile continues development of its Light Combat Aircraft to replace the MiG-21, and first flight could be in late 1996. Rollout was in November 1995.

Due to fly in 1997 and publicly announced at the 1995 Paris Airshow was China's Chengdu FC-1, a lightweight fighter to powered by a Klimov RD-93 (a derivative of the MiG-29's RD-33). The FC-1 replaces the Super 7, an advanced development of the J-7 MiG-21 copy. An IAI Lavi like multirole fighter called the F-10 is also under development, believed to have been designed with considerable

Many nations are upgrading their existing fighters with state of the art avionics instead of buying expensive new types. This capability enhancement can be obtained at a fraction of the cost of buying new aircraft and allows older generation airframes the ability to carry the latest smart weaponry. Pictured is the cockpit of an IAI upgraded MiG-21 featuring a new nav/comm suite, radar, weapons management computer and head up display. With these upgrades, a zero timed airframe and modern weapons, upgraded MiGs, F-5s and Mirages will be potent adversaries for many years to come. (IAI)

Israeli assistance. The F-10 is understood to be fitted with a Russian engine and radar and could be flying as early as 1996 or 1997. China is also though to be negotiating with Russia to build the Su-27 under licence.

Conceivably then in a decade's time China could be equipped with hundreds of advanced Su-27s, F-10s and FC-1s, giving it not only the numerically largest air force in Asia, but also the most capable – a far cry from today where the bulk of the fighter force is made up of obsolete MiG-19 and MiG-21 copies. This modernisation will dramatically alter the balance of power in Asia and how nations like Taiwan and Japan react remains to be seen.

So much for new aircraft production.

One of the few growth areas of the military aviation industry is upgrading existing aircraft in preference to procuring new build types. Although not a new phenomena, upgrades of fighters in particular are becoming an increasingly palatable alternative to buying new aircraft, and the end result is often a revitalised fighter nearly as capable as a new aircraft, but significantly cheaper to fund.

The main candidates for upgrade include the MiG-21, Northrop F-5, Dassault Mirage III and V, McDonnell's F-4 Phantom and Douglas' A-4. New radars, weaponry and cockpit displays, structural strengthening, and, in limited instances, re-engining, can give a 20 year old fighter modern capabilities unforeseen when it was built. This is particularly so given the leaps and bounds computers and electronics have taken over the past few decades.

Increasingly too it is the weapons that the aircraft carry, rather than the platform itself, that can determine the outcome of a battle. From long range an Amraam and APG-65 radar equipped F-4 will have as good a chance as shooting down a similarly armed F-15, while a tank can just as easily be plinked by a Maverick toting Skyhawk as a Maverick armed F-16. That is not to say that upgraded aircraft are as good as new in all cases, but upgrading can be very cost effective and for many nations represents good value for money.

See you in '98.

The Russians are willing to sell everything to almost anyone, although few are listening. Freed from the shackles of their political masters, ex-Soviet states are now looking to the west to acquire their aircraft, citing better build quality, technical reliability, spares support and lower long term maintenance cost as reasons for the change. However, the Russians might well prove viable in the long term at supplying relatively low cost theatre ground support attack aircraft such as the Sukhoi Su-25 (pictured here in Czech Air Force colours). (Paul Merritt)

Aeritalia G91

Country of origin: Italy

Type: Light strike fighter

Powerplants: G91Y – Two 12.1kN (2720lb) dry and 18.2kN (4080lb) afterburning General Electric J85-GE-13A turbojets.

Performance: G91Y – Max speed 1038km/h (560kt) at 30,000ft and 1110km/h (600kt) at sea level. Cruising speed 800km/h (432kt) at 30,000ft. Max initial rate of climb 17,000ft/min. Time to 40,000ft 4min 30sec. Service ceiling 41,000ft. Typical combat radius on a lo-lo-lo attack mission with a 1320kg (2910lb) payload 600km (325nm). Ferry range with drop tanks 3500km (1890nm).

Weights: G91Y – Empty equipped 3900kg (8598lb), max takeoff 8700kg (19,180lb).

Dimensions: G91Y – Wing span 9.01m (29ft 7in), length 11.67m (38ft 4in), height 4.43m (14ft 6in). Wing area 18.1m² (195.2sq ft).

Accommodation: Pilot only, except G91T which seats two in tandem.

Armament: G91Y – Two 30mm DEFA 532 cannon with 125 rounds per gun mounted in the forward fuselage. Disposable payload of up to 1815kg (4000lb), including Sidewinder AAMs, bombs and rockets.

Operators: Italy

History: The Fiat G91 was the result of an early 1950s design contest to produce a light attack fighter for NATO member countries.

Eight European companies responded to the 1953 NATO requirement to yield a light strike aircraft that was not reliant upon lengthy concrete runways. The winner of the competition was Fiat with its G91, which was designed by Giuseppe Gabrielli, although this decision was not made until 1957 when the prototype had been evaluated against three French contenders. The G91's first flight had earlier occurred on August 9 1956.

Although the single Bristol Orpheus powered G91 was selected as the clear winner of the design contest, interest in the concept had waned and the aircraft did not see the widespread European NATO service envisioned for it. Italy took delivery of the first production G91s (armed with four 12.7mm/0.5in Colt-Browning machine guns) in 1958.

Numerous variants followed including the G91R/1 reconnaissance variant with a suite of cameras mounted in a shortened nose. The G91R/1A had improved navaids and the 1B strengthened undercarriage. The G91R/3 meanwhile was similar but developed for the West German Air Force and built under licence in that country, some of which were later acquired by Portugal. It was equipped with a Doppler radar and twin 30mm cannon. The final single seat G91R variant was the G91R/4, it was similar to the German G91/R3 but had the original R/1 armament and some minor equipment changes.

The G91T was the two seat trainer version. It featured a lengthened forward fuselage to accommodate the extra cockpit, and retained the single seater's combat capability.

The ultimate expression of the G91 line was the G91Y. The result of a 1965 Italian requirement, the Yankee as its dubbed, differed in having two General Electric J85 turbojets mounted side by side in a revised fuselage, increasing total thrust by 60% and thus greatly improving performance. Only 67 were built, with Italy the only customer. The G91Y was retired from frontline service in early 1995.

Photo: The G91T two seat trainer. (MAP)

Aermacchi MB-326

Country of origin: Italy

Type: Two seat basic and advanced trainer

Powerplant: MB-326G – One 15.3kN (3410lb) Rolls-Royce Viper 11 turbojet.

Performance: MB-326G – Max speed 867km/h (468kt), max cruising speed 797km/h (430kt). Max initial rate of climb 6050ft/min. Service ceiling 47,000ft. Range with internal and tip tanks 1850km (1000nm), range with underwing tanks 2445km (1320nm). Combat radius (hi-lo-hi) with 770kg (1695lb) payload 650km (350nm).

Weights: MB-326G – Basic operating empty 2685kg (6920lb), max takeoff clean 4577kg (10,090lb), max takeoff armed 5215kg (11,500lb).

Dimensions: Wing span over tip tanks 10.85m (35ft 7in), length 10.67m (35ft 0in), height 3.72m (12ft 3in). Wing area 19.4m² (208.3sq ft).

Accommodation: Seating for two in tandem.

Armament: MB-326G – Provision for up to 1815kg (4000lb) of armaments, including bombs, rockets and gun pods on six underwing pylons.

Operators: Argentina, Australia, Brazil, Dubai, Ghana, Italy, Paraguay, South Africa, Togo, Tunisia, Zaire, Zambia.

History: Macchi initiated design of this classic two seat jet trainer in 1954 against an Italian Air Force requirement.

The 326 was designed by Dr-Ing Ermano Bazzochi (responsible for the B in the MB prefix) and a prototype flew for the first time on December 10 1957. The prototype MB-326 was powered by a 7.8kN (1750lb) thrust Bristol-Siddeley (later Rolls-Royce) Viper 8 turbojet and the aircraft was of the same basic configuration of almost every two seat jet trainer to follow it, with a low, straight wing, a single jet engine, tandem seating and pleasant handling characteristics.

Flight testing of the prototype revealed an aircraft that was highly suited to its intended role, displaying viceless flying characteristics and relatively snappy performance. The aircraft impressed the Italian Air Force which ordered the type into production, with the first examples arriving on strength in 1962.

The Italian Air Force took delivery of 100 basic, 11.1kN (2500lb) Viper 11 powered MB-326s (including 15 preproduction aircraft), and was offered the armed MB-326A with six underwing hardpoints, but did not order. Similar armed versions were built for other nations though, including Ghana (MB-326F) and Tunisia (MB-326B), while the Italian airline Alitalia took delivery of four unarmed MB-326Ds. Significant orders for the basic Viper 11 model meanwhile came from South Africa and Australia, the former taking delivery of 191, most of which were assembled locally by Atlas as Impala Mk 1s; the latter 97 MB-326Hs, the majority of which were built locally by CAC.

A more powerful and strengthened development with improved weapons payload was the successful MB-326G. Powered by a 15.2kN (3140lb) Viper 20 Mk.540 engine, examples were delivered to Argentina, Zaire and Zambia, while six similar but Viper 11 powered MB 326Es were delivered to Italy. Embraer meanwhile licence built MB-326G versions as Xavantes, delivered to Brazil, Paraguay and Togo.

The final two seater was the MB-326L, which included features introduced on the single seat MB-326K, described separately. Total MB-326 production was 761.

Photo: A Zambian MB-326GB. (Aermacchi)

Aermacchi MB-326K

Country of origin: Italy

Type: Single seat light attack aircraft

Powerplant: One 17.9kN (4000lb) Rolls-Royce Viper Mk 632-43 turbojet.

Performance: Max speed at 5000ft 890km/h (480kt), max speed with armament at 30,000ft 685km/h (370kt). Max initial rate of climb 6500ft/min. Time to 36,000ft 9min 30sec. Service ceiling 47,000ft. Ferry range with external fuel over 2130km (1150nm). Combat radius with 1280kg (2822lb) warload lo-lo-lo 268km (145nm), with a 1815kg (4000lb) on a lo-lo-lo mission 130km (70nm), radius on a hi-lo-hi photo reconnaissance mission with two external tanks and recce pod 1040km (560nm).

Weights: Empty equipped 2964kg (6534lb), normal takeoff 4210kg (9285lb), max takeoff 5900kg (13,000lb).

Dimensions: Wing span 10.85m (35ft 7in) with tip tanks, 10.15m (33ft 4in) without tip tanks, length 10.67m (35ft 0in), height 3.72 (12ft 2in). Wing area 19.4m² (208.3sq ft).

Accommodation: Pilot only.

Armament: Max payload of 1815kg (4000lb) on six hardpoints, comprising bombs, wire guided AS.12 ASMs, Matra R550 Magic AAMs, unguided rockets, cannon and reconnaissance pods. Fixed armament comprises two 30mm DEFA 553 cannon with 125 rounds per gun.

Operators: Dubai, Ghana, Tunisia, Zaire, South Africa (Impala Mk 2).

History: The MB-326K is the most successful single seat development of a two seat jet trainer, and has provided a number of third world nations with an effective light attack capability.

Right from the beginning of the MB-326 jet trainer program, its designer Dr-Ing Ermano Bazzochi intended that the aircraft also be an effective light strike platform, and this capability no doubt influenced a number of the two seat MB-326's customers to order it. The two seater proved to be a stable and effective weapons platform and a single seater optimised for light attack became a logical development.

The single seat MB-326K was developed well into the 326's career, given that the prototype two seater flew in 1957 and the single seat prototype flew on August 22 in 1970. The K was based on the MB-326G, which compared to earlier Macchis featured a strengthened airframe and more powerful Viper 20 engine. The first K prototype featured the 15.2kN (3410lb) Viper 20, while the second had the more powerful 18.8kN (4000lb) Viper Mk 632-43 intended for production aircraft which allowed an increased armament capability compared with two seaters and the fitting of two internal 30mm DEFA cannon. The second seat meanwhile gave way to avionics and fuel.

Despite a 1970 first flight, because of a lack of orders the first production machines were not built until 1974. The first customer was Dubai, which eventually took delivery of six MB-326KDs, while others were delivered to Zaire (MB-326KB), Ghana (MB-326KG) and Tunisia (MB-326KT).

South Africa was the MB-326Ks largest customer, taking delivery of seven Italian built MB-326KMs and 73 Atlas licence assembled 15.1kN (3360lb) Viper 540 powered Impala 2s.

Photo: Only about 20 Impala 2s survive in South African service. (MAP)

Aermacchi MB-339

Country of origin: Italy

Type: Advanced trainer, fighter lead-in trainer & light attack

Powerplant: MB-339A – One 17.9kN (4000lb) Rolls-Royce Viper Mk 632-43 turbojet (licence built in Italy). MB-339C – One 19.6kN (4400lb) Viper Mk 680-43.

Performance: MB-339A – Max speed at 30,000ft 817km/h (441kt), at sea level 898km/h (485kt). Max initial rate of climb 6595ft/min. Climb to 30,000ft 7min 6sec. Service ceiling 48,000ft. Ferry range with drop tanks 2110km (1140nm), range 1760km (950nm). Combat radius with four Mk 82 bombs and two drop tanks (hi-lo-hi) 393km (212nm). MB-339C – Max speed 902km/h (487kt). Max initial rate of climb 7085ft/min. Climb to 30,000ft 6min 40sec. Service ceiling 46,700ft. Ferry range with two drop tanks 2035km (1100nm). Combat radius with four Mk 82 bombs (hi-lo-hi) 500km (270nm).

Weights: MB-339A – Empty equipped 3125kg (6889lb), max takeoff 5895kg (13,000lb). MB-339C – Empty equipped 3310kg (7297lb), max takeoff 6350kg (14,000lb).

Dimensions: MB-339A – Wing span over tip tanks 10.86m (35ft 8in), length 10.97m (36ft 0in), height 3.99m (13ft 1in). Wing area 19.3m² (207.7sq ft). MB-339C – Same except wing span over tip tanks 11.22m (36ft 10in), length 11.24m (36ft 11in).

Accommodation: Seating for two in tandem.

Armament: MB-339A – Up to 2040kg (4500lb) of external stores on six hardpoints including bombs, rockets, cannon pods, Matre anti shipping missiles (MB-339AM), and Magic and Sidewinder AAMs. MB-339C – Up to 1815kg (4000lb) of external ordnance, as above, plus Maverick ASMs and Vinten recce pod.

Operators: Argentina, Ghana, Italy, Malaysia, New Zealand, Nigeria, Peru, UAE.

History: As the MB-326 was Aermacchi's most successful postwar design, an upgraded successor was a logical development.

The main change to the airframe was that the forward fuselage was reprofiled to feature stepped tandem cockpits (giving the instructor, who normally sits in the rear seat, greatly improved forward vision). Aermacchi also considered a number of new powerplant options, including turbofans and twins, but settled upon the familiar Viper turbojet for its performance, ease of maintenance and lower acquisition cost, despite higher fuel consumption.

The first of two prototypes flew on August 12 1976, since which time the basic aircraft has been developed into a small number of models. The base MB-339A has accounted for almost all sales and 101 were delivered to the Italian Air Force (some as MB-339PANS fitted with smoke generators for the Italian Air Force's Frecce Tricolori aerobatic team). The MB-339C meanwhile is optimised for lead-in fighter and light attack duties with advanced nav and attack systems, ability to carry missiles, a more powerful engine, lengthened nose and larger tip tanks. So far New Zealand is the only C customer.

Lockheed offered a development as the T-Bird II to meet the US's JPATS requirement, while the Italian Air Force MB-339CD (Viper 632) and export MB-339FD (Viper 680) feature a digital cockpit.

A single seat MB-339K Veltro 2 was built in prototype form only.

Photo: Dubai purchased seven MB-339As. (Aermacchi)

Aero L-29 Delfin

Country of origin: Czech Republic

Type: Two seat basic and advanced jet trainer

Powerplant: One 8.78kN (1960lb) Motorlet M 701c 500 turbojet.

Performance: Max speed at 16,400ft 655km/h (353kt), 620km/h (335kt) at sea level, cruising speed at 16,400ft 545km/h (294kt). Max initial rate of climb 2755ft/min. Time to 16,400ft 8min, time to 36,100ft 25min. Service ceiling 36,100ft. Ferry range with drop tanks 895km (482nm), range with standard fuel 640km (345nm).

Weights: Empty equipped 2365kg (5212lb), normal takeoff 3280kg (7230lb), max takeoff 3540kg (7805lb).

Dimensions: Wing span 10.29m (33ft 9in), length 10.81m (35ft 6in), height 3.13m (10ft 3in). Wing area 19.9m² (213sq ft).

Accommodation: Seating for two in tandem.

Armament: Max warload of 200kg on two underwing hardpoints (one per wing). Armament can include two 7.62mm gun pods, or two 100kg (220lb) bombs, eight light unguided rockets, or two drop tanks.

Operators: Bulgaria, Czech Republic, Egypt, Iraq, Mali, Nigeria, Romania, Syria.

History: One of the Czech aircraft industry's most successful aircraft designs, the L-29 Delfin saw widespread use in the Soviet Union as that country's primary advanced jet trainer for more than a decade from the early 1960s.

Early designs studies for a two seat jet engined trainer were conducted by K Tomas and Z Rubic in 1955. Features of the resulting L-29 Delfin (Dolphin) include its design concept of simplicity. Examples of this include easy construction and maintenance and docile handling qualities. Other design features are typical of jet trainers of the era, including a small turbojet engine, straight wing, tandem seating and lightweight ejection seats. Unlike many of its contemporaries and later jet trainers, the L-29 features a T tail and can operate from grass, waterlogged and dirt strips.

The first XL-29 prototype was powered by a Bristol Siddeley Viper engine and flew for the first time on April 5 1959. A second prototype flew in July 1960, powered by the indigenously developed M 701 turbojet. The following year the Delfin was pitted against the Yak-30 and PZL Mielec TS-11 Iskra in a competitive fly-off. The result of that competition saw the Delfin equip the air forces of every Warsaw Pact nation except for Poland. The Soviet Union alone took delivery of more than 2000 Delfins, while significant numbers also served with Czechoslovakia, East Germany and Hungary. In these countries the Delfin was used in all-through training from ab initio to advanced stages. The first Delfins were delivered in 1963, the last of over 3600 built rolled off the production line in 1974.

Almost all production was of the basic trainer variant (which was given the NATO codename 'Maya'), although two other variants did appear. Small numbers of single seat L-29A Delfin Akrobats were built for aerobatics while a prototype L-29R dedicated attack aircraft was also built. Total L-29 production was over 3000.

Photo: A Slovakian Air Force L-29. (MAP)

Aero Albatros

Country of origin: Czech Republic

Type: Two seat advanced trainer and light strike aircraft

Powerplant: L-39 C – One 16.9kN (3972lb) Progress (nee Ivchenko) AI-25 TL turbofan. L-59 – One 21.6kN (4850lb) Progress DV-2 turbofan.

Performance: L-39 C – Max speed at sea level 700km/h (378kt), at 16,400ft 750km/h (405kt). Max initial rate of climb 4130ft/min. Range with max internal fuel 1100km (595nm), with external fuel 1750km (945nm). Endurance with external fuel 3hr 50min. L-59 – Max speed at 16,400ft 876km/h (473kt). Max initial rate of climb 5120ft/min. Service ceiling 38,485ft. Ferry range with external fuel 1500km (810nm).

Weights: L-39 C – Empty equipped 3455kg (7617lb), max takeoff 4700kg (10,362lb). L-59 – Empty equipped 4150kg (9149lb), max takeoff 7000kg (15,432lb).

Dimensions: L-39 C – Wing span (incl tip tanks) 9.46m (31ft 0in), length 12.13m (39ft 10in), height 4.77m (15ft 8in). Wing area 18.8m² (202.4sq ft). L-59 – Same except wing span (incl tip tanks) 9.54m (31ft 4in), length 12.20m (40ft 0in).

Accommodation: Seating for two in tandem.

Armament: L-39 C – Unarmed. L-39ZA & L-59 – Max external warload of 1000kg (2205lb) comprising rockets and pods, plus a 23mm GSh-23 two barrel gun on centreline station.

Operators: L-39 – Afghanistan, Algeria, Bangladesh, Bulgaria, Congo, Cuba, Czech Republic, Egypt, Ethiopia, Hungary, Iraq, Libya, Nicaragua, Nigeria, North Korea, Russia, Slovakia, Syria, Thailand and various CIS republics. L-59 – Czech Republic, Egypt, Tunisia*.

History: The nimble Albatros series of jet trainers was developed as a follow-on successor to Aero's earlier Delfin design.

Design work on the Albatros, under the leadership of Dipl Ing Jan Vicek, began in 1966, just three years after the Delfin entered production. First flight of the second prototype took place on November 4 1968. Two other initial prototypes were built, both for structural testing, while a further four flying prototypes later joined the original aircraft in flight test duties. After a production decision was finally made in 1972 the L-39 was adopted for widespread use by Warsaw Pact countries (including the Soviet Union) and USSR client states.

One notable feature of the L-39 is its modular construction, it being designed to be easily manufactured and maintained.

Variants of the basic L-39 are numerous. The L-39 C is the basic two seat, unarmed trainer, and accounts for the majority of L-39 production. The L-39 V is a target tug, the L-39 ZO is an armed weapons trainer with a reinforced wing and four underwing hardpoints, while the L-39 ZO is similar to the ZA, but has reinforced undercarriage and can carry a reconnaissance pod. The L-39 ZA/ART was built for Thailand and features Israeli Elbit electronics. The L-139 is powered by a 18.2kN (4080lb) Garrett TFE731 turbofan, features Bendix King avionics and Flight Vision HUD and is offered for export.

The L-59 development is similar to the L-39 save for its more powerful engine, upgraded avionics and reinforced fuselage. The L-159 is being built for the Czech Air Force in single and two seat form and features Rockwell avionics and a AlliedSignal/ITEC F124 turbofan.

Photo: A Royal Thai Air Force L-39 ZE. (Aero)

Aerospatiale CM 170 Magister

Country of origin: France

Type: Two seat jet trainer

Powerplants: CM 170-1 – Two 3.94kN (880lb) Maborè IIA turbojets. CM 170-2 – Two 4.74kN (1058lb) Maborè VICs.

Performance: CM 170-1 – Max speed 715km/h (385kt) at 29,925ft, 650km/h (350kt) at sea level. Max initial rate of climb 3345ft/min. Service ceiling 36,090ft. Ferry range with auxiliary fuel 1200km (650nm), range with standard fuel 925km (500nm). CM 170-2 – Max speed clean 745km/h (402kt) at 30,000ft, 700km/h (378kt) at sea level. Max initial rate of climb 3540ft/min. Service ceiling 44,300ft. Range 1250km (675nm).

Weights: CM 170-1 – Empty equipped 2150kg (4740lb), max takeoff 3200kg (7055lb). CM 170-2 – Empty equipped 2310kg (5093lb), max takeoff 3200kg (7055lb).

Dimensions: Wing span over tip tanks 12.15m (39ft 10in), span without tip tanks 11.40m (37ft 5in), length 10.06m (33ft 0in), height 2.80m (9ft 2in). Wing area 17.3m² (186.1sq ft).

Accommodation: Standard seating for two in tandem.

Armament: Two 7.5mm or 7.62mm fixed machine guns mounted in the nose. Underwing hardpoints can carry bombs, rockets and Nord AS.12 air-to-ground missiles.

Operators: Bangladesh, Cameroon, France, Gabon, Ireland, Israel, Libya, Morocco, El Salvador, Senegambia, Togo.

History: The Magister was the first aircraft in the world specifically designed as a jet trainer, and was arguably postwar France's first successful world class military aircraft.

The Magister resulted from a French Air Force requirement for a jet powered trainer. The basic aircraft was conceived by Fouga designers Castello and Mauboussin (hence the CM prefix) in 1950. The first of three prototypes flew for the first time on June 27 1951, the type's promising performance leading to a French air force order for 10 pre production aircraft. Prolonged testing and development of the aircraft followed, with the first pre production aircraft not flying for the first time until June 1954 and the first production aircraft (for the French Air Force) on February 29 1956.

The Magister proved an ideal aircraft for its intended role as it was easy to fly with predictable flying characteristics, despite the unusual two surface butterfly tail. 387 were eventually built for the French Air Force while several hundred others were built in France and under licence in Finland, Germany and Israel for a large number of export customers including West Germany, Belgium, Austria, Belgium, Lebanon and Cambodia. Total French production amounted to 622 (built mainly by Fouga's successors Potez, Sud Aviation and Aerospatiale), while IAI built 36, Finland's Valmet 62 and Germany's Flugzeug Union Sud 188.

The Magister was built in three versions – the initial CM 170-1, the CM 170-2 Super Magister with more powerful engines and ejection seats, and the navalised, carrier capable CM 175 Zéphyr. The French Navy took delivery of 30 arrester hook equipped Zéphyrs. The Magister remains in service in fairly large numbers, a number of nations having acquired examples second hand.

Photo: An Algerian Magister.

Aerospatiale Alouette II & Lama

Country of origin: France

Type: Light utility helicopters

Powerplant: SA 313B Alouette II – One 270kW (360shp) Turboméca Artouste IIC6 turboshaft, driving a three bladed main rotor and two bladed tail rotor. SA 315B Lama – One 650kW (870shp) Turboméca Artouste IIIB turboshaft, derated to 410kW (550shp).

Performance: SA 313B – Max speed 185km/h (100kt), max cruising speed 165km/h (90kt). Max initial rate of climb 825ft/min. Hovering ceiling in ground effect 5400ft. Range with max fuel 300km (162nm), range with max payload 100km (54nm). SA 315B – Max cruising speed 192km/h (103kt). Max initial rate of climb 1080ft/min. Service ceiling 17,715ft. Hovering ceiling in ground effect 16,565ft, out of ground effect 15,090ft. Range with max fuel 515km (278nm).

Weights: SA 313B – Empty 895kg (1973lb), max takeoff 1600kg (3527lb). SA 315B – Empty 1020kg (2250lb), max takeoff 1950kg (4300lb), or 2300kg (5070lb) with external sling load.

Dimensions: SA 313B – Main rotor diameter 10.20m (33ft 5in), fuselage length 9.70m (31ft 10in), height 2.75m (9ft 0in). SA 315B – Main rotor diameter 11.02m (36ft 2in), length overall 12.92m (42ft 5in), fuselage length 10.26m (33ft 8in), height overall 3.09m (10ft 2in). Main rotor disc area 95.4m² (1026.7sq ft).

Accommodation: Typical seating for five. Can carry two stretchers in medevac role. Lama can lift a 1135kg (2500lb) external sling load.

Armament: None (officially).

Operators: Alouette II operators include Belgium, Benin, Cameroon, Central African Republic, Congo, Dominican Republic, France, Guinea-Bissau, Ivory Coast, Lebanon, Senegambia, Tunisia. Lama operators: Argentina, Chile, Ecuador, India (Cheetah), Togo.

History: For a time the most successful western European helicopter in terms of numbers built, the Alouette II was based on the original Sud-Est Alouette SA 3120 which first flew on March 12 1955.

Two prototypes were built and these were powered by Salmson 9 piston engines. Production deliveries of the turbine powered SE 313B Alouette II occurred from 1957, the first machines bound for the French Army. Most SA/SE 313B production was for military operators, many of whom had French links, while others went to civilian operators.

The Alouette II was soon followed by a more powerful Turboméca Astazou powered development. This aircraft was designated the SA 318C Alouette II Astazou, and flew for the first time on January 31 1961. Power was supplied by a 395kW (530shp) Astazou IIA derated to 270kW (360shp), which increased the type's maximum speed and max takeoff weight, but otherwise the Alouette II and Alouette II Astazou were similar.

The SA 315B Lama was developed initially as a utility helicopter for the Indian Army possessing excellent hot and high performance. Called Cheetah in Indian service, the Lama mated the Alouette II's airframe with the larger Alouette III's dynamic components including the Artouste IIIB engine. The Lama's first flight was on March 17 1969. Aerospatiale built 407 through to 1989, while HAL in India continues licence production.

Photo: A Belgian Alouette II. (MAP)

Aerospatiale Alouette III

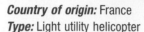

Country of origin: France

Type: Light utility helicopter

Powerplant: SA 316B – One 425kW (570shp) Turboméca Artouste IIIB turboshaft, driving a three bladed main rotor and three bladed tail rotor. SA 319B – One 450kW (600shp) derated Turboméca Astazou XIV.

Performance: SA 316B – Max speed 210km/h (113kt), max cruising speed 185km/h (100kt). Max initial rate of climb 885ft/min. Hovering ceiling in ground effect 7380ft/min. Range with max fuel 480km (260nm). SA 319B – Max cruising speed 197km/h (106kt). Max initial rate of climb 885ft/min. Hovering ceiling in ground effect 10,700ft, out of ground effect 5575ft. Range with six passengers 605km (327nm).

Weights: SA 316B – Empty 1122kg (2474lb), max takeoff 2200kg (4850lb). SA 319B – Empty 1140kg (2513lb), max takeoff 2250kg (4960lb).

Dimensions: SA 316B & SA 319B – Main rotor diameter 11.02m (36ft 2in), length overall 12.84m (42ft 2in), fuselage length 10.03m (32ft 11in), height 3.00, (9ft 10in). Main rotor disc area 95.4m² (1026.7sq ft).

Accommodation: Typical seating for seven.

Armament: Can carry one 7.62mm machine gun mounted on a tripod firing through right hand doorway, a 20mm cannon fixed to the left hand side of the fuselage, or four or two AS.11 anti tank missiles, or two Mk.44 torpedoes.

Operators: Operated by 45 countries including Argentina, Austria, Cameroon, France, Ghana, Iraq, Ireland, Malaysia, Mexico, Netherlands, Pakistan, Portugal, Romania, South Africa, Switzerland, Tunisia and Venezuela. Chetak in service with India and Nepal.

History: The popular Alouette III is an enlarged development of the Alouette II series and remains in widespread service worldwide.

Like the Alouette II, the Alouette III traces its development back to the Sud-Est SE 3101 piston powered prototypes, the first of which flew for the first time on July 31 1951. The largest member of the Alouette series, the III flew as the SE 3160 on February 28 1959. Compared with the Alouette II, the Alouette III is larger and seats seven, but in its initial SA 316A form is also powered by a Turboméca Artouste turboshaft.

This SA 316A Alouette III remained in production for almost a decade until 1969, when it was replaced by the improved SA 316B, with strengthened transmission and a greater max takeoff weight, but the same Artouste III turboshaft.

Further development led to the SA 319 Alouette III Astazou, which as its name suggests is powered by a 450kW (600shp) Turboméca Astazou XIV turboshaft. The more powerful Astazou engine conferred better hot and high performance and improved fuel economy. The SA 319 entered production in 1968.

The SA 319 and SA 316B remained in production side by side through the 1970s and into the 1980s. HAL of India continues to licence build Alouette IIIs as the Chetak, mainly for that country's military, while similarly 230 were built by ICA-Brasov in Romania through to 1989. The Romanians also developed a two seat anti tank attack helicopter based on the Alouette as the IAR-317 Skyfox, but this aircraft flew in prototype form only.

Photo: A ski equipped Austrian Alouette III. (Austrian MoD)

Aerospatiale SA 321 Super Frelon

Country of origin: France

Type: Multirole utility helicopter

Powerplants: SA 321G – Three 1100kW to 1215kW (1475shp to 1630shp) Turboméca Turmo IIIC turboshafts, driving a six bladed main rotor and five bladed tail rotor.

Performance: SA 321G – Max cruising speed at sea level 248km/h (134kt). Max initial rate of climb (inclined) 1214ft/min, 480ft/min on two engines. Hovering ceiling in ground effect 7120ft. Service ceiling 10,170ft. Range 1020km (550nm). Endurance in ASW role 4hr.

Weights: SA 321G – Empty 6700kg (14,775lb), max takeoff 13,000kg (28,660lb).

Dimensions: Main rotor diameter 18.90m (62ft 0in), length overall 23.03m (75ft 7in), fuselage length 19.40m (63ft 8in), height 6.66m (21ft 10in). Main rotor disc area 280.6m² (3019sq ft).

Accommodation: Flightcrew of two. Original SA 321G ASW configuration seats three tactical/sonar operators. Transport configured Super Frelons can seat 30 troops or carry 15 stretcher patients in a medevac configuration.

Armament: As originally configured, SA 321Gs could carry four homing torpedoes or two AM 39 Exocet anti shipping missiles. Various export aircraft configured to launch Exocet.

Operators: Argentina, China, France, Iraq, Syria.

History: While only built in relatively small numbers (though it is still built under licence in China), the Super Frelon has the distinction of being the largest helicopter to be built in quantity in western Europe.

The Super Frelon was developed from the smaller, mid size SA 3200 Frelon (Hornet), the first flight of which was on June 10 1959. The Frelon was intended to meet French military requirements for a mid size transport helicopter, and although four prototypes were built, it was not ordered into production. Instead the Frelon formed the basis for the much larger Super Frelon which Sud Aviation developed in conjunction with Sikorsky. Sikorsky helped primarily with the development of the main and tail rotor systems, while Fiat of Italy assisted with the gearbox and power transmission (and built those parts for production aircraft).

The SA 3210-01 prototype Super Frelon flew for the first time on December 7 1962, while 99 production aircraft were built in three basic models. The SA 321G was initially operated by the French Navy as an anti submarine warfare and sanitization aircraft for French nuclear armed submarines, equipped with radar, dunking sonar and torpedoes. Similar SA 321GMs and SA 321Hs were delivered to Syria and Iraq respectively. The SA 321F and SA 321J were civil variants, while the SA 321J is a utility transport. Non amphibious transport versions were exported to South Africa (SA 321L) and Israel (SA 321K), while Libya's SA 321Ms were delivered for SAR and logistics support.

French production ceased in 1983, while Changhe in China continues to licence build the multirole Z-8 development.

Photo: French Navy Super Frelons are now used for vertical replenishment. (MAP)

Aerospatiale TB 30 Epsilon

Country of origin: France

Type: Two seat basic trainer

Powerplant: TB 30B – One 225kW (300hp) Textron Lycoming AEIO-540-L1B5D fuel injected flat six piston engine, driving a two bladed constant speed Hartzell propeller.

Performance: TB 30B – Max speed at sea level 378km/h (204kt), cruising speed at 6000ft 358km/h (193kt). Max initial rate of climb 1850ft/min. Service ceiling 23,000ft. Range 1250km (675nm). Endurance at 60% power 3hr 45min.

Weights: TB 30B – Empty equipped 932kg (2055lb), max takeoff 1250kg (2755lb).

Dimensions: TB 30B – Wing span 7.92m (26ft 0in), length 7.59m (24ft 1in), height 2.66m (8ft 9in). Wing area 9.0m² (96.0sq ft).

Accommodation: Seating for two in tandem.

Armament: Togolese aircraft only – Maximum external ordnance of 300kg (660lb) with pilot only, comprising two twin 7.62mm machine gun pods, or four 68mm six rocket tubes or two 120kg (265lb) bombs, on four underwing hardpoints. Inner pylons stressed for 160kg (350lb), outer pylons 80kg (175lb).

Operators: France, Portugal, Togo.

History: The French Air Force's primary basic trainer, the Epsilon is based on the successful four seat TB 10 Tobago light aircraft.

Aerospatiale's General Aviation subsidiary Socata developed the Epsilon in response to meet an Armee d l'Air requirement for a basic trainer. Initially Socata looked at a jet powered aircraft, then a piston engined aircraft based on the Tobago with two seats side-by-side. When the French Air Force decided it wanted a tandem seating arrangement, the basic design was redeveloped and all commonality with the Tobago was lost.

Socata proposed the Epsilon in two variants differing in powerplant fitted. It offered the 195kW (260hp) powered TB 30A and the 225kW (300hp) powered TB 30B, with only the latter, higher powered aircraft selected for development and production. The French air force awarded the development contract in June 1979 and the resulting TB 30B prototype flew for the first time on December 22 that year.

Testing of the prototype revealed unacceptable pitch/yaw coupling characteristics, so Socata further refined the design to feature extended, rounded, upswept winglets and a redesigned rear fuselage and tail. The first and second prototypes were then modified and flew in this new, definitive configuration from late October 1980.

The first French Air Force production order was placed in March 1982 for 30 aircraft. Socata eventually delivered 150 Epsilons to the French Air Force through to 1989, while Togo took delivery of a total of four machines and Portugal 18, assembled locally by OGMA.

The fully aerobatic Epsilon's fuel system allows it to fly inverted for up to two minutes. Togo's aircraft meanwhile are equipped with four external hardpoints, which can carry gun pods, rockets and light bombs in a counter insurgency role.

The TB 30 also forms the basis for the turboprop powered TB 31 Omega, described separately.

Photo: The Epsilon is France's standard basic trainer. (Armée de l'Air)

Aerospatiale TB 31 Omega

Country of origin: France

Type: Two seat turboprop powered basic trainer

Powerplant: One 450kW (600shp) Turboméca Arrius turboprop, derated to 270kW (360shp) driving a three bladed Hartzell propeller.

Performance: Max speed at 16,000ft 520km/h (280kt), max cruising speed at 10,000ft 434km/h (234kt), economical cruising speed at 75% power 354km/h (191kt). Max initial rate of climb 2100ft/min. Time to 20,000ft 11min. Service ceiling 30,000ft. Range at economical cruising speed (75% power) with reserves 1308km (705nm).

Weights: Empty equipped 860kg (1896lb), average empty equipped with ejection seats 1080kg (2381lb), max takeoff 1450kg (3197lb).

Dimensions: Wing span 7.92m (26ft 0in), length overall 8.03m (26ft 4in), height 2.64m (8ft 8in). Wing area 9.0m² (96.88sq ft).

Accommodation: Seating for two in tandem.

Armament: None

Operators: None

History: The privately developed Socata TB 31 Omega turboprop trainer has yet to attract a single customer, despite having been available on the world market since the late 1980s.

The TB 31 Omega is a turboprop powered development of Socata's earlier, piston powered TB 30 Epsilon (described in the previous entry). The Omega originally flew as the Turbo Epsilon, which was essentially similar to the Epsilon from the firewall rearwards. The Turbo Epsilon flew for the first time on November 9 1985. Extensive engine development ensued, and the aircraft emerged as the Omega in 1989.

The Omega represents a substantial increase in performance to the Epsilon yet still retains 60% commonality with the earlier trainer. There are several significant and easily identifiable differences though. Most important of the changes is the substitution of the Epsilon's 225kW (300hp) Textron Lycoming AEIO-540 flat six piston engine with a Turboméca Arrius turboshaft. On the Omega the Arrius is flat rated to just 270kW (360shp), down from its original rating of 450kW (600shp) and features Full Authority Digital Electronic Control (FADEC). Power is delivered through a three bladed Hartzell prop, the original Turbo Epsilon featured a composite three bladed Ratier-Fagiec unit. (The Arrius is in use on the Eurocopter AS 555 Fennec/AS 355 Twin Ecureuil.)

Other changes include a new two piece moulded cockpit canopy, which significantly increases all round vision. Underneath the canopy customers can select the optional Martin Baker 15FC lightweight ejection seat, which has a zero height, 111km/h (60kt) speed capability. Changes to the airframe include a revised cowling shape and a dorsal fin. The aircraft avionics features CRT displays for radio and navigation data.

In its definitive form the Omega flew for the first time on April 30 1989. Successful flight testing followed, but Socata was unsuccessful in its attempts to sell the aircraft to the French Air Force, that service instead opting for the much larger, more powerful Embraer Tucano. Nevertheless Socata continues to market the aircraft for export.

Photo: The Omega is still on offer for export customers despite not yet having been ordered into production. (Aerospatiale)

Agusta A 109

Country of origin: Italy

Type: Multirole light helicopter

Powerplants: A 109K – Two 435kW (585shp) continuous operation rated Turboméca Arriel IK turboshafts, driving a four bladed main rotor and two bladed tail rotor.

Performance: A 109K – Max cruising speed at sea level clean 263km/h (142kt). Max initial rate of climb 2020ft/min. Service ceiling 20,000ft. Hovering ceiling in ground effect 18,600ft, out of ground effect 15,190ft. Max range at long range cruising speed 820km (442nm), max range with full payload 543km (293nm). Max endurance 4hr 16min.

Weights: A 109K – Empty 1650kg (3638lb), max takeoff 2850kg (6280lb).

Dimensions: A 109K – Main rotor diameter 11.00m (36ft 1in), length rotors turning 13.03m (42ft 9in), fuselage length 11.44m (37ft 6in), height 3.50m (11ft 6in). Main rotor disc area 95.0m² (1023sq ft).

Accommodation: Seats up to eight in passenger configuration.

Armament: Various weapons on two external hardpoints each side of the fuselage on pylons. Options include eight TOW anti armour missiles, Stinger air-to-air missiles, 7.62mm or 12.7m machine gun pods, 7.62mm or 12.7mm MGs pintle mounted in main cabin doorways, 70 or 80mm rocket launcher. Potential to carry anti ship missiles.

Operators: Argentina, Belgium, Italy, Syria, Yugoslavia, UK.

History: Although developed primarily for the civil market, the A 109 has been adopted for a range of military and quasi military roles.

The first of four prototype A 109s flew for the first time on August 4 1971, although the first production machines were not delivered until 1976. Basic models since then include the initial A 109A, the A 109A Mk II with improvements to the dynamic systems, and the A 109C with a further uprated transmission, composite rotor blades and greater width in the cabin with the fitment of bulged doors.

Early military use of the A 109 was confined to a small number procured for liaison and light transport. Argentina was an early operator, two of its four aircraft originally delivered being captured by the British during the Falklands War and then placed into service with the British Army in support of SAS operations.

The first major military A 109 customer was Italy, which initially ordered 24 A 109A based A 109EOA armed scout helicopters fitted with sliding main cabin doors, fixed landing gear, roof mounted day sight, laser range finder and the ability to carry a variety of weapons.

The A 109C based A 109CM is the current principal military model. Belgium has taken delivery of 18 scout and 24 anti armour variants as A 109BAs (designated by Belgium as A 109HO and HA respectively). Similar to the A 109EOA, the scouts feature a roof mounted Saab sight, the attack aircraft Saab/ESCO HeliTOW 2 sights and the capability to carry eight Hughes TOW-2A anti tank missiles.

The A 109K is designed for hot and high operations and is fitted with Turboméca Arrius turboshafts. The land based A 109KM has sliding doors and a fixed undercarriage, the naval A 109KN can be fitted with anti ship missiles, or be used as an over the horizon radar for its mother ship. No military A 109Ks have yet been ordered.

Photo: An Italian Army A 109EOA with mast mounted sight and grenade launchers. (Agusta)

Agusta A 129 Mangusta

Country of origin: Italy

Type: Two seat attack and scout helicopter

Powerplants: A 129 – Two 615kW (825shp) max continuous operation rated Rolls-Royce Gem 2 Mk 1004D turboshafts (licence built by Piaggio), driving a four bladed main rotor and two bladed tail rotor.

Performance: A 129 – Dash speed 294km/h (160kt), max speed at sea level 250km/h (135kt). Max initial rate of climb 2030ft/min. Hovering ceiling in ground effect 10,300ft, out of ground effect 6200ft. Combat radius with eight TOW missiles, reserves and a 90min loiter time on station 100km (55nm). Max endurance 3hr 5min.

Weights: A 129 – Empty equipped 2530kg (5575lb), max takeoff 4100kg (9040lb).

Dimensions: A 129 – Main rotor diameter 11.90m (39ft 1in), wing span 3.20m (10ft 6in), length overall rotors turning 14.29m (46ft 11in), fuselage length 12.28m (40ft 3in), height overall 3.35m (11ft 0in). Main rotor disc area 111.2m² (1197.0sq ft).

Accommodation: Crew of two seated in tandem, pilot in rear seat.

Armament: A 129 – Up to 1200kg of stores. Typical Italian loads can include up to eight TOW 2 or 2A wire guided anti tank missiles on outboard stations, and 7.62mm, 12.7mm or 20mm gun pods, or rocket pods with seven rockets each. Can carry Stinger, Hellfire or Mistral air-to-surface missiles or Sidewinder air-to-air missiles.

Operators: Italy

History: While the initial Italian Army specification for a light, two seat scout and attack helicopter was issued in 1972, it was not until much later in 1978 that project go-ahead was given for what became the A 129 Mangusta (Mongoose).

Even then it would be another five years before the prototype's first flight on September 11 1983. Features of the aircraft include two Rolls-Royce Gem turboshafts, seating for a gunner/copilot and pilot in separate, stepped cockpits, four blade main rotor with some use of composite construction, a computerised and fully redundant integrated management system designed to reduce crew workload, stub wings with two weapons pylons each, and a Saab/ESCO Helitow weapons system with nose mounted sight.

Following funding delays with the Helitow system, the A 129 entered service with the Italian Army in October 1990.

One proposed development of the Mangusta was the Tonal Joint European Light Attack Helicopter. Italy, Spain, the UK and the Netherlands were to have developed a more powerful, better equipped A 129 as Tonal, but the program was subsequently rejected. The A 139 meanwhile was to have been a utility transport derivative using the A 129 drive systems.

The only A 129 development to fly thus far has been the A 129 International, developed to attract export sales. Changes include the substitution of 20% more powerful LHTEC T800 turboshafts, uprated transmission, a higher max takeoff weight and optional three barrel 12.7mm gun turret. First A 129 International flight was in 1988, more latterly the prototype has flown with a five blade main rotor, while new armament and equipment options include Stinger AAMs, a Lockheed Martin/GIAT 20mm three barrelled cannon, FLIR and CCD displays.

Photo: An Italian Army A 129. (Bruce Malcolm)

AIDC Ching-Kuo

Country of origin: Taiwan

Type: Lightweight multirole fighter

Powerplants: Two 26.8kN (6025lb) dry and 42.1kN (9460lb) afterburning ITEC (Garrett/AIDC) TFE1042-70 (F125) turbofans.

Performance: Estimated max speed at 36,000ft approx Mach 1.7 or over 1275km/h (688kt). Max initial rate of climb 50,000ft/min. Service ceiling 55,000ft. Range figures not published.

Weights: Estimated internal fuel 1950kg (4300lb), max takeoff weight thought to be in the 9000kg (20,000lb) class.

Dimensions: All estimated – Wing span over wingtip missile rails 8.5m (28ft), length overall including nose probe 14.5m (47ft 6in), length overall excluding nose probe 13.3m (43ft 6in).

Accommodation: Pilot only, or two in tandem in trainers.

Armament: One 20mm M61A1 Vulcan cannon. Six hardpoints can carry a variety of missiles, bombs, guided bombs and cluster munitions including 500lb/225kg GBU-12, Rockeye, AGM-65B Maverick, Hsiung Feng II anti ship missile, Sky Sword I short range IR guided and Sky Sword II medium range radar homing AAMs.

Operators: Taiwan

History: The Ching-Kuo is by far Taiwan's most ambitious aircraft program thus far, and after more than a decade of development is now providing Taiwan with a capable multirole fighter.

Development of the Ching-Kuo, initially known as the Indigenous Defence Fighter (IDF), began in 1982 after a US arms embargo precluded Taiwan from ordering F-16s or Northrop F-20 Tigersharks to replace ageing F-5s and F-104s fighters for air superiority, anti shipping and ground attack roles. Despite the arms embargo, US companies were still able to provide technical support for the program, with the result that much of the aircraft's systems is based on US equipment. General Dynamics worked closely with AIDC to develop the airframe, and similarities to the F-16 are obvious, particular the blended fuselage/wing design. Other features such as the leading edge root extensions give the aircraft the appearance of a scaled down F/A-18.

The International Turbofan Engine Company (ITEC) TFE1042 afterburning turbofans were developed in partnership by Garrett and AIDC. The Golden Dragon 53 radar (which has a search range of 150km/80nm) is based on the GE AN/APG-67 originally developed for the F-20, with some elements based on the F-16A's APG-66 with air and sea search modes and lookdown, shootdown capability, while the specifically developed Sky Sword I and Sky Sword II AAMs closely resemble the AIM-9 Sidewinder and AIM-7 Sparrow, respectively. Other features include a side stick controller, two multi function displays, a HUD and fly-by-wire.

The first prototype Ching-Kuo, a single seater, flew for the first time on May 28 1989, while three other prototypes – one single seater and two two seaters – and 10 pre production aircraft followed. The first production Ching-Kuo was delivered to the Republic of China Air Force in January 1994, with production continuing through to 1999.

Taiwan's initial plan to buy 260 Ching-Kuos was halved when the lifting of arms embargoes during the early nineties allowed it to purchase F-16s and Mirage 2000-5s and cancel a developed version.

Photo: The first prototype Ching-Kuo.

AIDC AT-3 Tzu-Chiang

Type: Two seat advanced trainer and light attack aircraft

Country of origin: Taiwan

Powerplants: AT-3 – Two 15.6kN (3500lb) Garrett TPE731-2-2L non-afterburning turbofans.

Performance: AT-3 – Max speed at 36,000ft 904km/h (488kt), or 900km/h (486kt) at sea level, max cruising speed at 36,000ft 880km/h (475kt). Max initial rate of climb 10,100ft/min. Service ceiling 48,000ft. Range with internal fuel 2280km (1230nm). Endurance with internal fuel 3hr 12min.

Weights: AT-3 – Empty equipped 3855kg (8500lb), normal takeoff (trainer, clean) 5215kg (11,500lb), max takeoff 7940kg (17,500lb).

Dimensions: AT-3 – Wing span 10.46m (34ft 4in), length including nose probe 12.90m (42ft 4in), height 4.83m (15ft 10in). Wing area 21.9m² (236.1sq ft).

Accommodation: Seating for two in tandem. AT-3A seats pilot only.

Armament: Can be fitted with gun pods in an internal weapons bay. Disposable armament can be carried on one centreline pylon, four underwing hardpoints and two wingtip launch rails. Can carry bombs, rockets, wingtip mounted AAMs and training bombs.

Operators: Taiwan

History: The AT-3 Tzu-Chiang was AIDC's second indigenous design to enter Taiwanese service behind the turboprop powered Chung Tsing, and serves with the Taiwanese Air Force as an advanced/weapons trainer and light attack and close support aircraft. Up until the development of the Chung-Kuo fighter, the AT-3 was the most advanced aircraft to be developed by Taiwan's emerging aircraft industry.

Serious design of the AT-3 began in 1975 with the placement of a development contract. The first of two prototypes flew for the first time on September 16 1980, while the first production aircraft flew on February 6 1984. In all, AIDC built 60 AT-3s for the Republic of China Air Force, the last of which was delivered in 1990.

All 60 production aircraft were designated AT-3. The AT-3A Lui Meng meanwhile was a single seat dedicated light ground and maritime attack development. Two prototypes were known to have been built (the first one being converted from a two seat AT-3) and flown in the late 1980s, but the aircraft's current status is unclear, with development thought to have been suspended.

The AT-3A could have been suspended in favour of the two seat AT-3B, which features the nav/attack system initially developed for the Lui-Meng. Twenty AT-3s were converted to AT-3B standard which features a Westinghouse AN/APG-66 radar and an internal weapons bay that can carry semi recessed machine gun packs. The aircraft can carry a variety of weaponry, including wingtip mounted infrared guided AAMs, in addition to bombs and rockets on four underwing and a centreline pylon. The AT-3B's maximum external stores load is 2720kg (6000lb).

Power for the AT-3 is supplied by two Garrett TFE731 turbofans, while the airframe is of conventional construction. Other features include zero/zero ejection seats and the ability to carry and deploy an aerial target towing system.

Photo: An AT-3 in flight. The AT-3 has largely replaced the T-CH-1 Chung Tsing in Taiwanese service.

Airbus A310

Country of origin: European consortium

Type: VIP/strategic transport

Powerplants: Initially either two 213.5kN (48,000lb) Pratt & Whitney JT9D-7R4D1 or two 222.4kN (50,000lb) General Electric CF6-80A3 turbofans. Current choices of 238kN or 262kN (53,500lb or 59,000lb) GE CF6-80C2A2s or -80C2A8s, or 231kN or 249kN (52,000lb or 56,000lb) P&W PW4152 or PW4156 turbofans.

Performance: A310-200 – Max cruising speed 897kmh (484kt), long range cruising speed 850kmh (459kt). Range at typical airliner operating weight with reserves 6800km (3670nm). A310-300 (with CF6 80C2A2s) – Speeds same. Typical airliner range with reserves 7980km (4310nm), or up to 9580km (5170nm) for high gross weight version.

Weights: A310-200 with CF6-80C2A2s – Operating empty 80,142kg (176,683lb), max takeoff 142,000kg (313,055lb). A310-300 with CF6-80C2A8s – Operating empty 80,330kg (177,095lb), max takeoff up to 164,000kg (361,560lb).

Dimensions: Wing span 43.89m (144ft 0in), length 46.66m (153ft 1in), height 15.80m (51ft 10in). Wing area 219.0m² (2357.3sq ft).

Accommodation: Flightcrew of two. Max passenger capacity at nine abreast 280, max payload approx 30,000kg (66,080lb). Canadian and French A310s used as freighters, Germany's and Thailand's aircraft feature custom VIP layouts.

Armament: None

Operators: Canada, France, Germany, Thailand.

History: The A310, a shortened development of Airbus' original A300 widebody airliner, is now in limited military service as a transport.

While based on the larger A300 airliner, the A310 features a number of major differences including a shortened fuselage, a new higher aspect ratio wing of smaller span and greater area, new and smaller horizontal tail surfaces and a two crew flightdeck.

The first flight of an A310 occurred on April 3 1982, after the program was launched in July 1978. The basic passenger aircraft is the A310-200, while the A310-300 is a longer range development and has been in production since 1985.

The A310-200F freighter and A310-200C convertible are available as new build aircraft or as conversions of existing A310s. The A310-200F in particular could form the basis of a dedicated new build military freighter, possibly fitted with air-to-air refuelling pods. Airbus has established a division to study military derivatives of its commercial airliners, but it has yet to find a customer.

Military A310s currently in service operate in a variety of transport functions. Thailand became the first military A310 operator when its sole A310 was delivered in 1991. Germany inherited its A310s from the former East Germany's flag carrier Interflug, while France's have replaced DC-8s.

Canada was the largest operator of military A310s, with three, plus options on a further two ex Canadian Airlines aircraft to replace 707s. Designated CC-150 Polaris, two were converted for transport while the third was fitted with a VIP interior. The VIP A310 was subsequently sold off and the options on the other two aircraft were dropped because of defence budget cuts.

Photo: A Canadian Forces A310.

Airtech (CASA/IPTN) CN-235

Countries of origin: Indonesia & Spain

Type: Tactical transport and maritime patrol aircraft

Powerplants: Two 1305kW (1750shp) General Electric CT7-9C turboprops, driving four bladed Hamilton Standard propellers.

Performance: CN-235 M – Max cruising speed at 15,000ft 460km/h (248kt). Max initial rate of climb 1900ft/min. Service ceiling 26,600ft. Takeoff distance to 50ft at MTOW 1290m (4235ft). Range (srs 200) with max payload 1500km (810nm), with a 3550kg (7825lb) payload 4445km (2400nm).

Weights: CN-235 M – Operating empty 8800kg (19,400lb), max takeoff 16,500kg (36,375lb).

Dimensions: CN-235 M – Wing span 25.81m (84ft 8in), length 21.40m (70ft 3in), height 8.18m (26ft 10in). Wing area 59.1m² (636.1sq ft).

Accommodation: CN-235 M – Flightcrew of two, plus typically a loadmaster. Can accommodate 48 equipped troops or 46 paratroopers. CN-235MPA – Typical arrangement features two observer stations, two operator consoles and six passenger seats.

Armament: CN-235 MP & MPA – Six underwing hardpoints allow the carriage of anti shipping missiles such as Exocet and Harpoon. MPA can be armed with two Mk 46 torpedoes.

Operators: Botswana, Brunei, Chile, Ecuador, France, Gabon, Indonesia, Ireland, South Korea, Morocco, Panama, Papua New Guinea, Saudi Arabia, Spain, Turkey*, UAE.

History: CASA of Spain and Indonesia's IPTN specifically formed Airtech to jointly develop the CN-235 military transport and regional airliner.

With development shared equally between the two companies, prototypes, one in each country, were rolled out simultaneously on September 10 1983. The Spanish built prototype was the first to fly, taking to the skies for the first time on November 11 1983, while the Indonesian prototype flew for the first time on December 30 that year.

CN-235 final assembly lines are located in both Indonesia and Spain, but all other construction is not duplicated. CASA builds the centre and forward fuselage, wing centre section, inboard flaps and engine nacelles, while IPTN is responsible for the outer wings and flaps, ailerons, rear fuselage and tail.

Initial production was of the CN-235-10, subsequent and improved developments being the CN-235-100 and the current production -200, with more powerful engines and structural improvements respectively.

While commercial developments of the CN-235 (including the QC – quick change) have sold in modest numbers, the military CN-235 M transport has been quite successful with over 160 in service with 17 countries. Features of the M include good field performance, a rear loading ramp and spacious interior. IPTN markets the aircraft as the Phoenix.

Both CASA and IPTN have also developed maritime patrol derivatives. CASA's CN-235 MP Persuader and IPTN's CN-235 MPA both have a Litton APS-504 search radar and FLIR and ESM. The CN-235 MPA can be identified by its lengthened nose housing the radar.

Since the early 1990s CASA and IPTN have developed and marketed their own versions of the CN-235 separately. In mid 1995 CASA was studying a stretched CN-235.

Photo: Spain is one of the largest CN-235 operators.

Alenia G222

Country of origin: Italy

Type: Tactical transport

Powerplants: Two 2535kW (3400shp) General Electric T64-GE-P4D turboprops, licence built by Fiat, driving three bladed Hamilton Standard propellers.

Performance: Max speed 540km/h (292kt), economical cruising speed 440km/h (240kt). Max initial rate of climb 1705ft/min. Service ceiling 25,000ft. Takeoff run at MTOW 662m (2172ft). Ferry range 4630km (2500nm), range with max payload 1370km (740nm), range with 36 litters and four medical attendants 2500km (1350nm).

Weights: Empty equipped 15,400kg (33,950lb), max takeoff 28,000kg (61,728lb).

Dimensions: Wing span 28.70m (94ft 2in), length 22.70m (74ft 6in), height 9.80m (32ft 2in). Wing area 82.0m² (882.7sq ft).

Accommodation: Flightcrew of two with provision for a loadmaster. Typical accommodation for 46 fully equipped troops, or 40 fully equipped paratroops. Can carry a 9600kg (21,165lb) payload comprising light vehicles and artillery. Two Libyan G222s equipped for VIPs.

Armament: None

Operators: Argentina, Dubai, Italy, Libya, Nigeria, Somalia, Thailand, USA.

History: The G222's origins date back to an early 1960's NATO requirement for a V/STOL tactical transport.

The NATO requirement spawned a number of exotic V/STOL concepts, none of which were practical. The Italian Air Force placed a contract with Fiat to develop its G222 V/STOL concept, but importantly that contract was later extended to cover a conventionally configured STOL development, which laid the ground work for the definitive G222 transport. The Italian Air Force placed a contract for two prototype G222s in 1968, and, after a number of delays caused by external forces, the first G222 made the type's first flight on July 18 1970.

The two prototypes were unpressurised and powered by two lower rated CT64-820 engines, but otherwise the prototype and production aircraft were similar. Design features of the G222 include its good short field performance, large double slotted flaps, barrel shaped fuselage, rear freight ramp and tandem main undercarriage wheels with levered suspension. Much of the Italian aerospace industry was involved in the construction of the G222, with Aermacchi building the outer wings, Piaggio the wing centre sections and SIAI-Marchetti the tail.

Almost all of the G222s built were of the basic transport type, although 20 G222Ts built for Syria are powered by 3635kW (4860shp) Rolls-Royce Tynes. Other variants are the Chrysler C-27A Spartan, procured via Chrysler in 1990 from Alenia to fulfil transport duties with the US Air Force in South America; the Elint equipped G222VS; firefighting G222SAA; and the radio/radar calibration G222R/M.

Current G222 deliveries are to Thailand, which has ordered 10, while Australia is a prospective customer.

Photo: A taxying Italian Air Force G222 creates contrails with its spinning propellers. (Paul Merritt)

AMX International AMX

Countries of origin: Italy and Brazil

Type: Light attack aircraft

Powerplant: One 49.1kN (11,030lb) Rolls-Royce Spey Mk 807 non afterburning turbofan built under licence in Italy by Fiat, Piaggio and Alfa Romeo Avio, in cooperation with CELMA in Brazil.

Performance: Max speed 915km/h (493kt) at 36,000ft. Max initial rate of climb 10,250ft/min. Service ceiling 42,650ft. Combat radius at max takeoff weight with 2720kg (6000lb) of external payload lo-lo-lo 520km (205nm), hi-lo-hi 925km (500nm); combat radius at typical mission TO weight with 910kg (2000lb) of external stores lo-lo-lo 555km (300nm), hi-lo-hi 890km (480nm).

Weights: Operating empty 6700kg (14,770lb), max takeoff 13,000kg (28,660lb).

Dimensions: Wing span 8.87m (29ft 2in), length 13.58m (44ft 7in), height 4.58m (15ft 0in). Wing area 21.0m² (226.1sq ft).

Accommodation: Pilot only, seating for two in tandem in trainer.

Armament: Internal armament of a 20mm six barrel General Electric M61A1 Vulcan cannon in Italian aircraft, two 30mm DEFA cannons in Brazilian aircraft. External armament of up to 3800kg (8375lb) on four underwing, one centreline and two wingtip stations. Armaments include wingtip mounted AIM-9 Sidewinder or MAA-1 Piranha AAMs, unguided bombs, rockets and cluster munitions.

Operators: Brazil, Italy.

History: The AMX consortium resulted from similar air force specifications for a replacement for the G91 and F-104 (in ground attack roles) in Italian service, and the AT-26 Xavante (MB-326) in Brazilian service.

In the late 1970s Aermacchi was working with Embraer on the A-X, an Xavante replacement, while the Italian Air Force issued a formal requirement for a G91 replacement in 1977. Initial work on the AMX began in 1978 when Aeritalia (now Alenia) teamed with Aermacchi. Thus the involvement of Embraer, who joined the program in 1980 and who had been working with Aermacchi, was a logical development.

With an initial agreement for 266 production aircraft (79 for Brazil, 187 for Italy) reached in 1981, development of the AMX gathered pace and the first development prototype flew for the first time on May 15 1984. Construction of the first batch of 30 production aircraft and the design of a two seat AMX-T trainer began in mid 1986, while the first production aircraft, for Italy, first flew in May 1988.

Design of the AMX is fairly conservative, with power supplied by the proven Spey turbofan. Design features include HOTAS controls and HUD, multi function displays, INS navigation and ECM, with provision in the nose for FLIR or radar (Aermacchi has flown an AMX-T fitted with a GRIFO radar). In addition, three different Aeroelectronica of Brazil developed reconnaissance pallets can be fitted in the forward fuselage, while recce pods can be fitted on the external hardpoints. The AMX-T could also be adopted for ECR and anti shipping.

The workshare arrangements of AMX has Alenia as program leader with a 46.7% share of production, Aermacchi with a 23.6% share and Embraer with 29.7%. Component manufacture is not duplicated, however there are separate final assembly lines in Italy and Brazil. An export order from Thailand was subsequetly cancelled.

Photo: The AMX replaces G91s and Xavantes.

Antonov/PZL Mielec An-2

Country of origin: Ukraine

Type: General purpose utility biplane

Powerplant: An-2P – One 745kW (1000hp) PZL Kalisz ASz-61IR nine cylinder radial piston engine driving an AW-2 four bladed variable pitch propeller.

Performance: An-2P – Max speed 258km/h (139kt) at 5740ft, economical cruising speed 185km/h (100kt). Max initial rate of climb 690ft/min. Range at 3280ft with a 500kg (1100lb) cargo 900km (485nm).

Weights: An-2P – Empty 3450kg (7605lb), max takeoff 5500kg (12,125lb).

Dimensions: Upper wing span 18.18m (59ft 8in), lower 14.24m (46ft 9in), length (tail down) 12.40m (40ft 8in). Upper wing area 43.5m² (468.7sq ft), lower 28.0m² (301.2 sq ft).

Accommodation: Flightcrew of one or two pilots. Passenger accommodation for 12 at three abreast.

Armament: None, although some aircraft have been modified to carry a small bomb load.

Operators: An-2 – Operators include Afghanistan, Angola, Azerbaijan, Byelorussia, Bulgaria, Croatia, Cuba, Czech Republic, Georgia, Laos, Latvia, Mali, Mongolia, Nicaragua, Poland, Romania, Russia, Slovak Republic, Tadjikistan, Turkmenistan, Ukraine, Uzbekistan, Vietnam. Y-5 – Albania, China, North Korea.

History: The An-2 was originally designed to a USSR Ministry of Agriculture and Forestry requirement, and as well as large scale civil use was adopted in significant numbers by air arms of numerous Soviet aligned countries for a multitude of utility roles.

First flown on August 31 1947, the An-2 entered production and service the following year. The unusual biplane configuration was chosen for its good takeoff performance, docile low speed handling and excellent climb rates, and the wings were fitted with leading edge slats and double slotted flaps, further improving performance, while power was supplied by a 745kW (1000hp) ASh-62 radial. Soviet production continued through until 1960, by which time a number of variants had been developed, including the base model An-2P, An-2S and -2M crop sprayers, An-2VA water bomber, An-2M floatplane and the An-2ZA high altitude meteorological research aircraft.

Production responsibility was transferred to Poland's PZL Mielec in 1960, with the first Polish An-2 flying on October 23 1960. Aside from the An-2P, Polish versions include the An-2PK VIP transport, An-2PR for TV relay work, An-2S ambulance, An-2TD paratroop transport, An-2P cargo/passenger version and An-2 Geofiz geophysical survey version.

Chinese production as the Y-5 commenced with Nanchang in 1957, before being transferred to the Shijiazhuang Aircraft Plant. The main Chinese version is the standard Y-5N, while the latest development is the Y-5B specialist ag aircraft, which first flew in June 1989.

An Antonov turboprop powered version, the An-3, was developed in the late 1980s, but did not enter production.

In military service the An-2 is used in a wide variety of missions including paratroop transport, special forces insertion (North Korea in particular dedicates large numbers for this role), navigation trainer and general utility work, and it has even seen service as a light bomber.

Photo: The An-2 has the NATO reporting name of 'Colt'. (Paul Merritt)

Antonov An-12

Country of origin: Ukraine

Type: Tactical transport

Powerplants: An-12BP – Four 2985kW (4000ehp) Ivchenko (now Progress) AI-20K turboprops, driving four bladed constant speed propellers.

Performance: An-12BP – Max speed 777km/h (420kt), max cruising speed 670km/h (360kt). Max initial rate of climb 1970ft/min. Service ceiling 33,465ft. Takeoff run at max takeoff weight 700m (2296ft). Range with max fuel 5700km (3075nm), range with max payload 3600km (1940nm).

Weights: An-12BP – Empty 28,000kg (61,728lb), max takeoff 61,000kg (134,480lb).

Dimensions: An-12BP – Wing span 38.00m (124ft 8in), length 33.10m (108ft 7in), height 10.53m (34ft 7in). Wing area 121.7m² (1310sq ft).

Accommodation: Flightcrew of two pilots, flight engineer, navigator (in glazed nose) and radio operator, plus loadmasters. Can carry up to 20 tonnes (44,060lb) of freight such as artillery, light armoured vehicles and missile carriers, or alternatively up to 90 equipped troops or paratroopers.

Armament: Two tail mounted 23mm cannon (not on all aircraft).

Operators: China (Y-8), Czech Republic, Egypt, Ethiopia, Iraq, Russia, Sri Lanka (Y-8), Ukraine, Yemen.

History: For many years the An-12 (NATO codename 'Cub') provided the backbone of Soviet and Warsaw Pact air forces' medium lift transport capability, but the type, generally considered the Russian equivalent of the C-130, is now being replaced by more modern airlifters.

The origins of the An-12 lie in the original An-8, a twin turboprop powered military transport which featured the classical military freighter configuration of a high wing and rear loading ramp. About 100 An-8s were built and the type formed the basis for the stretched, four engined, An-10 airliner for Aeroflot. The An-10 in turn formed the basis for the An-12, the main differences between the two being the latter's more upswept rear fuselage and rear loading ramp.

The An-12 flew for the first time in 1958, powered by Kuznetsov NK-4 turboprops. The definitive production freighter meanwhile, the An-12BP, is powered by Ivchenko AI-20s. The An-12 remained in production until 1973, with a number also delivered to Aeroflot and Soviet aligned airlines. Its replacement in Russian service is the Il-76.

Various special missions variants of the An-12 have been developed, but details on these aircraft are sketchy. Many aircraft have been converted for Elint, festooned with various antennae, and these are covered by the NATO designations 'Cub-A', and 'Cub-B', while the 'Cub C' and more recently the 'Cub-D' are ECM aircraft. Unconfirmed reports have suggested the development of a command post variant, while others have been used for research and development tasks.

XIAN in China meanwhile developed the improved Y-8 from 1968. A number of variants have been developed (all built by Shaanxi Aircraft Company), including the Y-8A helicopter carrier, pressurised Y-8C (developed with assistance from Lockheed), Y-8D export aircraft with western avionics and Y-8E drone carrier. A single Y-8X maritime patrol and ASW aircraft has also flown. The Y-8 remains in production.

Photo: The Czech Air Force's sole An-12 transport at rest. (Paul Merritt)

Antonov An-22 Antheus

Country of origin: Ukraine

Type: Strategic turboprop freighter

Powerplants: Four 11,185kW (15,000shp) Kuznetsov (now Kuibyshev) NK-12MA turboprops, driving eight bladed counter rotating propellers.

Performance: Max speed 740km/h (400kt), cruising speed 520km/h (281kt). Range with max fuel and 45 tonne (99,200lb) payload 10,950km (5905nm), range with max payload 5000km (2692nm).

Weights: Typical empty equipped 114,000kg (251,325lb), max takeoff 250,000kg (551,160lb).

Dimensions: Wing span 29.2m (95ft 10in), length 25.53m (77ft 3in), height 8.32m (27ft 4in). Wing area 72.5m^2 (780.0sq ft).

Accommodation: Flightcrew of up to six, comprising two pilots, navigator, flight engineer and a communications specialist. Up to 29 passengers can be accommodated on the upper deck behind the flightdeck. Total An-22 payload is 80,000kg (176,350lb).

Armament: None

Operators: Russia

History: The massive An-22 (NATO reporting name 'Cock') is by far the largest turboprop powered aircraft yet built and was a remarkable technological achievement when it first appeared.

Antonov designed the An-22 in response to a Soviet military requirement for a strategic heavylift freighter, and when it made its first flight on February 27 1965 it was easily the largest aircraft in the world. Subsequent production of the An-22 lasted until 1974.

The An-22's NK-12 turboprops, which also power the Tu-95/Tu-142 'Bear' family of bombers, are the most powerful turboprop engines in service. Other notable An-22 features include comprehensive navigation and precision drop avionics complete with three separate radars, 14 wheel undercarriage (tyre pressures can be adjusted from the flightdeck to optimise the aircraft for different runway surfaces), integral rear loading ramp, twin tails and double slotted flaps.

After entering service, the An-22 set 14 payload to height records in 1967, the pinnacle of which was the carriage of 100 tonnes (220,500lb) of metal blocks to an altitude of 25,748ft (7848m). It also established the record for a maximum payload lifted to a height of 2000m (6562ft), carrying a payload of 104,445kg (221,443lb). A number of speed records were also set in 1972, including a speed of 608.5km/h (328kt) around a 1000km (540nm) circuit with a 50,000kg (110,250lb) payload. Further speed with payload records were established in 1974 and 1975.

Almost all An-22s, while primarily built for the Soviet air force, wear Aeroflot colours. The An-22s' 'civilian' colours and status allowed them much freer access to landing and overflight rights than had they been operated in military markings. The aircraft have also widely been used for civil operations.

While the An-22 has been superseded by the larger, turbofan powered An-124 (described separately), the surviving aircraft are still heavily utilised as they offer rare payload carrying characteristics.

Photo: Note the 14 wheel undercarriage of the An-22 as it is about to touch down. (Dave Fraser)

Antonov An-26 & An-32

Country of origin: Ukraine

Type: Tactical transport

Powerplants: An-24B – Two 2075kW (2780ehp) ZMKB Progress (formerly Ivchenko) AI-24VT turboprops driving four bladed propellers, and one auxiliary 7.85kN (1765lb) Soyuz (formerly Tumansky) RU-19A-300 turbojet. An-32 – Two 3760kW (5042ehp) ZMKB Progress AI-20D Series 5 turboprops.

Performance: An-24B – Cruising speed 435km/h (235kt). Max initial rate of climb 1575ft/min. Takeoff run on sealed runway 870m (2855ft). Range with max payload and no reserves 1240km (670nm), range with max fuel and no reserves 2660km (1435nm). An-32 – Max cruising speed 530km/h (285kt), economical cruising speed 470km/h (254kt). Service ceiling 30,840ft. Takeoff run on sealed runway 760m (2495ft/min). Range with max payload 1200km (645nm), range with max fuel 2520km (1360nm).

Weights: An-24B – Empty 14,750kg (32,518lb), max takeoff 24,000kg (52,910lb). An-32 – Empty 16,800kg (37,038lb), max takeoff 27,000kg (59,525lb).

Dimensions: An-24B – Wing span 29.20m (95ft 2in), length 23.80m (78ft 1in), height 8.58m (28ft 2in). Wing area 75.0m^2 (807.1sq ft). An-32 – Wing span 23.78m (78ft 0in), length 23.80m (78ft 1in), height 8.75m (28ft 9in). Wing area 75.0m^2 (807.1sq ft).

Accommodation: An-24B – Flightcrew of two pilots, flight engineer, navigator and radio operator, plus loadmaster. Seating for up to 40 troops or 24 stretcher patients. An-32 – Flightcrew of two pilots and navigator.

Armament: None, although some have been fitted with bomb racks.

Operators: An-24 – Afghanistan, Angola, Bangladesh, Benin, Bulgaria, Cape Verde, China, Cuba, Congo, Czech Republic, Germany, Ethiopia, Guinea Bissau, Hungary, Iraq, Laos, Libya, Madagascar, Mali, Mongolia, Mozambique, Nicaragua, Poland, Romania, Russia, Serbia, Slovakia, Ukraine, Vietnam, Yemen, Zambia. An-32 – Afghanistan, Bangladesh, Cuba, Czech Republic, India, Mongolia, Peru, Sri Lanka, Tanzania.

History: The An-26 has been the standard light tactical transport aircraft of almost every former Soviet Bloc country since the 1970s.

The An-26 (NATO reporting name 'Curl') is a militarised development of the An-24 airliner, which first flew in April 1963. The pressurised An-26 (first flight in 1968) differs from the An-24 in featuring a rear loading freight ramp, more powerful Ivchenko turboprops and a turbojet APU which can serve as an auxiliary engine for takeoff. More than 1000 An-26s and An-26Bs (with improved freight handling system) were built until the type was replaced in production by the improved An-32 (NATO reporting name Cline).

The An-32 first flew in the 1976 and features much more powerful engines for improved hot and high performance (the type finding favour with air forces which operate in such environments). The An-32 features improved systems and is visually identifiable by its above wing mounted engines, which give greater ground clearance for the increased diameter propellers.

Meanwhile Xian in China has developed the Y7 and the Y7H from the An-24, and some are in Chinese military service.

Photo: The An-26 remains the standard tactical transport of former Warsaw Pact nations, such as the Czech Republic. (Paul Merritt)

Antonov An-70

Country of origin: Ukraine

Type: Heavy freighter

Powerplants: Four 10,450kW (14,000hp) Progress D-27 turboprops driving all composite Stupino SV-27 14 bladed propellers.

Performance: Design cruising speed at 28,000 to 31,000ft 750 to 800km/h (405 to 430kt). Takeoff run at normal TO weight 1500m (4920ft), at max TOW 1800m (5905m). Range on typical transport mission carrying 20,000kg (44,100lb) of cargo 5350km (2885nm), or 3100km (1670nm) with a 30,000kg (66,135lb) payload.

Weights: Normal takeoff 112,000kg (246,900lb), max takeoff 130,000kg (286,600lb).

Dimensions: Wing span 44.06m (144ft 7in), length 40.25m (132ft 1in), height 16.10m (52ft 10in).

Accommodation: Flightcrew of two pilots and a flight engineer, plus accommodation for two loadmasters. Designed to accept a large percentage of NATO and CIS military equipment.

Operators: None

Armament: None

History: The An-70 was developed by Antonov as a replacement for its An-12 'Cub' freighter, which is currently in widespread military and civilian use with operators throughout the CIS. Originally designed to be in production in 1988, delays will now not see it enter service until some time in the late 1990s, if at all.

The An-70, as one of the most recent aircraft to be developed in the Commonwealth of Independent States, incorporates a range of modern technology design concepts. The most prominent feature of the An-70 is its four Russian designed propfans consisting of 14 bladed Stupino scimitar propellers and the Progress turboprops. These are designed to offer a very high speed combined with a very low fuel consumption, equivalent to burning 30% less fuel than the less powerful An-12. The Russian developed SV-27 all composite propellers are highly swept and are claimed to have a 90% efficiency in cruise, at near jet speeds.

Takeoff and landing speeds are also lower thanks to the propfans, while its ability to fly from relatively short fields means it can operate from 80% of all CIS airstrips, allowing shorter journeys and greater point to point flights.

Composite materials are used throughout the airframe, including the horizontal and vertical tails which are all composite. The An-70 also incorporates one of the most advanced electronic cockpits yet incorporated into a CIS designed aircraft including full colour digital displays and a head up display used for landings on short strips. The digital avionics are also linked via a databus equivalent to US 1553B standard, believed to be another first for a CIS aircraft, and allowing far easier integration of western avionics in the future.

The An-70 program was thrown into doubt in February 1995 when the sole prototype collided with its An-72 chase plane while on a test flight. At that time completion of a second prototype was still some time off. However, at least one report states that Russia remains committed to the program.

Photo: The crash of the sole An-70 prototype may have put an end to development of this promising aircraft.

Antonov An-72 & An-74

Country of origin: Ukraine

Type: STOL utility and (An-74) polar transport

Powerplants: Two 63.7kN (14,330lb) ZMKB Progress D-36 turbofans.

Performance: An-72 – Max speed 705km/h (380kt), cruising speed at 32,800ft 550 to 600km/h (295 to 325kt). Service ceiling 38,715ft. Range with max fuel and reserves 4800km (2590nm), with a 7500kg (16,535lb) payload 2000km (1080nm). An-74 – Range with a 1500kg (3310lb) payload 5300km (2860nm). An-72P – Patrol speed 300 to 350km/h (162 to 189kt). Service ceiling 33,135ft. Max endurance 5hr 18min.

Weights: An-72 – Empty 19,050kg (41,997lb), max takeoff (from a 1800m/5900ft runway) 34,500kg (76,060lb), max TO from a 1000m (3280ft) runway 27,500kg (60,625lb). An-72P – Max takeoff 37,500kg (82,670lb).

Dimensions: An-72 – Wing span 31.89m (104ft 8in), length 28.07m (92ft 1in), height 8.65m (28ft 5in). Wing area 98.6m² (1062sq ft).

Accommodation: An-72 flightcrew of two pilots and a flight engineer, An-74 has provision for a radio operator. Can carry a payload of 10 tonnes (22,045lb). An-72 can also seat 68 on removable seats.

Armament: An-72P – One 23mm gun pod, a UB-23M rocket launcher and four 100kg (220lb) bombs. Improved development offered by IAI can carry Griffin laser guided bombs.

Operators: Russia, Ukraine.

History: The An-72 (NATO came 'Coaler') was designed as a replacement for the An-26 tactical transport in service for the Soviet Air Forces.

The first of two An-72 prototypes flew for the first time on December 22 1977, although it was not until much later in 1985 that the first of eight extensively revised pre production An-72s flew. Included in this pre production batch were two An-74s, differing from the An-72s in their ability to operate in harsh weather conditions in polar regions because of an improved avionics suite.

Transport versions of the An-72 family include the An-72A base model with extended wings and fuselage compared to the prototypes, the An-72AT which can carry international standard containers, and the An-72S VIP transport. Versions of the An-74 include the base An-74A with enlarged nose radome, the An-74T freighter, the An-74TK convertible passenger/freighter model, and the An-74P-100 VIP transport. A prototype AEW An-74 has also flown. The An-72P maritime patrol aircraft meanwhile is based on the basic An-72 fuselage fitted with a 23mm gun, rocket pods, four light bombs carried internally, day and night downward looking and oblique optical cameras and an optical TV sight. The An-72P is intended for close-in coastal surveillance and Russia has ordered 20. Antonov is now offering an improved development of the An-72P in conjunction with Israel Aircraft Industries. Changes include a glass cockpit, Elta EL/M 2022A radar, Electro Optical day and night long range observation system and Elisra electronic warfare suite.

The most significant design feature of the An-72 and An-74 is the use of engine exhaust gases blown over the wing's upper surface to improve STOL performance and lift. Other features include multi slotted flaps, rear loading ramp and a multi unit landing gear system allowing operations from unprepared strips.

Photo: An An-72P demonstrator, note rocket launcher. (Paul Merritt)

Antonov An-124 Ruslan

Country of origin: Ukraine

Type: Heavy lift strategic transport

Powerplants: Four 229.5kN (51.590lb) ZMKB Progress (Lotarev) D-18T turbofans.

Performance: Max cruising speed 865km/h (468kt), typical cruising speeds between 800 and 850km/h (430 to 460kt). Range with max payload 4500km (2430nm), range with full fuel load 16,500km (8900nm).

Weights: Operating empty 175,000kg (385,800lb), max takeoff 405,000kg (892,875lb).

Dimensions: Wing span 73.30m (240ft 6in), length 69.10m (226ft 9in), height 20.78m (68ft 2in). Wing area 628.0m² (6760sq ft).

Accommodation: Flightcrew of six consisting of two pilots, two flight engineers, navigator and communications operator. Upper deck behind the flightdeck area comprises a galley, rest room and two relief crew cabins. Upper deck area behind the wing can accommodate up to 88 passengers. Main deck cargo compartment is designed to carry an extremely large range of bulky and oversized cargos including 12 ISO standard containers, heavy artillery, main battle tanks, SAM systems, helicopters, SS-20 mobile IRMB, etc. The An-124's total payload in weight is 150 tonnes (330,695lb).

Armament: None

Operators: Russia, Ukraine.

History: The massive An-124 for a time held the mantle of the world's largest aircraft before the arrival of the An-225, a stretched six engine derivative, and is the largest aircraft in the world to achieve full production status.

The An-124 was developed primarily as a strategic military freighter to replace the turboprop powered An-22 (described separately) but also for use by the Soviet state airline Aeroflot for carriage of bulky and oversize cargos. The first prototype An-124 flew on December 26 1982, while a second prototype, named Ruslan after Pushkin's mythical giant, made the type's first western public appearance at the Paris airshow in mid 1985, preceding the type's first commercial operations in January 1986. Since that time the An-124 set a wide range of payload records, its latest achievement being the heaviest single load ever transported by air – a 124 tonne powerplant generator and its associated weight spreading cradle, a total payload weight of 132.4 tonnes, set in late 1993.

Except for its low set tail, the An-124's configuration is similar to the United States Air Force's Lockheed C-5 Galaxy (described separately), which, with a maximum takeoff weight of 350 tonnes, is slightly smaller. Notable features include nose and tail cargo doors which allows simultaneous loading and unloading, 24 wheel undercarriage allowing operations from semi prepared strips, the ability to 'kneel' to allow easier front loading and a fly-by-wire control system.

Almost all An-124s built serve under Aeroflot markings, but these aircraft commonly perform military tasks, while a smaller number of Ruslans are assigned directly to the Russian Air Force. The An-124 has the NATO reporting name of 'Condor'.

Photo: While most An-124s operate in Aeroflot or other civil markings, this example wears the Russian Air Force's red star.

Antonov An-225 Myria

Country of origin: Ukraine

Type: Strategic heavy lift transport

Powerplants: Six 229.5kN (51,590lb) ZMKB Progress (Lotarev) D-18T turbofans.

Performance: Cruising speed range 800 to 850km/h (430 to 460kt). Range with a 200,000kg (440,900lb) internal payload 4500km (2425nm); with a 100,000kg (220,450lb) internal payload 9600km (5180nm); with max fuel 15,400km (8310nm).

Weights: Max takeoff 600,000kg (1,322,750lb).

Dimensions: Wing span 88.40m (290ft 0in), length 84.00m (275ft 7in), height 18.20m (59ft 9in). Wing area 905.0m² (9741sq ft).

Accommodation: Flight crew of six consisting of two pilots, a navigator, a communications specialist and two flight engineers. Accommodation for a relief crew plus a further 60 to 70 personnel provided in upper deck cabin behind the flightdeck. The maximum payload of 250 tonnes (551,150lb) can be carried internally in the 43m (141ft) long main cargo deck, or externally on two mounting beams.

Armament: None

Operators: None

History: The massive An-225 Myria (or Dream) is easily the world's largest aircraft, holds a raft of international lifting records and is the only aircraft in the world with a maximum takeoff weight in excess of 1,000,000lb (453,600kg).

The An-225 was designed to participate in the Soviet space program, with its primary use being the external carriage of the Buran space shuttle orbiter. Design work on the An-225 commenced in mid 1985, culminating in the first flight on December 21 1988. Early into the flight trails program on March 22 1989 the Myria set a total of 106 records, on a 3.5 hour flight on which it took off at a weight of 508,200kg (1,120,370lb), with a 156,300kg (344,576lb) payload, flying a 2000km (1080nm) closed circuit at an average speed of 813km/h (439kt), reaching an altitude of 40,485ft. The Myria subsequently made its first flight with the Buran orbiter mounted on its back in May of that year.

The An-225 is a stretch of the earlier An-124, which was itself the world's largest aircraft up until the appearance of the Myria. Changes over the Ruslan include a substantially lengthened fuselage, increased span wings, six (instead of four) Lotarev (now Progress) turbofans, twin fins, deletion of the rear loading ramp, seven instead of five pairs of wheels on each side, and longitudinal mounting beams and faired attachment points to carry external loads. Like the An-124, the Myria uses fly-by-wire, and the two types share similar avionics suites.

As the An-224 was conceived for use in the Soviet space program the aircraft has not been adopted for military service, despite its obvious attractions (although it has been allocated the NATO reporting name of 'Cossack'). Just one An-224 has been built and flown, but this aircraft may now have been retired. A second An-225 has also been under construction, but a lack of funding sees it uncompleted.

Photo: The only flying An-225. Despite its attractions, the An-225 has not yet been used for military applications. (Bruce Malcolm)

Atlas CSH-2 Rooivalk

Country of origin: South Africa

Type: Attack helicopter

Powerplants: Two 1490kW (2000shp) Topaz (uprated Turboméca Makila 1A1) turboshafts, driving a four bladed main rotor and five bladed tail rotor.

Performance: (ISA at S/L) – Max cruising speed 278km/h (150kt). Max initial rate of climb 2200ft/min. Service ceiling 20,000ft. Hovering ceiling in ground effect 18,200ft. Range with max internal fuel and no reserves 705km (380nm), range at max TO weight with external fuel 1260km (680nm). Endurance with max internal fuel 3hr 35min, endurance with external fuel 6hr 50min.

Weights: Empty 5910kg (13,030lb), typical mission takeoff 7500kg (16,535lb), max takeoff 8750kg (19,290lb).

Dimensions: Main rotor diameter 15.58m (51ft 2in), length overall 18.73m (61ft 5in), fuselage length (incl tail rotor, excluding gun) 16.39m (53ft 9in), height 5.12m (17ft 0in). Main rotor disc area 190.6m² (2051sq ft).

Accommodation: Copilot/weapons operator and pilot in tandem.

Armament: Steerable chin mounted gun, standard fit 20mm Kentron GA-1 Rattler, or 20mm Armscor MG 151 or 30mm DEFA gun. Four underwing stores pylons can carry rocket launchers or ZT-3 Swift or ZT-35 laser guided anti tank missiles. Wingtip stations can carry V3C Darter infra red air-to-air missiles.

Operators: South Africa*

History: Born out of necessity because of the now lifted UN arms embargo, the Rooivalk (or Red Kestrel) was designed in response to a South African Air Force requirement for a combat support helicopter.

The Rooivalk design is based on experience Atlas gained from building and flying the XH-1 Alpha concept demonstrator, a one-off attack helicopter configured testbed based on the Alouette III. Development of the XH-1 began in 1981, resulting in a first flight on February 27 1986. The XH-1 retained the Alouette's engine, rotor and transmission systems combined with a new tandem two seat fuselage.

Design of the Rooivalk began in 1984, and subsequent experience with the XH-1, plus two Puma testbeds modified as gunships and designated XTP-1 Beta, allowed a first flight of the XH-2 Rooivalk prototype on February 11 1990. The XH-2 was later redesignated XDM (Experimental Development Model) and was joined by a second flying prototype, the ADM (Advanced Development Model), which is tasked with avionics and weapons development.

The Rooivalk uses the same, although uprated, Turboméca Makila 1A1 turboshafts, transmission and rotor system of the SA 330 Puma. Otherwise the Rooivalk is an all new aircraft, featuring stepped cockpits, extensive armouring, a gyro stabilised nose mounted turret with FLIR and TV sensors, laser rangefinder which make up an automatic target detection and tracking system. Production aircraft will feature cheeks on the side of the aircraft (similar to those on the AH-64D) housing ammunition and avionics.

Despite a requirement for more due to funding restrictions, South Africa has ordered only 16 Rooivalks for one squadron.

Photo: The symbol of a new South Africa – Atlas is aggressively marketing the Rooivalk on the world market. (Bruce Malcolm)

Atlas Cheetah

Countries of origin: South Africa and France

Type: Upgraded multirole fighter

Powerplant: EZ – One 42.0kN (9435lb) dry and 60.8kN (13,670lb) with afterburning SNECMA Atar 9C turbojet. Some two seaters and R2Z recce aircraft are powered by a 49.0kN (11,025lb) dry and 70.6kN (15,875lb) with afterburning Atar 9K-50.

Performance: EZ – Max speed 2338km/h (1262kt), max cruising speed 956km/h (516kt). Range and payload radius figures unpublished.

Weights: Unpublished.

Dimensions: EZ – Wing span 8.22m (27ft 0in), length including nose probe 15.65m (51ft 4in), height 4.55m (14ft 11in). Wing area 34.8m² (374.6sq ft).

Accommodation: Pilot only in EZs and RZs, two in DZ trainers.

Armament: Fixed armament comprises two 30mm DEFA cannons. Disposable stores carried on four underwing and three underfuselage stations including indigenously developed Armscor V3B Kukri and V3C Darter air-to-air missiles, AS20 air-to-ground missiles, bombs, cluster bombs and rockets, plus AIM-9 Sidewinder and Matra R550 air-to-air missiles.

Operators: South Africa

History: The Atlas Cheetah is one of the most comprehensive upgrades of the venerable Mirage III yet, with significant changes and improvements to the airframe, avionics and, in the case of two seaters, powerplant.

Like a number of South African developed weapon systems, the Cheetah was born out of necessity. A 1977 United Nations arms embargo has prevented South Africa from buying military equipment from the rest of the world, thus preventing any South African Air Force plans for a replacement of its ageing fleet of 1960s vintage Mirage IIIs coming to fruition. Instead, South Africa instigated its own mid life update program, reportedly with assistance from IAI in Israel.

The Cheetah upgrade was first publicly announced in 1986 when Atlas unveiled an upgraded Mirage two seater, the Cheetah D (or DZ). Main aerodynamic features of the Cheetah upgrade include structural modifications to extend fatigue life, canards, a stretched nose to house new avionics, dog tooth leading edge extensions, small strakes on the nose and small fences on the wing replacing leading edge slats. The two seaters also feature strakes along the lower fuselage below the cockpit. Internally the Cheetah features new avionics, believed to be of Israeli origin and including a MIL-STD 1553B databus, a Head-Up Display, HOTAS (Hands On Throttle And Stick) controls and a new nav/attack system with inertial navigation. The extended nose houses avionics plus an Elta EL/M-2001B radar.

Single seat Cheetahs are known as Cheetah Es or EZs, and retain the original SNECMA Atar 9C turbojet. Some of the two seaters have been fitted with the more powerful Atar 9K-50 turbojet as on the Mirage F1, for which Atlas has a manufacturing licence. Reconnaissance Cheetah R2s are already powered by the 9K-50.

A prototype Cheetah ACW with an advanced combat wing flew for the first time in 1992, while 12 EZs will be fitted with the Israeli Elta EL/M-2035 fire control radar, and the Atar 9K-50.

Photo: A single seat Cheetah E. (Atlas)

Avioane IAR-99 Soim & IAR-109 Swift

Country of origin: Romania

Type: Two seat basic and advanced trainer

Powerplant: IAR-99 – One 17.8kN (4000lb) Turbomecanica licence built Rolls-Royce Viper Mk 632-41M turbojet.

Performance: IAR-99 – Max speed at sea level 865km/h (467kt). Max initial rate of climb 6890ft/min. Service ceiling 42,325ft. Max range with internal fuel (trainer) 1100km (593nm), ground attack 967km (522nm). Combat radius with pilot only, ventral gun and four rocket pods lo-lo-lo 350km (190nm); with ventral gun, two rocket pods and 500kg (1100lb) of bombs hi-lo-hi 345km (185nm); with ventral gun and four 250kg (550lb) bombs hi-hi-hi 385km (208nm). Max endurance (trainer mission) 2hr 40min, (ground attack) 1hr 45min.

Weights: IAR-99 – Empty equipped 3200kg (7055lb), max takeoff (trainer) 4400kg (9700lb), (ground attack) 5560kg (12,258lb).

Dimensions: IAR-99 – Wing span 9.85m (32ft 4in), length 11.01m (36ft 2in), height 3.90m (12ft 10in). Wing area 18.7m² (201.4sq ft).

Accommodation: Two in tandem, though pilot only when flying ground attack missions.

Armament: Removable ventral gun pod contains a 23mm GSh-23 gun. Four underwing hardpoints can carry a combined load of 1000kg (2205lb), including light bombs and rocket pods.

Operators: Romania

History: Romania's indigenously developed IAR-99 Soim (Falcon) is a two seat advanced trainer and light attack aircraft in a similar vein to the Aermacchi MB-339 and Aero Albatros.

Development of the Soim began at Romania's Institute de Aviatc at Bucharest in the early 1980s, while the program's existence was first made public to the west at the 1983 Paris airshow. Romania's state aviation enterprise IAv Croavia (renamed Avioane in 1991) was entrusted with Soim production, and IAv built the first prototype which flew for the first time on December 21 1985.

Production of the Soim began in 1987 against an initial order for 20 from the Romanian air force. A second order for 30 is believed to have been placed, with low rate production to meet this order continuing. No export orders have been placed.

The Soim replaced the Romanian air force's Aero L-29 Delfins, providing basic and advanced training, as well as a secondary close air support/ground attack role, supplementing IAR-93s.

The IAR-109 Swift is an upgraded development of the Soim, aimed primarily at export orders. The Swift differs from the Soim in having advanced Israeli developed nav/attack avionics and modern cockpit (including HUD and multi function displays), and expanded weapons carrying capability (including the capability to launch infrared guided AAMs and laser guided bombs), and Martin Baker lightweight ejection seats. The airframe and engine remain unchanged. It is offered in IAR-109T basic trainer configuration and IAR-109TF armed combat trainer form.

Avioane announced development of the Swift in 1993, a converted IAR-99 served as the first prototype, while the first new build Swift flew for the first time in November 1993.

Photo: Avioane is now marketing its IAR-109 Swift on the world market. (Keith Anderson)

Beechcraft T-34 Mentor & Turbo Mentor

Country of origin: United States of America

Type: Two seat primary trainer

Powerplant: T-34A & B – One 170kW (225hp) Continental O-470 flat six piston engine, driving a two bladed propeller. T-34C – One 535kW (715shp) Pratt & Whitney Canada PT6A-25 turboprop derated to 300kW (400shp) driving a three bladed prop.

Performance: T-34A & B – Max speed 302km/h (163kt), max cruising speed 270km/h (145kt). Max initial rate of climb 1210ft/min. Service ceiling 21,200ft. Range 1240km (667nm). T-34C – Max speed 414km/h (224kt), max cruising speed 398km/h (215kt). Max initial rate of climb 1480ft/min. Service ceiling 30,000ft plus. Range 1310km (708nm) at 333km/h (180kt) cruising speed.

Weights: T-34A & B – Empty 932kg (2055lb), max takeoff 1315kg (2900lb). T-34C – Empty 1193kg (2630lb), max takeoff 1938kg (4274lb).

Dimensions: T-34A & B – Wing span 10.01m (32ft 10in), length 7.87m (25ft 10in), height 2.92m (9ft 7in). Wing area 16.5m² (177.6sq ft). T-34C – Wing span 10.16m (33ft 4in), length 8.75m (28ft 9in), height 3.02m (9ft 11in). Wing area 16.71m² (179.9sq ft).

Accommodation: Seating for two in tandem.

Armament: T-34C-1 – Four underwing hardpoints can carry up to 545kg (1200lb) of practice and light bombs, rockets, miniguns, AGM-22A anti tank missiles or towed target equipment.

Operators: Mentor – Argentina, Colombia, Dominica, El Salvador, Philippines, Turkey, Uruguay, Venezuela. Turbo Mentor – Argentina, Ecuador, Gabon, Indonesia, Morocco, Peru, Taiwan, Uruguay, USA.

History: Perhaps the most successful western, postwar, basic trainer built, the T-34 is based on one of civil aviation's most successful light aircraft types, the Beech 35 Bonanza.

The prototype four seat Beech Bonanza flew for the first time on December 22 1945, predating a production run that began in 1947 and continues to this day. In 1948 Beech took the Bonanza design as the basis for a military basic trainer. The private venture Model 45 Mentor differed from the Bonanza in having seating for two in tandem and a conventional tail unit (the Model 35 Bonanza being famous for its V tail). The Model 45 Mentor flew for the first time on December 2 1948, arousing the interest of the newly formed US Air Force enough so that that service ordered three evaluation examples.

The three evaluation YT-34s were delivered in 1950, and successful testing led the USAF to order the first of an eventual 450 T-34As in 1953. That year the USN evaluated the T-34 and ordered 290 similar T-34Bs in mid 1954. Mentors were also built under licence in Canada and Japan and assembled in Argentina and in all over 1300 were built. USAF Mentors were retired in 1960.

The success of the Mentor led to a 1973 USN request for Beech to build a turboprop powered development to replace the T-34B and also the North American T-28 Trojan. The resulting Pratt & Whitney Canada PT6A powered T-34C Turbo Mentor (dubbed Tormentor) flew for the first time on September 21 1973. A total of 352 T-34Cs were built (the last of which, attrition replacements for the USN, were delivered in 1990), most of which were for the US Navy, but 129 armed T-34C-1s were exported.

Photo: A Morrocan Air Force T-34 Turbo Mentor.

Beechcraft King Air

Country of origin: United States of America

Type: Utility, VIP, Elint, ESM, Sigint & maritime patrol aircraft

Powerplants: B200T – Two 635kW (850shp) Pratt & Whitney Canada PT6A-42 turboprops, driving three bladed propellers.

Performance: B200T – Max cruising speed 490km/h (265kt) at 4990kg (11,000lb) AUW, typical patrolling speed 260km/h (140kt). Range with max fuel, patrolling at 420km/h (227kt) with reserves 3315km (1790nm). Typical endurance at 260km/h (140kt) patrolling speed with reserves 6hr 35min. Max time on station with wingtip fuel tanks fitted 9hr.

Weights: B200T – Empty 3745kg (8255lb), max takeoff 5670kg (12,500lb), max takeoff restricted category 6805kg (15,000lb).

Dimensions: Wing span over tip tanks 17.25m (56ft 7in), wing span 16.61m (54ft 6in), length 13.34m (43ft 9in), height 4.57m (15ft 0in). Wing area 28.2m² (303.0sq ft).

Accommodation: Flightcrew of two. Main cabin seating for up to eight in King Air 90 family, 13 in 100, 200, 300 and 350 series.

Armament: None

Operators: 90 series – Includes Bolivia, Chile, Colombia, Ecuador, Ivory Coast, Jamaica, Japan, Mexico, Morroco, Peru, Thailand, USA, Venezuela. 200 series – Includes Algeria, Argentina, Bolivia, Ecuador, Greece, Guatemala, India, Ireland, Israel, Ivory Coast, Japan, Libya, Morocco, Peru, Sudan, Sweden, Thailand, Togo, Turkey, USA, Venezuela. RC-12 – USA. B200T – Algeria, Malaysia, Peru, Puerto Rico, Uruguay.

History: A highly successful family of light corporate aircraft in civilian life, Beech's King Air series has also been adopted for a diverse range of military tasks, ranging from transport to Elint gathering.

The King Air series began life as a turboprop powered development of the piston engined Queen Air (itself developed from the civil Twin Bonanza) which today is in limited military service with Colombia, Dominica, Ecuador, Israel, Peru, Uruguay and the US Army. The initial 90 series King Air differed from the Queen Air primarily in having two Pratt & Whitney Canada PT6 turboprops and pressurisation. First flown in January 1964 it remains in military service with a number of nations. US military developments of the 90 King Air include the US Army's unpressurised U-21 Ute and the RU-21 Elint aircraft, and the US Navy's T-44 Pegasus trainer.

Beech stretched the King Air 90 in 1969 to come up with the King Air 100, but the by far the most important military King Airs are based on the 200. The Super King Air 200 used the stretched 100's fuselage, combined with a T tail and first flew in October 1972. Most Super King Airs are used as transports (designated C-12 in US service). A small number of Maritime Patrol B200Ts are in military service, fitted with a search radar, bubble observation windows and wings that can be fitted with tip tanks. Optional B200T equipment includes ESM, GPS, FLIR, sonobuoys and processor and a tactical navigation computer. The US Army's RC-12 Guardrail meanwhile has been developed in a number of progressively improved developments, used for intercepting enemy radio transmissions.

Military developments of the Super King Air 300 and stretched 350 series are also on offer.

Photo: A US Army RC-12 Guardrail Elint aircraft. (Paul Merritt)

Beech T-1A Jayhawk & T-400

Country of origin: United States of America

Type: Tanker & transport aircrew trainer

Powerplants: Two 12.9kN (2900lb) P&WC JT15D-5 turbofans.

Performance: Max level speed 867km/h (468kt) at 27,000ft, typical cruising speed at 12,500ft 835km/h (450kt), long range cruising speed 725km/h (392kt). Service ceiling 41,000ft. Range with max fuel and four passengers at long range cruising speed 3575km (1930nm).

Weights: Operating empty 4589kg (10,115lb), max takeoff 7157kg (15,780kg).

Dimensions: Wing span 13.25m (43ft 6in), length 14.75m (48ft 5in), height 4.24m (13ft 11in). Wing area 22.4m² (241.4sq ft).

Accommodation: T-1A – Student pilot and instructor side by side on flightdeck, with observer seated behind them on a jump seat. Main cabin can accommodate four passengers or waiting students.

Armament: None

Operators: T-1 – USA. T-400 – Japan.

History: The Jayhawk is an off-the-shelf development of the Beechjet 400A business jet acquired to meet a US Air Force requirement for a Tanker Transport/Training System (TTTS) aircraft.

The TTTS requirement was formulated as part of the US Air Force's Specialized Undergraduate Pilot Training system which is designed to make USAF pilot training more efficient and to ease strain on the Northrop T-38 Talon fleet. The TTTS requirement was issued in the late 1980s, with the USAF considering proposals from British Aerospace, Learjet, Cessna and Beech. In February 1991 the USAF ordered the first 28 of an eventual requirement for 168 Beechjet 400A based T-1A Jayhawks. The first was delivered in January 1992 and an initial operating capability (IOC) was achieved in January 1993. Deliveries are occurring at about a rate of three per month, through until 1997. Pilots training on the T-1 will go on to fly transports such as the C-17, C-5, KC-10 and KC-135.

The Beechjet 400 design began life as the Mitsubishi MU-300 Diamond, which first flew in August 1978. The improved Diamond 2 production aircraft flew in June 1984, but only 11 production aircraft were built before Beech acquired the manufacturing and development rights. Beech replaced the Diamond 2's JT15D-4s with -5s, improved the interior, moved production to the USA and renamed the aircraft the Beechjet 400.

The improved Beechjet 400A, on which the T-1 is based, first flew in September 1989 and introduced a number of improvements including EFIS, increased the weights and repositioned the rear fuselage fuel tank to increase cabin volume.

The T-1 differs from the 400A in having fewer cabin windows, the avionics relocated from the nose to the cabin, greater fuel capacity, single point refuelling, TACAN, reinforced windscreen protection against birdstrikes and strengthening of the wing carry through structure and engine pylons to handle increased low-level flight stresses.

The Japanese Air Self Defence Force also selected the Beechjet as the basis for a transport aircrew trainer, designated the T-400. Three T-400s (with six on option) are fitted with the optional thrust reversers, plus long range inertial navigation and direction finding systems.

Photo: A USAF T-1A Jayhawk. (Raytheon)

Bell 47G/H-13 Sioux

Country of origin: United States of America

Type: Light utility, training and observation helicopter

Powerplant: 47G-3B-2A – One 210kW (280hp) Lycoming TVO-435-F1A flat six piston engine, driving a two bladed main rotor and two bladed tail rotor.

Performance: 47G-3B-2A – Max speed 170km/h (91kt), cruising speed 135km/h (73kt) at 5000ft. Max initial rate of climb 880ft/min. Service ceiling 19,000ft. Hovering ceiling in ground effect 17,700ft, out of ground effect 12,700ft. Range 395km (215nm) at 6000ft.

Weights: 47G-3B-2A – Empty 858kg (1893lb), max takeoff 1340kg (2950lb).

Dimensions: 47G-3B-2A – Main rotor diameter 11.32m (37ft 2in), length overall 13.30m (43ft 8in), fuselage length 9.63m (31ft 7in), height 2.83m (9ft 4in). Main rotor disc area 100.8m² (1085sq ft).

Accommodation: Seating for two or three occupants, side-by-side. Can carry two stretchers, one on each skid.

Armament: None

Operators: Argentina, Greece, Indonesia, Malaysia, Malta, New Zealand, Pakistan, Peru, Taiwan, Thailand, Turkey, Uruguay, Zambia.

History: Both in the military and civil spheres, the Bell 47 is recognised as being one of the first practical helicopters, and was the first to see widespread military use.

The lineage of the Bell dates back to 1943 and the Bell Model 30, an experimental helicopter ordered by the US Army for evaluation. The US Army ordered 10 Model 30s for evaluation, and the type formed the basis for the improved Model 47. The Model 47's first flight was on December 8 1945. The prototype 47 featured seating for two side by side, with a car type cabin and was powered by a Franklin piston engine, and in this initial form the 47 became the first helicopter to be certificated by the USA's Civil Aeronautics Administration.

The promise the Bell helicopter showed soon translated into military orders from the US services, the USAAF ordering 28 as YR-13s in 1947 for evaluation, some of which went to the US Navy as HTL-1 trainers. In 1948 the US Army ordered 65, designated H-13Bs. The name Sioux was adopted later.

By 1953 Bell was producing the definitive Model 47 variant, the 47G, which featured progressively more powerful engines, plus the previously introduced goldfish bowl canopy and uncovered tail, the two features which make the Bell 47 probably the most recognised helicopter in the world. The 47G remained in production through to the 1970s, and was also licence built by Agusta in Italy and Kawasaki in Japan.

The H-13 saw widespread US military service during the Korean War, where the type was used for a range of roles such as medevac (fitted with stretchers on either skid), observation and utility transport, and proved beyond doubt the utility of the helicopter.

Today the Bell 47 remains only in limited military service, having largely been replaced by more modern and more capable types, with most in use as trainers or for light utility work.

Photo: New Zealand's Sioux are used for pilot training. (RNZAF)

Bell UH-1B & UH-1C Iroquois

Country of origin: United States of America

Type: Troop transport & utility helicopter

Powerplant: UH-1B & UH-1C – One 820kW (1100shp) Lycoming T53-L-9 or L-11 turboshaft, driving two bladed main rotor and tail rotors.

Performance: UH-1B – Max speed 222km/h (120kt), normal cruising speed 193km/h (104kt). Max initial rate of climb 1900ft/min. Service ceiling 16,7000ft. Hovering ceiling out of ground effect 11,800ft. Range 463km (250nm). UH-1C – Max speed and max cruising speed 238km/h (130kt), normal cruising speed 230km/h (124kt). Max initial rate of climb 1400ft/min. Service ceiling 11,500ft. Hovering ceiling in ground effect 10,600ft, hovering ceiling out of ground effect 10,000ft. Range 615km (332nm) with auxiliary fuel.

Weights: UH-1B – Empty 2050kg (4520lb), max takeoff 3855kg (8500lb). UH-1C – Empty 2300kg (5070lb), max takeoff 4310kg (9500lb).

Dimensions: Main rotor diameter 13.41m (44ft 0in), length overall rotors turning 16.15m (53ft 0in), fuselage length 11.70m (38ft 5in), height 3.84m (12ft 7in). Main rotor disc area 141.3m² (1520sq ft).

Accommodation: Pilot and copilot or passenger on flightdeck, with six troops in main cabin. Alternatively main cabin can accommodate three stretchers and a medical attendant.

Armament: UH-1B/C – Can be fitted with a variety of weaponry including a 7.62mm minigun. AB 204AS – Two Mark 44 torpedoes.

Operators: Austria, Indonesia, Japan, Panama, Singapore, South Korea, Spain, Sweden, Thailand, Uruguay, USA, Yemen.

History: The Iroquois has a very special place in modern military history. Produced in more numbers than any other western military aircraft since WW2, it is indelibly linked with the Vietnam War, where it proved beyond a doubt the importance and value of helicopter air mobility to land warfare.

The Iroquois, or Huey, began life in response to a 1954 US Army requirement for a turbine utility helicopter, primarily for medevac. Bell responded to the request with its Lycoming T53 powered Model 204, which was selected for development and the first of the XH-40 prototypes flew on October 22 1956. The XH-40s were followed by six larger, pre production YH-40s, basically representative of early production aircraft which up until 1962 were designated HU-1A, hence 'Huey'.

The HU-1B or UH-1B introduced a further enlarged cabin and a modified main rotor, and it was this model which was the first to see widespread service in Vietnam, both as a transport and fitted out as a gunship. War experience with gunship configured UH-1Bs led to the UH-1C with an improved rotor system and higher top speed. The UH-1E was similar but developed for the USMC as an assault support helicopter and also built in TH-1E (USMC) and TH-1L (USN) trainer versions. The UH-1F was developed for the USAF and used for missile range support duties and was powered by a General Electric T58 and featured the tailboom of the larger UH-1D (described separately).

Aside from Bell production, short fuselage UH-1s were built in Japan (Fuji) and Italy (by Agusta). Aside from the T53, Agusta built AB 204Bs were powered with the Bristol Siddeley Gnome or GE's T58. The T58 powered AB 204AS was developed specifically for ASW and was fitted with radar and sonar and could carry Mk 44 torpedoes.

Photo: An Austrian AB 204B. (Austrian AF)

Bell 205, UH-1D & UH-1H Iroquois

Country of origin: United States of America

Type: Utility and battlefield helicopters

Powerplant: UH-1H – One 1045kW (1400shp) Lycoming T53-L-13 turboshaft, driving a two bladed main rotor and two bladed tail rotor.

Performance: Max speed and max cruising speed 205km/h (110kt). Max initial rate of climb 1600ft/min. Service ceiling 12,600ft. Hovering ceiling out of ground effect 4000ft. Range with max fuel and typical payload 420km (225nm).

Weights: UH-1H – Empty equipped 2363kg (5210lb), normal takeoff 4100kg (9040lb), max takeoff 4310kg (9500lb).

Dimensions: UH-1H – Main rotor diameter 14.63m (48ft 0in), length overall rotors turning 17.62m (57ft 10in), fuselage length 12.77m (41ft 10in), height overall 4.41m (14ft 6in). Main rotor disc area 168.1m² (1809.6sq ft).

Accommodation: UH-1H – Flightcrew of one of two pilots, plus up to 14 equipped troops in main cabin. In medevac role can carry six stretcher patients and two medical attendants.

Armament: UH-1H – Pintle mounted machines guns, plus miniguns and rockets mounted on fuselage stub wings.

Operators: Bell 205, UH-1D/H & AB 205 – Argentina, Australia, Bahrain, Bangladesh, Bolivia, Brazil, Brunei, Canada, Chile, Colombia, Dominican Republic, Dubai, El Salvador, Germany, Greece, Guatemala, Honduras, Iran, Italy, Jamaica, Japan, Mexico, Morocco, Myanmar, New Zealand, Oman, Pakistan, Panama, Peru, Philippines, Saudi Arabia, Singapore, South Korea, Spain, Taiwan, Thailand, Tunisia, Turkey, Uganda, UAE, USA, Uruguay, Zambia, Zimbabwe.

History: With production of the UH-1B Huey in full swing in 1960, Bell approached the US Army about developing a larger and more powerful development.

The US Army ordered seven improved YUH-1D Iroquois, which had the Bell model number of 205, for trials and evaluation in July 1960. First flight of the improved Huey was on August 16 1961 and the type was subsequently ordered into production as the UH-1D.

Compared with the UH-1B and C, the D model featured an 820kW (1100shp) T53-L-11 turboshaft and an enlarged fuselage capable of seating 14 fully equipped troops, twice that of the earlier models. Deliveries of the first of 2008 UH-1Ds for the US Army began in August 1963. Further, Dornier licence built 352 for the West German military.

The improved UH-1H introduced a more powerful T53-L-13 turboshaft, but otherwise remained basically unchanged from the UH-1D. Deliveries of the definitive UH-1H to the US Army began in September 1967, while the final Bell built UH-1H was delivered almost two decades later in 1986. Licence built UH-1Hs were built in Italy (by Agusta as the AB 205), Taiwan (by AIDC) and Japan where Fuji continues low rate production of the improved UH-1J with uprated engine and transmission from the AH-1S, 212 main rotor and 212 style longer nose and wider fuselage.

The UH-1D and UH-1H both saw widespread service with the US military (and Australia) in Vietnam where it was used not only for transport but for a variety of special missions. In US Army service some 2900 Iroquois survive, and some may be upgraded in the future.

Photo: A US Army UH-1H.

Bell 214 Huey Plus, Isfahan & BigLifter

Country of origin: United States of America

Type: Utility & battlefield helicopter

Powerplant: 214A – One 2185kW (2930shp) Lycoming LTC4B-8D turboshaft, driving a two bladed main rotor and two bladed tail rotor.

Performance: 214A – Max cruising speed clean 260km/h (140kt), max cruising speed with slung load 185km/h (100kt). Service ceiling clean 16,400ft, with slung load 12,400ft. Hovering ceiling out of ground effect clean 12,200ft, out of ground effect with slung load 5400ft. Range clean with reserves 475km (255nm), with slung load 167km (90nm). Endurance 2hr 35min.

Weights: 214A – Empty 3442kg (7588lb), normal takeoff 6260kg (13,800lb), max takeoff with slung load 6805kg (15,000lb).

Dimensions: 214A – Main rotor diameter 15.24m (50ft 0in), fuselage length 14.63m (48ft 0in), height overall 3.90m (12ft 10in). Main rotor disc area 182.4m² (1963.5sq ft).

Accommodation: 214A – Flightcrew of two pilots plus 14 equipped troops. In medevac role can carry six stretcher patients and two medical attendants.

Armament: Usually none.

Operators: Dubai, Ecuador, Iran, Oman, Philippines.

History: A further development of the ubiquitous Bell Iroquois, the 214 is the most powerful single engined helicopter in military service anywhere.

Bell announced it was developing the 214 Huey Plus on October 12 1970. The private development 214 was based on the basic airframe of the UH-1H Iroquois, but introduced a significantly more powerful 1415kW (1900shp) T53-L-702 turboshaft, a new, longer diameter main rotor and a strengthened fuselage to cope with the new rotor and increased torque. A prototype 214 flew for the first time in 1970 and it demonstrated a number of performance improvements such as a top speed at max weight of 306km/h (165kt), but the type failed to attract orders from the US Army.

The 214 did however arouse the interest of Iran, who saw the 214 as being able to meet its requirement for a troop and supply transport able to operate in that country's hot environment. Iran ordered 287 Bell 214As, which featured the vastly more powerful 2185kW (2930shp) Lycoming LTC4B-8 turboshaft, on December 22 1972. In addition to the 214As, which were named Isfahan after the town near the Iranian Army's helicopter school, Iran also took delivery of 39 SAR configured 214Cs. Plans to establish a production line in Iran for the 214 and the larger 214ST (described separately) were terminated with the fall of the Shah in 1979 and the severing of diplomatic ties with the USA. The cutting of ties with the US also put an end to Bell's support for Iran's large fleet of 214s, and estimates suggest that more than half of the fleet is no longer serviceable.

Bell commercially marketed the 214 as the 214B Biglifter and promoted the helicopter's ability to lift large slung loads. Several countries purchased 214Bs for military use.

Photo: One of 287 Bell 214As delivered to Iran during the reign of the Shah. The 214 has a different air intake and exhaust arrangement compared with the 205/UH-1H.

Bell 212, UH-1N & AB 212

Countries of origin: United States of America & Canada

Type: Battlefield & utility helicopter & ASW helo (AB 212ASW)

Powerplants: 212 – One 1340kW (1800shp) TO rated Pratt & Whitney Canada PT6T-3 or PT6T-3B Turbo Twin-Pac (two coupled PT6 turboshafts) driving two bladed main and tail rotors.

Performance: 212 – Max cruising speed 206km/h (111kt), long range cruising speed 193km/h (104kt). Max initial rate of climb 1320ft/min. Range with standard fuel at long range cruising speed 450km (243nm).

Weights: 212 – Empty 2765kg (6097lb), max takeoff (with or without an external load) 5080kg (11,200lb).

Dimensions: 212 – Main rotor diameter 14.69m (48ft 2in), length overall rotors turning 17.46m (57ft 3in), fuselage length 12.92m (42ft 5in), height overall 4.53m (14ft 10in). Main rotor disc area 168.1m² (1809.6sq ft).

Accommodation: 212 – Total seating for 15, including one or two pilots. In medevac role can house six stretchers and two medical attendants. AB 212ASW – Typical crew of three or four.

Armament: 212 – Can be fitted with pintle mounted machine guns in main cabin doors. AB 212ASW – Two Mk 44, Mk 46 or MQ 44 torpedoes, or AS12 or Sea Killer ASMs.

Operators: Argentina, Austria, Bangladesh, Canada, Chile, Dominican Republic, Dubai, Ecuador, El Salvador, Ghana, Greece, Guatemala, Guyana, Iran, Israel, Italy, Japan, Lebanon, Libya, Malta, Mexico, Morocco, Panama, Philippines, Saudi Arabia, Singapore, South Korea, Spain, Sri Lanka, Sudan, Thailand, Tunisia, Turkey, Uganda, Venezuela, Yemen, Zambia.

History: Development of the Bell 212 was initiated in the late 1960s after Bell, Pratt & Whitney Canada and the Canadian Government agreed to jointly fund development of a twin engine version of the UH-1H Iroquois.

The early 1968 three way agreement paved the way to mate the basic UH-1H/205 fuselage with a Pratt & Whitney Canada PT6T Turbo Twin Pac to significantly boost performance. The Twin Pac mated two PT6 turboshafts through a single combining gearbox and single output shaft, and was fitted with torque sensors so that if one of the engines failed the other could be throttled up to compensate for the power loss. First flight was in 1968.

When the 1968 agreement was announced, Bell announced it held orders for the new helicopter from the Canadian Armed Forces for 50 CUH-1Ns (now CH-135 Twin Hueys) and the US military as UH-1Ns. The US Navy and Marines were the largest UH-1N operators, taking delivery of 221 between them. The USMC also converted two UH-1Ns to VIP transport VH-1N status.

The 212 is marketed commercially as the Twin Two-Twelve and it remains in production alongside other Bell civil helicopters in Canada.

In Italy, Agusta licence built the 212 as the AB 212, and developed the anti submarine warfare AB 212ASW. This unique 212 variant is the Italian Navy's primary shipborne helicopter. It is equipped with MM/APS-705 search radar, sonar and ESM and can be armed with homing torpedoes or anti ship missiles.

Photo: An Italian Navy AB 212ASW. (Agusta)

Bell 412, AB 412 Grifone & CH-146 Griffon

Countries of origin: United States of America & Canada

Type: Battlefield & utility helicopter

Powerplants: CH-146 – One 1425kW (1910shp) Pratt & Whitney Canada PT6T-3D Turbo Twin Pac (two coupled PT6s), driving a four bladed main rotor and two bladed tail rotor.

Performance: CH-146 – Max cruising speed 240km/h (130kt), long range cruising speed 230km/h (124kt). Hovering ceiling in ground effect 10,200ft, out of ground effect 5200ft. Range at long range cruising speed with standard fuel and no reserves 745km (402nm).

Weights: CH-146 – Empty equipped 3065kg (6760lb), max takeoff 5397kg (11,900lb).

Dimensions: CH-146 – Main rotor diameter 14.02m (46ft 0in), length overall rotors turning 17.12m (56ft 2in), fuselage length 12.92m (42ft 5in), height overall 4.57m (15ft 0in). Main rotor disc area 154.4m² (1661.9sq ft).

Accommodation: Total seating for 15, including one or two pilots. In medevac role can accommodate six stretcher patients and two medical attendants.

Armament: Military 412 – Offered with removable nose mounted turret gun, 7.62mm machine gun, 20mm cannon and rocket pods and pintle mounted machine guns in the main cabin doors.

Operators: 412 – Botswana, Canada, Honduras, Indonesia, Norway, Sri Lanka, Venezuela. AB 412 – Dubai, Finland, Italy, Venezuela, Zimbabwe.

History: The Bell 412 is the ultimate development of the world's most successful helicopter series which began in the late 1950s with the Bell 204 or UH-1A/B/C Iroquois.

The mating of the Pratt & Whitney Canada PT6T Turbo Twin Pac with the Bell 205 to produce the Bell 212 was a significant commercial success for Bell. However, by the mid 1970s Bell was looking at further improving the breed, and in particular improving the 212's speed and range performance.

Not wanting to re-engine the 212 or make any major structural changes, Bell instead decided to increase performance by developing a four bladed main rotor for the 212. The shorter diameter four blade main rotor is of composite construction except between the leading edge and spar, and has a longer fatigue life and produces less vibration than Bell's earlier two bladed units. First flight of the 412 was in August 1979, while production was transferred to Canada in early 1989.

Progressive development of the 412, spurred mainly by growing civil orders, led to the 412SP (Special Performance), 412HP (High Performance) and the current production 412EP (Enhanced Performance). The 412EP also forms the basis for the CH-146 Griffon, 100 of which have been ordered for the Canadian Forces.

Like the 204, 205 and 212, the 412 is licence built in Italy by Agusta-Bell as the AB 412. The military AB 412 Grifone features strengthened undercarriage skids to increase crash survivability, crew crash absorbing and armoured crew seats and can be fitted with impact absorbing seats for passengers. It is in service with the Italian Army as a battlefield transport and the Italian Navy for SAR.

Photo: An Indonesian Navy 412. The 412 is built under licence in Indonesia by IPTN as the NB 412.

Bell 206, OH-58, TH-67 & TH-57

Country of origin: United States of America

Type: Light observation (OH-58), utility transport and training helicopter (TH-67 & TH-57)

Powerplant: OH-58A – One 237kW (317shp) Allison T63-A-700 (Allison 250) turboshaft, driving two bladed main and tail rotors.

Performance: OH-58A – Max cruising speed at sea level 196km/h (106kt), economical cruising speed 188km/h (102kt), loiter speed for max endurance 91km/h (49kt). Max initial rate of climb 1780ft/min. Service ceiling 19,000ft. Hovering ceiling in ground effect 13,750ft, hovering ceiling out of ground effect 9000ft. Max range at sea level with reserves 480km (260nm). Endurance at sea level with no reserves 3hrs 30mins.

Weights: OH-58A – Empty equipped 718kg (1582lb), max takeoff 1360kg (3000lb).

Dimensions: OH-58A – Main rotor disc diameter 10.77m (35ft 4in), length overall with rotors turning 12.49m (41ft 0in), fuselage length 9.84m (32ft 4in), height overall rotors turning 2.91m (9ft 7in). Main rotor disc area 91.1m² (980.5sq ft).

Accommodation: Total seating for five including pilot.

Armament: Usually none, but can be fitted with pintle mounted MGs.

Operators: 206 – Includes Brazil, Brunei, Chile, Columbia, Cyprus, Ecuador, Guatemala, Guyana, Indonesia, Israel, Ivory Coast, Mexico, Myanmar, Pakistan, Peru, South Korea, Sri Lanka, Thailand, UAE, Venezuela. OH-58 – Australia, Austria, Canada, USA. TH-67 – USA. TH-57 – USA. 206L – Includes Bangladesh, Cameroon, Guatemala, Mexico, UAE, Venezuela.

History: The world's most successful light turbine helicopter grew out of Bell's failed submission to meet a US Army requirement for a four seat light observation helicopter in 1960.

While Bell lost that contract to Hughes with what became the OH-6 Cayuse (described separately), the company set about developing a five seat commercial light helicopter based on the general design of the four OH-4 prototypes which had flown for the first time in December 1962. The civil Bell 206 JetRanger flew for the first time on January 10 1966, and production aircraft were delivered from later that year. Since that time the JetRanger has been in continuous production in progressively modernised forms and has seen widespread military use, as has, to a lesser extent, the stretched 206L LongRanger.

The wheel turned full circle for Bell when in 1967 the US Army reopened the Light Observation Helicopter competition because of the rising costs and late deliveries of the OH-6, and ordered the 206A into production as the OH-58A Kiowa. In all, 2200 Kiowas were delivered to the US Army from May 1968. Many were upgraded to OH-58C standard with an uprated engine. Canada ordered 72 COH-58A Kiowas (subsequently redesignated CH-139), while Austria acquired 12 similar OH-58Bs. Finally Australia's Commonwealth Aircraft Corporation assembled 57 206B-1 Kiowas locally.

The US Navy and Army also use the 206 for training, the former's (delivered from 1968) aircraft designated TH-57 SeaRangers, the latter's, TH-67 Creeks (delivered from 1993).

Photo: An Australian Army Kiowa.

Bell Kiowa Warrior & Combat Scout

Country of origin: United States of America

Type: Armed observation & light attack helicopters

Powerplant: OH-58D – One 485kW (650shp) intermediate rating Allison T703-AD-700 (Allison 250-C30R) turboshaft, driving a four bladed main rotor and two bladed tail rotor.

Performance: OH-58D Kiowa Warrior – Max level speed at 4000ft 237km/h (128kt), max cruising speed at mission weight 211km/h (114kt), economical cruising speed 204km/h (110kt). Max initial rate of climb 1540ft/min. Service ceiling 15,000ft. Hovering ceiling out of ground effect 4000ft. Range 413km (223nm). Endurance 2hr 24min.

Weights: OH-58D Kiowa Warrior – Empty 1492kg (3289lb), max takeoff 2495kg (5500lb).

Dimensions: OH-58D – Main rotor diameter 10.67m (35ft 0in), length overall rotors turning 12.85m (42ft 2in), fuselage length 10.48m (34ft 5in), height overall 3.93m (7ft 10in). Main rotor disc area 89.4m² (962.0sq ft).

Accommodation: Seating for pilot and observer side by side in OH-58D Kiowa and Kiowa Warrior. Seating for five in Combat Scout.

Armament: OH-58D Kiowa Warrior – Four Stinger AAMs, or four AGM-114C Hellfire anti armour missiles, two seven round rocket pods, or podded 7.62mm or 0.50in machine guns.

Operators: OH-58D – USA. Combat Scout – Saudi Arabia.

History: The OH-58D development of the Kiowa resulted from the US Army's Army Helicopter Improvement Program of 1979.

The Army Helicopter Improvement Program (AHIP) was designed to result in a relatively low cost scout and observation helicopter to support attack AH-64 Apaches. The contract for the AHIP was awarded to Bell for a development of the OH-58 Kiowa.

The resulting OH-58D Kiowa flew for the first time on October 6 1983. Unlike the fairly basic Kiowa, the OH-58D introduced the McDonnell Douglas Astronautics developed mast mounted sight which features TV and infrared sensors, plus a new, four bladed main rotor to enhance performance. OH-58D deliveries began in December 1985. Initially the US Army planned to convert 592 OH-58A/Cs to OH-58D standard, this total now stands at 507.

Originally the OH-58D was to be unarmed, but all aircraft are being progressively upgraded to OH-58D Kiowa Warrior status, capable of carrying Stinger AAMs, Hellfire ASMs, rockets and gun pods. The Kiowa Warrior also features uprated transmission, higher max takeoff weight, RWR, IR jammer, laser warning receiver and lightened structure.

The Multi Purpose Light Helicopter (MPLH) development has squatting landing gear and quick folding rotors and is designed to fit into the cargo holds of C-130s and C-141s and be ready to fly 10 minutes after unloading. 81 conversions are on order.

A Stealth Kiowa Warrior with some stealth features (including chisel nose, blade root cuffs, composite main doors and RAM coating) has flown, as has a prototype OH-58X with night flying chin turret, colour digital maps, GPS and other improvements.

The 406CS Combat Scout is a downgraded export version of the OH-58D without the mast mounted sight (instead, Saudi aircraft are fitted with a Saab-Emerson HeliTow sight) and some sensitive avionics.

Photo: An armed US Army OH-58D Kiowa Warrior. (Bell)

Bell AH-1F & AH-1S HueyCobra

Country of origin: United States of America

Type: Attack helicopter

Powerplant: AH-1F – One 1340kW (1800shp) Textron Lycoming T53-L-703 turboshaft driving two bladed main and tail rotors.

Performance: AH-1F – Max level speed 227km/h (123kt). Max initial rate of climb 1620ft/min. Service ceiling 12,200ft. Hovering ceiling in ground effect 12,200ft. Range 507km (275nm).

Weights: AH-1F – Operating empty 2993kg (6598lb), normal takeoff 4525kg (9975lb), max takeoff 4535kg (10,000lb).

Dimensions: AH-1F – Main rotor diameter 13.41m (44ft 0in), length overall rotors turning 16.18m (53ft 1in), fuselage length 13.59m (44ft 7in), height to top of rotor head 4.09m (13ft 5in). Main rotor disc area 141.3m^2 (1520.2sq ft).

Accommodation: Copilot/gunner (in front cockpit) and pilot in tandem.

Armament: Eight Hughes TOW anti armour missiles on the outboard stations of two stub wings. Can carry rockets and machine gun pods. General Electric nose mounted three barrel 20mm gun turret can be slaved to helmet mounted sights.

Operators: Bahrain, Israel, Japan, Jordan, Pakistan, Romania*, South Korea, Thailand, Turkey, USA.

History: The world's first operational dedicated two seat helicopter gunship, the HueyCobra was initially intended to be an interim design pending the introduction into service of the subsequently cancelled Lockheed AH-56 Cheyenne.

The HueyCobra began life as a private venture when in 1965 Bell took the powerplant, transmission and rotor system of the UH-1B/C Iroquois and matched them to a new fuselage featuring seating for two in tandem, stub wings to carry weapons and a nose gun, to result in the Bell 209. The prototype flew for the first time on September 7 1965, just six months after design work had begun. The US Army subsequently ordered the 209 into production as the AH-1G HueyCobra to fulfil an urgent need for an attack helicopter primarily to escort troop carrying UH-1 Iroquois in Vietnam, pending delivery of the troubled AH-56. In all 1078 AH-1Gs were built, many of which saw service in Vietnam, while the AH-56 was cancelled.

The AH-1G was followed up by the AH-1Q, an interim anti armour version capable of firing Hughes TOW anti tank missiles. First flown in 1973, 92 AH-1Gs were converted to AH-1Qs. Combat experience found the AH-1Q's hot and high performance lacking, and resulted in the AH-1S. The AH-1S designation covers staged improvements to the AH-1's powerplant and transmission, armament, avionics and cockpit. New build production AH-1Ss and conversions of the AH-1Qs and AH-1Gs resulted in four separate AH-1S subvariants, the AH-1S(MC) being the definitive standard incorporating all the planned improvements.

In 1989 the US Army redesignated the AH-1S to reflect the different variants. Thus AH-1F covers the AH-1S(MC), while the AH-1S designation now covers AH-1S(MOD) aircraft (converted AH-1Qs), the AH-1P covers early build AH-1Ss, and the AH-1E covers AH-1Ss with improved weapon systems. In 1995 Bell and IAR Brasov signed an agreement covering the licence construction of 96 AH-1Fs in Romania. Deliveries will begin in 1999.

Photo: One of four AH-1F Cobras delivered to Thailand.

Bell AH-1W SuperCobra

Country of origin: United States of America

Type: Attack helicopter

Powerplants: AH-1W – Two 1285kW (1723shp) General Electric T700-GE-401 turboshafts driving a two bladed main rotor and two bladed tail rotor.

Performance: AH-1W – Max level speed 282km/h (152kt), max cruising speed 278km/h (150kt). Max initial rate of climb on one engine 800ft/min. Service ceiling 14,000ft plus. Hovering ceiling in ground effect 14,750ft, out of ground effect 3000ft. Range with standard fuel and no reserves 587km (317nm).

Weights: AH-1W – Empty 4635kg (10,215kg), max takeoff 6690kg (14,750lb).

Dimensions: AH-1W – Main rotor diameter 14.63m (48ft 0in), length overall rotors turning 17.68m (58ft 0in), fuselage length 13.87m (45ft 6in), height to top of rotor head 4.11m (13ft 6in), height overall 4.44m (14ft 7in). Main rotor disc area 168.1m^2 (1809.6sq ft).

Accommodation: Copilot/gunner (front cockpit) and pilot in tandem.

Armament: AH-1W – General Electric nose mounted turret houses three barrel 20mm M197 gun. Can carry up to eight Hughes TOW or AGM-114 Hellfire anti armour missiles on outboard stations of two stub wings, plus rocket or gun pods on inboard stations. Other armament options include fuel air explosives, iron bombs, two AIM-9L Sidewinder air-to-air missiles or AGM-122A Sidearm ASMs. Demonstrated ability to fire AGM-65D Maverick ASMs.

Operators: AH-1J – Iran. AH-1W – Turkey, USA.

History: The twin engine variants of the Cobra were developed specifically for the US Marine Corps, and have resulted in the ultimate Cobra development so far, the AH-1W SuperCobra.

The AH-1 HueyCobra aroused USMC interest early on in its career, and that service's evaluation of the US Army's AH-1G led to a 1968 order for 49 similar AH-1J SeaCobras. The AH-1J was similar to the AH-1G except for the powerplant, the Marines specifying the 1340kW (1800shp) (flat rated to 820kW/1100shp) Pratt & Whitney Canada T400-CP-400, the military version of the PT6T Turbo Twin Pac, an installation that combined two PT6 turboshafts through a combining transmission. The AH-1J also introduced the three barrel M197 20mm cannon in the nose turret. Iran also ordered 202 AH-1Js.

The improved AH-1T (initially known as the Improved Sea Cobra) was first ordered in 1974 and differed from the J in having a 1470kW (1970shp) T400-WV-402, a new rotor system based on that for the Bell 214, uprated transmission and lengthened fuselage and tail.

The AH-1W started life as a proposal to Iran for an AH-1T powered by two General Electric T700s. A so powered demonstrator was flown in 1983 and designated AH-1T+ and the type, with further improvements, was ordered into production for the USMC as the AH-1W SuperCobra, or Whiskey Cobra. Aside from new build AH-1Ws, AH-1Ts have been converted to the new configuration. USMC AH-1Ws saw service in the Gulf War and were also deployed to Somalia.

The AH-1W Cobra Venom was offered to meet a British requirement for an attack helicopter (won by the AH-64). It would have featured advanced avionics, colour CRTs, digital mapping, GPS and night vision equipment.

Photo: The twin T700 powered AH-1W. (Bell)

Bell 214ST

Country of origin: United States of America

Type: Medium transport helicopter

Powerplants: 214ST – Two 1215kW (1625shp) General Electric CT7-2A turboshafts linked through a combining gearbox driving a two bladed main rotor and two bladed tail rotor.

Performance: 214ST – Max cruising speed 260km/h (140kt) at 4000ft, or 264km/h (143kt) at sea level. Max initial rate of climb 1780ft/min. Service ceiling with one engine out 4800ft. Hovering ceiling in ground effect 6400ft. Ferry range with auxiliary fuel 1020km (550nm), range with standard fuel and no reserves 805km (435nm).

Weights: 214ST – Empty 4300kg (9481lb), max takeoff 7938kg (17,500lb).

Dimensions: 214ST – Main rotor diameter 15.85m (52ft 0in), length overall rotors turning 18.95m (62ft 2in), fuselage length 15.03m (49ft 4in), height overall 4.84m (15ft 11in). Main rotor disc area 197.3m² (2124sq ft).

Accommodation: 214ST – Pilot and copilot and up to 16 or 17 passengers. Freight volume of 8.95m³ (316cu ft). Can carry an external sling freight load of 3630kg (8000lb).

Armament: Typically none, but can be fitted with pintle mounted machine guns in main cabin door.

Operators: Brunei, Iraq, Oman, Peru, Thailand, Venezuela.

History: Despite sharing a common model number with the 214 Huey Plus and Big Lifter (described separately), the Bell 214ST is actually a much bigger helicopter.

Bell's biggest helicopter yet was developed in response to an Iranian requirement for a larger transport helicopter with better performance in its hot and high environment than its 214 Isfahans. Bell based its proposal on the 214 but made substantial design changes, resulting in what is essentially an all new helicopter with little commonality with the smaller 214 series.

The 214ST featured two General Electric CT7 turboshafts (the commercial equivalent of the military T700 which powers the UH-60), a stretched fuselage seating up to 17 in the main cabin and stretched main rotor blades from the 214 with composite construction. The 214ST designation originally stood for Stretched Twin, reflecting the changes over the 214, but this was later changed to stand for Super Transporter.

The 214ST was to have been built under licence in Iran as part of that country's plans to establish a large army air wing (other aircraft ordered in large numbers under this plan were the 214A Isfahan and AH-1J SeaCobra, both described separately), but the Islamic revolution and fall of the Shah in 1979 put paid to these plans.

Undeterred, Bell continued development of the 214ST for civil and military customers. The 214ST flew for the first time on July 21 1979 and 100 production aircraft were built through to 1990.

Most 214ST sales were to military customers. Ironically, Iraq was the 214ST's largest customer, taking delivery of 45 during 1987 and 1988, some most likely seeing service in the Gulf War. Other customers include Peru, Thailand and Venezuela.

Photo: The 214ST is the largest Bell helicopter thus far, and differs considerably from the similarly designated 214A and 214B. (Bell)

Bell/Boeing V-22 Osprey

Country of origin: United States of America

Type: Tilt rotor transport aircraft

Powerplants: Two 4590kW (6150shp) Allison T406-AD-400 turboshafts driving three bladed proprotors.

Performance: Max cruising speed in aeroplane mode 582km/h (314kt), at sea level in helicopter mode 185km/h (100kt). Service ceiling 26,000ft. Takeoff run in short takeoff mode less than 150m (500ft). Ferry range 3890km (2100nm). Range with a 5445kg (12,000lb) payload and vertical takeoff 2225km (1200nm). Range with a 9075kg (20,000lb) payload and short takeoff 3335km (1800nm).

Weights: Empty equipped 14,463kg (31,886lb), normal mission takeoff weight for a vertical takeoff 21,545kg (47,500lb), normal mission takeoff weight with short takeoff 24,947kg (55,000lb), max takeoff with short takeoff for self ferry 27,442kg (60,500lb).

Dimensions: Prop rotor diameter 11.58m (38ft 0in), wing span including nacelles 15.52m (50ft 11in), fuselage length excluding probe 17.47m (57ft 4in), height overall nacelles vertical 6.90m (22ft 8in), height at top of tail fins 5.28m (17ft 4in). Proprotor disc area each 105.4m² (1134sq ft), wing area 35.49m² (392.0sq ft).

Accommodation: Flightcrew of two plus loadmaster/crew chief. Seating for up to 24 fully combat equipped troops in main cabin.

Armament: None, although special mission aircraft would be armed.

Operators: None

History: Often delayed and criticised as overweight and overpriced, the revolutionary V-22 nevertheless is set to become the first operational tilt rotor aircraft in the world.

Development of the Osprey dates back to the early 1980s' joint services program to develop a tilt rotor transport based on the successful Bell/NASA XV-15 demonstrator. The US Navy awarded a teaming of Bell and Boeing an initial development contract in April 1983, while an order for six flying prototypes (later reduced to five) was signed in May 1986. First flight was on March 19 1989.

Since that time the Osprey program has suffered its share of problems, with two of the prototypes crashing, planned production orders reduced and the whole program coming close to cancellation in 1992. Construction of four production standard V-22s is now underway, and these will be evaluated from 1998 against conventional helicopters to meet the USMC's CH-46 replacement requirement. However, IOC for the first of the Marines MV-22s is still planned for 1998. Marines support for the Osprey remains steadfast because of the aircraft's ability to perform all the missions a helicopter can, yet it can cruise at twice the speed and carry twice the payload.

The V-22 features two Allison T400 turboshafts (with FADEC) mounted in tilting nacelles. The engines are also linked via a cross-shaft that allows both proprotors to be powered in the event of an engine failure. Other features include 59% composite construction by weight, fly-by-wire, and EFIS while the wings swivel to be parallel to the fuselage for stowage on ships.

Other than the USMC's MV-22s, other planned Osprey variants include the USAF's CV-22 special missions aircraft and the USN's HV-22 Combat SAR HH-3 replacement.

Photo: The US Marines remain committed to the V-22.

Beriev Be-12 Tchaika

Country of origin: Russia

Type: Maritime patrol and ASW amphibian

Powerplants: Two 3125kW (4190ehp) Ivchenko (now Progress) AI-20D turboprops, driving four bladed constant speed propellers.

Performance: Max level speed 608km/h (328kt), typical patrol speed 320km/h (173kt). Max initial rate of climb 2990ft/min. Service ceiling 37,000ft. Ferry range 7500km (4050nm), range with combat load 4000km (2160nm).

Weights: Empty 21,700kg (47,840lb), max takeoff 31,000kg (68,342lb).

Dimensions: Wing span 29.71m (97ft 6in), length 30.17m (99ft 0in), height 7.00m (23ft 0in). Wing area 105.0m^2 (1130.3sq ft).

Accommodation: Five crew complement consists of pilot, copilot, navigator, radar operator and MAD operator.

Armament: Internal weapons bay and two underwing hardpoints can carry a variety of weaponry including torpedoes, depth charges and mines.

Operators: Russia, Syria, Vietnam, Ukraine.

History: One of the few amphibians in military service, the Tchailka (or gull) still remains in Russian naval aviation service performing close in maritime patrol, ASW and SAR work.

The Be-12 (NATO name 'Mail') was developed as a replacement for the earlier piston powered Be-6, which first flew in 1949. The turboprop Be-12 meanwhile first flew during 1960, and made its public debut at the 1961 Soviet Aviation Day Display at Tushino, Moscow. The Be-12 was of the same basic configuration as the smaller Be-6, with twin tails and a high cranked wing to give the propellers and engine maximum clearance from the water. Other Be-12 features include the powerful Ivchenko AI-20D turboprops (AI-20s also power the land based Il-38 'May' maritime patrol and ASW aircraft), a stepped hull with spray dams along the nose to minimise engine water ingestion, retractable undercarriage, a nose mounted search radar and tail mounted Magnetic Anomaly Detector (MAD) boom.

The Be-12 was selected for Soviet naval service in 1964 ahead of another Beriev design, the jet powered Be-10. This aircraft established a number of seaplane world records, but only three or four are thought to have been built, mainly for trials purposes. The Be-12 itself set or broke all 44 FAI (Federation Aeronautique Internationale) records covering turboprop powered amphibians and seaplanes between 1964 and 1983.

Exact production of the Be-12 is unknown, though is thought to have run to around 100 aircraft. The main role of the Be-12 is ASW and maritime patrol within 370km (200nm) of shore bases, however Be-12s have performed a variety of different tasks including Arctic and Siberian exploration and resource exploration, geophysical mapping and search and rescue. While the brunt of Russian ASW and maritime patrol tasks are now borne by the Il-38 and Tu-142, the majority of Be-12s are still in service with the Russian northern fleet and probably with Ukraine. The Be-12 may also be in service in Syria.

Photo: This ex Russian Navy Be-12 was returned to Beriev in 1993 to serve as a demonstrator firebomber for civil/government use. (Beriev)

Beriev A-40 & Be-42 Albatross

Country of origin: Russia

Type: Maritime patrol & ASW (A-40) and SAR (Be-42) amphibian

Powerplants: A-40 – Two 117.7kN (26,455lb) Aviadvigatel D-30KPV turbofans and two 24.5kN (5510lb) RKBM (formerly Klimov) RD-60K booster turbojets.

Performance: A-40 – Max level speed 760km/h (410kt), max cruising speed 720km/h (388kt). Max initial rate of climb on one engine 5900ft/min. Service ceiling 31,825ft. Range with max payload 4100km (2210nm), range with max fuel 5500km (2965nm).

Weights: A-40 – Max payload 6500kg (14,330lb), max takeoff 86,000kg (189,595lb).

Dimensions: A-40 – Wing span 41.62m (136ft 7in), length overall including nose probe 43.84m (143ft 10in), fuselage length 38.92m (127ft 8in), height 11.07m (36ft 4in). Wing area 200.0m^2 (2153sq ft).

Accommodation: A-40 – Crew complement of eight consisting of pilot, copilot, flight engineer, radio operator, navigator/observer and three observers. Be-42 – Flightcrew of five, plus three medical attendants, and accommodation for 54 rescued survivors.

Armament: A-40 – Internal weapons bay could carry a range of weapons maritime such as torpedoes, mines and depth charges. Be-42 – None.

Operators: Russia*

History: The Beriev Albatross is the world's largest amphibious aircraft and was designed, initially at least, to replace the Be-12 and Il-38 in maritime patrol and ASW roles.

Design work on the Albatross (NATO identification name 'Mermaid') began in 1983, but it was not until 1988 that the type was made publicly known in the west when the US announced it had taken satellite photographs of a jet powered amphibian under development in Russia. The Albatross made its first flight in December 1986, while its first public appearance was a fly-by at the 1989 Soviet Aviation Day Display at Tushino, Moscow.

The exact future of the Albatross is in some doubt. As many as 20 A-40 Albatrosses have been ordered for CIS naval service, but the status of this order is unclear, and may have been converted to the Be-42, which is optimised for search and rescue. The aircraft does however form the basis of the slightly smaller civil Be-200, which is being promoted for various missions including firefighting. Other projected versions are the Be-40P 105 seat airliner and Be-40PT combi airliner/freighter.

Design features of the Albatross include its unique 'variable rise' single step hull, which is designed to improve stability and controllability in the water, and a unique powerplant combination of two D-30KPV turbofans with a booster turbojet in each of the engine pylons.

The Be-42 SAR aircraft would be able to take 54 survivors of a marine accident and would be equipped with liferafts, powerboats and a range of specialised medical equipment including a transfusion machine, refribillator and ECG. It would also be equipped with various infrared sensors and a searchlight.

Photo: The Albatross has the distinction of being the only jet powered amphibian currently flying. (Beriev)

Beriev/Ilyushin A-50

Country of origin: Russia

Type: Airborne Early Warning & Control aircraft

Powerplants: Four 117.7kN (26,455lb) Aviadvigatel (Soloviev) D-30KP turbofans.

Performance: Generally similar to the Il-76, described separately under Ilyushin, with cruising speed between 750 and 800km/h (405 and 432kt). Generally operates at 33,000ft flying figure of eight search tracks, with 100km (54nm) between the centre of each circle.

Weights: Unpublished, but similar to Il-76.

Dimensions: Wing span 50.50m (165ft 8in), length 46.59m (152ft 10in), height 14.76m (48ft 5in). Wing area 300.0m² (3229.2sq ft).

Accommodation: Normal crew complement of 15, including two pilots, flight engineer and navigator.

Armament: None

Operators: Russia

History: The A-50 (NATO name 'Mainstay') was developed to replace Russia's first operational AEW&C aircraft, the Tupolev Tu-126 'Moss'.

The Tu-126 was a conversion of the Tu-114 airliner (the Tu-114 was an airliner development of the Tu-95 bomber) and about a dozen Tu-126 conversions are thought to have seen service since the mid 1960s. Like other first generation AEW aircraft, the Tu-126s were limited in their effectiveness.

Development of an improved AEW&C aircraft to replace the Tu-126 began during the 1970s, resulting in the A-50. The A-50 is based on the Ilyushin Il-76 freighter, the most obvious difference being the large Sentry style rotating rotodome mounted above the fuselage. Other external features include a nose mounted refuelling probe (although refuelling is difficult because of the buffet caused by the rotodome), horizontal blade antennae mounted on each main undercarriage fairing, the glazed nose navigator station of the Il-76 has been deleted, a dorsal fin forward of the wing, an intake in the root of the tail to supply air to cool avionics, and a number of smaller antennae.

Inside the A-50, crew facilities are spartan, with no rest bunks and high noise levels. A single large colour CRT screen and station is used for controlling fighters, while other screens (also colour CRTs) display data about the air and ground tactical situations.

The A-50 represents the state of the art in Russian electronics, as its capabilities are reportedly comparable to that of the Sentry in some areas. The A-50 can detect low flying cruise missiles, control fighters, and download tactical information to ground stations and fighters automatically.

The A-50 first entered service in 1984 and around 20 have been built. During the Gulf War two A-50s maintained a round the clock patrol from the Black Sea, observing aircraft operations from Turkey and most of Iraq, and keeping watch for stray cruise missiles.

Iraq has independently developed two AEW versions of the Il-76. The failed Baghdad 1 featured a Thomson-CSF radar mounted in the lower tail, while the Adnan conversion features an A-50 style rotodome above the fuselage. Of the three Adnans converted, one was destroyed on the ground during the Gulf War, and the other two fled to Iran, where they are believed to still be.

Photo: A Russian Air Force A-50. (MAP)

Boeing B-52 Stratofortress

Country of origin: United States of America

Type: Strategic bomber

Powerplants: B-52H – Eight 75.6kN (17,000lb) Pratt & Whitney TF33-P-3 turbofans.

Performance: B-52H – Max level speed Mach 0.90 or 957km/h (516kt), cruising speed 820km/h (442kt), low level penetration speed 650 to 675km/h (352 to 365kt). Service ceiling 55,000ft. Range with max fuel without inflight refuelling over 16,095km (8685nm).

Weights: B-52H – Max takeoff 229,088kg (505,000lb).

Dimensions: B-52H – Wing span 56.39m (185ft 0in), length overall 49.05m (160ft 11in), height overall 12.40m (40ft 8in). Wing area 371.6m² (4000sq ft).

Accommodation: B-52H – Crew complement of five, comprising pilot, copilot, navigator, bombardier/radar navigator and ECM operator.

Armament: Tail mounted 20mm M61A1 Vulcan cannon no longer in use. In nuclear strike role can be fitted with 20 AGM-66B or AGM-129 cruise missiles in the internal bomb bay and two underwing stations. Can be fitted with free fall nuclear bombs. Conventional munitions include up to eight AGM-84 Harpoon or AGM-142A Have Nap ASMs, AGM-86C cruise missiles or up to 51 750lb (340kg) class bombs or mines.

Operators: USA

History: The mighty B-52 Stratofortress is the definitive symbol of the USA's manned bomber nuclear strike capabilities during the Cold War, and looks set to remain in service to past the turn of the century.

The B-52 began life in the 1940s as a proposed replacement for Strategic Air Command's B-50s (the B-50 was a development of the B-29 Superfortress). Originally the aircraft was to be powered by turboprops as they offered the best compromise between high performance and long range, but the availability of the Pratt & Whitney J57 turbojet (which offered a quantum leap forward in performance and economy over earlier jets) resulted in the definitive eight jet arrangement. A prototype XB-52 flew for the first time on April 15 1952. Successful evaluation of the B-52 led to the first production contracts and an entry into service in March 1955.

In all, 744 B-52s were built through to 1962 in eight major sub-types, the most important numerically being the B-52D (which saw extensive use as a conventional bomber in Vietnam), the B-52G which introduced a shorter vertical tail, remote control tail guns and a wet wing, and the B-52H with turbofan engines.

While all versions of the B-52 were progressively upgraded throughout their service lives to keep pace with new roles, mission profiles and technologies, the only model to remain in service in 1995 was the TF33 turbofan powered B-52H (the switch to more economical turbofan engines increased the B-52's range by a third). The B-52H also introduced a tail mounted 20mm cannon, although this is no longer used. B-52H features include a terrain following radar, comprehensive ECM protection and Electro-Optical Viewing System.

The 90 B-52Hs on Air Combat Command strength in 1995 are likely to remain in service past 2000, tasked with a variety of missions including standoff nuclear missile launching and conventional cruise missile launching.

Photo: A USAF B-52H – a symbol of US military might. (Boeing)

Boeing KC-135 Stratotanker

Country of origin: United States of America

Type: Air-to-air refuelling tanker

Powerplants: KC-135R – Four 97.9kN (22,000lb) CFM F108 turbofans.

Performance: KC-135R – Max speed 982km/h (530kt), cruising speed at 35,000ft 855km/h (462kt). Max initial rate of climb 1290ft/min. Service ceiling 45,000ft. Operational radius 4635km (2500nm).

Weights: KC-135R – Operating empty 48,220kg (106,305lb), max takeoff 146,285kg (322,500lb).

Dimensions: Wing span 39.88m (130ft 10in), length 41.53m (136ft 3in), height 12.70m (41ft 8in). Wing area 226.0m² (2433.0sq ft).

Accommodation: Standard crew complement for tanking of four, comprising pilot, copilot, navigator and boom operator. Fuel capacity 92,210kg (203,288lb).

Armament: None

Operators: France, Turkey*, USA.

History: The KC-135 Stratotanker is a very significant aircraft, having paved the way for Boeing's unparalleled success as the world's premier jet airliner manufacturer, while also considerably boosting the USAF's ability to conduct war by substantially increasing aircraft range.

In the early 1950s Boeing made the daring decision to develop as a private venture a four jet engined transport that could be developed into an airliner, but also meet a USAF requirement for an inflight refuelling tanker with jet aircraft speeds. The resulting 367-80 demonstrator flew for the first time on July 15 1954. Just one month later in August 1954 the USAF ordered it into production as the KC-135 Stratotanker inflight refueller with a Boeing developed flying boom. Features of the KC-135A included four J57 turbojets, fuel in belly and wing tanks and a side loading cargo door for freight on the main deck.

Some 820 KC-135s and variants were built, giving Boeing considerable experience in building jet transports, while the KC-135 (which has the Boeing model number of 717) forms the basis of the 707.

Aside from the KC-135A, 45 C-135 Stratolifter freighters were built without tanking equipment, pending the delivery of the Lockheed C-141 Starlifter. A handful survive as transports in support roles with special USAF units. The KC-135Q designation applies to 56 KC-135As modified to refuel SR-71s (now being re-engined with F108s as KC-135Ts), while France took delivery of 12 C-135F tankers (also later re-engined with F108s as C-135FRs).

The KC-135 has been the subject of two major re-engining programs. Over 160 Air Force Reserve and Air National Guard KC-135s were re-engined with TF33 turbofans sourced from retired 707 airliners as KC-135Es, while the KC-135R designation applies to KC-135s re-engined with CFM International F108 (CFM56) turbofans. More than 400 KC-135Rs had been delivered by late '95, mainly to active duty USAF units, while 33 will be modified with hose and drogue pods to refuel US Navy and NATO aircraft.

Both turbofan re-engining programs significantly increase the KC-135's takeoff performance, range and fuel offload capabilities, and, particularly in the case of the KC-135R, make the aircraft significantly quieter than the turbojet powered KC-135A. All surviving KC-135As that were not re-engined have been retired.

Photo: A CFM powered KC-135FR with boom extended. (Armée de l'Air)

Boeing EC-135 & RC-135

Country of origin: United States of America

Type: Series of special missions adaptations of basic C-135 airframe

Powerplants: EC-135C – Four 80.1kN (18,000lb) Pratt & Whitney TF33-P-9 turbofans.

Performance: EC-135C – Max speed 990km/h (535kt), cruising speed (at 35,000ft) 900km/h (485kt). Max initial rate of climb 2000ft/min. Service ceiling 40,600ft. Ferry range 9100km (4910nm), operational radius 4310km (2325nm).

Weights: EC-135 – Basic empty 46,403kg (102,300lb), max takeoff 135,625kg (299,000lb).

Dimensions: EC-135 – Wing span 39.88m (130ft 10in), length 41.53m (136ft 3in), height 12.70m (41ft 8in). Wing area 226.0m² (2433sq ft).

Accommodation: Various, depending on aircraft fit out and mission.

Armament: None

Operators: USA

History: The basic C-135 airframe forms the basis for one of the most prolific families of variants and subtypes in military aviation, with aircraft performing a diverse range of missions.

The EC-135 was originally developed to serve as an airborne command post for the then Strategic Air Command's B-52 nuclear bomber fleet, and some 40 C-135s were converted as EC-135s at various stages. The aircraft are fitted with a comprehensive communication suite which allows the battle commander to communicate with the national command structure, other command post and intelligence aircraft and ground forces. The EC-135s feature a trailing wire antenna which is reeled out behind it, various antennas along the fuselage, and in the case of four EC-135Cs, a Milstar satcom antenna mounted in a bulge on top of the fuselage. Most surviving EC-135s are EC-135Cs, most other subvariants have been retired because of a reduced requirement for these aircraft. The EC-135Cs themselves are scheduled to be retired, with most of their missions taken over by the US Navy's E-6 Mercury TACAMO platform. Another EC-135 variant is the EC-135E range instrumentation aircraft.

RC-135U, RC-135V Rivet Joint and RC-135W signals intelligence variants still form an important part of the USA's intelligence gathering assets. All three RC-135 variants feature slab sided cheek fairings covering the antennae for the Automatic Elint Emitter Locator System (AEELS) which intercepts transmissions on a broad range of frequencies and sorts out those which may be of interest to the aircraft's operators. The RC-135V and RC-135W also feature a thimble nose featuring further sensors. The TC-135W is a similar variant used for RC-135 crew training. The RC-135S Cobra Ball aircraft record foreign missile launches and testing.

The NC-135 and NKC-135 designations apply to aircraft used for various test and trials purposes, including inflight refuelling tests. The USN operates two NKC-135As electronic warfare aircraft, used to create simulated electronic warfare environments for fleet training.

Other variants on the C-135 theme include the WC-135M weather research platform and the OC-135 which is used for Open Skies treaty verification reconnaissance and is fitted with panoramic, oblique and vertical cameras.

Photo: One of two USAF RC-135U 'Combat Sent' aircraft. (Paul Merritt)

Boeing 707

Country of origin: United States of America

Type: Strategic & VIP transport, tanker and special mission aircraft

Powerplants: 707-320B – Four 80kN (18,000lb) Pratt & Whitney JT3D-3 or four 84.4kN (19,000lb) P&W JT3D-7 turbofans.

Performance: 707-320B – Max speed 1010km/h (545kt), max cruising speed 974km/h (525kt), long range cruising speed 885km/h (478kt). Max initial rate of climb 4000ft/min. Range with max passenger load 6920km (3735nm), range with max fuel and 147 passengers and reserves 9265km (5000nm).

Weights: 707-320B – Empty 66,408kg (146,400lb), max takeoff 151,315kg (333,600lb).

Dimensions: 707-320B – Wing span 44.42m (145ft 9in), length 46.61m (152ft 11in), height 12.94m (42ft 5in). Wing area 283m² (3050sq ft).

Accommodation: Flightcrew of two pilots and flight engineer. In passenger service could seat up to 190 passengers. Alternatively can carry freight on main deck in freighter and combi versions.

Armament: None

Operators: Angola, Argentina, Australia, Brazil, Canada, Chile, Columbia, Germany, India, Indonesia, Israel, Italy, Morocco, NATO, Pakistan, Peru, South Africa, Spain, Togo, Venezuela, Yugoslavia.

History: The 707 is widely recognised as one of the two most important postwar commercial airliners, and with almost 1000 built (over 1000 including military versions) was one of the most successful. Now largely retired from commercial service, it is not surprising that many are now in military service.

Boeing's model 707 was based on the Model 367-80 jet transport development aircraft, which flew for the first time on July 15 1954. The 367-80 or Dash 80 demonstrator led to the KC-135 tanker (described separately) and then the larger 707 airliner. The 707 flew for the first time on December 20 1957 and entered service the next year. Compared with the KC-135, the initial 707-120 featured a wider, longer fuselage capable of seating passengers six abreast. Power was supplied by JT3 turbojets, the commercial equivalent of the J57.

Military 707s are all converted 707-320Bsm or 320Cs. The -320B differs from the original 120 in having four JT3D turbofan engines (equivalent to the TF33) and a stretched fuselage. The 707-320B and the 707-320C convertible passenger/freighter aircraft are the definitive 707 models and were delivered to airlines around the world between 1962 and 1977. Most military 707s are ex civilian aircraft, although Canada, Germany and Iran purchased new build 707s direct from Boeing (the Iranian aircraft delivered with a KC-135 style flying boom refuelling equipment and Beech probe and drogue wingtip pods).

Aside from Iran, many other 707 operators have fitted their 707s with air-to-air refuelling equipment. Australia, Brazil, Canada, Israel, Italy, Morocco, Peru, Spain and Venezuela all operate 707 tankers.

Israel has taken the basic 707 transport and adapted it for Elint and AEW missions. Some serve as command posts, others combined tanker/Elint aircraft. The AEW Phalcon is the most extensive non US military development of the 707 with phased array radar mounted in a nose radome and conformal cheeks along the sides of the fuselage. Aside from Israel, Chile and possibly South Africa operate Phalcons.

Photo: An Italian Air Force 707 tanker – note wingtip refuelling pod.

Boeing E-6 Mercury, VC-137 & EC-18

Country of origin: United States of America

Type: E-6 – Submarine communications and airborne command post VC-137 – VIP transport. EC-18 – Range instrumentation & cruise missile control aircraft

Powerplants: E-6A – Four 97.9kN (22,000lb) CFM International F108-CF-100 turbofans.

Performance: E-6A – Dash speed 980km/h (530kt), max cruising speed at 40,000ft 842km/h (455kt). Patrol altitude between 25,000 and 30,000ft. Service ceiling 42,000ft. Mission range without inflight refuelling 11,760km (6350nm). Operational radius 1855km (1000nm) on a 10hr 30min without refuelling, or 28hr 55min with one refuelling, or 72hr with multiple refuellings. Unrefuelled endurance 15hr 25min.

Weights: E-6A – Operating empty 78,378kg (172,795lb), max takeoff 155,130kg (342,000lb).

Dimensions: E-6A – Wing span 45.16m (148ft 2in), length 46.61m (152ft 11in), height 12.93m (42ft 5in). Wing area 283.4m² (3050.0sq ft).

Accommodation: E-6A – Flightcrew of four. Has eight bunks in rest area for relief crew and four communications work stations.

Armament: None

Operators: USA

History: The E-6, EC-18 and VC-137 are military variants of the 707.

The first US military development of the 707 airliner to see service was the VC-137. Three VC-137As were first delivered for VIP transport use in 1959. These aircraft were based on the 707-120 airframe and were powered by J57 (JT3) turbojets, but later became VC-137Bs when re-engined with TF33 turbofans. The VC-137Bs were redesignated C-137Bs in the late 1970s. The VC-137C designation applies to two larger TF33 powered 707-320 based VIP transports, used as the presidential Air Force One aircraft until replaced by the 747 based VC-25.

The EC-18 designation applies to ex American Airlines 707-320Bs purchased in 1981. Eight were originally delivered as C-18s – of those one was scrapped for parts and one was retained for general transport duties. Four were converted as EC-18B Advanced Range Instrumentation Aircraft (ARIA) with a steerable telemetry-receiving antenna in a bulbous nose radome (similar to the EC-135E). The remaining two are EC-18D Cruise Missile Mission Control Aircraft, fitted with an APG-63 radar (as on the F-15) and telemetry receiver.

The E-6 Mercury was developed for the US Navy as a replacement for EC-130Q TACAMO (TAke Charge And Move Out) Hercules. These 16 new build aircraft are tasked with providing a communications link between the national command structure, other command post aircraft such as the E-4 and the US Navy's submarine fleet – primarily ballistic nuclear missile armed submarines. The E-6 (initially named Hermes) is powered by CFM F108 turbofans and is equipped with a comprehensive secure communications suite, including HF, VHF and UHF radio comms and UHF satellite comms (two underwing pods house ESM receivers and the UHF satellite antennas). The aircraft is also equipped with two trailing wire antennas. First flight was on February 19 1987. The E-6s are now being upgraded to E-6B standard, gaining some EC-135 equipment and gradually taking over the EC-135's airborne command post role.

Photo: One of four USAF EC-18Bs. (Keith Anderson)

Boeing E-3 Sentry

Country of origin: United States of America

Type: Airborne Warning & Control System (AWACS) aircraft

Powerplants: E-3A/C – Four 93.4kN (21,000lb) Pratt & Whitney TF33-P-100 turbofans. E-3D/F – Four 106.8kN (24,000lb) CFM56-2A-3s.

Performance: E-3C – Max speed 853km/h (460kt). Service ceiling over 29,000ft. Operational radius 1610km (870nm) for a 6 hour patrol without inflight refuelling. Endurance without inflight refuelling over 11 hours. E-3D/F – Service ceiling over 30,000ft. Endurance without inflight refuelling over 10 hours.

Weights: E-3C – Operating empty 77,995kg (171,950lb), max takeoff 147,420kg (325,000lb). E-3D – Max takeoff 150,820kg (332,500lb).

Dimensions: E-3A/C/F – Wing span 44.42m (145ft 9in), length 46.61m (152ft 11in), height 12.73m (41ft 9in). Wing area 283.4m² (3050.0sq ft). E-3D – Same except wingspan 44.98m (147ft 7in).

Accommodation: E-3C/D/F – Total crew complement of 17.

Armament: None, although could carry self defence AAMs.

Operators: France, NATO, Saudi Arabia, UK, USA.

History: The E-3 Sentry is a flying command post detecting enemy aircraft and missiles, and directing and warning friendly aircraft of their positions.

The Sentry was developed as a replacement for the ageing Lockheed Super Constellation based EC-121 Warning Star. Development of a replacement based upon Boeing's 707-320 airframe resulted in the first flight of a prototype EC-137 on February 5 1972. The first operational E-3A Sentry was delivered in March 1977.

The basis of the Sentry's detection abilities is the massive Westinghouse APY-1 (first 25 aircraft) or APY-2 radar mounted in the rotodome affixed above the rear fuselage. The rotodome rotates six times per minute and can be operated in various modes such as over the horizon, pulse doppler scan, passive and maritime. The APY-2 is capable of tracking up to 600 low flying aircraft.

Internally the Sentry is equipped with operator stations for the radar and comprehensive communications suite, galley, rest area and bunks for rest/relief crew.

The USAF's original EC-137s and 22 E-3A Core aircraft were upgraded to E-3B Block 20 standard with a limited maritime surveillance capability, provision for self defence measures, ECM resistant communications equipment, more UHF radios, five more operator stations and a more powerful central computer. A later upgrade was for 10 E-3A Standards to E-3C Block 25 level with more operator consoles, more UHF radios and provision for Have Quick anti jamming.

NATO operates 18 E-3A Standard Sentries, while Saudi Arabia took delivery of five E-3A Standards powered by CFM56 engines plus eight KE-3A tankers without AWACS equipment. British E-3D Sentry AEW.1s and French E-3Fs are powered by CFM56s and have a refuelling probe, while E-3Ds have wingtip mounted Loral ESM pods.

Boeing has developed a Multi Stage Improvement Programme which involves upgrading the communications suite, fitting GPS, upgrading the radar and the central computer. Additionally, US and NATO E-3s are to be fitted with ESM with sensors in side mounted canoe type fairings.

Photo: The first NATO E-3 with ESM upgrade. (Boeing)

Boeing 727 & C-22

Country of origin: United States of America

Type: Passenger & VIP transport

Powerplants: C-22B/727-100 – Three 62.3kN (14,000lb) Pratt & Whitney JT8D-7 turbofans.

Performance: C-22B/727-100 – Max speed 1017km/h (550kt), max cruising speed 960km/h (518kt). Range with max payload 5000km (2700nm).

Weights: C-22B/727-100 – Empty equipped 36,560kg (80,600lb), max takeoff 72,570kg (160,000lb).

Dimensions: C-22B/727-100 – Wing span 39.92m (108ft 0in), length 40.59m (133ft 2in), height 10.36m (34ft 0in). Wing area 157.9m² (1700sq ft).

Accommodation: C-22B/727-100 – Flightcrew of three (two pilots and flight engineer). Typical two class 727-100 airline seating for 94, max seating for 131. Most are configured with customised VIP/presidential transport interiors. C-22Bs configured to seat 90, including 24 in first class leather seats. All seats face rearwards.

Armament: None

Operators: 727-100 – Belgium, Mexico, New Zealand, Panama, Senegambia, Taiwan. C-22 – USA.

History: The 727 was built in greater numbers than any other jet engined airliner except the 737. When production was completed in 1984 more 727s had been built than any other commercial jetliner, although only a handful have ever seen military service.

The 727 began life as a short to medium range medium capacity airliner to slot beneath Boeing's four engined 707 (described separately) and 720. Initial design studies began as early as 1956, and the resulting Boeing Model 727, which first flew on February 9 1963, featured three engines (for good field performance), the 707's fuselage cross section but with a redesigned lower fuselage, and limited commonality with the 707 and 720. The first 727 was delivered in February 1964. Relatively slow initial sales led to various sub variants with higher gross weight options, the 727-100C Convertible and 727-200QC Quick Change.

The stretched 727-200 was announced in August 1965 in response to demand for a higher capacity model. The 6.10m (20ft) stretch involved equal length plugs fore and aft of the main undercarriage, but no increased fuel capacity, adversely affecting range. This issue was addressed with the higher gross weight and longer range Advanced 727-200, which entered service in June 1971. The 727-200F freighter flew in 1983 and was the last variant of this highly successful airliner.

While its success as an airliner is almost without parallel, only a small number have filtered down into military service. Nevertheless a number of nations use 727-100s for passenger transport, mainly equipped with customised VIP or presidential/head of state interiors.

The US Air Force's 201st Airlift Squadron operates four ex PanAm and National Airlines 727-100s as C-22B staff transports (a single ex Lufthansa 727-100 C-22A has recently been retired). A single ex Singapore Airlines 727-200 is operated as the C-22C.

Photo: New Zealand's two ex United Airlines 727-100Cs serve with 40 Squadron alongside C-130H Hercules. (RNZAF)

Boeing 737, CT-43 & Surveiller

Country of origin: United States of America

Type: 737 – VIP and general transport. CT-43 – Navigation trainer. Surveiller – Maritime reconnaissance/transport

Powerplants: 737-200 – Two 64.5kN (14,500lb) Pratt & Whitney JT8D-9A turbofans, or two 69.0kN (15,500lb) JT8D-15s, or two 71.2kN (16,000lb) JT8D-17s, or two 77.4kN (17,400lb) JT8D-17Rs.

Performance: 737-200 – Max speed 943km/h (509kt), max cruising speed 927km/h (500kt), economical cruising speed 795km/h (430kt). Max initial rate of climb 3760ft/min. Range with 155 passengers and reserves between 3520km (1900nm) and 4260km (2300nm) depending on weight options and engines.

Weights: 737-200 – Operating empty 27,690kg (61,050lb), max takeoff 58,105kg (128,100lb).

Dimensions: 737-200 – Wing span 28.35m (93ft 0in), length 30.48m (100ft 0in), height 11.28m (37ft 0in). Wing area 91.1m² (980sq ft).

Accommodation: Flight crew of two pilots. CT-43 – Configured for 12 students, four advanced students and three instructors. Surveiller – Indonesia's 737s fitted with 14 first class and 88 economy seats.

Armament: None

Operators: 737 – Brazil, India, Mexico, Niger, South Korea, Thailand, Venezuela. CT-43 – USA. Surveiller – Indonesia.

History: With over 3200 737s of all variants sold, Boeing's smallest airliner is the world's most successful jet airliner in terms of sales. A small number of these are in military service as transports, while the 737 also forms the basis of the USAF's CT-43 navigation trainer, and is in use for maritime patrol duties in Indonesia.

The 737 was conceived as a short range small capacity airliner to round out the Boeing jet airliner family, slotting beneath the 727 (described separately), 720 and 707 (described separately). Announced in February 1965, the 737 was originally envisioned as seating between 60 to 85, although a 100 seat design was finally settled upon. Design features included twin underwing mounted turbofans and 60% structure and systems commonality with the 727.

The first 737-100 made its first flight on April 9 1967. Further development led to the stretched 737-200, which became the main production model through to the mid 1980s. Current models are the CFM International CFM56 powered 110 seat 737-500, 130 seat 737-300 and 145 seat 737-400. The similarly sized 737-600, -700 and -800 respectively are currently under development.

The US Air Force took delivery of 19 T-43 navigation trainers from mid 1973. These aircraft are based on the 737-200 with a specialised trainer featuring accommodation for 12 student navigators, four advanced student navigators and three instructors. Navigation stations are fitted along the starboard side of the fuselage. The T-43 was later redesignated CT-43, reflecting the fact that many of these aircraft also have a passenger transport role.

Indonesia operates three 737-200 Surveillers for maritime reconnaissance, fitted with a Motorola Side Looking Airborne Modular Multi Mission Radar (SLAMMR), with antennae fitted in blade fairings on the rear fuselage.

Other nations operate 737s in VIP and staff transport roles.

Photo: One of three Indonesian 737-200 Surveillers. (Boeing)

Boeing 747, E-4 & VC-25

Country of origin: United States of America

Type: 747 – VIP transport, command post and strategic transport. E-4 – Command post aircraft. VC-25 – Presidential transport

Powerplants: E-4B – Four 233.5kN (52,500lb) GE F103-GE-100 turbofans.

Performance: E-4B – Max speed 970km/h (523kt), economical cruising speed 907km/h (490kt). Cruise ceiling 45,000ft. Ferry range 12,600km (6800nm). Mission endurance with reserves and without inflight refuelling 12 hours, with refuelling 72 hours.

Weights: E-4B – Max takeoff 362,875kg (800,000lb).

Dimensions: E-4B, VC-25 & 747-200 – Wing span 59.64m (195ft 8in), length 70.51m (231ft 4in), height 19.33m (63ft 5in). Wing area 511m² (5500sq ft).

Accommodation: E-4B – Flightcrew of four. Crew rest area in upper deck. Main deck fitted with command area, a conference room, battle staff area and command, control and communications area. VC-25 – Accommodation for the President with 70 passenger seats and accommodation for 23 crew. 747-200/400 – Seating for up to 400 troops.

Armament: None

Operators: 747 – Japan, Iran. E-4 – USA. VC-24 – USA.

History: Developed as a private venture at enormous financial risk, the 747 was the world's first widebody airliner and was over twice the size of any airliner preceding it.

The 747 went on to become one of the most important aircraft of all time, as it introduced massive reductions in the cost of travel, thus making international travel far more accessible.

The 747 first flew on February 9 1969. Since that time it has been produced in five basic versions, the initial 747-100, the heavier 747-200, long range, shorter fuselage 747SP (one is operated by the Saudi Royal Flight), the 747-300 which introduced the stretched upper deck, and the ultra long range, two crew 747-400.

The USAF selected the 747-200 as the basis for its E-4 Advanced Airborne National Command Post aircraft (alternatively the National Emergency Airborne Command Port – NEACP or Kneecap). Nicknamed the Doomsday Plane, the E-4 is tasked with providing an airborne base from which the US President and senior government officials can operate during war – in particular nuclear war. Three E-4As were delivered from late 1974, while a single E-4B with greatly improved communications and a revised interior was delivered in 1979. The E-4As were later modded to E-4B standard.

The VC-25 designation applies to two 747-200s delivered to the USAF in 1990 to serve as presidential transports – Air Force One when the US President is onboard. The VC-25 features a comprehensive communications fit, presidential stateroom, conference room and accommodation for senior staffers, press and flight and cabin crews.

The C-19 designation applies to US 747 airliners which are part of the Civil Reserve Air Fleet, a pool of transport aircraft that the military can call upon in time of war. The USAF may also acquire new 747-400 Freighters – C-33s – instead of acquiring additional C-17s.

Japan operates two 747-400s as VIP and troop transports. Iran meanwhile took delivery of three 747-100 tanker/transports and four 747-100F Freighters during the 1970s.

Photo: One of two USAF VC-25s over Mount Rushmore. (Boeing)

Boeing 757

Country of origin: United States of America

Type: Medium range VIP and government transport

Powerplants: Two 166.4kN (37,400lb) Rolls-Royce RB211-535C turbofans, or two 178.4kN (40,100lb) RB211-535E4s, or two 170kN (38,200lb) Pratt & Whitney PW2037s, or two 185.5kN (41,700lb) PW2040s.

Performance: Max cruising speed 914km/h (493kt), economical cruising speed 850km/h (460kt). Range with P&W engines and 186 passengers 5522km (2980nm), with RR engines 5226km (2820nm). Range at optional max takeoff weight with P&W engines 7410km (4000nm), with RR engines 6857km (3700nm).

Weights: Operating empty with P&W engines 57,040kg (125,750lb), with RR engines 57,180kg (126,050lb). Medium range max takeoff weight 104,325kg (230,000lb), long range max takeoff weight 113,395kg (250,000lb).

Dimensions: Wing span 38.05m (124ft 10in), length 47.32m (155ft 3in), height 13.56m (44ft 6in). Wing area 185.25m² (1994sq ft).

Accommodation: Flightcrew of two. Typical passenger arrangements vary from 16 first & 162 economy passengers to 214 to 239 in an all economy class configuration. Argentinean and Mexican aircraft have customised interiors.

Armament: None

Operators: Argentina, Mexico.

History: Just two 757s were in military service in 1995, however the type exhibits considerable potential as a VIP aircraft, transport and tanker.

Boeing bandied around a number of proposals for a successor to the 727 trijet airliner (described separately) during the 1970s, many of these designs featuring the nose and T tail of the earlier jet. It was not until later in that decade however that Boeing settled on a more conventional design featuring the same cross section as the 727, as well as the 737, 707 and 720, but considerably longer in length, with an all new wing, fuel efficient high bypass turbofan engines and a new nose section housing an advanced cockpit. Development of the 757 was launched in 1975 to be developed in tandem with the widebody 767 (described separately). The 767 first flew a few months earlier, but the two types share a number of systems and technology, including a common flightdeck.

First flight was on February 19 1982, entering service January the following year. Subsequent versions to appear are the 757-200PF Package Freighter, a pure freighter, and the 757-200M Combi. The standard passenger aircraft is designated the 757-200.

In terms of commercial orders, the 757 has been a great success story for Boeing, with over 870 ordered by late 1995. As yet though it has only found limited applications in the military role. Just two wore military colours in 1995, an example each serving with the air forces of Argentina and Mexico. Both these aircraft are used for VIP and government transport tasks, and are fitted with customised interiors. The 757 would appear to have great potential as a military transport in the years to come though, possibly as a replacement for the many transport and tanker 707s now in service.

Boeing also uses its prototype 757 for development for the F-22 fighter program in a number of roles, including avionics testing.

Photo: Mexico's 757 presidential transport. (Julian Green)

Boeing E-767

Country of origin: United States of America

Type: Airborne Early Warning & Control System (AWACS) aircraft

Powerplants: Two 273.6kN (61,500lb) General Electric CF6-80C2 turbofans.

Performance: Estimated – 767 airliner max cruising speed 914km/h (493kt), 767 airliner cruising speed 854km/h (461kt). Service ceiling 34,000 to 43,000ft. Unrefuelled range 8335 to 9260km (4500 to 5000nm). Endurance at 1850km (1000nm) patrol radius seven hours, endurance at 555km (300nm) 10 hours. Endurance with inflight refuelling 22 hours.

Weights: Max takeoff 171,005kg (377,000lb).

Dimensions: Wing span 47.47m (156ft 1in), length 48.51m (159ft 2in), height 15.85m (52ft 0in). Wing area 283.3m² (3050sq ft).

Accommodation: Full crew complement consists of two pilots, mission director, tactical director, fighter allocator, two weapon controllers, surveillance controller, link manager, seven surveillance operators, communications operator, radar technician, communications technician and computer display technician. Crew rest area and galley in rear of cabin. Reserve crew also carried.

Armament: None

Operators: Japan*

History: The Boeing E-767 is an adaptation of the 767-200 airliner fitted with the radar and systems of the E-3 Sentry for Japan.

Development of the E-767 was spurred by a Japanese requirement for four AWACS aircraft, with the natural choice being the E-3 Sentry (described separately). However, the closure of the 707/E-3 production line in 1991 led Boeing and Japan to look at developing an AWACS platform using the Sentry's core systems and the airframe of the 767-200ER airliner. Boeing announced it was performing definition studies of such a combination to meet the Japanese requirement in December 1991.

Japan ordered two E-767s in November 1993, and now has the required four on order. The first 'green' E-767 airframe was due to fly in December 1995. It will then be fitted with a dummy radome for aerodynamic testing, while the second E-767 will be the first fitted with the AWACS radar and avionics suite. The first two aircraft are scheduled to be delivered to Japan in 1998.

Central to the E-767 is the Westinghouse APY-2 surveillance radar, as on the E-3. Internally the E-767 will be configured with bays for communications, data processing, eight multifunction operator consoles in two rows, equipment bays, galley and crew rest area.

Aside from Japan, Boeing sees a small but significant market for further E-767 sales to countries such as Italy.

In addition, Boeing has also selected the 767 for development for a family of military transports to replace the large numbers of converted 707s currently in service. The most obvious roles are aerial tankers and strategic transports. Boeing studies found that the 767 was the best Boeing airliner platform suitable for adaption for the majority of anticipated military missions.

The US Army has also operated the prototype 767 as an airborne laboratory, fitted with a large dorsal cupola containing an infrared sensor as part of the Air and Strategic Defense programs.

Photo: An artist's impression of tanker and AWACS 767s. (Boeing)

Boeing Helicopters CH-46 Sea Knight

Boeing Helicopters CH-47 Chinook

Country of origin: United States of America

Type: Medium lift, multirole helicopter

Powerplants: CH-46E – Two 1395kW (1870shp) General Electric T58-GE-16 turboshafts, driving two three bladed rotors.

Performance: CH-46E – Max speed at sea level 267km/h (144kt), max cruising speed at sea level 266km/h (143kt). Max initial rate of climb 1715ft/min. Hovering ceiling in ground effect 9500ft, hovering ceiling out of ground effect 5750ft. Ferry range 1110km (600nm), range with a 1090kg (2400lb) payload 1020km (550nm).

Weights: CH-46E – Empty 5255kg (11,585lb), max takeoff 11,022kg (24,300lb).

Dimensions: CH-46E – Rotor diameter each 15.24m (50ft 0in), length overall with rotors turning 25.40m (83ft 4in), fuselage length 13.66m (44ft 10in), height to top of rear rotor head 5.09m (16ft 9in). Total rotor disc area 364.8m^2 (3927.0sq ft).

Accommodation: Crew of three, with 25 troops and troop commander. Standard USMC CH-46E load of 17 troops or 15 casualty litters. CH-46E max payload 3175kg (7000lb). Can carry external sling loads.

Armament: None

Operators: Canada, Japan, Saudi Arabia, Sweden, USA.

History: The United States Marine Corp's primary assault troop transport helicopter, the CH-46 Sea Knight began life as a private venture.

In the mid 1950s the Vertol company (later acquired by Boeing) began design studies of a medium lift twin engine transport helicopter, taking advantage of the lifting capabilities offered by turboshaft engines. The resulting Model 107 helicopter flew in prototype form for the first time on April 22 1958. This initial prototype was powered by two 640kW (860shp) Lycoming T53 turboshafts, tandem main rotors (negating the need for an anti torque tail rotor), an unobstructed main cabin and rear loading freight ramp.

The Model 107 originally aroused the interest of the US Army, who ordered three as YCH-1As for evaluation, but this service went on to order the larger CH-47 Chinook. Instead it was the US Marines who ordered the 107 into production in June 1961, as the HRB-1 (CH-46 after 1962), to replace its UH-34s.

The first of 160 USMC CH-46As entered service in June 1964, these aircraft powered by 935kW (1250shp) General Electric T58-GE-8 turboshafts. The US Navy took delivery of 14 similar UH-46As for vertical replenishment of ships at sea. The USMC's CH-46D and USN's UH-46D introduced 1045kW (1400shp) T58-GE-10s, while the similar CH-46F introduced more avionics.

The Marines' current CH-46 model is the E, an upgrade of CH-46D and F models with 1395kW (1870shp) T58-GE-16s, and improved crash survivability. Deliveries of upgraded Es began in 1977.

Canada took delivery of six CH-46A based CH-113 Labradors for SAR and 12 CH-113A Voyageurs for transport. Sweden's HKP-4s feature Rolls-Royce Gnome engines. In Japan Kawasaki has licence built (through to 1990) and further developed the 107 as the KV 107 for military and commercial operators. Uses include SAR, mine countermeasures and transport, while some were exported to Saudi Arabia and Sweden.

Photo: A US Navy UH-46 Sea Knight. (Wally Civitico)

Country of origin: United States of America

Type: Medium lift transport helicopter

Powerplants: CH-47D – Two 2795kW (3750shp) takeoff rated Textron Lycoming T55-L-712 turboshafts driving two three bladed rotors. MH-47E – two 3264kW (4378shp) takeoff rated T55-L-712s.

Performance: CH-47D – Max cruising speed at sea level 290km/h (156kt), cruising speed at sea level 265km/h (143kt). Max initial rate of climb 1522ft/min. Service ceiling 8450ft. Hovering ceiling in ground effect 8200ft, out of ground effect 4950ft/min. Range 425km (230nm). MH-47E – Ferry range 1380km (1200nm), operational radius 560km (300nm). Endurance 5hr 30min.

Weights: US Army CH-47D – Empty 10,615kg (23,400lb), max takeoff 22,680kg (50,000lb). Intl CH-47D – Empty 10,578kg (23,231lb), max takeoff 24,495kg (54,000lb). MH-47E – Empty 12,210kg (26,918lb), max takeoff 24,495kg (54,000lb).

Dimensions: CH-47D – Rotor diameter each 18.29m (60ft 0in), length overall rotors turning 30.18m (99ft 0in), fuselage length 15.55m (51ft 0in), height to top of rear rotor head 5.77m (18ft 11in). Total rotor disc area 525.3m^2 (5654.9sq ft). Intl CH-47E & MH-47E – Same except fuselage length 15.87m (52ft 1in).

Accommodation: Two flightcrew with main cabin seating for up to 44 troops or 24 casualty litters.

Armament: MH-47E – Two window mounted 0.50in M2 machine guns, with provision for Stinger AAMs, some mount miniguns.

Operators: Argentina, Australia, Canada, Egypt, Greece, Iran, Italy Japan, Libya, Morocco, Netherlands, Singapore, South Korea, Spain, Taiwan, Thailand, UK, USA.

History: The Chinook is the primary medium lift helicopter of the US Army and a number of other air arms, with no replacement in sight.

Although the US Army was originally interested in the smaller Vertol 107 (which became the CH-46 Sea Knight), in June 1959 the service selected the much larger Vertol Model 114 for development as its battlefield mobility helicopter. First flight was on September 21 1961, with service entry of the CH-47A Chinook in August 1962.

Large numbers of CH-47As and CH-47Bs (with uprated engines and larger diameter rotors) saw extensive service in Vietnam, as did to a lesser extent CH-47Cs (with further uprated engines and additional fuel capacity), which first flew in 1968. Large numbers of US Army CH-47As and Bs were upgraded to C standard, while new build Cs were widely exported and have also been built in Italy under licence by Agusta.

The current CH-47D Chinook first flew in February 1982. Improvements include yet more powerful T55-L-712 turboshafts, NVG compatible flightdeck and triple external cargo hooks. All US Army CH-47s have now been rebuilt to CH-47D standard while new build and upgraded CH-47D Internationals have been delivered to a number of countries.

The MH-47E is a US Army special operations aircraft used for covert troop insertion and extraction. Features include NVG compatible EFIS flightdeck, GPS, FLIR, terrain following radar, refuelling probe and a missile warning/countermeasures suite. Up to 51 will be built for the US Army and eight for the RAF as HC.3s.

Photo: An RAF Chinook HC.1. (Bruce Malcolm)

Boeing/Sikorsky RAH-66 Comanche

Country of origin: United States of America

Type: Two seat scout and reconnaissance attack helicopter

Powerplants: Two 1002kW (1344shp) LHTEC T800-LHT-801 turboshafts, driving a five bladed main rotor and eight blade fan-in-fin shrouded tail rotor.

Performance: Max level speed (dash) 328km/h (177kt). Max vertical rate of climb 1182ft/min. Time to turn 180° to target 4.7 seconds. Time to snap turn at target at 148km/h (80kt) 3.0 seconds. Ferry range with external fuel 2335km (1260nm). Endurance with standard fuel 2 hours 30 minutes.

Weights: Empty 3515kg (7750lb), empty equipped for combat 4167kg (9187lb), mission takeoff 4587kg (10,112lb), max takeoff 7790kg (17,175lb).

Dimensions: Main rotor diameter 11.90m (39ft 1in), length overall rotor turning 14.28m (46ft 10in), fuselage length excluding gun 13.22m (43ft 5in), height over tailplane 3.39m (11ft 2in). Main rotor disc area 111.2m² (1197.0sq ft).

Accommodation: Pilot (front) and Weapon Systems Operator (rear) in stepped, tandem cockpit.

Armament: One 20mm, three barrel General Electric/GIAT cannon in undernose turret. Two weapons bay doors can hold three Hellfire or Stinger missiles each, with four Hellfires or eight Stingers on optional stub wings.

Operators: USA*

History: Without doubt the most advanced (and most expensive) combat helicopter currently under development, the RAH-66 scout/reconnaissance helicopter may yet not make it into military service.

As early as 1982 the US Army devised the LHX (Light Helicopter Experimental) program to replace 5000 UH-1s, AH-1s, OH-6s and OH-58s. By 1988 though when a request for proposals was issued to the Boeing/Sikorsky First Team and Bell/McDonnell Douglas Super Team, the requirement had been refined to just a scout/reconnaissance helicopter, with the requirement brought back to 1292.

The Boeing Sikorsky teaming's proposal was selected for development as the RAH-66 Comanche in April 1991. Advanced features of the RAH-66 are many, and include: stealth with airframe faceting to reduce radar cross section; a five bladed, composite main rotor with swept tips and bearingless hub (based on a Daimler Benz Aerospace design); Sikorsky developed eight bladed fan-in-fin shrouded tail rotor; internal weapons bays; retractable undercarriage; two specially developed LHTEC (AlliedSignal and Allison) T800 turboshafts; detachable stub wings; NVG compatible EFIS cockpits with 3D digital moving map displays; triple redundant fly-by-wire controls; sidestick cyclics; helmet mounted sights; Longbow millimetre wave radar; FLIR and laser designator. First flight was due in the second half of 1995.

Unfortunately for Boeing, Sikorsky and the US Army, the RAH-66 program has suffered a number of delays and setbacks, mainly because of budget cutbacks. In December 1994 the US DoD deferred the decision whether or not to put in the RAH-66 into production until 2000, but in the meantime three YRAH-66 development aircraft are being built. Initial Operational Capability could be as far away as 2007.

Photo: A mock-up of the RAH-66 in desert camouflage. (Boeing)

Breguet Alizé

Country of origin: France

Type: Carrier borne anti submarine warfare aircraft

Powerplant: One 1475kW (1975shp) Rolls-Royce Dart RDa.7 Mk 21 turboprop, driving a four bladed propeller.

Performance: Max speed 520km/h (281kt) at 9900ft, 460km/h (248kt) at sea level, cruising speed 370km/h (200kt), patrol speed 232km/h (125kt). Max initial rate of climb 1380ft/min. Service ceiling above 20,500ft. Ferry range with auxiliary fuel 2870km (1550nm), or 2500km (1350nm) with standard fuel. Endurance with auxiliary fuel 7hr 40min, or 5hr 5min with standard fuel.

Weights: Empty 5700kg (12,565lb), max takeoff 8250kg (18,190lb).

Dimensions: Wing span 15.60m (51ft 2in), length 13.86m (45ft 6in), height 5.00m (16ft 5in). Wing area 36.0m² (387.5sq ft).

Accommodation: Crew of three, comprising pilot, radar operator and a sensor operator.

Armament: Internal weapons bay can carry a homing torpedo or three 160kg (353lb) depth charges. Two underwing hardpoints can carry an air-to-surface missile each, or rockets, bombs or depth charges.

Operators: France

History: That the Alizé looks set to see service in the harsh carrier environment past the turn of the century is a ringing tribute to the longevity of a design that was conceived in 1948, and flew for the first time in 1956.

Design work on what evolved into the Alizé began in 1948 against a French Navy requirement for a carrier based strike aircraft. Breguet's resulting Br.990 Vultur (vulture) featured a nose mounted Armstrong Siddeley Mamba turboprop plus an auxiliary Rolls-Royce Nene turbojet in the rear fuselage which would be shut down in cruise flight to boost endurance. Although the Vultur was successfully test flown, the French Navy never ordered it into production, and instead Breguet used the basic design as the basis for a carrier borne ASW platform.

The evolution to an ASW platform began in 1954 and involved dropping the Nene, substituting a Rolls-Royce Dart for the Mamba turboprop and the addition of a search radar mounted in a retractable radome. The changes to the Vultur justified the adoption of a new name – Alizé (tradewind). Other features of the Alizé design is that the main undercarriage retracts forward into underwing pods which also contain sonobuoys, while the pilot and radar operator sit side-by-side, with a sensor operator seated behind them.

The Alizé flew for the first time in prototype form on October 6 1956. Deliveries of production aircraft began in May 1959 and amounted to 75 for the French Navy and 12 for India. (Breguet merged with Dassault in December 1961.)

Since then France's surviving Alizé fleet has been upgraded twice. In 1980 they were fitted with a Thomson-CSF Iguane radar, plus new navigation and communications systems, and an ESM capability. In 1990 the 24 surviving French Alizés were fitted with a datalink and other minor modifications, extending their service life beyond 2000.

India's Alizés were retired in 1992, after having been shore based since 1987 (when the carrier *Vikrant* was fitted with a ski jump).

Photo: A French Navy Alizé at rest. (Paul Merritt)

British Aerospace 146

BAe/Hawker Siddeley HS.748

Country of origin: United Kingdom

Type: VIP transport

Powerplants: BAe 146-100 – Four 30.0kN (6700lb) Textron Lycoming ALF 502R-3s or four 31.0kN (6970lb) ALF 502R-5 turbofans.

Performance: BAe 146-100 – Cruising speed 767km/h (414kt), long range cruising speed 670km/h (361kt). Range with standard fuel 3000km (1620nm), range with max payload 1630km (880nm).

Weights: 146-100 – Operating empty 23,288kg (51,342lb), max takeoff 38,100kg (84,000lb).

Dimensions: 146-100 – Wing span 26.21m (86ft 0in), length 26.20m (86ft 0in), height 8.61m (28ft 3in). Wing area 77.3m² (832.0sq ft).

Accommodation: 146-100 – Flightcrew of two, plus seating for up to 94 passengers six abreast in an airliner configuration. Queen's Flight CC.Mk 2s and Saudi Statesman aircraft fitted with VIP interiors.

Armament: None

Operators: Saudi Arabia, UK.

History: The BAe 146 is only in limited military service.

The origins of the 146 date to August 1973 when the then Hawker Siddeley Aviation announced it was designing a short range quiet airliner powered by four small turbofans. Under the designation HS.146, large scale development was to last just a few months before a worsening economic recession made the risk of the project seem unjustifiable. Development then continued on a limited scale, but it was not until July 1978 when the project was relaunched, by which time Hawker Siddeley had been absorbed into the newly created British Aerospace.

The resulting BAe 146 thus made its first flight on September 3 1981. Certification was granted in early 1983, with first deliveries following shortly afterwards in May 1983. Initial deliveries were of the 146-100, later versions included the stretched, 85-100 seat 146-200 and further stretched, 100-112 seat 146-300. Because of the type's low noise characteristics the 146 series has been quite successful as a freighter, designated QT – Quiet Trader.

The 146QT also formed the basis of the 146STA Small Tactical Airlifter, which features a cargo door in the rear fuselage. Proposed payloads included up to 60 fully equipped paratroops, or 24 stretchers. Although a demonstrator 146STA was flown in the late 1980s, none were ordered.

The 146 series is now marketed by British Aerospace's Avro arm as the RJ series, with improved engines and other systems. The 146-100 is now the RJ70, the 146-200 the RJ85 and the 146-300 the RJ100 and RJ115.

Military use of the 146 is limited to the UK and Saudi Arabia. The RAF leased three BAe 146-100s as CC.1s for evaluation as replacement for Andovers for the Queen's Flight. Two 146-100s were then ordered as CC.2s for service with the Queen's Flight. These were delivered from 1986 and have been fitted with Loral Matador infrared jamming equipment. A third was delivered in 1990.

Saudi Arabia operates four 146s, named Statesman, as VIP transports with its Royal Flight.

Photo: The Royal Air Force's BAe 146 CC.2s are fitted with infrared jammers. (Wally Civitico)

Country of origin: United Kingdom

Type: Utility and VIP transport

Powerplants: Srs 2A – Two 1700kW (2280ehp) Rolls-Royce Dart RDa.7 Mk 534-2 or 535-2 turboprops, driving four bladed constant speed propellers.

Performance: Srs 2A – Cruising speed 452km/h (244kt). Max initial rate of climb 1320ft/min. Service ceiling 25,000ft. Range with max payload and reserves 1360km (735nm), range with max fuel and reserves 3130km (1690nm).

Weights: Srs 2A – Operating empty 12,160kg (26,805lb), max takeoff 21,092kg (46,500lb).

Dimensions: Srs 2A – Wing span 30.02m (98ft 6in), length 20.42m (67ft 0in), height 7.57m (24ft 10in). Wing area 75.4m² (810.8sq ft).

Accommodation: Flightcrew of two. Seating for up to 58 troops in airline style seating. Can carry 48 paratroopers or 24 stretcher patients and nine medical attendants. Can be fitted with VIP interior. Australian nav trainers fitted with side facing workstation for two students and an instructor, plus passenger seating.

Armament: None

Operators: Australia, Belgium, Brazil, Ecuador, India, Nepal, South Korea, Sri Lanka, Tanzania, Thailand.

History: The rugged HS.748 transport began life as an Avro design effort to re-enter the civil market in anticipation of a decline in military business.

The HS.748 has proven to be reasonably successful sales wise, and popular in third world nations with poor facilities, mainly as an airliner, but also as a military transport. Of the 382 built, 52 were delivered new to military customers.

First surfacing as the Avro 748 in 1958, Hawker Siddeley took over the 748 design in 1959 (Avro being a part of the Hawker Siddeley Group). The new aircraft made a successful maiden flight on June 24 1960.

The Series 2, in its 2, 2A and 2C variants, was the most successful of the line, the first flying on November 6 1961. The Series 2 differed from the 1 in having progressively higher weights and more powerful engines. The Series 2B appeared in 1977, offering a range of aerodynamic and other improvements, including an increased wing span.

The most advanced variant of the 748 to appear, the Super 748, made its first flight in July 1984. It introduced an advanced flight deck, improved efficiency and hushkitted engines, and new interior fitout.

Two specific military versions offered were the BAe 748 Military Transport and the Coast Guarder. The Military Transport features a large cargo door in the rear fuselage, strengthened floor for freight and optional higher max takeoff weights. Customers included Belgium, Brazil and Ecuador. 20 similar aircraft were licence built in India.

The Coastguarder was optimised for maritime patrol and SAR and fitted with a search radar, but was never sold. India meanwhile has tested a 748 modified for AEW with a rotodome above the fuselage.

Australia is one of the largest 748 operators. The RAAF operates two as light transports and eight as navigation trainers. The Royal Australian Navy operates a further two configured as EW trainers to simulate an electronic warfare environment as a training aid for training ships and aircraft.

Photo: This Australian 748 serves as a nav trainer. (Keith Anderson)

BAe/Hawker Siddeley Andover

Country of origin: United Kingdom

Type: Tactical transport

Powerplants: Two 2420kW (3245ehp) Rolls-Royce RDa.12 Dart turboprops, driving four bladed constant speed propellers.

Performance: Max speed 490km/h (265kt), normal cruising speed 450km/h (243kt). Max initial rate of climb 1200ft/min. Service ceiling 24,000ft. STOL takeoff run 315m (1030ft). Range with max fuel and reserves 3620km (1955nm), range with max payload 795km (430nm).

Weights: Basic operating 12,550kg (27,665lb), max takeoff 22,680kg (50,000lb).

Dimensions: Wing span 29.87m (98ft 0in), length 23.75m (77ft 11in), height 8.97m (29ft 5in). Wing area 77.2m² (831.4sq ft).

Accommodation: Flightcrew of two pilots, can also carry a navigator/radio operator. Main cabin can seat up to 52 troops, or 40 paratroops or 25 stretcher patients plus medical attendants or up to three Land Rover 4WDs. Some New Zealand aircraft fitted with a customised VIP interior.

Armament: None

Operators: New Zealand, UK.

History: The Andover is a dedicated STOL capable military tactical transport, complete with rear loading ramp, developed from the basic HS.748 transport.

Avro began design work on its Model 780 to meet a Royal Air Force requirement for a STOL tactical transport capable of operating from dirt or roughly prepared 275m length airstrips from 1963. The resulting aircraft was based closely on the HS.748 Series 2 airliner, but differed in a number of key areas to tailor it to its military role. The most obvious change was to the rear fuselage, which was redesigned to feature a rear loading ramp. The fuselage was also stretched slightly, and the tailplane repositioned (with dihedral added to the horizontal tail) to allow for the rear ramp. One innovative feature was the Dowty Rotol kneeling main undercarriage, designed to allow the cabin floor sill to be adjusted in height and horizontally to align with the trays of loading/unloading trucks.

The Andover also features more powerful Dart turboprops compared with the HS.748, and larger diameter propellers.

The first Andover was in fact the HS.748 prototype converted to the new configuration, and it flew for the first time on December 21 1963. In all, 31 were built and all were delivered to the RAF's Air Support Command. Apart from UK based squadrons, RAF Andovers were based in Singapore and Aden (Yemen).

The UK's 1975 budget cuts resulted in a number of the Andover fleet becoming surplus, and 10 were sold to New Zealand. Nine still serve with the RNZAF, used for tactical and VIP transport.

Numbers of RAF Andovers are dwindling, but includes four HS.748s delivered originally for the Queen's Flight and confusingly designated Andover CC.Mk 2. RAF Andovers are still used for a variety of roles including test duties and for Open Skies verification flights.

Photo: A New Zealand Andover in Somalia.

British Aerospace Bulldog

Country of origin: United Kingdom

Type: Two seat basic trainer

Powerplant: T.1 – One 150kW (200hp) Lycoming IO-360-A1B6 fuel injected flat four piston engine, driving a two bladed constant speed propeller.

Performance: T.1 – Max speed 240km/h (130kt), max cruising speed 222km/h (120kt), economical cruising speed 195km/h (105kt). Max initial rate of climb 1035ft/min. Service ceiling 16,000ft. Range with max fuel at 55% power 1000km (540nm). Endurance with max fuel 5 hours.

Weights: T.1 – Empty equipped 650kg (1430lb), normal and semi aerobatic max takeoff 1065kg (2350lb), fully aerobatic max takeoff 1015kg (2238lb).

Dimensions: T.1 – Wing span 10.06m (33ft 0in), length 7.09m (23ft 3in), height 2.28m (7ft 6in). Wing area 12.0m² (129.4sq ft).

Accommodation: Seating for two side-by-side, with room for an observer behind them.

Armament: Provision for weapons on four optional underwing hardpoints, including rocket and gun pods, practice and live bombs.

Operators: Ghana, Jordan, Kenya, Lebanon, Malaysia, Sweden, UK.

History: The Bulldog two seat primary trainer has its origins in the civil Beagle B.121 Pup, a two place light aircraft.

The Beagle Pup flew for the first time on April 8 1967 and established the basis design and configuration that was to characterise the Bulldog. While the Pup was popular with pilots for its good flying characteristics the Beagle company was experiencing continuing financial difficulties that forced it to close its doors in January 1970, with production of the Pup ceasing after just 150 had been built.

Before then though, Beagle had flown a military trainer variant called the Bulldog on May 19 1969. Based closely on the Pup, features of the Bulldog included a rearward sliding cockpit canopy with seating for two side by side (with room for an observer behind them), a Lycoming IO-360 four cylinder piston engine driving a two bladed constant speed prop and fixed undercarriage.

Following the collapse of Beagle, Scottish Aviation (since merged into British Aerospace) purchased the Bulldog's design rights, and flew its own Bulldog prototype on February 14 1971. The first Series 100 production aircraft flew on June 22 1971 and a total of 98 was built for Kenya, Malaysia and Sweden (both air force and army).

The Series 120 was built in larger numbers, and introduced increased aerobatic capability at maximum weight, and full aerobatic capability up to a higher weight. The largest Bulldog customer was the RAF, who took delivery of 130 Model 121s designated the T.1. The survivors equip University Air Squadrons to train sponsored undergraduate students, plus other miscellaneous units. The 120 was also widely exported, and production ceased in 1981.

A developed version of the Bulldog was the Bullfinch, which featured a retractable undercarriage. It was flown in 1976 but was not put into production.

Photo: An RAF Bulldog T.1. Note the good visibility offered by the rearward sliding canopy. (Bruce Malcolm)

British Aerospace Harrier T.4 & AV-8S

Country of origin: United Kingdom

Type: STOVL light attack aircraft

Powerplant: One 95.6kN (21,500lb) Rolls-Royce Pegasus Mk 103 turbofan (designated F402 on AV-8).

Performance: AV-8S – Max speed 1175km/h (635kt). Max initial rate of climb 29,000ft/min. Time to 40,000ft after vertical takeoff 2min 23sec. Service ceiling 51,000ft. Takeoff run with 2270kg (5000lb) warload 305m (1000ft). Ferry range with external fuel 3430km (1850nm). Combat radius with 1995kg (4400lb) warload, hi-lo-hi, 665km (360nm).

Weights: AV-8S – Empty equipped 5530kg (12,190lb), normal VTO 7735kg (17,050lb), max takeoff STO 10,115kg (22,300lb).

Dimensions: AV-8S – Wing span 7.70m (25ft 3in), length 13.87m (45ft 6in), height 3.63m (11ft 11in). Wing area 18.7m² (201.1sq ft).

Accommodation: Pilot only in AV-8S. Seating for two in tandem in T.4 and TAV-8S.

Armament: Two 30mm Aden cannon mounted in underfuselage fairings. Four underwing stations can carry up to 2270kg (5000lb) of ordnance, including AIM-9 Sidewinder AAMs, rockets and bombs.

Operators: Spain, Thailand*, UK.

History: The revolutionary Harrier was the world's first practical V/STOL (vertical takeoff and landing) fixed wing aircraft.

The origins of the Harrier lie in the Hawker P.1127, design of which began in 1957 to take advantage of the Bristol BS.53 turbofan engine. The BS.53, which evolved into the Rolls-Royce Pegasus, was able to vector or direct thrust from its four exhaust nozzles which could pivot more than 90° from the horizontal.

The first of six P.1127 prototypes successfully made its first hovering flight on October 21 1960, while the first transition from vertical to horizontal flight occurred on September 12 1961. The P.1127s were followed by nine pre production development aircraft named Kestrel, which were operated for a time by a special tri nation squadron with pilots from the RAF, Germany and the USA. Britain ordered a further six development aircraft in February 1965, which it named Harrier. The first of these original Harriers first flew in August 1966.

While the planned P.1154 multirole supersonic fighter development for the RAF and RN was scrapped, the Harrier entered production for the RAF as a light strike aircraft, the first of these, designated GR.1, flying on December 28 1967. 132 were ordered, including T.2 trainers. RAF Harriers were delivered as GR.3s and T.4s from 1976 when the aircraft were fitted with a Marconi laser ranger/designator in an lengthened nose. In 1995 only T.4s survived for Harrier training.

The US Marines have been keen proponents of the Harrier since the program's inception and took delivery of 110 McDonnell Douglas built AV-8A and two seat TAV-8As, these aircraft have similar specification to the GR.1. Later upgraded to AV-8C standard, the last of these earlier Harriers was retired in 1987.

The only other customer for early Harriers was the Spanish navy, who ordered 11 AV-8A(S) single seaters and two TAV-8(S) two seaters from MDC. Designated VA.1 and VAE.1 respectively and named Matador, these aircraft remain in service alongside newer EAV-8B Matador IIs.

Photo: A Spanish AV-8A(S). Note deployed airbrake. (Paul Merritt)

British Aerospace Sea Harrier

Country of origin: UK

Type: STOVL naval multirole fighter

Powerplant: One 95.6kN (21,500lb) Rolls-Royce Pegasus Mk 104 turbofan.

Performance: FRS.1 – Max speed 1185km/h (640kt) plus at low level, cruising speed at 36,000ft 850km/h (460kt), cruising speed at low level 640 to 835km/h (350 to 450kt). Combat radius on a high altitude interception mission 750km (405nm), combat radius on a low level attack mission 465km (305nm).

Weights: FRS.1 – Operating empty 6375kg (14,052lb), max takeoff 11,880kg (26,200lb).

Dimensions: FRS.1 – Wing span 7.70m (25ft 3in), length overall 14.50m (47ft 7in), height 3.71m (12ft 2in). Wing area 18.7m² (201.1sq ft).

Accommodation: Pilot only.

Armament: FRS.1 – Two underfuselage pod mounted 30mm Aden cannons. Four underwing pylons can carry up to 3630kg (8000lb) but cleared for 2270kg (5000lb) of armament including AIM-9 Sidewinders, bombs, rockets and BAe Sea Eagle antishipping missiles. Indian FRS.51s wired for Matra AAMs.

Operators: India, UK.

History: The Sea Harrier has one of the best air-to-air combat records in recent military history, shooting down 28 Argentinean warplanes in the Falklands War for no loss.

The suitability of the basic Harrier design for use from small aircraft carriers was obvious from the program's inception. A P.1127 (Harrier predecessor) first demonstrated the type's suitability for carrier operations by flying off HMS *Ark Royal*, although official Royal Navy interest was not forthcoming until the mid 1970s when it became obvious that its conventional Phantom and Buccaneer equipped aircraft carriers would not be replaced. Instead the RN sanctioned development of a navalised Harrier for operation off the forthcoming ASW helicopter carriers (fitted with ski jump ramps), with 24 Sea Harrier FRS.1s ordered in May 1975. This far sighted decision was to pay huge dividends, the Sea Harrier coming into its own during the 1982 Falklands War, as they provided vital air cover for British ground forces and ships, and consistently outclassed Argentinean Mirage fighters in air-to-air engagements.

The FRS.1 Harrier is similar to the GR.3 except for the forward fuselage. The cockpit was raised, increasing room for additional avionics in the forward fuselage and giving the pilot much greater all round vision, while the FRS.1's nose contains an oblique reconnaissance camera and a Ferranti Blue Fox multimode radar (a development of the Lynx helicopter's Sea Spray radar). The FRS.1's Pegasus Mk 104 engine is a navalised version of the GR.3's Mk 103 with minor changes for operations in a marine environment, including anti corrosive coatings on some ferrous components.

The RN took delivery of a total of 57 FRS.1s plus four T.4N two seat conversion trainers which are similar to the RAF's T.4 and do not feature the Blue Fox radar. The FRS.1s are currently being upgraded to the improved F/A.2 standard (described next entry).

India is the only Sea Harrier export customer, ordering 24 Sea Harrier FRS.51s, plus four T.60 two seat trainers in 1978.

Photo: An FRS.1 hovers above HMS *Invincible*. (BAe)

British Aerospace Sea Harrier F/A.2

Country of origin: United Kingdom

Type: STOVL naval multirole fighter

Powerplant: One 95.6kN (21,500lb) Rolls-Royce Pegasus Mk 106 turbofan.

Performance: F/A.2 – Max speed 1185km/h (640kt) plus, cruising speed at 36,000ft 850km/h (460kt). Max initial rate of climb 50,000ft/min. Service ceiling 51,000ft. Takeoff run without ski ramp approx 305m (1000ft). Combat radius on a 90min time on station CAP with four AIM-120s and two drop tanks 185km (100nm), hi-lo-hi combat radius with two Sea Eagle missiles and two 30mm cannon 370km (200nm), hi-lo-hi reconnaissance mission radius with two drop tanks 970km (525nm).

Weights: Unpublished but similar to the FRS.1.

Dimensions: F/A.2 – Wing span 7.70m (25ft 3in), length overall 14.17m (46ft 6in), height 3.71m (12ft 2in). Wing area 18.7m² (201.1sq ft).

Accommodation: Pilot only.

Armament: Stressed to carry up to 3630kg (8000lb) of external ordnance, although only cleared for 2270kg (5000lb) on four underwing and two underfuselage hardpoints. Can carry up to four AIM-120 Amraams on outboard and underfuselage stations, or two AIM-120s and four AIM-9 Sidewinders. Underfuselage stations can also carry 30mm Aden cannon. Other weapons include bombs, rockets and BAe Sea Eagle ASM.

Operators: UK

History: The Sea Harrier F/A.2 is a midlife upgrade of the FRS.1, with changes to the airframe, cockpit, avionics, radar and armament.

Work on a midlife upgrade of the Sea Harrier first began in January 1985 when BAe was contracted to do a project definition study. British Aerospace initially proposed a number of aerodynamic refinements plus wingtip Sidewinder rails that were not adopted, with changes focusing around a new radar and modernised cockpit.

The first modified Sea Harrier, designated FRS.2, was an aerodynamic prototype without radar installed and it flew for the first time in its new configuration on September 19 1988. In all, British Aerospace has been contracted to convert 35 FRS.1s to the new standard (the FRS.2 designation was dropped in favour of F/A.2 in May 1994), while 10 new build F/A.2s were ordered to cover attrition losses. The first production conversions were delivered from April 1993.

The most obvious change of the F/A.2 is the Blue Vixen radar mounted in a new, rounded radome. The GEC-Marconi Blue Vixen is a pulse doppler multimode radar featuring all weather lookdown/shootdown capability, track-while-scan, multiple target tracking and improved surface target detection abilities. The F/A.2's nose contains an additional avionics bay, while the upgrade to the cockpit involves fitting HOTAS controls and multi function CRT displays. The fuselage is also stretched slightly, via the insertion of a 35cm (1ft 2in) plug behind the wing.

The F/A.2 program suffered a number of delays and an increase in cost of 20%, due largely to problems with integrating the Blue Vixen radar with the AIM-120 Amraam. However these problems have been overcome, giving the Royal Navy a very capable medium range fire and forget missile armed fighter.

Photo: The F/A.2 Sea Harrier features a more rounded radome. (BAe)

British Aerospace Strikemaster

Country of origin: United Kingdom

Type: Advanced jet trainer and light attack aircraft

Powerplant: Mk 80 – One 15.2kN (3140lb) Rolls-Royce Viper Mk 535 turbojet.

Performance: Mk 80 – Max speed at 18,000ft 775km/h (418kt), at sea level 725km/h (320kt). Max initial rate of climb 5250ft/min. Time to 30,000ft 8min 45sec. Service ceiling 40,000ft. Combat radius on a hi-lo-hi attack mission with 1360kg (3000lb) payload 397km (215nm), with a 455kg (1000lb) payload 925km (500nm). Combat radius on a lo-lo-lo attack mission with 455kg (1000lb) payload 445km (240nm).

Weights: Mk 80 – Operating empty 2810kg (6195lb), max takeoff 5215kg (11,500lb).

Dimensions: Mk 80 – Wing span 11.23m (36ft 10in), length 10.27m (33ft 9in), height 3.10m (10ft 2in). Wing area 19.9m² (213.7sq ft).

Accommodation: Seating for two, side by side.

Armament: Mk 80 – Two internal 7.62mm FN machine guns. Max permissible external stores load 1360kg (3000lb) on four underwing hardpoints, including rockets, bombs, practice bombs, gun and cannon pods, plus reconnaissance pods.

Operators: Botswana, Kenya, Oman, Saudi Arabia, Sudan.

History: The Strikemaster is the final and most potent development of a family of two seat trainers that began with the radial piston engine powered Percival Provost.

The Strikemaster is a direct development of the Hunting Percival (later BAC) Jet Provost. The Jet Provost began life as a low cost, minimum change development of the piston engined Provost, although the metamorphosis to jet power involved a much greater redesign than first planned. The Jet Provost (or JP) established the basic configuration of the Strikemaster, and flew for the first time on June 26 1954. The first major production JP was the T.3, the T.4 introduced two Martin Baker ejection seats and wingtip tanks. The definitive Jet Provost, the T.5 featured a redesigned, longer nose with a larger canopy, and forms the basis for the Strikemaster.

The development of an armed Jet Provost T.5 was a logical development, considering the JP's reasonable success with export customers. The resulting private venture Strikemaster was based closely on the Jet Provost T.5, but introduced a more powerful Viper turbojet, structural strengthening and four underwing hardpoints. BAC gave the Strikemaster its model number 167. The first Strikemaster made its first flight in October 1967 and production of the Mk 80 began a year later. All but 10 of the 146 built were Mk 80s, Sudan took delivery of 10 similar Mk 90s in 1984.

The Strikemaster appealed to a number of air arms because of its versatile ability to conduct advanced weapon training and light attack missions. The largest current Strikemaster operator is Saudi Arabia, where the aircraft is used for refresher training and liaison tasks now that Hawks have been delivered. Other important Strikemaster customers who have since retired their aircraft include New Zealand (its Strikemasters were nicknamed Bluntys), Kuwait and Singapore.

Photo: New Zealand replaced its Strikemasters with MB-339Cs. (Richard Kuluz)

British Aerospace Hawk

Country of origin: United Kingdom

Type: Two seat advanced trainer and light attack aircraft

Powerplant: 60 – One 25.4kN (5700lb) Rolls-Royce Turboméca Adour 861 turbofan. 100 – One 26.0kN (5845lb) Adour 871.

Performance: 60 – Max level speed at sea level 1010km/h (545kt). Max initial rate of climb 11,800ft/min. Service ceiling 46,000ft. Combat radius with 907kg (2000lb) external load 1448km (781nm), with a 2270kg (5000lb) external load 1000km (538nm). 100 – Max speed 1038km/h (560kt) at 36,000ft, at sea level 1001km/h (540kt). Max initial rate of climb 11,800ft/min. Service ceiling 44,500ft. Combat radius on a hi-lo-hi mission with seven BL755 cluster bombs 510km (275nm).

Weights: 60 – Empty 4012kg (8845lb), max takeoff 9100kg (20,060lb). 100 – Empty 4400kg (9700lb), max takeoff 9100kg (20,060lb).

Dimensions: 60 – Wing span 9.39m (30ft 10in), length 11.85m (38ft 11in), height 3.98m (13ft 1in). Wing area 16.7m^2 (179.6sq ft). 100 – Wing span 9.94m (32ft 8in) with wingtip AIM-9 missiles, length including nose probe 11.68m (38ft 4in), height 3.99m (12ft 1in). Wing area 16.7m^2 (179.6sq ft).

Accommodation: Seating for two in tandem.

Armament: 60 & 100 – Up to 3000kg (6615lb) of external ordnance, including rocket pods, bombs and cluster bombs, AIM-9 Sidewinder AAMs and a centreline 30mm Aden cannon.

Operators: Brunei, Finland, Indonesia, Kenya, Kuwait, Malaysia, Oman, Saudi Arabia, Switzerland, South Korea, UAE, UK, Zimbabwe.

History: One of the most successful trainer families of the past 25 years, the Hawk has also been adopted for use by the US Navy and as a single seat attack aircraft (both described separately).

Hawker Siddeley began initial design studies of a two seat jet trainer in 1968 under the designation P.1182, at a time when the RAF had a marked shortfall in trainer aircraft. Hawker's design was subsequently formally adopted by the RAF in 1970, and the first aircraft (a production standard T.1 – there being no prototype or pre production aircraft) flew for the first time on August 21 1971.

In all the RAF took delivery of 176 Hawk T.1s, the first of which was delivered in 1976. In the mid 1980s 89 RAF Hawks were modified as T.1As, wired to accept Sidewinders on the inboard pylons for emergency wartime use as air defence fighters alongside radar equipped Phantoms (since retired) and Tornado F.2/F.3s.

The first export Hawk was the Mk 50 which introduced a more powerful engine, a higher max takeoff weight and greater stores carriage on four underwing pylons. The Mk 60 features a further increase in engine power, an improved wing with leading edge fences and a revised flap layout, giving improved airfield performance, and Sidewinder and Matra AAM capability.

The ultimate Hawk two seat development is the 100, with improvements primarily aimed at enhancing its ground attack abilities. Changes are many and include a more powerful Adour 871 turbofan; a revised wing with fixed leading edge droop to improve manoeuvrability, full width flaps and optional wingtip missile rails; an extended nose, optionally housing FLIR and/or a laser designator; and revised avionics, including multi function displays, plus HUD and HOTAS controls.

Photo: A United Arab Emirates Hawk Mk 63. (BAe)

British Aerospace Hawk 200

Country of origin: United Kingdom

Type: Light multirole single seat fighter

Powerplant: One 26.0kN (5845lb) Rolls-Royce/Turboméca Adour Mk 871 turbofan.

Performance: Max speed at sea level 1017km/h (550kt), economical cruising speed 795km/h (430kt). Max initial rate of climb 11,510ft/min. Service ceiling 45,000ft. Ferry range with two drop tanks over 2590km (1400nm). Combat radius with a recce pod and two drop tanks, hi-hi-hi 1600km (862nm); combat radius with 1360kg (3000lb) ordnance hi-lo-hi 945km (510nm); combat radius on a hi-hi-hi interception with two AIM-9s and two drop tanks 1335km (720nm).

Weights: Basic empty 4450kg (9810lb), max takeoff 9100kg (20,060lb).

Dimensions: Wing span 9.94m (32ft 8in) with wingtip missiles, normal wingspan 9.39m (30ft 10in), length 11.34m (37ft 3in), height 4.13m (13ft 7in). Wing area 16.7m^2 (179.6sq ft).

Accommodation: Pilot only.

Armament: Up to 3495kg (7700lb) of ordnance externally on one centreline, four underwing and two wingtip stations. Weapon options include up to four AIM-9 Sidewinder AAMs, a centreline Aden 30mm cannon, bombs and rockets.

Operators: Indonesia*, Malaysia, Oman*.

History: The ultimate expression of the Hawk family so far, the single seat Hawk 200 fighter is finding a small but ready market from existing two seat Hawk customers.

The original two seat Hawk flew for the first time on August 21 1971, since which time over 450 have been ordered. This commercial success in part contributed to British Aerospace's announcement in 1984 that it was to build a single seat light fighter development known as the Hawk 200. This demonstrator first flew on May 19 1986.

While the first Hawk 200 demonstrator crashed two months after its first flight (through g-induced loss of consciousness), a preproduction 200 flew in April 1987, and a production representative, radar equipped Hawk 200RDA demonstrator flew in February 1992.

Compared with the two seater Hawks, the Hawk 200 differs mainly in the redesigned forward fuselage and nose to accommodate the single seat cockpit. Otherwise the Hawk 200 and equivalent Hawk 100 two seater retain 80% commonality. Like the 100, the single seater features the advanced combat wing with leading edge droop for improved manoeuvrability, full span flaps and wingtip rails for air-to-air missiles (typically the Sidewinder). The wingtip rails, four underwing and one centreline station can carry between them over three tonnes of ordnance.

The redesigned nose houses a Westinghouse APG-66H multimode radar (similar to that fitted to the F-16). The FLIR/laser designator nose of the Hawk 100 was also offered as an option for the single seater for a time, but this has now been dropped. In the cockpit the 200 features modern avionics, a single colour multi function display, a HUD and optional HOTAS controls.

So far all Hawk 200 orders have been placed in conjunction with two seat orders. Oman was the first customer, and its initial 200 flew for the first time in September 1993.

Photo: A Royal Malaysian Air Force Hawk 200. (BAe)

British Aerospace Nimrod

Country of origin: United Kingdom

Type: Maritime patrol and Elint aircraft

Powerplants: Four 54.0kN (12,140lb) Rolls-Royce RB.168-20 Spey Mk 250 turbofans.

Performance: MR.2 – Max cruising speed 880km/h (475kt), economical cruising speed 787km/h (425kt), typical patrol speed at low level on two engines 370km/h (200kt). Service ceiling 42,000ft. Typical endurance 12 hours. Max endurance without refuelling 15 hours, with one refuelling 19 hours. Ferry range 9265km (5000nm).

Weights: MR.2 – Typical empty 39,010kg (86,000lb), max normal takeoff 80,515kg (177,500lb), max overload takeoff 87,090kg (192,000lb).

Dimensions: Wing span 35.00m (114ft 10in), length 38.63m (126ft 9in), height 9.08m (29ft 9in). Wing area 197.0m² (2121.0sq ft).

Accommodation: Normal crew of 12 comprising two pilots and flight engineer on flightdeck with navigator, tactical navigator, radio operator, two sonic system operators, ESM/MAD operator and two observers/stores loaders in main cabin.

Armament: Total of 6125kg (13,500lb) of ordnance can be carried in the internal weapons bay and on two underwing hardpoints. Options include AGM-84 Harpoon ASMs, Stingray torpedoes, bombs and depth charges, plus up to four AIM-9 Sidewinders for self defence.

Operators: UK

History: The Nimrod (or mighty hunter) was developed to meet an RAF requirement for a replacement for the ageing Avro Shackleton.

In 1964 two unsold Comet 4 airliners were selected as prototype airframes for the new maritime patrol aircraft. These two prototypes were given the Hawker Siddeley model number 801, and the first flew in converted form on May 23 1967. Changes to the Comet included the replacement of the airliner's RR Avon turbojets with Spey turbofans (increasing fuel efficiency, and thus range – the Nimrod can cruise while on patrol on two of its four Speys) and a new lower fuselage with an internal weapons bay and extended nose to contain a search radar. Other changes included a Magnetic Anomaly Detector (MAD) mounted in a boom extending from the rear fuselage, and ESM sensors mounted in a fairing on top of the tail. The first of 46 Nimrod MR.1s ordered entered service in October 1969.

The MR.2 designations applies to an upgrade applied to 32 Nimrods from 1975. The upgrade involved a new central tactical system with a new computer and processors, new communications suite and EMI's Searchwater radar. Subsequently the fleet was modified to MR.2P standard with the addition of an inflight refuelling probe, and more recently Nimrods have been fitted with Loral wingtip ESM pods.

In the mid 1980s a failed attempt was made to adapt the Nimrod as an AEW aircraft, with the designation AEW.3. Seven surplus Nimrods were fitted with Marconi radars in bulbous radomes in the nose and tail, but the program was defeated by technical problems.

Two further Nimrods (a third made one of the few successful ditchings of a jet transport off the coast of Scotland in May 1995) serve as R.1P Elint platforms. Identifiable by the lack of MAD boom, the R.2s are still officially identified as radar calibration aircraft, but are fitted with sensors to detect and record electronic emissions.

Photo: A Nimrod MR.2P launches from RAF Fairford. (Paul Merritt)

Canadair CT-114 Tutor

Country of origin: Canada

Type: Two seat advanced jet trainer

Powerplant: CL-41A – One 13.1kN (2950lb) Orenda licence built General Electric J85-CAN-J4 turbojet. CL-41G – One 11.8kN (2633lb) J85-CAN-40.

Performance: CL-41A – Max speed at 28,500ft 801km/h (432kt). Service ceiling 43,000ft. Range 1000km (540nm).

Weights: Empty equipped 2220kg (4895lb), max takeoff 3532kg (7788lb).

Dimensions: Wing span 11.13m (36ft 6in), length 9.75m (32ft 0in), height 2.84m (9ft 4in). Wing area 20.4m² (220.0sq ft).

Accommodation: Seating for two, side-by-side.

Armament: Usually none in Canadian service. Malaysian (CL-41G) aircraft were fitted with six hardpoints which could carry a total 1815kg (4000lb) of ordnance, including bombs, rockets, gun pods and air-to-air missiles.

Operators: Canada

History: Despite flying for the first time in 1960, and with the average age of those remaining in service being over three decades, the Canadair Tutor looks set to remain Canada's primary advanced trainer through to the end of the decade.

The Tutor was initially developed as a private venture due to a lack of official Canadian Government interest in the project. Regardless of the lack of support, development continued, resulting in a first flight on January 13 1960. This first prototype CL-41 was powered by a 10.8kN (2400lb) Pratt & Whitney JT12A-5 turbojet, while the design as a whole differed from most of its contemporaries in having side-by-side seating and a T tail. Another design feature is the two airbrakes on either side of the rear fuselage.

The Canadian Government ordered 190 production CL-41s for the then Royal Canadian Air Force in September 1961 after evaluation of contemporary trainers. Unlike the prototype these production aircraft are powered by a General Electric J85 turbojet, built under licence in Canada by Orenda. In Canadian service the CL-41 is designated the CT-114 Tutor.

The 190 production Tutors were delivered between December 1963 and September 1966. More than 130 remain in Canadian Forces service, although a number are in storage. Principle operator of the Tutor is 2 Flying Training School at Moose Jaw in Saskatchewan, with whom pilots are trained up to 'wings' standard. Those pilots bound for fast jets then have further Tutor training. Other CT-114s are in service with the Central Flying School for instructor training. The most famous operator of the Tutor is the Snowbirds aerobatic display team whose aircraft are fitted with smoke generators.

The only country outside Canada to operate the Tutor was Malaysia. The Royal Malaysian Air Force took delivery of 20 CL-41Gs, which compared with the basic CL-41 were equipped with six hardpoints capable of carrying a range of armaments including rockets and bombs. Named the Tebuan, or Wasp, the CL-41Gs were delivered in 1967-68, but were retired from service in the mid 1980s, due to fatigue and corrosion problems.

Photo: Canada's Tutors look set to soldier on in the training role for some time. (Canadian Forces)

Canadair CL-215, CL-215T & CL-415

Country of origin: Canada

Type: Firefighting, SAR and multirole transport amphibian

Powerplants: CL-215 – Two 1565kW (2100hp) Pratt & Whitney R-2800-CA3 18 cylinder radial piston engines, driving three bladed constant speed propellers.

Performance: CL-215 – Max cruising speed 290km/h (157kt). Max initial rate of climb 1000ft/min. Takeoff run from water at 17,100kg (37,700lb) all up weight 800m (2625ft). Range with a 1590kg (3500lb) payload at max cruising speed 1715km (925nm), or 2095km (1130nm) at long range cruise power.

Weights: CL-215 – Empty 12,220kg (26,940lb), typical operating empty 12,740kg (28,080lb), max takeoff from water 17,100kg (37,700lb), max takeoff from land 19,730kg (43,500lb).

Dimensions: CL-215 – Wing span 28.60m (93ft 10in), length 19.82m (65ft 1in), height 8.98m (29ft 6in) on land or 6.88m (22ft 7in) on water. Wing area 100.3m² (1080sq ft).

Accommodation: Flightcrew of two, plus accommodation in special missions variants for a third flightdeck member, a mission specialist and two observers. Passenger configuration for 30, or in a combi configuration for 11, with firebombing tanks retained and freight in forward fuselage. Fire retardant capacity of 6125kg (13,500lb).

Armament: None

Operators: CL-215 – Greece, Spain, Thailand, former Yugoslavia, Venezuela.

History: While most production CL-215/415s have been for civilian/government agency work where they serve as firebombers, a number have also been acquired for a range of military roles including maritime patrol, search and rescue and transport.

The CL-215 first flew on October 23 1967, and 125 were built in different batches through to 1990. Primary customers were government agencies, including various Canadian province governments and France, plus the air forces of Greece, Italy and Yugoslavia. The status of the aircraft delivered to what was then Yugoslavia is unclear, while the Italian AF CL-215s have been transferred to a government agency. In the firefighting role the CL-215's capabilities are impressive, it can scoop up 5455 litres (1200 Imp gal/1440US gal) of water from a flat water source such as a lake in 12 seconds.

Spain took delivery of a total of 20 CL-215s, of which eight were configured for maritime patrol and search and rescue work, while the Thai Navy operates two CL-215s, also configured for SAR. The final military CL-215 operator is Venezuela, its two aircraft are configured as passenger transports.

Canadair offers retrofit kits for CL-215s to the new Pratt & Whitney Canada PW123 turboprop powered CL-215T standard. Spain has ordered 15 retrofit kits for its aircraft.

The improved, new build CL-415 features the PW123s, but also an EFIS cockpit, higher weights and an increased capacity firebombing system. Its principle mission is that of a firebomber, but various special mission (including SAR and maritime patrol) and transport configurations are offered. The first CL-415 flew on December 6 1993.

Photo: The status of the five CL-215 firebombers delivered to Yugoslavia in the mid 1980s is unclear. (Bombardier)

Canadair Challenger

Country of origin: Canada

Type: Special missions and VIP transport

Powerplants: 600 – Two 33.6kN (7500lb) Avco Lycoming ALF 502L turbofans. 601 – Two 40.66kN (9140lb) General Electric CF34-3As.

Performance: 600 – Max speed 904km/h (488kt), max cruising speed 890km/h (480kt), long range cruising speed 800km/h (432kt). Range with reserves (latter build aircraft) 6300km (3402nm). 601-1A – Max cruising speed 851km/h (460kt), typical cruising speed 820km/h (442kt), long range cruising speed 786km/h (424kt). Range with max fuel and reserves 6208km (3352nm).

Weights: 600 latter build aircraft – Empty 8370kg (18,450lb), operating empty 10,285kg (22,675lb), max takeoff 18,200kg (40,125lb). 601-1A – Empty 9050kg (19,950lb), operating empty 11,605kg (25,585lb). Max takeoff 19,550kg (43,100lb).

Dimensions: 600 – Wing span 18.85m (61ft 10in), length 20.85m (68ft 5in), height 6.30m (20ft 8in). Wing area 41.8m² (450sq ft). 601 – Same except wing span 19.61m (64ft 4in). Wing area 48.3m² (520.0sq ft).

Accommodation: Flightcrew of two. Various seating options available depending on customer preference, max seating for 19.

Armament: None

Operators: Canada, China, Croatia, Germany, Malaysia.

History: The Challenger family of business jets has seen limited military service, mainly as a VIP transport.

Canadair purchased the rights to an all new business jet developed by Bill Lear, original designer of the Lear Jet, in 1976. Known as the LearStar 600 this design was notable for its large cabin, long range and good operating economics. As the CL-600, Canadair launched development of the LearStar design in October 1976.

The first CL-600 flew on November 8 1978. Unfortunately for Canadair the aircraft suffered a number of early problems. Overweight, a major weight and drag reduction programme paired back the CL-600's weight, improving range, while the troubled ALF 502 turbofans failed to meet predicted performance levels.

Troubles with the ALF 502 powered CL-600 led Canadair to develop a vastly improved variant in the form of the General Electric CF34 powered Challenger 601 (the CF34 also powers the USAF A-10 Thunderbolt II and USN S-2 Viking). Other detail changes included winglets, which are also offered as a retrofit to earlier aircraft. The 601 first flew on April 10 1982 and for a time was offered alongside the CL-600. The CL-600 was dropped from the model line in 1983. The 601 has been offered in progressively improved variants, the latest is the 604.

Canada is the largest Challenger military operator with 15 on strength. The Canadian Forces uses the CE-144s as high speed, high altitude threat simulators for developing fighter pilot interception skills. One is a CX-144 electronics and avionics testbed while four serve as CC-144 VIP transports. All Canadian CL-600s have been fitted with the winglets of the 601.

Other military operators are Malaysia (CL-600), Germany (601) and China (601), all these countries' aircraft are used as VIP transports.

Photo: A Canadian Forces CE-144. (Bombardier)

CASA C-101 Aviojet

Country of origin: Spain

Type: Two seat basic and advanced trainer and light attack aircraft

Powerplant: C-101CC/DD – One 20.9kN (4700lb) with max reserve power or 19.1kN (4300lb) without reserve Garrett TFE731-5-IJ turbofan.

Performance: C-101CC/DD – Max speed with max reserve power 835km/h (450kt) at 15,000ft, max speed at sea level 785km/h (423kt), economical cruising speed 612km/h (330kt). Max initial rate of climb 6360ft/min (with max reserve power), normal max initial rate of climb 4975ft/min. Time to 25,000ft 6min 30sec. Service ceiling 44,000ft. Lo-lo-lo attack radius with four 250kg bombs and 30mm cannon with 5min over target and reserves 482km (260nm). Ferry range with reserves 3705km (2000nm). Max endurance 7 hours.

Weights: C-101CC – Empty equipped 3470kg (7650lb), max takeoff 6300kg (13,890lb).

Dimensions: Wing span 10.60m (34ft 10in), length 12.50m (41ft 0in), height 4.25m (14ft 0in). Wing area 20.0^{2}m (215.3sq ft).

Accommodation: Two in tandem.

Armament: C-101CC – Can carry a 30mm DEFA 533 cannon or twin 12.7mm Browning M3 machine gun pod in lower fuselage. Six underwing hardpoints can carry a total of 2250kg (4960lb) of ordnance, including bombs, rocket pods, plus up to two AGM-65 Maverick ASMs, or two AIM-9 Sidewinder of Matra Magic AAMs on C-101DD.

Operators: Chile, Honduras, Jordan, Spain.

History: At the lower end of the jet trainer/light attack platform spectrum, the CASA C-101 Aviojet is nevertheless a relatively inexpensive and capable aircraft.

Design of the Aviojet began in 1975 to replace the Hispano Saeta after CASA signed a development contract with the Spanish Air Ministry. As CASA's first foray into the jet engined trainer field, the company enrolled the help of Northrop of the USA and Germany's MBB (now Northrop Grumman and Daimler Benz Aerospace respectively). Northrop designed the unswept wing and inlet area, but CASA assumed all design responsibility after the first flight of the first of four prototypes on June 27 1977.

Notable features of the Aviojet include modular construction, the Garrett TFE731 high bypass turbofan, an engine widely used on business jets and known for its reliability and fuel efficiency (conversely the high bypass contributes to ordinary high altitude performance), and a weapons bay in the forward fuselage which can house cannon or gun packs, a reconnaissance pod, an ECM package or a laser designator.

Initial production of the C-101 was for Spain, whose C-101EB trainers are designated E.25 Mirlo, or Blackbird. The C-101BB features a more powerful engine was sold to Chile as the T-36 (subsequently fitted with a ranging radar) and Honduras. The C-101CC introduced a more powerful engine than the C.101BB which features a five minute military reserve power thrust rating of 20.9kN (4700lb). It has sold to Chile as the A-36 Halcón and Jordan. The C-101DD features nav/attack avionics improvements, including a HUD, HOTAS controls, weapon aiming controls, and AGM-65 compatibility. First flown in May 1985, none have been ordered.

Photo: One of 16 C-101CC Aviojets delivered to Jordan. (Paul Merritt)

CASA C-212 Aviocar & Patrullero

Country of origin: Spain

Type: Aviocar – STOL utility transport. Patrullero – Maritime patrol and Elint/ECM platform

Powerplants: 200 – Two 670kW (900shp) TPE311-10-501Cs turboprops driving four bladed constant speed propellers. 300 – Two 670kW (900shp) Garrett TPE331-10R-513Cs.

Performance: 200 – Max cruising speed 365km/h (197kt), cruising speed 346km/h (187kt). Range with max payload 410km (220nm), range with max fuel 1760km (950nm). 300 – Max cruising speed 354km/h (190kt), economical cruising speed 300km/h (162kt). Max initial rate of climb 1630ft/min. STOL takeoff run 385m (1260ft). Range with 25 passengers at max cruising speed 440km (237nm), range with a 1700kg (3770lb) payload 1435km (775nm).

Weights: 200 – Empty 3780kg (8333lb), max takeoff 7450kg (16,424lb). 300 – Empty 3780kg (8333lb), max takeoff 7700kg (16,975lb).

Dimensions: 200 – Wing span 19.00m (62ft 4in), length 15.16m (49ft 9in), height 6.30m (20ft 8in). Wing area 40.0m^2 (430.6sq ft). 300 – Wing span 20.28m (66ft 7in), length 16.15m (53ft 0in), height 6.60m (21ft 8in). Wing area 41.0m^2 (441.3sq ft).

Accommodation: Aviocar – Flightcrew of two. Max passenger seating for 26 troops or 12 stretchers and four medical attendants. Patrullero – Four systems operators in maritime patrol configuration, or radar operator and two observers in ASW configuration.

Armament: Aviocar – Two underwing hardpoints of 250kg (550lb) capacity each can carry light gun or rocket pods. Patrullero – Can carry torpedoes (such as Mk 46s or Stingray), rockets and anti shipping missiles (including Aerospatiale AS15TT and Sea Skua).

Operators: Abu Dhabi, Angola, Bolivia, Chad, Chile, Columbia, Djibouti, Equatorial Guinea, France, Ghana, Indonesia, Jordan, Mexico, Myanmar, Nicaragua, Panama, Paraguay, Portugal, South Africa, Spain, Sweden, Sudan, Uruguay, Venezuela, Zimbabwe.

History: Initially conceived as a light STOL transport for the Spanish Air Force, the CASA C-212 has found a large military market worldwide and is particularly popular in underdeveloped regions.

The C-212 was designed to replace the Spanish Air Force's mixed fleet of Douglas C-47 Dakotas and Junkers Ju 52s still in service in the 1960s. Design work began in the late 1960s (features including good STOL performance and a rear cargo ramp), the first prototype flying on March 26 1971. The type entered air force service in 1974.

The initial civil version was designated the C-212C, the military version the C-212-5. Production of these models ceased in 1978, CASA switching to the Series 200 with more powerful engines and higher operating weights. The Series 200 first flew in converted C-212C prototype form on April 30 1978.

A third development of the Aviocar is the Series 300 which first flew in 1984 and was certificated in late 1987. Improvements to this model are newer engines and winglets.

The Series 300 is also offered in special mission Patrullero form, and is offered in radar and sonobuoy equipped 300MP maritime patrol form, and signal interception, classification, identification and jamming equipment in 300DE ECM/Elint form.

Photo: A Spanish Air Force C-212. (Spanish AF)

Cessna O-1 Bird Dog

Country of origin: United States of America

Type: Observation, liaison and forward air control aircraft

Powerplant: O-1E – One 159kW (213hp) Continental O-470-11 flat six piston engine, driving a two bladed constant speed propeller.

Performance: O-1E – Max speed at sea level 243km/h (131kt), economical cruising speed 167km/h (90kt). Max initial rate of climb 1150ft/min. Service ceiling 18,500ft. Range 853km (460nm).

Weights: O-1E – Empty 732kg (1614lb), max takeoff 1102kg (2430lb).

Dimensions: O-1E – Wing span 10.97m (36ft 0in), length 7.85m (25ft 9in), height 2.22m (7ft 4in). Wing area 16.2m² (174.0sq ft).

Accommodation: Pilot and observer in tandem. Stretcher patient (with no observer) alternatively can be carried.

Armament: O-1E – None. O-1C – Two underwing hardpoints for a 113kg (250lb) bomb each, or unguided rockets.

Operators: Austria, Indonesia, Italy, Malta, Pakistan, South Korea, Thailand.

History: Of the more than 3500 Bird Dogs built from 1950, over 200 remain in military service today, testament to the utility of this Korean and Vietnam wars veteran.

During WW2 the US Army successfully employed many thousands of light aircraft, mainly Piper L-4s and Taylorcraft L-2 'Grasshoppers', for observation, artillery direction, tactical reconnaissance and liaison duties. Both the L-2 and L-4 were simple conversions of existing civil aircraft, and their success in their many roles led the US Army postwar to seek a standard observation aircraft, tailored closely to its specific needs.

Anticipating such a requirement, Cessna developed its Model 305 as a private venture, and this flew for the first time in December 1949. In April 1950 the official US Army competition for an observation aircraft saw Cessna's 305 selected over designs from a number of other manufacturers. The US Army ordered an initial 418 Model 305s as L-19As (O-1A from 1962).

The 305 was based loosely on the Cessna 170, a taildragger that formed the basis for the Cessna 172 (from which was developed the T-41 Mescalero – described separately). Compared with the 170 though, Cessna cut down the rear fuselage, giving 360° vision, while a transparency was fitted in the wing centre section above the main fuselage. Seating was for two in tandem. At the US Army's request the 305 was also fitted with electrically operated, slotted trailing edge flaps (later fitted to civil Cessnas) to improve STOL performance.

Bird Dog variants included the instrument trainer L-19A-ITs and TL-19Ds (TO-1D – many of these were later converted to O-2D and O-2F standards), the US Marines OE-1 (O-1B) and improved OE-2 (O-1C), the TL-19A (TO-1A) dual control trainer (many of which were converted to O-1G FAC standard), and the definitive L-19E/O-1E, and improved L-19A/O-1A with more modern equipment. L-19E production initially ceased in 1959, but a further batch was built from 1961.

The O-1A saw service in the Korean War, while the O-1E saw extensive service in Vietnam, primarily directing air strikes.

Photo: An O-1A Bird Dog in Thai markings. Note the cut down rear fuselage. (Bill Lines)

Cessna T-41 Mescalero & 172

Country of origin: United States of America

Type: Basic trainer, liaison and observation aircraft

Powerplant: T-41A – One 108kW (145hp) Continental O-300-C flat six piston engine, driving a two bladed fixed pitch propeller.

Performance: T-41A – Max speed 224km/h (121kt), max cruising speed at 9000ft 211km/h (114kt). Max initial rate of climb 645ft/min. Service ceiling 13,100ft. Ferry range 1030km (555nm), standard range 990km (535nm).

Weights: T-41A – Operating empty 565kg (1245lb), max takeoff 1043kg (2300lb).

Dimensions: T-41A – Wing span 10.92m (35ft 10in), length 8.20m (26ft 11in), height 2.68m (8ft 10in). Wing area 16.2m² (174.0sq ft).

Accommodation: Seating for pilot and instructor side-by-side, with seats for two passengers behind them.

Armament: None

Operators: Includes Angola, Bolivia, Chile, Columbia, Dominican Republic, Ecuador, El Salvador, Greece, Guatemala, Honduras, Indonesia, Ireland, Liberia, Pakistan, Peru, Philippines, Saudi Arabia, South Korea, Trinidad and Tobago, Turkey.

History: The Cessna 172 is by far and away the most successful light aircraft built, and so it is not surprising that a significant portion of the nearly 42,000 built found their way into military service.

The 172 began life as a tricycle undercarriage development of the four place Cessna 170, the aircraft that also formed the basis of the O-1 Bird Dog (described separately). The prototype 170 flew in September 1947, the prototype 172 in November 1955. The type was a success almost instantly, and through to 1986 the 172 was built in successively improved variants. An improved 172, aimed principally at civil customers, is due to enter production in 1996.

US military interest resulted in the July 1964 US Air Force order for Cessna 172Fs for pilot flight screening performed by civil firms under contract, designated the T-41A Mescalero. These aircraft differ little from the civil 172F, and production took place between 1964 and 1967. The US Army also ordered 172s for pilot training, its T-41Bs based on the R172E with a 155kW (210hp) Continental IO-360 driving a constant speed prop. The USAF's T-41C was similar to the T-41B except for its fixed pitch propeller, and 52 were built for the USAF Academy. The T-41D, based on the T-41C but with a 28 volt electrical system, was procured for a number of countries under the US's Military Assistance Program (MAP). 311 T-41Ds were built between 1968 and 1978. In 1995 50 T-41s remained in service with the US Air Force, although replacement with T-3 Fireflies was near completion.

Apart from 172s built as T-41s, several other countries procured civil 172s direct from Cessna, or from Reims-Cessna in France, which built several thousand FR172s under licence. In all, over 30 countries have operated military 172s or T-41s.

Apart from basic pilot training, the 172 is also widely used for a number of secondary duties such as observation, liaison and border patrol.

Photo: One of Peru's T-41Ds. (MAP)

Cessna T-37 Tweet

Country of origin: United States of America

Type: Two seat basic and advanced trainer

Powerplants: T-37B/C – Two 4.56kN (1025lb) Continental J69-T-25 turbojets.

Performance: T-37B – Max speed 684km/h (370kt) at 25,000ft, cruising speed 612km/h (330kt). Max initial rate of climb 3370ft/min. Service ceiling 39,200ft. Range 1500km (810nm). T-37C – Max speed 650km/h (350kt), cruising speed 575km/h (310kt). Max initial rate of climb 2390ft/min. Service ceiling 29,900ft. Ferry range 1517km (820nm) with tip tanks, range with standard fuel 1367km (738nm).

Weights: T-37B – Empty 1755kg (3870lb), max takeoff 2993kg (6600lb). T-37C – Max takeoff 3402kg (7500lb).

Dimensions: Wing span 10.30m (33ft 9in), length 8.92m (29ft 3in), height 2.80m (9ft 2in). Wing area 17.1m² (183.9sq ft).

Accommodation: Seating for two, side-by-side.

Armament: T-37C – Up to 227kg (500lb) of armament on two underwing hardpoints, comprising two 113kg (250lb) bombs or rockets.

Operators: Bangladesh, Chile, Columbia, Germany, Greece, Pakistan, Peru, Portugal, Thailand, Turkey, USA.

History: Cessna's viceless T-37 Tweet has almost four decades of service behind it, and seems likely to see out the 1990s in service with a number of operators.

In 1952 the US Air Force devised a requirement for an 'all through' jet trainer that would train pilots from basic right through to wings standard. The winner of this contest was Cessna, whose Model 318 featured seating for two side-by-side, two small turbojets and a straight wing. The first of two prototype Model 318s, designated XT-37, flew for the first time on October 12 1954.

The initial production model was the 4.1kN (920lb) Continental J69-T-9 turbojet (licence built Turboméca Mabore) powered T-37A, which first flew in September 1955, although some problems with the aircraft delayed service entry until 1957. In all 534 T-37As were built, all of which were delivered to the USAF. In 1959 production switched to the T-37B, which introduced more powerful J69-T-25s, improved avionics and optional wingtip tanks. 449 T-37Bs were built. Surviving T-37As were subsequently upgraded to T-37B standard.

The final production Tweet or 'Tweetie Bird' (named after the cartoon character) model was the T-37C, 269 of which were built specifically for export. It differs from the T-37B in having a higher max takeoff weight and two underwing hardpoints for bombs or rockets.

The US Air Force began all through jet training with the T-37 in 1961, however the cost of operations led that service to reintroduce piston engined T-41 Mescaleros for initial training in 1965.

Plans to replace the USAF's T-37s with an all new jet trainer faltered when the Fairchild T-46 Eaglet (disparagingly dubbed the Thunderpiglet) was cancelled in 1986 due to program management problems. Cessna then proposed substantially upgrading the T-37 to Garrett turbofan powered T-48 standard, but instead the aircraft's replacement will be the long awaited JPATS winner, the Beech Mk II (PC-9).

In the meantime, USAF T-37s have been undergoing a service life extension program (SLEP) engineered by Sabreliner.

Photo: T-37Cs of Portugal's aerobatic display team. (Paul Merritt)

Cessna A-37 Dragonfly

Country of origin: United States of America

Type: Two seat light attack aircraft

Powerplants: A-37B/OA-37B – Two 12.7kN (2850lb) General Electric J85-GE-17A turbojets.

Performance: A-37/OA-37B – Max speed 816km/h (440kt) at 16,000ft, max cruising speed 787km/h (425kt). Max initial rate of climb 6990ft/min. Service ceiling 41,765ft. Range with max fuel and reserves 1630km (880nm), range with max payload including 1860kg (4100lb) of external ordnance 740km (400nm).

Weights: A-37B – Empty equipped 2817kg (6211lb), max takeoff 6350kg (14,000lb).

Dimensions: Wing span 10.93m (35ft 11in), length excluding refuelling probe 8.93m (29ft 4in), height 2.71m (8ft 11in). Wing area 17.1m² (183.9sq ft).

Accommodation: Seating for two, side-by-side.

Armament: One 7.62mm GAU-2 minigun in forward fuselage. Eight underwing hardpoints can carry a total ordnance load of 1860kg (4100lb), including bombs, rockets and gun pods.

Operators: Chile, Columbia, Ecuador, El Salvador, Guatemala, Honduras, Peru, South Korea, Thailand, Uruguay.

History: The US Air Force's decision to evaluate the suitability of an armed version of the T-37 Tweet jet trainer for light attack/counter insurgency work was a fruitful one, as the resulting A-37 saw widespread active service in Vietnam where it was well suited to the type of conflict fought there.

In 1962 the USAF's Special Air Warfare centre began evaluating two T-37Bs to test the type's suitability for the counter insurgency (COIN) role. After initial testing the two T-37Bs were modified to YAT-37D standard (first flight October 22 1963) and fitted with two 10.7kN (2400lb) General Electric J85-GE-5 turbojets. Testing proved positive but initially nothing came of the concept until the Vietnam War intensified. In 1966 the USAF contracted Cessna to convert 39 T-37Bs to light attack A-37A Dragonfly standard. Apart from the GE turbojets, the A-37As introduced eight underwing hardpoints, extra fuel capacity in wingtip tanks, armour protection, attack avionics, larger wheels and tyres and an internal 7.62mm minigun.

Twenty five A-37As were successfully evaluated in operational conditions in Vietnam from mid 1967, these aircraft were later transferred to full operational service, and were passed to the South Vietnamese AF in 1970.

The success of the A-37A led to the definitive A-37B, with uprated engines, an inflight refuelling probe and increased internal fuel capacity, while the airframe was stressed for 6g rather than 5g. In all 577 A-37Bs were delivered to the USAF and export customers between May 1968 and 1975. A-37Bs saw widespread service with the US and South Vietnamese air forces during the Vietnam War, and captured examples even saw brief service with the North Vietnamese air force during the closing stages of that conflict.

The USAF fitted 130 A-37Bs as OA-37Bs with avionics for forward air control work, although the last of these was retired in 1992. Ex USAF A-37 and OA-37s serve widely in South America.

Photo: An A-37B Dragonfly.

Chengdu J-7 & F-7

Country of origin: China (based on Russian designed MiG-21)

Type: Single seat fighter

Powerplant: F-7M – One 43.2kN (9700lb) dry and 64.7kN (14,550lb) with afterburner Chengdu WP-7BM turbojet.

Performance: F-7M – Max speed 2175km/h (1175kt). Max initial rate of climb 35,433ft/min. Service ceiling 59,700ft. Max ferry range with external fuel 2230km (1203nm). Combat radius with two 150kg (330lb) bombs and drop tanks on a hi-lo-hi interdiction mission 600km (325nm), combat radius on a long range intercept mission with two AAMs and three drop tanks 650km (350nm).

Weights: F-7M – Empty 5275kg (11,630lb), max takeoff 8888kg (19,577lb).

Dimensions: F-7M – Wing span 7.15m (23ft 6in), length (excl probe) 13.95m (45ft 9in), height 4.10m (13ft 6in). Wing area 23.0m² (247.6sq ft).

Accommodation: Pilot only, except for two in tandem in JJ-7/FT-7.

Armament: F-7M – Two Type 30-1 30mm cannon. Max external ordnance of 1000kg (2205lb) on four underwing hardpoints and on centreline fuel tank station. Two inner hardpoints can carry PL-2, -2A or -7 infrared guided AAMs, or Matra R550 Magic AAMs. Inner and outer pylons can carry rockets and bombs.

Operators: Albania, Bangladesh, China, Egypt, Iran, Iraq, Myanmar, Pakistan, Sri Lanka, Tanzania, Zimbabwe.

History: China's copy of the MiG-21 forms an important part of the Peoples Liberation Army Air Force inventory and has been widely exported to a number of non aligned countries.

In 1961 China acquired a licence to build the MiG-21F-13 ('Fishbed C') and its Tumansky R-11F-300 turbojet. However, the severing of ties with Russia left the Chinese with incomplete technical drawings, and they instead were forced to reverse engineer pattern aircraft. This meant the first Chinese built aircraft, designated J-7 didn't fly until January 17 1966. The J-7 entered production the following year with Shenyang despite the turmoil of the cultural revolution, and some were exported as the F-7A to Albania and Tanzania.

Production was subsequently transferred to Chengdu as the J-7I. In 1975 development work began on the improved J-7II, which introduced a more powerful engine with double the time between overhaul. It was exported to Egypt and Iraq in the early 1980s as the F-7B.

The export F-7M Airguard features a GEC-Marconi HUD and weapons aiming computer, an improved ranging radar, radar altimeter, IFF and an improved engine. It has been exported to Bangladesh, Iran and Zimbabwe. The F-7P and F-7MP are similar, but with a number of minor modifications (including Martin-Baker ejection seat and Sidewinder compatibility) specifically for the Pakistan Air Force. Pakistan is also seen as the prime customer of the FC-1 development which will feature a multi mode radar in a solid nose, lateral air intakes and probably a Klimov RD-33 turbofan as on the MiG-29.

Other variants include the J-7E, thought to have first flown in 1990 and featuring a cranked delta wing, more powerful engine and extra hardpoints, and the J-7III, loosely equivalent to the MiG-21M and featuring an all weather radar in an enlarged radome. Two seater JJ-7s and FT-7s meanwhile are built by Guizhou.

Photo: Pakistan's F-7Ms were initially dubbed Skybolt. (Chengdu)

Dassault Atlantic & Atlantique 2

Country of origin: France

Type: Maritime patrol aircraft

Powerplants: ATL2 – Two 4550kW (6100ehp) Rolls-Royce Tyne RTy.20 Mk 21 turboprops, driving four bladed propellers.

Performance: ATL2 – Max level speed 648km/h (350kt) at altitude or 592km/h (320kt) at sea level, max cruising speed 555km/h (300kt), normal patrol speed 315km/h (170kt). Max initial rate of climb at 30,000kg (66,140lb) AUW 1200ft/min, or at 40,000kg (88,185lb) AUW 700ft/min. Service ceiling 30,000ft. Ferry range with max fuel 9075km (4900nm). Combat radius with two hours on station on anti shipping mission with one AM 39 Exocet missile 3333km (1800nm). Radius with 8hr patrol and four torpedoes 1110km (600nm), or with 5hr patrol 1850km (1000nm). Max endurance 18hr.

Weights: ATL2 – Empty equipped standard mission 25,700kg (56,660lb), max takeoff 46,200kg (101,850lb).

Dimensions: Wing span incl wingtip pods 37.42m (122ft 9in), length 33.63m (110ft 4in), height 10.89m (35ft 9in). Wing area 120.3m² (1295.3sq ft).

Accommodation: Normal crew complement of 10 to 12, comprising pilot, copilot, flight engineer, nose observer, radio navigator, ESM/ECM/MAD operator, radar & IFF operator, tactical coordinator, two acoustic operators and optionally two observers in rear fuselage.

Armament: ATL2 – Up to eight Mk 46 torpedoes, or seven Murène torpedoes or two AM 39 Exocet or AS 37 Martel ASMs (typical load three torpedoes and one missile), or NATO standard bombs in weapons bay. Four underwing hardpoints for ASMs and AAMs.

Operators: France, Germany, Italy, Pakistan.

History: The Atlantic resulted from a NATO requirement to find a replacement for the Lockheed P-2 Neptune, and is an early example of international collaboration on a military aircraft program.

The NATO requirement for a long range maritime patrol aircraft was issued in 1958. Breguet (who merged with Dassault in 1971) was the successful bidder, with its Br 1150 design selected over 24 other designs from nine countries.

The Atlantic first flew in prototype form on October 21 1961, and entered service with the navies of France and Germany in 1965. In all, 87 production Altantics were built through to 1974 by a European consortium led by Breguet (other partners were SABCA and SONACA of Belgium, Aeritalia, Aerospatiale, Dornier, Fokker and MBB). Other customers were Italy and the Netherlands while Pakistan's three ex French Navy Atlantics were delivered in the mid 1970s.

Design features of the basic Atlantic include a double bubble fuselage, the lower portion of which is unpressurised and includes the weapons bay, US sourced ASW equipment and a Thomson-CSF search radar in a retractable radome. Germany also operates five Atlantics modified for Elint, while Thomson-CSF is upgrading Pakistan's aircraft.

Twenty eight new build Atlantique 2s have been ordered for the French Navy. These aircraft feature modern avionics and systems including a Thomson-CSF Iguane radar, a pod mounted FLIR in the nose, a new MAD, new ESM equipment, processors, and navigation equipment. First flight was in 1981, with deliveries beginning in 1988.

Photo: A French Navy Atlantique 2. (Dassault)

Dassault Mystère/Falcon 200 & Gardian

Country of origin: France

Type: VIP transport, ECM trainer, maritime patrol and utility transport.

Powerplants: 200 – Two 23.1kN (5200lb) Garrett ATF 3-6A-4C turbofans.

Performance: 200 – Max cruising speed 870km/h (470kt) at 30,000ft, economical cruising speed 780km/h (420kt). Service ceiling 45,000ft. Range with max fuel, eight passengers and reserves 4650km (2510nm).

Weights: 200 – Empty 8250kg (18,290lb), max takeoff 14,515kg (32,000lb).

Dimensions: Wing span 16.32m (53ft 7in), length 17.15m (56ft 3in), height 5.32m (17ft 6in). Wing area 41.0m² (441.3sq ft).

Accommodation: Flightcrew of two. Typical main cabin seating for between eight and 10 passengers, or up to 14 in a high density configuration. Aerial ambulance can be fitted with three stretchers.

Armament: The Gardian was offered with the capability of carrying two AM 39 Exocet anti shipping missiles.

Operators: Belgium, Central African Republic, Chile, Egypt, France, Iran, Morocco, Norway, Pakistan, Peru, Portugal, Spain, Sudan, Syria.

History: The Mystère or Falcon 20 and 200 constitutes Dassault's most successful business jet program thus far, with more than 500 built. Many of these serve as VIP transports, while others are used in a variety of special missions roles.

Development of the original Mystère 20 traces back to joint collaboration between Sud Aviation (which later merged into Aerospatiale) and Dassault in the late 1950s. Development progressed to the stage where prototype construction began in January 1962, progressing to a first flight on May 4 1963. This prototype shared with production aircraft the type's overall configuration, but differed in that it was powered by 14.8kN (3300lb) Pratt & Whitney JT12A-8 turbojets, whereas production Mystère 20s (or Falcon 20s outside France) were powered with General Electric CF-700 turbofans.

The 200, or initially the 20H, features Garrett turbofans, greater fuel tankage and much longer range. This version remained in production till 1988, while production of the 20 ceased in 1983.

The majority of military Falcon 20 and 200 operators use them as VIP transports. However, France's sizeable fleet is an exception. The French Navy operates five maritime patrol Gardians from its New Caledonia and Tahiti territories in the Pacific. These aircraft are fitted with a Thomson-CSF Varan radar and large observation windows. Chile has also upgraded two ex civil Falcon 200s to a similar standard. The French Air Force meanwhile operates a variety of combat radar and navigation system equipped Mystère 20NAs to train crews bound for Mirage IVs and 2000s, while a single Mystère 20NR trains pilots bound for the Mirage F1CR.

Other military applications include target towing, aerial ambulance and electronic warfare training aircraft. In the USA the Coast Guard operates a number of HU-25s Gardians for Search and Rescue. A number are equipped with Motorola SLAR and Texas Instruments linescan for maritime pollution detection, while others are fitted with a Westinghouse APG-66 radar (as on the F-16) and FLIR used for tracking suspicious sea and air traffic.

Photo: A French Navy maritime patrol Gardian. (Julian Green)

Dassault Falcon 50

Country of origin: France

Type: VIP & government transport

Powerplants: Three 16.5kN (3700lb) Garrett TFE731-3 turbofans.

Performance: Max cruising speed 880km/h (475kt), long range cruising speed 797km/h (430kt). Max operating altitude 45,000ft. Range at Mach 0.75 with eight passengers and reserves 6400km (3500nm).

Weights: Empty equipped 9150kg (20,170lb), standard max takeoff weight 17,600kg (38,800lb), or optionally 18,500kg (40,780lb).

Dimensions: Wing span 18.86m (61ft 11in), length 18.52m (61ft 9in), height 6.97m (22ft 11in). Wing area 46.8m² (504.1sq ft).

Accommodation: Flightcrew of two pilots. A number of cabin seating arrangements are available, depending on the toilet location. Seating for eight or nine with aft toilet, or for up to 12 with forward toilet. Can accommodate three stretchers, two doctors or attendants and medical equipment in a medevac role.

Armament: None

Operators: France, Italy, Morocco, Portugal, Spain, South Africa, Sudan.

History: The long range trijet Falcon 50 is based loosely on the earlier twinjet Mystère/Falcon 20 and 200 family, and like the 20 and 200, has found a military market as a VIP transport.

The Dassault Falcon 50 was developed for long range trans Atlantic and transcontinental flight sectors, using the Falcon 20 as the design basis. To meet the required 6440km (3475nm) range requirement though significant changes mean that the Falcon 50 is for all intents and purposes an all new aircraft.

Key new features to achieve the range were the selection of three 16.6kN (3700lb) Garrett TFE731 turbofans, mounted on a new rear tail section, plus a new supercritical wing of greater area than that on the 20 and 200. The triple redundancy of three engines also allows overflight of oceans and uninhabited regions. Many Falcon 20 components were retained, the most obvious of these being the nose and fuselage cross section.

The prototype Falcon 50 flew in November 1976, but it wasn't until 1979 that production deliveries began. In the meantime the wing design had been changed to incorporate a supercritical wing that still retained the original wing's planform. A second prototype flew on February 18 1978, and the first preproduction aircraft flew on June 13 1978.

Like others in the Falcon family, Aerospatiale participates in the Falcon 50 manufacturing program, building the fuselage and tail surfaces. Dassault also announced in 1991 that the tail surfaces would be built in Russia by the same company that assembles the Mikoyan MiG-29.

All military operated Falcon 50s serve as VIP and government transports, fitted with four or five seats in the main cabin. Italy's Falcon 50s are also convertible to an air ambulance configuration.

Photo: An Italian Air Force (Aeronautica Militare Italiana) Falcon 50 in landing configuration. Italy flies four Falcon 50s on VIP duties alongside two DC-9-30s and two Gulfstream IIIs. (MAP)

Dassault Falcon 900

Country of origin: France

Type: VIP & head of state transport & maritime patrol

Powerplants: 900 – Three 20.0kN (4500lb) Garrett TFE731-5AR-1C turbofans. 900B – Three 21.1kN (4750lb) Garrett TFE731-5BRs.

Performance: 900 – Max cruising speed 927km/h (500kt), economical cruising speed Mach 0.75. Max cruising altitude 51,000ft. Range with max payload and reserves 6412km (3460nm), range with 15 passengers and reserves 6968km (3760nm), with eight pax and reserves 7227km (3900nm). 900B – Same except for range with 15 pax and reserves 7115km (3840nm).

Weights: 900 – Empty equipped 10,545kg (23,248lb), max takeoff 20,640kg (45,500lb). 900B – Empty equipped 10,240kg (22,575kg), max takeoff 20,640kg (45,500lb).

Dimensions: Wing span 19.33m (63ft 5in), length 20.21m (66ft 4in), height 7.55m (24ft 9in). Wing area 49.0m2 (527.4sq ft).

Accommodation: Flightcrew of two. Main passenger cabin accommodation for between eight or 15 passengers, or as many as 18 in a high density configuration.

Armament: None

Operators: Algeria, Australia, France, Gabon, Japan, Malaysia, Nigeria, South Africa, Spain, Syria, United Arab Emirates.

History: Of the more than 150 transcontinental Falcon 900s built so far, a significant number are operated as military VIP transports.

Dassault announced it was developing a new intercontinental range large size business jet based on its Falcon 50 trijet at the 1983 Paris Airshow. Development culminated in the prototype, *Spirit of Lafayette*, flying for the first time on September 21 1984. A second prototype flew on August 30 1985, and this aircraft demonstrated the type's long range potential by flying nonstop from Paris to Little Rock, Arkansas in the USA for a demonstration tour.

While of similar overall configuration to the Falcon 50, the Falcon 900 features an all new widebody fuselage, which can seat three passengers abreast, and is also considerably longer and wider. The main commonality with the Falcon 50 is the wing, which despite being originally designed for a considerably lighter aircraft, was adapted almost directly unchanged (and incidentally also appears on the new Falcon 2000 twin). Design of the Falcon 900 made extensive use of computer aided design, while the aircraft's structure incorporates a high degree of composite material.

From 1991 the standard production model was the Falcon 900B, which differs from the earlier 900 in having more powerful engines, increased range and the ability to operate from unprepared strips and Category II visibility approach clearance. A further improved development is the 900EX with longer range.

Like the smaller Falcons (Mystères in France), the 900 has proven popular with a number of countries as military VIP transports, particularly so for its large cabin and transcontinental range. Japan operates a unique maritime surveillance version of the Falcon 900 with a US sourced search radar, HU-25 Guardian/Gardian like large observation windows, a dedicated operator station, and a hatch to drop sonobuoys, markers and flares. Two are in JASDF service.

Photo: South Africa's sole Falcon 900. (Richard Siudak)

Dassault Mirage III

Country of origin: France

Type: Multirole fighter

Powerplant: IIIE – One 41.2kN (9435lb) dry and 60.8kN (13,670lb) afterburning SNECMA Atar 9C-3 turbojet, plus optional (although rarely used) 14.7kN (3305lb) SEPR jettisonable booster rocket.

Performance: IIIE – Max speed 2350km/h (1268kt), cruising speed at 36,100ft 955km/h (516kt). Time to 26,090ft 3min 0sec. Service ceiling 55,775ft, or 75,460ft with booster rocket. Ferry range with three drop tanks 4000km (2150nm). Combat radius on a hi-lo-hi attack mission 1200km (647nm).

Weights: IIIE – Empty 7050kg (15,542lb), max takeoff 13,700kg (30,205lb).

Dimensions: Wing span 8.22m (27ft 0in), length 15.03m (49ft 4in), height 4.50m (14ft 9in). Wing area 35.0m^2 (376.8sq ft).

Accommodation: Pilot only, or two in tandem in IIIB and IIID.

Armament: Two 30mm DEFA 552A cannon in lower fuselage. IIIE has four underwing and one centreline hardpoints capable of carrying up to 4000kg (8818lb) of armaments, including one radar guided Matra R.350 AAM, Matra R.550 Magic or AIM-9 Sidewinder infrared guided AAMs, AS30 and AS37 ASMs, bombs and rockets.

Operators: Argentina, Brazil, France, Pakistan, South Africa, Switzerland.

History: The first of Dassault's famous Mirage series of fighters to achieve production, the Mirage III enjoyed considerable export success, and propelled France to the forefront of combat aircraft design.

The Mirage name was first applied to a design to meet a 1952 French Air Force requirement for a light, high speed interceptor. The Mirage I was a small delta wing design powered by two Armstrong Siddeley Viper turbojets and first flew in June 1955. While the Mirage I was too small to be practical, test experience was invaluable for the much larger SNECMA Atar powered Mirage III. The prototype Mirage III-001 flew for the first time on November 17 1956 and later became the first western European aircraft to reach Mach 2 in level flight. Ten pre production Mirage IIIAs were built before the first Mirage IIICs were delivered to the French Air Force in July 1961. IIICs were also built for South Africa (IIICZ) and Israel (IIICJ – veterans of Israel's Middle East wars, survivors were sold to Argentina in 1982). The equivalent two seater is the IIIB.

The multirole Mirage IIIE retains the Thomson-CSF Cyrano II radar but with nav/attack avionics and Doppler navigation radar (in a bulge beneath the cockpit), while French aircraft had the ability to carry a AN52 nuclear bomb. The two seat IIID does not have the Cyrano radar.

The IIIE was a significant export success, and was built under licence in Australia and Switzerland (as the IIIS with a Hughes TARAN 18 radar). The reconnaissance Mirage IIIR is based on the IIIE, but features cameras (and no radar) in a modified nose (four South African IIIR2Zs were delivered with Atar 9K-50s).

Most of France's Mirage IIIs have been retired, while most other remaining Mirage III operators have upgraded their aircraft. The radar-less, ground attack optimised Mirage 5 is described separately.

Photo: Swiss Mirages have been retrofitted with canards. (Swiss MoD)

Dassault Mirage 5 & 50

Country of origin: France

Type: Ground attack and day fighter

Powerplant: 50M – One 49.0kN (11,025lb) dry and 70.8kN (15,875lb) afterburning SNECMA Atar 9K-50 turbojet.

Performance: 50M – Max speed 2338km/h (1262kt) at 39,370ft, cruising speed at 36,100ft 955km/h (516kt). Max initial rate of climb 36,615ft/min. Time to 45,000ft 4min 42sec. Service ceiling 59,055ft. Interception combat radius with two AAMs and three drop tanks, hi-hi-hi 1315km (710nm). Combat radius with two 400kg (880lb) bombs and three drop tanks, hi-lo-hi 1260km (680nm), or with same load and lo-lo-lo 630km (340nm).

Weights: 50M – Empty equipped 7150kg (15,763lb), max takeoff 14,700kg (32,407lb).

Dimensions: 50M – Wing span 8.22m (27ft 0in), length 15.56m (51ft 1in), height 4.50m (14ft 9in). Wing area 35.0m² (376.8sq ft).

Accommodation: Pilot only, except two in tandem in two seaters.

Armament: 5 – Two 30mm DEFA 552A cannon in lower fuselage. Can carry up to 4000kg (8818lb) of armament on four underwing and three underfuselage hardpoints, comprising rockets, bombs and infrared guided missiles. Cyrano radar equipped 5s can fire radar guided Matra R.350. Venezuelan and some Pakistani aircraft can fire AM39 Exocet anti shipping missiles.

Operators: Argentina, Chile, Columbia, Egypt, Gabon, Libya, Pakistan, Peru, UAE (Abu Dhabi), Venezuela, Zaire.

History: Dassault developed the Mirage 5 at the request of Israel, who was seeking a low cost, day ground attack fighter version of the Mirage III.

First flown in May 1969, the Mirage 5 originally differed from the IIIE in the deletion of the Cyrano radar, which allowed simplified avionics to be carried in a slimmer and longer nose, and thus creating space for extra internal fuel, and the addition of two extra hardpoints under the fuselage. Otherwise the Mirage 5 was identical to the III. Variants other than the basic single seater were the two seat 5D and reconnaissance 5R.

Ironically France's then president Charles de Gualle embargoed the delivery of the 50 Mirage 5Js on order for Israel, and instead these aircraft were delivered to the French Air Force as Mirage 5Fs. Other customers were soon attracted to the Mirage 5 and in all 525 were built.

The Mirage 5 was offered with increasingly more sophisticated avionics and systems (including ranging radar and laser designators) as production progressed, and a number were fitted with lightweight Cyrano IV, Agave or Aida 2 radars.

The last major production version on the line that began with the Mirage III was the Mirage 50, which features a 20% more powerful Atar 9K-50 turbojet, as fitted on the Mirage F1. First flown on April 15 1979, customers were Chile and Venezuela. Dassault also offers the 50M as an upgrade of existing Mirage III and 5s.

Like the Mirage III, several nations have Mirage 5 upgrade programs, new features usually including modern avionics and canards.

Photo: Dassault's demonstrator Mirage 50M, rebuilt from a Mirage III.

Dassault Mirage IV

Country of origin: France

Type: Strategic nuclear bomber

Powerplants: Two 49.0kN (11,025lb) dry and 70.6kN (15,875lb) afterburning SNECMA Atar 9K-50 turbojets.

Performance: Max speed 2338km/h (1262kt) at 36,100ft, max speed at sea level approx 1350km (728kt), normal penetration speed 1913km/h (1172kt). Time to 36,100ft 4min 14sec. Service ceiling 65,615ft. Ferry range with drop tanks 4000km (2158nm). Typical combat radius 1240km (668nm).

Weights: Empty equipped 14,500kg (31,965lb), max takeoff 31,600kg (69,665lb).

Dimensions: Wing span 11.85m (38ft 11in), length 23.50m (77ft 1in), height 5.65m (18ft 6in). Wing area 78.0m² (839.6sq ft).

Accommodation: Crew of two in tandem.

Armament: One 30kT or 150kT yield 900kg (1985lb) Aerospatiale ASMP standoff supersonic nuclear ASM. Alternatively can carry up to 7200kg (15,873lb) of conventional ordnance, including bombs or AS 37 Martel anti radar missiles on underwing and underfuselage hardpoints.

Operators: France

History: The Mirage IV was the end result of France's 1954 decision to field a nuclear deterrent force.

Dassault looked at a number of proposals for a strategic nuclear bomber before settling on the Mirage IVA, including developments of the Vautour through to a design approaching the B-58 Hustler in size and powered by two Pratt & Whitney J75 turbojets. In the end the much smaller Mirage IVA design was settled upon, to be powered by two SNECMA Atar turbojets and incapable of launching a strike to the Soviet Union and returning without the aid of inflight refuelling. First flight was on June 17 1959.

Resembling a scaled up Mirage III, the Mirage IV features a delta wing, a crew of two in tandem, an inflight refuelling probe extending from the nose (for refuelling either from KC-135FRs or Mirage IV buddy tankers), surveillance and doppler radars for navigation more latterly augmented by dual INS, while the original 60kT nuclear bomb would be carried semi recessed under fuselage). Twelve booster rockets (six under each wing) are often used to improve field performance.

The successful flight trials of one prototype and three revised pre production Mirage IVs led to a French Air Force order for 50 production aircraft. In all France took delivery of 62 production Mirage IVAs, and these have been subjected to numerous upgrades and modifications throughout their service lives. Twelve IVs were modified for reconnaissance with the fitment of semi recessed cameras and SLAR. In the late 1980s 19 Mirage IVs were modified to IVP standard, which involved fitting modern avionics including the dual INS, plus new RWR and the ability to launch the Aerospatiale ASMP standoff nuclear missile (which has a range of 80km/43nm at low level, or 250km/135nm from high altitude). All other IVAs have been retired.

Photo: A rocket assisted Mirage IV takeoff. Note the nose inflight refuelling probe and large underwing drop tanks. (Armée de l'Air)

Dassault Mirage F1

Country of origin: France

Type: Multirole fighter

Powerplant: F1C – One 49.0kN (11,025lb) dry and 70.2kN (15,785lb) afterburning SNECMA Atar 9K-50 turbojet.

Performance: F1C – Max speed 2338km/h (1262kt). Max initial rate of climb 41,930ft/min. Service ceiling 65,600ft. Combat radius with 14 250kg (550lb) bombs, hi-lo-hi 425km (230nm), or lo-lo-lo with one AM39 Exocet anti shipping missile and two drop tanks 700km (378nm). Combat air patrol with two Super 350 AAMs, one underfuselage tank and one combat engagement 2hr 15min.

Weights: F1C – Empty 7400kg (16,315lb), max takeoff 16,200kg (35,715lb).

Dimensions: F1C – Wing span without wingtip missiles 8.40m (27ft 7in), length 15.30m (50ft 3in), height 4.50m (14ft 9in). Wing area 25.0m² (269.1sq ft). F1C-200 – Same except length 15.30m (50ft 3in).

Accommodation: Pilot only, or two in tandem in F1B.

Armament: F1C – Two 30mm DEFA 553 cannon in lower fuselage. Theoretically can carry 6300kg (13,890lb), or in practice 4000kg (8818lb) of ordnance on four underwing, one centreline and two wingtip hardpoints including wingtip AIM-9 or Magic infrared guided AAMs, R.530 or Super 530F radar guided AAMs, rockets, bombs and ASMs, including the AM 39 Exocet, or Armat anti radiation missile.

Operators: Ecuador, France, Greece, Iraq, Jordan, Kuwait, Libya, Morocco, South Africa, Spain.

History: When developing a successor for the popular Mirage III, Dassault dropped the tailless delta configuration and instead adopted a conventional swept wing for its Mirage F1.

In 1964 the French Government awarded a development contract to begin work on an all weather interceptor. Work was initially on the Mirage F2, a 20 tonne class fighter powered by a TF306 turbofan. At the same time though Dassault worked on a private venture fighter that was similar to the F2, but smaller overall and to be powered by an Atar turbojet. This design was the Mirage F1, which flew in a privately funded prototype form on December 23 1966.

The Mirage F1 was not a great technological advance, yet it was quite a big improvement over the Mirage III, in that the Atar 9K-50 was considerably more powerful, it had 43% more internal fuel (doubling the ground attack radius), improved manoeuvrability, 30% better field performance, slower approach speed and an improved Cyrano IV radar.

Production of the F1 began with 100 F1C interceptors for the French Air Force, which were delivered from May 1973. From 1977 deliveries to the French Air Force were of the F1C-200 which introduced a fixed refuelling probe and a minor fuselage stretch. Fifty five F1Cs have now been modified for ground attack as F1CTs.

France also took delivery of 64 reconnaissance F1CRs fitted with infrared linescan installed in place of cannon, optical cameras in a small nose fairing, and various centreline recce pods. Also in French service are two seat F1Bs – with less external fuel and a slight stretch.

The Mirage F1 has been exported widely, mostly F1Cs. The F1A is simplified for day ground attack without the Cyrano radar, while the multirole F1E and equivalent F1D two seater achieved some success.

Photo: A French F1 fitted with a Thomson-CSF ASTAC Flint pod.

Dassault Mirage 2000

Country of origin: France

Type: Multirole fighter

Powerplant: 2000C – One 64.3kN (14,460lb) dry and 95.1kN (21,835lb) afterburning SNECMA M53-P2 turbofan.

Performance: 2000C – Max speed over 2338km/h (1262kt). Max initial rate of climb 56,000ft/min. Service ceiling 54,000ft. Time to 49,215ft 4min. Ferry range with drop tanks 3335km (1800nm). Combat range with four 250kg (550lb) bombs 1480km (800nm) without drop tanks, or over 1850km (1000nm) with drop tanks.

Weights: 2000C – Empty 7500kg (16,535lb), max takeoff 17,000kg (37,478lb).

Dimensions: 2000C – Wing span 9.13m (30ft 0in), length 14.36m (47ft 1in), height 5.20m (17ft 1in). Wing area 41.0m² (441.3sq ft).

Accommodation: Pilot only, or two in tandem in 2000B.

Armament: 2000C – Two 30mm DEFA 554 cannon in lower fuselage. Up to 6300kg (13,890lb) of external ordnance can be carried on four underwing and five underfuselage hardpoints, including Matra Magic 2 and Super 530D AAMs, laser guided bombs, dumb bombs, anti runway bombs, cluster bombs, two AS 30L ASMs, two Armat anti radiation missiles or two AM 39 Exocet anti ship missiles. Typical interceptor load two Magic 2 and two Super 530Ds.

Operators: Egypt, France, Greece, India, Peru, Taiwan*, UAE.

History: The Mirage 2000 combines the proven benefits of the delta wing layout with technological improvements such as fly-by-wire.

A delta wing configuration boasts a number of advantages such as a large wing area and large internal fuel volume, but has also a number of shortcomings including poor field performance and manoeuvrability due to wing sweep angle. The Mirage 2000's use of fly-by-wire with inherent instability and leading edge slats dramatically improves manoeuvrability and field performance compared with the Mirage III.

Development work on the Mirage 2000 began when a lack of funding forced the cancellation of the larger, twin engined Super Mirage in 1975. Even though the Mirage 2000 was intended as a smaller and simpler fighter than the Super Mirage, the program was highly ambitious, as the aircraft was to incorporate advances in radar, cockpit, armament, airframe and powerplant technologies. The official specification written for the Mirage 2000 was issued in 1976, with the first prototype flying for the first time on March 10 1978, and with deliveries of production 2000Cs (and later two seat 2000B) occurring from April 1983, only a year behind the original schedule.

Apart from fly-by-wire (a technology in which France had little prior experience), the Mirage 2000 introduced the new SNECMA M53 turbofan, a Thomson-CSF RDM multimode radar, a CRT, HUD and HOTAS.

Other than Taiwan, all export customers have ordered the 2000E (and recce pod carrying 2000R), a multirole development powered by the SNECMA M53-P2. Taiwan has ordered the 2000-5, a modernised multirole development and France is upgrading 23 Mirage 2000s to 2000-5 standard.

The 2000-5 features five LCD cockpit displays (as developed for Rafale), a multimode Thomson-CSF RDY radar, Matra Mica AAM compatibility and an uprated M53-P20 powerplant.

Photo: French Air Force Mirage 2000Cs. (Armée de l'Air)

Dassault Mirage 2000N, 2000D & 2000S

Country of origin: France

Type: Nuclear & conventional strike fighters

Powerplant: 2000D – One 64.3kN (14,460lb) dry and 95.1kN (21,385lb) afterburning SNECMA M53-P2 turbofan.

Performance: 2000D – Max speed 2390km/h (1290kt). Penetration speed at 195ft 1112km/h (600kt). Max initial rate of climb 59,055ft/min. Service ceiling 59,055ft. Range with max external fuel 3335km (1800nm), combat radius with two Magic 2 AAMs, 1000kg (2205lb) of ordnance and two drop tanks 1500km (810nm).

Weights: 2000D – Empty equipped 7750kg (17,085lb), max takeoff 17,300kg (38,140lb).

Dimensions: 2000D – Wing span 9.13m (30ft 0in), length 14.55m (47ft 9in), height 5.15m (16ft 11in), Wing area 41.0m² (441.3sq ft).

Accommodation: Crew of two in tandem.

Armament: Nine hardpoints (one centreline, four underfuselage and four underwing) can carry a total payload of 6300kg (13,890lb). Weapon options include Matra BGL laser guided bombs, Aerospatiale AS 30L laser guided ASMs, Matra Armat anti radiation missiles, two AM 39 Exocet anti ship missiles, bombs, cluster bombs, gun pods with two 30mm cannon each and dispensers with anti runway and anti armour munitions. Two Matra Magic 2 AAMs typically carried on outboard wing stations. 2000N can carry a single Aerospatiale 150kT or 300kT yield ASMP 850kg (1875lb) standoff guided nuclear missile.

Operators: France

History: The two seat strike variants of Dassault's Mirage 2000 originate from efforts to find a replacement for the Mirage IV nuclear bomber.

As early as 1979 Dassault received a contract to build a nuclear attack development of the 2000, designated the 2000P (Pénétration). This designation was subsequently changed to 2000N (Nucléaire), to better reflect its role, and the first of the two prototypes flew for the first time on February 3 1983.

The 2000N is closely based on the airframe of the 2000B conversion trainer. Changes to the airframe were restricted mainly to structural strengthening for low level operations. The 2000N though does have a considerably different avionics suite to reflect its offensive roles. The key difference is the Dassault Electronique/Thomson-CSF Antilope 5 radar, with terrain following (down to 300ft and speeds of 1110km/h/600kt), ground mapping, navigation, air-to-sea and air-to-air modes. The primary weapon of the 2000N is the Aerospatiale ASMP standoff guided nuclear missile which is carried on the centreline station. A typical nuclear attack configuration would be the ASMP, two 2000 litre (440Imp gal/528US gal) tanks and two Magic 2 AAMs.

To augment the Mirage IVP, France ordered 75 2000Ns in two variants, the nuclear only 2000N-K1 and nuclear and conventional capable 2000N-K2. These were delivered between the late 1980s and 1993.

The 2000D is basically similar to the 2000N-K2 except that it can only carry conventional munitions (it can be identified by its lack of nose probe). It first flew on February 19 1991, and France has 90 on order. Finally the 2000S (Strike) is an export version of the 2000D, with Antilope 5 radar. None have been ordered.

Photo: A rocket armed Mirage 2000N. (Armée de l'Air)

Dassault Super Etendard

Country of origin: France

Type: Carrier borne strike fighter

Powerplant: One 49.0kN (11,025lb) SNECMA Atar 8K-50 non afterburning turbojet.

Performance: Max speed 1118km/h (603.5kt), max speed at sea level 1180km/h (637kt). Max initial rate of climb 19,685ft/min. Service ceiling over 45,000ft. Combat radius on an anti shipping mission with one AM39 Exocet and two drop tanks, hi-lo-hi 850km (460nm).

Weights: Empty equipped 6500kg (14,330lb), max takeoff 12,000kg (26,455lb).

Dimensions: Wing span 9.60m (31ft 6in), length 14.31m (47ft 0in), height 3.86m (12ft 8in). Wing area 28.4m² (305.7sq ft).

Accommodation: Pilot only

Armament: Two internal 30mm DEFA cannon. Up to 2100kg (4630lb) of ordnance can be carried on two under fuselage and four underwing hardpoints, including rocket pods, bombs, laser guided bombs, Magic AAMs, two AM 39 Exocet anti ship missiles, or one ASMP guided standoff nuclear missile (under one wing, offset by a fuel tank under the other wing).

Operators: Argentina, France.

History: As its name suggests, the Super Etendard is a developed version of the now retired Etendard IV.

The original Etendard (meaning standard, as in flag) was designed in response to the same NATO requirement for a light attack fighter as the Fiat G91. While the original Bristol Orpheus powered Etendard was looked over in favour of the G91, Dassault, convinced of the design's potential, launched the Etendard IV powered by a SNECMA Atar turbojet (first flight July 24 1956). The IV attracted the attention of the French Navy, who, after some delays, took delivery of the attack IVM and reconnaissance IVR. The Etendard IVR has only recently been retired from service.

The early 1970s Etendard replacement requirement was originally to be met by about 100 navalised SEPECAT Jaguar Ms. However politics and cost interfered, and instead, after evaluation of the Skyhawk and Corsair, the French Navy ordered Dassault's proposed Super Etendard.

The Super Etendard introduced a more powerful Atar 8K-50 turbojet, a non afterburning version of the Mirage F1's 9K-50, a strengthened and revised structure for operations at higher speeds and weights, a Thomson-CSF/Dassault Agave radar, inertial navigation, improved avionics and a retractable inflight refuelling probe.

The first of three converted Etendard IVM Super Etendard prototypes flew for the first time on October 29 1974, while the first of 71 production Super Etendards were delivered from June 1978. In the mid 1980s France's Super Etendards were subjected to an upgrade that featured a life extension out to 2008, the ability to launch the ASMP standoff nuclear missile, a new Dassault Electronique Anemone radar, new cockpit instrumentation, HUD, HOTAS and other systems.

While Iraq leased five Super Etendards pending the delivery of Mirage F1EQs from 1983, the only export customer was Argentina. Argentinean Navy Super Etendards gained some notoriety when they sunk HMS *Sheffield* and the *Atlantic Conveyer* with Exocets during the Falklands War in 1982.

Photo: Rafale Ms will replace French Super Etendards. (Paul Merritt)

Dassault Rafale

Country of origin: France

Type: Advanced multirole fighter

Powerplants: Two 87.0kN (19,555lb) with afterburning SNECMA M88-3 turbofans.

Performance: Rafale C – Max speed 2125km/h (1147kt), max speed at low level 1390km/h (750kt). Combat radius on a low level penetration mission with 12 250kg (550lb) bombs, four Mica AAMs and three drop tanks 1095km (590nm). Air-to-air combat radius with eight Mica AAMs and four tanks 1850km (1000nm).

Weights: Rafale C – Empty equipped approx 9060kg (19,975lb), max takeoff 21,500kg (47,400lb).

Dimensions: Rafale C – Wing span incl wingtip missiles 10.90m (35ft 9in), length 15.30m (50ft 3in), height 5.34m (17ft 6in). Wing area 46.0m² (495.1sq ft).

Accommodation: Pilot only in Rafale C & M, two crew in Rafale B.

Armament: One internal 30mm GIAT DEFA 791B cannon. Up to 6000kg (13,230lb) of ordnance can be carried on six underwing, two wingtip, two centreline and four underfuselage stations. Options include an ASMP nuclear standoff missile, up to eight Matra Mica AAMs, AM 39 Exocet anti shipmissiles, laser guided bombs, AS30L laser guided ASMs, or Apache dispensers with anti armour or anti runway munitions.

Operators: France*

History: When the Mirage 2000 was just entering service in the early 1980s France was already casting its eye on a successor fighter program.

When France withdrew as a participant of the EFA (now Eurofighter) consortium on the grounds that the EFA was too big and France wanted to be the lead partner, development instead focused on Dassault's Avions de Combat Experimentale (ACX) design.

As the Rafale A, the ACX was built in demonstrator form which first flew on July 4 1986. The Rafale A was used to validate much of the design of the definitive Rafale, including the airframe, fly-by-wire system and SNECMA M88 turbofan (the Rafale A initially flew with two GE F404s, a M88 was installed in the port engine station in 1990).

The definitive Rafale is slightly smaller than the Rafale A, has some stealth measures and greater use of composite materials by weight. It will be built in three versions, the single seat Rafale C (first flight May 19 1991) and two seat Rafale B for the French Air Force (the two types have the generic Rafale D designation), and the navalised Rafale M single seater for the French Navy. Current orders stand at 95 Cs and 135 Ds (for ground attack – Gulf War experience proving the value of two crew) to replace Mirage F1s and Jaguars, and 78 Ms to replace French Navy Super Etendards and F-8EN Crusaders.

Features of the Rafale include its blended fuselage/wing airframe, comprehensive Spectra integrated defensive aids subsystems, Dassault Electronique/Thomson-CSF RBE2 radar (with electronic scanning, air-to-air, air-to-ground, navigation and terrain following functions), LCD cockpit displays, a helmet mounted sight, voice commands, and FLIR, IRST and laser rangefinder. (Early production Rafales will not have full Spectra suite, terrain following capability, helmet mounted sight or voice commands). Rafale Ms will be the first to enter service, currently planned for 1999.

Photo: The Rafale B prototype in flight. (Dassault)

Dassault/Dornier Alpha Jet

Countries of origin: France and Germany

Type: Two seat advanced trainer and close support aircraft

Powerplants: Alpha Jet A – Two 14.1kN (3175lb) SNECMA/Turboméca Larzac 04-C20 turbofans. E – Two 13.2kN (2975lb) Larzac 04-C6s.

Performance: A – Max speed Mach 0.86. Max initial rate of climb 12,000ft/min. Time to 30,000ft less than 7min. Service ceiling 48,000ft. Ferry range with four external tanks over 4000km (2160nm). Combat radius with gun pod and underwing weapons hi-lo-hi 585km (315nm), or lo-lo-lo 390km (210nm). Combat radius with gun pod, weapons and two tanks hi-lo-hi 1075km (580nm), or lo-lo-lo 630km (340nm). E – Same except max speed 1000km/h (540kt). Radius on a lo-lo-lo training mission with two drop tanks 670km (360nm). Endurance with internal fuel over 3hr 30min.

Weights: A – Empty equipped 3515kg (7750lb), max takeoff 8000kg (17,637lb). E – Empty equipped 3345kg (7375lb), max takeoff same.

Dimensions: A – Wing span 9.11m (29ft 11in), length 13.23m (43ft 5in), height 4.19m (13ft 9in). Wing area 17.5m² (188.4sq ft). E – Same except length 11.75m (38ft 7in).

Accommodation: Two in tandem.

Armament: More than 2500kg (5510lb) of external ordnance, including centreline 30mm DEFA or 27mm Mauser cannon pod, bombs and rockets, AAMs (such as Sidewinder or Magic) and ASMs (such as Maverick).

Operators: Belgium, Cameroon, Egypt, France, Germany, Ivory Coast, Morocco, Nigeria, Portugal, Qatar, Togo.

History: France and Germany agreed to jointly develop a new subsonic advanced trainer in the late 1960s.

The TA501 design, which was submitted by Dassault, Breguet (the two French companies merged in 1971) and Dornier, was chosen in 1970 over two other competing designs, all of which were to be powered by two small Larzac turbofans, a legacy of Germany's bad experiences with single engine F-104 Starfighters. The TA501 was named Alpha Jet, and a change in Germany's requirement for the aircraft saw it being developed in advanced trainer and close support/battlefield reconnaissance forms.

Official development go-ahead for the program was given in February 1972, resulting in the first flight of a prototype on October 26 1973. French Alpha Jet E (Ecole – school) deliveries to replace Magisters began in 1978, while Germany's first Alpha Jet A (Appui-tactique) first flew in April 1978. Most new build Alpha Jet export customers took delivery of aircraft similar to the French standard.

Germany's were fitted with a comprehensive nav/attack suite including twin gyro INS and a doppler navigation radar. Germany took delivery of 175 Alpha Jets which primarily replaced G91s for close air support. These aircraft were subsequently re-engined with uprated engines. All but 35 retained for Tornado lead-in training were retired in 1993, of which 50 went to Portugal.

The Alpha Jet NGEA (new generation attack/trainer) was launched in 1980 and features a HUD, cockpit CRTs, laser rangefinder and compatibility with the Matra Magic AAM. It was sold to Cameroon and Egypt. The current offering Alpha Jet ATS would feature LCD displays, HOTAS controls, a small radar and FLIR.

Photo: Moroccan and French Alpha Jet Es in formation. (Dassault)

De Havilland Canada DHC-4 Caribou

Country of origin: Canada

Type: STOL tactical transport

Powerplants: DHC-4A – Two 1080kW (1450shp) Pratt & Whitney R-2000-7M2 14 cylinder twin row radial piston engines driving three bladed propellers.

Performance: DHC-4A – Max speed 347km/h (187kt), normal cruising speed 293km/h (158kt). Max initial rate of climb 1355ft/min. Service ceiling 24,8000ft. Takeoff run to 50ft at MTOW 360m (1185ft). Range with max payload 390km (210nm), range with max fuel 2105km (1135nm).

Weights: DHC-4A – Basic operating 8293kg (18,260lb), standard max takeoff 12,930kg (28,500lb), military overload max takeoff 14,195kg (28,500lb).

Dimensions: DHC-4A – Wing span 29.15m (95ft 8in), length 22.13m (72ft 7in), height 9.68m (31ft 9in). Wing area 84.7m² (912.0sq ft).

Accommodation: Crew of two and a loadmaster. Can carry almost 4 tonnes (8000lb) of cargo (including two jeeps or Land Rovers, or light artillery pieces). Can seat 32 equipped troops, or 22 stretcher patients plus medical attendants in air ambulance configuration.

Armament: None

Operators: Australia, Cameroon, Liberia, Malaysia, Uganda, Zambia.

History: De Havilland Canada's fourth design was a successful attempt at combining the payload of the DC-3 with the STOL performance of the earlier single engine DHC-2 Beaver and DHC-3 Otter.

De Havilland Canada (DHC) originally designed the DHC-4 as a private venture with an eye on Canadian and US military requirements. DHC built a prototype demonstrator (with assistance from Canada's Department of Defence Production) that flew for the first time on July 30 1958. Impressed with the DHC-4's STOL capabilities and potential, the US Army ordered five for evaluation as the YAC-1 to meet its requirement for a tactical airlifter to supply the battlefront with troops and supplies and evacuate casualties on the return journey.

The US Army went on to become the largest Caribou operator, taking delivery of 159. The initial AC-1 designation was later changed to CV-2, and then C-7 when the US Army's CV-2s were transferred to the US Air Force in 1966 (the Caribou was the largest aircraft ever operated by the US Army up to that time). Caribou production ended in 1973 after 307 had been built, mostly for military customers.

US Army CV-2s, Air Force C-7s and Australian DHC-4A Caribou saw extensive service during the Vietnam conflict, where the type came into its own. The Caribou was well suited to Vietnam's demanding conditions and its STOL performance (unmatched by few types before or since) saw it operate into areas otherwise the domain of helicopters. Interestingly many US Caribou were captured by North Vietnamese forces in 1975 and remained in service with that country through the late 1970s. Other former military operators included Canada, Colombia, India, Spain and Tanzania.

Today a dwindling number of Caribou survive in military service, notably with Australia and Malaysia. Malaysia already has IPTN built CN-235s on order as a replacement, while Australia is evaluating the Alenia G222 and the CN-235 to replace its long serving fleet.

Photo: An Australian Caribou. (Julian Green)

De Havilland Canada DHC-5 Buffalo

Country of origin: Canada

Type: STOL tactical transport

Powerplants: DHC-5D – Two 2335kW (3133shp) General Electric CT64-820-4 turboprops driving three bladed propellers.

Performance: DHC-5D – Max cruising speed 467km/h (252kt). Max initial rate of climb 2330ft/min. Service ceiling 31,000ft. Takeoff run with a 5445kg (12,000lb) payload 290m (950ft). Max range with ferry tanks 6115km (3300nm).

Weights: DHC-5D – Operating empty 11,410kg (25,160lb), max takeoff weight from an unprepared strip 18,597kg (41,000lb), max takeoff from prepared strip 22,315kg (49,200lb).

Dimensions: DHC-5D – Wing span 29.26m (96ft 0in), length 24.08m (79ft 0in), height 8.73m (28ft 8in). Wing area 87.8m² (945sq ft).

Accommodation: Crew of two pilots plus loadmaster. Cabin can seat 41 equipped troops, or 35 paratroops, or 24 stretcher patients and six medical attendants. Max payload 8165kg (18,000lb). Max airdroppable unit 2720kg (6000lb).

Armament: None

Operators: Cameroon, Canada, Ecuador, Kenya, Mauritania, Mexico, Peru, Sudan, Tanzania, Togo, Zaire, Zambia, UAE.

History: The Buffalo is a turboprop powered development of the earlier Caribou, and was developed specifically to meet a 1962 US Army requirement.

The US Army selected the Buffalo for development ahead of 24 other contenders for the STOL transport requirement. Funding for the development of the DHC-5 (initially called Caribou II) was split equally between de Havilland Canada, the Canadian Government and the US Army. The resulting aircraft was closely based on the Caribou, but introduced two General Electric CT64 turboprops, an increased maximum lift coefficient, a T tail and a significantly higher max takeoff weight.

The US Army funded the development of four CV-7A evaluation Buffalos, the first of which flew for the first time on April 9 1964. Unfortunately for de Havilland Canada, the same change of US policy that saw the US Army transfer its CV-2s to the US Air Force saw the cancellation of plans to procure production CV-7s. The four CV-7As were thus transferred to the USAF as the C-8.

A Canadian Armed Forces order for 15 CC-113 Buffalos for search and rescue saved the program from an uncertain future, and export orders soon flowed in (the first coming from Brazil). In all 59 Buffalos were built through to 1972 when production ceased for the first time.

Proposed but unbuilt Buffalo variants were the DHC-5B with CT64-P4Cs and the DHC-5C with either CT64-P4Cs or Rolls-Royce Darts.

DHC reopened the Buffalo line in 1974 when it introduced the improved DHC-5D. The DHC-5D features more powerful CT64-820-4s (in place of the DHC-5A's 2280kW (3055ehp) CT64-820-1s), increasing payload range. DHC-5D production continued for a number of overseas customers through to 1986, by which time total Buffalo production reached 126.

Photo: Canada's 14 surviving CC-115 Buffalos are used for SAR. Note the nose mounted weather radar. (Bombardier)

De Havilland Canada DHC-6 Twin Otter

Country of origin: Canada

Type: STOL utility transport

Powerplants: 100 – Two 430kW (579shp) Pratt & Whitney Canada PT6A-20 turboprops.

Performance: 100 – Max cruising speed 297km/h (160kt). Range with max fuel 1427km (770nm), range with a 975kg (2150lb) payload 1344km (727nm). 300 – Max cruising speed at 10,000ft 338km/h (182kt). Max initial rate of climb 1600ft/min. STOL takeoff run 104m (304ft). Range with 1135kg (2500lb) payload 1297km (700nm), range with a 860kg (1900lb) payload and wing tanks 1705km (920nm).

Weights: 100 – Basic operating empty 2653kg (5850lb), max takeoff 4765kg (10,500lb). 300 – Operating empty 3363kg (7415lb), max takeoff 5670kg (12,500lb).

Dimensions: 100 – Wing span 19.81m (65ft 0in), length 15.09m (49ft 6in), height 5.94m (19ft 6in). Wing area 39.0m² (420sq ft). 300 – Same except for length 15.77m (51ft 9in), or 15.09m (49ft 6in) for floatplane variants.

Accommodation: Flightcrew of two. Standard airliner interior seats 20 at three abreast.

Armament: None, although DHC-6-300M(COIN) offered with a cabin mounted machine gun and the ability to carry underwing ordnance.

Operators: Argentina, Canada, Chile, Ecuador, Ethiopia, France, Haiti, Nepal, Norway, Paraguay, Peru, Uganda, USA.

History: De Havilland Canada's most successful design in terms of sales, the Twin Otter has sold widely to the world's military air arms due to its rugged construction and STOL performance.

Development of the Twin Otter dates back to January 1964 when de Havilland Canada started design work on a new STOL twin turboprop commuter airliner (seating between 13 and 18) and utility transport. Designated the DHC-6, construction of the prototype began in November that year, resulting in the type's first flight on May 20 1965.

The first production aircraft were known as Series 100, design features including double slotted trailing edge flaps and ailerons on the wings that act in unison to boost STOL performance. In comparison with the later Series 200 and 300s, the 100s are distinguishable by their blunt noses, while in common with the later aircraft skis and floats can be fitted. Canada was the only military customer for the Series 100, taking delivery of eight CC-138s for search and rescue.

The main addition to the Series 200, which was introduced in April 1968, featured the extended nose, which together with a reconfigured storage compartment in the rear cabin greatly increased baggage stowage area. The Series 300 was introduced from the 231st production aircraft in 1966. It too features the lengthened nose, but also introduced more powerful engines, thus allowing a 450kg (1000lb) increase in takeoff weight. Production ceased in 1988 and comprised 115 Series 100 aircraft, 115 Series 200s and 614 Series 300s.

Dedicated military variants of the 300 were offered in 1982. The DHC-6-200M was a 15 seat troop transport with optional air ambulance and paratroop configurations; armed and armoured DHC-6-300M (COIN) for counter insurgency missions; and the DHC-6-300MR maritime patrol variant fitted with searchlight and radar.

Photo: A Canadian Forces CC-138 (DHC-6-100). (Paul Merritt)

De Havilland Dash 8 & E-9

Country of origin: Canada

Type: Utility transport, navigation trainer and range support aircraft

Powerplants: 100 – Two 1490kW (2000shp) Pratt & Whitney Canada PW120A turboprops driving four bladed propellers.

Performance: 100A – Max cruising speed 491km/h (265kt), long range cruising speed 440km/h (237kt). Max initial rate of climb 1560ft/min. Certificated service ceiling 25,000ft. Range with full passenger load, max fuel and reserves 1520km (820nm), range with a 2720kg (6000lb) payload 2040km (1100nm).

Weights: 100A – Operating empty 10,251kg (22,600lb), max takeoff 15,650kg (34,500lb).

Dimensions: Wing span 25.91m (85ft 0in), length 22.25m (73ft 0in), height 7.49m (24ft 7in). Wing area 54.4m² (585.0sq ft).

Accommodation: Flightcrew of two. Typical passenger seating for 37 at four abreast, or max seating for 40.

Armament: None

Operators: Canada, Kenya, USA.

History: De Havilland's Dash 8 has carved itself a handy niche in the fiercely competitive regional airliner market, but has also found its way in small numbers into military colours.

De Havilland began development of the Dash 8 in the late 1970s in response to what it saw as a considerable market niche for a new generation 30 to 40 seat commuter airliner. The first flight of the first of the new airliners was on June 20 1983, while the first airline customer delivery took place on October 23 1984.

Like the four engined 50 seat Dash 7 before it, the Dash 8 features a high mounted wing and T tail, and has an advanced flight control system and large full length trailing edge flaps. Power is supplied by two Pratt & Whitney Canada PW120 (originally PT7A) turboprops.

The initial Dash 8 production model was the Series 100, which was followed by the PW120A powered Series 100A in 1990. The Series 100B has been on offer since 1992 and has more powerful PW121s for better climb and airfield performance. Significant performance benefits are offered by the Series 200 which was announced in 1992 and has been available for delivery since 1994. It features more powerful PW123C engines, and thus has a higher cruising speed, plus greater commonality with the stretched Dash 8 300. The 200B has PW123Bs for better hot and high performance. Four Dash 8 200s are being fitted with search radar and FLIR for Australian Customs use.

The stretched, 50 seat Dash 8 300 is powered by PW123s and is greater in length by 3.43m (11ft 3in). A future development is the Dash 8 400, a 70 seat regional airliner which could be available from 1998.

Dash 8 military service is currently limited to variants of the Dash 8 100. Canada is the largest operator with two CC-142 transports (Dash 8M) and three modified CT-142 navigation trainers, which feature a mapping radar housed in a bulged nose radome. Kenya meanwhile operates three standard Dash 8s as transports.

The US Air Force uses two modified Dash 8s for missile range control, designated E-9A. These two aircraft feature a large phased array radar mounted along the right hand side of the fuselage, telemetry equipment and an APS-128D surveillance radar in a ventral dome.

Photo: One of two USAF E-9As. (Bombardier)

Dornier Do 27

Country of origin: Germany

Type: Light STOL utility transport, trainer and liaison aircraft

Powerplant: Do 27H-2 – One 255kW (340hp) Lycoming GSO-480-B1B6 flat six piston engine, driving a three bladed propeller. Do 27Q-5 – One 200kW (270hp) GSO-480-B1A6 driving a two bladed prop.

Performance: Do 27H-2 – Max speed 245km/h (132kt), high speed cruise 212km/h (115kt), economical cruising speed 180km/h (97kt). Max initial rate of climb 965ft/min. Service ceiling 22,000ft. Range with max fuel 1360km (735nm). Do 27Q-5 – Max speed 232km/h (125kt), 75% power cruising speed 211km/h (114kt), 60% power cruising speed 190km/h (103kt), economical cruising speed 175km/h (95kt). Max initial rate of climb 650ft/min. Service ceiling 10,800ft. Range with max fuel and no reserves 1102km (595nm).

Weights: Do 27H-2 – Empty equipped 1170kg (2580lb), max takeoff 1848kg (4070lb). Do 27Q-5 – Empty equipped 1130kg (2490lb), max takeoff 1848kg (4070lb).

Dimensions: Do 27H-2 & Q-5 – Wing span 12.00m (39ft 5in), length 9.60m (31ft 6in), height 2.80m (9ft 2in). Wing area 19.4m² (208.8sq ft).

Accommodation: Pilot and passenger with between four and six passengers behind them. Can be configured for freight or stretchers.

Armament: Usually none.

Operators: Angola, Burundi, Switzerland, Togo.

History: The Dornier Do 27 was the first military aircraft to be built in any numbers in West Germany since World War 2 (577 in all), and marked the re-emergence of Dornier as an aircraft designer and manufacturer.

The Do 27 traces back to the Do 25, which Professor Claude Dornier (Dornier was responsible for the Do 17 medium bomber in WW2) designed in Spain for a Spanish military requirement for a light general purpose utility aircraft. Two prototype Do 25s were built, the first was powered by a 110kW (150hp) ENMA Tigre G-IVB engine and flew for the first time on June 25 1954. Subsequently CASA built 50 production aircraft, as Do 27As for the Spanish Air Force (Spain designated the type the C-127).

Following this success the German army and air force ordered the Do 27 in large numbers. A total of 428 were delivered to German forces from the mid 1950s to 1960, although these aircraft have now been retired. Small numbers were built for other military customers, while many of the ex German aircraft went to other military customers, including the air arms of Portugal, Nigeria, Israel, Sudan and Turkey. In turn some of the Portuguese aircraft ended up in Angolan military service, while other second hand Do 27s have been delivered to a number of African nations.

Features of the Do 27 design include a flat six Lycoming engine, a wide and relatively roomy cabin, wide track tricycle undercarriage and excellent STOL performance. The STOL performance in particular suited the Do 27 for use in undeveloped countries, hence the large list of operator nations with mountainous and rough terrain.

Models of the Do 27 include the initial Do 27A and dual control Do 27B for Germany; the Do 27-H series that was based on the A-4 but with a more powerful engine and three bladed prop; and the Do 27Q series, equivalent to the Do 27A.

Photo: Germany's Do 27 have long been retired. (Dornier)

Dornier Do 28 & 128

Country of origin: Germany

Type: STOL utility and transport and liaison aircraft

Powerplants: Do 28 D-2 – Two 285kW (380hp) Lycoming IGSO-540-A1E flat six piston engines driving three bladed constant speed propellers. 128-6 – Two 300kW (400shp) Pratt & Whitney Canada PT6A-110 turboprops.

Performance: Do 28 D-2 – Max speed 325km/h (175kt), max cruising speed 306km/h (165kt), economical cruising speed 241km/h (130kt). Max initial rate of climb 1160ft/min. Service ceiling 25,200ft. Takeoff run 280m (920ft). Range with max payload 1050km (566nm). 128-6 – Max speed 340km/h (183kt), max cruising speed 330km/h (178kt), economical cruising speed 256km/h (138kt). Max initial rate of climb 1260ft/min. Service ceiling 32,600ft. Takeoff run to 50ft altitude 554m (1820ft). Range with max fuel 1825nm (985nm), with a 805kg (1774lb) payload 1460km (788nm).

Weights: Do 28 D-2 – Empty 2328kg (5132lb), max takeoff 3842kg (8470lb). 128-6 – Empty 2540kg (5600lb), max takeoff 4350kg (9590lb).

Dimensions: Do 28 D-2 – Wing span 15.55m (51ft 0in), length 11.41m (37ft 5in), height 3.90m (12ft 10in). Wing area 29.0m² (312sq ft). 128-6 – Same except for wing span 15.85m (52ft 0in).

Accommodation: One or two pilots on flightdeck and up to 13 troops on inward facing folding seats. In air ambulance configuration can accommodate five stretchers. Also used to carry freight.

Armament: Usually none.

Operators: Do 28 – Croatia, Germany, Greece, Israel, Kenya, Malawi, Morocco, Niger, Turkey, Zambia. Do 128 – Cameroon, Nigeria.

History: The Skyservant followed from the success of the Do 27 single in the liaison and light transport roles, and over 200 were built almost exclusively for military customers.

The Do 28 Skyservant was the second aircraft to bear the Do 28 designation, but is similar only in configuration to the original Do 28 (the first Do 28 flew in 1959 and was a twin engine development of the Do 27). The Do 28 Skyservant first flew on February 23 1966, and while it retained the earlier Do 28's high wing and side mounted engine configuration, was an all new and much larger aircraft. Other design features were the fixed tailwheel undercarriage and the faired mainwheels mounted beneath the engines.

The Do 28 was developed into a number of progressively improved variants, from the original D, through the D-1 and D-2, to the 128-2, introduced in 1980. Each variant introduced a number of detail changes. Most Do 28 production was for military customers, notably Germany, although a small number were sold to commercial operators.

A turboprop version of the Do 28, designated the DO 28 D-5X, first flew in April 1978, fitted with two Avco Lycoming LTP 101-600-1As derated to 298kW (400shp). Production turboprop Dornier 128-6s however feature Pratt & Whitney PT6As, the first such configured aircraft flying in March 1980. Only a small number were built between then and 1986, notably for Peru, which ordered 16, and Cameroon, whose three Do 128s were fitted with a MEL Marec search radar for maritime patrol.

Photo: Germany was the largest Do 28 operator, although most have now been sold. (Dornier)

Country of origin: Germany

Type: Utility transport and maritime patrol aircraft

Powerplants: 100 – Two 535kW (715shp) Garrett TPE 331-5 turbo-props, driving four bladed propellers. 212 – Two 560kW (776shp) Garrett TPE 331-5-252Ds.

Performance: 100 – Max cruising speed 432km/h (233kt). Max initial rate of climb 2050ft/min. Service ceiling 29,600ft. Range at max cruising speed 1730km (935nm), or 1970km (1065nm) at long range cruising speed. Patrol time close to base 7hr 45min, or at 740km (400nm) from base 3hr 45min. 212 – Max cruising speed 434km/h (234kt), cruising speed 408km/h (220kt). Max initial rate of climb 1870ft. Service ceiling 28,000ft. Range with 19 passengers at max cruising speed 1037km (560nm), range with a 775kg (1710lb) payload at long range cruising speed 2445km (1320nm).

Weights: 100 – Operating empty 3235kg (7132lb), max takeoff 5700kg (12,570lb). 212 – Operating empty 3739kg (8243lb), max takeoff 6400kg (14,110lb).

Dimensions: 100 – Wing span 16.97m (55ft 7in), length 15.03m (49ft 3in), height 4.86m (15ft 9in). Wing area 32.0m² (345sq ft). 212 – Same except for length 16.56m (54ft 4in).

Accommodation: Flightcrew of two. 100 – Seating for 15. Maritime patrol configuration crew of three with a radar operator. 212 – Typical passenger seating for 19. 228-212 based 228 Cargo has a max payload of 2340kg (5159lb). 228-212 based ambulance accommodates six stretchers and up to nine attendants or passengers.

Armament: None

Operators: Germany, India, Italy, Malawi, Niger, Nigeria, Oman, Thailand.

History: Although primarily designed as a commuter airliner, the Dornier 228 series also serves as a light military transport and in various maritime patrol configurations.

The Dornier 228 incorporates the fuselage cross section of the earlier Do 28 and 128, combined with an all new high technology supercritical wing and Garrett turboprops. Two fuselage length versions, the 100 and 200 were developed concurrently, the 100 offering better range, the 200 more payload. The 100 was the first to fly taking to the skies for the first time on March 28 1981, the first 200 followed on May 9 1981.

Dornier 228 developments include the 228-101 with reinforced structure and landing gear for higher weights, the corresponding 228-201 version of the -200, the 228-202 version under licence production in India with HAL (over 50 are being acquired for all three military services), and the 228-212. The -212 is the current Dornier production model with higher operating weights, improvements to enhance short field performance and modern avionics.

India is by far the largest military 228 operator, with several maritime patrol configured aircraft in service with its air force and coast guard. These aircraft are fitted with a MEL Marec II search radar and linescan equipment, while the Royal Thai Navy operates 228s fitted with a Bendix 1500 radar. The German Navy meanwhile operates a 228 configured for maritime pollution patrol. Most other military operated 228s serve as transports.

Photo: A Royal Thai Navy Dornier 228. Note search radar.

Douglas C-47 Skytrain/Dakota

Country of origin: United States of America

Type: Tactical transport, gunship and utility transport

Powerplants: C-47A – Two 895kW (1200hp) Pratt & Whitney R-1830-92 14 cylinder two row radial piston engines, driving three bladed propellers. Jet Prop DC-3 – Two 1060kW (1425shp) Pratt & Whitney Canada PT6A-65AR turboprops, driving five bladed propellers.

Performance: C-47A – Max speed 346km/h (187kt), max cruising speed 298km/h (161kt), economical cruising speed 280km/h (151kt). Max initial rate of climb 1160ft/min. Service ceiling 24,000ft. Range 2415km (1305nm). Jet Prop DC-3 – Max cruising speed 343km/h (185kt). Max initial rate of climb 1000ft/min. Range with max payload 648km (350nm), max range 3705km (2000nm). Max endurance 14hr.

Weights: C-47A – Empty equipped 8250kg (18,190lb), max takeoff 13,290kg (29,300lb). Jet Prop DC-3 – Empty 7257kg (16,000lb), max takeoff 12,202kg (26,900lb).

Dimensions: C-47A – Wing span 28.95m (95ft 0in), length 19.62m (64ft 6in), height 5.15m (16ft 11in). Wing area 91.7m² (987sq ft). Jet Prop DC-3 – Same except length 20.68m (67ft 10in).

Accommodation: C-47 – Flightcrew of two. Up to 28 troops on inward facing seats, or 18 stretchers and three medical attendants. Jet Prop DC-3 – Up to 40 troops.

Armament: AC-47 – Three 7.62mm MGs through left side windows.

Operators: In service with over 25 countries including Australia, Bolivia, Cameroon, Colombia, Greece, Honduras, Mexico, Israel, Paraguay, Salvador, South Africa, Taiwan, Thailand, Turkey, Zaire.

History: The C-47 was the most important military transport of WW2, and yet today, five decades later, it remains in service with the air arms of more than 25 countries around the world.

The C-47 traces back to the DC-3 airliner, an improved development of the earlier DC-2 which made its first flight in 1934. The DC-3 flew for the first time on December 17 1935 and went on to become the mainstay of US domestic airlines in the years prior to World War 2.

The entry of the US into WW2 in December 1941 would have a profound effect on the fortunes of the already successful DC-3 (more than 400 had been built by then). The US Army Air Force's requirements for transport aircraft were well met by the in-production DC-3, with the result that as the C-47 Skytrain it became the standard USAAF transport during the war. More than 10,000 were built for service with US and foreign air arms; in British service it was named Dakota.

Postwar surplus C-47s became the standard equipment of almost all the world's airlines, while many US surplus C-47s were also sold or donated to the world's air forces. In the USSR it was built in quantity as the Lisunov Li-2.

The C-47's longevity has resulted in a number of turboprop conversion programs to improve its performance. Two notable conversions are the Basler Turbo-67 and Professional Aviation Jet Prop DC-3, both of which feature a small fuselage stretch and two Pratt & Whitney Canada PT6A turboprops. A small number of operators have converted their C-47s to Turbo-67 standard, while South Africa is converting 30 or so to Jet Prop standard.

Photo: Australia's surviving C-47s are used for various trials, this one wears a grey colour scheme tested for P-3 Orions. (92WG RAAF)

Douglas DC-8 & EC-24

Country of origin: United States of America

Type: Strategic & VIP transport, ECM and Elint aircraft

Powerplants: Series 50 – Four 80.6kN (18,000lb) Pratt & Whitney JT3D-3 turbofans. Super 70 Series – Four 97.9kN (22,000lb) CFM International CFM56-2-C5 turbofans.

Performance: Series 50 – Max recommended cruising speed 933km/h (504kt). Range with max payload 9205km (4970nm), max range 11,260km (6078nm). Super 70 – Max cruising speed 887km/h (479kt), economical cruising speed 850km/h (460kt). Range with max payload (Super 73) 8950km (4830nm).

Weights: Series 50 – Operating empty 60,020kg (132,325lb), max takeoff 147,415kg (325,000lb). Super 73 – Operating empty 75,500kg (166,500lb), max takeoff 162,025kg (355,000lb).

Dimensions: Wing span 43.41m (142ft 5in), length 45.87m (150ft 6in), height 12.91m (42ft 4in). Wing area 257.6m2 (2773sq ft) on early aircraft, or 266.5m² (2868sq ft) on later aircraft. Super 63 & 73 – Wing span 45.23m (148ft 5in), length 57.12m (187ft 5in), height 12.92m (45ft 5in). Wing area 271.9m² (2927sq ft).

Accommodation: Flightcrew of three. Series 50 can seat up to 179, and Series 71 and 73 can seat up to 220 in high density passenger configurations. Some of the French and Peruvian aircraft configured as VIP transports.

Armament: None

Operators: France, Peru, USA.

History: The DC-8 was Douglas' first jet powered airliner, and arch rival of the more successful Boeing 707. Compared with the 707, only a small number have ever seen military service.

Douglas was slower and more cautious to move into the then radical field of jet powered transports than Boeing, the project was announced in 1955, the year after Boeing had flown its Dash 80 707/KC-135 predecessor. The first DC-8 flew on May 30 1958, and after a concentrated certification program the first production aircraft entered airliner service in September 1959, a year later than the 707.

Over 550 DC-8s were in built in a number of different variants, and two distinct fuselage lengths. Original short fuselage models included the turbojet powered Series 10, 20, 30 and 40, and the turbofan powered 50 series. The stretched Super 60 series was built from the late 1960s, and comprised the long range 47.98m (157ft 5in) length 62, and the 57.12m (187ft 5in) length 61 and 63. When re-engined with CFM56s, the Super 60 series are known as Super 70s.

France continues to be the largest military operator, currently with a Series 55 and three Series 72s used for strategic and VIP transport duties, while a modified Series 53, the DC-8 SARIGUE, is used for ECM/Elint reconnaissance. It features wingtip pods and a dorsal fairing. All current French Air Force DC-8s are ex civil airliners, as are Peru's two DC-8-62CFs which are used as VIP transports.

In the USA Chrysler Technologies operates a single converted DC-8-54F freighter for the US Navy for ECM training. Designated EC-24, the DC-8 is used to simulate a realistic Electronic Warfare (EW) environment for fleet training exercises.

Photo: A French Air Force DC-8-72CF transport. (Armée de l'Air)

EH Industries EH 101 Merlin & Cormorant

Countries of origin: Italy and the United Kingdom

Type: Medium lift utility transport and shipborne ASW helicopter

Powerplants: Merlin – Three 1725kW (2312shp) Rolls-Royce/Turboméca RTM322-01 turboshafts, driving a five bladed main rotor and four bladed tail rotor.

Performance: Merlin – Cruising speed 296km/h (160kt), long range cruising speed 260km/h (140kt), best endurance speed 167km/h (90kt). Ferry range with auxiliary tanks 1853km (1000nm). Endurance with max weapon load, 5hr on station.

Weights: Merlin – Basic empty (estimated) 7120kg (15,700lb), max takeoff 13,000kg (28,660lb) or 13,530kg (29,830lb).

Dimensions: Main rotor diameter 18.59m (61ft 0in), length overall rotors turning 22.81m (74ft 10in), length main rotor and tail folded (Merlin) 16.00m (52ft 6in), height overall rotors turning 6.65m (21ft 10in), height main rotor and tail folded (Merlin) 5.21m (17ft 1in). Main rotor disc area 271.5m² (2922.5sq ft).

Accommodation: Flightcrew of one or two. Merlin will have a crew comprising one or two pilots, an acoustic sensor operator and observer. Utility version will accommodate 30 equipped troops, or 16 stretchers and medical attendants. Max external slung load 5445kg (12,000lb).

Armament: Merlin can be fitted with four homing torpedoes in addition to anti shipping missiles. Utility version can be fitted with stub wings for rocket pods and a 12.7mm machine gun in a nose turret.

Operators: Italy*, UK*.

History: The three engined EH 101 was initially conceived as a replacement for the Sikorsky/Westland Sea King, but is also on offer in a number of civil and military versions.

EH (or European Helicopter) Industries is a collaborative venture between Westland of the UK and Agusta of Italy, and was formed primarily to develop an anti submarine warfare helicopter for the Royal Navy and Italian Navy, plus utility and civil variants. The partnership was formed in 1980, and both companies have a 50% holding. The development history of this aircraft is protracted and dates back to the late 1970s when Westland was working on its WG 34 Sea King replacement. The WG 34 was cancelled, paving the way for the joint Anglo Italian EH 101 program, which was formed in 1980. Full scale program go ahead of the EH 101 was announced in March 1984. First flight of an EH 101 (the Westland built PP1) was on October 9 1987.

The lead customer for the EH 101 is the Royal Navy, which takes delivery of the ASW configured Merlin HAS.1 (equipped with Blue Kestrel search radar, dipping sonar and ESM) from 1996. The RAF has ordered 22 utility EH 101s for delivery from 1998, while the Italian Navy has ordered eight ASW EH 101s similar in configuration to the Merlin and four EH 101 utility transports. Canada meanwhile has cancelled an order for utility (CH-149 Chimo) and ASW (CH-148 Petrel) EH 101s in which it had significant industrial input. Export EH 101s have been dubbed Cormorant.

The EH 101 is offered with a choice of engines, either the Rolls-Royce Turboméca RTM322 or General Electric T700. British EH 101s will have RTM322s, civil EH 101s have General Electric CT7 engines.

Photo: A pre production EH 101 in Italian Navy markings.

Embraer EMB-110 & EMB-111

Country of origin: Brazil

Type: Light utility transport & maritime patrol aircraft (EMB-111)

Powerplants: Two 560kW (750shp) Pratt & Whitney Canada PT6A-34 turboprops, driving three bladed Hartzell propellers.

Performance: EMB-111 – Max cruising speed 360km/h (194kt), economical cruising speed 347km/h (187kt). Max initial rate of climb 1190ft/min. Service ceiling 25,500ft. Range 2945km (1590nm).

Weights: EMB-111 – Empty equipped 3760kg (8289lb), max takeoff 7000kg (15,432lb).

Dimensions: EMB-111 – Wing span over tip tanks 15.95m (52ft 4in), length 14.91m (48ft 11in), height 4.91m (16ft 2in). Wing area 29.1m² (313sq ft).

Accommodation: Flightcrew of two. Can carry up to 18 troops or six stretchers.

Armament: EMB-111 – Four underwing pylons can carry rockets, smoke bombs, flares, chaff dispenser and a searchlight.

Operators: EMB-110 – Australia, Brazil, Chile, Colombia, Gabon, Peru, Senegambia, Uruguay. EMB-111 – Angola, Brazil, Chile, Gabon.

History: The EMB-110 Bandeirante, or 'Bandit', was Embraer's first and thus far most successful indigenous aircraft program and is in widespread civil and military service.

Design of the EMB-110 was undertaken in response to a Brazilian Ministry of Aeronautics specification for a general purpose light transport suitable for both military and civilian duties. The new design was developed with the assistance of well known French designer Max Holste, and the first of three prototypes, designated YC-95s, flew for the first time on October 26 1968. Embraer (or Empresa Brasilera de Aeronáutica SA) was established the following year, and development and production of the YC-95 became one of the company's first responsibilities.

The first of the larger production standard EMB-110 Bandeirantes (or Pioneer) flew on August 9 1972 and the type entered Brazilian Air Force service in February 1973.

Brazilian military transport versions of the basic EMB-110 are designated C-95, including 60 early build, 12 seat C-95s and 31 stretched C-95Bs, equivalent to the EMB-110P, the definitive civil version. Brazil also operates a small number of navigation aid calibration EC-95s and photographic survey RC-95s.

The most heavily modified Bandeirante is the EMB-111 maritime patrol variant, which features an Eaton-AIL APS-128 Sea Patrol radar mounted in a nose radome, ESM, wingtip tanks and four underwing hardpoints. The last 10 EMB-111s built for Brazil feature improved avionics including a MEL Super Searchmaster radar and EFIS. Brazil's EMB-111s are designated P-95.

Production of the Bandeirante ceased in May 1990 (the last aircraft was delivered to the Brazilian Air Force). In all over 500 Bandeirantes were built, including 29 EMB-111s.

Photo: A Brazilian Navy EMB-111. In Brazilian service these aircraft are nicknamed Bandeirulha, a contraction of Bandeirante Patrulha.

Embraer EMB-120 Brasilia

Country of origin: Brazil

Type: Twin turboprop VIP transport and surveillance platform

Powerplants: Two 1340kW (1800shp) Pratt & Whitney Canada PW118 or PW118A turboprops, driving four bladed Hamilton Standard propellers.

Performance: EMB-120 with PW118As – Max cruising speed 574km/h (310kt), long range cruising speed 482km/h (260kt). Max initial rate of climb 2120ft/min. Service ceiling 32,000ft. Range with max passengers and reserves 926km (500nm). EMB-120ER with PW118As – Max cruising speed 580km/h (313kt), long range cruising speed 500km/h (270kt). Max initial rate of climb 2500ft/min. Service ceiling 32,000ft. Range with max pax and reserves 1500km (810nm).

Weights: EMB-120 – Empty equipped 7100kg (15,655lb), max take-off 11,500kg (25,353lb). EMB-120ER – Empty equipped 7140kg (15,741lb), max takeoff 11,990kg (26,433lb).

Dimensions: EMB-120 – Wing span 19.78m (64ft 11in), length 20.00m (65ft 8in), height 6.35m (20ft 10in). Wing area 39.4m² (424.42sq ft). EMB-120ER – Same except for length 20.07m (65ft 10in).

Accommodation: Flightcrew of two. Standard main cabin seating for 30 at three abreast. Brazilian VC-97s configured as VIP transports. EMB-120AEWs will feature three multi function work stations.

Armament: None

Operators: Brazil, Peru.

History: Although in only limited military service, the Brasilia, a high speed yet relatively inexpensive to operate and purchase commuter, is proving to be a considerable sales success, following in the highly successful footsteps of the earlier and smaller Bandeirante.

Design work of the Brasilia dates back to the late 1970s when Embraer investigated stretching its EMB-121 Xingu corporate turbo-prop to a 25 seat regional airliner. While this was the first aircraft to bear the EMB-120 designation (it was named the Araguia), the resulting EMB-120 is an all new aircraft. Design studies began in September 1979, first flight of a PW115 powered prototype took place on July 27 1983, and entry into service was in October 1985.

Brazil operates 10 VIP transport configured Brasilias, designated VC-97. These were delivered to the Brazilian air force from 1987.

Brazil has also ordered five Airborne Early Warning and three Synthetic Aperture Radar configured Brasilias for its Amazon Surveillance System program. The EMB-120AEWs will be fitted with an Ericsson Erieye phased array surveillance radar and three multi function operator work stations and an onboard command and control system. The EMB-120SRs will be fitted with a Synthetic Aperture Radar, an ultraviolet/visible/infrared line scanner and a high sensitivity TV/FLIR. The Brazilian AirForce will use the EMB-120AEWs to detect and track illegal aircraft movements over the Amazon, while the EMB-120SRs will be used for resource exploration, pollution detection and control and illegal activities surveillance. First deliveries are planned for 1997.

Photo: A Brazilian Air Force VC-97 (EMB-120RT) VIP transport.

Embraer EMB-121 Xingu

Country of origin: Brazil

Type: Liaison, VIP transport and multi engine trainer aircraft

Powerplants: Xingu I – Two 505kW (600shp) Pratt & Whitney Canada PT6A-28 turboprops, driving three bladed props. Xingu II – Two 635kW (850shp) PT6A-42s driving four bladed props.

Performance: Xingu I – Max cruising speed 450km/h (243kt), economical cruising speed 365km/h (197kt). Max initial rate of climb 1400ft/min. Service ceiling 26,000ft. Range with max fuel 2352km (1270nm). Xingu II – Max cruising speed 465km/h (251kt), economical cruising speed 380km/h (205kt). Max initial rate of climb 1800ft/min. Range with max fuel 2278km (1230nm), with max payload 1630km (880nm).

Weights: Xingu I – Empty equipped 3620kg (7984lb), max takeoff 5670kg (12,500lb). Xingu II – Empty equipped 3500kg (7716lb), max takeoff weight 6140kg (13,536lb).

Dimensions: Xingu I – Wing span 14.45m (47ft 5in), length 12.25m (40ft 2in), height 4.74m (15ft 7in). Wing area 27.5m² (296.0sq ft). Xingu II – Wing span 14.83m (48ft 8in), length 13.44m (44ft 1in). Wing area 27.9m² (300.3sq ft).

Accommodation: Xingu I – Flightcrew of one or two, plus typical main cabin seating for five or six passengers. Xingu II – Flightcrew of two. Main cabin seating for seven, eight or nine passengers.

Armament: None

Operators: Brazil, France.

History: The sleek looking Xingu coupled the Bandeirante's wing and engines with an all new fuselage and was intended as a fast corporate transport for the civil market, but in the end almost half of all EMB-121 production was for the Brazilian and French militaries.

The Xingu flew for the first time on October 10 1976, with a production aircraft following on May 20 1977 and customer deliveries starting later that year.

Several derivatives of the Xingu design were proposed, including the original EMB-120, the Araguia, a commuter airliner which would have seated 25, and the EMB-123 Tapajós. The Tapajós would have had more powerful 835kW (1120shp) PT6A-45 engines (which also would have powered the Araguia), increased wing span and lengthened fuselage.

A more modest development did enter production, the EMB-121B Xingu II. This features more powerful engines, four bladed props, increased fuel tankage and greater seating capacity courtesy of a slightly stretched fuselage. The Xingu II made its first flight on September 4 1981. Xingu production ceased in August 1987 after 105 had been built.

The first six production Xingus were all delivered to the Brazilian Air Force in late 1977, designated VU-9 and used for VIP transport. Brazil later acquired a further six second hand EMB-121s, and these are designated EC-9.

Some 41 EMB-121s, almost half of all Xingu production were delivered to the French Air Force and Navy where they are used for aircrew training and liaison duties. They were ordered in September 1980 and the last were delivered in 1983.

Photo: French Air Force and Navy Xingus fly in formation.

Embraer EMB-312 Tucano

Country of origin: Brazil

Type: Two seat basic/advanced trainer

Powerplant: EMB-312 – One 560kW (750shp) Pratt & Whitney Canada PT6A-25C turboprop, driving a three bladed propeller.

Performance: EMB-312 – Max speed 448km/h (242kt), max cruising speed 411km/h (222kt), economical cruising speed 319km/h (172kt). Max initial rate of climb 2330ft/min. Service ceiling 30,000ft. Ferry range with two underwing tanks 3330km (1797nm), typical range on internal fuel 1845km (995nm). Endurance on internal fuel approx 5hr.

Weights: EMB-312 – Basic empty 1810kg (3990lb), max takeoff 3175kg (7000lb).

Dimensions: EMB-312 – Wing span 11.14 (36ft 7in), length 9.86m (32ft 4in), height 3.40m (11ft 2in). Wing area 19.4m² (208.8sq ft).

Accommodation: Seating for two in tandem, except in ALX single seater.

Armament: EMB-312 – Up to 1000kg (2205lb) on four underwing pylons, including bombs, rockets, gun pods and practice bombs.

Operators: Argentina, Brazil, Columbia, Egypt, France, Honduras, Iran, Iraq, Kenya, Kuwait, Paraguay, Peru, Venezuela, UK.

History: What started as a replacement program for Brazil's fleet of T-37 trainers has resulted in South America's most successful military aircraft program, with over 600 sold to 14 different nations.

Development of the Tucano (Toucan) began in late 1978 when the Brazilian Ministry of Aeronautics awarded Embraer a development contract to design and fly a turboprop powered trainer to replace the Brazilian Air Force's Cessna T-37s. What resulted was the Tucano, a tandem two seater (with ejection seats) powered by a Pratt & Whitney Canada PT6A turboprop, featuring four underwing hardpoints for light armament or practice bombs. First flight was on August 16 1980.

Brazil originally ordered 133 Tucanos which were delivered between 1983 and 1986. Egypt became the first export customer, when in 1983 it ordered a total of 134, all but 10 of which were to be assembled by Helwan in Egypt. Of those 134, 80 were built for Iraq.

In 1985 the British RAF selected a Garrett TPE331 powered variant of the Tucano to replace its Jet Provosts. These aircraft were licence built by Shorts in Northern Ireland as the S312 (Tucano T.1 in RAF service), and feature a significantly more powerful 820kW (1100shp) TPE331-12B engine, improved systems and structural strengthening for improved fatigue life. Kuwait and Kenya have also ordered Shorts built, Garrett powered Tucanos.

France is another major Tucano customer, ordering 80 Embraer built EMB-312F Tucanos in 1991 to replace Magisters. Delivered from 1993, these aircraft feature structural strengthening and French avionics.

The EMB-312H Super Tucano is a stretched (11.41m/37ft 6in long), more powerful development (featuring a 930kW/1250shp PT6A-68 driving a five bladed prop). This aircraft was an unsuccessful contender in the USA's JPATS competition, but the armed single and two seat Tucano ALX versions are being developed for the Brazilian Air Force. They will be used for anti narcotics and anti smuggling operations.

Photo: An Argentinean Tucano on a pre delivery test flight.

ENAER T-35 Pillán

Country of origin: Chile

Type: Two seat basic trainer

Powerplant: T-35A – One 225kW (300hp) Textron Lycoming IO-540-K1K5 fuel injected flat six piston engine driving a three bladed constant speed propeller. T-35TD – One 315kW (420shp) Allison 250-B17D turboprop driving a three bladed constant speed propeller.

Performance: T-35A – Max speed 311km/h (268kt), max cruising speed 266km/h (144kt). Max initial rate of climb 1525ft/min. Time to 10,000ft 8min 48sec. Service ceiling 19,160ft. Range at 55% power 1205km (650nm), range at 75% power 1095km (590nm). Endurance at 55% power 5hr 35min, endurance at 75% power 4hr 25min. T-35DT – Max speed 425km/h (230kt), 75% power cruising speed 337km/h (182kt), 55% power cruising speed 313km/h (170kt). Max initial rate of climb 2850ft/min. Time to 9850ft 5min 36sec. Service ceiling 25,000ft. Range at 55% power 760km (410nm), range at 75% power 648km (350nm).

Weights: T-35A – Empty equipped 930kg (2050lb), max takeoff 1338kg (2950lb). T-35DT – Empty 943kg (2080lb), max takeoff 1338kg (2950lb).

Dimensions: T-35A – Wing span 8.84m (29ft 0in), length 8.00m (26ft 3in), height 2.64m (8ft 8in). Wing area 13.7m² (147.3sq ft). T-35DT – Same except length 8.60m (28ft 3in).

Accommodation: Seating for two in tandem.

Armament: Usually none.

Operators: Chile, Panama, Paraguay, Spain.

History: The Pillán (devil) basic trainer resulted from a Chilean Air Force requirement for a two seat, aerobatic basic trainer.

Responding to the requirement Piper designed a new trainer based on its PA-28R Saratoga, a six seater with retractable undercarriage itself based on the PA-28 four seater family. Piper designated its new two seater the PA-28R-300, and while based on the Saratoga it featured a new fuselage centre section and structural strengthening for aerobatics. Like the Saratoga it featured a 225kW (300hp) six cylinder Lycoming IO-540 engine.

Piper built two prototypes, the first flying on March 6 1981, while the first of three ENAER assembled prototypes flew in January 1982. From 1979 ENAER (Empresa Nacional de Aeronáutic de Chile) had assembled under licence 27 Piper PA-28 Dakota four seat light aircraft for the Chilean Air Force and various local flying clubs and so was already experienced in building Piper aircraft.

ENAER production of the T-35 began in 1985. In all 60 were built for Chile, 60 T-35As and 20 IFR equipped T-35Bs. The most significant export customer for the T-35 was Spain, who ordered 41 T-35Cs. Designated the E.26 Tamiz in Spanish service, these aircraft were assembled in Spain by CASA from ENAER built kits. Other customers were Panama (10 IFR equipped T-35Ds) and Paraguay (15 T-35Ds). Final T-35 deliveries were completed in 1991.

The turboprop T-35DT Turbo Pillán is a development of the original T-35TX Aucán which first flew in February 1986. The T-35DT features a new one piece canopy, oxygen system and improved instrumentation. None have been sold thus far.

Photo: One of Spain's CASA built E.26 Tamiz. (MAP)

English Electric Canberra

Country of origin: United Kingdom

Type: Bomber, target tug and reconnaissance aircraft

Powerplants: B(I).8 – Two 33.2kN (7400lb) Rolls-Royce Avon 109 turbojets.

Performance: B(I).8 – Max speed 871km/h (470kt) at 40,000ft, max speed at sea level 827km/h (447kt). Max initial rate of climb 3400ft/min. Service ceiling 48,000ft. Range with max fuel 5840km (3155nm), range with max load and 10 minutes over target 1295km (700nm).

Weights: B(I).8 – Basic operating 12,678kg (27,950lb), max takeoff 24,925kg (54,950lb).

Dimensions: B(I).8 – Wing span over tip tanks 19.96m (65ft 6in), wing span 19.51m (64ft 0in), length 19.96m (65ft 6in), height 4.77m (15ft 8in). Wing area 89.2m^2 (960sq ft).

Accommodation: B(I).8 – Flightcrew of two. Pilot seated under fighter style canopy, navigator in nose.

Armament: Up to six 1000lb (455kg) bombs in weapons bay, or alternatively one 4000lb (1815kg) and four 1000lb (455kg) bombs, or eight 500lb (227kg) bombs, or three 1000lb (455kg) bombs and four Hispano cannon. Two underwing wingtip stations can carry 455kg (1000lb) each.

Operators: Argentina, Chile, India, Peru, UK.

History: The Canberra was Britain's primary medium bomber during the 1950s and into the 1960s, in addition to being widely exported, and today continues to serve, albeit in dwindling numbers.

As far back as 1944 English Electric (a large British industrial company that had built Halifax bombers under licence in WW2) was shortlisted along with a number of higher profile British aircraft manufacturers to design the RAF's first jet bomber. English Electric's design was selected and it flew for the first time on Friday May 13 1949. Features of the Canberra included its very large, broad wing which was designed for high altitude operations but gave the aircraft fighter like agility, plus its two Rolls-Royce Avon turbojets (one in each wing) and an internal bomb bay. In all, 27 variants were built, including those built under licence in the USA by Martin as the B-57 Canberra (one of which is still in service with NASA), and 48 in Australia by GAF. Significant models include the B.2 bomber, PR.3 and PR.7 reconnaissance aircraft, and the B.6 bomber.

In October 1994 the RAF retired its last T.17s, originally built as trainers but later used for Electronic Warfare training. However other Canberras remain in RAF service for test and trials duties and reconnaissance.

The Shorts developed PR.9 remains in RAF service as a reconnaissance platform. Features of this aircraft include more powerful engines, an offset fighter style tear drop canopy under which sat the pilot (with the navigator enclosed in the nose) and increased span wings. The B(I).8 Interdictor also featured the offset fighter style canopy.

India is the largest current Canberra operator with a mixed fleet including B(I).58s (B(I).8s) and PR.57s (PR.7s). Argentina and Peru also operate Canberras as bombers, while until recently Germany operated two PR.9s and Chile a B.2.

Photo: The RAF's five PR.9s are used for photo survey work and should remain in service through to 2000. (Paul Merritt)

Eurocopter Gazelle

Country of origin: France

Type: Reconnaissance, training, anti tank and multirole helicopter

Powerplant: SA 342L – One 640kW (858shp) Turboméca XIVM turboshaft, driving a three bladed main rotor and fenestron shrouded tail rotor.

Performance: SA 342L – Max cruising speed at sea level 260km/h (140kt). Max initial rate of climb 1535ft/min. Service ceiling 13,450ft. Hovering ceiling in ground effect 9975ft, out of ground effect 7775ft. Range at sea level with standard fuel 710km (383nm).

Weights: SA 342L – Empty 999kg (2202lb), max takeoff 2000kg (4410lb).

Dimensions: SA 342L – Main rotor diameter 10.50m (34ft 6in), length overall 11.97m (39ft 3in), fuselage length 9.53m (31ft 3in), height overall 3.19m (10ft 6in). Main rotor disc area 86.6m^2 (932.1sq ft).

Accommodation: Seating for five including pilot.

Armament: Armament options include rocket pods, four or six HOT wire guided anti armour missiles, two forward firing 7.62mm machine guns, and a single 20mm GIAT cannon on starboard side. Former Yugoslav SA 342Ls equipped four AT-3 'Sagger' ASMs and two SA-7 AAMs.

Operators: Military operators include Angola, Burundi, Cameroon, Cyprus, Ecuador, Egypt, France, Gabon, Guinea Republic, Iraq, Ireland, Kenya, Kuwait, Lebanon, Libya, Morocco, Qatar, Senegambia, Syria, Trinidad and Tobago, Tunisia, UAE, UK, former Yugoslavia.

History: Widely sold around the world to various military air arms, the Gazelle was developed as a replacement to the Alouette II.

The Gazelle pioneered a number of significant technological features, namely a rigid main rotor head, composite construction rotor blades and the shrouded tail rotor, a feature of a number of Aerospatiale/Eurocopter helicopters since.

The prototype was designated SA 340-01, had conventional rotor blades and first flew on April 7 1967. A second prototype introduced composite blades, while improved pre production aircraft with a larger cabin were designated the SA 341 and named Gazelle.

The 1967 Anglo French agreement between Sud Aviation (Aerospatiale from 1970) and Westland covering the Gazelle, Lynx and Puma helicopters resulted in the Gazelle becoming a joint production effort between both nations. Initial production Gazelles were the SA 341B Gazelle AH.1 for the British Army, SA 341C Gazelle HT.2 for the Royal Navy, SA 341D Gazelle HT.3 trainer and SA 341E Gazelle HCC.4 transport for the RAF, the French Army's SA 341F, civil SA 341G and military export SA 341H.

Over 600 SA 341s of different versions were built before production switched to the more powerful Astazou XIVH powered SA 342. Versions are the civil SA 342J and export optimised SA 342K. Final versions are the export military SA 341L and French Army SA 342M, which remain in low rate production. French SA 342Ms are equipped with HOT anti armour missiles, while earlier SA 341Fs have been converted to fire HOTs. France is also equipping 30 Gazelles (the SA 342M ATAM) to fire Matra Mistral AAMs.

Photo: An RAF Gazelle HT.3 trainer. (Paul Merritt)

Eurocopter/Aerospatiale SA 330 Puma

Country of origin: France

Type: Multirole medium lift helicopter transport

Powerplants: SA 330L – Two 1175kW (1575shp) Turboméca Turmo IVC turboshafts, driving a four bladed main rotor and five bladed tail rotor.

Performance: SA 330L – Max cruising speed 271km/h (146kt). Max initial rate of climb 1810ft/min. Service ceiling 19,685ft. Hovering ceiling in ground effect 13,940ft, hovering ceiling out of ground effect 13,940ft. Range 572km (309nm).

Weights: SA 330L – Empty 3615kg (7970lb), normal MTOW 7405kg (16,315lb), max takeoff with sling load 7500kg (16,534lb).

Dimensions: SA 330L – Main rotor diameter 15.00m (49ft 3in), length overall rotors turning 18.15m (59ft 7in), fuselage length 14.06m (46ft 2in), height overall 5.14m (16ft 11in). Main rotor disc area 176.7m² (1902.2sq ft).

Accommodation: Flightcrew of two plus jumpseat on flightdeck. Up to 20 combat equipped troops or six stretchers and six seated patients or medical attendants in main cabin.

Armament: Options include 7.62mm gun pods, rockets and ASMs mounted on the fuselage sides, and pintle mounted machine guns in cabin doors.

Operators: Military operators include Argentina, Chile, Ecuador, France, Gabon, Indonesia, Ivory Coast, Kuwait, Lebanon, Malawi, Morocco, Nepal, Nigeria, Portugal, Romania, Senegambia, South Africa, Spain, Togo, UAE, UK, Zaire.

History: The Puma was designed to meet a French Army requirement for a medium lift helicopter capable of operating in all weather conditions.

The first of two SA 330 prototypes flew for the first time on April 15 1965, with the first production aircraft flying in September 1968. A 1967 Royal Air Force decision to order the Puma as its new tactical helicopter transport resulted in substantial Westland participation in design and construction. This was a result of the Westland/Sud Aviation helicopter cooperation agreement covering the Puma, Gazelle and Lynx signed in 1967.

Early military versions of the Puma were the French Army SA 330B, export SA 330C, SA 330E Puma HC.1 transport for the RAF, and the hot and high Turmo IVC powered SA 330H (designated SA 330Ba in French service). The initial civil variants were the SA 330F passenger and SA 330G freight versions The SA 330L is the definitive military version, and compared to the earlier models has composite main rotors and an increased maximum takeoff weight. The SA 330J is the civil equivalent.

IPTN of Indonesia assembled a small number of SA 330Js as the NSA-330 before switching to the SA 332 Super Puma (described separately), and after Aerospatiale ceased production in 1987, the sole source for the Puma became IAR of Romania.

Since it was isolated by a UN arms embargo, South Africa has developed its own Puma derivatives. Two Makila powered, armed XTP-1 Beta prototypes were used as testbeds during the 1980s for the Rooivalk attack helicopter program, while the Oryx is a Makila powered upgrade of South Africa's Puma fleet. The Oryx was originally named Gemsbok, and entered service in 1988. Other changes include single pilot operation, weather radar and Super Puma style tail.

Photo: An RAF Puma HC.1. (Paul Merritt)

Eurocopter Super Puma & Cougar

Country of origin: France

Type: Multirole medium lift helicopter transport

Powerplants: AS 532U2 – Two 1375kW (1845shp) takeoff rated Turboméca Makila 1A2 turboshafts driving a four bladed main rotor and four bladed tail rotor.

Performance: AS 532U2 – Fast cruising speed 273km/h (147kt), economical cruising speed 242km/h (131kt). Rate of climb 1260ft/min. Service ceiling 13,450ft. Hovering ceiling in ground effect 8333ft, out of ground effect 6235ft. Range with standard fuel 795km (430nm), range with max fuel 1175km (635nm). Endurance 4hr 12min.

Weights: AS 535U2 – Empty 4760kg (10,493lb), max takeoff 9750kg (21,495lb).

Dimensions: AS 532U2 – Main rotor diameter 16.20m (53ft 2in), length overall 19.50m (63ft 11in), length overall main rotor folded 16.79m (55ft 1in), height overall 4.97m (16ft 4in). Main rotor disc area 206.0m² (2217.4sq ft).

Accommodation: AS 532U2 – One pilot VFR or two pilots IFR operations. Main cabin seats up to 29 troops, or 14 stretchers, four seated patients and a medical attendant. Max slung load 4500kg (9920lb).

Armament: Options include 7.62mm gun pods, rockets and ASMs (including AM 39 Exocet anti ship missiles) mounted on the fuselage sides, and pintle mounted machine guns in cabin doors.

Operators: Military operators include Argentina, Brazil, Cameroon, Chile, China, Ecuador, France, Indonesia, Japan, Jordan, Kuwait, Mexico, Nepal, Netherlands*, Nigeria, Qatar, Saudi Arabia, Singapore, South Korea, Spain, Sweden, Switzerland, Thailand*, Togo, Turkey, UAE, Venezuela, Zaire.

History: The Super Puma and Cougar are stretched and re-engined developments of the Puma.

The original Super Puma first flew in September 1978 and was simply a more powerful version of the original Puma, featuring 1270kW (1700shp) Turboméca Makila turboshafts, new avionics and composite rotor blades. Military versions were designated AS 332Bs, commercial versions AS 332Cs.

The AS 332M Super Puma (and civil AS 332L) introduced the stretched fuselage and was first flown on October 10 1980. Uprated Makila 1A1 engines were introduced in 1986. Indonesia's IPTN has licence built a small number of AS 332Ls for that country's military.

In 1990 Aerospatiale (Eurocopter from 1992) renamed military Super Pumas the AS 532 Cougar Mk I series. Various suffixes denote the different military versions – U for unarmed, A for armed, C for the shorter version, L for the slightly stretched fuselage variant. Further variants are the SAR/surveillance AS 532MC and ASW AS 532SC – both feature the shorter fuselage.

The AS 532L remains in production but is progressively being replaced by the AS 532U2 Cougar Mk II. The unarmed U2, armed A2 and civil L2 feature a further fuselage stretch allowing an extra row of seats (and making them the longest members of the Super Puma/Cougar family), EFIS cockpit and longer main rotor blades with parabolic tips. It has been available since 1993.

Photo: A Brazilian AF AS 332M Super Puma. (Jim Thorn)

Eurocopter Ecureuil & Fennec

Country of origin: France

Type: Multirole light helicopter

Powerplants: AS 555N – Two 340kW (455shp) takeoff rated Turboméca TM 319 Arrius turboshafts, driving a three bladed main rotor and two bladed tail rotor.

Performance: AS 555N – Max cruising speed 225km/h (121kt). Max initial rate of climb 1340ft/min. Service ceiling 13,125ft. Hovering ceiling in ground effect 8530ft, out of ground effect 5085ft. Range 722km (390nm). Endurance with one torpedo 2hr 20min.

Weights: AS 555N – Empty 1382kg (3046lb), max takeoff 2600kg (5732lb).

Dimensions: AS 555N – Main rotor diameter 10.69m (35ft 1in), length overall 12.94m (42ft 6in), fuselage length 10.93m (35ft 11in), height overall 3.34m (11ft 0in). Main rotor disc area 89.8m² (966.1sq ft).

Accommodation: Seating for up to six.

Armament: Options include a pintle mounted 7.62mm machine gun, a 20mm GIAT gun pod, twin 7.62mm gun pods, rockets, HeliTOW anti tank missiles, and up to two torpedoes on naval variants.

Operators: Australia, Benin, Botswana, Brazil, Central African Republic, Denmark, Djibouti, Ecuador, France, Malawi, Paraguay, Peru, Sierra Leone, Singapore, UAE.

History: The Ecureuil was conceived as a replacement for the Alouette II (described under Aerospatiale).

Development in the early 1970s culminated in the first flights of the Lycoming LTS 101 powered prototype on June 27 1974, and the Turboméca Arriel powered prototype on February 14 1975. Customer deliveries began in April 1978.

Initial models offered were the Arriel powered AS 350B, which was marketed outside North America, and the LTS 101 powered AS 350C and A350D Astar sold in the USA.

Developments include the AS 350BA (certificated in 1991) fitted with the larger main rotors of the AS 350B2 and the AS 350B2 with a more powerful Arriel 1D1 turboshaft, and the main and tail rotors developed for the AS 355F Ecureuil 2.

The twin engined Ecuriel 2 first flew on September 28 1979. Powered by two Allison 250-C20F turboshafts, the Ecureuil 2 entered production as the AS 355E. In common with the AS 350, the AS 355 features the maintenance free Starflex main rotor hub and main rotor blades of composite construction.

The AS 355F replaced the AS 355E from early 1982, while the current production model is the AS 350N (TwinStar in the US) with Turboméca Arrius turboshafts. Deliveries took place from early 1992.

Aerospatiale adopted the name Fennec for dedicated military Ecureuils in 1990. Single engine military versions are based on the AS 350B2 and include the utility AS 550U2, gun and rocket armed AS 550A2, Heli-TOW missile armed AS 550C2, unarmed maritime AS 350M2 and armed anti shipping AS 550S2. Twin engine Fennec variants include the AS 555UN utility, armed AS 555AN, missile armed AS 555CN, unarmed maritime AS 555MN (with optional chin mounted radar) and armed maritime AS 555SN.

Photo: An Australian AS 350B. (RAN)

Eurocopter Dauphin 2 & Panther

Country of origin: France

Type: Multirole helicopter

Powerplants: AS 565UA – Two 585kW (783shp) Turboméca Arriel 1M1 turboshafts driving a four bladed main rotor and Fenestron shrouded tail rotor.

Performance: AS 565UA – Max cruising speed at sea level 278km/h (150kt). Max initial rate of climb 1378ft/min. Hovering ceiling in ground effect 8530ft, out of ground effect 6070ft. Range with standard fuel 875km (472nm).

Weights: AS 565UA – Empty 2193kg (4835lb), max takeoff 4250kg (9040lb).

Dimensions: AS 565UA – Main rotor diameter 11.94m (39ft 2in), length overall 13.68m (44ft 11in), fuselage length 12.11m (39ft 9in), height 3.99m (13ft 1in). Main rotor disc area 112.0m² (1205.3sq ft).

Accommodation: AS 565 – Two pilots and eight to 10 troops in assault transport role. Can carry four stretchers plus medical attendants.

Armament: AS 565AA – Two rocket packs, or 20mm GIAT M621 gun pods, or up to eight Matra Mistral AAMs in four two round packs, on two fuselage outriggers. AS 565SA – Can carry four side mounted AS15TT radar guided ASMs.

Operators: Angola, Brazil, Cameroon, China, Dominican Republic, France, India, Ireland, Ivory Coast, Malawi, Saudi Arabia.

History: The Dauphin 2 is a twin engined development of the original single Turboméca Astazou powered SA 360 and SA 361 Dauphin, which first flew on June 2 1972.

A dedicated military anti tank variant of the SA 361 was offered, the HOT anti tank missile equipped SA 361F, however none were sold.

Compared with the SA 360, the SA 365 Dauphin 2 introduced twin Turboméca Arriel turboshafts and a new engine fairing, Starflex main rotor hub and higher max takeoff weight, but retained the same basic fuselage. The Dauphin 2's first flight was on January 24 1975, while production deliveries of SA 365Cs began in early 1978. Few SA 365Cs are in military service, Sri Lanka being a notable operator.

The SA 365 was soon replaced by the AS 356N, with more powerful Arriel 1C turboshafts, enlarged tail surfaces, revised transmission and main rotor, new rotor mast fairing and engine cowling, and retractable tricycle undercarriage. The US Coast Guard took delivery of 99 AS 365N based HH-65 Dolphins, optimised for Search and Rescue. These aircraft are powered by two Lycoming LTS 101s.

Current civil production is of the AS 365N2, on which the military AS 565 Panther family is based. Released in 1990, features of the AS 365N2 and Panther include upgraded Arriel engines, increased max takeoff weights, redesigned cabin doors and optional EFIS displays.

Panther models include the AS 565UA unarmed assault transport AS 565AA armed transport, and the AS 565CA anti tank variant equipped with a roof mounted sight and HOT missiles. Naval variants comprise the unarmed AS 565SA and armed AS 565SA. Equipment options include sonar, MAD, searchlight, and search radar. A final military variant is the AS 565 Panther 800, a twin LHTEC T800 powered variant offered to the US Army by Vought and Sikorsky as a UH-1H Iroquois replacement.

Photo: The French Navy uses the Panther for plane guard duty.

Eurocopter BO 105

Country of origin: Germany

Type: Observation, utility and anti tank helicopter

Powerplants: BO 105 CB – Two 320kW (429shp) Allison 250-C20B turboshafts, driving a four bladed main rotor and two bladed tail rotor.

Performance: BO 105 CB – Max cruising speed 245km/h (137kt), cruising speed 232km/h (125kt). Max initial rate of climb 1773ft/min. Service ceiling 17,000ft. Hovering ceiling out of ground effect 6500ft, inside ground effect 9515ft. Range with max payload 655km (354nm), ferry range 1110km (600nm).

Weights: BO 105 CB – Empty equipped 1280kg (2820lb), max takeoff 2400kg (5290lb).

Dimensions: BO 105 CB – Main rotor diameter 9.84m (32ft 4in), length overall 11.86m (38ft 11in), fuselage length 8.56m (28ft 1in), height 3.00m (9ft 10in). Main rotor disc area 76.1m² (818.6sq ft).

Accommodation: Pilot and observer/copilot side by side, with three passengers or two stretchers behind them. Behind rear seats and below the engine is a cargo compartment, accessible by two clamshell doors in the rear fuselage.

Armament: PAH-1 – Six Euromissile HOT anti tank missiles in two three-tube launchers mounted on fuselage outriggers. Majority have been modified to fire HOT 2. Swedish BO 105 CBS can fire ESCO Helitow anti tank missiles.

Operators: Bahrain, Brunei, Chile, Colombia, Germany, Indonesia, Iraq, Kenya, Mexico, Netherlands, Peru, Philippines, Sierra Leone, Spain, Sweden, Trinidad and Tobago, UAE.

History: Well regarded for its agility, twin engine safety and performance, the BO 105 serves widely as a multirole observation and anti tank attack helicopter.

The first of three BO 105 prototypes made the type's maiden flight on February 16 1967. This aircraft was powered by two 236kW (317shp) Allison 250-C18 turboshafts and featured a conventional main rotor hub, but the subsequent prototypes incorporated a new rigid hub with feathering hinges, composite blades and MAN-Turbo 6022 engines. The BO 105 reverted to Allison 250 power with the second of two preproduction aircraft, flying in this form in January 1971. Initial production was of the BO 105 C, available from 1970, while Allison 250-C20 turboshafts became standard from 1973.

The BO 105 CB was introduced in 1975 and remains the basic production model. It introduced uprated engines and a strengthened transmission. The BO 105 is also available in BO 105 CBS form with a slight 25cm (10in) fuselage stretch and an additional window, allowing an extra passenger to be carried. The BO 105 L has more powerful engines and a higher takeoff weight. The BO 105 LS is a hot and high version with Allison 250-C28C engines and built exclusively in Canada by Eurocopter Canada.

Easily the largest BO 105 operator is the German Army, which took delivery of 212 HOT armed BO 105 Ps as PAH-1s and 100 BO 105 M scouts as the VBH. Both these models are similar to the BO 105 CB, and have now been upgraded with new rotor blades and other improvements. These modifications also form the basis of the civil EC Super Five.

Photo: A German Army PAH-1.

Eurocopter/Kawasaki BK 117

Countries of origin: Germany and Japan

Type: Multirole helicopter

Powerplants: BK 117 A – Two 450kW (600shp) Avco (Textron) Lycoming LTS 101-650B-1 turboshafts driving a four bladed main rotor and two bladed tail rotor.

Performance: BK 117 A – Max speed 275km/h (150kt), cruising speed 264km/h (143kt). Max initial rate of climb 1970ft/min. Hovering ceiling in ground effect 13,450ft. Range with max payload 545km (295nm).

Weights: BK 117 A – Empty 1520kg (3351lb), max takeoff 2800kg (6173lb).

Dimensions: Main rotor diameter 11.00m (36ft 1in), length overall 13.00m (42ft 8in), fuselage length 9.91m (32ft 6in), height rotors turning 3.85m (12ft 8in). Main rotor disc area 95.0m² (1023sq ft).

Accommodation: One pilot and maximum seating for 10 passengers.

Armament: Usually none, although the BK 117A-3M was offered with eight HOT 2 or four TOW anti tank missiles.

Operators: Japan, Iraq, South Africa.

History: The BK 117 was developed under a joint collaborative effort between MBB of Germany (now part of Eurocopter) and Kawasaki of Japan.

The BK 117 program replaced the separate MBB BO 107 and Kawasaki KH-7 design studies. Retaining the former's overall configuration, Eurocopter is responsible for the helicopter's rotor system (which uses a scaled up version of the BO 105's four blade rigid main rotor), tail unit, hydraulic system and power controls, while Kawasaki is in charge of the fuselage, transmission and undercarriage.

Development led to the BK 117's first flight on June 13 1979, the first production aircraft (built in Japan) flew December 1981, civil certification was awarded in December 1982, and first deliveries took place early in 1983. Initial production was of the BK 117 A-1, while the BK 117 A-3 with higher max takeoff weight and enlarged tail rotor with twisted blades was certificated in March 1985.

The BK 117 A-3 also formed the basis of the only specific military development offered, the BK 117 A-3M. It was offered with a roof mounted sight, either TOW or HOT 2 anti tank missiles, a trainable nose mounted machine gun, rocket pods, RWR and ECM. However, the BK 117 A-3M was dropped in 1988 due to a lack of interest.

The BK 117 A-4 introduced from 1987 features enhanced performance through an increased transmission limit at takeoff power, improved tail rotor head and on German built aircraft increased fuel. The BK 117 B-1 (certificated in 1987) has more powerful engines and better performance, the BK 117 B-2 is currently in production and has an increased max takeoff weight, while the BK 117 C-1 is a German development with a new cockpit and Turboméca Arriel engines. Indonesian licence built aircraft are known as the NBK-117.

The BK 117 has not emulated the military sales success of its smaller BO 105 brother, and is only in small scale military use. The largest operator is Iraq, which took delivery of 16 SAR configured BK 117 B-1s. Others are in government and quasi military service.

Photo: MBB's BK 117 A-3M armed with four TOW anti tank missiles.

Eurocopter Tiger

Countries of origin: France and Germany

Type: Anti tank and battlefield reconnaissance helicopter

Powerplants: Two 960kW (1285shp) takeoff rated MTU/Turboméca/Rolls-Royce MTR 390 turboshafts, driving a four bladed main rotor and three bladed tail rotor.

Performance: Estimated – Cruising speed range 250 to 280km/h (135 to 150kt). Max initial rate of climb 1970ft/min. Hovering ceiling out of ground effect over 6560ft. Endurance 2hr 50min.

Weights: Basic empty 3300kg (7275lb), max overload takeoff 6000kg (13,227lb).

Dimensions: Main rotor diameter 13.00m (42ft 8in), fuselage length 14.00m (46ft 0in), height overall 4.32m (14ft 2in). Main rotor disc area 132.7m² (1428.8sq ft).

Accommodation: Pilot and weapons systems operator in tandem.

Armament: HAP – One 30mm GIAT cannon in chin turret, four Matra Mistral AAMs and two rocket pods, or six rocket pods and no Mistrals. HAC – Up to eight HOT 2 or Trigat anti tank missiles and four Matra Mistral AAMs on two wing pylons. UHU – Up to Eight HOT 2 or Trigat missiles, plus four Stinger AAMs, or rocket and gun pods.

Operators: No production aircraft funded at time of writing.

History: Arguably the most advanced combat helicopter to be designed in Europe, the Tiger (or Tigre) has its genesis in similar German and French Army helicopter programs.

In the early 1980s the German Army had begun looking at options to replace its sizeable fleet of MBB PAH-1 (BO 105) anti tank helicopters, while the French Army at the same time had a very similar requirement to replace its Gazelle anti tank force. Thus the two countries signed a memorandum of understanding covering the joint development of such a helicopter in 1984.

The aim and direction of the program was subsequently reviewed, leading to an amended MoU being signed in 1987. In December that year full scale development was approved, while in late 1989 the main development contract was awarded and the name Tiger (or Tigre in French) adopted. 1989 also saw Aerospatiale and MBB form the jointly owned Eurocopter to cover development of the helicopter. (In 1992 Aerospatiale and MBB merged all their helicopter activities under the Eurocopter banner).

The Tiger is currently being developed in three versions, differing in equipment and weapons fit. The HAP is the French Army's escort/fire support version (called Gerfaut until 1993), the HAC is the French anti tank version, while Germany's UHU is a multirole anti tank/support helicopter (replacing the previously planned PAH-2).

The Tiger is of conventional attack helicopter configuration (although the pilot sits in the front cockpit). Features include redundant electrical, fuel and hydraulic systems, two MTR 390 turboshafts, advanced cockpit displays and extensive use of composites

First flight was on April 22 1993, with five development aircraft funded. Deliveries to France and Germany are planned for 1999 and 2000 respectively. France requires about 215 Tigers, Germany 138. Major losses for the Tiger program were the Dutch and British selections of the rival AH-64 Apache to meet their attack helicopter requirements.

Photo: The first Tiger prototype, fitted with mast mounted sight.

Eurofighter EF 2000

Countries of origin: Germany, Italy, Spain and the UK

Type: Advanced multirole fighter

Powerplants: Two 60.0kN (13,490lb) dry and 90.0kN (20,250lb) afterburning Eurojet EJ200 turbofans. First two development aircraft powered by two Turbo Union RB199 turbofans.

Performance: Max speed approx Mach 2.0. Combat radius with unspecified load 465 to 555km (250 to 300nm).

Weights: Empty 9750kg (21,495lb), max takeoff 21,000kg (46,297lb).

Dimensions: Wing span 10.50m (34ft 6in), length 14.50m (47ft 7in), height approx 4.00m (13ft). Wing area 50.0m² (538.2sq ft).

Accommodation: Pilot only, or two in tandem in trainer

Armament: One 27mm Mauser cannon. 13 hardpoints can carry AIM-120, Skyflash, Future MRAAM, Aspide, AIM-9 or ASRAAM AAMs, and a variety of air-to-ground ordnance.

Operators: No production aircraft funded at time of writing.

History: The EF 2000 is one of Europe's most drawn out, controversial and expensive collaborative aircraft development programs.

In December 1983 the air chiefs of Germany, France, Italy, Spain and the UK signed an air staff requirement for a new multirole fighter, leading to the launch of an initial feasibility study in July 1984. In 1985 France took the controversial step of leaving the studies to develop its own, slighter smaller fighter, which resulted in the Rafale.

The Eurofighter consortium was then formed in June 1986 to manage the European Fighter Aircraft (or EFA) program. Development work share is split to Germany and the UK 33% each, Italy 21% and Spain 13%. The specific concept of the EFA, a medium size (9.5 tonne) air superiority fighter with considerable air-to-ground capabilities was formalised in December 1987.

By this time BAe had flown its EAP (Experimental Aircraft Programme) technology demonstrator. The EAP is of similar overall configuration (canard delta with fly-by-wire) to the Eurofighter and the results from its five year flight test program have played an important part in Eurofighter development.

In 1992 Germany's new defence minister reacted to the EFA's extremely high $US83m approx system unit price and threatened to withdraw Germany from the program unless ways were found of containing costs. Various variants of the EFA were proffered (including a single engine development), however in the end Germany decided on fewer numbers of a lower spec version of the relaunched Eurofighter EF 2000, featuring reduced capability or off the shelf equipment.

Controversy over the EF 2000 overshadows the fact that is should prove to be a highly capable fighter. Features include its specifically developed EJ200 engines (developed by Rolls-Royce, MTU, Fiat Avio and ITP of Spain), ECR90 radar (although German aircraft will most likely feature the APG-65), an infrared search and tracking system (IRST), an advanced Defensive Aids SubSystems or DASS, at least in British and Italian aircraft, and an advanced cockpit.

The EF 2000's first flight occurred on March 29 1994, after much delay. Britain still requires 250 EF 2000s, Germany about 130, Italy 130, and Spain 87. Service entry is planned for 2002.

Photo: Alenia built EF 2000 DA3. (BAe)

Fairchild C-123 Provider

Country of origin: United States of America

Type: Tactical transport

Powerplants: C-123K – Two 1865kW (2500hp) Pratt & Whitney R-2800-99W Double Wasp radial piston engines driving three bladed propellers and two auxiliary 12.7kN (2850lb) General Electric J85-GE-17 turbojets.

Performance: C-123K – Max speed at 10,000ft 365km/h (198kt), max cruising speed 278km/h (150kt). Takeoff run at max takeoff weight 355m (1165ft). Ferry range 5280km (2850nm), range with max payload 1665km (900nm).

Weights: C-123K – Empty 16,040kg (35,365lb), max takeoff 27,215kg (60,000lb).

Dimensions: C-123K – Wing span 33.53m (110ft 0in), length 23.93m (76ft 3in), height 10.63m (34ft 1in). Wing area 113.6m² (1223sq ft).

Accommodation: Flightcrew of two. Main cabin can accommodate up to 60 equipped troops or 50 stretcher patients and four medical attendants, or light vehicles and artillery pieces.

Armament: Usually none, although AC-123 gunship was armed with various cannon and miniguns.

Operators: El Salvador, Laos, South Korea, Thailand.

History: Widely used during the Vietnam War, the veteran Provider tactical transport still soldiers on in service principally in Thailand and South Korea.

The Provider is unique in that its origins lie in a glider, the Chase Aircraft XG-20. The XG-20 was an all metal design intended mainly for troop transport. One of the two prototypes was fitted with two Pratt & Whitney R-2800 Double Wasp piston radial engines as the XC-123 Avitruc to evaluate the design for assault transport.

The Avitruc flew for the first time on October 14 1949 and the type soon proved itself to the US Air Force, who, suitably impressed, ordered five pre production C-123s from Chase and 300 production C-123s (including aircraft for Saudi Arabia and Venezuela) from the Kaiser-Frazier Corporation. Kaiser-Frazier was unable to fulfil the massive order and instead Fairchild took over the contract. Fairchild refined the basic design, resulting in the C-123B Provider. Fairchild built 302 production C-123Bs between 1954 and 1958.

To improve airfield performance Fairchild fitted the Provider with two auxiliary turbojets, initially the C-123H with Fairchild J44s mounted on the wingtips. Ten C-123Hs were converted. The definitive jet augmented Provider model was the C-123K, fitted with two General Electric J85 turbojets in underwing pods. The C-123K flew for the first time on May 27 1966. In all, 183 C-123Bs were converted to jet augmented C-123K standard between 1966 and 1968.

C-123Bs and C-123Ks served widely in the Vietnam War with US Forces (including the AC-123 gunship variant, fitted with various sensors, cannon and miniguns) and with the Republic of South Vietnam Air Force. Several other Asian nations have operated ex USAF and RSVAF C-123Bs and C-123Ks, including Laos, the Philippines, Thailand, Taiwan and South Korea. Of those nations, Thailand, Laos and South Korea operate small numbers of C-123s, while two examples survive in El Salvador.

Photo: Thailand continues to fly C-123s alongside C-47s. (Glyn Jones)

Fairchild C-26 & Metro

Country of origin: United States of America

Type: Multirole light transport

Powerplants: C-26A/B – Two 835kW (1120shp) Garrett TFE331-121UAR turboprops, driving four bladed propellers.

Performance: C-26A/B – Max cruising speed 517km/h (280kt), economical cruising speed 467km/h (252kt). Max initial rate of climb 2370ft/min. Service ceiling 27,500ft. Range at optional MTOW 1970km (1063nm), range at standard MTOW 710km (385nm).

Weights: C-26A/B – Operating empty 4165kg (9180lb), max takeoff 6577kg (14,500lb), or optionally 7257kg (16,000lb).

Dimensions: C-26A/B – Wing span 17.37m (57ft 0in), length 18.09m (59ft 4in), height 5.08m (16ft 8in). Wing area 28.7m² (309.0sq ft).

Accommodation: Flightcrew of two. Main cabin can be configured to seat 19 passengers, or less with a VIP interior. Cabin can be configured to accept freight or stretchers.

Armament: None

Operators: Argentina, Sweden, Thailand, USA.

History: The popular Metro series of commuter airliners has found its way into military service in a variety of utility roles.

Design work on Swearingen's first complete in house design began in the late 1960s, culminating in the SA-226TC Metro's first flight on August 26 1969. The design was similar in appearance and layout to the earlier Merlins, and featured a pressurised fuselage, Garrett TPE331 turboprop engines and double slotted trailing edge flaps on the wings. It entered commercial service in 1973.

The Metro II quickly superseded the I from 1975, its improvements focusing on reducing cabin noise levels, plus changes to the flightdeck. The equivalent executive aircraft to the Metro II is the Merlin IV. Following the Metro II from 1981 was the III (by which time Fairchild had taken over Swearingen), which was certificated to a higher standard which allowed greater takeoff weights, while more efficient engines and greater wing span made the III more economical to operate. The Expediter civil freighter is based on the III.

Argentina operates three VIP equipped Merlins IVAs, and Thailand two. Sweden operates a VIP configured Merlin IVC, plus a Merlin III which serves as the testbed for the Ericsson Erieye phased array AEW radar mounted above the aircraft's fuselage. Sweden is buying 10 Saab 340s with the Erieye radar system fitted.

The USA though is the largest military Metro customer. The first of 13 C-26As was ordered in 1988 for the US Air National Guard for use as a general light transport/VIP aircraft. Up to 53 C-26Bs (with TCAS, GPS and MLS) will be ordered for the Army and Air National Guards.

A single UC-26C meanwhile is fitted with an APG-66 radar (as on the F-16) and FLIR, and is used in anti drug missions. All C-26 models are based on the Metro III, but with some changes.

The current production Metro model is the 23. It features higher takeoff weights, more powerful engines and systems improvements first introduced on the C-26. Merlin and Expediter models are also offered, while Fairchild offers the 23 as its Multi Mission Surveillance Aircraft (MMSA) platform, fitted with a reconnaissance pod jointly developed with Lockheed Martin.

Photo: The Swedish Erieye radar Metro demonstrator.

Fairchild A-10A Thunderbolt II

Country of origin: United States of America

Type: Anti armour/close air support attack aircraft

Powerplants: Two 40.3kN (9065lb) General Electric TF34-GE-100 non afterburning turbofans.

Performance: Max speed 835km/h (450kt). Max initial rate of climb 6000ft/min. Ferry range with drop tanks 3950km (2130nm), combat radius on a deep strike mission 1000km (540nm), combat radius on a close air support mission with 1hr 42min loiter 465km (250nm).

Weights: Basic empty 9770kg (21,540lb), max takeoff 22,680kg (50,000lb).

Dimensions: Wing span 17.53m (57ft 6in), length 16.26m (53ft 4in), height 4.47m (14ft 8in). Wing area 47.0m² (506.0sq ft).

Accommodation: Pilot only.

Armament: One 30mm General Electric GAU-8 Avenger seven barrel cannon mounted in the nose. 11 underwing and underfuselage hardpoints can carry a total external ordnance load of 7257kg (16,000lb), options including AGM-65 Maverick anti armour missiles, cluster bombs, laser guided bombs, conventional bombs and AIM-9 Sidewinders.

Operators: USA

History: Nicknamed the Warthog, the A-10 Thunderbolt II was conceived during the Vietnam War as a close support aircraft for low intensity conflicts, but grew into a dedicated anti armour platform optimised for war in western Europe.

The unsuitability of its supersonic tactical fighters in close air support roles in the Vietnam War saw the US Air Force formulate its AX specification. This called for an aircraft that could haul a heavy load of ordnance, had good endurance to loiter for long periods and could survive damage from ground fire. Originally it was envisaged that a twin turboprop design would fill the role, although the concept grew to a larger, more powerful aircraft powered by twin turbofans.

In the early 1970s designs from Northrop and Fairchild Republic were selected for a competitive fly-off, which occurred in late 1972. The A-10 (first flight April 5 1972) was selected over Northrop's YA-9, with the result that 707 production A-10A Thunderbolts were built.

More than any other aircraft, the A-10's design layout was dictated by survivability. The large, low set straight wing provides good agility and a degree of shielding for the two high mounted engines. The engines themselves are separated by the fuselage so a hit to one will not necessarily damage the other, while the aircraft can fly with substantial damage to one of its twin vertical tails. The pilot is also protected in a titanium armour bathtub.

The heart of the A-10's weapon system is the massive GE GAU-8 seven barrel 30mm cannon, the most powerful gun to be fitted to an aircraft in this class. This and the AGM-65 Maverick missile are the A-10's primary anti armour weapons.

Debate continues about the subsonic A-10's survivability in the modern battlefield and it is being progressively replaced by F-16s. During the Gulf War the A-10 was ideally suited to operations there where Iraqi air opposition was minimal, allowing the A-10s to range at will.

A number of A-10s have been redesignated OA-10 for the Forward Air Control role. These aircraft differ from the A-10 in designation only and carry smoke rockets and Sidewinder AAMs for self defence.

Photo: An A-10A on approach to land.

FFA AS 202 Bravo

Country of origin: Switzerland

Type: Two seat basic trainer

Powerplants: AS 202/15 – One 110kW (150hp) Lycoming O-320-E2A flat four piston engine, driving a two bladed fixed pitch propeller. AS 202/18A4 – One 135kW (180hp) Textron Lycoming AEIO-360-B1F fuel injected flat four driving a two bladed constant speed propeller, or optionally a three bladed prop.

Performance: 15 – Max cruising speed 210km/h (114kt), economical cruising speed 203km/h (110kt). Max initial rate of climb 633ft/min. Service ceiling 14,000ft. Range with max fuel and no reserves 890km (480nm). 18A4 – Max speed 240km/h (130kt), max cruising speed 226km/h (122kt), economical cruising speed 205km/h (110kt). Max initial rate of climb 800ft/min. Service ceiling 17,000ft. Range with max fuel and no reserves 1140km (615nm).

Weights: 15 – Empty equipped 630kg (1388lb), max takeoff 999kg (2202lb) for Utility, 885kg (1951lb) for Acrobatic. 18AF – Operating empty 710kg (1565lb), max takeoff 1080kg (2380lb) for Utility, 1050kg (2315lb) for Acrobatic.

Dimensions: Wing span 9.95m (31ft 12in), length 7.50m (24ft 7in), height 2.81m (9ft 3in). Wing area 13.9m² (149.2sq ft).

Accommodation: Student and instructor side by side, with room for one passenger/observer behind them.

Armament: Usually none.

Operators: Indonesia, Iraq, Jordan, Morocco, Oman, Uganda.

History: In service with a diverse, if small number of air arms around the world, the Bravo is a basic pilot trainer.

Design of the Bravo dates back to the late 1960s, with original design work actually undertaken by SIAI Marchetti of Italy as the S.202, but with production and subsequent development work the responsibility of FFA (originally established by Dornier as its Swiss subsidiary). The first prototype to fly was Swiss built, it took to the air for the first time on March 7 1969. An Italian built prototype followed soon after on May 7, while the first production standard aircraft flew on December 22 1971.

The first production model was the AS 202/15 and 34 were built through to the early 1980s. The current production model is the AS 202/18AF, which first flew in August 1974 and received certification in late 1975. This version differs from the original 15 principally in having a more powerful 135kW (180hp) engine. The AS 202/18 is operated by all the countries listed above (Iraq and Indonesia, with 48 and 40 delivered respectively, are the largest customers). A significant civil operator is the British Aerospace Flying College in Scotland which operates 11 as the Wren.

Two other models have been developed, although single examples of each have flown only. The first was the 195kW (260hp) Textron Lycoming AEIO-540 powered Bravo 26A1, which first flew in 1979. The second was the 240kW (320shp) Allison 250-B17C turbine powered Bravo 32TP which flew in 1991.

The Bravo is still offered for sale despite the fact that none have been delivered since 1989.

Photo: An AS 202/18A4 wearing Royal Flight of Oman markings.

FMA IA-58 Pucará

Country of origin: Argentina

Type: Counter insurgency/light ground attack aircraft

Powerplants: IA-58A – Two 730kW (978shp) Turboméca Astazou XVIG turboprops, driving three bladed propellers.

Performance: Max speed 500km/h (270kt), max cruising speed 480km/h (260kt), economical cruising speed 430km/h (232kt). Max initial rate of climb 3545ft/min. Service ceiling 32,800ft. Ferry range with three drop tanks 3710km (2002nm). Combat radius with a 1500kg (3307lb) warload, lo-lo-lo 225km (120nm), radius with a 1500kg (3307lb) warload, hi-lo-hi 350km (190nm). Combat radius with a 1000kg (2205lb) warload lo-lo-lo 400km (215nm), with a 1000kg (2205lb) warload hi-lo-hi 650km (350nm).

Weights: IA-58A – Empty equipped 4020kg (8862lb), max takeoff 6800kg (14,990lb).

Dimensions: IA-58A – Wing span 14.50m (47ft 7in), length 14.25m (46ft 9in), height 5.36m (17ft 7in). Wing area 30.3m² (326.2sq ft).

Accommodation: Pilot and observer in tandem.

Armament: IA-58A – Two 20mm Hispano HS-284 cannon and four 7.62mm Browning machine guns in the forward fuselage. One underfuselage and two underwing hardpoints can carry a total of 1500kg (3307lb) of external ordnance, including bombs and rocket pods.

Operators: Argentina, Colombia, Sri Lanka, Uruguay.

History: Made famous by its participation in the Falklands War in 1982, the Pucará was developed to meet a 1960s Argentinean requirement for a counter insurgency aircraft.

Design and production responsibility fell to Argentina's government controlled Fabrica Militar de Aviones (FMA), with work culminating in the prototype's first flight on August 20 1969. This prototype was powered by two 675kW (905eshp) AiResearch TPE331 turboprops, whereas production Pucarás feature Turboméca Astazous. A second prototype, the first to be powered by Astazous, first flew in September 1970, while the first production Pucará flew in November 1974. Production deliveries did not begin until 1976.

It was also in 1976 that the Pucará had its baptism of fire against rebel guerrillas in Argentina's north west. However the Pucará is better known for its participation in the Falklands War against the British in 1982. In these actions it was less than successful, and all 24 deployed were either destroyed by ground fire or sabotage by the SAS, or captured when Argentina was evicted from the islands. One captured example was subsequently evaluated by the RAF before it was retired to a museum.

The Pucará was built to be manoeuvrable, survivable and carry an effective offensive punch. However its poor showing in the Falklands meant that the type fell out of favour, and 40 of the survivors were made surplus in 1986.

Two planned Pucará variants were flown in prototype form but failed to see production. The IA-58B featured improved avionics and twin 30mm DEFA cannon, and first flew in May 1979. The single seat IA-58C had a faired over front cockpit, improved avionics and two 30mm cannon, and could carry Matra Magic AAMs and Martin Pescador ASMs. The prototype flew in December 1985.

Photo: One of 108 Pucarás built for the Argentinean Air Force.

FMA IA-63 Pampa

Country of origin: Argentina

Type: Trainer and light ground attack aircraft

Powerplant: One 15.6kN (3500lb) Garrett TFE731-2-2N turbofan.

Performance: Max speed 750km/h (405kt). Max initial rate of climb 5120ft/min. Service ceiling 42,325ft. Air-to-air gunnery training mission radius with 250kg (550lb) of external ordnance 440km (237nm). Air-to-ground combat radius with 1000kg (2205lb) external load 360km (195nm). Ferry range with max internal and external fuel 1000km (1850nm). Max endurance at 555km/h (300kt) 3hr 48min.

Weights: Empty 2820kg (6220lb), max takeoff 5000kg (11,025lb).

Dimensions: Wing span 9.67m (32ft 9in), length 10.90m (35ft 10in), height 4.29m (14ft 1in). Wing area 15.6m² (168.3sq ft).

Accommodation: Student and instructor in tandem.

Armament: Four underwing and one underfuselage hardpoint can carry a combined ordnance load of 1550kg (3415lb), including 30mm DEFA cannon pod on the centreline station, and light bombs.

Operators: Argentina

History: Developed against an Argentinean Air Force requirement for a modern armed trainer, the IA-63 Pampa is South America's only indigenous jet powered military aircraft program.

FMA (Fabrica Militar de Aviones) began development work on what would result in the Pampa in 1979, against the Argentinean Air Force's requirement to replace its ageing Morane-Saulnier MS.760 four place jets. To design the new trainer FMA teamed with Dornier of Germany, who had gained considerable experience in developing and building jet trainers through its co-development of the Alpha Jet along with Dassault. The FMA/Dornier teaming came up with seven joint designs, the selected one resembling the Alpha Jet in configuration.

Like the Alpha Jet, the IA-63 Pampa features a high wing, stepped tandem cockpits and side mounted air intakes. The Pampa differs in having a single turbofan (a Garrett TFE731) and unswept wing and tailplane. Dornier's technical assistance also including construction of the wings and tailplanes for the first three flying prototypes and two static test airframes. The first prototype (EX-01) took to the air for the first time on October 6 1984, while the first production aircraft's first flight was in October 1987.

The Argentinean Air Force has placed firm orders for 18 Pampas, the first of which was delivered in April 1988, while a follow-on order for 46 is anticipated. Aside from training, the Pampas have a secondary ground attack role. They are equipped with five hardpoints and are being fitted with a HUD and an Elbit developed Weapon Delivery and Navigation System.

Development of a navalised Pampa capable of operating off the Argentinean aircraft carrier *25 de Mayo* has lapsed due to a lack of funding, although Argentina's navy has now expressed an interest in unmodified Pampas.

The Pampa program was dealt a blow when in early 1995 it was eliminated form the lucrative USAF/USN JPATS contest (which was subsequently won by the PC-9). The Pampa 2000 was being offered by Northrop Grumman (originally by Vought), but was ruled out due to "technical deficiencies related to spin recovery."

Photo: The first Pampa prototype at Farnborough. (Jim Thorn)

Fokker F27, Maritime & Troopship

Country of origin: Netherlands

Type: Tactical transport and maritime patrol aircraft

Powerplants: Maritime – Two 1770kW (2370eshp) with water methanol injection and 1505kW (2020eshp) dry Rolls-Royce Dart RDa7 Mk 536-76 turboprops, driving four bladed props.

Performance: Maritime – Max speed 474km/h (256kt), cruising speed 463km/h (250kt), typical search speed range 270 to 325km/h (145 to 175kt) at 2000ft. Service ceiling 25,000ft. Max range with 30min loiter 5000km (2700nm), time on station 370km (200nm) from base 8hr, or 740km (400nm) from base 6hr, or 1205km (650nm) from base 4hr.

Weights: Maritime – Empty 12,520kg (27,600lb), max overload takeoff 21,545kg (47,500lb).

Dimensions: Maritime – Wing span 29.00m (95ft 2in), length 23.56m (77ft 4in), height 8.70m (28ft 7in). Wing area 70.0m² (754sq ft).

Accommodation: Maritime – Flightcrew of two. Crew complement would usually include a tactical commander/navigator, a radar operator and two observers. Troopship – Up to 46 troops, or alternatively 24 stretchers and nine medical attendants.

Armament: None, although the armed Maritime Enforcer was offered.

Operators: Algeria, Argentina, Bolivia, Cote d'Ivoire, Finland, Ghana, Guatemala, Indonesia, Iran, Mexico, Myanmar, Netherlands, Pakistan, Philippines, Senegambia, Sudan, Thailand, Uruguay. Maritime – Netherlands, Pakistan, Spain, Thailand.

History: The Fokker F27, together with the Fairchild built F-27 and FH-227, was ordered in greater numbers than any other western built turboprop airliner, and their military derivatives serve in tactical transport and maritime patrol roles.

The Fokker F27 began life as a 1950 32 seat design study known as the P.275. A prototype first flew on November 24 1955, while a larger prototype representative of production aircraft flew in January 1957. By this stage Fokker had signed an agreement with Fairchild that would see F27s, as F-27s, built in the USA, and later the stretched FH-227.

Friendship developments included the Mk 200/F-27A with more powerful engines, the Mk 300/F-27B, the Mk 400 Combiplane and military Mk 400M Troopship tactical transport. The Troopship first flew in 1965 and features a large freight door and enlarged parachuting doors. The definitive Mk 500 airliner has a 1.50m (4ft 11in) fuselage stretch taking seating to 52, and also forms the basis for the Mk 600 quick change freight/pax aircraft.

The 400M (the Troopship name was dropped after a time) was particularly successful, and accounted for the majority of military sales with over 110 built, while other air arms have acquired ex civil examples.

The most developed military variant of the ubiquitous Friendship is the maritime patrol Maritime, which provided a low cost alternative to the likes of the Atlantic and Orion. It features a Litton APS-504 search radar, bulged observation windows, a crew rest area and comprehensive navigation equipment. The armed Maritime Enforcer would also have featured sonobuoys, ESM, an infrared searcher and a MAD, although none were ordered. F27 production ceased in 1986.

Photo: Spain was one of the customers for the Fokker Maritime.

Fokker 50 & 60

Country of origin: Netherlands

Type: Multirole twin turboprop transport

Powerplants: 50 – Two 1865kW (2500shp) Pratt & Whitney Canada PW125B turboprops, driving six bladed propellers. 60 Utility – Two 2050kW (2750shp) P&WC PW127Bs.

Performance: 50 – Normal cruising speed 480km/h (260kt), typical search speed 277km/h (150kt) at 2000ft. Service ceiling 25,000ft. Max radius of action with pylon tanks 3150km (1700nm). Max time on station with pylon tanks 14hr 20min. 60 Utility – Typical cruising speed 520km/h (280kt). Max operating altitude 25,000ft. Range with 50 troops 2965km (1600nm), range with 27 stretchers 3150km (1700nm).

Weights: 50 Maritime Enforcer 2 – Operating empty 13,560kg (29,895lb), max takeoff 21,545kg (47,500lb). 60 Utility – Typical operating empty 12,500kg (27,855lb), max takeoff 21,950kg (48,390lb), or optionally 22,950kg (50,595lb).

Dimensions: 50 – Wing span 29.00m (95ft 2in), length 25.25m (82ft 10in), height 8.32m (27ft 4in). Wing area 70.0m² (753.5sq ft). Same except length 26.87m (88ft 2in).

Accommodation: 50 Utility – Seating for 40 troops. Maritime Enforcer 2 – Crew complement of two flightcrew, tactical coordinator, acoustic sensor operator, sensor operators and two observers. 60 Utility – Seating for up to 50 troops.

Armament: Maritime Enforcer 2 – Two fuselage and six underwing hardpoints can carry a range of armament including mines, torpedoes, depth charges and up to four anti ship missiles such as Harpoon, Exocet, Sea Eagle or Sea Skua.

Operators: 50 – Singapore, Taiwan. 60 – Netherlands*.

History: The Fokker 50 and 60 are modernised developments of the basic F27 Friendship, and are offered in a range of military configurations.

Fokker announced development of the basic Fokker 50 airliner in November 1983. The updated turboprop airliner is based on the fuselage of the F27-500, but features Pratt & Whitney Canada PW120 series engines with six bladed props, modern avionics including EFIS instrumentation, small winglets, square main cabin windows and some use of composites. First flight was on December 28 1985.

Around 220 Fokker 50s had been ordered at the time of writing, although almost all of these have been from airlines. Nevertheless, Fokker offers a range of military derivatives. The unarmed Fokker 50 Maritime Mk 2 and armed Fokker 50 Maritime Enforcer Mk 2 are offered with a Texas Instruments APS-134 search radar, FLIR, MAD and sonobuoys. The Enforcer can carry torpedoes, mines, and anti ship missiles such as Exocet and Harpoon. Singapore is an operator.

The Kingbird Mk 2 is an AEW variant offered with the Ericsson Erieye phased array radar mounted above the fuselage, while the Sentinel Mk 2 is a reconnaissance aircraft fitted with either sideways looking or synthetic aperture radar. The Fokker 50 is also offered in Elint/communications Black Crow Mk 2 form. Finally transport versions are covered by the Utility title.

The Fokker 60 Utility (first flight November 2 1995) is a stretched version with a large cargo door whose development was launched by the Netherlands Air Force. Deliveries are due from mid 1996.

Photo: A Singapore Air Force Fokker 50 transport. (Doug Mackay)

Fokker F28 Fellowship

Country of origin: Netherlands

Type: VIP and government transport

Powerplants: Mk 3000 & 4000 – Two 44kN (9900lb) Rolls-Royce RB183-2 Spey Mk 555-15P turbofans.

Performance: Mk 3000 – Max cruising speed 843km/h (455kt), economical cruising speed 678km/h (366kt). Max cruising altitude 35,000ft. Range at high speed cruise with 65 passengers 2743km (1480nm), at long range cruise with 65 pax 3170km (1710nm). Mk 4000 – Speeds same. Range at high speed cruise with 85 pax 1900km (1025nm), at long range cruising speed with 85 pax 2085km (1125nm).

Weights: Mk 3000 – Operating empty 16,965kg (37,400lb), max takeoff weight 33,110kg (73,000lb). Mk 4000 – Operating empty 17,645kg (38,900lb), max takeoff 33,110kg (73,000lb).

Dimensions: Mk 3000 – Wing span 25.07m (82ft 3in), length 27.40m (89ft 11in), height 8.47m (27ft 10in). Wing area 79.00m² (850sq ft). Mk 4000 – Same except for length 29.61m (97ft 2in).

Accommodation: Flightcrew of two. Max passenger seating for 85 at five abreast in Mk 4000, or 65 in Mk 3000. Both marks offered with a 15-20 seat VIP interior.

Armament: None

Operators: Argentina, Colombia, Ecuador, Gabon, Ghana, Indonesia, Ivory Coast, Malaysia, Netherlands, Peru, Tanzania, Togo.

History: The commercially successful F28 Fellowship was Fokker's first jet engined design. Small numbers have been acquired for military service, mainly as VIP and government transports.

Fokker began development of the F28 in 1960 after perceiving a market requirement for a jet engined and greater capacity airliner to complement its turboprop powered F27. The first of three prototypes flew for the first time on May 9 1967 and customer deliveries were made from February 24 1969.

The F28 was developed into a range of models, starting with the initial production model, the Mk 1000. The 1000 would typically seat between 55 and 65, and was powered by 44kN (9850lb) Spey Mk 555-15 turbofans. The Mk 2000 introduced a 2.21m (7ft 3in) fuselage stretch, increasing maximum seating to 79.

The longer span 5000 and 6000 were based on the 1000 and 2000 respectively, but attracted little sales interest and no 5000s and just two 6000s were built. Another version that did not come to fruition was the Mk 6600, which would have been stretched by a further 2.21m (7ft 3in), allowing for seating for 100 in a high density layout. However the F28 does form the basis for the 100 seat Tay powered Fokker 100, two of which serve in the Ivory Coast as government transports.

The final production models were the 3000 and 4000, again based on the 1000 and 2000 respectively. Both introduced a number of improvements, while the addition of two extra above wing emergency exits on the 4000 increased max seating to 85. Freight door equipped convertible versions of each model are identified by a C suffix.

Given its size and performance the F28 has been a popular choice as a VIP, Presidential and government transport, and several remain in military and quasi military service in these roles.

Photo: Ghana flies this F28-3000 on VIP tasks. (Keith Gaskell)

GAF Nomad & Searchmaster

Country of origin: Australia

Type: STOL multirole light transport

Powerplants: Two 315kW (420shp) Allison 250-B17C turboprops driving three bladed propellers.

Performance: N22B – Typical cruising speed 311km/h (165kt). Take-off run at max takeoff weight 225m (730ft). Max initial rate of climb 1460ft/min. Service ceiling 21,000ft. Range with standard fuel at 90% power 1350km (730nm). Searchmaster – Mission endurance at 260km/h (140kt) at 5000ft up to 8 hours.

Weights: N22B – Operating empty 2150kg (4741lb), max takeoff 3855kg (8500lb). N24A – Operating empty 2377kg (5241lb), max takeoff 4173kg (9200lb).

Dimensions: N22B – Wing span 16.52m (54ft 2in), length 12.56m (41ft 2in), height 5.52m (18ft 1.5in). Wing area 30.1m² (324.0sq ft). N22A – Same except length 14.36m (47ft 1in).

Accommodation: Flightcrew of one or two pilots. Seating in main cabin at two abreast for 12 (N22) or 16 (N24). Searchmaster B – Normal crew complement of one or two pilots, a tactical navigator and one or two observers.

Armament: Four underwing hardpoints can carry up to 910kg (2000lb) between them, although this capability is rarely used. Thai aircraft thought to be armed with machine guns as mini gunships.

Operators: Indonesia, Papua New Guinea, Philippines, Thailand.

History: The Nomad was developed by Australia's Government Aircraft Factory during the late 1960s as a means of providing the facility with work after construction of licence built Mirage III fighters was completed, allowing it to offer a new rugged STOL utility transport suited to military and civil operators.

Developed as project N, first flight of the prototype Nomad N2 occurred on July 23 1971. A second prototype flew on December 5 that year. First deliveries of the production N22 aircraft (to the Philippines military) occurred in 1975. The N22 was followed up by the N22B with an increased max takeoff weight, this version being certificated in 1975. The military utility transport version was marketed as the Missionmaster, although most are now simply called Nomads.

The N22 also formed the basis for the Searchmaster coastal patrol aircraft. It was offered in two variants, the Searchmaster B with a nose mounted forward looking Bendix RDR 1400 search radar, and the more sophisticated Searchmaster L, with a more capable chin mounted Litton LASR (APS-504), with 360° coverage. Papua New Guinea, Indonesia and the Philippines all operate Searchmasters in the coastal patrol role.

Stretching of the N22 fuselage by 1.14m (3ft 9in) led to the N24. Aimed mainly at commuter airlines (known as the Commuterliner), this version increased passenger capacity to 16. Versions of the N24 included the Cargomaster freighter and the Medicmaster aerial ambulance. Both the Australian Army and Air Force operated N24s.

Nomad production ceased in late 1984 after 172 had been built.

By far the largest military Nomad operator was the Australian Army. However its fleet of N22Bs and N24As was permanently grounded in mid 1995 due to concerns over the type's safety and suitability.

Photo: A Philippines Air Force N22 Nomad. (Bob Livingstone)

General Dynamics F-111

Country of origin: United States of America

Type: Long range strategic and tactical strike aircraft

Powerplants: F-111F – Two 111.7kN (25,100lb) with afterburning Pratt & Whitney TF30-P-100 turbofans.

Performance: F-111F – Max speed Mach 2.5 or 2655km/h (1433kt), cruising speed at high altitude 920km/h (495kt). Range with internal fuel over 4705km (2540nm).

Weights: F-111F – Operating empty 21,537kg (47,480lb), max takeoff 45,360kg (100,000lb).

Dimensions: Wing span fully extended 19.20m (63ft 0in), wing span fully swept 9.74m (31ft 11in), length 22.40m (73ft 6in), height 5.22m (17ft 1in). Wing area with wings spread 48.8m² (525.0sq ft), wing area with wings swept 61.6m² (657.1sq ft).

Accommodation: Pilot & WSO/navigator side by side.

Armament: F-111F – Max weapons load of 14,228kg (31,500lb) including laser guided GBU-12, GBU-10 & GBU-24 bombs, electro optically guided GBU-15 bombs, conventional bombs, and AIM-9s.

Operators: Australia, USA.

History: Highly controversial and expensive at the time of its birth, the F-111 (nicknamed Aardvark) has evolved into perhaps the world's most capable medium range strike bomber.

The F-111 was conceived in the early 1960s as the TFX, a misguided attempt by the US Defense Department, under Defense Secretary Robert McNamara, to combine into a single aircraft the US Air Force's requirement for a new fighter bomber and the US Navy's need for a new air defence fighter. First flight was on December 21 1964. The USN's overweight F-111B interceptor was cancelled in 1968.

The Air Force's F-111 showed considerably more promise. The F-111 was the first operational aircraft to feature swing wings and afterburning turbofans, while in a clean configuration it could cruise supersonically without afterburner. Other design features include a small internal bomb bay, a cockpit escape capsule and terrain following radar. Initially problems persisted with the complex swing wing mechanism and air inlets, but these were eventually resolved.

USAF F-111 models comprise the initial production F-111A, the F-111E with revised air inlets, the F-111D with digital avionics (a first for a tactical fighter), the F-111F with more powerful engines and improved analog avionics, and the nuclear FB-111 strategic bomber (with longer span wings and strengthened undercarriage). In the early 1990s the FB-111s had their nuclear role removed, becoming the F-111G. Only the F-111F (with upgraded digital avionics and Pave Tack pod in the bomb bay for autonomous laser guided bomb launching) and the EF-111 (described separately) survived in USAF service in 1996.

Australia operates 22 F-111Cs which combine the engines and avionics of the F-111A with the FB-111B's heavier undercarriage and longer span wings. Four have been modified as RF-111C reconnaissance aircraft, with a similar equipment fit in the bomb bay as in the USN's F-14 TARP pod. These aircraft are undergoing a comprehensive avionics upgrade program and are unique in their ability to carry HARM and Harpoon. An additional 15 ex USAF F-111Gs delivered from 1993 will help to extend the RAAF F-111 fleet life to 2015.

Photo: Note the Pack Tack pod on this F-111F. (Paul Merritt)

Grumman/GD EF-111 Raven

Country of origin: United States of America

Type: Electronic warfare aircraft

Powerplants: Two 82.3kN (18,500lb) with afterburning Pratt & Whitney TF30-P-3 turbofans.

Performance: Max speed 2272km/h (1226kt), max combat speed 2215km/h (1195kt), average speed in combat area 940km/h (507kt). Max initial rate of climb 3300ft/min. Service ceiling 45,000ft. Combat radius 1495km (807nm). Endurance unrefuelled over 4hr.

Weights: Operating empty 25,073kg (55,275lb), max takeoff 40,347kg (88,948lb).

Dimensions: Wing span fully extended 19.20m (63ft 0in), wing span fully swept 9.74m (31ft 11in), length 23.16m (76ft 0in), height 6.10m (20ft 0in). Wing area with wings fully spread 48.8m² (525.0sq ft), wing area with wings swept 61.6m² (657.1sq ft).

Accommodation: Pilot and Electronic Warfare Officer side-by-side.

Armament: Usually none, although can carry two AIM-9 Sidewinders for self defence.

Operators: USA

History: The Grumman EF-111A Raven is a highly specialised electronic warfare conversion of over 40 General Dynamics F-111A strike bombers.

Grumman has considerable experience in designing, integrating and building electronic warfare aircraft, specifically the EA-6A and EA-6B Prowler variants of its Intruder for the US Navy. Thus Grumman was the logical choice as lead contractor to develop surplus F-111As as electronic warfare aircraft for the US Air Force. Development work of an EW aircraft, or Tactical Jamming System, based on the F-111 airframe began in 1972, and the US Department of Defense awarded Grumman an initial contract to build two prototypes in 1975. An aerodynamic prototype flew in late 1975, while the first production standard prototype flew in May 1977. Extensive testing ensued, and the first production conversion flew on June 26 1981. In all, the USAF took delivery of 42 EF-111 conversions.

The Raven conversion is based on the basic F-111A airframe, featuring a Tactical Jamming System based on the ALQ-99 system in the EA-6B Prowler, but with a higher degree of automation, requiring one Electronic Warfare Operator (rather than three in the Prowler).

The jamming system's antennae are housed in the System Integrated Receiver pod, the bulbous fairing on top of the fin, plus further receivers on the fin, and the two blade antennae protruding from the lower fuselage. The jamming transmitters are housed in a canoe fairing (with 10 transmitters, five exciters and six receivers) on the aircraft's underside, occupying the internal weapons bay space. A central computer processes and analyses all data received, either presenting its findings to the EWO, or carrying out automatic jamming.

The Raven's principle mission types are to provide a standoff jamming barrage to disguise incoming air raids, direct escort of strike aircraft, and battlefield jamming support. The EF-111's success in these roles in the Gulf War staved off premature retirement, although their role is due to be handed over to US Navy EA-6Bs in 1996.

Photo: The EF-111 is the USAF's prime dedicated EW platform.

Grumman HU-16 Albatross

Country of origin: United States of America

Type: SAR amphibian

Powerplants: HU-16B – Two 1060kW (1425hp) Wright R-1820-76A Cyclone radial piston engines, driving three bladed propellers.

Performance: HU-16B – Max speed 380km/h (205kt), max cruising speed 362km/h (195kt), long range cruising speed 200km/h (108kt). Max initial rate of climb 1450ft/min. Service ceiling 21,500ft. Range with max fuel and reserves 4587km (2477nm). Max endurance with external tanks 22hr 55min.

Weights: HU-16B – Empty 10,380kg (22,883lb), max takeoff from land 17,010kg (37,500lb), or 15,422kg (34,000lb) from water.

Dimensions: HU-16B – Wing span 29.46m (96ft 8in), length 19.15m (62ft 10in), height 7.87m (25ft 10in). Wing area 96.2m² (1035sq ft).

Accommodation: Crew of four in ASW configuration. Crew of up to five in SAR configuration with room for 12 stretcher patient survivors. Seats 22 when modified for transport.

Armament: In ASW configuration could carry four Mk 43 torpedoes or two Mk 43s and two depth charges.

Operators: Greece

History: The Albatross has enjoyed a long military career being used for a variety of tasks including ASW patrol and search and rescue.

The Albatross resulted from a mid 1940s US Navy requirement for a general purpose amphibious transport. First flight (the prototype was designated XJR2F-1) was on October 24 1947, paving the way for a 418 unit production run and then conversion program that lasted through to 1961.

The Albatross is by far the largest of Grumman's family of amphibians (several hundred Widgeons and Gooses were built for service during WW2). Design features include its stepped hull, retractable undercarriage, fixed outrigger floats, large cabin and two Wright Cyclone radial engines.

Initial Albatross production was of the US Navy's UF-1, plus the UF-1L optimised for Antarctic operations and the UF-1T trainer. From 1962 these models were redesignated HU-16C, LU-16C and TU-16C respectively. The US Air Force bought 170 SA-16A Albatrosses for air sea rescue (redesignated HU-16A from 1962). A number of these were converted to SA-16B/HU-16B standard when fitted with the Albatross's definitive larger tail and greater span wing.

US Navy UF-1s were similarly modified, becoming the UF-2, or from 1962 the HU-16D. Another major customer was the US Coast Guard which took delivery of 34 UF-1Gs, which were modified with the larger tail and longer span wing to UF-2G standard (HU-16E from 1962).

The Albatross was also exported to a dozen nations (many under the auspices of MAP). Norway and Spain took delivery of HU-16B Albatrosses modified for anti submarine warfare fitted with a nose mounted search radar. Twelve Norwegian aircraft were subsequently transferred to Greece where the survivors continue to serve with the Hellenic Air Force. Indonesia also operated four HU-16s until quite recently, but these aircraft are now believed to be in storage.

Photo: Greece uses its HU-16s for search and rescue and coastal patrol duties. (Greek MoD)

Grumman S-2 Tracker

Country of origin: United States of America

Type: Maritime patrol and anti submarine patrol aircraft

Powerplants: S-2E – Two 1135kW (1525hp) Pratt & Whitney R-1820-82WA Cyclone radial piston engines driving three bladed propellers. TS-2F – Two 1225kW (1645shp) Garrett TPE331-15 turboprops driving five bladed props.

Performance: S-2E – Max speed 425km/h (230kt), cruising speed 333km/h (180kt), patrol speed at 1500ft 240km/h (130kt). Max initial rate of climb 1390ft/min. Service ceiling 21,000ft. Ferry range 2095km (1130nm), range 1855km (1000nm). Endurance 9hr. TS-2F – Max speed 482km/h (260kt), cruising speed 467km/h (252kt). Service ceiling 24,000ft. Max range 1200km (648nm).

Weights: S-2E – Empty 8505kg (18,750lb), max takeoff 13,222kg (29,150lb). TS-2F – Empty 6278kg (13,840lb), max takeoff 13,155kg (29,000lb).

Dimensions: S-2E – Wing span 22.13m (72ft 7in), span wings folded 8.33m (27ft 4in), length 13.26m (43ft 6in), height 5.06m (16ft 7in). Wing area 46.1m² (496.0sq ft).

Accommodation: Normal crew complement of four comprising pilot, copilot, radar operator and MAD operator.

Armament: Internal weapons bay can hold two homing torpedoes, depth charges or mines. Six underwing pylons for bombs and rockets.

Operators: Argentina, Brazil, Peru, South Korea, Taiwan, Thailand, Turkey, Uruguay.

History: The veteran S-2 Tracker still provides a number of nations with a useful maritime patrol and ASW capability.

The origins of the Tracker date back to the late 1940s when the US Navy devised a requirement to replace the hunter/killer team of Grumman TBM-3W and TBM-3S Avengers then used for anti submarine warfare. Responding to the requirement, Grumman devised its G-89, featuring a high wing, large cabin area for four crew and avionics, a search radar, extendable MAD, sonobuoys stored in the rear of each engine nacelle and an internal weapons bay. The G-89 was selected for development in June 1950, resulting in the first flight of the prototype XS2F-1 on December 4 1952. Initial production S2F Trackers entered service in February 1954. The S2F also formed the basis for the WF Tracer AEW aircraft and the TF Trader carrier onboard delivery aircraft. With the rationalisation of US designations in 1962 the S2F became the S-2, the WF the E-1 and the TF the C-1.

More than 600 Trackers were built in progressively improved variants including the S-2C with an enlarged bomb bay and the S-2D and S-2E with various equipment improvements. The S-2B was an upgrade of the S-2A, the S-2G a rebuilt S-2E. The last USN Trackers were retired from 1976.

Most surviving Trackers are S-2As and S-2Es, while Argentina and Taiwan are upgrading their aircraft with turboprops.

A number of turboprop upgrades have flown, using either Garrett TFE331s (Marsh Aviation's TFE331 program is described above) or Pratt & Whitney Canada PT6As. IAI offers a comprehensive S-2UP upgrade with modern systems and avionics, plus Marsh Aviation's TFE331 re-engine.

Photo: IAI has re-engined Argentine S-2Es with TFE331s. (IAI)

Grumman A-6 Intruder

Country of origin: United States of America

Type: Carrier borne strike fighter

Powerplants: A-6E – Two 41.4kN (9300lb) non afterburning Pratt & Whitney J52-P-8B turbojets.

Performance: A-6E – Max speed 1037km/h (560kt), cruising speed 763km/h (412kt). Max initial rate of climb 7620ft/min. Service ceiling 42,400ft. Max ferry range 5222km (2818nm), range with max warload 1627km (878nm).

Weights: A-6E – Empty 12,525kg (27,613lb), max takeoff from carrier 26,580kg (58,600lb), max takeoff from land 27,397kg (60,400lb).

Dimensions: A-6E – Wing span 16.15m (53ft 0in), span wings folded 7.72m (25ft 4in), length 16.69m (54ft 9in), height 4.93m (16ft 2in). Wing area 49.1m² (528.9sq ft).

Accommodation: Pilot and navigator/bombardier side by side.

Armament: Total external ordnance of 8165kg (18,000lb) on one centreline and four underwing hardpoints. Options include bombs, Harpoon, HARM and SLAM standoff missiles, laser guided bombs, and the AGM-123 Skipper laser guided missile.

Operators: USA

History: The long serving Intruder was developed to meet a US Navy requirement for a carrier based long range, low level attack aircraft.

Grumman's G-128 design proposal was selected from 10 designs from seven other manufacturers submitted in 1957. The first of six initial A2F-1 development aircraft flew on April 19 1960 (the A2F designation change to A-6 in 1962). Interestingly this and other development Intruders featured jet pipes which could vector downwards to boost lift during takeoff, a feature which was deleted from production aircraft. In all, 482 production A-6As were delivered between 1963 and 1969, and the type saw extensive service over Vietnam from 1965. In addition to the Intruder's good payload range, its effectiveness was further increased by the all-weather effectiveness of the Digital Integrated Attack Navigation Equipment, or DIANE.

Variants of the A-6A include: 19 A-6Bs, converted A-6As able to carry HARM anti radar missiles; 12 A-6Cs, A-6As fitted with FLIR and Low Light TV; and 78 A-6As converted to KA-6D tanker configuration.

The A-6E first flew on February 27 1970 and introduced upgraded powerplants, a Norden APQ-148 nav/attack radar and an IBM/Fairchild ASQ-133 nav/attack computer. The US Navy and Marines between them took delivery of 445 A-6Es, comprising 240 new build aircraft and 205 conversions. The A-6Es were upgraded to A-6E TRAM (Target Recognition Attack Multi sensor) standard from the mid 1970s. TRAM comprises a pod mounted FLIR and laser equipment, CAINS (Carrier Airborne INS) with automatic carrier landing capability and compatibility with guided bombs and missiles. The SWIP or Systems Weapon Integration Program began in 1990 to provide compatibility with missiles such as Harpoon, SLAM, HARM and Maverick.

The GE F404 and digital avionics equipped A-6G first flew in 1987, but this program was cancelled when the USN switched development to the A-12 Avenger, which itself was cancelled in 1992. All USMC A-6s have been retired, while USN A-6s will be withdrawn from 1997, their capability filled by F/A-18s and air-to-ground capable F-14s.

Photo: A US Navy A-6E aboard USS *Abraham Lincoln*. (Keith Anderson)

Grumman EA-6 Prowler

Country of origin: United States of America

Type: Electronic warfare aircraft

Powerplants: EA-6B – Two 49.8kN (11,200lb) Pratt & Whitney J52-P-408 turbojets.

Performance: EA-6B – Max speed with five jammer pods 982km/h (530kt), cruising speed at optimum altitude 774km/h (418kt). Max initial rate of climb with five jammer pods 10,030ft/min. Service ceiling with five jammer pods 38,000ft. Max ferry range 3860km (2085nm), range with max external load 1770km (955nm).

Weights: EA-6B – Empty 14,320kg (31,572lb), normal takeoff from carrier in standard jammer configuration 24,705kg (54,460lb), max takeoff 29,895kg (65,000lb).

Dimensions: EA-6B – Wing span 16.15m (53ft 0in), span wings folded 7.87m (25ft 10in), length 18.24m (59ft 10in), height 4.95m (16ft 3in). Wing area 49.1m² (528.9sq ft).

Accommodation: Pilot and three ECM officers.

Armament: EA-6B – Up to four (usually two) AGM-88A HARM anti radar missiles on four inboard (of six) underwing hardpoints.

Operators: USA

History: The Prowler is the US Navy's standard tactical electronic warfare aircraft, designed to provide electronic jamming support to Navy strike aircraft.

The original EA-6A Intruder was developed for the US Marine Corps in the early 1960s to replace Douglas EF-10B Skynights. The EA-6A was based on the A-6A and had a crew of two. It was identifiable via its fin top bulge which housed a series of antennae, while jammers were carried in underwing pods. Of the 27 built, 15 were new build aircraft. After seeing service over Vietnam the majority of the survivors were retired in the late 1970s, having been replaced by EA-6B Prowlers. A few survived into the 1990s as EW aggressors.

The definitive EW development of the Intruder is the EA-6B Prowler. Grumman developed the Prowler from 1966 to replace Douglas EKA-3B Skywarriors on US carrier decks. The EA-6B is based on the A-6, but with a stretched forward fuselage with a four seat cockpit for the pilot and three Electronic Warfare Officers. The other airframe mod is the bulbous fin tip antenna housing, while the jammers are carried in underwing pods. First flight was on May 25 1968, with service entry from 1971. In all, 170 were built for the USN and USMC through to 1991.

The Prowlers EW systems are collectively called the TJS, or Tactical Jamming System. The TJS incorporates antennae, processing computer and the jammers. These systems have been progressively updated under a number of programs, with changes to software and hardware.

Update programs were: EXCAP (Expanded Capability); ICAP-1 (Improved Capability 1); ICAP-2; ICAP-2/Block 86 which gave the Prowler the ability to carry HARMs, a capability put to good use in the Gulf War; ADVCAP, or Advanced Capability; and ADVCAP/Block 91. ADVCAP aircraft feature improvements to the jamming system plus GPS, while ADVCAP Block 91 upgraded aircraft, which should be delivered in the late 1990s, will feature new avionics and displays. The VEP, or Vehicle Enhancement Program is a series of aerodynamic improvements.

Photo: A Prowler moments before touchdown. (Wally Civitico)

Grumman OV-1 Mohawk

Country of origin: United States of America

Type: Battlefield surveillance aircraft

Powerplants: OV-1D – Two 820kW (1100shp) Lycoming T53-L-15 turboprops driving three bladed propellers.

Performance: OV-1D – Max speed 478km/h (258kt), max cruising speed 444km/h (240kt), economical cruising speed 334km/h (180kt). Max initial rate of climb 2350ft/min. Service ceiling 30,300ft. Takeoff distance to 50ft 268m (880ft). Ferry range with drop tanks 1980km (1068nm). Max endurance 4hr plus.

Weights: OV-1D – Empty equipped 5020kg (11,067lb), max takeoff 8722kg (19,230lb).

Dimensions: OV-1D – Wing span 14.63m (48ft 0in), length 12.50m (41ft 0in), height 3.86m (12ft 8in). Wing area 33.5m² (360.0sq ft).

Accommodation: Crew of two (pilot and observer) side by side.

Armament: Usually none, although guns and rocket pods have occasionally been carried on the two underwing hardpoints.

Operators: Argentina, USA.

History: The Mohawk resulted from simultaneous requirements from the US Army and US Marines for a battlefield surveillance aircraft.

The similarity of the two services' requirements – rough field STOL performance and the ability to carry a range of reconnaissance sensors – led to the creation of a joint program. The US Navy acted as program manager for the new aircraft and Grumman's G-134 design was selected for development. Nine G-134s were ordered for evaluation, and the first of these flew for the first time on April 14 1959. Initially the evaluation aircraft were designated YAO-1, but this was changed to YOV-1.

Early experience with the G-134 proved its suitability for the battlefield surveillance role, but despite this the US Marines pulled out from the program (USMC aircraft would have been designated OF-1 pre 1962). Regardless, the US Army placed contracts for what would become the OV-1A and OV-1B in 1959.

The Mohawk became the first twin turboprop powered aircraft to enter US Army service. Other notable design features include considerable crew armouring including bullet resistant glass, a mid set wing and a three tail unit (with horizontal tailplane dihedral). The side cockpit glass is bulged outwards to improve downwards visibility.

The basic OV-1A was equipped for day and night visual reconnaissance using conventional reconnaissance cameras. The OV-1B was similar except for its SLAR (side looking airborne radar) which was carried in a large pod carried under the fuselage, while it lacked optical cameras. The OV-1C was similar to the OV-1B but with an AAS-24 infrared surveillance system. The definitive OV-1D features more powerful engines, a side loading door to accept a pallet with optical (KS-80), IR (AAS-24), or SLAR (APD-7) reconnaissance sensors. Aside from new build OV-1Ds, over 110 OV-1B and OV-1C Mohawks were converted to D status. RV-1Cs and RV-1Ds were Mohawks permanently converted to electronic surveillance configuration. Other RV-1D Quick Look II aircraft were converted for Elint, while the US Army denies of the existence of EV-1D Quick Look III Mohawks.

Photo: Surviving US Army Mohawks are due to be replaced by Beech RC-12 Guardrails during 1996. Note SLAR pod. (Bruce Malcolm)

Grumman C-2 Greyhound

Country of origin: United States of America

Type: Carrier onboard delivery aircraft

Powerplants: C-2A – Two 3665kW (4912ehp) Allison T56-A-425 turboprops, driving four bladed propellers.

Performance: C-2A – Max speed 575km/h (310kt), max cruising speed 482km/h (260kt). Max initial rate of climb 2610ft/min. Service ceiling 33,500ft. Ferry range 2890km (1560nm), range with a 4535kg (10,000lb) payload over 1930km (1040nm).

Weights: C-2A – Empty 16,485kg (36,345lb), max takeoff 26,080kg (57,500lb).

Dimensions: C-2A – Wing span 24.56m (80ft 7in), span wings folded 8.94m (29ft 4in), length 17.32m (56ft 10in), height 4.84m (15ft 11in). Wing area 65.0m² (700.0sq ft).

Accommodation: Flightcrew of two. Can carry alternatively 39 passengers, or 20 stretcher patients plus medical attendants, or up to 4540kg (10,000lb) of freight.

Armament: None

Operators: USA

History: The US Navy's small fleet of Greyhounds plays a very important although unsung role in supplying the carriers while they are at sea.

The Greyhound is probably the last in a line of Grumman aircraft adapted for Carrier Onboard Delivery (COD) aircraft since WW2. Immediately after WW2 this role fell to conversions of the Avenger, while the Greyhound's immediate predecessor was the C-1 Trader, a conversion of the S-2 Tracker.

Like the COD Avengers and Traders, the Greyhound is an adaption of an existing Grumman design, in this case the E-2 Hawkeye (described under Northrop Grumman). Unlike the earlier two aircraft, the Greyhound differs significantly from its donor airframe. The C-2 retains the Hawkeye's powerplants and wing, but features a new, much broader fuselage with an upturned tail and rear loading cargo ramp. Apart from passengers the fuselage can carry a range of cargo, including jet engines. Another change is to the tailplane, the Greyhound's unit lacks dihedral (as it does not have to contend with unusual airflows caused by the Hawkeye's radome).

Two converted Hawkeyes served as YC-2A prototypes, the first of these flew for the first time on November 18 1964. An initial batch of 17 production C-2As was built, the first of these was delivered in early 1966, the last was delivered in 1968. At that time the USN had planned to acquire a further 12 C-2s, but this order was cancelled due to budget cuts. The survivors of the 17 C-2As and two prototypes underwent a Service Life Extension Program (SLEP) from 1978.

To replace its remaining C-1 Traders and to make good C-2 attrition losses the US Navy ordered an additional 39 Greyhounds in 1982. The first of these were delivered in 1985, the last rolled off the line in 1989.

The C-2 fleet is split between three operational units while other examples are on strength with the two E-2 training units.

Photo: The Greyhound provides a vital transport link between carriers at sea and shore bases. (Howard Geary)

Grumman F-14A Tomcat

Country of origin: United States of America

Type: Carrier borne air defence/air superiority fighter

Powerplants: F-14A – Two 93.0kN (20,900lb) with afterburning Pratt & Whitney TF30-P-412 or -414A turbofans.

Performance: F-14A – Max speed at altitude Mach 2.4 or 2485km/h (1342kt), max speed at low level 1468km/h (792kt). Max initial rate of climb over 30,000ft/min. Service ceiling over 50,000ft. Max range with internal and external fuel 3220km (1735nm). Radius on a combat air patrol mission with six AIM-7s and four AIM-9s 1233km (665nm).

Weights: F-14A – Empty (with -414A engines) 18,190kg (40,105lb), max takeoff (with six AIM-54 Phoenix) 32,098kg (70,764lb), max overload 33,724kg (74,349lb).

Dimensions: F-14A – Wing span extended 19.54m (64ft 2in), span wings swept 11.65m (38ft 3in), length 19.10m (62ft 8in), height 4.88m (16ft 0in). Wing area 52.5m² (565.0sq ft).

Accommodation: Pilot and radar intercept officer (RIO) in tandem.

Armament: F-14A – One internal GE M61A1 Vulcan 20mm cannon. Typical intercept configuration of two AIM-54 Phoenix (the world's longest ranging air-to-air missile), two AIM-7 Sparrows and two AIM-9 Sidewinders, or combinations thereof. In ground attack configuration can carry up to 6577kg (14,500lb) of conventional bombs.

Operators: Iran, USA.

History: Arguably the most capable air defence fighter currently in service, the Tomcat emerged from the embers of the failed F-111B program.

The cancellation of the overweight F-111B left the US Navy without a successor for the F-4 Phantom, which it flew primarily in the air defence role. Grumman acted as the lead contractor for the US Navy's version of General Dynamics' F-111, but had begun design studies on a new air defence fighter even before the F-111B's cancellation. One of Grumman's design concepts, the G-303, was thus selected in January 1969 to fill the gap left by the demise of the F-111B. The two crew G-303 was designed from the outset for carrier operations, although it retained many of the features of the F-111, including the powerful AWG-9 radar system and AIM-54 Phoenix compatibility, the P&W TF30 afterburning turbofans, and swing wings. Other design features included the twin tails and moveable foreplanes, or glove vanes.

The first prototype F-14 flew for the first time December 12 1970 (this aircraft subsequently crashed due to hydraulic failure), while a total of 556 production aircraft were delivered to the USN from 1972. Pre revolutionary Iran was the only Tomcat export customer, although the serviceability of the survivors of 79 delivered is questionable.

Apart from air defence and a limited ground attack capability, the Tomcat is also used for reconnaissance, carrying a Tactical Air Reconnaissance Pod System (TARPS) camera pod under the fuselage.

The F-14's TF30 turbofans have proved troublesome, and a number of blade failures have caused F-14 loses. Problems with the engines were largely overcome with the TF30-P-414A version, which has been adapted as standard. The re-engined F-14B and F-14D are described separately.

Photo: A US Navy F-14A. The F-14's combination of AWG-9 radar, AIM-9, AIM-7 and AIM-54 AAMs and M61 cannon means that it can handle short to long range threats.

Grumman F-14B & F-14D Tomcat

Country of origin: United States of America

Type: Carrier borne air defence/air superiority fighter

Powerplants: F-14D – Two 62.3kN (14,000lb) dry and 102.8kN (23,100lb) with afterburning General Electric F110-GE-400 turbofans.

Performance: F-14D – Max speed at altitude Mach 1.88 or 1997km/h (1078kt), cruising speed 764km/h (413kt). Max initial rate of climb over 30,000ft/min. Service ceiling over 53,000ft. Max range with internal and external fuel approximately 2965km (1600nm). Combat radius on a combat air patrol with four AIM-7s and four AIM-9s 1995km (1075nm).

Weights: F-14D – Empty 18,950kg (41,780lb), max takeoff 33,725kg (74,350lb).

Dimensions: F-14D – Wing span spread 19.54m (64ft 2in), span wings swept 11.65m (38ft 3in), length 19.10m (62ft 8in), height 4.88m (16ft 0in). Wing area 52.5m² (565.0sq ft).

Accommodation: Pilot and radar intercept officer (RIO) in tandem.

Armament: One GE M61A1 Vulcan 20mm cannon. Typical intercept configuration of two AIM-54 Phoenix, two AIM-7 Sparrows and two AIM-9 Sidewinders, or combinations thereof. Can carry conventional bombs.

Operators: USA

History: The Grumman F-14B and F-14D are the long planned re-engined variants of the F-14A Tomcat, although funding restrictions means they serve only in small numbers.

The TF30 turbofan has long been recognised as the F-14A's achilles heal – not only has it suffered from a number of catastrophic blade failures, it is not considered powerful enough for the Tomcat's massive 30 tonne plus max weight. As early as 1973 a prototype F-14 flew powered by two Pratt & Whitney F401-PW-400 turbofans as the F-14B. However this original F-14B program was cancelled due to technical and budgetary problems.

Development of a re-engined Tomcat was thus suspended until 1984 when Grumman was contracted to develop the F-14A (Plus) Interim, basically a General Electric F110-GE-400 (with extended jetpipes) powered F-14A intended as an interim aircraft until the arrival of the F-14D. The F-14A (Plus) flew for the first time in September 1986. Redesignated the F-14B, and featuring some minor avionics improvements, 38 new build F-14Bs and 32 F-14As converted to B standard were delivered from 1988.

The F-14D features two GE F110s like the F-14B, but also significant equipment changes. The primary changes are digital avionics with digital radar processing linked to the AWG-9 radar, which is redesignated APG-71, the twin IRST/TV pods under the nose, NACES ejection seats and improved radar warning receiver. Only 37 of a planned total of 127 new build F-14Ds were funded, while plans to convert the remainder of the USN's F-14A fleet to D standard were dropped due to budget cuts, with only 18 being rebuilt.

Other proposed but unfunded Tomcat variants/programs have included Quickstrike, with enhanced air-to-ground capability; the Super Tomcat-21 naval ATF alternative; Attack Super Tomcat-21 an interim A-12 replacement; and ASF-14 naval ATF alternative.

Photo: An F-14D. Tomcats will be used more widely in air-to-ground missions with the retirement of the Intruder from 1997. (Paul Merritt)

Gulfstream II & III, C-20 & SRA-1

Country of origin: United States of America

Type: VIP transport & reconnaissance platform (SRA-1)

Powerplants: Gulfstream II & III – Two 51.1kN (11,400lb) Rolls-Royce Spey turbofans.

Performance: GII – Max cruising speed 936km/h (505kt), economical cruising speed 796km/h (430kt). Max initial rate of climb 4350ft/min. Range with max fuel 6880km (3715nm). GIII – Max cruising speed 928km/h (501kt), economical cruising speed 818km/h (442kt). Max initial rate of climb 3800ft/min. Max operating ceiling 45,000ft. Range with eight passengers 7600km (4100nm).

Weights: GII – Operating empty 16,740kg (36,900lb), max takeoff 29,710kg (65,500lb). GIII – Empty 14,515kg (32,000lb), operating empty 17,235kg (38,000lb), max takeoff 31,615kg (69,700lb).

Dimensions: GII – Wing span 20.98m (68ft 10in), length 24.36m (79ft 11in), height 7.47m (24ft 6in). Wing area 75.2m² (809.6sq ft). GIII – Wing span 23.72m (77ft 10in), length 25.32m (83ft 1in), height 7.43m (24ft 5in). Wing area 86.8m² (41ft 4in).

Accommodation: Flightcrew of two. Main cabin seating for up to 19 in GII or 21 in GIII in a high density configuration, or eight to 12 in a typical corporate/VIP configuration. SRA-1 seats five to 10 operators depending on equipment fit.

Armament: None

Operators: Denmark, India, Italy, Mexico, Morocco, Saudi Arabia, USA, Venezuela.

History: The popular Gulfstream series is widely used as VIP/government transports, while a number also operate in special mission roles.

The Gulfstream II and Gulfstream III are jet powered developments of the original turboprop powered Gulfstream I. The Rolls-Royce Dart turboprop powered Grumman Gulfstream I proved to be quite successful as a large long range corporate transport, and a number have seen military service. The availability of the Rolls-Royce Spey turbofan allowed the development of a jet successor, which Grumman launched as the Gulfstream II or GII, in May 1965.

While based on the original Gulfstream I, the GII shares the same forward fuselage and cross section, there are more differences than similarities. Apart from the two Spey turbofans, the GII has a new swept wing and T tail. The GII's first flight was on October 2 1966.

The improved Gulfstream III followed Gulfstream American's purchase of Grumman's civil aircraft lines in 1978. The Gulfstream III first flew on December 2 1979. Changes compared with the GII include a revised wing of greater span and area with drag reducing winglets, more fuel tankage and thus range, and a 97cm (3ft 2in) fuselage stretch. Gulfstream IIBs meanwhile are GIIs retrofitted with the GIII's wing.

Production deliveries of GIIIs began in late 1980 and continued until 1986 when production ceased in preference to the Gulfstream IV.

The Gulfstream III in particular has been popular as a military VIP transport (designated C-20 in US service). Gulfstream also used the GIII as the basis of its SRA-1 (Surveillance and Reconnaissance Aircraft), which was offered in a variety of Elint, reconnaissance and maritime patrol configurations.

Photo: A Mexican Air Force Gulfstream III. (David Daw)

Gulfstream IV, C-20 & SRA-4

Country of origin: United States of America

Type: VIP & utility transport & multirole surveillance platform

Powerplants: Two 61.6kN (13,850lb) Rolls-Royce Tay Mk 611-8 turbofans.

Performance: IV – Normal cruising speed 850km/h (460kt). Max initial rate of climb 4000ft/min. Range with max payload 6730km (3633nm), range with eight passengers 7820km (4220nm). IV-SP – Normal cruising speed 850km/h (460kt). Max initial rate of climb 3970ft/min. Range with max payload and reserves 6186km (3338nm), range with eight passengers and reserves 7820km (4220nm). SRA-4 (maritime patrol) – Time on station 1110km (600nm) from station 6hr. Anti shipping radius with two missiles, hi-lo-hi 2500km (1350nm).

Weights: IV – Empty 16,102kg (35,500lb), max takeoff 33,203kg (73,200lb). IV-SP – Same except for max takeoff 33,838kg (74,600lb).

Dimensions: Wing span 23.72m (77ft 10in), length 26.92m (88ft 4in), height 7.45m (24ft 5in). Wing area 88.3m² (950.39sq ft).

Accommodation: Flightcrew of two. Main cabin seating for between 14 and 19, plus attendant. SRA-4 – Five to 10 operators depending on configuration, or 15 stretchers plus medical attendants.

Armament: SRA-4 ASW – Two anti shipping missiles on two underwing hardpoints.

Operators: Ireland, Sweden, USA.

History: The Gulfstream IV is a significantly improved and advanced development of the earlier Spey powered Gulfstream II and III, and its long range and large cabin make it a popular choice as a VIP transport.

The most significant improvement over the earlier Gulfstream models are the Rolls-Royce Tay turbofans, which have a much lower fuel burn and dramatically lower noise emissions, despite higher thrust than the GII's and GIII's Speys. Other changes include a stretched fuselage and structurally revised wing with 30% fewer parts, greater fuel capacity (and hence range), increased span tailplane and modern EFIS displays and avionics.

Design work on the IV began in early 1983, and the first of four production prototypes made the type's first flight on September 19 1985. The improved Gulfstream IV-SP, with higher weights and improved payload range performance, replaced the IV in production from September 1992.

Like earlier Gulfstreams, the GIV has been ordered for the US services. Single examples of the C-20G and C-20H transports serve with the US Army and Air Force respectively. The US Navy (four) and US Marines (one) operate C-20G Operational Support Aircraft, with a convertible interior for passengers or freight, with a large freight door. Meanwhile two of Sweden's three GIVs are equipped for Elint.

Gulfstream offers the GIV for a variety of military roles, under the designation SRA-4. The SRA-4 is offered in a variety of configurations, including electronic warfare support, ASW and maritime patrol (can be armed with two anti shipping missiles), Elint and medical evacuation.

Photo: A US Navy C-20G Operational Support Aircraft. (Gulfstream)

Harbin H-5

Countries of origin: Russia and China

Type: Tactical bomber

Powerplants: II-28 – Two 26.5kN (5950lb) Klimov VK-1A turbojets.

Performance: II-28 – Max speed at 14,765ft 900km/h (485kt), max speed at sea level 800km/h (432kt), typical cruising speed at altitude 875km/h (472kt). Max initial rate of climb 2950ft/min. Service ceiling 40,350ft. Range at 32,810ft 2400km (1295nm), range at 3280ft 1135km (612nm).

Weights: II-28 – Empty equipped 11,890kg (28,415lb), max takeoff 21,200kg (46,738lb).

Dimensions: II-28 – Wing span without tip tanks 21.45m (70ft 5in), fuselage length 17.65m (57ft 11in), height 6.70m (22ft 0in). Wing area 60.8m² (654.4sq ft).

Accommodation: Crew of three – pilot under fighter style canopy, bombardier/navigator in nose and rear gunner/radio operator in tail.

Armament: Two NR-23 23mm cannon in lower forward fuselage, two NR-23 cannon in rear turret and up to 3000kg (6615lb) of bombs, or two torpedoes in internal weapons bay.

Operators: H-5 – China, North Korea, Romania.

History: The Harbin H-5 is China's unlicenced built copy of the Ilyushin II-28 'Beagle' light tactical jet bomber.

Ilyushin first began design work on the II-28 in December 1947 as a private venture. The first of three prototypes, powered by two Rolls-Royce Nenes (at the time the most powerful turbojets in the world and donated to the USSR by the UK Government during the late 1940s as 'technical aid'), flew for the first time on July 8 1948. After competitive evaluation against Tupolev's larger but similarly powered Tu-73 the II-28 was selected for production to meet a Russian Air Force need for a medium sized jet bomber.

Several thousand II-28s were built for the Soviet Air Force and various Warsaw Pact nations, with deliveries beginning in 1950. Over 500 were exported to China in the 1950s, while other II-28 operators included Egypt, Indonesia, Iraq, North Vietnam, Syria and Yemen. Small numbers were also built in Czechoslovakia as the B-228.

II-28 variants include the basic II-28 bomber, II-28T torpedo bomber, reconnaissance II-28R and the II-28U trainer with a second cockpit in the nose (forward of the standard cockpit). Several served through to the late 1980s as target tugs and ECM platforms.

After Russia and China severed ties in the 1960s China began a program to build the II-28 unlicenced. The Harbin Aircraft Factory was responsible for reverse engineering the II-28 and consequently the first Chinese built 'Beagle', designated H-5, first flew on September 25 1966.

H-5 production began the following year and continued into the 1980s (although late production was at a low rate primarily for attrition replacements). As many as 2000 H-5s may have been built (including HJ-5 two seaters and H-5R or HZ-5 reconnaissance platforms) for China's Air Force and Navy. Several hundred still serve, despite their obsolescence. North Korea also operates Chinese II-28s, with the export designation B-5.

Photo: Poland was one of a number of Warsaw Pact nations to operate the II-28. (MAP)

Hawker 800/BAe 125 Srs & HS Dominie

Country of origin: United Kingdom

Type: VIP transport, navigation trainer (Dominie) and SAR aircraft

Powerplants: 700 – Two 16.6kN (3700lb) Garrett TFE731-3-RH turbofans. 800 – Two 19.1kN (4300lb) Garrett TFE731-5R-1Hs.

Performance: 700 – Max cruising speed 808km/h (436kt), economical cruising speed 723km/h (390kt). Service ceiling 41,000ft. Range with max payload 4725km (2500nm). 800 – Max cruising speed 845km/h (456kt), economical cruising speed 741km/h (400kt). Max initial rate of climb 3100ft/min. Service ceiling 43,000ft. Range with max payload 5318km (2870nm), range with max fuel 5560km (3000nm).

Weights: 700 – Empty 5826kg (12,845lb), max takeoff 11,567kg (25,500lb). 800 – Empty 6676kg (14,720lb), max takeoff 12,430kg (27,400lb).

Dimensions: 700 – Wing span 14.33m (47ft 0in), length 15.46m (50ft 9in), height 5.36m (17ft 7in). Wing area 32.8m² (353.0sq ft). 800 – Wing span 15.66m (51ft 5in), length 15.60m (51ft 2in), height 5.36m (17ft 7in). Wing area 34.8m² (374.0sq ft).

Accommodation: Flightcrew of two. Typical seating for nine in VIP layout, or max seating for 14. Dominie crew complement of two pilots, instructor and three students.

Armament: None

Operators: Botswana, Brazil, Japan, Malawi, Saudi Arabia, UK.

History: The Hawker 800 is one of the latest versions and names for the longest running corporate jet production run in history. Limited numbers serve as VIP transports and the basic type forms the basis for the RAF's Dominie navigation trainer.

What is now the Hawker 800 started life as the de Havilland DH.125, which flew for the first time on August 13 1962. For a time named the Jet Dragon, initial production was of the Series 1 and improved Series 1A and 1B.

The similar Series 2 meanwhile was the basis for the Dominie T.1, the Royal Air Force's standard navigator trainer since 1966. Twenty Dominies were built, while from 1993 11 were updated with modern systems to make the aircraft more representative of current frontline aircraft. Subsequent Viper powered 125 models were the Series 3; Series 4, or Series 400 when de Havilland merged into Hawker Siddeley; and the Series 600 with a stretched fuselage and standard seating for eight.

The much improved British Aerospace 125-700 with new fuel efficient Garrett turbofans flew for the first time in 1976. The 700 remained in production until replaced by the 125-800 in the early 1980s. The 125-800 first flew in May 1983 and introduced aerodynamic changes including a reprofiled nose and windscreen; a larger ventral fuel tank, more powerful engines and a redesigned interior.

The 125-800 became the Hawker 800 from mid 1993 when Raytheon purchased BAe's Corporate Jets division. Production was transferred to the US in 1995. Raytheon delivered five SAR equipped Hawker 800s to the Japan Air Self Defence Force as the U-125 from 1995. These aircraft feature a search radar, FLIR and observation windows.

Photo: One of four RAF BAe 125 CC.3s (BAe 125-700), fitted with a infrared countermeasures unit in the tail. (Paul Merritt)

Hawker Hunter

Country of origin: United Kingdom

Type: Multirole fighter

Powerplant: FGA.9 – One 48.7kN (10,150lb) Rolls-Royce Avon 207 turbojet.

Performance: FGA.9 – Max speed at sea level 1150km/h (622kt), max speed at 36,000ft 1010km/h (545kt), economical cruising speed 740km/h (400kt). Max initial rate of climb 16,500ft. Time to 40,000ft 5min 30sec clean or 12min 30sec loaded. Service ceiling 50,000ft. Combat radius with two drop tanks and rockets 875km (472nm), combat radius with two 455kg/1000lb bombs and two drop tanks 352km (190nm). Max ferry range 2955km (1595nm).

Weights: FGA.9 – Empty 6610kg (14,572lb), max takeoff 11,078kg (24,422lb).

Dimensions: FGA.9 – Wing span 10.26m (33ft 8in), length 13.98m (45ft 11in), height 4.01m (13ft 2in). Wing area 32.4m² (349sq ft).

Accommodation: Pilot only, or two side-by-side in trainers.

Armament: Four 30mm Aden cannon in lower forward fuselage. Four underwing pylons can carry a combined total of 3355kg (7400lb) of ordnance, including rockets and bombs. Some wired for AIM-9 AAMs.

Operators: India, Lebanon, Oman, UK, Zimbabwe.

History: Perhaps the most famous British jet fighter, the Hawker Hunter has seen four decades of frontline service and yet is still regarded as a capable ground attack platform.

The Hunter's origins lie in the Hawker P.1067 design penned by Sydney Camm to meet an RAF requirement for a replacement for the Gloster Meteor. Three P.1067 Hunter prototypes (two powered by the Rolls-Royce Avon and one by the Armstrong Siddeley Sapphire) were ordered in May 1948 for evaluation, and the first of these flew for the first time on July 20 1951.

Production Hunter F.1s were delivered from 1953, although these early aircraft suffered from a severe lack of range and engine surge when the four cannon were fired. Nevertheless, the problems with early production Hunter models were resolved in time, leaving a very capable fighter.

Early Hunter models, including the Sapphire powered F.2 and F.5, served primarily as interceptors. Most went to the RAF, although the F.4 and F.6 were the subject of some significant export orders, and were built under licence in the Netherlands and Belgium. The T.7 and T.8 were two seat side by side trainers for the RAF and RN respectively.

The definitive Hunter model, and the basis for all single seaters remaining in service, is the FGA.9, a true multirole aircraft with strengthened structure and greater payload. All FGA.9s were in fact conversions of earlier aircraft, with significant operators including the RAF, India and Switzerland (whose aircraft were retired in 1994).

In 1995 Oman and Zimbabwe were the only countries using the Hunter for frontline tasks, while India's Hunters are used as lead-in fighters. In the UK the Royal Navy operates (in late 1995) nine T.7 and T.8 two seaters and with the Fleet Requirements and Direction Unit (FRADU). Chile retired its last Hunters in 1995 while Lebanon is returning three to service.

Photo: A Sidewinder armed Hunter FGA.9 of Oman.

Helio Courier & U-10

Country of origin: United States of America

Type: STOL light utility transport

Powerplants: H-295 – One 230kW (295hp) geared Lycoming GO-480-G1D6 flat six piston engine driving a three bladed propeller.

Performance: H-295 – Max speed 270km/h (145kt), max cruising speed 265km/h (143kt), long range cruising speed 240km/h (130kt). Max initial rate of climb 1150ft/min. Service ceiling 20,500ft. Takeoff run at max STOL weight 102m (335ft). Conventional takeoff run at max weight 215m (700ft). Range with standard fuel 1060km (575nm), with optional fuel 2220km (1200nm).

Weights: H-295 – Empty 943kg (2080lb), max takeoff 1542kg (3400lb).

Dimensions: H-295 – Wing span 11.89m (39ft 0in), length 9.45m (31ft 0in), height 2.69m (8ft 10in). Wing area 21.5m² (231sq ft).

Accommodation: Early models up to the H-250 could seat four, the H-395 five or six, the H-250 and subsequent models six.

Armament: Usually none.

Operators: Columbia, Peru, Thailand.

History: The Helio Courier has proven to be a highly versatile family of utility aircraft types, renowned for superb STOL abilities.

The Courier lineage traces back to a much modified development of the two seat Piper Vagabond known as the Koppen-Bolinger Helioplane. This Helioplane featured numerous aerodynamic improvements to enhance low speed handling capabilities and STOL ability. While the subsequent Courier was an all new and much larger design, it did incorporate features pioneered on the Helioplane.

The Courier was initially known as the Helioplane Four and first appeared in 1952, in its first form it was powered by a 197kW (264hp) Lycoming GO-435 and seated four. First flight occurred during 1953. Subsequent development led to a number of derivatives, beginning with the H-392 Strato Courier of 1957. Intended for high altitude photographic work, it was powered by a 255kW (340hp) supercharged GSO-435. The H-395, featuring a 220kW (295hp) GO-485 and seating for five or six, was the first major production version and appeared in 1957. The H-395 was similar but its engine could operate on 80 octane fuel, making it suitable for operations in remote areas. The H-395 served as the basis for the US Air Force's U-10. The USAF procured 130 U-10As, U-10Bs and U-10Ds in the mid 1960s, some of which saw service in Vietnam, although the majority were passed onto Asian allies under the Military Assistance Program (MAP). A turboprop powered development, the AU-24 Stallion also saw USAF service in Vietnam in the armed recce and COIN roles.

The next civil model was the H-250 (with a 185kW/250hp O-540) and H-295 Super Courier (220kW/295hp GO-480) from 1965, and the tricycle undercarriage HT-295 from 1974. The H-250 remained in production until 1972, the H-295 1976. Developments of the H-295 with a eight cylinder 300kW (400hp) Lycoming IO-720, the Courier 800, and 260kW (350hp) TIO-540 powered Courier 700 were put into production by the newly established Helio Aircraft Company from 1983, but production was limited, and delivered to civil customers only.

Small numbers of U-10s remain in service with Thailand and Peru.

Photo: Peru's Army Air Arm operates five U-10s. (MAP)

Hindustan Advanced Light Helicopter

Country of origin: India

Type: Troop transport/ship borne multirole helicopter

Powerplants: Two 745kW (1000shp) Turboméca TM 333-2B turbo-shafts, driving four bladed main and bladed tail rotors.

Performance: Max level speed 290km/h (156kt), max cruising speed 245km/h (132kt). Max initial rate of climb 2360ft/min. Service ceiling 19,685ft. Hovering ceiling in ground effect over 9850ft. Range with max fuel 800km (430nm), range with a 700kg (1543lb) payload 400km (215nm). Endurance 4hr.

Weights: Army version – Empty equipped 2500kg (5511lb), max takeoff 4000kg (8818lb). Naval version – Empty 2500kg (5511lb), max takeoff 5000kg (11,023lb).

Dimensions: Main rotor diameter 13.20m (43ft 4in), length overall rotors turning 15.87m (42ft 1in), fuselage length tail rotor turning 12.89m (42ft 4in), height overall tail rotor turning army version 4.98m (16ft 4in), naval version 4.81m (15ft 10in). Main rotor disc area 136.9m² (1473.0sq ft).

Accommodation: Flightcrew of two. Main cabin seating for 10 to 14, depending on configuration. Max external sling load army variant 1000kg (2205lb), naval variant 1500kg (3307lb).

Armament: Two stub wings can carry a variety of armaments, includ-ing up to four torpedoes or depth charges on naval variant, or two anti armour missiles and two rocket pods, or air-to-air missiles (land variant). Army versions can be fitted with a ventral 20mm gun pod.

Operators: Production not funded at time of writing.

History: The Advanced Light Helicopter is the first indigenous heli-copter of the growing Indian aircraft industry, and will be built in different versions for the Indian Army, Navy, Coast Guard and Air Force, plus civil customers.

In the early 1980s India approached Germany's MBB (now Euro-copter Deutschland) to help it design and build a mid size multirole helicopter for both military and civil use. Subsequently a cooperation agreement was signed in July 1984, covering design support, devel-opment and production. Actual design work began in November that year, while the first flight of the first of four prototypes was on August 20 1992.

ALH design features include, a hingeless four blade main rotor with swept back tips and composite construction main and tail rotor blades.

The Advanced Light Helicopter will be built in two distinct military versions, one for the Indian Air Force and Army, and one for the Navy. Army and air force versions will feature skids, and will be used for a number missions including ground attack, troop transport and SAR. Naval versions will be fitted with retractable tricycle undercarriage, and a folding tail boom. A civil version is also planned, possibly powered by General Electric CT7s.

The Indian Government plans to buy around 250 ALHs for its mili-tary, to replace a variety of helicopters including Chetaks and Chee-tahs, although no firm orders had been placed by late 1995.

The ALH also serves as the basis for the Light Attack Helicopter (LAH) development, which would feature the ALH's dynamic systems coupled to a new fuselage with seating for two crew in tandem cockpits.

Photo: The first prototype ALH, Z 3182. (Hindustan)

Hindustan HJT-16 Kiran

Country of origin: India

Type: Advanced trainer & light attack aircraft

Powerplant: Mk II – One 18.4kN (4130lb) HAL licence built Rolls-Royce Orpheus 701-01 turbojet.

Performance: Mk II – Max speed at sea level 704km/h (380kt), max cruising speed at 15,000ft 620km/h (335kt), economical cruising speed 417km/h (225kt). Max initial rate of climb 5250ft/min. Service ceiling 39,375ft. Range with standard fuel 615km (332nm).

Weights: Mk II – Empty equipped 2965kg (6540lb), max takeoff 4950kg (10,913lb).

Dimensions: Mk II – Wing span 10.70m (35ft 1in), length 10.25m (33ft 8in), height 3.64m (11ft 11in). Wing area 19.0m² (204.5sq ft).

Accommodation: Crew of two side by side.

Armament: Mk II – Two 7.62mm Aden guns in nose. Four underwing pylons can carry rocket pods, a single 250kg (550lb) bomb each, various practice bombs or fuel tanks.

Operators: India

History: While the last production examples were only delivered in 1989, the Hindustan Kiran (Ray of Light) was first developed in the early 1960s to replace India's sizeable fleet of two seat licence built de Havilland Vampire advanced trainers.

Design of the Kiran began at Hindustan's Bangalore facilities under the leadership of Dr V M Chatage in 1961. Dr Chatage's team came up with a design similar in some respects to the contemporary Jet Provost, as the Kiran featured a straight wing, side by side seating and a Bristol (now Rolls-Royce) Viper turbojet. The first prototype Kiran flew for the first time on September 4 1964, the second in August 1965.

A batch of 24 Kiran Mk Is was built, the first of these were deliv-ered to the Indian Air Force from 1968. As well as the 24 pre produc-tion aircraft, 118 production Kiran Is were built, some as Kiran IAs with two underwing hardpoints for weapons training. The Kiran Mk I entered service with Indian Air Force Academy in 1973, while a small number have also been transferred to the Indian Navy.

The improved Kiran Mk II first flew on July 30 1976. Compared with the Kiran I, the Mk II introduced a more powerful Rolls-Royce Orpheus turbojet in place of the Viper, four underwing hardpoints for light ground attack/COIN work, two 7.62mm Aden guns in the forward fuselage and an improved hydraulic system.

The Mk II featured performance and payload improvements over the Kiran Mk I, but the Indian Air Force deemed it unsuitable for night flying and it had poor payload range. These findings delayed Kiran production by many years and it was not until 1983 that official development work was completed. Deliveries of the first of 61 pro-duction Kiran Mk IIs began in March 1985, with the line closing in 1989. Aside from the Indian Air Force, six Kiran Mk IIs were also delivered to the Indian Navy.

Hindustan is currently developing the turboprop powered HTT-35 to replace the Kiran and piston powered Deepak from the late 1990s.

Photo: India is the only Kiran operator.

IAI Arava

Country of origin: Israel

Type: STOL utility transport

Powerplants: 201 – Two 560kW (750shp) Pratt & Whitney Canada PT6S-34 turboprops, driving three bladed propellers.

Performance: 201 – Max speed 326km/h (176kt), max cruising speed 320km/h (172kt), economical cruising speed 311km/h (168kt). Max initial rate of climb 1290ft/min. Service ceiling 25,000ft. Takeoff run at max takeoff weight 295m (960ft). Range with max payload 260km (140nm), max range with a 1585kg (3500lb) payload 1000km (540nm).

Weights: 201 – Operating empty 4000kg (8816lb), max takeoff 6804kg (15,000lb).

Dimensions: 201 – Wing span 20.96m (68ft 9in), length 13.03m (42ft 9in), height 5.21m (17ft 1in). Wing area 43.7m² (470.2sq ft).

Accommodation: Flightcrew of two. Seating for 24 passengers four abreast in 201. Configurations offered included freight, aerial ambulance, Elint and maritime patrol.

Armament: Can be fitted with fuselage mounted 12.7mm gun pods or up to 12 rockets.

Operators: Bolivia, Cameroon, Colombia, Ecuador, El Salvador, Guatemala, Honduras, Mexico, Israel, Swaziland, Thailand, Venezuela.

History: The Arava STOL utility transport was developed to meet an Israel Defence Force requirement to replace Douglas DC-3s, but it has also proved popular with export customers in underdeveloped and rugged regions of the world.

IAI began design work on the Arava in 1966. Design objectives included STOL performance, the ability to operate from rough strips and the ability to carry 25 troops or bulky payloads. To achieve this the Arava design was of a fairly unusual configuration, featuring a barrel-like short but wide fuselage, the rear of which is hinged and swings open for easy loading and unloading; plus long span wings; twin tails (to compensate for the loss of moment arm due to the short fuselage) mounted on booms that run from the engine nacelles; and two Pratt & Whitney Canada PT6A turboprops.

The Arava first flew on November 27 1969, while a second prototype flew for the first time on May 8 1971. The initial Arava 101 was not put into production, but it formed the basis for the 101B, 102 and 201 production models. The 101B differed from the 101 in having an improved 19 seat interior and more powerful PT6A-36s. The 102 had a 20 seat passenger interior.

The 201 is the primary military version, and has sold in the most numbers. More than 70 were built, mainly for Israel and customers in Latin America. Israeli aircraft are used for a variety of roles other than transport, including maritime patrol (fitted with a search radar) and Elint. Thailand uses its Aravas for Elint/border surveillance.

The final Arava development is the 202, which is easily recognised by its large Whitcomb winglets, boundary layer fences inboard of each wingtip and slightly stretched fuselage. The winglets and boundary layer fences were offered as a kit for retrofitting to existing Aravas.

Photo: Papua New Guinea retired its Aravas in 1989. (Warwick Henry)

IAI Kfir

Country of origin: Israel

Type: Multirole fighter

Powerplant: C7 – One 52.9kN (11,890lb) dry and 79.4kN (17,860lb) with afterburning IAI licence built General Electric J79-JIE turbojet.

Performance: C7 – Max speed over 2440km/h (1315kt), or Mach 2.3, max sustained speed Mach 2.0, max speed at sea level 1390km/h (750kt). Max initial rate of climb 45,930ft/min. Interception radius with two Shafrir AAMs and three drop tanks (3425 l/904 US gal) 775km (420nm). Radius with two 363kg/800lb and three 180kg/400lb bombs, two Shafrir AAMs and three drop tanks (4700 l/1241 US gal) hi-lo-hi 1185km (640nm). Ferry range with three drop tanks 2990km (1615nm).

Weights: C7 – Empty approx 7285kg (16,060lb), max takeoff 16,500kg (36,375lb).

Dimensions: C7 – Wing span 8.22m (27ft 0in), length overall 15.65m (51ft 4in), height 4.55m (14ft 11in). Wing area 34.8m² (374.6sq ft).

Accommodation: Pilot only, or two in tandem in trainer variants.

Armament: Two IAI built DEFA 30mm cannon. Five under fuselage and two underwing hardpoints can carry two AIM-9 Sidewinder, Python 3 or Shafrir 2 AAMs on outer wing stations, bombs, rockets, Shrike and Maverick ASMs, or GBU-15 laser guided bombs.

Operators: Colombia, Ecuador, Israel.

History: The Israeli developed Kfir is arguably the most potent member of the basic Dassault Mirage III/5 fighter series.

France cancelled the deliveries of paid for Mirage 5Js to Israel in 1967, leading IAI to develop and build the Nesher, an unlicensed Mirage 5 copy. After building 100 or so Neshers (some of which were subsequently sold to Argentina as the Dagger and used in the 1982 Falklands War), IAI switched to building the Kfir.

With the Kfir (Lion Cub) IAI was able to make major improvements compared with the basic Mirage, the most important of which was the use of the significantly more powerful General Electric J79 turbojet (necessitating larger intakes and dorsal airscoop), plus Israeli developed avionics (but no radar) in an extended nose. The first Kfir, a converted French built Mirage, first flew in October 1970, while the first IAI built Kfir flew in September 1971.

Initial production Kfirs were delivered from April 1975, but these were soon followed by the Kfir C2, the first major production model and the first to introduce canards. Early Kfirs meanwhile were subsequently upgraded to C1 standard, fitted with small canards. Between 1985 and 1989 some were operated by the US Navy and Marines as the F-21 for aggressor training.

The C2 introduced airframe modifications to improve manoeuvrability, including larger canards, nose strakes and dogtooth wing leading edges, as well as improved avionics and a HUD. 185 C2s and two seat TC2s were built, with small numbers delivered to Ecuador and Columbia in the 1980s. Most Israeli C2s were upgraded to C7 standard during the 1980s with a modern cockpit including HOTAS controls.

Surplus Israeli Kfir C2s and C7s are now offered for export. IAI is also offering the Kfir 2000 (or C10) upgrade for these aircraft, with new avionics, including the multimode radar developed for the Lavi.

Photo: An Israeli Kfir TC7. (IAI)

IAI Lavi

Country of origin: Israel

Type: Multirole fighter/technology demonstrator

Powerplant: One 55.5kN (12,500lb) dry and 82.7kN (18,600lb) with afterburning (approx ratings) Pratt & Whitney PW1120 afterburning turbojet (the PW1120 is a turbojet development of the F100).

Performance: Estimated – Max speed above 36,000ft 1969km/h (1063kt) or Mach 1.85. Low level penetration speed with two AAMs and eight 340kg/750lb bombs 997km/h (538kt). Combat radius on an air-to-ground mission, lo-lo-lo 1110km (600nm), or hi-lo-hi with six 113kg/250lb bombs 2130km (1150nm). Combat air patrol radius 1850km (1000nm).

Weights: Empty approx 7030kg (15,500lb), max takeoff 18,370kg (40,500lb).

Dimensions: Wing span 8.78m (28ft 10in), length 14.57m (47ft 10in), height 4.78m (15ft 8in). Wing area 33.1m² (355.8sq ft).

Armament: One internal 30mm cannon. Two wingtip pylons for AAMs. Four underwing and seven underfuselage hardpoints can carry air-to-surface missiles, bombs, laser guided bombs and rockets.

Accommodation: Two in tandem Lavi TD.

Operators: Project terminated prior to service entry.

History: The Lavi (Young Lion) was originally developed as a multirole fighter for the Israeli Defence Forces, before program cancellation saw the prototypes used as technology demonstrator airframes.

The Lavi story begins in the early 1980s when IAI began development work on a multirole fighter to meet an IDF requirement for 300 or so such aircraft. Program go-ahead was given in 1980, while full scale development began in October 1982. The first prototype (B-1) flew for the first time on December 31 1986, the second (B-2) flew on March 30 1987. Both prototypes were two seaters, with test avionics occupying the second seat.

Despite promising results, the Lavi program was cancelled in August 1987, due mainly to budget restrictions, coupled with some US opposition (the Lavi was developed with considerable US support) and the availability of extra, cheaper F-16s.

Design features of the Lavi include F-16 style ventral air intake, canard delta configuration, a single PW1120 turbojet (also planned to power the proposed IAI Phantom upgrade), an Elta multimode radar, HUD, HOTAS and three multi function displays.

Following cancellation IAI elected to use the Lavi as a technology demonstrator and testbed for Israeli avionics and systems. To this end the third prototype (B-3) was completed as the Lavi TD. Another two seater (but this time with no test avionics in the second seat), it first flew on September 25 1989.

The Lavi TD is flown on a variety of test tasks, one more notable item tested is the Elta EL\M-2032 multimode radar which is offered as part of a number of IAI fighter upgrade programs.

In the mid 1990s a number of reports have suggested that IAI is cooperating with China to develop the F-10, a new Lavi lookalike multirole fighter based on Lavi technologies (including the EL\M-2032 radar). The F-10 is apparently in an advanced stage of development, and could fly during 1996.

Photo: IAI's Lavi TD technology demonstrator. (IAI)

Ilyushin Il-18, Il-20, Il-22 & Il-38

Country of origin: Russia

Type: Il-18 – VIP & general transport. Il-20 – Elint platform. Il-22 – Command Post. Il-38 – Maritime patrol and ASW aircraft

Powerplants: Il-38 – Four 3125kW (4190ehp) ZMKB Progess (Ivchenko) AI-20M turboprops, driving four bladed propellers.

Performance: Il-38 – Max speed at 21,000ft 722km/h (390kt), max cruising speed at 27,000ft 610km/h (330kt), patrol speed at 2000ft 400km/h (216kt). Range with max fuel 7200km (3887nm). Patrol endurance with max fuel 12hr.

Weights: Il-38 – Empty 36,000kg (79,367lb), max takeoff 63,500kg (140,000lb).

Dimensions: Il-38 – Wing span 37.42m (122ft 9in), length overall 36.90m (129ft 10in), height 10.17m (33ft 4in). Wing area 140.0m² (1506.9sq ft).

Accommodation: Flightcrew of two pilots and flight engineer. Operational crew believed to be nine, which would include a tactical coordinator, sensor operators, MAD operator and observers.

Armament: Forward and aft internal weapons bays can carry homing torpedoes, sonobuoys and nuclear and conventional depth charges.

Operators: Il-18 – China, Congo, North Korea, Romania, Syria, Vietnam. Il-20 & 22 – Russia. Il-38 – India, CIS.

History: Ilyushin's Il-18 turboprop airliner played a significant role in developing the USSR's air services in the 1960s and 1970s, but it has also been adopted for a variety of military roles, ranging from transport, to command post, Elint and maritime patrol.

The Il-18 was originally developed against a mid 1950s Aeroflot requirement for an economical 75 to 100 seat airliner. The Il-18 first flew on June 4 1957, and entered airline service with Aeroflot in 1959. Some 600 were built mainly for USSR and Soviet client state airlines, with a smaller number delivered for military service as VIP and general transports. Given the NATO reporting name 'Coot', a small number remain in military service.

The Il-18 airframe also serves as the basis of the Il-20 Elint/reconnaissance platform. The Il-20 ('Coot-A') was first observed in 1978 and features a variety of antennae, with a large ventral canoe presumed to contain a side looking radar. Blisters on either side of the forward fuselage are another obvious external feature.

Several Il-22 ('Coot-B') airborne command post aircraft were converted from surplus Il-18 airliners, and again feature a variety of antennae and external protuberances.

The most well known military adaption of the Il-18 is the maritime patrol/ASW Il-38 'May'. The Il-38 is believed to have flown for the first time in 1967 and about three dozen serve with Russian Naval Aviation, while five were delivered to India in 1975. Details of the Il-38 are limited, but the airframe is stretched by 4m (13ft) over the Il-18 and the wings are moved forward. The tail contains a MAD, while under the forward fuselage a search radar (named 'Wet Eye' by NATO) housed in a bulged radome. There are two internal weapons bays, one forward and one rear of the wing.

Photo: A Russian Navy Il-38.

Ilyushin Il-76 & Il-78

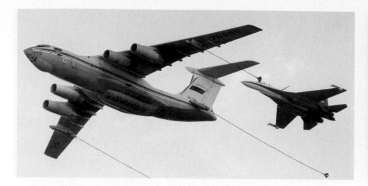

Country of origin: Russia

Type: Strategic freighter. Il-78 – Aerial refueller

Powerplants: Four 117.7kN (26,455lb) Aviadvigatel (Soloviev) D-30KP turbofans. Il-76MF – Four 156.9kN (35,275lb) PS-90ANs.

Performance: Il-76M – Max speed 850km/h (460kt), cruising speed 750 to 800km/h (405 to 432kt). Max range 6700km (3617nm), range with a 40 tonne (88,185lb) payload 5000km (2700nm). Il-76MD – Speeds same. Range with max payload 3650km (1970nm), range with 20 tonne (44,090lb) payload 7300km (3940nm). Il-76MF – Range with 40 tonne (88,185lb) payload 5200km (2805nm).

Weights: Il-76M – Max takeoff 170,000kg (374,785lb). Il-78 – Empty 98,000kg (216,050lb), max takeoff 190,000kg (418,875lb).

Dimensions: Il-76M & Il-76MF – Wing span 50.50m (165ft 8in), length 46.59m (152ft 10in), height 14.76m (48ft 5in). Wing area 300.0m² (3229.2sq ft). Il-76MF – Same except length approx 53m (174ft).

Accommodation: Il-75M & Il-76MF – Crew of seven comprising two pilots, flight engineer, navigator and radio operator, plus two freight handlers. Can carry up to 140 troops or 120 paratroops.

Armament: Il-76 – Provision for two 23mm twin barrel GSh-23L guns in tail.

Operators: Cuba, India, Iraq, Libya, North Korea, Russia, Syria.

History: The Ilyushin Il-76 (NATO name 'Candid') was developed as a replacement for the turboprop powered Antonov An-12 (described separately).

Il-76 development under the leadership of G V Novozhilov began in the late 1960s, resulting in the type's first flight on March 25 1971. Series production commenced in 1975.

In the now classic military freighter configuration, the Il-76 features a high mounted wing passing above the fuselage with four engines, a T tail, rear loading ramp and freight doors. For enhanced short field performance the Il-76 features wide span triple slotted trailing edge flaps, upper surface spoilers and near full span leading edge slats, while the aircraft rides on a total of 20 low pressure tyres, the front nose unit features four wheels, the main wheel bogies having two rows of four tyres each.

Military versions developed from the basic Il-76 include the Il-76M with additional fuel and the Il-76MD with increased takeoff and payload weights and D-30KP-2s which retain their power output to higher altitudes. The stretched PS90 powered Il-76MF first flew on August 1 1995. The A-50 AEW&C development is described under Beriev.

The Il-78 'Midas' is an air-to-air refuelling development of the Il-76, developed to replace Myasischev 'Bison' tankers. The Il-78 is based on the Il-76MD and features two internal fuel tanks which can be removed, allowing the aircraft to revert to a freighter. The more developed Il-78M features three permanent tanks capable of holding up to 35 tonnes of fuel. Fuel is transferred via three hose drum units, one under each wing and one on the rear starboard fuselage, a rangefinding radar is built into the rear fuselage and the observer is located in the tail. Service entry was in 1987.

Photo: Most Il-78 tankers serve in civil colours. This one refuels an Su-27 Flanker during an airshow routine. (Gerard Frawley)

Kaman SH-2 Seasprite

Country of origin: United States of America

Type: Shipborne ASW helicopter

Powerplants: SH-2G – Two 1285kW (1723shp) General Electric T700-GE-401 turboshafts, driving four bladed main and tail rotors.

Performance: SH-2G – Max speed 256km/h (138kt), normal cruising speed 222km/h (120kt). Max initial rate of climb 2500ft/min. Service ceiling 23,900ft. Hovering ceiling in ground effect 20,800ft, out of ground effect 18,000ft. Max range with two external tanks 885km (478nm). Time on station 65km (35nm) from ship with two torpedoes 1hr 30min. Max endurance with two external tanks 5hr.

Weights: SH-2G – Empty 4173kg (9200lb), max takeoff 6125kg (13,500lb).

Dimensions: SH-2G – Main rotor diameter 13.41m (44ft 0in), length overall rotors turning 16.00m (52ft 6in), fuselage length 12.34m (40ft 6in), height overall rotors turning 4.62m (15ft 2in), height blades folded 4.14m (13ft 7in). Main rotor disc area 141.3m² (1521.1sq ft).

Accommodation: Crew of three, comprising pilot, copilot/tactical co-ordinator and sensor operator. Can carry one passenger, or four passengers or two stretchers with sonobuoy launcher removed.

Armament: SH-2G – One or two Mk 46 or Mk 50 torpedoes. Can carry a 7.62mm pintle mounted MG in each cabin doorway.

Operators: Argentina (unconfirmed), Egypt*, USA.

History: The Kaman SH-2 Seasprite has for several decades been one of the US Navy's primary shipborne transport and ASW helicopters.

The Seasprite was designed in response to a 1956 US Navy requirement for a long range, all weather multirole utility helicopter. Kaman's K-20 was selected for development as the HU2K-1 (UH-2A from 1962), and it flew in prototype form on July 2 1959. The UH-2A and improved UH-2B were powered by a single General Electric T58 turboshaft, and could carry up to 11 passengers or a 1815kg (4000lb) sling load. 190 were built and used for utility transport, SAR and Vertrep. From 1968 all surviving UH-2s were re-engined with two T58s.

The UH-2 was selected as the basis for an interim ASW LAMPS (Light Airborne Multi-Purpose System) helicopter in October 1970 as the SH-2D. Twenty Seasprites were converted to SH-2D standard with a Litton search radar, a MAD on the starboard fuselage pylon and a removable sonobuoy launcher.

From May 1973 Kaman converted 88 Seasprites (almost all surviving UH-2 and SH-2D airframes) to LAMPS 2 SH-2F Seasprite standard, fitted with uprated engines, a Marconi search radar and a towed MAD. Kaman delivered 52 new build SH-2Fs from 1981, many with RWRs and chaff and flare dispensers. Sixteen were fitted with countermeasures and a FLIR for operations in the Persian Gulf.

The SH-2G Super Seasprite is the final SH-2 development and is powered by two General Electric T700s, which are 10% more powerful than the SH-2F's two T58s but more fuel efficient. Other changes include multi function displays and a new acoustic processor and a new tactical management system. The first YSH-2G prototype first flew on April 2 1985. Six new build SH-2Gs were delivered from 1991, alongside 18 converted SH-2Fs. These aircraft equip two US Navy Reserve units, and are the only SH-2s remaining in service.

Photo: An SH-2G at rest with the rotors folded back. (Keith Anderson)

Kamov Ka-25

Country of origin: Russia

Type: Shipborne ASW & multirole helicopter

Powerplants: Ka-25PL – Two 670kW (900shp) Glushenkov (OMKB Mars) GTD-3F turboshafts, driving two three bladed coaxial rotors.

Performance: Ka-25PL – Max speed 209km/h (113kt), normal cruising speed 193km/h (104kt). Service ceiling 11,000ft. Range with standard fuel 400km (217nm), range with external tanks 650km (350nm).

Weights: Ka-25PL – Empty 4765kg (10,505lb), max takeoff 7500kg (16,535lb).

Dimensions: Ka-25PL – Rotor diameter (each) 15.74m (51ft 8in), fuselage length 9.75m (32ft 0in), height to top of rotor head 5.37m (17ft 8in). Rotor disc area (each) 194.6m² (2095sq ft).

Accommodation: Pilot and copilot side by side. Main cabin can carry up to 12 passengers on folding seats when so equipped.

Armament: Some aircraft equipped with internal weapons bay which can contain two torpedoes or nuclear or conventional depth charges.

Operators: India, Russia, Syria, Vietnam, Yugoslavia.

History: The Kamov Ka-25 was built in large numbers for the Soviet Navy and export customers as a ship based ASW and utility helicopter, but it is progressively being replaced by the Ka-32.

The Ka-25 was the end result of a 1957 Soviet Navy requirement for a shipborne anti submarine warfare helicopter. In response Kamov developed the Ka-20 which flew for the first time during 1960. The Ka-20 was displayed in the 1961 Soviet Aviation Day flypast at Tushino carrying two mock air-to-surface missiles. The Ka-20 formed the basis for the production Ka-25 (NATO name 'Hormone'), 460 or so production aircraft being delivered between 1966 and 1975. In the Soviet Navy the Ka-25 replaced the Mil Mi-4 as the service's primary shipborne helicopter.

The most prominent design feature of the Ka-25 is Kamov's trademark counter rotating coaxial main rotors, which do away with the need for a tail rotor, and means the tail can be kept short and thus saving space, an important consideration for naval operations. Other features include a search radar mounted beneath the nose, a downward looking electro optical sensor in the tailboom, a MAD which can be mounted either in the fuselage or tail, and retractable undercarriage. The Ka-25 was usually flown unarmed, but can be fitted with an underfuselage weapons bay that can carry torpedoes and mines.

While up to 25 separate Ka-25 variants may have been built, major identified variants include the Ka-25PL 'Hormone-A', the Ka-25Ts 'Hormone-B', the Ka-25PS 'Hormone-C', and the Ka-25BShZ. The Ka-25Bsh is the primary ASW variant and has largely been replaced in Russian service by the Ka-27. The Ka-25Ts was used for target acquisition and mid course guidance for ship launched missiles, with most now retired. The Ka-24PS is a dedicated search and rescue aircraft. It is stripped of all ASW equipment and can also be used for troop transport (carrying up to 12 passengers), vertrep and utility transport. Many Ka-25PSs were fitted with a searchlight and a rescue winch. The Ka-25BShZ was developed to tow minesweeping gear.

Photo: The Yugoslav Navy continues to operate Ka-25s alongside Ka-27s and Mi-14s. (MAP)

Kamov Ka-27, Ka-28 & Ka-32

Country of origin: Russia

Type: ASW & multirole shipborne helicopter

Powerplants: Ka-27PL – Two 1645kW (2205shp) Klimov (Isotov) TV3-117V turboshafts driving two three bladed counter rotating co-axial main rotors.

Performance: Ka-27PL – Max speed 250km/h (135kt), max cruising speed 230km/h (124kt). Max initial rate of climb 2460ft/min. Service ceiling 16,405ft. Hovering ceiling out of ground effect 11,485ft. Ferry range with auxiliary fuel 800km (432nm). Radius of action tracking a submarine moving at up to 75km/h (40kt) at a depth of 500m (1640ft) 200km (108nm). Endurance 4hr 30min.

Weights: Ka-27PL – Basic empty 6100kg (13,338lb), operating empty 6500kg (14,330lb), max takeoff 12,600kg (27,778lb).

Dimensions: Ka-27PL – Rotor diameter (each) 15.90m (52ft 2in), length rotors folded 12.25m (40ft 2in), fuselage length 11.30m (37ft 1in), height to top of rotor head 5.40m (17ft 9in). Rotor disc area each 198.5m² (2138sq ft).

Accommodation: Ka-27PL – Normal crew complement of three, comprising pilot, tactical coordinator and ASW systems operator. Ka-32 – Main cabin can accommodate up to 16 passengers or freight.

Armament: Torpedoes or depth charges carried in a ventral weapons bay.

Operators: Ka-27 – Russia. Ka-28 – India, Yugoslavia.

History: The Kamov Ka-27 was developed to replace the Ka-25 in Soviet naval service, and is now the Russian Navy's standard ship based ASW helicopter.

The Kamov design bureau began work on a successor for its Ka-25 in 1967, when Sergei Mikheyev became chief designer following Nikolai Kamov's death. The Soviet Navy required a replacement for its Ka-25s, which could not operate dunking sonar at night or in poor weather. The result was the Ka-27 (NATO name 'Helix'), an all new helicopter of similar overall dimensions to the Ka-25 and featuring Kamov's signature counter rotating coaxial main rotors. The Ka-27 flew for the first time in 1973.

The Ka-27's similar overall dimensions to the Ka-25 means it requires only the same amount of deck space to operate from as the older helicopter. However the Ka-27 features more powerful Isotov turboshafts which turn redesigned, although similar diameter rotors, giving greater performance and allowing higher weights.

The basic Ka-27PL anti submarine warfare helicopter features an under nose mounted search radar, dipping sonar and disposable sonobuoys. The Ka-27PL usually operates in 'hunter killer' teams, with one aircraft tracking the target sub, the other dropping depth charges. The Ka-28 is a down spec export version of the Ka-27PL, while the Ka-27PS is a naval SAR helicopter with some ASW equipment deleted, an external winch, and fuselage side mounted fuel tanks. The Ka-29 assault transport derivative is described separately.

The Ka-32 is the civil version of the Ka-27, and while none have been sold to military operators, some Ka-32s in Aeroflot markings have been observed operating off Russian naval vessels.

Photo: A Ka-27PL on display at the 1995 Moscow Airshow. (Alex Radetski)

Kamov Ka-29

Country of origin: Russia

Type: Assault transport & radar picket helicopter

Powerplants: Ka-29 – Two 1635kW (2190shp) Klimov (Isotov) TV3-117V turboshafts, driving two three bladed counter rotating coaxial main rotors.

Performance: Ka-29 – Max level speed at sea level 280km/h (151kt), cruising speed 235km/h (127kt). Max initial rate of climb 3050ft/min. Service ceiling 14,100ft. Hovering ceiling out of ground effect 12,140ft. Ferry range 740km (400nm), range with max standard fuel 460km (248nm). Combat radius with six to eight attack passes 100km (54nm).

Weights: Ka-29 – Empty 5520kg (12,170lb), max takeoff 12,600kg (27,775lb).

Dimensions: Ka-29 – Main rotor diameter (each) 15.90m (52ft 2in), length overall excluding nose probes and rotors 11.30m (37ft 1in), height to top of rotor hub 5.40m (17ft 9in). Main rotor disc area each 198.5m² (2138sq ft).

Accommodation: Crew of two. Main cabin can accommodate up to 16 combat equipped troops, or four stretcher patients and six seated patients in medevac configuration.

Armament: One 7.62mm four barrel gatling machine gun mounted underneath right side door. Two pylons on each stub wing can carry rocket pods, or two four round clusters of 9M114 Shturm (AT-6 Spiral) ASMs and two rocket pods. Can carry a 30mm gun above left side stub wing.

Operators: Russia

History: The Ka-29 development of the Ka-27 was designed specifically for use providing fire support of Russian Navy amphibious landing operations.

The Ka-29 'Helix-B' was initially thought to be a non radar equipped transport version of the Ka-27, although this observation has since been proven to be untrue. The basic Ka-29 variant is the Ka-29TB attack helicopter, of which around 30 are thought to have entered Russian Navy service. Service entry was in 1985.

While the Ka-29 is based on the Ka-27, there are a number of substantial changes. The Ka-29's forward fuselage is widened, with changes to the nose profile including a five piece flat windscreen and bluntened nose. Armament is carried on two stub wings with two hardpoints each, typically carrying rocket pods or air-to-surface missiles. The Ka-29 also features a small radar thought to be for missile targeting, and an electro optical sensor under the nose, thought to be a combined TV/FLIR unit.

The Ka-29RLD is a radar picket development of the Ka-29 and features a large rotating radar mounted beneath the fuselage. The radar folds flat against the fuselage bottom for transit flight and stowage, and extends and rotates beneath the fuselage when operated. As on other Kamov helicopters, the undercarriage retracts upwards, so it doesn't interfere with the radar. The Ka-29RLD was first observed in 1988 when two were observed operating off the carrier *Admiral of the Fleet Kuznetsov*, although its present status is unclear.

Photo: The Ka-29 naval assault transport. (Kamov)

Kamov Ka-50 Werewolf

Country of origin: Russia

Type: Attack helicopter

Powerplants: Ka-50 – Two 1635kW (2190shp) Klimov TV3-117VK turboshafts, driving two three bladed counter rotating coaxial main rotors.

Performance: Ka-50 – Max speed 310km/h (167kt). Max vertical rate of climb from 8200ft 1970ft/min. Hovering ceiling out of ground effect 13,125ft. Combat radius estimated at 250km (135nm). Endurance with standard fuel 1hr 40min, endurance with auxiliary fuel 4hr.

Weights: Ka-50 – Normal takeoff 9800kg (21,605lb), max takeoff 10,800kg (23,810lb).

Dimensions: Ka-50 – Rotor diameter (each) 14.50m (47ft 7in), length overall rotors turning 16.00m (52ft 6in), height overall 4.93m (16ft 2in). Rotor disc area each 165.1m² (1777.4sq ft).

Accommodation: Pilot only in Ka-50, or crew of two in Ka-52.

Armament: One single barrel 30mm 2A42 gun on right side of the fuselage. Two hardpoints on each stubwing can carry a variety of weaponry, including up to 80 S-8 rockets in four packs, or 12 Vikhr (AT-12) tube launched laser guided air-to-surface missiles. Other options include gun pods and AAMs.

Operators: Russia

History: The Ka-50 Werewolf (or 'Hokum' in NATO parlance) is one of two attack helicopters (the other being the Mi-28) that were developed against a Russian Army requirement for a new close air support helicopter.

Design work on Kamov's first helicopter for the then Soviet Army began in 1977, and the first prototype Ka-50, the V.80, flew for the first time on July 27 1982. Characteristic of a Kamov helicopter, the Ka-50 features two counter rotating coaxial main rotors, which negates the need for a tail rotor and allows the construction of a simpler, more compact airframe. Unusually for an attack helicopter though, the Ka-50 is also a single seater, Kamov introducing some of the advanced autohover systems developed for its naval helicopters to reduce pilot workload. Another unique Ka-50 feature is the ejection seat – the main rotors are jettisoned before the pilots seat is ejected. More than 35% of the Ka-50's structure by weight is of composite materials.

The Ka-50 was reportedly selected in preference to the Mil Mi-38 in 1986, although in early 1994 new competitive evaluation trials between the two types began. Low rate series production began in early 1994.

The Russian Army has not been overly impressed with the heavy workload imposed on the pilot of the Ka-50 and so has sanctioned the development of a two seater with all weather, day and night capability, the Ka-52. The Ka-52 will be unique among dedicated attack helicopters in that it will seat two side by side. Approximately 85% of airframe remains unchanged from the Ka-50.

Kamov is actively marketing the Ka-50 on the world market and it may yet find its way into service with Middle Eastern or African nations who are attracted to its relatively low purchase price.

Photo: A Ka-50 with its weaponry on display. The wingtips of the stub wings house chaff and flare dispensers. (Jim Thorn)

Kawasaki C-1

Country of origin: Japan

Type: Tactical transport

Powerplants: Two 64.5kN (14,500lb) Pratt & Whitney JT8D-M-9 turbofans, licence built in Japan by Mitsubishi.

Performance: Max speed 805km/h (435kt), max cruising speed 704km/h (380kt), economical cruising speed 658km/h (355kt). Max initial rate of climb 3495ft/min. Takeoff run at max TO weight 640m (2100ft). Range with max fuel and a 2200kg (4500lb) payload 3355km (1810nm), range with a 7900kg (17,415lb) payload 1295km (700nm).

Weights: Empty equipped 24,300kg (53,570lb), max takeoff 45,000kg (99,205lb).

Dimensions: Wing span 30.60m (100ft 5in), length 29.00m (95ft 2in), height 9.99m (32ft 9in). Wing area 120.5m² (1297.1sq ft).

Accommodation: Flightcrew of four, comprising two pilots, flight engineer and navigator. Can carry up to 60 equipped troops, or 45 paratroops or 36 stretchers plus medical attendants.

Armament: None

Operators: Japan

History: Japan's first large jet powered transport was developed specifically for the Japan Air Self Defence Force (JASDF) to replace an ageing fleet of Curtiss C-46 Commandos.

The JASDF formulated its C-X specification for a Japanese developed tactical transport for its C-46 replacement requirement. NAMC, a consortium of Japanese aerospace companies which had developed the YS-11 turboprop powered airliner, began work on the C-X in 1966. Kawasaki was responsible for the construction of the first three prototype XC-1 aircraft (one was a static test article) and the first of these flew for the first time on November 12 1970.

Kawasaki subsequently assumed overall responsibility for the C-1, although the construction remained a collaborative venture. Fuji built the outer wings, Mitsubishi the centre and rear fuselage and tail, Nihon the control surfaces and engine pods. Kawasaki built the forward fuselage and the wing centre section, as well as being responsible for final assembly and flight testing.

Just 31 C-1s were built, including prototypes and two preproduction aircraft. The first C-1 production delivery to the JASDF was in February 1974, while the last production aircraft was delivered in 1981.

The C-1 is of conventional military freighter configuration, with a T tail, rear loading freight ramp and a high wing that does not obstruct the fuselage. Power is supplied by Mitsubishi licence built JT8D turbofans. The last five production C-1s had an additional fuel tank in the wing centre section.

The C-1 was not developed beyond its basic form and no export sales were sought. Two notable C-1 conversions though are the C-1Kai and the Asuka STOL research platform. The C-1Kai is an one-off ECM trainer and features flat bulbous nose and tail radomes, plus various antennae underneath the fuselage. The Asuka was fitted with four above wing turbofans and blown flaps.

Photo: The Japan Air Self Defence Force operates two squadrons of C-1 transports.

Kawasaki T-4

Country of origin: Japan

Type: Two seat advanced jet trainer

Powerplants: Two 16.3kN (3660lb) Ishikawajima-Harima F3-IHI-30 turbofans.

Performance: Max speed at altitude 956km/h (516kt), max speed at sea level 1038km/h (560kt), cruising speed 797km/h (430kt). Max initial rate of climb 10,000ft/min. Service ceiling 50,000ft. Ferry range with drop tanks 1760km (900nm), range with standard fuel 1295km (700nm).

Weights: Empty 3700kg (8157lb), max takeoff 7500kg (16,535lb).

Dimensions: Wing span 9.94m (32ft 8in), length 13.00m (42ft 8in), height 4.60m (15ft 1in). Wing area 21.0m² (226.1sq ft).

Accommodation: Student and instructor in tandem.

Armament: Usually none, although theoretically could carry up to 2000kg (4410lb) of external ordnance. Two underwing pylons designed to carry fuel tanks.

Operators: Japan

History: Very similar in overall configuration to the Alpha Jet, The T-4 is Japan's new intermediate and advanced pilot trainer, and has replaced the Fuji T-1 and Lockheed T-33 in service.

With Japan looking increasingly to its own industry to meet its requirements for military aircraft, Kawasaki headed up a design team of various Japanese aerospace companies to develop a new advanced trainer from the early 1980s. Kawasaki was selected as the prime contractor to develop the new trainer in September 1981. The T-4 was designed by a team led by Kohki Isozaki. Four XT-4 prototypes were built, and the first of these first flew on July 29 1985.

The T-4 features as much Japanese content as possible, including the engines, locally designed and built Ishikawajima-Harima turbofans. Other design features are the high mounted wing with dogtooth leading edges and a single hardpoint each for drop tanks, stepped tandem cockpits with excellent visibility from the rear seats, Japanese ejection seats and a small rear baggage compartment for liaison duties. A centreline hardpoint beneath the fuselage can carry a target towing winch, an air sampling pod or an ECM pod, reflecting the T-4's the secondary utility roles.

Construction of the T-4 is a collaborative venture. Fuji constructs the rear fuselage, wings and tail unit, while Mitsubishi builds the centre fuselage including the air intakes. Fuji and Mitsubishi each have a 30% share of the T-4 construction program. Kawasaki builds the forward fuselage, as well as being responsible for final assembly and flight testing.

The Japanese Air Self Defence Force has a requirement for 200 T-4s to replace ageing Fuji T-1s and Lockheed T-33s, and slotting beneath the Mitsubishi T-2. Construction of production T-4s began in 1986 while production deliveries began in late 1988. Aside from training units, a small number serve with operational squadrons as liaison/hack aircraft, and a small number of these wear camouflage. A developed version may be procured to replace the T-2.

Photo: The Kawasaki T-4 is now the JASDF's primary intermediate and advanced trainer. (MAP)

Learjet 35, 36 & C-21

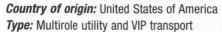

Country of origin: United States of America

Type: Multirole utility and VIP transport

Powerplants: Two 15.6kN (3500lb) Garrett TFE731-2-2B turbofans.

Performance: 35A/36A – Max speed 872km/h (471kt), max cruising speed 852km/h (460kt), econ cruising speed 774km/h (418kt). Max initial rate of climb 4350ft/min. Service ceiling 41,000ft. Range with four passengers and max fuel 4070km (2195nm) for 35A; 4673km (2522nm) for 36A.

Weights: 35A/36A – Empty equipped 4590kg (10,119lb), max take-off weight 8300kg (18,300lb).

Dimensions: 35/36 – Span over tip tanks 12.04m (39ft 6in), length 14.83m (48ft 8in), height 3.73m (12ft 3in). Wing area 23.5m² (253.3sq ft).

Accommodation: Flightcrew of two. Seating for up to eight in main cabin in 35 and 31, or up to six in 36A. Can carry light freight.

Armament: None

Operators: Argentina, Bolivia, Brazil, Chile, Ecuador, Finland, Japan, Mexico, Peru, Saudi Arabia, Switzerland, Thailand, USA, Venezuela.

History: The Learjet series is one of the world's best known family of business jets, and serves widely with a number of military air arms as utility and VIP transports.

The original six to eight seat turbojet powered Learjet 23 first flew on October 7 1963. It was replaced by the Lear 24 in 1966, while the Learjet 25 introduced a 1.27m (4ft 2in) fuselage stretch allowing seating for up to eight passengers. The Learjet 28 and 29 Longhorns were based on the 25 but introduced a new increased span wing with drag reducing winglets.

The Learjet 35 and 36 are larger, turbofan powered developments of the initial Learjet models. The availability of the Garrett AiResearch TFE731 turbofan in the late 1960s led to the development of the stretched Learjet 35, which first flew on August 22 1973. The Learjet 36 is similar, but sacrifices seating capacity for range. The improved 35A and 36A appeared in 1976.

Further development of the 35 and 36 has resulted in the 31 which combines the 35/36's fuselage and powerplants with the wing of the Learjet 55.

A small number of Lear 24s and 25s survive in military service, although most military Lears are 35s and 36s. Around 200 are used for a variety of missions ranging from VIP transport, to photo survey and reconnaissance, light freight, staff transport, medevac, target towing and EW training.

The US Air Force and Air National Guard have taken delivery of a total of 85 Learjet 35As as the C-21. These are used as Operational Support Aircraft transporting priority freight and for medevac and staff transport.

Learjet has also marketed a range of military developments of the 35 and 36. The PC-35A maritime patrol aircraft is offered with a search radar, ESM, FLIR, MAD and sonobuoys; the RC-35A and RC-36A are reconnaissance platforms offered with a variety of sensors; while the UC-35A is a utility transport. Japan operates four modified U-36As for target towing, EW training and anti ship missile simulation.

Photo: A Swiss Learjet 35A. (Paul Merritt)

Let L 410 Turbolet

Country of origin: Czech Republic

Type: Light tactical & utility transport

Powerplants: 410 UVP-E – Two 560kW (751shp) Motorlet M 601 E turboprops, driving five bladed propellers.

Performance: 410 UVP-E – Max cruising speed 380km/h (205kt), economical cruising speed 365km/h (197kt). Max initial rate of climb 1420ft/min. Service ceiling 19,700ft. Takeoff run at max takeoff weight 445m (1460ft). Range with max fuel (including wingtip tanks) and a 920kg (2030lb) payload and reserves 1318km (707nm).

Weights: 410 UVP-E – Empty (without tip tanks) 4020kg (8662lb), max takeoff 6400kg (14,109lb).

Dimensions: 410 UVP-E – Wing span (with tip tanks) 19.98m (65ft 7in), length 14.42m (47ft 4in), height 5.83m (19ft 2in). Wing area 34.9m² (375.2sq ft).

Accommodation: Flightcrew of one or two. Standard seating for 15 at three abreast. Alternatively seats 12 paratroops and loadmaster. Can be configured for freight. Air ambulance version configured for six stretcher patients and six sitting passengers, either injured or medical attendants.

Armament: None.

Operators: Bulgaria, Czech Republic, Germany, Hungary, Latvia, Libya, Lithuania, Russia, Slovakia, Slovenia.

History: This very successful Czech commuter was first built in response to Soviet requirements for a commuter airliner, but has also seen military service with a number of Eastern European countries

Initial design studies of the original 15 seat L 410 began in 1966. The resulting design, named the Turbolet, was conventional, but was designed with operations from unprepared strips in mind. The powerplant chosen was the all new Czech designed Walter (now Motorlet) M 601, but this engine was not developed enough to power the prototypes and so Pratt & Whitney Canada PT6A-27s were fitted in their place. First flight occurred on April 16 1969 and series production began in 1970. Initial production L 410s were also powered by the PT6A and it was not until 1973 that production aircraft featured the M 601, these being known as the L 410M.

The L 410 was first superseded from 1979 by the L 410 UVP with a 0.47m (1ft 7in) fuselage stretch, M 601B engines and detail refinements. The UVP was in turn replaced by the UVP-E in which featured a reconfigured interior to allow seating for up to 19 passengers and M 601E powerplants. The UVP-E is the current production version.

The L 410 proved to be quite popular as a commuter, and over 1000 have been built. While most of those aircraft were delivered to Aeroflot and various east European state owned airlines, others were delivered for military use as a utility transport. Military duties include freight and troop transport, liaison and communications, and paradropping.

The L 420 is an improved civil variant with more powerful M 601F engines, higher weights and improved performance designed to meet western certification requirements. It first flew in November 1993.

Photo: A Czech Republic Air Force L 410. (Paul Merritt)

Lockheed T-33 Shooting Star

Country of origin: United States of America

Type: Advanced trainer, light attack, liaison aircraft & EW trainer

Powerplant: T-33A – One 24.0kN (5400lb) Allison J33-A-35 turbojet.

Performance: T-33A – Max speed 965km/h (520kt), cruising speed 732km/h (395kt). Max initial rate of climb 4870ft/min. Service ceiling 48,000ft. Ferry range with tip tanks 2050km (1105nm), range with internal fuel 1650km (890nm).

Weights: T-33A – Empty equipped 3795kg (8365lb), max takeoff 6830kg (15,060lb).

Dimensions: T-33A – Wing span 11.85m (38ft 11in), length 11.51m (37ft 9in), height 3.55m (11ft 8in). Wing area 21.8m² (234.0sq ft).

Accommodation: Two in tandem. Pilot only in RT-33.

Armament: Can be fitted with two 12.7mm (0.50in) M-3 machine guns mounted in the nose. Can carry up to 910kg (2000lb) of external armament including bombs or rockets.

Operators: Bolivia, Canada, Ecuador, Greece, Guatemala, Iran, Japan, Mexico, Pakistan, Philippines, Sth Korea, Thailand, Turkey, Uruguay.

History: The T-33 is the most successful jet trainer in history, with more than 6000 built. More remarkable than that, significant numbers survive in service in the mid 1990s, more than 45 years after its first flight.

The T-33 is a development of the F-80 Shooting Star, the USAAF's first operational jet fighter. The T-33 arose from a USAF requirement for an advanced two seat jet trainer, which Lockheed was easily able to meet by stretching the F-80 and adding a second seat under a lengthened canopy. The first prototype, designated TF-80C, first flew on March 22 1948.

Subsequent Lockheed T-33 production between 1948 and 1959 amounted to 5771 aircraft. The largest T-33, or T-bird, operator was the USAF, while just under 700 modified examples were delivered to the US Navy as the TV-2 SeaStar (or T-33B from 1962). Several thousand T-birds were built under the auspices of the US's MAP (Military Assistance Program) and were delivered to friendly nations around the world.

Lockheed built variants of the T-33 included the AT-33, an armed close air support version delivered to various nations under MAP, and the RT-33, a single seat variant with various reconnaissance sensors in the nose. Limited numbers of AT-33s remain in service, while Thailand and the Philippines still operate RT-33s.

Aside from Lockheed the T-33 was also built under licence in Japan by Kawasaki (210 built) and in Canada. Canadair built 656 Rolls-Royce Nene powered CL-30 Silver Stars, designated CT-133 in Canadian Forces service. Around 60 CT-133s survive in CF service, used as EW aggressors, or for various test duties. Japan meanwhile remains the largest T-33 operator, with about 100 aircraft used for training, as hacks and for various liaison tasks.

The Skyfox was a substantially reworked and modernised development of the T-33 with two Garrett TFE731 turbofans designed by Skyfox in the USA. A demonstrator flew in 1983, although no customers were found.

Photo: A Canadian CT-133 EW trainer. (Canadian Forces)

Lockheed U-2

Country of origin: United States of America

Type: High altitude electronic and optical reconnaissance aircraft

Powerplant: U-2R – One 75.6kN (17,000lb) Pratt & Whitney J75-P-13B turbojet.

Performance: U-2R – Max cruising speed at 70,000ft over 690km/h (373kt). Max initial rate of climb 5000ft/min. Time to 65,000ft 35min. Operational ceiling 90,000ft. Max range over 4830km (2605nm). Max endurance 12hr.

Weights: U-2R – Empty weight without powerplant and underwing pods under 4355kg (10,000lb), operating empty approx 7030kg (15,500lb), max takeoff 18,735kg (41,300lb).

Dimensions: U-2R – Wing span 31.39m (103ft 0in), length 19.13m (62ft 9in), height 4.88m (16ft 0in). Wing area approx 92.9m² (1000sq ft).

Accommodation: Pilot only, except two in tandem in U-2RT.

Armament: None

Operators: USA

History: Perhaps the most famous spyplane in history, the U-2 remains an important part of the US's intelligence gathering capabilities.

In the early 1950s reconnaissance of the USSR was performed by modified B-36 and B-47 bombers, however these aircraft were increasingly successfully intercepted by MiG-15s. Thus in 1954 the US initiated development of a purpose built spyplane which could fly at extreme altitude where it would be hopefully immune to interception. Development was entrusted to Lockheed's Skunk Works, the nature of the black program being responsible for the U-2 designation (U for utility) to hide the aircraft's true role.

The U-2 first flew in August 1955. Subsequent production comprised 48 U-2A/B/C single seaters and five two seat U-2Ds. These aircraft had outstanding high altitude performance and good endurance despite payload restrictions and they were successfully used by the USAF and CIA for a number of years. One such CIA operated aircraft, piloted by Gary Powers, gained infamy when it was shot down by a SAM while operating over the USSR in April 1960.

The early U-2s were airframe hour limited, so Lockheed developed the larger U-2R. The U-2R first flew on August 28 1967 and 12 production aircraft were operated by the USAF and the CIA. The U-2R features a larger airframe than earlier models, allowing the carriage of more sensors and greater fuel capacity. Two seaters are designated U-2RT.

The U-2 line was reopened again in 1979, this time to build 37 new TR-1As (including two TR-1B and a U-2RT – both two seaters). The TR-1 was designed for tactical reconnaissance (hence the TR prefix), and combined the U-2R's airframe with the ASARS-2 battlefield surveillance radar. The TR-1s have since been redesignated U-2Rs in recognition of the fact that the two aircraft are basically identical. NASA operates three similar ER-2s.

U-2R sensors are carried in detachable noses, in the forward fuselage and in underwing pods, while some aircraft carry Senior Span satellite communications equipment for real time global data transmission in a teardrop shaped dorsal mounted pod.

From 1992 Lockheed has been re-engining the surviving U-2R fleet with a more powerful yet more efficient GE F101 turbofan.

Photo: U-2Rs are operated from Beale AFB in California. (Paul Merritt)

Lockheed C-130 Hercules

Country of origin: United States of America

Type: Tactical & multirole transport

Powerplants: C-130H – Four 3362kW (4508shp) Allison T56-A-15 turboprops, driving four bladed propellers.

Performance: C-130H – Max cruising speed 602km/h (325kt), economical cruising speed 555km/h (300kt). Max initial rate of climb 1900ft/min. Service ceiling 33,000ft. Takeoff run 1090m (3580ft). Range with max fuel including external tanks with a 7080kg (15,610lb) payload and reserves 7870km (4250nm), range with a 18,145kg (40,000lb) payload 2945km (1590nm).

Weights: C-130H – Operating empty 34,685kg (76,470lb), max normal takeoff 70,310kg (155,000lb), max overload takeoff 79,380kg (175,000lb). Max payload 19,355kg (42,675lb).

Dimensions: C-130H – Wing span 40.41m (132ft 7in), length 29.79m (97ft 9in), height 11.66m (38ft 3in). Wing area 162.1m² (1745.0sq ft).

Accommodation: Typical crew of five comprising two pilots, flight engineer, navigator and loadmaster. Standard layouts seat 92 troops, or 64 paratroops, or 74 stretcher patients and two medical attendants. Can carry light armoured vehicles, artillery pieces and 4WDs.

Armament: None, except on AC-130, described separately.

Operators: In service with over 60 countries including Algeria, Argentina, Australia, Brazil, Canada, Egypt, Indonesia, Israel, Japan, Morocco, Pakistan, Saudi Arabia, Taiwan, Thailand, Turkey, UK, USA.

History: With over 2200 built over four decades, the C-130 Hercules is the world's most successful and prolific postwar military transport.

The Hercules was developed against a 1951 US Air Force requirement for a new tactical transport to equip the Military Air Transport Service (MATS). The USAF ordered two YC-130 prototypes from Lockheed in July 1951 and the first of these flew for the first time on August 23 1954. The first production C-130A flew in April 1955.

The Hercules established the basic military transport configuration, with a high wing with minimal obstruction of the fuselage and a rear loading freight ramp. Other features included Allison T56 turboprops, pressurisation and limited STOL performance. Apart from the blunt, radar-less nose of early production C-130As, the Hercules's external configuration has remained largely unchanged.

The improved C-130B entered service in mid 1959. Compared with the C-130A, the B introduced more powerful engines driving four bladed props, strengthened undercarriage and greater fuel capacity. In 1961 production switched to the C-130E with more powerful engines with greater hot and high performance, increased max takeoff weight, some structural strengthening and larger external fuel tanks, mounted between the engines (rather than outboard of them). Most of the USAF's fleet of 400 plus Hercules are C-130Es.

The C-130H was first introduced in 1965. Early C-130Hs featured more powerful engines, while changes introduced to the H over the following 20 years include structural strengthening and updated avionics. The C-130H-30 is stretched by 4.57m (15ft), but is otherwise similar to the C-130H. Civil Hercules are designated L-100 and have been built in standard length L-100, stretched L-100-20 and further stretched L-100-30 (equivalent to the C-130H-30) versions.

Photo: One of Singapore's five C-130Hs. (Doug Mackay)

Lockheed Martin C-130J Hercules II

Country of origin: United States of America

Type: Tactical & multirole transport

Powerplants: Four 4475kW (6000shp) Allison AE 2100D3 turboprops rated at 3693kW (4591shp), driving six bladed propellers.

Performance: Max cruising speed 645km/h (348kt), economical cruising speed 628km/h (339kt). Max initial rate of climb 2100ft/min. Time to 20,000ft 14min. Max effort takeoff run 550m (1800ft), normal takeoff run 955m (3125ft). Range with a 18,155kg (40,000lb) payload 5250km (2835nm).

Weights: C-130J – Operating empty 32,615kg (71,902lb)..

Dimensions: Wing span 40.41m (132ft 7in), length 29.79m (97ft 9in), height 11.66m (38ft 3in). Wing area 162.1m² (1745.0sq ft). C-130J-30 – Same except length 34.37m (112ft 9in).

Accommodation: Flightcrew of two pilots, provision for flight engineer if required. C-130J can seat 92 troops, or 64 paratroops, or 74 stretcher patients and two medical attendants.

Armament: None

Operators: Australia*, UK*, USA*.

History: The C-130J Hercules II is the most comprehensive update of the Hercules airlifter yet, with changes to the cockpit, engines and systems.

Development of the private venture C-130J began primarily to offer the US Air Force a replacement for its ageing fleet of C-130E Hercules. The USAF was unprepared to fund the development of a new Hercules variant and so began procuring new build C-130Hs instead. This spurred Lockheed to developing an improved C-130 as a private venture, aimed at both USAF and export requirements.

The driving requirement behind the C-130J was to keep operation and acquisition costs as low as possible. Lockheed has worked to reduce assembly costs, adopting a modular assembly process, and has also kept pressure on its suppliers (who also have a financial stake in the program through funding the development of their own products for the C-130J) to keep costs down.

The C-130J and stretched C-130J-30 airframes differ little from their predecessor C-130H and C-130H-30 donors. The J features composite flaps and leading edge surfaces, and the external fuel tanks are deleted (although they can be added to extend range), but the airframe is otherwise unchanged. The engines though are new generation Allison AE 2100 turboprops, a development of the T406 turboshaft which powers the V-22 Osprey, and drive six blade, swept Dowty propellers. The J can be optionally fitted with a refuelling probe and underwing air-to-air refuelling pods.

Inside the Hercules II simplified wiring and systems reduce acquisition and operating costs. Some of the biggest savings though come from the new two crew cockpit. The cockpit will be amongst the most modern of any aircraft, military or civil, with two HUDS, four large multifunction displays, five monochrome displays and fighter style controls on the control columns.

The first of five development C-130Js (two C-130Js for the USAF and three C-130J-30s for the RAF) rolled out in October 1995. At late 1995 the USAF had ordered two Js for evaluation, the UK 25 C-130J-30s to replace C-130Ks, and Australia 12 C-130J-30s.

Photo: The first C-130J-30 Hercules II for the RAF. (Lockheed)

Lockheed C-130 Special Mission Variants

Country of origin: United States of America

Type: Special mission adaptations of the C-130 Hercules

Powerplants: MC-130E – Four 3020kW (4050shp) Allison T56-A-7 turboprops, driving four bladed propellers. AC-130H – Four 3362kW (4508shp) T56-A-15s.

Performance: MC-130E – Max speed 590km/h (318kt). Max initial rate of climb 1600ft/min. Range 3705km (2000nm). AC-130H – Max speed 612km/h (330kt), cruising speed 592km/h (320kt). Max initial rate of climb 1830ft/min. Endurance 5hr.

Weights: MC-130E – Empty 33,065kg (72,882lb), max takeoff 70,310kg (155,000lb). AC-130H – Empty 33,065kg (72,892lb), max takeoff 70,310kg (155,000lb).

Dimensions: Wing span 40.41m (132ft 7in), length 29.79m (97ft 9in), height 11.66m (38ft 3in). Wing area 162.1m² (1745.0sq ft).

Accommodation: Flightcrew of four.

Armament: AC-130H – Armament mounted in the left side of the fuselage comprises two M61 Vulcan 20mm, two 7.62mm miniguns (not usually carried), two 40mm Bofors cannon and a 105mm Howitzer.

Operators: Special Mission – USA. KC-130 – Argentina, Brazil, Canada, Indonesia, Israel, Saudi Arabia, Singapore, Spain, UK, USA.

History: The versatility and longevity of the basic Hercules airframe is reflected in the multitude of special mission adaptations.

The USAF began modification work on a C-130A to gunship configuration in 1965. A further 17 were modified to AC-130As (equipment fit including two 7.62mm miniguns, two 20mm cannon and two 40mm Bofors cannon, plus a beacon tracker and radar), and their combat success in Vietnam led to the procurement of 11 similar AC-130Es. From 1973 the 10 survivors were upgraded to AC-130H standard with T56-A-15s, and then subsequently fitted with a 105mm Howitzer. The latest Spectre variant is the Rockwell AC-130U with modern sensors and a 25mm GAU-12 cannon in place of the M61s.

The US Navy operates three drone carrying DC-130s, while the USAF operates a similar NC-130H. The EC-130 designation covers a number of EW Hercules adaptations. EC-130E variants include the ABCCC (Airborne Command & Control Centre); the Elint EC-130E(CL); and the EC-130E(RR) 'Rivet Rider', which apart from Comint and Sigint, can be used for TV and radio broadcasts. The EC-130H Compass Call is a standoff jammer.

The HC-130 designation covers USAF SAR aircraft. 43 HC-130Hs were delivered with the ARD-117 Cook Aerial Tracker in a blunt radome. The HC-130N is similar but equipped for inflight refuelling (hose & drogue). New build HC-130H(N)s have modern avionics and systems.

KC-130 tankers are in service with a number of nations, although the USMC is the largest operator, with KC-130Fs, KC-130Rs, KC-130Ts and stretched KC-130T-30s. Ski equipped US Navy LC-130s are used for Antarctic support operations.

Finally the USAF's MC-130 Combat Talons are used in support of special forces operations. MC-130Es are fitted with a weather/nav radar with a terrain following function in a blunt nose, STAR nose forks, and a retractable FLIR pod. The current MC-130H has a APQ-170 radar in a reprofiled nose.

Photo: A Fulton STAR personnel recovery system equipped MC-130E.

Lockheed C-141 Starlifter

Country of origin: United States of America

Type: Strategic transport

Powerplants: C-141B – Four 93.4kN (21,000lb) Pratt & Whitney TF33-P-7 turbofans.

Performance: C-141B – Max cruising speed at altitude 910km/h (492kt), economical cruising speed at altitude 795km/h (430kt). Max initial rate of climb 2920ft/min. Service ceiling 41,600ft. Takeoff distance to 50ft at MTOW 1770m (5800ft). Ferry range 10,280km (5550nm), range with max payload 4725km (2550nm).

Weights: C-141B – Operating empty 67,185kg (148,120lb), max takeoff 155,580kg (343,000lb).

Dimensions: C-141B – Wing span 48.74m (159ft 11in), length 51.29m (168ft 4in), height 11.96m (39ft 3in). Wing area 299.8m² (3228.0sq ft).

Accommodation: Flightcrew of four comprising two pilots, a flight engineer and navigator. Can be configured to seat 205 equipped troops, or 168 paratroops or 103 stretchers. Max payload 41,220kg (90,880lb). Can carry a variety of cargoes including five HMMWV 4WDs, or a single Sheridan tank, or 13 standard pallets.

Armament: None

Operators: USA

History: The C-141 Starlifter was the USA's first purpose designed jet powered strategic freighter, giving the US military the capability to airlift large amounts of equipment to a war zone in as short a time as possible.

The Starlifter was designed against Specific Operational Requirement 182 for a turbofan powered strategic freighter for the then Military Airlift Command. Lockheed was selected to develop the new airlifter ahead of Boeing, Douglas and General Dynamics. Lockheed's design took the basic cross section of the C-130 Hercules, combined with swept, high mounted wings with high lift devices for good field performance, four TF33 turbofans and a rear loading ramp.

The first C-141A flew for the first time on December 17 1963 (there was no C-141 prototype). Service entry was in 1965, replacing C-124s, C-97s and interim C-135s. 285 C-141As were built through to 1968.

The Starlifter was soon used for trans Pacific transport flights to Vietnam and the type has been used in support of almost every US military deployment since. In service though it was soon found that the C-141A cargo volume would easily be filled (or bulked out) without reaching the type's max payload limit, thus prompting development of the stretched C-141B.

The prototype YC-141B conversion flew for the first time on March 24 1977, and through to May 1982 271 Starlifters were converted to C-141B standard. Apart from the fuselage stretch the C-141B also gained an inflight refuelling receptacle above the flightdeck.

Apart from standard transport C-141Bs, the USAF also operates 13 C-141Bs equipped for special missions support, with defensive countermeasures and a retractable FLIR pod, while four short fuselage NC-141As are used for various test duties.

Photo: A C-141B in the old MAC grey and white scheme. (Bill Lines)

Lockheed Electra

Country of origin: United States of America

Type: Maritime patrol and transport aircraft

Powerplants: Four 2800kW (3750shp) Allison 501-D13 turboprops, driving four bladed propellers.

Performance: L-118C – Max speed 720km/h (390kt), max cruising speed 652km/h (352kt), economical cruising speed 602km/h (325kt). Service ceiling 27,000ft. Range with max payload 3450km (1910nm), with max fuel 4023km (2180nm).

Weights: L-118C – Operating empty 27,895kg (61,500lb), max take-off 52,664kg (116,000lb).

Dimensions: Wing span 30.18m (99ft 0in), length 31.90m (104ft 6in), height 10.01m (32ft 10in). Wing area 120.8m² (1300sq ft).

Accommodation: Flightcrew of two pilots and flight engineer. Max payload in freighter configuration is approximately 12 tonnes (26,000lb). Seating for up to 98 in passenger configuration.

Armament: None

Operators: Argentina, Bolivia, Honduras.

History: The Electra is one of the world's first turboprop airliners and ex civil examples have found their way into limited military service with Argentina, Bolivia and Honduras.

The Lockheed L-188 Electra resulted from an America Airlines requirement for a domestic short to medium range airliner. In June 1955 Lockheed was awarded an order for 35 such aircraft. Lockheed's design, designated the L-188, featured a low wing and four turboprops. By the time the first prototype flew on December 6 1957 it had gained 144 orders. However, any optimism Lockheed would have felt about a healthy sales future would have been short lived, the onset of the jet age and two mysterious crashes soon after the Electra had entered service contributing to the order book drying up.

As an interim measure following the crashes speed restrictions were imposed on Electras while the problem was resolved. Strengthened nacelles, nacelle mountings and a stronger wing structure overcame the problems, but it was not until 1961 that the speed restrictions were lifted.

Two basic versions of the Electra were built. The L-118A was the basic production aircraft and accounted for most Electra sales. The L-188C also entered service in 1959 and had more fuel and higher weights. From 1967 Lockheed converted 41 Electras to freighters or convertible freighter/passenger aircraft, fitting a strengthened floor and a large cargo door forward of the wing on the left side. Other companies have also converted Electras to freighters. In all 170 production Electras were built.

In the early 1980s the Argentine Navy acquired four L-118A Electras which it converted for maritime patrol, with the primary change being the installation of an APS-705 search radar in an under-fuselage radome. Subsequently Israel Aircraft Industries has converted one of these for Elint and Sigint reconnaissance. The Argentine Navy operates a further four Electra freighters. Bolivia and Honduras are the only other current military Electra operators, with a single example in service each.

Photo: One of the Argentine Navy's converted Electras.

Lockheed Martin P-3 Orion

Country of origin: United States of America

Type: Maritime patrol aircraft

Powerplants: P-3C – Four 3660kW (4910ehp) Allison T56-A-14 turboprops, driving four bladed propellers.

Performance: P-3C – Max speed 760km/h (411kt), economical cruising speed 608km/h (328kt), patrol speed at 1500ft 380km/h (206kt). Service ceiling 28,300ft. Ferry range 8945km (4830nm). Mission radius with 3hr on station at 1500ft 2495km (1345nm). Max endurance with four engines 12hr 20min, with two engines running 17hr 10min.

Weights: P-3C – Empty 27,890kg (61,490lb), max normal takeoff 61,235kg (135,000lb), max permissible weight 64,610kg (142,000lb).

Dimensions: P-3B/C – Wing span 30.37m (99ft 8in), length 35.61m (116ft 10in), height 10.27m (33ft 9in). Wing area 120.8m² (1300.0sq ft).

Accommodation: Normal crew complement of 10 comprises two pilots, flight engineer and navigator on flightdeck, with a tactical coordinator, two acoustic sensor operators, a MAD operator and two observers/sonobuoy loaders. Has seating/bunks for a relief crew.

Armament: Internal weapons bay can carry eight torpedoes or eight depth bombs. A total of 10 underwing hardpoints can carry up to eight AGM-86 Harpoons, or 10 torpedoes, or 10 mines.

Operators: Australia*, Chile, Greece, Iran, Japan, Netherlands, New Zealand, Norway, Portugal, South Korea, Spain, Thailand.

History: The Orion was developed against a 1957 US Navy requirement to replace the Lockheed P2V/SP-2 Neptune.

Lockheed's submission was based on a shortened Electra airliner and this aircraft was selected for development in April 1958. The first Orion prototype flew for the first time on November 25 1959.

Features of the Orion (which entered service in 1962) include a MAD mounted in a boom extending from the tail and an internal weapons bay forward of the wing. Initial production was of the P-3A, while the P-3B, with more powerful engines, was delivered from 1965.

The current P-3C was first introduced in 1969. While retaining the P-3B's engines and airframe, the C introduced a new radar (APS-115), MAD and processing equipment. The P-3C was built in progressively improved Update I, II, II.5 and III form, while Australian P-3Cs feature a British designed AQS-901 acoustic processing suite and carry locally developed Barra sonobuoys.

The US Navy also employs a number of special missions developments. The VP-3 is a VIP/staff transport conversion of early P-3A/Bs, the EP-3E 'Aries' is an Elint platform, the TP-3A is a crew trainer, the UP-3A a utility transport, WP-3As perform weather reconnaissance, RP-3As are designed for oceanographic reconnaissance and NP-3As are used for trials work. Two EP-3As and three RP-3As are used for range support work, while the EP-3J is an EW trainer.

Three significant Orion upgrades have all been cancelled or dropped for budgetary reasons – the Lockheed P-7, Boeing P-3C Update IV and the Lockheed P-3H. USN Orions are instead being fitted with a new radar (APS-134). Australia is upgrading its P-3Cs to AP-3C standard with new radar, MAD and processing equipment, while Lockheed Martin is now proposing the Orion 2000. Over 700 Orions have been built, including 100 under licence by Kawasaki in Japan.

Photo: One of eight P-3Cs recently delivered to South Korea.

Lockheed CP-140 Aurora & Arcturus

Country of origin: United States of America

Type: Maritime patrol aircraft

Powerplants: Four 3660kW (4910ehp) Allison T56-A-14 turboprops, driving four bladed propellers.

Performance: CP-140 – Max cruising speed 732km/h (395kt). Max initial rate of climb 2980ft/min. Service ceiling 28,250ft. Ferry range 8340km (4500nm). Operational radius for an 8hr 10min patrol 1850km (1000nm).

Weights: CP-140 – Empty 27,892kg (61,491lb), max permissible load 64,610kg (142,000lb).

Dimensions: Wing span 30.37m (99ft 8in), length 35.61m (116ft 10in), height 10.27m (33ft 9in). Wing area 120.8m² (1300.0sq ft).

Accommodation: Crew complement of 11, including flightcrew of four comprising two pilots, a flight engineer and navigator.

Armament: Theoretical armament as for P-3C, including eight torpedoes or eight depth bombs in internal weapons bay. A total of 10 underwing hardpoints can carry up to eight AGM-86 Harpoons, or 10 torpedoes, or 10 mines. Can be fitted with two AIM-9 Sidewinder AAMs for self defence.

Operators: Canada

History: The CP-140 Aurora is a unique development of the Orion which combines the P-3's airframe with the electronic systems of the US Navy S-3 Viking, while the CP-140A Arcturus is a down spec Aurora optimised specifically for training and fishery patrols.

In 1976 the Canadian Armed Forces ordered the Aurora to replace the CP-107 Argus. While the resulting aircraft closely resembles the P-3 Orion physically, internal changes have made the Aurora a significantly different aircraft. The Aurora was fitted with the Texas Instruments APS-116 search radar, a Texas Instruments ASQ-501 MAD and an AYK-10 processing computer, all equipment featured on the S-3A Viking (described separately). Other equipment allows the Aurora to fly a number of secondary missions including pollution patrol, aerial survey, shipping, fishing and Arctic surveillance and search and rescue. The Aurora also carries a crew of 11, rather than 10 on the Orion.

Canada ordered 18 Auroras and the first of these flew for the first time on March 22 1979. The last example was delivered in July 1981. They currently serve with four squadrons, three at CFB Greenwood and one at CFB Comox.

The CP-140A Arcturus is a stripped down development of the Aurora and has the twin roles of Aurora crew training (thus increasing the amount of actual patrol hours Auroras can fly, and increasing their service lives) and environmental, Arctic sovereignty and fishery patrols. The Arcturus feature no ASW equipment, but are fitted with APS-134 radar.

Canada ordered the three CP-140As in 1989. These were the last Orion family aircraft to be built at Lockheed's Burbank assembly line before production was transferred to Marietta, alongside the C-130. The final CP-140A was delivered in September 1991.

Photo: This CP-140 Aurora is flying low along the Australia coastline during its participation in an Australian/Canadian/NZ/UK Fincastle ASW exercise. (Bruce Homewood, 92WG RAAF)

Lockheed S-3 & ES-3 Viking

Country of origin: United States of America

Type: Carrier borne ASW aircraft

Powerplants: Two 41.3kN (9275lb) General Electric TF34-GE-2 turbofans.

Performance: S-3A – Max speed 815km/h (440kt), patrol speed at optimum altitude 295km/h (160kt). Max initial rate of climb 4200ft/min. Service ceiling 40,000ft. Max ferry range 6085km (3230nm), range with max payload 3705km (2000nm). Operational radius over 1750km (945nm). Endurance 7hr 30min.

Weights: S-3A – Empty 12,088kg (26,650lb), max takeoff 23,832kg (52,540lb).

Dimensions: Wing span 20.93m (68ft 8in), length 16.26m (53ft 4in), height 6.93m (22ft 9in). Wing area 55.6m² (598.0sq ft).

Accommodation: Crew complement of four, consisting of two pilots, a tactical coordinator and a sensor operator.

Armament: The internal weapons bay can house four torpedoes, or four Mk 36 destructors, or four Mk 82 bombs, or four Mk 53 Mines. Two underwing hardpoints can carry a torpedo each, or an AGM-84 Harpoon anti ship missile each (S-3B only), or rocket pods.

Operators: USA

History: The Viking was developed to replace the S-2 Tracker and in the face of increasingly difficult to detect Soviet missile submarines.

In 1967 the USN invited US manufacturers to submit designs for its consideration, with Convair, Grumman, McDonnell Douglas, North American Rockwell and Lockheed/Ling Temco Vought responding. In 1969 the USN selected Lockheed's proposal, and the first of eight service evaluation YS-3A aircraft flew for the first time on January 21 1972 (eight YS-3As were funded to expedite the aircraft's service entry).

Lockheed developed the Viking in cooperation with Vought, who was responsible for the design and manufacture of the aircraft's wings, tail unit, landing gear and engine nacelles. The S-3A Viking's design features a high wing, two turbofan engines, an internal weapons bay, seating for four crew, a Univac AYK-10 digital computer, Texas Instruments APS-116 search radar and a retractable FLIR pod. ASW systems comprise an extendable tail MAD boom and sonobuoys. The S-3A entered service in July 1974 and 187 were built.

Development of the improved S-3B was initiated in 1980. The S-3B gained an improved acoustic processing suite, expanded ESM coverage, better radar processing, a new sonobuoy receiver system and the ability to carry and fire the AGM-84 Harpoon anti ship missile. The first converted S-3B development aircraft flew in September 1984, and subsequently almost all S-3As were converted to S-3B configuration.

The USN also operates four US-3A Carrier Onboard Delivery (COD) aircraft, stripped of all ASW equipment. A single KS-3A dedicated tanker was evaluated, and while S-3As can buddy tank, no KS-3s were ordered.

The ES-3E first flew in 1991 and is an Elint variant which replaced the EA-3B Skywarrior, which was retired in 1987. The 16 ES-3As were converted from S-3As, and feature EW equipment in a dorsal fairing, a new radome, direction finding antenna and an array of antennae beneath the fuselage.

Photos: A Viking with hook, gear and flaps down moments before recovery aboard its carrier. (Wally Civitico)

Lockheed F-104 Starfighter

Country of origin: United States of America

Type: Multirole fighter

Powerplant: F-104ASA – One 52.8kN (11,870lb) dry and 79.6kN (17,900lb) with afterburning General Electric J79-GE-19 turbojet.

Performance: F-104ASA – Max speed at 36,000ft Mach 2.2 or 2333km/h (1260kt), max speed at sea level 1465km/h (790kt), max cruising speed at 36,000ft 980km/h (530kt). Max initial rate of climb 55,000ft. Service ceiling 58,000ft. Ferry range with drop tanks 2920km (1575nm), combat radius with max fuel 1247km (673nm).

Weights: F-104ASA – Empty 6760kg (14,903lb), max takeoff 14,060kg (30,995lb).

Dimensions: F-104ASA – Wing span without tip tanks 6.68m (21ft 11in), length 16.69m (54ft 9in), height 4.11m (13ft 6in). Wing area 18.2m² (196.1sq ft).

Accommodation: Pilot only, or two in tandem in TF-104.

Armament: F-104ASA – One 20mm T171ES Vulcan six barrel cannon. Can carry up to 3400kg (7495lb) of ordnance including AIM-9L Sidewinders, Selenia Aspide medium range AAMs, conventional bombs and rockets.

Operators: Italy, Taiwan, Turkey.

History: The controversial Starfighter was intended as a day fighter, but grew into a capable fighter bomber, with 2406 built.

Lockheed's Kelly Johnson and the company's Skunk Works began work on the F-104 in 1952 after evaluating the experiences of American fighter pilots in Korea. In designing the new fighter performance was considered the overriding factor, with a small size and powerful single engine allowing Mach 2 performance in an aircraft that defied the trends for greater complexity, weight and hence cost.

The resulting aircraft was quite remarkable in that it featured incredibly small, straight wings (only 10cm/4in deep at its thickest point) with blown flaps and a single J79 turbojet engine (the most advanced engine of the day) giving a max speed of Mach 2.2.

The XF-104 prototype flew for the first time on February 7 1954 powered by a Wright XJ65 (Sapphire) turbojet. Service entry was in 1958, although the USAF had transferred the survivors of its F-104A/B/C/D fleet to the Air National Guard by 1968. USAF experience with the F-104 was less than favourable, with high attrition.

The F-104 gained a new lease of life with the F-104G, which was redesigned as a fighter bomber. The F-104G first flew on February 17 1956 and introduced a more powerful engine and a multirole nav/attack system. In what was termed the 'Sale of the Century' the F-104G was selected in 1959 by Belgium, Germany, Italy and the Netherlands for a joint production program. Germany was the largest customer, taking delivery of 750, although attrition was very high. The F-104G was also built under licence in Japan as the F-104J and in Canada as the CF-104G. Taiwan flies recce RF-104 'Stargazers'.

Aeritalia (now Alenia) in Italy built 246 (including 40 for Turkey) AIM-7 Sparrow capable F-104S Starfighters through to 1979. As the F-104ASA Italian aircraft were further upgraded with FIAR Setter radar and Selenia Aspide compatibility. Around 180 survivors will remain in service until the arrival of the EF 2000.

Photo: A Turkish Air Force F-104S. (Paul Merritt)

Lockheed SR-71

Country of origin: United States of America

Type: High speed & high altitude reconnaissance platform

Powerplants: Two 145.6kN (32,500lb) with afterburning Pratt & Whitney J58-1 continuous bleed turbojets.

Performance: SR-71A (estimated) – Max speed over Mach 3, or approximately 3220km/h (1735kt) at high altitude. Operating ceiling above 80,000ft. Approximate range at Mach 3 and 79,000ft 4830km (2605nm). Max endurance at Mach 3 1hr 30min.

Weights: SR-71A (estimated) – Empty 27,215kg (60,000lb), max takeoff 77,110kg (170,000lb).

Dimensions: Wing span 16.95m (55ft 7in), length 37.74m (107ft 5in), height 5.64m (18ft 6in).

Accommodation: Crew of two, pilot and reconnaissance systems operator in tandem in SR-71A. The SR-71B trainer seats two in tandem, with the second cockpit raised behind the first.

Armament: None

Operators: USA

History: The incredible SR-71 'Blackbird' is the pinnacle of aircraft performance, it flies faster than any other production aircraft and is able to cruise at a sustained Mach 3.0.

The SR-71 program began life in 1959 as the A-12, a CIA sponsored program to develop a high speed high flying reconnaissance platform to supplement the U-2. The A-12 was developed in complete secrecy by Lockheed's Skunk Works under the stewardship of Kelly Johnson. It flew for the first time on April 26 1962 powered by interim J75 turbojets (less than three years after program go-ahead). Some 18 A-12s were built for reconnaissance, and these aircraft could also carry the Lockheed GTD-21 drone (they were retired in 1968).

The A-12 also served as the basis for the F-12, a high speed interceptor intended for the defence of continental US airspace. Three A-12s served as YF-12As, although production of the F-12B was not funded due to cost.

The definitive SR-71 has a longer fuselage than the A-12, and first flew on December 22 1964. Thirty one SR-71s (including three SR-71B two seaters) were built, and served with the 9th Strategic Reconnaissance Wing at Beale AFB in California through to 1990.

The SR-71 was initially withdrawn from service in 1990 due to budget constraints (and rumoured introduction of the Aurora successor) and their reconnaissance role was handed to satellites. However three aircraft (including an SR-71B) were transferred to NASA for research tasks.

In 1995 the SR-71 was reactivated to plug the gap in US reconnaissance capabilities left by its premature retirement. Two SR-71As (one reactivated from storage, the other transferred back from NASA) returned to USAF service in 1995, with pilot conversion training performed on NASA's SR-71B.

The secret to the SR-71's high performance lies in its aerodynamic design, titanium construction and the J58 engine installation. At high speed more thrust is produced by the suction at the intakes and from the ejector nozzles than from the engines themselves.

Photo: The SR-71 gained its Blackbird nickname from its black finish.

Lockheed C-5 Galaxy

Country of origin: United States of America

Type: Heavylift strategic freighter

Powerplants: C-5B – Four 191.3kN (43,000lb) General Electric TF39-GE-1C turbofans.

Performance: C-5B – Max speed 920km/h (496kt), max cruising speed at 25,000ft 890 to 910km/h (460 to 480kt). Max initial rate of climb 1725ft/min. Service ceiling at 278,960kg (615,000lb) AUW 35,750ft. Takeoff distance to 50ft at MTOW 2985m (9800ft). Range with max fuel 10,410km (5618nm), range with max payload 5525km (2982nm).

Weights: C-5B – Operating empty 169,643kg (374,000lb), max takeoff 379,655lb (837,000lb).

Dimensions: Wing span 67.88m (222ft 9in), length 75.54m (247ft 10in), height 19.85m (65ft 2in). Wing area 576.0m² (6200.0sq ft).

Accommodation: Crew complement of five comprising two pilots, a flight engineer and two loadmasters. Accommodation for 15 relief crew on upper deck rear of flightdeck. C-5 can accommodate up to 350 troops, with 75 on upper deck. Max payload on C-5B 118,385kg (261,000lb), can carry two M1A1 Abrams tanks, or one CH-47, or four Sheridan lights tanks and five HMMVW 4WDs, or 10 LAV 25s.

Armament: None

Operators: USA

History: The C-5 Galaxy was the world's largest aircraft for over a decade and was a remarkable engineering accomplishment.

The Galaxy was born out of the US Air Force's Cargo Experimental Heavy Logistics System (CX-HLS) requirement, which called for an enormous freighter (for the day) capable of airlifting payloads of 113,400kg (250,000lb) over 4830km (2605nm) without inflight refuelling. Boeing, McDonnell Douglas and Lockheed were awarded initial contracts for the airframe, while Pratt & Whitney and General Electric were awarded initial contracts to develop a suitable engine, something that would have to be substantially more powerful than anything then available.

In August 1965 GE's TF39 high bypass turbofan was selected, while Lockheed was selected as the C-5 prime contractor two months later. The Galaxy flew for the first time on June 30 1968 and entered service in December 1969, although cost overruns earned the C-5 the nickname FRED – Fantastic Ridiculous Economic Disaster.

Design features include the high wing, T tail, rear ramp and upward lifting nose freight door, allowing roll on, roll off loading and unloading. The Galaxy also features a complex four leg main undercarriage system, designed to allow operation from semi prepared runways.

In all, 81 C-5As were delivered between 1969 and 1973 (structural problems meant 77 C-5As were rewinged in the 1980s), while the production line was reopened in the early 1980s for 50 new build C-5Bs which were delivered between 1986 and 1989. The B differs little from the C-5A except it features simplified landing gear and an improved automatic flight control system. Two Galaxies modified for satellite carriage are designated C-5C, while Lockheed has offered the C-5D to meet future USAF airlift requirements. The C-5D would feature a modern two crew flightdeck and new engines among other changes.

Photo: A 'Proud Grey' painted Galaxy. (Keith Anderson)

Lockheed L-1011 TriStar

Country of origin: United States of America

Type: Strategic freighter and tanker

Powerplants: K.1 – Three 222.4kN (50,000lb) Rolls-Royce RB211-524B or -525B4 turbofans.

Performance: K.1 – Max cruising speed 964km/h (520kt), economical cruising speed 890km/h (480kt). Max initial rate of climb 2820ft/min. Service ceiling 43,000ft. Range with max pax payload 7785km (4200nm).

Weights: K.1 – Operating empty 110,165kg (242,684lb), max takeoff 244,955kg (540,000lb).

Dimensions: K.1/KC.1/C.2 – Wing span 50.09m (164ft 4in), length 50.05m (164ft 3in), height 16.87m (55ft 4in). Wing area 329.0m² (3540sq ft).

Accommodation: Flightcrew of three. Total fuel capacity in K.1 136,080kg (300,000lb).

Armament: None

Operators: Jordan, UK.

History: The TriStar was the second widebody commercial airliner to be launched and the UK has successfully adopted and modified it as a strategic tanker transport.

The L-1011 TriStar was Lockheed's last commercial airliner, and was launched in March 1968 in response to an American Airlines requirement (that also spawned the DC-10) for a large capacity medium range airliner. Lockheed initially studied a twin engined layout, but it was felt that three would be necessary to ensure it could takeoff at max weights from existing runways. Engine choice was Rolls-Royce's advanced three shaft design RB211, which after initial troubles (including bankrupting RR) eventually proved to be extremely reliable and efficient in service.

First flight was on November 16 1970 with service entry in 1972. The basic L-1011-1 was soon followed by a number of progressively improved models, the most significant being the destretched L-1011-500. The L-1011-500 was developed for long range missions and sacrificed seating capacity for range. The first L-1011-500 flew on October 16 1978 and entered service in May 1979. Only 50 L-1011-500s were built of a total TriStar production run of 250.

In the early 1980s the UK Ministry of Defence acquired six ex British Airways and three ex PanAm L-1011-500s for conversion into tanker transports. Marshall of Cambridge converted four of the BA aircraft to TriStar K.1s with extra fuel tanks in the cargo holds, a refuelling probe and twin retractable refuelling drogues mounted under the rear fuselage. The first K.1 conversion flew in July 1985.

Two K.1s and two additional L-1011-500s were converted to KC.1 configuration, gaining a forward freight door, structural strengthening of the main cabin door and a freight handling system allowing the carriage of palletised cargo and 35 passengers.

Two of the ex PanAm aircraft serve as C.2 troop transports without any refuelling capability, while the third is a C.2A, which is identical save for some military avionics and a new interior. All RAF TriStars have been fitted with radar warning receivers.

A single L-1011 equips Jordan's Royal Flight.

Photo: The RAF's nine TriStars equip No 216 Squadron. Pictured is a KC.1. (Paul Merritt)

Lockheed Martin F-16A Fighting Falcon

Country of origin: United States of America

Type: Multirole fighter

Powerplant: F-16A – One 65.3kN (14,670lb) dry and 106.0kN (23,830lb) with afterburning Pratt & Whitney F100-PW-100 turbofan.

Performance: F-16A – Max speed at 40,000ft over Mach 2.0 or 2125km/h (1145kt), at sea level 1472km/h (795kt). Max initial rate of climb over 50,000ft/min. Service ceiling above 50,000ft. Combat radius with six 1000lb bombs, hi-lo-hi 545km (295nm).

Weights: F-16A – Operating empty 6607kg (14,567lb), max takeoff 14,968kg (33,000lb).

Dimensions: F-16A – Span with AAMs 10.00m (32ft 10in), length 15.03m (49ft 4in), height 5.01m (16ft 5in). Wing area 28.9m² (300.0sq ft).

Accommodation: Pilot only, except two in tandem in F-16B.

Armament: One internal M61A1 Vulcan 20mm cannon. Six underwing, one centreline and two wingtip hardpoints can carry up to 5435kg (12,000lb) of ordnance. Options include AIM-9 Sidewinder or AIM-120 Amraam AAMs (can be mounted on wingtip pylons), bombs, rockets, AGM-65 Maverick ASMs and Penguin anti shipping missiles.

Operators: Belgium, Denmark, Egypt, Indonesia, Israel, Netherlands, Norway, Pakistan, Portugal, Singapore, Taiwan*, Thailand, USA, Venezuela.

History: The F-16 was conceived as a lightweight, highly agile and relatively inexpensive fighter.

The F-16 evolved from the USAF sponsored Lightweight Fighter (LWF) program to evaluate the concept of a small and manoeuvrable fighter. In April General Dynamics and Northrop were selected ahead of Boeing, LTV and Lockheed to build two prototypes each of their respective designs for a competitive fly-off. The first General Dynamics YF-16 first flew on January 20 1974, and after almost a year of evaluation against the twin engine Northrop YF-17 (forerunner to the F/A-18) the type was selected for further development. Eight development F-16As were then built, including two dual seat F-16Bs, while the first production F-16A flew in 1978.

The F-16 (or 'Viper' as it's nicknamed) was the first production fighter to feature fly-by-wire and relaxed stability. It also features wing/fuselage blending, a Westinghouse APG-66 radar, an advanced (for the time) cockpit with sidestick controller and a 30° reclined seat.

The USAF selected the F-16 for production in early 1975. Later that year Belgium, Denmark, the Netherlands and Norway jointly selected the F-16 to build under licence in Europe and replace their F-104Gs.

The inferior GE J79 turbojet powered F-16/79 was offered for export to secondary status nations until the full F100 powered F-16A was released for wider export. Production F-16As were built to Block 1, 5, 10 and 15 standard. Block 15 introduced the most noteworthy changes, including the extended horizontal stabilator and a track while scan mode for the radar. All USAF pre Block 15s are being retired.

The USAF also took delivery of 272 Block 15s converted to ADF (Air Defense Fighter) standard. The F-16A ADFs are interceptors assigned for air defence of US airspace and feature an upgraded radar, AIM-7 compatibility and a searchlight, and can be identified by their bulged fin/fuselage fairing. Apart from these, all other USAF F-16s are used primarily for ground attack.

Photo: Dutch F-16As are being upgraded under the MLU program.

Lockheed Martin F-16C Fighting Falcon

Country of origin: United States of America

Type: Multirole fighter

Powerplant: F-16C Blk 30/40 – One 122.8kN (27,600lb) with afterburning General Electric F110-GE-100 turbofan.

Performance: F-16C – Max speed at 40,000ft above Mach 2.0 or 2125km/h (1145kt), at sea level 1472km/h (795kt). Service ceiling above 50,000ft. Ferry range with drop tanks over 3890km (2100nm). Blk 40 radius with two AIM-9s, four 910kg/2000lb bombs and external fuel, hi-lo-lo-hi 630km (340nm). Blk 40 radius with two AIM-9s, two AIM-7s and external fuel with 2hr 10min CAP 370km (200nm).

Weights: F-16C Blk 30/40 – Empty 8665kg (19,100lb), max takeoff 19,190kg (42,300lb).

Dimensions: F-16C – Span with wingtip AAMs 10.00m (32ft 10in), length 15.03m (49ft 4in), height 5.01m (16ft 5in). Wing area 28.9m² (300.0sq ft).

Accommodation: Pilot only, or two in tandem in F-16D.

Armament: One internal M61A1 Vulcan 20mm cannon. Six underwing, one centreline and two wingtip hardpoints can carry up to 5435kg (12,000lb) of ordnance. Options include AIM-9 Sidewinder or AIM-120 Amraam AAMs (can be mounted on wingtip pylons), bombs, rockets, AGM-65 Maverick ASMs, Penguin anti shipping missiles, GBU-10 and GBU-12 laser guided bombs and on Block 50D/52D AGM-88 HARM anti radiation missiles.

Operators: Bahrain, Egypt, Greece, Israel, South Korea, Turkey, USA.

History: Various avionics, radar and cockpit changes mark the evolution of the F-16A into the more capable and heavier F-16C.

The F-16C first flew on June 19 1984. Changes to the F-16C came under the Multi Stage Improvement Program (MSIP), which aimed to increase the F-16's ground attack and all weather capabilities and introduce BVR missile compatibility. Initial production F-16C Block 25 introduced the F-16C's improved Westinghouse APG-68 radar (with increased range, more operating modes and better ECCM), an improved cockpit with a wide angle HUD, compatibility with AGM-65D and AIM-120 missiles and provision for future greater max takeoff weight. Externally the F-16C's fin base is extended forward, which made room for the since cancelled ALQ-165 jamming suite.

Subsequent F-16C/D Block Models comprise: the General Electric F110-GE-100 powered Block 30 and the PW F100-PW-220 powered Block 32; the GE powered Block 40 and PW powered Block 42 Night Falcon with upgraded APG-68(V) radar and compatibility with Lockheed Martin's LANTIRN (Low Altitude Navigation and Targeting InfraRed for Night) pods giving all weather navigation and attack capability with precision guided missions; the more powerful Improved Performance Engine (IPE) F110-GE-229 Block 50 and F100-PW-220 Block 52; and the Block 50D and 52D with AGM-88 HARM compatibility.

The F-16N designation applies to 26 Block 30s (including two seat TF-16Ns) modified for aggressor training for the US Navy. Changes include the deletion of the gun, an APG-66 radar and some structural strengthening. The two seat F-16ES (Enhanced Strike) with dorsal conformal fuel tanks was offered to Israel, but was not ordered.

F-16C licence assembly continues in South Korea and Turkey.

Photo: An F-16C Block 50D with HARM targeting sensor and missile.

Lockheed Martin F-16XL & F-16U

Country of origin: United States of America

Type: Multirole fighter

Powerplant: F-16XL – One 65.3kN (14,670lb) dry and 106.0kN (23,830lb) Pratt & Whitney F100-PW-100 turbofan, or one 122.8kN (27,600lb) afterburning General Electric F110-GE-100 turbofan.

Performance: F-16XL – Max speed at 36,000ft Mach 2.0 or 2125km/h (1145kt). Range over 4630km (2500nm).

Weights: F-16XL – Design mission takeoff 19,505kg (43,000lb), max takeoff 21,775kg (48,000lb).

Dimensions: F-16XL – Wing span 10.43m (34ft 3in), length 16.51m (54ft 2in), height 5.36m (17ft 7in). Wing area 61.6m² (663.0sq ft).

Accommodation: Pilot only, or two in tandem in two seaters.

Armament: One internal General Electric M61A1 Vulcan 20mm cannon. Total external ordnance of 6800kg (15,000lb) can be carried on two wingtip, underwing and centreline hardpoints. Weapons options on F-16E would have included AIM-9 Sidewinder and AIM-120 Amraam AAMs, AGM-65 Maverick ASMs, GBU-10 and GBU-12 laser guided bombs and conventional bombs.

Operators: None

History: The F-16XL and F-16U are rewinged and stretched developments of the basic F-16 fighter, intended to increase payload and range for long range strike missions.

The F-16XL started life as the SCAMP (Supersonic Cruise and Manoeuvring Prototype). The SCAMP was a research project intended to increase the F-16's load carrying abilities, range and penetration speed. Two full scale development F-16s were converted to SCAMPs, a single seater and a two seater. The conversion centred around a stretched fuselage and an enlarged cranked delta wing with 17 stores stations and no horizontal tailplane.

The first converted F-16XL flew on July 3 1982 (the single seater), the two seater (powered by the GE F110) flew in October that year. The F-16XL was evaluated against the F-15 to meet a USAF requirement for a long range strike fighter development of an aircraft already in service, although the F-15E Eagle was selected in 1984. If the F-16XL had been selected, the single seater would have been designated F-16E, the two seater F-16F. The two F-16XLs are now on strength with NASA where they are presently used for supersonic laminar flow testing.

The F-16XL showed considerable promise and would no doubt have been much less expensive than the F-15E. Lockheed Martin (Lockheed acquired General Dynamics Fort Worth in 1992) has recognised the F-16XL's potential and has produced a number of studies of similarly stretched F-16s fitted with an F-22 style wing. Such an F-16, Lockheed Martin says, would be able to perform most F/A-18E missions, yet cost two thirds less to acquire. The so configured F-16U was offered to meet a United Arab Emirates requirement for a long range strike fighter.

Other development F-16s include the AFTI/F-16 Advanced Fighter Technology Integration demonstrator, and the NF-16D VISTA Variable Stability Inflight Simulator Test Aircraft.

Photo: The single seat F-16XL SCAMP demonstrator.

Lockheed F-117 Night Hawk

Country of origin: United States of America

Type: Low observable precision strike fighter

Powerplants: Two 48.0kN (10,800lb) non afterburning General Electric F404-GE-F1D2 turbofans.

Performance: Max level speed 1040km/h (560kt), normal max operating speed Mach 0.9. Unrefuelled mission radius with a 2270kg (5000lb) weapon load 1055km (570nm).

Weights: Estimated empty 13,380kg (29,500lb), max takeoff 23,815kg (52,500lb).

Dimensions: Wing span 13.20m (43ft 4in), length overall 20.08m (65ft 11in), height overall 3.78m (12ft 5in). Wing area 84.8m² (913.0sq ft).

Accommodation: Pilot only.

Armament: Usually two 910kg/2000lb bombs, either BLU-109B low level laser guided bombs or GBU-10 or GBU-27 laser guided bombs, in internal weapons bay. Can also carry AGM-65 Maverick or AGM-88 HARM ASMs and AIM-9 Sidewinder AAMs. No provision for external stores carriage.

Operators: USA

History: Lockheed's 'Black Jet', the F-117 Night Hawk was designed in utmost secrecy from the ground up as a stealthy attack fighter.

Development of the F-117 traces back to the mid 1970s when the US Air Force awarded Lockheed's Advanced Development Company – 'Skunk Works' – a contract under the Have Blue program to develop an attack aircraft that would be very difficult to detect with radar. Two XST (Experimental Stealth Technology) Have Blue prototypes were built, and the first of these flew for the first time from Groom Lake in Nevada in December 1977. The two Have Blue demonstrators were powered by two small General Electric CJ610 turbojets and were similar in overall configuration to the ensuing F-117 except for inward canted tailplanes. Both XSTs had crashed by 1980.

Development of the operational F-117A began in November 1978 under the Senior Trend program, with the first of five preproduction F-117s flying for the first time on June 18 1981, while the first of an eventual 59 production F-117As was delivered in August 1982.

The F-117s were operated by the 4450 Tactical Group in complete secrecy at the remote Tonopah Test Range and all flights were undertaken at night. It was not until late 1988 that the veil of secrecy surrounding the F-117 was lifted when the US Department of Defense confirmed the aircraft's existence and the type began flying daylight missions. Today they equip they 37th Fighter Wing, based in New Mexico.

The F-117 uses a range of features to defeat radar and to remain undetected, or to be detected too late. Most obvious is the Night Hawk's faceted airframe construction and the avoidance of straight lines on doors and panels, so that radar energy is reflected in all directions. The airframe is also covered in a range of radar absorbent material (RAM) coatings. The two non afterburning F404 engines' gases mix with bypass air and exit through platypus exhausts to reduce the infrared signature.

Lockheed has also proposed the navalised F-117N 'Seahawk' to the US Navy to augment the F/A-18E.

Photo: The F-117A. These aircraft were used with devastating effect during the Gulf War in early 1991.

Lockheed Martin/Boeing F-22

Country of origin: United States of America

Type: Advanced tactical fighter

Powerplants: Two 155kN (35,000lb) class Pratt & Whitney F119-PW-100 afterburning turbofans.

Performance: YF-22 – Max speed at 30,000ft with afterburning Mach 1.7, max speed with supercruise Mach 1.58. Service ceiling 50,000ft. F-22A – Estimated max speed at sea level 1480km/h (800kt).

Weights: YF-22 – Empty more than 13,610kg (30,000lb), max takeoff 26,310kg (58,000lb). F-22A – Max takeoff approx 27,215kg (60,000lb).

Dimensions: YF-22 – Wing span 13.11m (43ft 0in), length 19.56m (64ft 2in), height 5.36m (64ft 2in). Wing area approx 78.0m² (840.0sq ft). F-22A – Wing span 13.56m (44ft 6in), length 18.92m (62ft 1in), height 5.00m (16ft 5in).

Accommodation: Pilot only, or two in tandem in F-22B.

Armament: Internal long barrel GE M61A1 Vulcan 20mm cannon. Two side weapons bays can carry two AIM-9 Sidewinders each. Ventral weapons bay can carry four AIM-120 Amraams or JDAM PGMs. Four underwing hardpoints can carry a variety of weaponry.

Operators: No production aircraft ordered at time of writing.

History: The next generation Lockheed/Boeing F-22 is destined to become the United States' premier fighter aircraft of the next century.

The F-22 resulted from the USAF's Advanced Tactical Fighter (ATF) program to develop a replacement for the F-15 Eagle. In October 1986 the USAF selected Lockheed and Northrop to build two proto-types each of their respective ATF designs for evaluation, allowing the subsequent selection of a single aircraft for full scale development. At the same time competing engines for the ATF from General Electric (YF120) and Pratt & Whitney (YF119) would be compared.

Lockheed teamed with General Dynamics and Boeing and their YF-22 flew for the first time on September 29 1990. The rival Northrop McDonnell Douglas YF-23 had earlier flown on August 27. The USAF announced its selection of the P&W F119 powered F-22 in April 1991.

Currently seven F-22As and two F-22B two seater development aircraft are funded, and the first of these is due to fly in mid 1996. The USAF now plans to acquire 442 F-22s, due to be funded from 1997. These will be delivered between 2000 and 2011, with an initial operational capability (IOC) planned for 2004.

The F-22 is designed to defeat all current and projected fighters in air-to-air combat (first look first kill), while it will have a secondary precision ground attack function with PGMs. The F-22 is designed to be extremely agile and has low observable (stealth) technology (in-cluding RAM and serrated edges on doors and panels) as an integral part of the design. The low bypass two shaft F119 engines give the F-22 a thrust to weight ratio of 1.4 to 1 and the aircraft can cruise at supersonic speeds without afterburner (supercruise) with the exhaust exiting through vectoring nozzles. The integrated avionics system featuring a Westinghouse developed low probability of intercept radar, a HUD and four LCD displays is designed to reduce pilot workload, allowing the pilot to concentrate on fighting rather than flying.

Photo: One of two YF-22 prototypes. Production F-22s will feature a revised configuration with a modified wing planform and with the intakes moved further aft.

LTV (Vought) A-7 Corsair II

Country of origin: United States of America

Type: Attack aircraft

Powerplant: A-7E – One 66.7kN (15,000lb) dry Allison TF41-A-2 turbofan (licence built Rolls-Royce Spey).

Performance: A-7E – Max speed 1112km/h (600kt), max speed at 5000ft 1102km/h (595kt). Ferry range with external fuel 4605km (2485nm), ferry range with max internal fuel 3670km (1980nm).

Weights: A-7E – Empty 8668kg (19,111lb), max takeoff 19,050kg (42,000lb).

Dimensions: A-7E – Wing span 11.80m (38ft 9in), span wings folded 7.24m (23ft 9in), length 14.06m (46ft 2in), height 4.90m (16ft 1in). Wing area 34.8m² (375sq ft).

Accommodation: Pilot only, or two in tandem in TA-7.

Armament: One M61A1 Vulcan 20mm cannon mounted in port side forward fuselage. Two side fuselage (AIM-9 compatible only) and six underwing hardpoints can carry a total ordnance load of over 6805kg (15,000lb). Weapon options include AIM-9 Sidewinders, bombs, laser guided bombs, AGM-65 Maverick ASMs and rockets.

Operators: Greece, Portugal, Thailand*, USA.

History: The A-7 Corsair is one of a select number of US Navy aircraft to be purchased by the US Air Force, and while it is no longer in frontline US service, it remains an important part of the inventories of Portugal and Greece.

The US Navy's 1963 VAL (light attack aircraft) specification aimed to find a 'light' attack aircraft with roughly twice the payload of the A-4 Skyhawk then in service for an in service date of 1967. Vought's proposal was selected ahead of those from North American, Douglas and Grumman, and seven development aircraft and 35 production A-7As were ordered on March 19 1964.

Vought's design, named Corsair II in honour of the WW2 F4U, was very similar in configuration to its F-8 Crusader fighter, however the A-7 was smaller and shorter, with fixed incidence wings, and only had subsonic performance. Power for the A-7A was supplied by a non afterburning 54.7kN (12,200lb) Pratt & Whitney TF30-P-8 turbofan. First flight was on September 27 1965, while production deliveries took place from October 1966.

It was also in 1966 that the USAF ordered its own version of the A-7 to fill a requirement for a tactical attack aircraft (a role usually perfor-med by superseded fighters). The USAF's A-7D introduced the Allison TF41 turbofan, a licence built development of the Rolls-Royce Spey. The USN's developed A-7E was also powered by the TF41. The USAF's mid 1980s A-7F close air support upgrade program was cancelled.

USAF and USN Corsairs were used widely during the Vietnam War, while US Navy Corsairs were again used in anger during the Gulf War. Both these services have now retired the A-7 from frontline service, although a small number survive with the USN on test duties.

The first Corsair II export customer was Greece, who ordered 60 A-7Hs and five TA-7Hs in the mid 1970s. The survivors can fire AGM-65 Maver-icks and are used primarily for anti shipping strike. Portugal's A-7Ps are refurbished TF30 powered A-7As, and were delivered from 1981.

Finally, Thailand is acquiring 18 ex USN A-7Es for its Navy.

Photo: A Portuguese TA-7P two seater. (Paul Merritt)

McDonnell Douglas A-4 Skyhawk

Country of origin: United States of America

Type: Light attack fighter and advanced two seat trainer (TA-4J).

Powerplant: A-4M – One 50kN (11,200lb) non afterburning Pratt & Whitney J52-P-408 turbojet.

Performance: A-4M – Max speed with a 1815kg (4000lb) bomb load 1038km/h (560kt), max speed at sea level 1100km/h (595kt). Max initial rate of climb 10,300ft/min. Service ceiling 38,700ft. Ferry range 3305km (1785nm), combat radius with a 1815kg (4000lb) bomb load 545km (295nm).

Weights: A-4M – Empty 4747kg (10,465lb), normal takeoff 11,115kg (24,500lb).

Dimensions: A-4M – Wing span 8.38m (27ft 6in), length 12.27m (40ft 4in), height 4.57m (15ft 0in). Wing area 24.2m² (260.0sq ft).

Accommodation: Pilot only, or two in tandem in TA-4.

Armament: Two 20mm Colt Mk 12 cannon in wing roots. A-4M max external ordnance of 4155kg (9155lb) can be carried on one centre-line and four underwing hardpoints. Weapon options include bombs, cluster bombs, AIM-9 Sidewinders, Bullpup and Maverick ASMs.

Operators: Argentina, Indonesia, Israel, Kuwait, Malaysia, New Zealand, Singapore, USA.

History: Affectionately dubbed the Scooter and Heinemann's Hot Rod, the A-4 Skyhawk enjoyed a three decade 2960 unit production run.

In the early 1950s Douglas had been working on its turboprop powered A2D Skyshark to replace the piston powered AD (A-1) Skyraider, but development was terminated due to problems with the powerplant. At the same time Douglas' Ed Heinemann had been working on a compact jet powered light attack aircraft and in early 1952 the US Navy ordered this aircraft for further development. The first of nine XA4D-1 development aircraft first flew on August 14 1954. Deliveries of production A4D-1s began in September 1956.

The Skyhawk's dimensions are such that it can fit on an aircraft carrier lift without the need for folding wings. Power for initial A-4A, A-4B and A-4C Skyhawks was from a Wright J65, a licence built Armstrong Siddeley Sapphire.

The A-4C was followed into USN service by the much improved A-4E, a heavier development powered by a Pratt & Whitney J52. The final Skyhawk for the US Navy was the A-4F, characterised by its dorsal avionics hump. The ultimate production Skyhawk was the A-4M Skyhawk II, which introduced a larger canopy for better pilot vision, a more powerful J52-P-408 and a max takeoff weight double that of initial A-4As. The A-4M was developed specifically for the US Marines. The M first flew in 1970 and remained in production until 1979.

Only two seat TA-4Fs used as advanced trainers survive in US service, although the Skyhawk has been widely exported. Argentina was the first, taking delivery of 50 A-4Ps (modified A-4Bs) in 1966, while more recently it has ordered ex US A-4Ms. Israel is also an important A-4 customer having ordered A-4E based A-4Hs and A-4M based A-4Ns. Malaysia operates modified ex USN A-4Es, while Singapore's A-4S is described separately. New Zealand's Kahu upgraded A-4Ks feature a HUD, HOTAS, two CRTs and an APG-66 radar, and AIM-9L, AGM-65 Maverick and laser guided bomb compatibility.

Photo: A New Zealand A-4K Skyhawk. (Bill Lines)

McDonnell Douglas F-4 Phantom II

Country of origin: United States of America

Type: Multirole fighter

Powerplants: F-4E – Two 52.5kN (11,810lb) dry and 79.6kN (17,900lb) with afterburning General Electric J79-GE-17A turbojets.

Performance: F-4E – Max speed at 36,000ft Mach 2.2 or 2390km/h (1290kt), cruising speed at MTOW 920km/h (495kt). Max initial rate of climb 61,400ft/min, air intercept mission rate of climb 49,800ft. Service ceiling 62,250ft. Ferry range 3185km (1720nm). Area intercept combat radius 1265km (683nm), defensive counter air combat radius 795km (430nm), interdiction combat radius 1145km (618nm).

Weights: F-4E – Empty 13,757kg (30,328lb), max takeoff 28,030kg (61,795lb).

Dimensions: F-4E – Wing span 11.77m (38ft 8in), length 19.20m (63ft 0in), height 5.02m (16ft 6in). Wing area 49.2m² (530.0sq ft).

Accommodation: Pilot and weapon system operator in tandem.

Armament: F-4E – One M61A1 20mm Vulcan cannon. One centreline and four underwing hardpoints can carry 7255kg (16,000lb) of ordnance including AIM-9 Sidewinder AAMs, bombs, rockets and laser guided bombs. Four AIM-7 Sparrows can be carried in semi recessed underfuselage stations.

Operators: Egypt, Germany, Greece, Iran, Israel, Japan, South Korea, Turkey, USA.

History: The most important western fighter of the postwar period, more than 5000 F-4 Phantoms were built between 1957 and 1981.

What became the Phantom began life as a private venture, the F3H naval strike fighter, which would have been powered by Wright J65s. In 1954 the US Navy issued a letter of intent for two F3Hs for evaluation as the AH-1, to be powered by General Electric's promising J79 turbojet. Later in 1955 the AH-1 was adapted to meet a Navy requirement for a fleet defence fighter, and with suitable changes the AH-1 became the F4H Phantom II. Development go-ahead was given in May 1955. Aside from the then advanced J79s, design characteristics included the upturned outer wings and anhedral on the horizontal tail.

The first prototype XF4H-1 made the type's first flight on May 27 1958, and it revealed performance levels far above anything then flying. Indeed Navy Phantoms set a series of speed, altitude and time to height records in the late 1950s and early 1960s.

Initial production was of the Navy's F-4B fleet defence fighter. In 1965 the US Air Force took the unprecedented step of ordering a USN fighter when it ordered the F-4C. Subsequent Navy and Marine Phantoms comprise the F-4J, F-4N and F-4S. These models, the USAF's F-4C and F-4Ds, and British Spey powered F-4Ks and F-4Ms have all been retired. Small numbers of F-4Ds survive with South Korea and Iran.

The definitive Phantom variant is the gun equipped F-4E. It first flew on August 7 1965 and almost 1500 were built. Israeli F-4Es are being upgraded to Kurnass 2000 status with improved avionics. Japan's F-4EJs were built under licence by Mitsubishi and 96 are being upgraded to F-4EJ Kai standard with a Westinghouse APG-66J radar. Meanwhile Germany's Improved Combat Efficiency (ICE) upgrade to its F-4Fs adds a Hughes APG-65 radar and AIM-120 Amraam compatibility.

Photo: A Japanese F-4EJ. Big, powerful and able to lift a large payload, F-4s have seen combat in Vietnam, the Middle East and the Gulf.

McDonnell Douglas RF-4 Phantom II

Country of origin: United States of America

Type: Tactical reconnaissance fighter

Powerplants: RF-4C – Two 48.5kN (10,900lb) dry and 75.6kN (17,000lb) with afterburning General Electric J79-GE-15 turbojets.

Performance: RF-4C – Max speed at 40,000ft 2348km/h (1267kt), max speed at sea level 1445km/h (780kt). Max initial rate of climb 48,000ft/min. Service ceiling 59,400ft. Ferry range with external fuel 2815km (1520nm). Combat radius 1355km (730nm).

Weights: RF-4C – Empty 12,825kg (28,275lb), max takeoff 26,308kg (58,000lb).

Dimensions: RF-4C – Wing span 11.77m (38ft 8in), length 19.17m (62ft 11in), height 5.03m (16ft 6in). Wing area 49.2m² (530.0sq ft).

Accommodation: Pilot and Reconnaissance Officer in tandem.

Armament: None, although max theoretical external load is 7255kg (16,000lb). Many RF-4s wired to carry two AIM-9s for self defence.

Operators: Germany, Greece, Japan, Israel, South Korea, Spain, Turkey, USA.

History: A number of factors made the F-4 Phantom suitable for conversion as a reconnaissance platform, including its speed (hence survivability), range and availability.

Development of the reconnaissance Phantom was done at the beckon of the US Air Force, who ordered the RF-4C in 1965 to replace its RF-101 Voodoos (also a McDonnell product). The RF-4C retained the basic airframe and systems of the F-4C fighter but introduced a lengthened nose containing an APQ-99 forward looking radar for mapping and terrain clearance plus an APQ-102 side looking radar and various optical cameras. Cameras to be fitted to RF-4Cs include the KS-72 and KS-87 forward looking oblique cameras, the KA-56A low altitude camera, the KA-55A high altitude panoramic camera and the 167cm (66in) focal length KS-127. Other systems fitted to the RF-4 include the ARN-101 digital navigation and reconnaissance system, infrared linescan cameras, Elint and ESM sensors.

The YRF-4C prototype first flew on August 9 1963, while production RF-4Cs were delivered from the following year. In all McDonnell built 505 RF-4C Phantoms for the USAF through to December 1973, and these have served widely including during the Vietnam and Gulf Wars. By 1995 however just two Air National Guard units operated the RF-4C and retirement was imminent with their role due to be taken over by pod equipped F-15s or F-16s. Surplus USAF RF-4Cs were supplied to Spain in the early 1970s and to South Korea from 1988, and the type looks set to remain in service with these nations for some years.

Similar to the RF-4C were the 46 RF-4Bs built for the US Marines from 1965. The survivors were retired in the early 1990s.

The export RF-4E was developed initially for Germany and flew for the first time in September 1970. Compared with the RF-4C, the RF-4E was based on the F-4E and did not feature some of the RF-4C's more sensitive systems. New build RF-4Es were delivered to Germany, Japan, Israel, Greece and Turkey (the latter two now also operate ex Luftwaffe RF-4Es). Israeli RF-4Es are fitted with indigenous sensors and avionics and can fire the Shafir and Python AAMs for self defence.

Photo: A Nevada ANG RF-4C Phantom. (Keith Anderson)

McDonnell Douglas F-4G Wild Weasel

Country of origin: United States of America

Type: Suppression of Enemy Air Defences (SEAD) aircraft

Powerplants: Two 52.5kN (11,810lb) dry and 79.6kN (17,900lb) with afterburning General Electric J79-GE-17A turbojets.

Performance: Max speed at 36,000ft Mach 2.2 or 2390km/h (1290kt), cruising speed at MTOW 920km/h (495kt). Service ceiling 62,250ft. Ferry range 3185km (1718nm). Combat radius 965km (520nm).

Weights: Empty equipped 13,300kg (29,320lb), max takeoff 28,300kg (62,390lb).

Dimensions: Wing span 11.77m (38ft 8in), length 19.20m (63ft 0in), height 5.02m (16ft 6in), Wing area 49.2m^2 (530.0sq ft).

Accommodation: Pilot and Weapon Systems Operator in tandem.

Armament: One centreline and four underwing hardpoints can carry 7255kg (16,000lb) of ordnance. Current typical fit is two AGM-88 HARM anti radiation missiles on inboard wing pylons. Can also carry AGM-45 Shrike anti radiation missiles and AGM-65 Maverick ASMs, plus two AIM-7s in rear underfuselage stations and AIM-9 Sidewinders for self defence.

Operators: USA

History: The F-4G Wild Weasel is designed to detect, locate, identify and destroy enemy radar, and hence is the USAF's only specialised SEAD (Suppression of Enemy Air Defences) aircraft.

During the course of the Vietnam War US tactical fighters encountered a growing threat from SA-2 SAMs. To counter this the USAF sponsored the development of optimised aircraft for anti radar attack – the Wild Weasels. Initially anti radar attacks were flown by Douglas EB-66s, then by modified F-100 Super Sabres and F-105 Thunderchiefs.

To replace these aircraft in the early 1970s the USAF ordered the development of an anti radar Phantom. By this time the multirole Phantom was well and truly established as the USAF's primary tactical fighter and had replaced a range of specialised fighters in roles ranging from air defence to ground attack to reconnaissance.

The initial Wild Weasel Phantoms were converted F-4Cs, carrying a Westinghouse ECM pod and AGM-45 Shrike missiles. These Phantoms were unofficially referred to as EF-4Cs.

The success of the F-4C Wild Weasels led the USAF to develop the definitive F-4G Wild Weasel IV (initially called Advanced Wild Weasel). The 116 F-4Es converted to F-4G standard from the mid 1970s had their M61 cannon removed (with that space now occupied by mission specific avionics) and were fitted with the McDonnell Douglas APR-38 RHAWS (components of which are installed in a fin tip fairing). Initially the F-4Gs were armed with the Shrike, however the HARM is now the Wild Weasel's standard offensive weapon (the G is currently the only aircraft that can utilise all of the HARM's operating modes).

The F-4G played an important part in Gulf War operations in early 1991, and their operations there staved off then imminent retirement. However in 1995 the F-4G's future was again uncertain and just two Air National Guard units operated the type.

Photo: The F-4G was highly successful in operations during the Gulf War, and played a pivotal part in early air operations. This one is armed with an AGM-88 HARM and fitted with an ECM pod. Note raised refuelling boom receptacle.

MDC/BAe AV-8B/GR.7 Harrier II

Countries of origin: United States of America and United Kingdom

Type: STOVL ground attack fighter

Powerplant: AV-8B – One 95.4kN (21,450lb) Rolls-Royce F402-RR-406A turbofan, or a 105.9kN (23,800lb) F402-RR-408 from 1990.

Performance: AV-8B – Max speed 1065km/h (575kt). Max initial rate of climb 14,715ft/min. Service ceiling over 50,000ft. Short takeoff run at MTOW 435m (1437ft). Ferry range with external fuel 3640km (1965nm). Combat radius from a STO with 12 500lb Mk 82 Snakeye bombs with a 1hr loiter 167km (90nm). Combat radius from a STO with seven Mk 82 Snakeye bombs and external fuel, hi-lo-hi 1100km (595nm). Endurance with two AIM-9 Sidewinders on a CAP 185km (100nm) from the carrier 3hr.

Weights: AV-8B – Operating empty 6336kg (13,968lb), max takeoff (with a STO) 14,060kg (31,000lb).

Dimensions: AV-8B – Wing span 9.25m (30ft 4in), length 14.12m (46ft 4in), height 3.55m (11ft 8in). Wing area with LEXes from 1990 22.6m^2 (243.4sq ft).

Accommodation: Pilot only, or two in tandem in TAV-8B and T.10.

Armament: AV-8B – One 25mm GAU-12/A Equaliser cannon in ventral pod. Max external stores load of 6003kg (13,235lb) can include AIM-9 Sidewinders, AGM-65 Mavericks and various bombs.

Operators: Italy, Spain, UK, USA.

History: Experience with the GR.3 and AV-8A Harriers proved beyond doubt the utility of this unique STOVL fighter, although at the same time illustrated its restrictive payload/range performance, thus providing the spur for the development of an enlarged derivative.

Hawker Siddeley (Now BAe) pulled out of initial Anglo/America development of the 'big wing' Harrier in 1975. Instead later that decade McDonnell Douglas (under a new collaborative agreement with Hawker Siddeley) began development of the Super Harrier for the US Marines, with a much larger supercritical wing with two additional underwing hardpoints. The new wing was flown for the first time on an AV-8A as the YA-V8B on November 9 1978. The raised cockpit was introduced on the first of four full scale development aircraft, the first of which flew on November 5 1981.

After a batch of 12 pilot production AV-8Bs were built, production AV-8Bs were delivered to the US Marines from early 1984. That same year the first full scale development GR.5 Harrier for the British RAF had its first flight. AV-8Bs and GR.5s differed only in that the British Harriers have two 25mm cannon, rather than one in the AV-8B.

Also in 1984 development work began on the AV-8B Night Attack for the US Marines, which differs in having a GEC FLIR mounted on the nose, a head down display and a colour moving map. Deliveries were from 1989. Similarly the RAF has upgraded all its aircraft to GR.7 standard, with a nose mounted FLIR for night attack.

The ultimate Harrier development is the AV-8B Plus, fitted with the multimode Hughes APG-65 radar giving AIM-120, AIM-7 and AGM-84 compatibility. Apart from 24 production aircraft, 114 AV-8Bs are being upgraded to plus standard.

The USMC has ordered a total of 280 AV-8Bs (including 24 TAV-8Bs), while the RAF has ordered 109 GR.5/GR.7s, including 13 T.10s.

Photo: One of two Italian Navy TAV-8Bs. (Julian Green)

McDonnell Douglas F-15 Eagle

Country of origin: United States of America

Type: Air superiority fighter

Powerplants: F-15C – Two 65.3kN (14,670lb) dry and 105.7kN (23,770lb) with afterburning Pratt & Whitney F100-PW-220 turbofans.

Performance: F-15C – Max level speed over Mach 2.5, or approx 2655km/h (1433kt). Max initial rate of climb over 50,000ft/min. Service ceiling 60,000ft. Ferry range with external fuel and conformal fuel tanks over 5745km (3100nm). Combat radius on an intercept mission 1965km (1060nm). Endurance with conformal fuel tanks 5hr 15min.

Weights: F-15C – Operating empty 12,793kg (28,600lb), max takeoff 30,845kg (68,000lb).

Dimensions: Wing span 13.05m (42ft 10in), length 19.43m (63ft 9in), height 5.63m (18ft 6in). Wing area 56.5m² (608.0sq ft).

Accommodation: Pilot only, or two in tandem in F-15B/D.

Armament: One M61A1 20mm Vulcan cannon. Can carry total external ordnance load of 7257kg (16,000lb). Typical CAP fit of four AIM-7 Sparrows on fuselage corner stations and two AIM-9 Sidewinder or AIM-120 Amraams on each wing pylon.

Operators: Japan, Israel, Saudi Arabia, USA.

History: Without doubt the pre-eminent air superiority fighter since the mid 1970s (backed by a 70+ to nil kill ratio), the F-15 Eagle's air-to-air abilities are only challenged by the Sukhoi Su-27.

Design work on a new fighter for the USAF first began in the mid 1960s, although the program gained fresh impetus later that decade when US spy satellites revealed the existence of the MiG-23 and the fast, high flying MiG-25. The FX requirement took in the hard learnt air combat lessons of Vietnam and called for a fighter with a thrust to weight ratio in excess of unity and that could out turn any potential adversary to bring its missiles to bear first.

McDonnell Douglas's design was chosen ahead of proposals from Fairchild-Republic and North American Rockwell, with the result that the first development F-15 Eagle took to the skies for the first time on July 27 1972. Design features of the F-15 include the specifically developed P&W F100 turbofans (selected ahead of a GE design), the Hughes APG-63 radar, a high wing of great area and then advanced cockpit displays, including a HUD.

The F-15 subsequently entered service in January 1976, and 355 F-15As and 57 two seat F-15Bs were built. Israel was the first F-15 export customer, and that nation's Eagles were the first to be used in combat. Production switched to the improved F-15C/D in 1979. Changes are minor but include the ability to carry the conformal fuel tanks (CFTs) on each fuselage side, uprated engines and improved radar. The C was exported to Israel and Saudi Arabia and Mitsubishi built it under licence in Japan as the F-15J. US F-15C/D production ceased in 1992 (622 built). Saudi and US F-15s flew extensive combat air patrols during the Gulf War in 1991, claiming 32 Iraqi aircraft without loss.

Both the F-15A and F-15C are being upgraded under the Multi Stage Improvement Program (MSIP) to feature the Hughes APG-70 radar, a colour CRT in the cockpit and AIM-120 compatibility. Once the F-22 is introduced into service next century its likely that surplus F-15s will be converted for the SEAD or Wild Weasel role.

Photo: An F-15C of the Kadena, Japan based 18th TFW. (Nick Sayer)

McDonnell Douglas F-15E Eagle

Country of origin: United States of America

Type: Long range strike fighter

Powerplants: F-15E (later aircraft) – Two 79.2kN (17,800lb) dry and 129.4kN (29,100lb) with afterburning Pratt & Whitney F100-PW-229 turbofans.

Performance: F-15E – Max speed at altitude Mach 2.5 or approx 2655km/h (1433kt), cruising speed 917km/h (495kt). Service ceiling 60,000ft. Max range 4445km (2400nm). Combat radius 1270km (685nm).

Weights: F-15E – Operating empty 14,515kg (32,000lb), max takeoff 36,740kg (81,000lb).

Dimensions: Wing span 13.05m (42ft 10in), length 19.43m (63ft 9in), height 5.63m (18ft 6in). Wing area 56.5m² (608.0sq ft).

Accommodation: Pilot and Weapon Systems Operator in tandem.

Armament: One M61A1 20mm Vulcan cannon. Max weapon load of 11,115kg (24,500lb). Options include AIM-9 Sidewinder, AIM-7 Sparrow and AIM-120 Amraam AAMs, GBU-10, GBU-12 and GBU-24 laser guided bombs, electro optically guided GBU-15 and powered AGM-130 bombs, conventional bombs, cluster munitions, B51 and B61 nuclear bombs and AGM-88 HARM (from 1996) and AGM-65 ASMs.

Operators: Israel (F-15I), Saudi Arabia (F-15S), USA.

History: While 'not a pound for air to ground' epitomised the role of the F-15A/C, the multirole F-15E was developed specifically to supplant the long ranging F-111 strike bomber.

McDonnell Douglas had long promoted the bomb carrying ability of the F-15, even though an official requirement for an air-to-ground capability was dropped in 1975. In the early 1980s the USAF had a requirement for a new multirole fighter the ETF (Enhanced Tactical Fighter) to supplement the F-111. The USAF selected a two seat development of the F-15, the F-15E, in preference to the General Dynamics F-16XL (an enlarged F-16 featuring a cranked delta wing) in February 1984. First flight was on December 11 1986.

Changes to the F-15E over the F-15D reflect not only the change in role but also advances in technology. Features include the APG-70 radar with synthetic aperture ground mapping, a wide angle HUD, three colour multi function CRTs in the front cockpit and four in the rear, permanent CFTs (conformal fuel tanks) fitted with tangential stores stations, more powerful F100-PW-229 engines (-220s in initial aircraft) and removable Martin Marietta (now Lockheed Martin) LANTIRN navigation and target designation pods. The AAQ-13 LANTIRN pod beneath the port intake comprises a wide angle FLIR and Texas Instruments terrain following radar. The AAQ-14 (underneath the starboard intake) features FLIR and a laser rangefinder/designator.

The last of 209 USAF F-15Es was delivered in mid 1994. Many saw extensive service during the Gulf War in 1991.

F-15E derivative production continues for Saudi Arabia and Israel. The Saudi F-15S features downgraded avionics, a simplified APG-70 without ground mapping and a Lockheed Martin Sharpshooter targeting pod in place of the AAQ-14. First flight was in June 1995 and 72 are on order. The 21 Israeli F-15Is to be delivered from mid 1997 will be generally similar to the F-15E. The single seat air-to-air F-15F has not been sold.

Photo: The F-15E has the nickname Beagle (Bomber Eagle). (MDC)

McDonnell Douglas F/A-18 Hornet

Country of origin: United States of America

Type: Multirole fighter

Powerplants: F/A-18C – Two 71.2kN (16,000lb) with afterburning General Electric F404-GE-400 turbofans, or since 1992 two 78.7kN (17,700lb) F404-GE-402 EPEs.

Performance: F/A-18C – Max speed over Mach 1.8 or approx 1915km/h (1033kt). Max initial rate of climb 45,000ft/min. Combat ceiling approx 50,000ft. Unrefuelled ferry range over 3335km (1800nm). Interdiction combat radius hi-lo-hi 537km (290nm), attack mission combat radius 1065km (575nm), combat radius on an air-to-air mission 740km (400nm). CAP endurance from an aircraft carrier 1hr 45min.

Weights: F/A-18C – Empty 10,810kg (23,832lb), max takeoff approx 25,400kg (56,000lb).

Dimensions: Wing span 11.43m (37ft 6in), length 17.07m (56ft 0in), height 4.66m (15ft 4in). Wing area 37.2m² (400.0sq ft).

Accommodation: Pilot only, or two in tandem in F/A-18B/D.

Armament: One M61A1 Vulcan 20mm cannon. F/A-18C can carry 7030kg (15,500lb) of ordnance, including AIM-9 Sidewinder, AIM-7 Sparrow and AIM-120 Amraam AAMs, AGM-65 Maverick ASMs, AGM-88 HARM anti radiation missiles, AGM-84 Harpoon anti ship missiles, bombs, cluster bombs, rockets and laser guided bombs.

Operators: Australia, Canada, Finland*, Kuwait, Malaysia*, Spain, Switzerland*, USA.

History: Designed for both air-to-air and air-to-ground missions, the multirole Hornet is a potent fighter and accurate attack aircraft.

In August 1974 the US Congress cancelled the US Navy's VFAX program for a new low cost lightweight multirole fighter, and instead recommended that the service should study developments of the General Dynamics YF-16 and Northrop YF-17 developed for the US Air Force. Neither of these companies had experience building carrier aircraft, so McDonnell Douglas teamed with Northrop to offer a developed F-17 while Vought teamed with GD.

McDonnell Douglas, with Northrop as a major associate (major contractor from 1985), was selected to develop its enlarged YF-17 proposal on May 2 1975. Initially the aircraft was to be built in F-18 fighter and ground attack A-18 versions, but the two roles were combined into the one airframe, resulting in the F/A-18 Hornet. The first of 11 development Hornets first flew on November 18 1978.

The F/A-18 is bigger and heavier than the YF-17. Features include fly-by-wire, an advanced cockpit with a HUD and HOTAS, a multi mode Hughes APG-65 radar, folding wingtips and two GE F404 turbofans.

The improved F/A-18C first flew in 1986. Changes include improved avionics, a new central computer and AIM-120 and AGM-65 compatibility. The US Marines operate Night Attack F/A-18C/Ds with NVG compatibility and carrying FLIR and laser designator pods. Marine F/A-18D two seaters have a dedicated mission capable rear cockpit with two large colour multi function displays and a colour moving map with no flight controls (although these can be added), while USMC F/A-18D(RC)s are wired to carry a reconnaissance pod. Uprated GE F404-GE-402 engines were introduced from 1992, the improved APG-73 radar from 1994.

Photo: A US Marines F/A-18C Night Attack Hornet. (MDC)

McDonnell Douglas F/A-18E Super Hornet

Country of origin: United States of America

Type: Multirole fighter

Powerplants: Two 98.0kN (22,000lb) approx with afterburning General Electric F414-GE-400 turbofans.

Performance: F/A-18E – Max level speed more than Mach 1.8 or approx 1915km/h (1033kt). Service ceiling 50,000ft. Required combat radius specification on a hi-lo-lo-hi interdiction mission with four 455kg/1000lb bombs, two AIM-9 Sidewinders and external fuel 720km (390nm). Fighter escort combat radius with two AIM-9s and two AIM-120s 760km (410nm). Maritime air superiority endurance with six AAMs and external fuel 280km (150nm) from the ship 2hr 15min.

Weights: F/A-18E – Design target empty weight 13,387kg (29,574lb), TO weight on an attack mission 29,937kg (66,000lb).

Dimensions: Span over missiles 13.62m (44ft 9in), length 18.31m (60ft 1in), height 4.88m (16ft 0in). Wing area 46.5m² (500.0sq ft).

Accommodation: Pilot only or two in tandem in F/A-18F and F/A-18C²W.

Armament: One M61A1 Vulcan 20mm cannon. 11 external hardpoints (three underwing, one centreline and two fuselage side) can carry 8050kg (17,750lb) of stores. Armaments would be similar to those carried on the F/A-18A/C.

Operators: USA*

History: The success of the multirole Hornet on US carrier decks meant development of an improved and heavier version was logical.

McDonnell Douglas proposed an enlarged Hornet as a successor for the cancelled General Dynamics/McDonnell Douglas A-12 Avenger II (which was to have been a stealthy successor to the A-6) in 1991. Official interest was such that in 1992 a $US3.8bn contract covering the development of the F/A-18E and two seat F/A-18F and the construction of seven development aircraft was signed on December 7 1992. The first of these aircraft was rolled out on September 18 1995 (when the Super Hornet name was adopted), with first flight on November 18 that year.

Compared with the F/A-18C the F/A-18E is significantly larger (and in fact is broadly comparable in size and weight to the F-4 Phantom – some distance from the F/A-18's lightweight beginnings). The fuselage is stretched 86cm (2ft 10in) while the wings are of the same layout but are 1.31m (4ft 4in) longer and 9.3m² (100.0sq ft) greater in area. The LEXes have been enlarged to retain the Hornet's excellent high alpha performance and the horizontal tails are bigger. The larger airframe substantially increases fuel capacity so much that range is increased by 40% over the F/A-18C. The engine intakes have also been redesigned to increase the airflow to the more powerful GE F414 engines (a development of the F404).

Internally the E's avionics suite is based on the F/A-18C's, including the APG-73 radar, although the cockpit has been improved to feature a large touch panel LCD display, a second LCD colour display and three monochrome displays.

The USN intends to acquire as many as 1000 F/A-18E/Fs, delivered from 1998. This number may be further boosted if the USN orders the McDonnell Douglas/Northrop Grumman proposed F/A-18C²W electronic warfare variant of the F/A-18F to replace the EA-6B Prowler.

Photo: The F/A-18E first flew on November 18.

McDonnell Douglas/BAe T-45 Goshawk

Countries of origin: United Kingdom and United States of America

Type: Advanced carrier-capable trainer.

Powerplant: T-45A – One 26.0kN (5845lb) Rolls-Royce Turboméca F405-RR-401 (navalised Adour).

Performance: T-45A – Max speed at 8000ft 1005km/h (543kt). Max initial rate of climb 8000ft/min. Time to 30,000ft clean 7min 40sec. Service ceiling 40,000ft. Ferry range with internal fuel 1532km (826nm).

Weights: T-45A – Empty 4460kg (9834lb), max takeoff 6387kg (14,081lb).

Dimensions: T-45A – Wing span 9.39m (30ft 10in), length incl nose probe 11.99m (39ft 4in), fuselage length 10.89m (35ft 9in), height 4.08m (13ft 5in). Wing area 17.7m² (190.1sq ft).

Accommodation: Two in tandem.

Armament: Usually none. One hardpoint under each wing can be used to carry practice bomb racks, rocket pods or fuel tanks.

Operators: USA

History: One of the rare instances where the US military has ordered a foreign aircraft, albeit heavily modified and built under licence in the USA, the T-45 Goshawk is a navalised carrier-capable variant of the British Aerospace Hawk (described separately).

The lengthy evolution of the basic Hawk into the Goshawk dates back to the late 1970s. The US Navy's VTXTS (later T45TS) program to find a replacement for both the TA-4J Skyhawk and T-2 Buckeye evaluated a number of aircraft including the BAe Hawk and the Dassault/Dornier Alpha Jet in 1978. This evaluation proved the Hawk's relatively economic operation and it was selected for development to tailor it to US Navy requirements in November 1981, with McDonnell Douglas as prime contractor and British Aerospace as principal subcontractor.

The redesign of the Hawk 60 to make it capable of carrier operations was fairly extensive, and involved strengthening of the airframe and undercarriage with a twin wheel nose gear that retracts into a slightly enlarged forward fuselage, adding a tail arrester hook, two side mounted airbrakes, a ventral fin and US Navy standard cockpit displays and radios. The crew sit on two Martin-Baker Mk 14 NACES ejection seats. The Hawk's Adour turbofan has been modified for operations from carriers and under the US system is designated F405.

The first full scale development T-45 first flew on April 16 1988. Deliveries were originally planned for 1989, but this was delayed when the USN requested further changes to the airframe and engine. Production aircraft were delivered from January 1992. These aircraft are built at St Louis, while BAe builds the wings, centre and rear fuselage, tail, canopy and flying controls.

From the 73rd production aircraft in 1997 the Goshawk will be fitted with the 'Cockpit 21' glass cockpit, with two Elbit multi function displays in each cockpit. Another possible future change is the substitution of the Adour with the AlliedSignal F124 turbofan, although this proposal had no official support at the time of writing.

The US Navy plans to acquire 268 production T-45As, 42% fewer aircraft than currently used for advanced training. McDonnell Douglas is also promoting the Goshawk for export.

Photo: The T-45 replaces TA-4s and T-2s. (MDC)

McDonnell Douglas C-9 & DC-9

Country of origin: United States of America

Type: Multirole transport and medical evacuation aircraft

Powerplants: C-9A – Two 64.5kN (14,500lb) Pratt & Whitney JT8D-9 turbofans.

Performance: C-9A – Max speed 935km/h (505kt), typical cruising speed 810km/h (437kt). Max initial rate of climb 2900ft/min. Time to 35,000ft 25min. Service ceiling 35,820ft. Range with max payload 1690km (913nm), ferry range 4700km (2538nm).

Weights: C-9A – Basic equipped 28,235kg (62,247lb), max takeoff 48,990kg (108,000lb).

Dimensions: C-9A – Wing span 28.47m (93ft 5in), length 36.37m (119ft 4in), height 8.38m (27ft 6in). Wing area 93.0m² (1000.7sq ft).

Accommodation: Flightcrew of two. Crew on C-9A comprises two flightcrew, flight observer, senior flight nurse, nurse, senior medical technician and two medical attendants. Can carry 40 ambulatory patients or 30 stretcher patients, or combinations thereof. DC-9-30 max seating in passenger configuration for 115.

Armament: None

Operators: Italy, Kuwait, USA, Venezuela.

History: The DC-9 series is a highly successful (2400 built) family of twinjet airliners ranging in size from 80 to 150 seats. In its DC-9-30 form it has been adopted for military operations as an aeromedical transport (C-9A) and staff and utility transport (C-9B/C-9C).

The DC-9 was developed as a short range airliner complementing the much larger DC-8, and filling a market sector that at the time Boeing was neglecting. Development was launched on April 8 1963.

The DC-9 was an all new design, featuring rear fuselage mounted engines, a T tail, moderately swept wings and seats for up to 80 passengers. Construction of the prototype began in July 1963 and first flight occurred on February 25 1965. Certification and service entry occurred on November 23 1965 and December 8 1965 respectively.

The DC-9 had been designed with stretched larger capacity developments in mind, and such versions of the basic DC-9-10 soon followed. The first stretch resulted in the 4.54m (14ft 11in) longer DC-9-30, which entered service in February 1967. Subsequent stretched versions are the DC-9-40, DC-9-50, JT8D-200 powered MD-80 series and the V2500 powered, 150 seat MD-90.

The DC-9-30 is the major DC-9 development adopted for military use. In August 1967 the USAF selected the DC-9-30 to meet its requirement for an off the shelf airliner suitable for development as an aeromedical transport. Designated C-9A, USAF aeromedical DC-9s are appropriately named Nightingale. The 21 C-9As delivered feature a large forward freight door, provision for a therapeutic oxygen supply and an isolated care section. In addition, the USAF acquired three DC-9-30s as C-9C VIP/staff transports.

The US Navy and Marines acquired a total of 15 freight door equipped staff/logistical transport C-9B Skytrain IIs from 1972. Similarly Kuwait operates a single freight door fitted DC-9-32CF as a VIP transport, plus an MD-83. Finally, Italy operates two DC-9-30s as VIP transports, while Venezuela flies a single DC-9-15.

Photo: A USAF C-9A Nightingale. (Paul Merritt)

MDC KC-10 Extender & DC-10

Country of origin: United States of America

Type: Strategic tanker transport

Powerplants: KC-10 – Three 233.5kN (52,500lb) General Electric F103-GE-100 (CF6-50C2) turbofans.

Performance: KC-10 – Max speed at 25,000ft 982km/h (530kt), max cruising speed at 30,000ft 908km/h (490kt), long range cruising speed 870km/h (470kt). Max initial rate of climb 2900ft/min. Range with max payload 7030km (3797nm). Max ferry range unrefuelled 18,505km (9990nm). Can transfer 90,720kg (200,000lb) of fuel 3540km (1910nm) from base.

Weights: KC-10 – Operating empty 108,890kg (240,065lb), max takeoff 267,620kg (590,000lb).

Dimensions: Wing span 47.34m (155ft 4in), length 55.35m (181ft 7in), height 17.70m (58ft 1in). Wing area 358.7m² (3861.0sq ft).

Accommodation: KC-10 – Crew complement of five, with six seats provided for a relief crew. Can be configured with 75 passenger seats. Max payload 76,845kg (169,410lb), max fuel is 161,510kg (356,065lb).

Armament: None

Operators: KC-10 – USA. DC-10 – Netherlands.

History: The KC-10 Extender tanker transport is a military development of the DC-10 widebody airliner.

Development of the DC-10 airliner was launched in February 1968 with orders from American and United Airlines. The second widebody to fly (behind the 747), the DC-10 began life as a twinjet, but gained a third engine to meet the field performance American Airlines demanded. The prototype first flew on August 29 1970.

DC-10 variants include the initial production DC-10-10, the intercontinental range DC-10-30 (with extra fuel and a third main undercarriage unit) and the P&W JT9D powered DC-10-40.

In December 1977 the US Air Force selected the DC-10 as its Advanced Tanker Cargo Aircraft (ATCA), ahead of the Boeing 747. The ATCA program aimed to procure an off the shelf jet transport suitable for use as both a strategic transport and an air-to-air refueler.

Initially the USAF ordered 16 modified DC-10s as the KC-10A Extender. The first of these flew on July 12 1980. In May 1982 the total KC-10 order was increased to 60. The final Extender was delivered in 1988.

The KC-10 is based on the DC-10-30CF (convertible freighter) and features a large forward freight door, an air-to-air receptacle above the cockpit, a McDonnell Douglas Advanced Aerial Refuelling Boom and a hose and reel refuelling unit, both beneath the rear fuselage. In addition 20 KC-10s feature two underwing hose and reel refuelling units. As well as the basic fuel tanks, fuel is stored in seven bladder tanks in the lower cargo holds. The main deck accommodates freight and up to 75 passengers.

The only other DC-10 military operator is the Royal Netherlands Air Force, who in 1995 took delivery of the first of two ex Martinair DC-10-30CFs that McDonnell Douglas had converted with refuelling boom to KDC-10 configuration.

Photo: A KC-10 cleans up after takeoff. Extenders regularly support long range fighter deployments as they can carry fighter units' support crews and equipment while also providing inflight refuelling. (Nick Sayer)

McDonnell Douglas C-17 Globemaster III

Country of origin: United States of America

Type: Strategic and intratheatre transport

Powerplants: Four 181.0kN (40,700lb) Pratt & Whitney F117-PW-100 turbofans.

Performance: Normal cruising speed at 28,000ft Mach 0.77, max cruising speed at low altitude 648km/h (350kt) CAS. Airdrop speed at sea level 215 to 465km/h (115 to 250kt) CAS. Max ferry range 8705km (4700nm). Operational radius with a 36,785kg (81,000lb) payload and a 975m (3200ft) TO, land in 823m (2700ft), takeoff again with a similar payload in 853m (2800ft) – 925km (500nm). Unrefuelled range with a 68,040kg (150,000lb) payload, a 2320m (7600ft) TO run and a 885m (2900ft) landing – 5000km (2700nm).

Weights: Target operating empty 122,015kg (269,000lb), target max takeoff 265,352kg (585,000lb), peacetime takeoff 263,083kg (580,000lb).

Dimensions: Wing span over winglets 51.76m (169ft 10in), length 53.04m (174ft 0in), height 16.79m (55ft 1in). Wing area 353m² (3800.0sq ft).

Accommodation: Flightcrew of two, plus loadmaster. Max payload 76,657kg (169,000lb) can comprise standard freight pallets, air droppable pallets, 100 passengers on seating pallets, 48 stretcher patients, or 75 troops on temporary fuselage side and centreline seats, or 102 paratroops, 4WD vehicles, an M1A1 Abrams MBT plus other vehicles, and up to three AH-64 Apaches.

Armament: None

Operators: USA

History: Highly expensive and highly controversial, the C-17 airlifter suffered a prolonged and often troublesome development, but in service is proving to be highly reliable and very versatile.

The USAF selected the McDonnell Douglas C-17 to meet its C-X requirement for a heavy airlifter in August 1981. The C-X requirement called for a transport capable of strategic and intratheatre missions, with good STOL performance from semi prepared strips, good ground manoeuvrability and a voluminous cargo hold capable of accommodating attack helicopters and the M1 Abrams main battle tank.

The original C-17 full scale development contract was cancelled in 1982 and replaced with low priority development. The first flying prototype was ordered in late 1985 while the first production contract was signed in January 1988. First flight was on September 15 1991.

The C-17 is of conventional military freighter configuration with a high wing, T tail and rear loading freight ramp. Power is supplied by four Pratt & Whitney F117 turbofans, developments of the commercial PW2000 series used for the Boeing 757 airliner. Notable design features include fly-by-wire flight controls (the first on a US transport aircraft), a two crew glass cockpit with HUDs, externally blown flaps and STOL performance equivalent to the C-130's.

At late 1995 40 of the planned total of 120 C-17s had been ordered. In November 1995 the USAF elected to procure the remaining 80 C-17s following evaluation of the C-33 (Boeing 747-400F) and improved C-5D as alternatives. At the time of writing this decision had yet to be passed by Congress.

Photo: A head-on view of the C-17 Globemaster III. (MDC)

MDC/Hughes OH-6 & MD 500

Country of origin: United States of America

Type: Observation, light attack, training and utility helicopter

Powerplant: 530MG – One 485kW (650shp) Allison 250-C20B turboshaft driving a five bladed main rotor and two bladed tail rotor.

Performance: 530MG – Max cruising speed 228km/h (123kt), max cruising speed at sea level 224km/h (121kt). Max initial rate of climb 2055ft/min. Service ceiling over 16,000ft. Hovering ceiling in ground effect (ISA) 14,300ft, out of ground effect (ISA) 12,000ft. Range with standard fuel 370km (200nm). Endurance with standard fuel 2hr 7min.

Weights: 530MG – Empty equipped 850kg (1870lb), max takeoff 1405kg (3100lb), max overload takeoff 1700kg (3750lb).

Dimensions: 530MG – Main rotor diameter 8.33m (27ft 4in), length overall rotors turning 8.97m (29ft 5in), fuselage length 7.29m (23ft 11in), height to top of rotor head 2.62m (8ft 7in). Main rotor disc area 50.9m^2 (547.8sq ft).

Accommodation: Can seat up to seven, including pilot. Alternatively can carry pilot, a medical attendant and two stretcher patients.

Armament: 500MG – Options include four TOW 2 anti tank missiles, FN Herstal pods with two 7.62mm or 0.50in machine guns each and rocket pods. To be cleared for Stinger AAMs and MDC's 7.62mm Chain Gun.

Operators: OH-6 – Brazil, Colombia, Taiwan, USA. 500 – Argentina, Bahrain, Bolivia, Colombia, Costa Rica, Cyprus, Dominican Republic, El Salvador, Finland, Greece, Indonesia, Israel, Italy, Japan, Jordan, Kenya, Mauritania, Mexico, North Korea, Philippines, South Korea, Spain, USA.

History: One of the most successful and useful light turbine helicopters built, the Hughes/McDonnell Douglas 500 series began life in response to a US Army requirement for an observation helicopter.

Hughes won the US Army observation helicopter contest against competition from Bell and Hiller, resulting in the Allison 250 powered OH-6 Cayuse, which first flew in February 1963. Although now largely retired from US Army service, several thousand OH-6s (or Loaches) served widely in observation and special mission roles since the mid 1960s (including in Vietnam). The OH-6 was marketed in civil guise as the Hughes 500, which formed the basis for a number of export orientated military variants.

The first Hughes 500 export military variant was the 500M Defender, which was delivered to Colombia and built under licence by Kawasaki in Japan as the OH-6J. The 500M was followed by the 500MD Defender in 1976, an improved variant with a more powerful engine, small T tail and new five bladed main rotor. Apart from the basic Defender, it was offered in 500D Scout Defender, anti tank 500MD/TOW Defender and torpedo carrying 500MD/ASW Defender (with search radar and towed MAD) variants.

The 500MG Defender is the military variant of the 500E (with a recontoured nose and an Allison 250-C20B). The 530F is a more powerful version optimised for hot and high work and the equivalent military model is the 530MG Defender. Current production 500MG and 530MGs are offered with a FLIR, mast mounted TOW sight and a laser rangefinder. Built alongside these models is the revolutionary NOTAR equipped MD 520N, although none are in military service.

Photo: A Mexican Air Force 530MG Defender. (MDHS)

McDonnell Douglas AH-64 Apache

Country of origin: United States of America

Type: Attack helicopter

Powerplants: AH-64A – Two 1265kW (1696shp) General Electric T700-GE-701 turboshafts, or from 1990 two 1410kW (1890shp) T700-GE-701Cs, driving four bladed main and tail rotors.

Performance: AH-64A (with T700-GE-701s) – Max speed and max cruising speed 293km/h (158kt), cruising speed approx 278km/h (150kt). Max vertical rate of climb 2500ft/min. Service ceiling 21,000ft. Hovering ceiling in ground effect 15,000ft, out of ground effect 11,500ft. Ferry range with and external fuel 1900km (1025nm). Max range with internal fuel 480km (260nm). Max endurance 3hr 9min.

Weights: AH-64A – Empty 5165kg (11,387lb), max takeoff 9525kg (21,000lb).

Dimensions: Main rotor diameter 14.63m (48ft 0in), wing span 5.23m (17ft 2in), length overall rotors turning 17.76m (58ft 3in), fuselage length 14.97m (49ft 2in), height overall 4.66m (15ft 4in). Main rotor disc area 168.1m^2 (1809.1m^2).

Accommodation: Copilot/gunner in front cockpit, with pilot behind.

Armament: One M230 Chain Gun 30mm automatic cannon under forward fuselage with 1200 rounds. Four underwing hardpoints can carry up to 16 AGM-114 Hellfire anti armour missiles, or rocket pods, Stinger or Sidewinder AAMs, or Sidearm anti radiation missiles.

Operators: Egypt, Greece, Israel, Netherlands*, Saudi Arabia, UAE, UK*, USA.

History: The most capable attack helicopter currently in service was developed to meet the US Army's Advanced Attack Helicopter requirement.

To meet the AAH requirement the US Army sponsored the development of the Bell YAH-63 and the Hughes YAH-64 for a competitive fly-off. Hughes' YAH-64 flew for the first time on September 30 1975, and it was selected ahead of the Bell design for further development in December 1976. Full scale development followed, although it was not until March 1982 that final production approval was given, with a US Army order for an initial 11 AH-64 Apaches. The first Apaches were delivered in 1984 and the first unit became operational in 1986.

Apache design features include two shoulder mounted GE T700 turboshafts, crew armour, aerobatic capability, a high degree of survivability and the nose mounted Lockheed Martin (Martin Marietta) AAQ-11 TADS/PNVS (Target Acquisition and Designation Sight/Pilot Night Vision Sensor). TADS comprises a FLIR, TV camera, laser spot tracker and laser rangefinder and is used for target location and designation. The PNVS FLIR allows nap of the earth flying.

Over 800 AH-64As have been built for the US Army and export and the type proved very successful in combat in the Gulf War. The interim AH-64B with improvements from combat experience was cancelled.

More than 500 US Army AH-64A Apaches are being upgraded to AH-64D standard, of which 227 will be to AH-64D Longbow Apache standard. The AH-64D features improved avionics housed in enlarged cheek fairings, while full standard AH-64D Longbow Apaches will feature the Westinghouse mast mounted millimetre wave radar, able to guide a radio frequency seeker Hellfire missile. Deliveries are due from 1996. UK built WAH-64Ds will feature RTM332s.

Photo: A US Army AH-64A Apache. (MDHS)

Mikoyan-Gurevich MiG-15 & MiG-15UTI

Country of origin: Russia

Type: Lead-in fighter and advanced trainer

Powerplant: MiG-15UTI – One 22.3kN (5000lb) Klimov RD-45F turbojet.

Performance: MiG-15UTI – Max speed at sea level 1015km/h (549kt), max speed at 9600ft 1010km/h (547kt). Time to 16,400ft 2min 35sec, time to 32,800ft 6min 48sec. Service ceiling 48,640ft. Max range with external fuel 1425km (770nm), range with internal fuel 950km (513nm). Max endurance 2hr 30min.

Weights: MiG-15UTI – Empty 3720kg (8200lb), max takeoff 5415kg (11,938lb).

Dimensions: MiG-15UTI – Wing span 10.13m (33ft 3in), length 11.15m (36ft 7in), height 3.39m (11ft 2in). Wing area 20.6m² (221.8sq ft).

Accommodation: Pilot only in MiG-15, or two in tandem in MiG-15UTI.

Armament: None usually carried, but can be fitted with one 23mm NR-23 cannon or one 12.4mm UBK-E machine gun, or one 12.7mm A – 12.7 machine gun.

Operators: MiG-15 – Albania, China, Cuba, Romania. MiG-15UTI – Albania, Angola, Congo, Guinea Bissau, Guinea Republic, Mali, Mongolia, Romania, Syria, Vietnam, Yemen.

History: The MiG-15 shattered western beliefs of the standard of Russian aircraft design when it appeared in combat in the skies of Korea over four decades ago, while today it still survives in service in single and two seat forms.

The MiG-15 (NATO codename 'Fagot') resulted from Project S – a 1946 requirement for a new jet powered high altitude day fighter capable of speeds over 1000km/h (540kt) with a ceiling of 46,000ft. The Lavochkin, Yakovlev and Mikoyan-Gurevich design bureaus responded with fairly similar aircraft, all with swept wings and tail surfaces, a stubby fuselage with nose air intake, and, probably most important of all, a Klimov RD-45 turbojet. The RD-45 was an unlicenced copy of the Rolls-Royce Nene centrifugal turbojet and was far more advanced than any contemporary Russian turbojet design.

Mikoyan-Gurevich's design, the I-310, flew for the first time in December 1945. Following evaluation both the Mikoyan-Gurevich and Lavochkin designs were ordered into production, as the MiG-15 and La-15 respectively. Around 500 La-15s were built, compared with at least 3000 single seat MiG-15s (many under licence in Poland and Czechoslovakia).

Chinese MiG-15s were used widely in combat during the Korean War. The MiG's excellent performance came as something of a shock to the western world, although it was ably countered by experienced and well trained pilots flying North American F-86 Sabres.

Aside from the basic MiG-15, the single seater was also built in improved MiG-15bis form. MiG-15bis improvements included a more powerful engine (redesignated VK-1), lower empty weight, greater fuel capacity and some aerodynamic changes.

Finally over 5000 two seat MiG-15UTIs (or 'Midgets') were built for operational conversion and advanced training from 1949. Today several nations have MiG-15UTIs (or Chinese built FT-2s) on strength, although their serviceability may be questionable.

Photo: Soviet/Russian MiG-15UTIs were retired in the 1970s, although several third world nations continue to operate the type.

Mikoyan-Gurevich MiG-17 & Chengdu JJ-5

Country of origin: Russia

Type: Light attack fighter

Powerplant: MiG-17F – One 29.5kN (5732lb) dry and 33.14kN (7450lb) with afterburning Klimov VK-1F turbojet.

Performance: MiG-17F – Max speed at 16,400ft Mach 0.98 or 1130km/h (610kt), max speed at 32,810ft Mach 0.93 or 1071km/h (578kt). Max initial rate of climb 12,795ft/min. Service ceiling 54,460ft. Range with external fuel at 32,810ft 1470km (794nm), range with internal fuel at 32,810ft 970km (524nm).

Weights: MiG-17F – Empty equipped 3930kg (8665lb), max takeoff 6070kg (13,380lb).

Dimensions: MiG-17F – Wing span 9.63m (31ft 7in), length 11.26m (37ft 0in), height 3.80m (12ft 6in). Wing area 22.6m² (243.3sq ft).

Accommodation: Pilot only, or two in tandem in Chengdu JJ-5/FT-5.

Armament: MiG-17F – Three 23mm NR-23 cannon. Four underwing hardpoints can carry a single 250kg (550lb) bomb each, or a UV-16-57 rocket pod (with 16 x 50mm rockets) each.

Operators: MiG-17 – Albania, Congo, Cuba, Guinea Bissau, Guinea Republic, Madagascar, Mali, Mongolia, Romania, Sudan, Syria, Uganda, Vietnam, Yemen. JJ 5/FT-5 – Albania, China, Sri Lanka, Sudan, Zimbabwe.

History: The MiG-17 was designed to overcome some of the performance and design shortcomings of the MiG-15.

Design work on the improved MiG-15 began in early 1949 under the designation I-330. The developed MiG-15 (Mikoyan-Gurevich's Project SI) aimed in particular to overcome the MiG-15's poor high Mach number handling characteristics (a lack of directional control limited the MiG-15's top speed to Mach 0.92). While the MiG-17 looks very similar to the MiG-15, the -17 introduced a new longer span, wider chord wing with greater sweepback angle and a redesigned tailplane. The tail is taller while the horizontal surfaces have greater sweepback.

The prototype MiG-17 first flew on February 1 1950 and the type was ordered into production in August 1951. Initial production was of the MiG-17 (NATO 'Fresco-A'), while the MiG-17F ('Fresco-C') introduced an afterburning VK-1F turbojet (still derived from the RR Nene). The MiG-17PF featured radar, the MiG-17PFU radar and four radar guided AAMs.

At least 8000 MiG-17s were built in Russia, Poland (as the Lim-6) and China (as the J-5). The MiG-17 served widely with Soviet client state air forces, initially as an interceptor and later as a light attack/close support platform armed with bombs and rockets. Several third world nations use it for ground attack and weapons training.

The only two seat MiG-17s were built in China, as the USSR deemed the MiG-15UTI suitable for conversion training for the MiG-17 and MiG-19. The Chinese two seat MiG-17, the JJ-5, was built by Chengdu. Design changes include the two cockpits in tandem under a similar canopy as that on the MiG-15UTI and a slightly stretched fuselage. The JJ-5 first flew on May 8 1966 and Chengdu built more than 1060 through to 1986. The JJ-5 was exported widely as the FT-5 and several nations continue to operate it as an advanced trainer.

Photo: Poland retired its MiG-17s (Lim-6s) in 1992. (Alan Scoot)

Mikoyan MiG-21

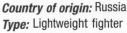

Country of origin: Russia

Type: Lightweight fighter

Powerplant: MiG-21MF – One 39.9kN (8792lb) dry and 63.7kN (14,307lb) with afterburning Tumansky (now Soyuz) R-13-300 turbojet.

Performance: MiG-21MF – Max speed at 36,090ft 2230km/h (1203kt), max speed at sea level 1300km/h (703kt). Max initial rate of climb 23,620ft/min. Service ceiling (theoretical) 59,710ft. Ferry range with three drop tanks 1800km (970nm). Combat radius with four 250kg (550lb) bombs hi-lo-hi 370km (200nm), combat radius with two 250kg (550lb) bombs and external fuel hi-lo-hi 740km (400nm).

Weights: MiG-21MF – Empty 5350kg (11,795lb), max takeoff 9400kg (20,723lb).

Dimensions: MiG-21MF – Span 7.15m (23ft 6in), length inc probe 15.76m (51ft 9in), height 4.13m (13ft 6in). Wing area 23.0m² (247.5sq ft).

Accommodation: Pilot only, or two in tandem in MiG-21U/UM.

Armament: MiG-21MF – One 23mm GSh-23L cannon. Max external ordnance load of 2000kg (4410lb) on four underwing hardpoints.

Operators: Afghanistan, Algeria, Angola, Bulgaria, Cambodia, Congo, Croatia, Cuba, India, Iraq, Laos, Mongolia, Mozambique, Nigeria, North Korea, Poland, Slovakia, Sudan, Vietnam, Yemen, Yugoslavia, Zambia.

History: More MiG-21s were built (8000+), they served with more nations and fought in more wars than any other jet fighter.

The MiG-21 ('Fishbed' in NATO parlance) was conceived as a lightweight day interceptor, with design emphasis on performance, simplicity, ease of construction and maintainability, at the expense of cost and complexity. Prototype MiG-21s were flown in swept wing 'Faceplate' and tailed delta forms in 1955.

The tailed delta configuration was selected for development. Consequently 40 pre production MiG-21Fs were built. Initial production was of the MiG-21F-13 ('Fishbed-C'). Primary armament was a cannon and two AA-2 'Atoll' AAMs. The MiG-21F-13 also formed the basis for the MiG-21U ('Mongol') two seater.

Further early model MiG-21s, characterised by their forward opening single piece cockpit canopies, included the gun-less MiG-21P ('Fishbed-D'), the RP-21 Shafir radar equipped MiG-21PF and export MiG-21FL with down spec radar and less powerful engine. The MiG-21P and MiG-21PF were called 'Fishbed-E' by NATO and later subvariants featured a ventral cannon. The MiG-21PFS and PFM (both 'Fishbed-F') were similar but introduced a two piece canopy, upgraded radar and more powerful engine.

The reconnaissance MiG-21R ('Fishbed-H') was based on the MiG-21PFM and carried a centreline recce pod which could contain a variety of sensors including optical or TV cameras, infrared sensors or a Sideways Looking Airborne Radar (SLAR).

Development of fighter MiG-21s continued with the MiG-21S with a RP-22 radar and ventral gun pod. The export MiG-21M and more powerful R-13-300 powered MiG-21SM reintroduced an internal cannon. Improvement continued with the R-13-300 powered MiG-21MF ('Fishbed-J') with RP-22 radar and AAM missile capability on all four underwing hardpoints, plus the MiG-21SMT with an oversize dorsal fairing containing fuel.

Photo: Vietnam's MiG-21PFs operate alongside the MiG-21bis.

Mikoyan MiG-21bis

Country of origin: Russia

Type: Light multirole fighter

Powerplant: One 40.2kN (9038lb) dry and 69.7kN (15,653lb) with afterburning (and 97.1kN/21,825lb emergency rating) Tumansky (now Soyuz) R-25-300 turbojet, with provision for two 24.5kN (5510lb) SPRD-99 rocket boosters.

Performance: Max speed at 42,650ft Mach 2.1 or 2175km/h (1177kt), max speed at sea level 1150km/h (620kt). Max initial rate of climb with two AAMs and 50% fuel 45,275ft/min. Service ceiling 57,415ft. Range at 32,800ft with one drop tank 2175km/h (1177kt). Typical combat radius 450 to 500km (245 to 270nm).

Weights: Empty 5450kg (12,015lb), max takeoff 9800kg (21,605lb).

Dimensions: Wing span 7.15m (23ft 6in), length inc probe 15.76m (51ft 9in), height 4.13m (13ft 6in). Wing area 23.0m² (247.5sq ft).

Accommodation: Pilot only.

Armament: One 23mm GSh-23 cannon. One centreline and four underwing hardpoints can carry a total ordnance load of 2000kg (4410lb). Options include four rocket pods, or two 500kg (1100lb) and two 250kg (550lb) bombs, AA-2 'Atoll' and R-60 AA-8 'Aphid' AAMs. Egyptian MiG-21s were wired for AIM-9P Sidewinder and Matra R550 AAMs.

Operators: MiG-21bis – Afghanistan, Algeria, Angola, Croatia, Cuba, Finland, Guinea Republic, Hungary, India, Mozambique, Poland, Romania, Russia, Syria, Vietnam, Yemen, Yugoslavia.

History: The MiG-21bis was developed as a multirole fighter for the Soviet Union's Frontal Aviation and was the most important and capable MiG-21 variant. Most MiG-21s surviving in service today are MiG-21bis.

Like earlier variants before it, the MiG-21bis introduced further improvements to the airframe, engine, avionics and weaponry. The MiG-21bis is powered by a Tumansky R-25-300 turbojet, over a third more powerful than in the original MiG-21s. This increase in power allowed Mikoyan to increase the MiG-21's fuel capacity in an enlarged dorsal fairing. The MiG-21bis entered Russian service in early 1972, and was allocated the NATO reporting name 'Fishbed-L'. NATO's 'Fishbed-N' designation covers later production MiG-21bis fitted with an undernose ILS antenna and improved avionics.

As well as Russian production, several hundred MiG-21s were built under licence by HAL in India between 1980 and 1987. India remains an important operator of MiG-21bis and earlier model MiG-21s with 400+ in service.

With the large numbers of MiG-21bis remaining in service the type is a logical candidate for an upgrade program. A number of MiG-21 upgrades are on offer, most notably from Mikoyan-MAPO and Israel's IAI (ironically a country that had been on the receiving end of the MiG-21 in several wars). IAI's upgrade package is offered in varying levels of equipment, including airframe overhaul, avionics upgrade and new radar. IAI is upgrading MiG-21bis for both Romania and Cambodia and the first upgraded aircraft flew for the first time in May 1995.

Mikoyan-MAPO meanwhile is offering an upgraded MiG-21 featuring Russian avionics, a new radar and compatibility with current generation Russian AAMs. A demonstrator was exhibited at the 1995 Paris Airshow.

Photo: Hungary operates a single squadron of MiG-21bis. (Paul Merritt)

Mikoyan MiG-23

Country of origin: Russia

Type: Multirole fighter

Powerplant: MiG-23ML – One 83.8kN (18,850lb) dry and 127.5kN (28,660lb) with afterburning Tumansky (now Soyuz) R-35-300 turbojet.

Performance: MiG-23ML – Max speed with weapons Mach 2.35 or 2500km/h (1349kt). Max initial rate of climb 47,250ft/min. Service ceiling 59,055ft. Combat radius with six AAMs 1150km (620nm), combat radius with 2000kg (4410lb) of bombs 700km (378nm).

Weights: MiG-23ML – Empty 10,200kg (22,485lb), max takeoff 17,800kg (39,250lb).

Dimensions: MiG-23ML – Span wings spread 13.97m (45ft 10in), span wings swept 7.78m (25ft 6in), length overall exc probe 15.88m (52ft 1in), height 4.82m (15ft 10in). Wing area wings spread 37.3m² (401.5sq ft), wing area wings swept 34.2m² (368.1sq ft).

Accommodation: Pilot only, or two in tandem MiG-23UM and UB.

Armament: One twin barrel 23mm GSh-23 cannon. Five external hardpoints (one centreline, two underfuselage and two underwing) can carry a max external load of 2000kg (4410lb) on MiG-23ML. Typical air-to-air configuration of two R-60 (AA-8 'Aphid') and two R-23 (AA-7 'Apex') AAMs.

Operators: Afghanistan, Algeria, Byelorussia, Bulgaria, Cuba, Czech Republic, Ethiopia, Hungary, India, Iraq, Libya, North Korea, Poland, Romania, Russia, Sudan, Syria, Ukraine, USA, Vietnam, Yemen.

History: From the mid 1970s and into the 1980s the MiG-23 (NATO reporting name 'Flogger') was the Soviet Unions' most capable tactical fighter.

The MiG-23 was developed to replace the MiG-21, with improvements in overall performance and in particular short field performance. Two Mikoyan designed prototypes were built, the swept wing 23-01 'Faithless' and the swing wing 23-11. The 23-11 first flew on April 10 1967 and was ordered into production as the MiG-23S, fitted with the MiG-21S' RP-22 radar. Fifty were built for evaluation.

The MiG-23M ('Flogger-B') was the first model to introduce the specially designed Sapfir-23 pulse doppler radar in a larger nose radome and also featured a more powerful engine and IRST and R-23 missile compatibility. The down spec export MiG-23MS ('Flogger-E') was similar, while the export and further down spec MiG-23MF ('Flogger-B') features the RP-22 radar and smaller nose.

Subsequent fighter MiG-23s were the lightened MiG-23ML ('Flogger-G') with less fuel and no dorsal fin extension, the MiG-23P interceptor that could be automatically guided to its target by ground controllers and the MiG-23MLD ('Flogger-K') with aerodynamic changes. The MiG-23UB ('Flogger-C') meanwhile is the two seat conversion trainer.

Various MiG-23 models were also built specifically for ground attack. The first to appear was the MiG-23B with a pointy, radar-less nose and a Lyulka AL-21 turbojet. The improved MiG-23BN returned to the Tumansky turbojet. NATO called both the MiG-23B and MiG-23BN the 'Flogger-F'. Further improved MiG-23 attack variants were the MiG-23BK and MiG-23BM, both of which borrowed nav attack systems from the MiG-27.

Photo: A Russian MiG-23ML (note lack of dorsal fin).

Mikoyan MiG-27

Country of origin: Russia

Type: Ground attack aircraft

Powerplant: MiG-27 – One 78.5kN (17,637lb) dry and 112.8kN (25,353lb) Tumansky (now Soyuz) R-29B-300 turbojet.

Performance: MiG-27 – Max speed at 26,200ft 1885km/h (1017kt), max speed at sea level 1350km/h (728kt). Max initial rate of climb 39,370ft/min. Service ceiling 45,930ft. Combat radius with two Kh-29 ASMs and three drop tanks lo-lo-lo 540km (290nm), radius with two Kh-29s and no external fuel 225km (120nm).

Weights: MiG-27 – Empty equipped 11,910kg (26,252lb), max takeoff 20,300kg (44,753lb).

Dimensions: MiG-27 – Span wings spread 13.97m (45ft 10in), span wings swept 7.78m (25ft 6in), length 17.08m (56ft 0in), height 5.00m (16ft 5in). Wing area wings spread 37.4m² (402.1sq ft), wings swept 34.2m² (367.7sq ft).

Accommodation: Pilot only.

Armament: One GSh-6-30 30mm cannon. Max external weapons load of over 4000kg (8820lb). Options include laser, TV and electro optically guided ASMs and PGMs, conventional bombs, rockets, gun and cannon pods and tactical nuclear bombs.

Operators: India, Kazakhstan, Russia, Ukraine.

History: The MiG-27 family are the strike and ground attack optimised variants of the MiG-23, and as such forms an important part of Russia's offensive inventory.

The MiG-27 designation originally applied to a range of Mikoyan design studies aimed to meet a requirement for a modern day Shturmovik that was eventually met by the Sukhoi Su-25. Instead the MiG-27 is the definitive strike/ground attack member of the 'Flogger' MiG-23/27 family.

The ground attack MiG-23s, as described in the previous entry, were regarded as interim ground attack aircraft pending the arrival of the optimised MiG-27. Compared with the MiG-23, the MiG-27 features simplified air intakes (as opposed to the F-4 style variable intake ramps of the MiG-23 optimised for high end performance) and simplified two stage afterburner nozzles. An extra external hardpoint and strengthened main undercarriage permit the carriage of over 4000kg (8820lb) of armament. Perhaps its most distinctive feature is the duckbill nose (which it shares with ground attack MiG-23s) which features a laser rangefinder and other sensors. The MiG-27 features advanced nav attack systems allowing all weather operations, and can be used in the tactical reconnaissance role carrying various recce pods.

The MiG-27 first flew in prototype form in 1972. The initial production MiG-27 was soon followed by the MiG-27K ('Flogger-D'). NATO's 'Flogger-J' designation covers the improved MiG-27D, MiG-27M and MiG-27K ('Flogger-J2') with a TV/laser designator.

Outside the CIS India is the only MiG-27 export customer, where it has been built under licence. India calls its aircraft MiG-27M Bahadur, although Mikoyan refers to them as MiG-27Ls.

Photo: The duckbill nose, stronger undercarriage, simpler intakes and a shorter exhaust nozzle differentiate the MiG-27 from the MiG-23. (MAP)

Mikoyan MiG-25

Country of origin: Russia

Type: Interceptor and reconnaissance aircraft

Powerplants: MiG-25PDS – Two 109.8kN (24,690lb) with afterburning Tumansky (now Soyuz) R-15BD-300 turbojets.

Performance: MiG-25PDS – Max speed Mach 2.8 or 3000km/h (1620kt), max speed at sea level 1200km/h (647kt). Time to 65,615ft 8min 55sec. Service ceiling 67,915ft. Range with internal fuel 1730km (933nm). Endurance 2hr 5min.

Weights: MiG-25PDS – Normal takeoff with four R-40 AAMs and max internal fuel 36,720kg (80,950lb).

Dimensions: MiG-25PDS – Wing span 14.02m (46ft 0in), length 23.82m (78ft 2in), height 6.10m (20ft 0in). Wing area 61.4m² (660.9sq ft).

Accommodation: Pilot only, or two in separate cockpits in MiG-25PU.

Armament: Four underwing hardpoints can carry a total ordnance load of 4000kg (9635lb). Typical interceptor configuration of two R-40 (AA-6 'Acrid') and four R-60 (AA-8 'Aphid') AAMs, or alternatively can carry four R-40s, or two R-23s (AA-7 'Apex') and four R-73A (AA-11 'Archer') AAMs. MiG-25BM can carry for Kh-58 (AS-11 'Kilter') anti radiation missiles.

Operators: Algeria, India, Iraq, Libya, Russia, Syria.

History: The MiG-25 high altitude, high speed interceptor was initially developed to counter the Mach 3 XB-70 Valkyrie bomber under development in the US in the late 1950s and early 1960s.

Although the XB-70 as a bomber was cancelled in 1961, work on the new high speed interceptor and reconnaissance platform continued. The two main design considerations for the new aircraft were speed and high altitude performance, something that was attained at the expense of manoeuvrability. Design of the MiG-25 was also a remarkable feat, given that it had to withstand the high temperatures of high speed flight. The airframe is made mainly of nickel steel, with some titanium used in areas such as leading edges.

The first MiG-25 prototype to fly was the Ye-155R-1 reconnaissance prototype and it flew for the first time on March 6 1964. The interceptor Ye-166P-1 had its first flight that September. Under the designation Ye-266 and Ye-266M, two MiG-25s have set a range of speed and altitude records, many of which remain unbroken.

Initial 'Foxbat' production was of the MiG-25P interceptor. Service entry was in 1973. Subsequent MiG-25 interceptors were the new build MiG-25PD 'Foxbat-E' with new look down shoot down radar, more powerful engines and an IRST, and the similar MiG-25PDS to which standard MiG-25Ps were rebuilt from 1979. The MiG-25PU 'Foxbat-C' two seat conversion trainer has stepped separate cockpits.

Initial reconnaissance variant production was of the MiG-25R, which was soon replaced by the MiG-25RB 'Foxbat-B', which also had a ground attack capability. Variants with different equipment were the MiG-25RBS, BSh and RBV. The MiG-25RBK is fitted with SLAR rather than optical cameras, as is the MiG-25RBF. The MiG-25RU is a two seater. Finally the MiG-25BM ('Foxbat-F') is a dedicated defence suppression platform that carries up to four Kh-58 (AS-11 'Kilter') anti radiation missiles.

Photo: The nose dielectric panel identifies this 'Foxbat' as a SLAR equipped, camera-less MiG-25RBK. (MAP)

Mikoyan MiG-31

Country of origin: Russia

Type: Interceptor

Powerplants: MiG-31 – Two 151.9kN (34,170lb) with afterburning Aviadvigatel (nee Soloviev) D-30F6 turbofans.

Performance: MiG-31 – Max speed Mach 2.83 or 3000km/h (1620kt), max speed at sea level 1500km/h (810kt), max cruising speed at altitude Mach 2.35, economical cruising speed Mach 0.85. Time to 32,800ft 7min 54sec. Service ceiling 67,600ft. Combat radius with four R-33 AAMs and max internal fuel at Mach 2.35 720km (388nm), radius with four R-33s and external fuel at Mach 0.85 1400km (755nm). Ferry range with external fuel 3300km (1780nm). Endurance with external fuel 3hr 35min.

Weights: MiG-31 – Empty 21,825kg (48,115lb), max takeoff 46,200kg (101,850lb).

Dimensions: MiG-31 – Wing span 13.46m (44ft 2in), length 22.69m (74ft 5in), height 6.15m (20ft 2in). Wing area 61.6m² (663.0sq ft).

Accommodation: Pilot and weapon systems operator in tandem.

Armament: One GSh-6-23 23mm cannon. Four R-33 (AA-9 'Amos') long range AAMs carried under the fuselage. Four underwing hardpoints (two earlier) can carry two R-40T (AA-6 'Acrid') AAMs on inner pylons and four R-60 (AA-8 'Aphid') AAMs on outboard pylons (carried two in tandem).

Operators: Russia

History: The advanced MiG-31 two seat interceptor is designed to counter low flying strike aircraft and cruise missiles.

Development of this massive interceptor began in the 1970s, although the MiG-31 was first conceived as a single tail swing wing design, and then a tailless canard delta. In the end a design based on the MiG-25 was settled upon and a development aircraft, the Ye-155MP, flew for the first time on September 16 1975. Production MiG-31 'Foxhound-A's were delivered from 1979 and 280 were built to replace Su-15s and MiG-23s.

While the MiG-31's airframe is based on the MiG-25, it is a really a new aircraft, with several design changes and differences. Unlike the MiG-25, the MiG-31 is powered by afterburning turbofans. Its airframe construction is made up of nickel steel (50%), light alloy (33%) and titanium (16%). The MiG-31 is also the first production aircraft to feature an electronically scanned phased array radar – the SBI 16 Zalson ('Flash Dance') – which is operated from the second cockpit by the dedicated weapon systems operator. It can track up to 10 targets and engage four simultaneously. Via datalink the MiG-31 can be controlled automatically by a ground control interceptor. Other changes include a retractable inflight refuelling probe (on later production aircraft), an internal gun and tandem main undercarriage.

The improved MiG-31M has been under development since 1984 and has flown in prototype form, but not been ordered into production. It features a new radar, no gun, two centreline hardpoints, R-37 (a derivative of the R-33) and R-77 (AA-12) AAM compatibility, a massive 52,000kg (114,638lb) max takeoff weight and three colour CRTs in the rear cockpit. One has been observed with wingtip ECM pods. The MiG-31D designation covers new and converted aircraft similar to the M but with the original radar.

Photo: Mikoyan's MiG-31 demonstrator. (Doug Mackay)

Mikoyan MiG-29

Country of origin: Russia

Type: Tactical counter-air fighter

Powerplants: MiG-29 – Two 49.4kN (11,110lb) dry and 81.4kN (18,300lb) with afterburning Klimov/Sariskov RD-33 turbofans.

Performance: MiG-29 – Max speed at altitude Mach 2.3 or 2445km/h (1320kt), max speed at sea level Mach 1.06 or 1300km/h (700kt). Max initial rate of climb 65,000ft/min. Service ceiling 65,000ft. Service ceiling 55,775ft. Range with external fuel 2100km (1133nm), range with max internal fuel 1500km (810nm).

Weights: MiG-29 – Operating empty 10,900kg (24,030lb), max takeoff 18,500kg (40,785lb).

Dimensions: MiG-29 – Wing span 11.36m (37ft 3in), length inc nose probe 17.32m (56ft 10in), height 4.73m (15ft 6in). Wing area 38.0m² (409.0sq ft).

Accommodation: Pilot only, or two in tandem in MiG-29UB.

Armament: MiG-29 – One 30mm GSh-301 cannon. Six underwing hardpoints can carry a max weapon load of 3000kg (6615lb), including six R-60MK (AA-8) AAMs, or four R-60MKs and two R-27R1 (AA-10A)s. Alternatively can carry R-73E (AA-11) AAMs, bombs, cluster bombs and rockets pods.

Operators: Bulgaria, Cuba, Germany, Hungary, India, Iran, Iraq, North Korea, Malaysia, Moldova, Poland, Romania, Slovakia, Syria, Yugoslavia.

History: The highly capable MiG-29 is Russia's most important tactical fighter.

Serious development of the MiG-29 began in 1974 against a Soviet Air Force requirement for a highly manoeuvrable lightweight fighter capable of outperforming new western fighters in dogfights and to replace a range of aircraft in Frontal Aviation service including the MiG-21, MiG-23 and Su-15. The first of 14 prototypes flew on October 6 1977, although service entry was not until 1984. Some 500 are believed to be in Russian service and several hundred have been exported.

The MiG-29 features the same overall configuration as the much larger Sukhoi Su-27 which was developed concurrently. It features excellent high angle of attack performance and low speed handling and a thrust to weight ratio greater than unity. Additionally the MiG-29 features a RP-29 pulse doppler look down shoot down radar and an IRST unit which allows it to passively detect, track and engage other aircraft, while a helmet mounted sight can cue IR guided AAMs to off boresight targets. In addition the MiG-29 is designed for operations from primitive airfields and doors seal the main intakes to protect the engines from foreign object damage (FOD) during start-up and taxying, with air drawn from louvred intakes in the wingroots. The intake doors open on rotation.

The basic MiG-29 'Fulcrum' was joined in production by the 'Fulcrum-C' with a larger dorsal spine containing extra fuel. The 'Fulcrum-C' was built only for Russia and forms the basis for the MiG-29S with a modified flight control system, improved radar, compatibility with the advanced AAM-AE radar guided AAM and greater weapons load. It is offered for export as the MiG-29SE while earlier MiG-29s could be rebuilt to MiG-29S standard.

Photo: Germany continues to operate the former East German MiG-29s inherited on re-unification in 1989. (Luftwaffe)

Mikoyan MiG-29M & MiG-33

Country of origin: Russia

Type: Multirole fighter

Powerplants: Two 96kN (19,355lb) with afterburning Klimov/Sariskov RD-33K turbofans.

Performance: Max speed at altitude Mach 2.35 or 2445km/h (1320kt), max speed at sea level Mach 1.06 or 1500km/h (810kt). Max initial rate of climb 64,960ft/min. Service ceiling 55,775ft. Range with external fuel 3200km (1728nm), range with max internal fuel 2000km (1080nm).

Weights: Max takeoff approx 20,000kg (44,050lb).

Dimensions: Wing span 11.36m (37ft 3in), length inc probe 17.37m (57ft 0in), height 4.73m (15ft 6in). Wing area 38.0m² (409.0sq ft).

Accommodation: Pilot only.

Armament: One GSh-301 30mm cannon. Max external ordnance of 4500kg (9920lb) on eight underwing hardpoints can include R-60MK (AA-8), R-27R1 (AA-10A), R-73E (AA-11) and R-77 (AA-12) AAMs, plus laser guided Kh-25ML (AS-10 'Karen'), Kh-29L (AS-14 'Kedge') ASMs, radar homing Kh-31P/A (AS-17 'Krypton') ASMs, TV guided Kh-29T (AS-14 'Kedge') ASMs, TV guided bombs, bombs and rockets.

Operators: India*, Russia*.

History: The MiG-29M is an advanced multirole development of the basic MiG-29.

Development of the MiG-29M dates to the mid 1980s. Six prototypes were built and the first of these flew for the first time on April 25 1986 (although powered by RD-33s rather than RD-33Ks). The first prototype powered by the definitive, more powerful RD-33K powerplants first flew in late 1989. However it was not until 1995 that the MiG-29M was ordered into late production. Export versions would have been designated MiG-29ME, although both versions have recently been redesignated MiG-33.

The MiG-33 features significant changes over the basic MiG-29. The MiG-33 has greatly increased internal fuel capacity courtesy of the bulged dorsal spine (different than that of the 'Fulcrum-C'), a smaller cannon ammunition tank and the deletion of the overwing air intakes (the MiG-33 instead features retractable meshed intake FOD doors). The MiG-33's chaff and flare dispensers are housed in the spine rather than in the extended fins of earlier models, while the M also features redesigned leading-edge root extensions, tail, and, to a lesser extent, wing.

Internally the MiG-33 introduces an analog fly-by-wire flight control system and a slight aft centre of gravity for relaxed stability, a new N-010 radar with vastly improved processing capabilities and new operating modes expanding air-to-ground capabilities, and a revised cockpit with two CRT displays and HOTAS controls. The MiG-33 can fire an expanded range of advanced AAMs and ASMs, while the more powerful RD-33K engines have an increased (and much needed) TBO (time between overhaul).

The MiG-29K is similar to the MiG-29M but was designed for carrier operations with strengthened undercarriage for ski jump takeoffs, an arrester hook and folding wings. It was passed over in preference for a navalised Su-27.

Photo: Takeoff for a MiG-29M demonstrator/prototype. (Dave Fraser)

Mikoyan MiG-AT

Country of origin: Russia

Type: Two seat advanced trainer

Powerplants: Two 14.1kN (3175lb) Turboméca-SNECMA Larzac 04-R20 turbofans (production engines will be built under licence in Russia by Chernyshov).

Performance: Estimated – Max speed at 8200ft 1000km/h (540kt), max speed at sea level 850km/h (460kt). Service ceiling 50,820ft. Range approx 2600km (1405nm).

Weights: Normal takeoff 4610kg (10,155lb), max takeoff 7000kg (15,420lb).

Dimensions: Wing span 10.16m (33ft 4ft), length overall including nose probe 12.01m (39ft 5in), height 4.62m (15ft 2in).

Accommodation: Two in tandem.

Armament: Six underwing and one centreline hardpoints can carry a max external load of 2000kg (4410lb), including missiles and bombs.

Operators: Russian decision on whether to acquire the MiG-AT or Yak-130 pending at late 1995. Requirement for up to 250 aircraft.

History: The Mikoyan MiG-AT is one of two competitors for a Russian Air Force requirement for a new advanced jet trainer to replace the Czech designed L-29 Delphin and L-39 Albatros.

The MiG-AT and Yak-130 were selected for further development and competitive evaluation from a number of design proposals from Russian aircraft designers. In 1992 Mikoyan reached an agreement with engine manufacturer SNECMA of France that the first two prototypes would be powered by two Larzac turbofans (the Larzac powers the Alpha Jet). Production MiG-ATs are also due to powered by Larzacs, built under licence in Russia by Chernyshov.

The MiG-AT is of conventional configuration and features a large degree of composite construction and fly-by-wire flight controls. The wing is straight and the two engines are mounted either side of the fuselage. One early design change was the repositioning of the tailplane from the top of the fin to lower down on the tail.

If the MiG-AT is selected for the Russian trainer program it will feature Russian avionics. Regardless of the competition's outcome though Mikoyan is offering the MiG-AT for export with either Russian or French avionics. The MiG-ATF features advanced avionics built by Sextant Avionique. The MiG-ATF's cockpit would feature LCD colour displays, a wide angle HUD and HOTAS controls with all avionics connected through a MIL STD 1553B databus, allowing future integration of further western equipment and weaponry.

The first prototype (which was publicly displayed at the 1995 Paris Airshow and was due to make its first flight by the end of that year) is equipped with French avionics, while the second prototype will be equipped with Russian avionics. If selected for production the MiG-AT would be built by MAPO (Moscow Aircraft Production Organisation), the aircraft factory which has merged with the Mikoyan bureau and which also builds the MiG-29.

A single seat attack version of the MiG-AT is also under development under the designation MiG-ATB (B for Boyevoy or combat). It will be marketed internationally.

Photo: The MiG-AT prototype at the 1995 Moscow Airshow. (Alex Radetski)

Mil Mi-4 & Harbin Z-5

Country of origin: Russia

Type: Utility helicopter

Powerplant: One 1270kW (1700hp) Shvetsov ASh-82V eighteen cylinder radial piston engine, driving a four bladed main rotor and three bladed tail rotor.

Performance: Max speed at 3280ft 200km/h (108kt), max speed at sea level 175km/h (95kt), max cruising speed 160km/h (65kt). Service ceiling 18,045ft. Hovering ceiling out of ground effect 2295ft. Range 650km (650km).

Weights: Empty 4900kg (10,802lb), max takeoff 7550kg (16,645lb).

Dimensions: Main rotor diameter 21.00m (68ft 11in), length overall rotors turning 25.02m (82ft 1in), fuselage length 16.80m (55ft 1in), height overall 4.40m (14ft 5in). Main rotor disc area 349.5m² (3761.9sq ft).

Accommodation: Two pilots in flightdeck. Main cabin can accommodate up to 12 combat equipped troops or 1600kg (3525lb) of freight.

Armament: Some army assault Mi-4s were fitted with a fixed or movable machine gun in a ventral gondola designed to accommodate a navigator/observer. Optional weapon pylons could carry gun and rocket pods.

Operators: Mi-4 – Afghanistan, Algeria, Cuba, Guinea, Mali, North Korea, Sudan, Vietnam, Yemen. Z-5 – Albania, China.

History: The Mi-4 ('Hound' to NATO) was one of Russia's first effective and useful helicopters with over 3500 built. Harbin of China built several hundred more as the Z-5 and these still form the backbone of China's helicopter force.

Development of the Mi-4 began at the direct request of Soviet Premier Josef Stalin in 1951. Hurried development resulted in the prototype Mi-4 making its first flight in August 1951, while production deliveries began the following year, initially to the state airline Aeroflot (as the passenger carrying Mi-4P). Early production Mi-4s were fitted with wooden rotor blades.

The Mi-4 is close in appearance and configuration to Sikorsky's S-55 (H-19) but larger overall and closer in weights and size to the later S-58 (described under the Westland Wessex entry). Like the S-58 the Mi-4 is powered by a radial piston engine mounted in the nose which drives the four bladed main rotor via a shaft which passes between the raised cockpit and the main cabin.

The cabin can accommodate 12 fully equipped troops, while the rear fuselage is formed by two clamshell doors.

Apart from the basic troop transport Mi-4 'Hound-A' troop transport, the Mi-4 was also built in ASW 'Hound-B' form fitted with a search radar and the 'Hound-C' ECM platform. Soviet production continued until 1969.

The first Chinese built Mi-4 had its maiden flight on December 14 1959, with deliveries of Harbin built H-5s commencing in the mid 1960s. Over 500 were built through to 1979 and several hundred remain in service. The Z-6 designation applies to at least one Z-5 fitted with two Pratt & Whitney PT6T turboshafts. It flew in 1979.

Photo: Hungary was one of the more than 25 nations to have operated the Mi-4. (MAP)

Mil Mi-6 & Mi-22

Mil Mi-26

Country of origin: Russia

Type: Heavylift transport helicopter

Powerplants: Mi-6 – Two 4045kW (5425shp) Soloviev (now Aviadvigatel) D-25V (TV-2BM) turboshafts, driving a five bladed main rotor and two bladed tail rotor.

Performance: Mi-6 – Max speed 300km/h (162kt), max cruising speed 250km/h (135kt). Service ceiling 14,750ft. Hovering ceiling in ground effect 8200ft. Max ferry range with auxiliary fuel 1450km (780nm), range with external fuel and a 4500kg (9920lb) payload 1000km (540nm), range with a 8000kg (17,635lb) payload 620km (335nm).

Weights: Mi-6 – Empty 27,240kg (60,055lb), max takeoff for a VTO 42,500kg (93,700lb).

Dimensions: Main rotor diameter 35.00m (114ft 10in), wing span 15.30m (50ft 3in), length overall rotors turning 41.74m (137ft 0in), fuselage length exc nose gun 33.18m (108ft 11in), height overall 9.86m (32ft 4in). Main rotor disc area 962.1m² (10,356sq ft).

Accommodation: Crew of five comprising two pilots, flight engineer, navigator and radio operator. Main cabin can accommodate 65 to 90 passengers or 70 combat equipped troops or 41 stretcher patients and two medical attendants in medevac configuration. Max slung cargo load of 8000kg (17,637lb), max internal payload 12,000kg (26,450lb).

Armament: Some Mi-6s are fitted with nose 12.7mm machine gun.

Operators: Iraq, Laos, Peru, Poland, Russia, Syria.

History: At the time of its first flight the Mi-6 ('Hook') was the world's largest and fastest helicopter.

The Mi-6 was developed against a joint Soviet Air Force/Aeroflot requirement for a heavylift helicopter. The resulting Mi-6 is a behemoth, its 42 tonne max takeoff weight approaching that of the Lockheed C-130 Hercules. The Mi-6 was also the first turboshaft powered helicopter in the USSR to reach production, and, remarkably for its size, became the first helicopter to break 300km/h (162kt).

The Mi-6 flew for the first time in late 1957 and around 800 production 'Hook's were built through to 1981. The basic military transport Mi-6 'Hook-A' was joined by the civilian Mi-6P with square windows, while the type formed the basis of the civil Mi-10 flying crane.

Two specialised variants are the Mi-6VKP 'Hook-B' and the Mi-22 'Hook-C'. The Mi-6VKP and Mi-22 are both command support aircraft that seem to act as portable command posts. The Mi-6VKP can be identified by a U shaped antenna under the tailboom and a number of T shaped antennae around the tailboom. The Mi-22 can be distinguished by its single blade antenna on the tailboom and assortment of antennae under the fuselage. Little is known of their precise equipment or roles.

While such a large helicopter may seem an anomaly in the west the lack of suitable airfields in the underdeveloped regions of Russia makes helicopters particularly useful. Indeed the Mi-6 has been superseded by an even larger helicopter, the Mi-26, although the Mi-6 still remains in widespread use.

Photo: The Mi-6's wings provide 20% of total lift in cruising flight. (MAP)

Country of origin: Russia

Type: Heavylift helicopter

Powerplants: Mi-26 – Two 8267kW (11,086shp) ZKMB Progress (Lotarev) D-136 turboshafts, driving an eight bladed main rotor and five bladed tail rotor.

Performance: Mi-26 – Max speed 295km/h (160kt), typical cruising speed 255km/h (137kt). Service ceiling 15,100ft. Hovering ceiling in ground effect 14,765ft. Range with max internal fuel at max takeoff weight with reserves 800km (432nm), range with four auxiliary fuel tanks 1920km (1036nm).

Weights: Mi-26 – Empty 28,200kg (62,170lb), normal takeoff 49,600kg (109,350lb), max takeoff 56,000kg (123,450lb).

Dimensions: Mi-26 – Main rotor diameter 32.00m (105ft 0in), length overall 40.03m (131ft 4in), fuselage length 33.73m (110ft 8in), height to top of rotor head 8.15m (26ft 9in). Main rotor disc area 804.25m² (8657sq ft).

Accommodation: Flightcrew of four comprising two pilots, flight engineer and navigator, plus load master. Four seat passenger compartment behind flightdeck. Main cabin accommodates freight typically (max payload 20 tonnes/44,090lb), or up to 80 combat equipped troops or in medevac role 60 stretcher patients and four or five medical attendants. Medical version comprehensively equipped with operating theatre and accommodation for stretcher patients and medical attendants.

Armament: None

Operators: India, Russia.

History: One word describes the Mi-26 (NATO reporting name 'Halo') ... big. The largest helicopter in the world by a large margin, the Mi-26 has a maximum takeoff weight greater than that of the Transall C-160 and an internal freight hold close in size to that in the C-130 Hercules.

Development of the Mi-26 began in the early 1970s and resulted in a first flight on December 14 1977. The original design requirement called for a helicopter for military and civil use with a maximum takeoff weight one and a half times that of any previous helicopter. Pre production machines were built from 1980, production machines sometime after that. The first Mi-26s are understood to have become operational with the Soviet military during 1983.

Notable for its eight bladed main rotor, powerful turboshaft engines, massive size, rear loading freight door and twin internal hoists, several Mi-26 versions have been developed or proposed. These include the basic Mi-26 'Halo-A' freighter, the equivalent civil Mi-26T, Mi-26MS medevac version, civil Mi-26P 63 passenger airliner, Mi-26TM flying crane and Mi-26TZ fuel tanker. The improved Mi-26M is under development and features new ZKMB Progress D-127 turboshafts, composite main rotor blades, improved aerodynamics, better hot and high performance and EFIS cockpit displays. The Mi-26 or Mi-26M could also form the basis of a replacement for command support Mi-6s.

Photo: The Mi-26TM flying crane demonstrator at a Paris Airshow. It features a gondola under the fuselage for a pilot/sling supervisor. (Julian Green)

Mil Mi-8 & Mi-17

Country of origin: Russia

Type: Multirole transport helicopter

Powerplants: Mi-8 – Two 1255kW (1700shp) Klimov (Isotov) TV2-117A turboshafts driving a five bladed main rotor and three bladed tail rotor.

Performance: Mi-8 – Max speed at 3280ft 260km/h (140kt), max cruising speed 225km/h (122kt). Service ceiling 14,760ft. Hovering ceiling in ground effect 6235ft, out of ground effect 2625ft. Ferry range 1200km (650nm), range with standard fuel 465km (250nm).

Weights: Mi-8 – Empty 7600kg (16,007lb), max takeoff 12,000kg (26,455lb).

Dimensions: Mi-8 – Main rotor diameter 21.29m (69ft 11in), length overall rotors turning 25.24m (82ft 10in), fuselage length 18.17m (59ft 7in), height overall 5.65m (18ft 7in). Main rotor disc area 356.0m² (3823.1sq ft).

Accommodation: Mi-8 – Two pilots and loadmaster. Main cabin can accommodate 28 troops, or twelve stretcher patients.

Armament: Most variants fitted with outriggers either side of the fuselage with two hardpoints each typically for rocket pods, although Mi-8TB equipped for M17P (AT-2 'Sagger') anti armour missiles.

Operators: In service with at least 50 nations including Afghanistan, Angola, Byelorussia, Bulgaria, China, Cuba, Czech Republic, Egypt, Finland, Hungary, India, Iraq, North Korea, Pakistan, Peru, Poland, Romania, Russia, Slovakia, Ukraine, Vietnam, Yemen, Yugoslavia.

History: The rugged and useful Mi-8 and Mi-17 transports have been built in more numbers than any other helicopter in Russia.

Work on the Mi-8 began in 1960 with the aim of finding a successor for the piston engined 14 seat Mi-4 'Hound'. The resulting aircraft featured the Mi-4's dynamic systems coupled to a new fuselage and powered by a turboshaft engine. The first prototype Mi-8 ('Hip-A') flew during June 1961 and was powered by a single 2015kW (2700shp) Soloviev turboshaft, but when the Mi-8 was found to be underpowered two Isotov TV2 turboshafts and a five bladed main rotor were substituted instead. The Mi-8 first flew in this configuration in August 1962, and since that time more than 10,000 have been built.

Initial production Mi-8s including the Mi-8T are covered by the NATO designation 'Hip-C' and include the basic military transport plus civil versions with square windows. The Mi-8TB 'Hip-E' is a dedicated assault version with three (instead of two) outrigger hardpoints either side of the fuselage for rockets or 9M17 (AT-2 'Swatter') anti armour missiles, while the export Mi-8TBK 'Hip-F' was armed with 9M14M (AT-3 'Sagger') missiles.

There have been numerous Mi-8 special mission variants including the Mi-8PS 'Hip-D' radio relay/command post aircraft, the similar Mi-9 'Hip-G' with hockey stick antennae under the tailboom and fuselage, the Mi-8SMV 'Hip-J' ECM jammer, and the Mi-8PPA 'Hip-K' communications jammer with a unique antenna array either side of the fuselage (with six cross dipole antennae each).

The Mi-17 'Hip-H' introduced uprated TV3 turboshafts and can be identified by its port side tail rotor. Several Mi-8s were also rebuilt to this standard under the designations Mi-8MT or Mi-8TV. The Mi-171 and Mi-172 have more powerful TV3s.

Photo: Six Mi-8s remain in German service. (Luftwaffe)

Mil Mi-14

Country of origin: Russia

Type: ASW, mine countermeasures and SAR amphibious helicopter

Powerplants: Mi-14PL – Two 1270kW (1700shp) Klimov (Isotov) TV3-117A turboshafts driving a five bladed main rotor and three bladed tail rotor.

Performance: Mi-14PL – Max speed 230km/h (125kt), max cruising speed 215km/h (116kt), economical cruising speed 205km/h (110kt). Max initial rate of climb 1535ft/min. Service ceiling 13,125ft. Time to 3280ft 2min 18sec. Ferry range with auxiliary fuel 1135km (612nm), range with standard fuel 925km (500nm). Endurance 5hr 55min.

Weights: Mi-14PL – Empty 8900kg (19,625lb), max takeoff 14,000kg (30,865lb).

Dimensions: Mi-14PL – Main rotor diameter 21.29m (69ft 11in), length overall rotors turning 25.32m (83ft 1in), fuselage length 18.37m (60ft 3in), height overall 6.93m (22ft 9in). Main rotor disc area 356.0m² (3832.1sq ft).

Accommodation: Mi-14PL has a crew of four. The Mi-14PS has a crew of three and can accommodate 10 rescued survivors in the main cabin including two on stretchers.

Armament: The Mi-14PL can carry torpedoes, bombs and depth charges in an enclosed weapons bay in the lower hull.

Operators: Bulgaria, Cuba, Libya, Poland, Romania, Syria, Yugoslavia.

History: The Mi-14 is an amphibious development of the Mi-8/Mi-17, used for a variety of maritime tasks including anti submarine warfare, search and rescue and mine countermeasures.

The Mi-8 presented itself as the logical replacement for a number of Mi-4 variants in Soviet naval service, and so development began on a navalised variant in 1968. Under the preliminary designation V-14 the first Mi-14 prototype flew for the first time in 1968. This first prototype featured the TV2 turboshafts and right hand side tail rotor of the Mi-8, while production Mi-14s feature the more powerful TV3s and left hand side tail rotor of the Mi-17. The most notable feature of the Mi-14 (NATO name 'Haze') is the boat like hull, floatation equipment and retractable undercarriage.

The Mi-14 has been built in three basic variants. The Mi-14PL 'Haze-A' is the ASW variant and features a large undernose radome, dunking sonar, sonobuoys, a towed MAD bird and a weapons bay which can house torpedoes, bombs and depth charges. An improved model is designated Mi-14PLM.

The Mi-14BT 'Haze-B' is a dedicated mine countermeasures variant. The Mi-14BT was introduced into service in the early 1980s and can carry three towed sleds to counter magnetic, acoustic or contact mines. The Mi-14BT retains the nose radome but lacks the MAD bird of the Mi-14PL.

Finally the search and rescue Mi-14PS 'Haze-C' features an enlarged sliding door, a retractable rescue hoist, a searchlight either side of the nose and carries 10 20-place liferafts. The cabin can accommodate 10 rescued survivors, while others can be towed in liferafts. It is designated Mi-14PW in Polish service.

Photo: Former East German Mi-14BTs (including this SAR converted example) were retired after reunification. (MAP)

Mil Mi-24, Mi-25 & Mi-35

Country of origin: Russia

Type: Armed assault/attack helicopter

Powerplants: Two 1635kW (2190shp) Klimov TV3-117 turboshafts driving a five bladed main rotor and three bladed tail rotor.

Performance: Mi-24P – Max speed 335km/h (180kt), cruising speed 270km/h (145kt), economical cruising speed 217km/h (117kt). Max initial rate of climb 2460ft/min. Service ceiling 14,750ft. Hovering ceiling out of ground effect 4920ft. Range with auxiliary fuel 1000km (540nm), range with standard internal fuel 500km (270nm). Combat radius with max military load 160km (85nm), radius with two external fuel tanks 225km (120nm), radius with four tanks 288km (155nm).

Weights: Mi-24P – Empty 8200kg (18,078lb), max takeoff 12,000kg (26,455lb).

Dimensions: Mi-24P – Main rotor diameter 17.30m (56ft 9in), length overall rotors turning 21.35m (70ft 1in), fuselage length exc gun 17.51m (57ft 5in), height to top of rotor head 3.97m (13ft 1in). Main rotor disc area 235.1m² (2530.2sq ft).

Accommodation: Weapon operator and pilot in tandem stepped cockpit. Main cabin can accommodate eight troops or four stretchers.

Armament: One 12.7mm four barrel YakB machine gun in undernose turret or 23mm or 30mm cannon. Two anti armour missiles on each stub wing endplate. Four underwing hardpoints for rockets and guns.

Operators: Afghanistan, Algeria, Angola, Armenia, Azerbaijan, Bulgaria, Croatia, Cuba, Czech Republic, Hungary, India, Iraq, Libya, Mozambique, Peru, Poland, Russia, Slovakia, Syria, Ukraine, USA, Yemen.

History: Mil's feared 'Devil's Chariot' is unique in that it is a combined armed assault/attack helicopter, although the latter is its primary role.

The Mi-24 is based on the dynamic systems of the Mi-8 transport helicopter, although almost all production aircraft featured the uprated TV3 turboshafts and port side tail rotor of the Mi-17. Design considerations were speed and firepower.

First flight of the V-24 prototype was in 1973, while production Mi-24 'Hind-A's entered service in 1973. Early production 'Hind-A's, 'Hind-B's and 'Hind-C's feature a glasshouse style cockpit for the pilot and weapons operator which offered poor visibility and protection. The Mi-24D 'Hind-D' and export Mi-25 introduced the definitive stepped and armoured cockpits, plus the four barrel 12.7mm machine gun in an undernose turret plus undernose missile guidance and electro optical pods. The similar Mi-24V 'Hind-E' (or Mi-35 for export) introduced the stubwing endplates for 9M114 (AT-6 'Spiral') anti armour missiles and a HUD for the pilot. The Mi-24VP introduced a twin barrel GSh-23L cannon in the turret as operational experience in Afghanistan found the original gun ineffective against some targets, while the Mi-24P 'Hind-F' (and export Mi-35P) has a twin 30mm cannon. The Mi-24R and Mi-24K NBC reconnaissance platforms.

Finally Mil is developing an upgraded Mi-24/Mi-35 featuring the Mi-28's rotors and transmission, a 23mm cannon and 9K114-9 Attacka advanced anti armour missiles. A version could have advanced avionics and displays provided by Sextant Avionique of France.

Photo: The Czech Republic operates Mi-24Ds and Mi-24Vs. (Bruce Malcolm)

Mil Mi-28

Country of origin: Russia

Type: Two seat attack helicopter

Powerplants: Two 1545kW (2070shp) Klimov TV3-117VM turboshafts driving a five bladed main rotor and four bladed tail rotor.

Performance: Max speed 300km/h (162kt), max cruising speed 270km/h (145kt). Max initial rate of climb 2675ft/min. Service ceiling 19,025ft. Hovering ceiling out of ground effect 11,810ft. Ferry range with reserves 1100km (595nm), max range with standard fuel 460km (250nm). Combat radius with standard fuel, 10min loiter and reserves 200km (110nm). Endurance with max fuel 2hr.

Weights: Empty equipped 8095kg (17,845lb), max takeoff 11,660kg (25,705lb).

Dimensions: Main rotor diameter 17.20m (56ft 5in), length exc rotors 17.01m (55ft 9in), height to top of rotor head 3.82m (12ft 7in). Main rotor disc area 232.3m² (2501sq ft).

Accommodation: Navigator/weapons operator and pilot in stepped tandem cockpit with navigator in front cockpit. A rear fuselage compartment can accommodate two or three people – intended for emergency recovery of personnel only.

Armament: One NPPU-28 30mm cannon in undernose turret. Four underwing hardpoints can carry a combined ordnance load of 1920kg (4230lb). Typical configuration of two rocket pods and up to 16 9P149 Shturm C (AT-6 'Spiral') radio guided tube launched anti armour missiles.

Operators: Russia*

History: Manoeuvrable, well armed, armoured and fast, the Mi-28 is Mil's first dedicated two seat attack helicopter and is in heated competition with the Kamov Ka-50 to meet Russian Army requirements.

Design of the Mi-28 (NATO reporting name 'Havoc') began as early as 1980 and the first of three prototypes flew for the first time on November 10 1982. Development of the basic Mi-28 is now largely complete with only a small number built for service evaluation.

The Mi-28 is of conventional dedicated attack helicopter configuration with tandem stepped cockpits with energy absorbing crew seats, an undernose turret containing a 30mm cannon, stubwings with two hardpoints each and twin TV3 turboshafts (the TV3 also powers the Ka-50, plus Mil's Mi-17 and Mi-24). The original three bladed tail rotor unit has been replaced by a four blade X shape unit, similar to that on the AH-64 Apache. The cockpits feature ceramic and titanium armour, while the entire airframe is designed to absorb and survive small arms fire. Countermeasures are carried in the wingtip pods. The thimble nose radome contains a missile guidance radar, beneath are two fixed infrared sensors.

The Mi-28N is an improved night/all weather development featuring a mast mounted millimetre wave radar, a FLIR ball turret under the nose radome, a low light TV and night vision compatible cockpit lighting. The Russian Army has ordered the Mi-28N into production, with service entry in 1997 or 1998. First flight was due during 1995.

Photo: The mast mounted sight equipped Mi-28N debuted at the 1995 Moscow Airshow. (Alex Radetski)

Mitsubishi T-2

Country of origin: Japan

Type: Two seat advanced trainer and weapons trainer

Powerplants: Two 22.8kN (5115lb) dry and 32.5kN (7305lb) with afterburning Ishikawajima-Harima TF40-IHI-801A (licence built Rolls-Royce Turboméca Adour Mk 801) turbofans.

Performance: Max speed at 36,000ft Mach 1.6 or 1700km/h (917kt). Max initial rate of climb 35,000ft. Service ceiling 50,000ft. Ferry range 2595km (1400nm).

Weights: Operating empty 6305kg (13,905lb), max takeoff 12,800kg (28,220lb).

Dimensions: Wing span 7.88m (25ft 10in), length overall inc probe 17.86m (58ft 7in), fuselage length 17.31m (56ft 10in), height 4.33m (14ft 3in). Wing area 21.2m² (227.9sq ft).

Accommodation: Two in tandem.

Armament: T-2A – One licence built JM61 Vulcan 20mm cannon in lower fuselage. AIM-9 Sidewinder or Mitsubishi AAM-1 AAMs on wingtips, plus bombs, rocket pods and fuel tanks on one centreline and four underwing hardpoints.

Operators: Japan

History: The T-2 is Japan's first indigenously developed supersonic aircraft and serves as the Japan Air Self Defence Force's primary advanced trainer and weapons trainer.

The Japanese Defence Ministry selected Mitsubishi as prime contractor to develop a supersonic advanced and weapons trainer in September 1967. The T-2 was designed by a team led by Dr Kenji Ikeda and the resulting aircraft was similar in configuration and philosophy to the Northrop T-38 Talon and the SEPECAT Jaguar. First flight of the first of four flying XT-2 prototypes was on July 20 1971. Service entry was in 1976.

The Mach 1.6 T-2 was designed as a lead-in trainer for F-4EJ and F-104J fighters. It features two afterburning licence built Rolls-Royce Turboméca Adour turbofans (licence built by Ishikawajima-Harima as the TF40-IHI-801A), a high mounted wing (which lacks ailerons, lateral control is instead provided by differential spoilers ahead of the flaps), an airbrake on either side of the fuselage, tandem seating under separate canopies and licence built ejection seats. About 10% of the T-2's structure by weight is titanium, in particular around the engine bays.

A total of 90 production T-2s were ordered, comprising 28 standard T-2 trainers and 62 T-2A armament trainers. The T-2A features wingtip missile rails for Sidewinder of Mitsubishi AAM-1 infrared guided air-to-air missiles, a JM61 Vulcan 20mm cannon, four underwing hardpoints for weaponry, a HUD and a Mitsubishi Electric J/AWG-11 search and ranging radar.

A single T-2 was converted to act as the T-2CCV control configured vehicle, with a triplex digital fly-by-wire flight control system and canards with test equipment in the rear cockpit. In addition, two T-2s were converted to act as prototypes for the F-1 ground attack fighter (which is described in the next entry).

Photo: Six T-2As equip the Japan Air Self Defence Force's Blue Impulse aerobatic display team. These aircraft have a secondary wartime air defence role. (MAP)

Mitsubishi F-1

Country of origin: Japan

Type: Close support/ground attack fighter

Powerplants: Two 22.8kN (5115lb) dry and 32.5kN (7305lb) with afterburning Ishikawajima-Harima TF40-IHI-801A (licence built Rolls-Royce Turboméca Adour Mk 801) turbofans.

Performance: Max speed at 36,000ft Mach 1.6 or 1700km/h (917kt). Max initial rate of climb 35,000ft/min. Service ceiling 50,000ft. Combat radius with eight 500lb/227kg bombs, hi-lo-hi 350km (190nm), combat radius with two ASM-1 anti ship missiles and two drop tanks, hi-lo-hi 555km (300nm).

Weights: Operating empty 6358kg (14,017lb), max takeoff 13,700kg (30,203lb).

Dimensions: Wing span 7.88m (25ft 10in), length overall inc probe 17.86m (58ft 7in), fuselage length 17.31m (56ft 10in), height 4.33m (14ft 3in). Wing area 21.2m² (227.9sq ft).

Accommodation: Pilot only.

Armament: One licence built JM61 Vulcan 20mm internal cannon. AIM-9L Sidewinder or Mitsubishi AAM-1 AAMs on wingtip and outboard underwing hardpoints. One centreline and four underwing hardpoints for bombs, rocket pods and fuel tanks. Can carry a ASM-1 radar guided ASM on each inboard underwing pylon.

Operators: Japan

History: The T-2 advanced trainer based Mitsubishi F-1 is Japan's first supersonic fighter and is tasked primarily with anti shipping strike.

The Japan Air Self Defence Force ordered development of a single seat ground attack development of the Mitsubishi T-2 under the provisional designation FS-T2-Kai in 1972. The second and third XT-2 prototypes were converted to act as F-1 prototypes, and the first of these flew in modified form on June 3 1975 (the second flew four days later).

The F-1 prototypes were largely unchanged from the T-2 except that the faired over rear cockpit contained a fire control system and test equipment. In mid 1975 they were delivered to the JASDF's Air Proving Wing at Gifu for a year of service testing. Following the successful completion of service trials the F-1 designation was adopted and the type was ordered into production. In all, 77 F-1s were built, delivered between September 1977 and March 1987, replacing elderly F-86 Sabres.

The only major change from the T-2 to the F-1 was the faired over second cockpit which contains the bombing computer, inertial navigation system and radar warning system. From 1982 the Mitsubishi J/AWG-12 search and ranging radar replaced the earlier J/AWG-11, introducing compatibility with the radar guided ASM-1 air-to-surface missile. With this weapon the F-1 is primarily tasked with anti shipping strike. The F-1 is now cleared to fire the AIM-9L Sidewinder and is due to be equipped with the newly developed longer range ASM-2 anti ship missile.

The F-1 is due to remain in service to around the turn of the century, when it is due to be replaced with the Mitsubishi FS-X. In the meantime the survivors are undergoing a service life extension program. They equip three hikotais (squadrons).

Photo: Compared with its predecessor the T-2, the F-1 features avionics in the faired over rear cockpit and a higher max takeoff weight. (MAP)

Mitsubishi FS-X

Country of origin: Japan and the USA

Type: Ground attack & maritime strike fighter

Powerplants: One 129.0kN (29,000lb) with afterburning General Electric F110-GE-129 turbofan.

Performance: No performance figures published at time of writing.

Weights: Empty 9525kg (21,000lb), max takeoff 22,100kg (48,722lb).

Dimensions: Wing span over missile rails 11.13m (36ft 6in), length overall 15.27m (50ft 1in), height 4.97m (16ft 4in). Wing area 33.2m² (357.0sq ft).

Accommodation: Pilot only, or two in tandem in TFS-X.

Armament: One M61A1 Vulcan 20mm internal cannon. Sidewinders and forthcoming AAM-3 AAMs on wingtip rails. One centreline and four underwing hardpoints for a variety of weaponry, such as the radar guided Mitsubishi ASM-1 anti ship missile, the forthcoming Mitsubishi ASM-2 anti ship missile and AIM-7M Sparrow AAMs.

Operators: Japan*

History: The hugely expensive Mitsubishi FS-X is a Japanese development of the Lockheed Martin F-16 to replace the F-1 for maritime strike, ground attack and counter air missions.

Following on from the success of the T-2 trainer and F-1 fighter Japan originally planned to develop an all new aircraft to meet the F-1 replacement requirement. In the early 1980s Japan's Technical Research and Development Institute had been studying designs for a new fighter to meet the Japan Air Self Defence Force's particular design requirements, including long range and manoeuvrability. However the USA exerted considerable pressure on Japan to continue to buy US sourced weapons and to reduce the large trade imbalance between the two countries. Thus plans to develop an indigenous fighter were dropped in 1987 with the Japan Defence Agency (JDA) instead compromising on developing an existing US fighter with considerable US industrial participation.

The then General Dynamics F-16 was selected to form the basis of a Japanese developed support fighter in October 1987. Mitsubishi was appointed prime contractor for the FS-X program in November 1988 while the General Electric F110-GE-129 Improved Performance Engine was selected as the FS-X's powerplant in December 1990. Four FS-X prototypes are being built, and the first of these flew for the first time in October 1995.

Compared with the F-16 the FS-X features a 25% larger wing constructed of co-cured composites (for increased strength and reduced weight), a longer fuselage, conventional cockpit canopy, a Mitsubishi Electric developed active phased array radar and Japanese avionics including the integrated electronic warfare system, LCD displays and a HUD. In addition the FS-X features a Japanese developed fly-by-wire flight control system (developed on the T-2CCV) because of US refusal to release F-16 fly-by-wire software source codes.

The JASDF originally required 130 FS-Xs, including some two seat TFS-X conversion trainers, although funding cuts and spiralling development costs (over $US3bn) saw this number reduced to around 80. The JDA now wants to acquire 83 FS-X fighters and TFS-X conversion trainers, plus 58 further TFS-Xs to replace the T-2 advanced trainer.

Photo: The FS-X first flew in October 1995.

Morane-Saulnier MS-760 Paris

Country of origin: France

Type: Basic trainer, light strike, fast liaison/communications and target simulation aircraft.

Powerplants: MS-760B – Two 4.74kN (1058lb) Turboméca Maboré VI turbojets.

Performance: MS-760B – Max speed at 25,000ft 695km/h (375kt), max cruising speed at 16,400ft 633km/h (342kt), economical cruising speed 550km/h (297kt). Max initial rate of climb 2460ft/min. Service ceiling 39,370ft. Max range 1740km (940nm).

Weights: MS-760B – Empty equipped 2067kg (4557lb), max takeoff 3920kg (8642lb).

Dimensions: MS-760B – Wing span 10.15m (33ft 3in), length overall 10.24m (33ft 7in), height 2.60m (8ft 6in). Wing area 18.0m² (193.7sq ft).

Accommodation: Seating for four.

Armament: For weapons training and light strike two underwing hardpoints (one under each wing) for 7.5m machine gun pods, rockets or light bombs.

Operators: Argentina, France.

History: The four seat Paris jet was designed primarily as a high speed military liaison/communications aircraft but was also offered in civil forms. A significant number remain in service with the French Air Force plus the French Navy and the Argentine Air Force.

The Paris was based on Morane-Saulnier's MS-755 Flueret, a two seat jet trainer which flew in 1953. The larger MS-760 Paris features seating for four under a rearwards sliding canopy with dual controls for pilot training, a straight wing, two Turboméca Maboré turbojets (fed through air inlets in the wingroots) and a T tail. It can be armed with four 3.5in rockets, gun pods or 50kg bombs for a weapons training missions.

The prototype Paris, designated MS-760-01, took to the air for the first time on July 29 1954. The Paris was then subsequently adopted by the French Air Force for communications and liaison duties. Initial production was of the 3.94kN (880lb) Maboré IIC turbojet powered MS-760A, which first flew on February 7 1958. The production total of 150 MS-760As includes 48 assembled in Argentina (by FMA).

About half of the MS-760s delivered to Argentina remain in service, although these have been upgraded to improved MS-760B standard. The MS-760B flew for the first time on December 12 1960 and introduced more powerful Maboré VI turbojets and wingtip fuel tanks. Sixty three new production MS-760Bs were built, including 48 assembled in Brazil for that country's air force. In all 219 MS-760s were manufactured. A stretched six seat development was offered for civil use.

Despite their age about 30 MS-760s remain in service with the French Armée de l'Air and Aéronavale (air force and naval air arm) where they are used for liaison, continuation training and target simulation.

Argentina's surviving MS-760s are used by two units for weapons training, while Brazil's MS-760s have long been retired.

Photo: Three French Air Force units continue to fly the Paris, while smaller numbers survive with the French Navy. (Armée de l'Air)

Mudry CAP 10, 20, 21 230, 231 & 323

Country of origin: France

Type: Basic trainer and aerobatics aircraft

Powerplant: CAP 10B – One 135kW (180hp) Lycoming AEIO-360-B2F fuel injected flat four piston engine, driving a two bladed propeller.

Performance: CAP 10B – Max speed 270km/h (146kt), max cruising speed at 75% power 250km/h (135kt). Max initial rate of climb 1575ft/min. Service ceiling 16,400ft. Range with max fuel 1000km (540nm).

Weights: 10B – Empty equipped 550kg (1213lb), max takeoff in aerobatic category 760kg (1675lb), or 830kg (1829lb) in utility category.

Dimensions: 10B – Wing span 8.06m (26ft 5in), length 7.16m (23ft 6in), height 2.55m (8ft 5in). Wing area 10.9m² (116.8sq ft).

Accommodation: Two side by side in CAP 10, pilot only in other models.

Armament: None

Operators: CAP 10 – France, Mexico, Morocco. CAP 230 – France, Morocco. CAP 231 – Morocco.

History: The Mudry CAP series serves as an initial flight screener/basic trainer with the French and Mexican air forces and as an aerobatic display mount for French and Moroccan teams.

The successful CAP series dates back to the Piel C.P.30 Emeraude of the early 1960s. More than 200 two seat Emeraudes (first flight 1962) were built in four different factories across Europe.

One of the companies to build the Emeraude was CAARP, a company owned by Auguste Mudry. CAARP used the basic Emeraude design as the basis for the CAP 10, which was a similar aircraft other than its 135kW (180hp) Lycoming IO-360 engine and stressing for aerobatic flight. The prototype CAP 10 first flew in August 1968. CAARP built 30 CAP 10s for the French Air Force before Mudry started CAP 10 production for civil orders in 1972 at his other aviation company, Avions Mudry.

The CAP 10 remains in production today in 10B form with an enlarged tail. Twenty six CAP 10Bs were delivered to the French Armée de l'Air. All French Air Force CAP 10s serve with the Ecole de l'Air at Salon de Province and the Ecole de Formation Initiale du Personnel Navigant at Avord.

Other CAP 10 military operators are Morocco, the Mexican Air Force which took delivery of 20 for aerobatic training, and the French Navy, which operates 10 for pilot screening and grading.

The CAP 20 meanwhile is a single seat development with a 150kW (200hp) AEIO-360 engine designed for civil aerobatic competition. The Armée de l'Air took delivery of six CAP 20s for its Equipe de Voltage aerobatic team.

The revised CAP 21 replaced the CAP 20 in 1981. The CAP 21 is of the same basic overall configuration to the CAP 20 but introduced a new wing and undercarriage. The following CAP 230 was heavier, stronger and powered by an uprated AEIO-540 flat six. Four were delivered to the French Air Force's Equipe de Voltage team. The 230 was followed by the 231, which first flew in April 1990. Seven CAP 231s were delivered to the Moroccan Air Force's aerobatic display team, Marche Verte (Green March). The CAP 231 EX introduced a carbon fibre wing, while production is due to switch to the further improved CAP 232, which first flew in July 1994.

Photo: French Air Force CAP 10 basic trainers. (Armée de l'Air)

NAMC YS-11

Country of origin: Japan

Type: Utility transport, ECM trainer and Elint platform

Powerplants: YS-11A-200 – Two 2280kW (3060shp) Rolls-Royce Dart Mk 542-10K turboprops, driving four bladed propellers.

Performance: -200 – Max cruising speed 470km/h (253kt), economical cruising speed 452km/h (244kt). Service ceiling 22,900ft. Range with max payload and no reserves 1090km (590nm), range with max fuel and no reserves 3215km (1736nm).

Weights: -200 – Operating empty 15,419kg (33,993lb), max takeoff 24,500kg (54,010lb).

Dimensions: Wing span 32.00m (105ft 0in), length 26.30m (86ft 4in), height 8.98m (29ft 6in). Wing area 94.8m² (1020.4sq ft).

Accommodation: Flightcrew of two. Typical seating in main cabin for 60. JMSDF YS-11M-As have seating for 48 with a rear cargo compartment. The combi YS-11A-300 was designed for freight in the forward fuselage and seating for 46 behind that.

Armament: None

Operators: Gabon, Greece, Japan.

History: The NAMC YS-11 is postwar Japan's only indigenously developed airliner. Several serve with the Japanese military and the Greek Air Force.

The YS-11 was a product of the Nihon Aircraft Manufacturing Company, a consortium of Fuji, Kawasaki, Mitsubishi, Nippi, Shin Meiwa and Showa. NAMC formed on June 1 1959 specifically to design and develop a short to medium range airliner, with particular attention paid to meeting the requirements of Japanese domestic airlines.

Within NAMC Fuji was given responsibility for the tail unit, Kawasaki the wings and engine nacelles, Mitsubishi the forward fuselage and final assembly, Nippi the ailerons and flaps, Shin Meiwa the rear fuselage and Showa the light alloy honeycomb structural components.

The YS-11 first flew on August 30 1962. Airline service entry was in April 1965. Initial production was of the YS-11-100, while the YS-11A-200 was designed for export and had an increased max takeoff weight. The YS-11A-300 was a combi passenger/freight model, while the YS-11A-400 was a pure freighter with a forward freight door. The YS-11A-500, -600 and -700 were equivalent to the -200, -300 and -400, but with a 500kg (1100lb) greater max takeoff weight. Production ceased in February 1974 after 182 were built.

The Japan Air Self Defence Force acquired four YS-11-100s as YS-11Ps for VIP transports, a YS-11-300 combi as the YS-11PC, seven YS-11-400 freighters as YS-11Cs (one subsequently converted to a YS-11NT nav trainer), and a YS-11-200 as a YS-11FC for flight check duties. In 1976 two YS-11Cs were converted to YS-11E ECM trainers (festooned with various antennae and a large chaff/flare dispenser fairing behind the starboard wing). A third YS-11C was converted as a YS-11E(EL) in 1982 for Elint reconnaissance.

The Japanese Maritime Self Defence Force meanwhile acquired two YS-11-100s as YS-11M transports and two YS-11-400 combis as YS-11M-As. Four YS-11-200s and two YS-11-600s serve as YS-11T-A ASW crew trainers, fitted with a search radar in an underbelly radome.

Greece operates six ex Olympic Airways YS-11s as transports.

Photo: One of Greece's six YS-11s. (Greek MoD)

Nanchang CJ-5 & CJ-6/PT-6

Country of origin: China

Type: Two seat basic trainer

Powerplant: CJ-6 – One 215kW (285hp) Zhuzhou (SMPMC) HS6A nine cylinder radial piston engine, driving a two bladed propeller.

Performance: CJ-6 – Max speed 297km/h (160kt), cruising speed 260km/h (160kt). Max initial rate of climb 1250ft/min. Service ceiling 20,500ft. Range with max fuel 690km (372nm). Endurance 3hr 35min.

Weights: CJ-6 – Empty 1095kg (2414lb), max takeoff 1400kg (3086lb).

Dimensions: CJ-6 – Wing span 10.22m (33ft 7in), length overall 8.46m (27ft 9in), height overall 3.25m (10ft 8in).

Accommodation: Two in tandem.

Armament: CJ-6 – None, although 10 armed CJ-6Bs built could carry light armament.

Operators: Albania, Bangladesh, Cambodia, China, North Korea.

History: The Nanchang CJ-6 is a Chinese development of the Yak-18 and is that country's primary basic trainer.

During the 1950s China had built the Yak-18 under licence as the CJ-5. China began development of its own version of the Yak-18/CJ-5 optimised specifically for its requirements and incorporating a number of improvements in the mid 1950s. Design work was carried out at Shenyang during the late 1950s. The first prototype flew for the first time on August 27 1958 and it was powered by a 110kW (145hp) Mikulln M-11ER engine. However the CJ-6 prototype soon proved underpowered and a re-engined aircraft powered by a 195kW (260hp) Ivchenko AI-14R first flew in July 1960.

CJ-6 design and production was subsequently transferred to Nanchang where further design changes were incorporated and a production standard CJ-6 first flew October 15 1961. Production go-ahead was announced the following year.

Compared with the CJ-5, the CJ-6 differed in its retractable undercarriage and more powerful engine. Initial production CJ-6s were powered by the 195kW (260hp) Chinese HS6 version of the Ivchenko AI-14. The CJ-6 was superseded in production by the definitive CJ-6A in 1965. The CJ-6A introduced the 215kW (285hp) HS6A. In addition, 10 armed CJ-6Bs were built between 1964 and 1966. Interestingly the type was also considered the basis for a civil agricultural spraying aircraft, and a single prototype flew in this form as the Haiyan-A.

In all, over 1800 CJ-6As were built through to 1986. It was exported to several non-aligned nations – Bangladesh, Cambodia, North Korea, Tanzania and Zambia – where it carries the westernised PT-6A designation.

The CJ-6 is reportedly easy to fly, rugged, easy to maintain and well suited to its training role. Design features include the two bladed constant speed prop, dihedral on the outer wing panels and a framed glasshouse style canopy covering the two occupants and giving good all round visibility.

Photo: One of more than 1800 CJ-6A/PT-6A trainers built. About 1500 remain in Chinese service.

Nanchang Q-5/A-5

Country of origin: China

Type: Ground attack aircraft

Powerplants: Two 25.5kN (5732lb) dry and 31.9kN (7165lb) with afterburning Shenyang WP6 turbojets.

Performance: A-5C – Max speed at 36,000ft Mach 1.12 or 1190km/h (643kt), max speed at sea level 1210km/h (653kt). Max rate of climb at 16,400ft, 16,430 to 20,275ft/min. Service ceiling 52,000ft. Range with max internal and external fuel 2000km (1080nm). Combat radius with max external stores hi-lo-hi 600km (325nm), lo-lo-lo 400km (215nm).

Weights: A-5C – Empty 6375kg (14,054lb), max takeoff 12,000kg (26,455lb).

Dimensions: A-5C – Wing span 9.70m (31ft 10in), length overall inc nose probe 16.26m (53ft 4in), length exc nose probe 15.42m (50ft 7in), height 4.52m (14ft 10in). Wing area 28.0m² (300.9sq ft).

Accommodation: Pilot only.

Armament: Q-5 II/A-5C – Two Norinco Type 23 23mm cannon. Ten external hardpoints for a max ordnance load of 2000kg (4410lb) including bombs, rockets, air-to-surface and air-to-air missiles. Some Chinese aircraft believed to be modified to carry a five to 20kT nuclear bomb.

Operators: Bangladesh, China, Myanmar, North Korea, Pakistan.

History: The Nanchang Q-5 (Westernised designation A-5) is a close air support/ground attack fighter developed from China's MiG-19 copy.

Development of the Q-5 (NATO reporting name 'Fantan') began in 1958, with Shenyang undertaking initial work and mock-up construction and assisting Nanchang (who had no previous experience with jet designs) with subsequent detail design. Construction of the prototype began in May 1960 although the Chinese Cultural Revolution intervened and the prototype program was cancelled in 1961. Between then and 1963 when development was officially reinstated a small team continued work on the aircraft. First flight was on June 4 1965 and subsequent testing revealed the need for a number of modifications. The first of two prototypes with the required modifications flew in late 1969 and production aircraft were delivered from 1970.

The Q-5 retained the Shenyang J-6's (MiG-19's) rear fuselage and powerplants but features a stretched area ruled fuselage with an internal weapons bay, side mounted air intakes, a new conical nose and larger wings with less sweepback.

Initial production was of the Q-5. The longer range Q-5 I has extra fuel in place of the internal bomb bay. Chinese Navy Q-5 Is may be fitted with a radar and can carry C-801 anti ship missiles and torpedoes. The Q-5 IA gained two extra underwing hardpoints and the Q-5 II is fitted with a radar warning receiver.

The A-5C was developed for Pakistan (and subsequently sold to Bangladesh) and is based on the Q-5 I but with upgraded western avionics and compatibility with western weapons (including the AIM-9 Sidewinder). The export A-5K Kong Yun with Thomson-CSF laser range finder was cancelled in 1990.

Also designed for export is the A-5M which features improved engines and Alenia avionics including a ranging radar, INS, HUD and RWR. It first flew in 1988 and has been sold to Myanmar.

Photo: Note underfuselage mounted bombs on this Q-5.

Nanchang K-8 Karakorum

Country of origin: China

Type: Two seat basic/advanced trainer

Powerplant: One 16.0kN (3600lb) AlliedSignal (Garrett) TFE731-2A-2A turbofan.

Performance: Max speed at sea level 807km/h (435kt). Max initial rate of climb 5315ft/min. Service ceiling 42,650ft. Range with max internal fuel 1400km (755nm), range with max internal and external fuel 2200km (1890nm). Endurance with max internal fuel 3hr, endurance with max internal and external fuel 4hr 25min.

Weights: Empty equipped 2687kg (5924lb), max takeoff with external stores 4330kg (9545lb).

Dimensions: Wing span 9.63m (31ft 7in), length overall inc probe 11.60m (38ft 1in), height 4.21m (13ft 10in). Wing area 17.0m^2 (183.2sq ft).

Accommodation: Two in tandem.

Armament: One centreline and four underwing hardpoints can carry max weapons load of 945kg (2080lb). Centreline hardpoint can carry a 23mm gun pod, other weapon options include light bombs and rockets. Two outboard pylons can carry a PL-7 AAM each.

Operators: China*, Pakistan*.

History: The Karakorum is China's first locally designed jet trainer and has been developed in co-operation with Pakistan.

Development of the Karakorum, initially designated L-8, was announced at the 1987 Paris Airshow. At the time of the new trainer's launch Nanchang (or NAMC – Nanchang Aircraft Manufacturing Company) sought international partners to develop the aircraft for export. Subsequently a development and co production deal was signed with Pakistan, which took a 25% share in the program.

When Pakistan joined the trainer project the aircraft was redesignated K-8 and named Karakorum, after the mountain range that forms the China/Pakistan border. Pakistan, through PAC (Pakistan Aeronautical Complex), had some design input into the K-8 and is responsible for the manufacture of the K-8's fin and tailplane. Pakistan has, however, decided not to establish its own K-8 assembly line.

The first of three flying Karakorum prototypes flew for the first time on November 21 1990. These were followed by 15 pre production development aircraft, the first of which flew in 1993. Pakistan is understood to have a total requirement for 75 K-8s – a first batch of nine was handed over in late 1994 and another eight are on order. The Chinese K-8 requirement is unknown, but could involve several hundred airframes (it is likely to replace JJ-7s and CJ-6s).

The K-8 is of conventional design for a jet trainer, with a straight wing and tandem seating. It is powered by an AlliedSignal (nee Garrett) TFE731 turbofan (55 engines are on order, while the remainder required may be built under licence in China). Other western origin equipment in the K-8 includes the two Collins CRTs in each cockpit. The crew sits on two Martin-Baker zero/zero ejection seats. Five hardpoints, one centreline and four under the wing, give the K-8 a light ground attack/weapons training capability.

Photo: An early Karakorum development aircraft.

NH Industries NH 90

Countries of origin: France, Germany, Italy and the Netherlands

Type: Medium lift tactical transport and naval helicopter

Powerplants: Two 1255kW (1680shp) max continuous rated Rolls-Royce Turboméca RTM332 turboshafts or in Italian aircraft two similarly rated GE T700-T6Es, driving four bladed main and tail rotors.

Performance: TTH – Dash speed at sea level 300km/h (162kt), max cruising speed at sea level 290km/h (155kt), normal cruising speed 260km/h (140kt). Service ceiling 13,945ft, absolute ceiling 19,685ft. Hovering ceiling in ground effect 11,810ft, out of ground effect 9850ft. Ferry range 1205km (650nm). NFH – Time on station 110km (60nm) from base 3hr. Max endurance at 140km/h (75kt) 5hr 5min.

Weights: TTH – Empty 5400kg (11,905lb), max takeoff 10,000kg (22,045lb). NFH – Empty equipped 6430kg (14,170lb), max takeoff same.

Dimensions: Main rotor diameter 16.30m (53ft 6in), length overall rotors turning 19.60m (64ft 4in), fuselage length tail rotor turning 16.11m (52ft 10in), height overall rotors turning 5.44m (17ft 10in). Main rotor disc area 208.7m^2 (2246.1sq ft).

Accommodation: TTH – One or two pilots and up to 20 combat equipped troops or a two tonne 4WD. NFH – Pilot, copilot/tacco and sensor operator, or two pilots, tacco and sensor operator.

Armament: TTH – To be fitted with area suppression and defensive armament. NFH – Anti ship missiles and torpedoes.

Operators: To be built for France, Germany, Italy and the Netherlands.

History: The NH 90 is an advanced 10 tonne class helicopter designed for tactical transport and anti ship and ASW naval operations.

The NH 90 results from a 1985 teaming of five European nations to jointly develop a NATO Helicopter for the 90s. The UK withdrew from the program in 1987, leaving France, Germany, Italy and the Netherlands the four partners. The first prototype was rolled out at Eurocopter France's Marignane plant in September 1995, and first flight was due by the end of that year.

The most significant design feature of the NH 90 is its quadruplex fly-by-wire flight control system with sidestick controllers. In addition the entire fuselage and rotor blades (with curved tips) are made of composites. It is designed to be easy to maintain and difficult to detect.

The NH 90 will be built in two basic versions, the land TTH (tactical transport helicopter) and naval NFH (NATO Frigate Helicopter). TTH features include a rear loading ramp to allow it to carry a two tonne vehicle, ECM, NVG and FLIR compatibility and accommodation for up to 20 fully equipped troops.

The NFH is designed for autonomous anti ship, anti submarine warfare and other general naval helicopter tasks (SAR and vertrep etc). Equipment includes a search radar in an undernose radome and a crew of three or four.

NH Industries' partners are Eurocopter France (43%), Agusta (26%), Eurocopter Deutschland (23%) and Fokker (7%). Provisional requirements are France 160 TTHs and 60 NFHs, Germany 234 TTHs and 38 NFHs, Italy 150 TTHs and 64 NFHs and the Netherlands 20 NFHs, although these numbers are expected to be reduced. Production deliveries are planned for 2001.

Photo: The first NH 90 prototype. (Eurocopter France)

North American T-6 Texan/Harvard

Country of origin: United States of America

Type: Advanced piston engined trainer

Powerplant: T-6G – One 410kW (550hp) Pratt & Whitney R-1340-AN-1 Wasp nine cylinder radial piston engine driving a two bladed propeller.

Performance: T-6G – Max speed at 5000ft 340km/h (184kt), max cruising speed 274km/h (148kt), economical cruising speed 235km/h (127kt). Max initial rate of climb 1643ft/min. Service ceiling 24,750ft. Normal range 1400km (755nm).

Weights: T-6G – Empty 1938kg (4271lb), max takeoff 2546kg (5617lb).

Dimensions: Wing span 12.80m (42ft 0in), length 8.99m (29ft 6in), height 3.56m (11ft 9in). Wing area 23.6m² (253.7sq ft).

Accommodation: Seating for two in tandem.

Armament: Could be fitted with machine guns in the wings, a rearward firing manually operated machine gun in rear cockpit, and with underwing bomb racks for light bombs.

Operators: Bolivia, Paraguay, South Africa.

History: North American's Texan/Harvard/SNJ series was the most important Allied trainer of World War 2.

This prolific aircraft family started as the NA 16, which was similar in appearance to subsequent models but featured fixed undercarriage, open cockpits and fabric covering around the fuselage. First flight was in April 1935. The US Army Air Corp adopted the NA-16 as the BT-9 basic trainer. Similar variants included the BT-14, Canada's Yale and the retractable undercarriage BC-1 and British Harvard I. Another variant was the Australian built Wirraway, with three bladed propeller, fabric covered fuselage and retractable undercarriage. The Wirraway (755 built) saw widespread use in advanced trainer, army cooperation, light bomber, dive bomber and even fighter roles (one even shot down a Japanese Zero in December 1942).

The AT-6 Texan (AT = advanced trainer) was introduced in 1939 and features retractable undercarriage, a two bladed prop and metal fuselage covering. The initial Texan model was the AT-6A, supplied to the US Navy as the SNJ-3 and built in Canada (by Noorduyn) as the Harvard IIB (over 2000 went to Britain). The similar AT-6C/SNJ-4/Harvard III were redesigned to eliminate high value aluminium alloys and high alloy steels, although fears of shortages of these materials proved groundless and they were reintroduced into production.

Other wartime models were the AT-6D/SNJ-5/Harvard III and the AT-6F/SNJ-6. In all 15,000 T-6s/SNJs/Harvards were built through to 1945. In addition, small numbers of single seat AT-6 based fighters were built for Peru and Siam (Thailand).

Cancar in Canada built a further 555 T-6Gs for the US and Canadian air forces between 1951 and 1954, bringing total production of all variants to approximately 20,300.

Postwar, thousands of refurbished surplus Texans (designated T-6 by the USAF from 1948) and Harvards etc served on every continent. By 1980 still more than 20 nations operated T-6s/Harvards for advanced training and light strike. In 1995 South Africa had begun to replace its 50 Harvards with Pilatus PC-7 Mk II Astras, while smaller numbers operated in Bolivia and Paraguay.

Photo: Brazil was one of more than 20 nations to fly T-6s into the 1980s, although they have since been replaced by Tucanos. (Bill Lines)

North American T-28 Trojan

Country of origin: United States of America

Type: Two seat advanced trainer/light attack aircraft

Powerplant: T-28D – One 1065kW (1425hp) Wright R-1820-86 Cyclone 14 cylinder radial piston engine driving a three bladed propeller.

Performance: T-28D – Max speed at 10,000ft 552km/h (598kt). Max initial rate of climb 3540ft/min. Service ceiling 35,500ft. Ferry range 1705km (920nm).

Weights: T-28D – Empty equipped 2915kg (6424lb), max takeoff 3855kg (8500lb).

Dimensions: T-28D – Wing span 12.22m (40ft 1in), length 10.06m (33ft 0in), height 3.86m (12ft 8in). Wing area 24.9m² (268.0sq ft).

Accommodation: Two in tandem.

Armament: Six underwing hardpoints can carry a total weapons load of 1815kg (4000lb), including rockets, 12.7mm/0.5in machine gun pods and 500lb/230kg bombs.

Operators: South Korea, Uruguay.

History: The big T-28 Trojan was designed as a successor to the T-6 Texan/Harvard and served widely with the US Air Force and Navy and numerous South East Asian and South American air arms.

North American Aviation's NA-159 design won the US Air Force's late 1940s contest to develop a new advanced trainer to replace T-6 Texans. Although, like the Texan, the Trojan was powered by a large radial piston engine, the new aircraft differed in having a tricycle undercarriage and was significantly more powerful and larger overall.

The first of two XT-28 prototypes flew for the first time on September 26 1949. Subsequently production deliveries of the first of 1194 T-28As for the US Air Force (with a 595kW/800hp Wright R-1300 driving a two bladed variable pitch prop) began in January 1950. Production for the US Navy and Marine Corps comprised 489 1065kW (1425hp) Wright R-1820 powered T-28Bs with three bladed props, plus 299 similarly powered T-28Cs, fitted with an arrester hook and structurally strengthened for landing on dummy aircraft carrier decks.

Total T-28 production reached 1984, with many Trojans delivered to South East Asian and South American nations under the auspices of the US's Military Assistance Program.

The T-28D Trojan was produced by conversion of surplus USAF T-28As and was also supplied widely under MAP. The T-28D conversion involved re engining with a 1065kW (1425hp) R-1820 (driving a three bladed prop), six underwing hardpoints and some crew armour. T-28D conversions were performed by Fairchild (some as AT-28Ds) and North American. Sud Aviation in France converted 245 T-28As to Fennecs (desert rat), a similar standard to the T-28D and many of these served extensively in Algeria with the French Air Force. Meanwhile US and South Vietnamese T-28Ds saw combat in Laos and Vietnam.

In Taiwan AIDC used the T-28 as the basis for its T-CH-1 Chung Tsing advanced trainer, which was powered by a Lycoming T53 turboprop. Most have been retired from service.

Photo: Laos was one of several Asian nations to operate T-28Ds supplied under MAP. (Steve Death)

North American F-86 Sabre

Country of origin: United States of America

Type: Fighter/light ground attack aircraft

Powerplant: F-86F – One 26.5kN (5910lb) General Electric J47-GE-27 turbojet.

Performance: F-86F – Max speed at sea level 1118km/h (604kt), max speed at 35,000ft 980km/h (530kt). Max initial rate of climb 9300ft/min. Service ceiling 48,000ft. Combat radius with max external fuel 740km (400nm), combat radius with two 1000lb/450kg bombs 510km (275nm). Range with internal fuel 1265km (683nm). Ferry range with max external fuel 2455km (1327nm).

Weights: F-86F – Empty 4965kg (10,950lb), max takeoff 9235kg (20,357lb).

Dimensions: F-86F – Wing span 11.31m (37ft 1in), length 11.44m (37ft 7in), height 4.49m (14ft 9in). Wing area 28.1m² (303sq ft).

Accommodation: Pilot only.

Armament: F-86F – Six 0.50in Browning M-3 machine guns in nose. Four underwing hardpoints, innermost can carry 1000lb/450kg bombs, plus rockets. Some Sabres carried two AIM-9 Sidewinders.

Operators: Bolivia

History: The legendary Sabre was built in more numbers than any other postwar western fighter and served in numerous wars (including Korea) and skirmishes.

North American first looked at designing a jet powered fighter in late 1943, early studies including a jet powered Mustang. In 1944 the company received contracts from both the US Navy and Army Air Force for jet fighters, the Navy program resulting in the straight wing FJ Fury. NAA elected to delay development of the Army Air Force's jet (which initially was to have been closely based on the Fury) while the company studied captured German data on swept wings. The end result was the swept wing P-86 (F-86 from June 1948) Sabre, which first flew in prototype XP-86 form on October 1 1947.

The F-86 was far in advance of any American fighter before it. Powered by a General Electric axial flow turbojet and featuring a swept wing and tail surfaces it was the fastest fighter then flying (an unmodified F-86 broke the World Speed Record in September 1948 by reaching 671mph – 1080km/h/583kt).

Initial production was of the F-86A. The F-86E had a powered flying tail and more powerful engine, while the F-86F with a further increase in power, extended and fixed wing leading edge and small wing fences. The F-86D all weather fighter was fitted with a nose radar and complex avionics (some were later converted to F-86L), while the F-86K was similar but had simplified avionics. The F-86H fighter bomber had a revised airframe and four 20mm cannon. The US Navy's FJ-2 and FJ-3 Furies were based on the F-86, while the FJ-4 (AF-1E from 1962) was much modified.

In all, 9502 Sabres were built in the USA and under licence in Australia (RR Avon powered CA-27s), Canada (including Avro Orenda powered Sabre Mk.5s and Mk.6s), Italy and Japan. Thirty seven nations have operated the Sabre, however in late 1995 the only military Sabre operator was Bolivia. Three F-86Fs are that country's only fighters, although they are flown only rarely.

Photo: Japan was one of 37 nations to fly the Sabre. (MAP)

Northrop T-38 Talon

Country of origin: United States of America

Type: Two seat advanced trainer

Powerplants: Two 11.9kN (2680lb) dry and 17.1kN (3850lb) with afterburning General Electric J85-GE-5 turbojets.

Performance: Max speed at 36,000ft Mach 1.22 or 1295km/h (700kt), max cruising speed 930km/h (502kt). Max initial rate of climb 33,600ft/min. Service ceiling 53,600ft. Ferry range 1760km (950nm), typical range 1385km (747nm).

Weights: Empty 3255kg (7175lb), max takeoff 5465kg (12,050lb).

Dimensions: Wing span 7.70m (25ft 3in), length 14.14m (46ft 5in), height 3.92m (12ft 11in). Wing area 15.8m² (170.0sq ft).

Accommodation: Two in tandem.

Armament: Usually none, although Portuguese T-38s were equipped to fire AIM-9 Sidewinder AAMs. T-38B LIFT aircraft (AT-38Bs) were equipped to carry practice bombs and rockets, plus a minigun pod.

Operators: Germany, Portugal, Taiwan, Turkey, USA.

History: The supersonic Talon is the US Air Force's primary advanced trainer and is a development of Northrop's N-156 light fighter proposal.

Northrop began private venture development of its N-156 light fighter concept in the mid 1950s. Part of Northrop's N-156 design was the N-156T two seater which it offered to the USAF as an advanced trainer. In 1956 that service ordered three N-156Ts for evaluation and the first of these YT-38s (powered by non afterburning YJ85-GE-1s) flew for the first time on April 10 1959. In all, six YT-38s were built, the final three with afterburning YJ85-GE-5s. Testing of these latter aircraft in particular was very promising, and the YT-38 was ordered into production as the T-38 Talon. Deliveries began in March 1961. Production ceased in 1972 after 1187 had been built.

The T-38 possesses fighter like supersonic performance but is still a good trainer with a relatively low stalling speed and manageable handling. The USAF expects its T-38s to remain in service until 2010 to 2015. To extend their airframe lives future USAF transport and tanker pilots now undergo advanced training on the Beech T-1 rather than the T-38. An avionics upgrade is also planned.

Apart from Air Education and Training Command, the Talon is in service with Air Combat Command and Air Mobility Command for the Companion Trainer Program. Others are used as chase aircraft for various test programs. Previous USAF T-38 operators included aggressor squadrons and the Thunderbirds.

The USAF also operates 46 German funded T-38s to train Luftwaffe pilots. Ex USAF aircraft meanwhile were supplied to Turkey and Portugal (Portugal's aircraft had an air defence role and were armed with AIM-9 Sidewinders prior to the delivery of F-16s). Finally Taiwan is leasing 40 T-38s to make up for a shortfall in fast jet numbers pending the delivery of F-16s in 1997.

The T-38A was the basic Talon production model. For a time the US Navy operated some QT-38 drones and DT-38 drone controllers and NASA flies T-38A(N)s on astronaut training duties. Finally 132 T-38As were converted to T-38 LIFT configuration, able to carry practice bombs, rockets and a minigun for weapons training. These were unofficially dubbed AT-38Bs.

Photo: A T-38A of the 64th FTW based in Texas. (Paul Merritt)

Northrop F-5A/B Freedom Fighter

Country of origin: United States of America

Type: Lightweight multirole fighter

Powerplants: Two 12.1kN (2720lb) dry and 18.2kN (4080lb) with afterburning General Electric J85-GE-13 turbojets.

Performance: F-5A – Max speed at 36,000ft Mach 1.4 or 1488km/h (802kt), cruising speed at 36,000ft 1030km/h (556kt). Max initial rate of climb 28,700ft/min. Service ceiling 50,500ft. Ferry range 2595km (1400nm). Combat radius with two 240kg (530lb) bombs and max fuel hi-lo-hi 990km (485nm), radius with max external bomb load (1995kg/4400lb) hi-lo-hi 315km (170nm).

Weights: F-5A – Empty equipped 3667kg (8085lb), max takeoff 9380kg (20,677lb).

Dimensions: F-5A – Wing span over tip tanks 7.87m (25ft 10in), span without tip tanks 7.70m (25ft 3in), length 14.38m (47ft 2in), height 4.01m (13ft 2in). Wing area 15.8m² (170.0sq ft).

Accommodation: Pilot only in F-5A, two in tandem in F-5B.

Armament: Two M39A2 20mm cannons. Max external weapons load of 1995kg (4400lb) including bombs, rockets and AIM-9 Sidewinders on four underwing hardpoints (AIM-9s also on wingtip stations).

Operators: Brazil, Canada, Greece, Morocco, Norway, Philippines, Saudi Arabia, South Korea, Spain, Thailand, Turkey, Venezuela, Yemen.

History: Northrop's N-156 lightweight fighter was adopted by the USA to supply to friendly European and Asian nations under the Military Assistance Program, resulting in the F-5 Freedom Fighter.

As early as 1952 Northrop designed its first lightweight jet fighter, the N-102 Fang to be powered by a single GE J79 turbojet. While the USAF rejected the Fang its interest in a lightweight fighter was aroused and in 1954 it conducted a study into the concept of a lightweight high performance fighter that could be supplied under MAP. This study prompted Northrop to design a new lightweight fighter to meet such a requirement, resulting in the N-156 powered by two small J85 turbojets (originally developed for a decoy drone).

US official interest was initially for the two seat N-156T which became the T-38 Talon, while Northrop continued development of the single seat N-156 and a privately funded prototype flew for the first time on July 30 1959 (Mach 1 was reached on this first flight).

Due to a disinterested USAF the first production F-5A Freedom Fighter did not fly until May 1963. The USAF operated a squadron of F-5As in Vietnam for combat evaluation (Skoshi Tiger) but that service never intended to acquire the F-5 in any numbers.

However Northrop built 879 F-5As and two seat F-5Bs for over a dozen MAP customers, while Canadair built 250 (with uprated engines and an inflight refuelling probe as the CF-5A and CF-5D for Canada, NF-5A/B for the Netherlands) and CASA of Spain 70 under licence. The RF-5A is a reconnaissance variant with four KS-92A cameras in a reprofiled nose.

Several countries have upgraded their F-5A/B fleets, including Canada, Venezuela and Norway. Canada's upgrade was the most comprehensive, with an airframe refurbishment, a HUD, advanced avionics and HOTAS controls. However, all but two have been retired and they have been offered for sale.

Photo: Norway's F-5s are used as lead-in fighters. (Paul Merritt)

Northrop F-5E/F Tiger II

Country of origin: United States of America

Type: Lightweight multirole fighter

Powerplants: Two 15.5kN (3500lb) dry and 22.4kN (5000lb) with afterburning General Electric J85-GE-21B turbojets.

Performance: F-5E – Max speed at 37,000ft Mach 1.63 or 1730km/h (935kt), cruising speed at 36,000ft 1040km/h (562kt). Max initial rate of climb 34,300ft/min. Service ceiling 51,800ft. Ferry range with max external fuel and empty tanks dropped 3720km (2010nm). Combat radius with two AIM-9s 1405km (760nm).

Weights: F-5E – Empty 4350kg (9558lb), max takeoff 11,187kg (24,664lb).

Dimensions: F-5E – Wing span with tip mounted AIM-9s 8.53m (28ft 0in), length 14.45m (47ft 5in), height 4.08m (13ft 5in). Wing area 17.3m² (186.0sq ft).

Accommodation: Pilot only in F-5E, two in tandem in F-5F.

Armament: Two M39A2 20mm cannon. Up to 3195kg (7000lb) of ordnance on two wingtip, one centreline and four underwing hardpoints including AIM-9 Sidewinders, bombs, rockets, cluster bombs and ASMs (including AGM-65 Maverick).

Operators: Bahrain, Brazil, Chile, Honduras, Indonesia, Iran, Jordan, Kenya, Malaysia, Mexico, Morocco, Saudi Arabia, Singapore, South Korea, Sudan, Switzerland, Taiwan, Thailand, Tunisia, USA, Yemen.

History: Northrop's F-5E Tiger II was selected as the USA's International Fighter Aircraft (IFA), an export lightweight fighter.

Northrop began work on an improved F-5 as a private venture. This resulted in the first flight of a converted F-5A prototype powered by two GE J85-GE-21 turbojets in March 1969. This aircraft was submitted for the US Government's International Fighter Competition (previously Advanced International Fighter), which was managed by the USAF. To conform with government procedures for selecting and procuring a new fighter the F-5E had to be evaluated against other US fighters before it could be accepted, these being versions of the Vought F-8 Crusader, Lockheed F-104 Starfighter and even the F-4 Phantom. The F-5E was officially selected in November 1970.

Compared with the F-5A, the F-5E Tiger II features more powerful engines, enlarged leading edge extensions, permanent wingtip AAM stations and more capable avionics and systems. First flight was on August 11 1972. The F-5F two seater first flew in September 1974. The RF-5E Tigereye features four KS-121A 70mm cameras in a modified nose section.

Like the F-5A, the F-5E was extremely popular and over 1300 (including two seater F-5Fs) were built. Licence production was undertaken in Taiwan, South Korea and Switzerland, while large numbers have seen USAF and USN service as DACT aggressors. Several companies now offer F-5 upgrade programs, including IAI who upgraded Chilean aircraft with a new radar, avionics and HUD, and Northrop Grumman who offers a staged upgrade.

The ultimate expression of the F-5 line was the F-5G, or F-20 Tigershark, powered by a GE F404 and fitted with a modified APG-66 radar. It was offered for sale in the early 1980s but the free availability of F-16s damaged its sales prospects and the program was cancelled.

Photo: Switzerland is the only European F-5E operator.

Northrop Grumman B-2 Spirit

Country of origin: United States of America

Type: Low observables strategic bomber

Powerplants: Four 84.5kN (19,000lb) General Electric F118-GE-110 turbofans.

Performance: Max speed at sea level approx 915km/h (495kt). Service ceiling 50,000ft. Range with eight SRAMs and eight B83 bombs (total weapons weight 16,920kg/37,300lb) hi-hi-hi 11,665km (6300nm), hi-lo-hi with 1850km (1000nm) at low level 8150km (4400nm). Range with eight SRAMs and eight B61s (total weapons weight 10,885kg/24,000lb) hi-hi-hi 12,225km (6600nm), hi-lo-hi with 1850km (1000nm) at low level 8335km (4500nm).

Weights: Empty in 45,360kg to 49,900kg (100,000lb to 110,00lb) class, max takeoff 170,550kg (376,000lb).

Dimensions: Wing span 52.43m (172ft 0in), length 21.03 (69ft 0in), height 5.18m (17ft 0in).

Accommodation: Crew of two with provision for a third member.

Armament: Two Boeing rotary launcher assemblies (RLAs), one in each bomb bay, can carry a total of 16 AGM-131 SRAM IIs, or AGM-129 ACMs or AGM-137 TSSAMs (Triple Service Standoff Attack Missiles). Can also carry 16 B61 tactical/strategic or B83 strategic freefall nuclear bombs, or 80 Mk 82 1000lb/450kg bombs, or 16 JDAMs, or 16 Mk 84 2000lb/910kg bombs, plus cluster bombs.

Operators: USA

History: Highly controversial for its more than $US1bn unit cost, the B-2 was designed from the outset to be almost invisible to radar and is without doubt the most capable strategic bomber yet devised.

Concept work on a totally new strategic bomber incorporating low observable or stealth technology was already underway in 1977 when the Rockwell B-1A was cancelled. The resulting Advanced Technology Bomber (ATB) program was launched in 1978, while a Northrop design (with Boeing as principal subcontractor) was selected over a rival concept from Lockheed/Rockwell in June 1981. Work on the aircraft continued under complete secrecy and only the existence of the program and that the aircraft was a flying wing had been officially recognised until the B-2 was rolled out in November 1988. First flight was on July 17 1989. The USAF originally planned to acquire 133 B-2s, although the aircraft's massive cost and the end of the Cold War has seen this figure reduced to 20, although more could be funded.

The B-2 is unlike anything before it. Its flying wing design harks back to Northrop's revolutionary postwar XB-35 and XB-49, and features a double W trailing edge with eight flying control services. The flying wing design has an inherently low radar cross section, the airframe is largely constructed of graphite/epoxy, which forms a honeycomb radar absorbent structure. Exterior surfaces are designed to minimise radar returns and heat radiation. Other features include four GE F118-GE-110 turbofans (modified non afterburning GE F110s), fly-by-wire flight controls, two side by side internal weapons bays, a Hughes APG-181 low probability of intercept radar (for terrain following and last minute target position updates) behind two dielectric panels beneath the nose, a 90,720kg (200,000lb) internal fuel capacity and seating for two crew on ejection seats side by side.

Photo: B-2s are being delivered to the 509th Bomb Wing in Missouri.

Northrop Grumman E-2 Hawkeye

Country of origin: United States of America

Type: Carrier borne AEW aircraft

Powerplants: E-2C – Two 3805kW (5100ehp) Allison T56-A-425 turboprops, driving four bladed propellers.

Performance: E-2C – Max speed 625km/h (338kt), max cruising speed 602km/h (325kt), ferry cruising speed 480km/h (260kt). Service ceiling 37,000ft. Ferry range 2855km (1540nm). Time on station 320km (175nm) from base 4hr 25min. Endurance with max fuel 6hr 15min.

Weights: E-2C – Empty 17,860kg (39,373lb), max takeoff 24,160kg (53,267lb).

Dimensions: Wing span 24.56m (80ft 7in), length 17.54m (57ft 7in), height 5.58m (18ft 4in). Wing area 65.0m^2 (700.0sq ft).

Accommodation: Crew complement of five – pilot, copilot, combat information centre officer, air control operator and radar operator.

Armament: None

Operators: Egypt, France*, Japan, Israel, Singapore, Taiwan, USA.

History: Grumman has had a long history of supplying AEW aircraft to the US Navy, starting with developments of the WW2 Avenger.

The Hawkeye was developed to replace another Grumman design, the E-1 Tracer, an AEW development of the S-2 Tracker. Grumman was announced the winner of a US Navy requirement to develop a twin turboprop AEW aircraft with a crew of five, digital processing computers and a General Electric APS-96 surveillance radar in March 1957. The resulting W2F (E-2 from 1962) Hawkeye featured the APS-96 in an above fuselage rotodome, two Allison T56 turboprops, a high wing and a widespan tailplane with considerable dihedral with four fins including two rudders (providing the necessary directional control while conforming to carrier hangar height limitations. First flight was October 21 1960. Production E-2As (59 aircraft in all) saw widespread service in the Vietnam theatre.

From 1969 the E-2As were upgraded to E-2B standard with an improved computer and provision for inflight refuelling. Taiwan originally planned to acquire four E-2Bs which it planned to upgrade to a similar standard to the E-2C as the E-2T, but these plans were dropped in preference for acquiring four new build E-2Cs. All E-2Bs have been retired from USN service.

The definitive Hawkeye is the E-2C, which first flew in January 1970. The main new feature of the E-2C was the APS-125 radar and improved signal processing capability. It can be identified by its large air intake ahead of the wing. The E-2C has been continually updated and fitted with increasingly capable radars, in the form of the APS-138, APS-139 and now the APS-145. The APS-145 has a greater resistance to jamming, better overground performance and the ability to track up to 2000 targets at one time. Other recent E-2C features include more powerful engines (as described above) and JTIDS software. The TE-2C is a trainer.

Over 170 Hawkeyes have been ordered, primarily for the US Navy, but also for export. Low rate production continues for the US Navy (procuring new build aircraft was found to be more cost effective than upgrading early E-2Cs) and against fresh export orders.

Photo: The E-2C Hawkeye patrols at an altitude of 30,000ft and can detect and assess targets out to a range of 555km (300nm).

Northrop Grumman E-8 J-STARS

Country of origin: United States of America

Type: Long range battlefield reconnaissance platform.

Powerplants: E-8C – Four 80.1kN (18,000lb) Pratt & Whitney JT8D-3B turbofans.

Performance: E-8C – Max speed 1010km/h (545kt), max cruising speed 974km/h (525kt), long range cruising speed 885km/h (478kt). Service ceiling 42,000ft. Endurance with internal fuel 11hr, endurance with one inflight refuelling 20hr.

Weights: E-8C – Empty 77,565kg (171,000lb), max takeoff 152,407kg (336,000lb).

Dimensions: Wing span 44.42m (145ft 9in), length 44.61m (152ft 11in), height 12.95m (42ft 6in). Wing area 283.4m² (3050.0sq ft).

Accommodation: Two pilots and flight engineer. E-8A fitted with consoles for 10 operators. E-8C fitted with 18 operator consoles, one of which is for navigation/self defence.

Armament: None

Operators: USA*

History: The Northrop Grumman developed E-8 J-STARS, or Joint STARS is a Joint Strategic Target Attack Radar System, a long range battlefield surveillance platform fitted with a side looking radar.

Grumman was awarded a full scale development J-STARS contract, covering the conversion of two Boeing 707 airliners to serve as prototypes, in September 1985. The first of these prototypes first flew in converted E-8A J-STARS configuration on December 22 1988. Originally the USAF planned to acquire 22 new build E-8B production J-STARS, powered by F108 turbofans (CFM56s), and one airframe was built (and flown in 1990) before the US instead opted to convert second hand Boeing 707 airliners into E-8Cs. The two E-8A prototypes will be upgraded to E-8C standard to serve alongside 18 production E-8C conversions. The first E-8C production aircraft first flew in March 1994, although it will used as a permanent testbed. The E-8Cs will be operated by the USAF on behalf of the US Army, with first deliveries due in 1996.

The heart of the E-8 is the Norden APY-3 side looking phased array multimode radar, which is housed in a canoe fairing beneath the forward fuselage. In synthetic aperture radar mode the APY-3 can image targets up to 175km distant and can survey one million km² in one eight hour sortie. Pulse doppler modes gather moving target information allowing the operators to track moving vehicles and convoys.

Joint STARS provides ground commanders with a complete overview of the battlefield and can also be used for specific target reconnaissance and for individual targeting functions. E-8 gathered information is relayed to mobile ground stations (with operator stations similar to those onboard the aircraft) via datalink, allowing individual ground commanders to access specific information they require.

The two E-8As were hastily deployed to the Gulf War in 1991 where they flew 49 operational missions, providing invaluable information to ground commanders and proving the concept in a real war environment.

Photo: The first production E-8C, which is destined to spend its life as a testbed. (Northrop Grumman)

Pacific Aerospace CT-4 Airtrainer

Country of origin: New Zealand

Type: Two/three seat light basic trainer

Powerplant: CT-4A – One 155kW (210hp) Teledyne Continental IO-360-D fuel injected flat six piston engine, driving a two bladed propeller. CT-4B – One 155kW (210hp) IO-360-HB9.

Performance: CT-4A – Max speed 290km/h (157kt), cruising speed 240km/h (130kt), long range cruising speed 235km/h (127kt). Max initial rate of climb 1345ft/min. Range at long range cruising speed 1300km (700nm). CT-4B – Max speed 267km/h (144kt), cruising speed 260km/h (140kt). Max initial rate of climb 1250ft/min. Range with max fuel at normal cruising speed 1110km (600nm).

Weights: CT-4A – Empty 690kg (1520lb), max takeoff 1088kg (2400lb). CT-4B – Max takeoff 1202kg (2650lb).

Dimensions: Wing span 7.92m (26ft 0in), length 7.06m (23ft 2in), height 2.59m (8ft 6in). Wing area 12.0m² (129.0sq ft).

Accommodation: Two side by side, with optional third seat behind.

Armament: None

Operators: New Zealand, Thailand.

History: Affectionately dubbed the Plastic Parrot, the CT-4 Airtrainer is a two seat basic trainer contemporary to the BAe/Scottish Aviation Bulldog.

The CT-4 is developed from the Australian Victa Airtourer, a light two seat GA aircraft. The Airtourer was designed in 1953 by Henry Millicer, then chief aerodynamicist at Australia's Government Aircraft Factory. Victa had developed a larger four place Aircruiser, but development work was not continued with and instead the production rights for the Aircruiser were purchased by Aero Engine Services Ltd (or AESL) of New Zealand in 1974, which by then already had the rights to the Airtourer series. AESL made a number of changes to the basic Aircruiser design, including a new clamshell canopy, structural strengthening for aerobatic work and stick controls, making it suitable for military basic training.

The first such CT-4A Airtrainer flew on February 23 1972. Primary customers were the Australian (51 aircraft), New Zealand (24) and Thai (26) air forces. Production by NZAI (New Zealand Aircraft Industries), as AESL had become, continued until 1977.

In 1991 Pacific Aerospace Corporation (the successor to NZAI) resumed production of the CT-4B against an order from the BAe/Ansett Flying College in Tamworth, Australia. Using these aircraft the college provides flight screening and basic training for Australian and Papua New Guinea military pilots under contract. Australia's CT-4As were retired in early 1993. Five CT-4Bs were also built for the Royal Thai Air Force, while that service's surviving CT-4As are being rewinged to extend their service lives.

Three other CT-4 developments have been offered but have not been ordered into production. The turboprop Allison 250 powered CT-4C flew on January 21 1991, and a retractable version, the CT-4CR, was proposed. The 225kW (300hp) IO-540 powered CT-4E was aimed at the US Air Force's Enhanced Flight Screening competition (won by the Slingsby Firefly).

During 1994 Pacific Aerospace announced it would cease aircraft production unless fresh orders were forthcoming.

Photo: An Airtrainer in service with its home country's air force. (RNZAF)

Panavia Tornado IDS & ECR

Countries of origin: Germany, Italy and UK

Type: Strike/ground attack aircraft

Powerplants: IDS (from 1983) – Two 40.5kN (9100lb) dry (downrated to 38.5kN/8650lb for RAF aircraft) and 71.5kN (16,075lb) with afterburning Turbo-Union RB199-34R Mk 103 turbofans.

Performance: IDS – Max speed Mach 2.2 (Mach 1.3 for RAF aircraft), max speed with external stores Mach 0.92 or 1112km/h (600kt). Time to 30,000ft less than 2min. Combat radius with a heavy weapon load hi-lo-lo-hi 1390km (750nm). Ferry range approx 3890km (2100nm).

Weights: IDS – Basic empty approx 13,890kg (30,620lb), max takeoff approx 27,950kg (61,620lb).

Dimensions: Span wings extended 13.91m (45ft 8in), span wings swept 8.60m (28ft 3in), length 16.72m (54ft 10in), height 5.95m (19ft 6in). Wing area (25° sweepback) 26.6m² (286.3sq ft).

Accommodation: Pilot and weapons system operator/navigator in tandem.

Armament: Two IWKA-Mauser 27mm cannon. Max external load over 9000kg (19,840lb), including AIM-9s, bombs, laser guided bombs, ALARM (RAF) and HARM (ECR) anti radiation missiles, WE177B (RAF) and B61 (Luftwaffe) nuclear bombs, JP 233 (RAF) and MW-1 (Luftwaffe) area denial weapons, Sea Eagle (GR.1B) and Kormoran (Marineflieger) anti ship missiles.

Operators: Germany, Italy, Saudi Arabia, UK.

History: A veteran of combat over Iraq, the Tornado is the most advanced European military aircraft currently in service.

The Tornado resulted from a late 1960s feasibility study for such an aircraft conducted by Belgium, Canada, Germany, Italy, the Netherlands and the UK (Belgium, Canada and the Netherlands subsequently withdrew). Panavia was formed in March 1969 to develop and build the aircraft, dubbed the MRCA – Multi Role Combat Aircraft, with formal development beginning in mid 1970. Germany and the UK each hold a 42.5% holding in Panavia, and Italy 15%.

The first of nine prototypes flew for the first time on August 14 1974, while production aircraft were delivered from July 1980. Orders stand at 828 including ECRs and dual control trainers.

The Tornado features variable geometry wings, two Turbo-Union RB199 engines (developed specifically by a consortium of Rolls-Royce, MTU and FiatAvio), a Texas Instruments radar with terrain following and ground mapping, fly-by-wire and a Ferranti built digital INS.

UK aircraft are designated GR.1 and feature a laser rangefinder in an undernose pod, while their intakes have been fixed and engines downrated. Twelve GR.1As are used for reconnaissance and are fitted with a BAe SLIR (side looking infrared) and Vinten IR linescan. The 24 converted GR.1Bs are used for maritime strike and can carry up to five Sea Eagle anti ship missiles. The GR.4 upgrade (involving 142 GR.1s) will comprise a new HUD, undernose FLIR, new avionics and ECM. Italy and Germany are upgrading their IDS aircraft under the MDI (Mid Life Improvement) program with FLIR, ECM and new avionics.

The Tornado ECR (Electronic Combat Reconnaissance) for Germany and Italy is a dedicated Suppression of Enemy Air Defence (SEAD) variant of the IDS fitted with a Emitter Location System (ELS) and can fire the AGM-88 HARM anti radiation missile.

Photo: A German Navy Tornado IDS. (Paul Merritt)

Panavia Tornado ADV

Countries of origin: Germany, Italy and UK

Type: Air defence fighter/interceptor

Powerplants: F.3 – Two 40.5kN (9100lb) dry and 73.5kN (16,520lb) with afterburning Turbo-Union RB199-34R Mk 104 turbofans.

Performance: F.3 – Max speed Mach 2.2. Operational ceiling approx 70,000ft. Combat radius supersonic 555km (300nm), subsonic over 1850km (1000nm). CAP endurance 555 to 740km (300 to 400nm) from base with time for interception and 10min combat, 2hr.

Weights: F.3 – Operating empty approx 14,500kg (31,970lb), max takeoff 27,895kg (61,700lb).

Dimensions: Span wings spread 13.91m (45ft 8in), span wings swept 8.60m (28ft 3in), length 18.68m (61ft 4in), height 5.95m (19ft 6in). Wing area (25° sweepback) 26.6m² (286.3sq ft).

Accommodation: Pilot and radar operator in tandem.

Armament: One IKMA-Mauser 27mm cannon. Four underfuselage Skyflash AAMs and two AIM-9L Sidewinders on each underwing pylon. Italian F.3s modified to carry Alenia Aspide AAMs under fuselage.

Operators: Italy, Saudi Arabia, UK.

History: An air-to-air Tornado model had always been envisioned in early planning, and a feasibility study of an air defence variant was first conducted in 1968.

The Tornado was subsequently selected to meet the UK's 1971 requirement for an advanced air defence fighter armed with BAe's Skyflash medium range air-to-air missile and fitted with an advanced radar. Formal development of the Tornado ADV or Air Defence Variant, as the Tornado fighter was designated, was authorised in March 1976.

The first of three Tornado ADV prototypes flew for the first time on October 27 1979, while the first production Tornado F.2 first flew in March 1984.

Compared with the Tornado IDS, the ADV features a 1.36m (4ft 6in) fuselage stretch, allowing the underfuselage carriage of four Skyflash missiles in semi recessed stations, while also increasing internal fuel capacity to 7143 litres. The ADV features the GEC-Marconi AI.24 Foxhunter radar, which was designed to track up to 20 targets while scanning, with a search range out to 185km (100nm). Development of the Foxhound however has been troubled and early production Tornado F.2s and F.3s were fitted with Foxhounds completed to X and Y standards, not meeting the full RAF requirement. AA standard Foxhounds fully meeting the RAF requirement have been installed in production aircraft since 1989, while all radars are now being upgraded to much improved AB standard with a new data processor.

The RAF ordered 173 Tornado ADVs, the first 18 of which were delivered in interim F.2 standard with less powerful Mk 103 engines, while the definitive F.3 features the RB199 Mk 104. F.2s have been retired from service, and the fuselages from 16 F.2s are being used to rebuild F.3s damaged by a contractor while undergoing maintenance.

Saudi Arabia is the only Tornado ADV export customer, with 24 delivered from 1989. Saudi and RAF Tornados flew combat air patrols during the Gulf War, but without seeing combat. Finally Italy has leased 24 RAF Tornado F.3s (modified to fire the Alenia Aspide) to bolster its fighter force pending the delivery of the Eurofighter.

Photo: A Skyflash and Sidewinder armed Saudi Tornado ADV. (BAe)

Pilatus Britten-Norman Islander/Defender

Country of origin: United Kingdom

Type: STOL utility transport

Powerplants: BN-2B-20 – Two 225kW (300hp) Textron Lycoming IO-540K1B5 flat six piston engines, driving two bladed props.

Performance: BN-2B-20 – Max speed 280km/h (151kt), max cruising speed 264km/h (142kt), economical cruising speed 245km/h (132kt). Max initial rate of climb 1130ft/min. Service ceiling 17,200ft. Takeoff run at sea level 352m (1155ft). Range at economical cruising speed with standard fuel 1136km (613nm), with optional fuel 1965km (1061nm).

Weights: BN-2B-20 – Empty equipped 1925kg (4244lb), max takeoff 2993kg (6600lb).

Dimensions: Wing span 14.94m (49ft 0in), length 10.86m (35ft 8in), height 4.18m (13ft 9in). Wing area 30.2m^2 (325.0sq ft).

Accommodation: Flightcrew of one or two, with seating for eight in main cabin.

Armament: Defender fitted with four underwing hardpoints for bombs, rockets and gun pods.

Operators: Belgium, Belize, Botswana, Cyprus, Guyana, India, Indonesia, Jamaica, Madagascar, Mauritania, Oman, Panama, Pakistan, Philippines, Seychelles, South Africa, Surinam, Turkey, UAE, UK, Venezuela, Zaire, Zimbabwe.

History: More than 1200 Islanders, Defenders and Turbine Islander/Defenders have been built for civil and military customers.

The BN-2 Islander was Britten-Norman's second original design, work on which began during 1963. Emphasis was on producing a rugged and durable aircraft that had good field performance and operating economics and was easy to maintain. One unusual feature was that there was no centre aisle between seats in the main cabin, instead there was three doors along each side of the fuselage for passenger boarding. The prototype BN-2 Islander (powered by two 155kW/210hp Continental IO-360s) first flew on June 13 1965.

The first production machines were powered by 195kW (260hp) Lycoming O-540s and were simply designated the BN-2, the first flew in 1967. Since then it has been built in improved BN-2A and BN-2B forms, the BN-2B still remaining in production with Pilatus Britten-Norman. The military specific Defender differs little from the Islander except for its four underwing hardpoints.

The BN-2T Turbine Islander/Defender is powered by two Allison 250 turboprops, and flew for the first time in August 1980. The BN-2T is not in as wide scale service as its piston powered brothers, but has spawned a range of military special mission derivatives.

The maritime patrol ASW/ASV Islander flew in demonstrator form in 1984, but was not built. The CASTOR Islander battlefield surveillance platform is intended for the British Army while the MASTOR is similar. Various AEW Defenders have also been marketed including the current MSSA (Multi Sensor Surveillance Aircraft), fitted with an APG-66 radar in a bulbous radome, plus FLIR and GPS.

The Defender 4000 features the larger wing of the Islander's three engined brother, the Trislander, plus an enlarged nose for a search radar, more powerful engines and increased weights. It first flew in August 1994.

Photo: Botswana's Defenders have a counter insurgency role.

Pilatus PC-6 Porter & Turbo-Porter

Country of origin: Switzerland

Type: STOL utility transport

Powerplant: PC-6/B2-H4 – One 410kW (550shp) flat rated Pratt & Whitney Canada PT6A-27 turboprop driving a three bladed propeller.

Performance: PC-6/B2-H4 (Utility version) – Economical cruising speed 213mk/h (115kt). Max initial rate of climb 940ft/min. Max operating altitude 25,000ft. Takeoff run at sea level 127m (415ft). Range with max payload at economical cruising speed and no reserves 730km (395nm), range with max internal fuel 925km (500nm), with external fuel 1610km (870nm).

Weights: PC-6/B2-H4 – Empty equipped 1270kg (2800lb), max takeoff 2800kg (6173lb).

Dimensions: PC-6/B2-H4 – Wing span 15.87m (52ft 1in), length 10.90m (35ft 9in), height tail down 3.20m (10ft 6in). Wing area 30.2m^2 (324.5sq ft).

Accommodation: Pilot and passenger on flightdeck, with max seating for nine in main cabin. Standard seating for six in main cabin. Alternative layouts include two stretchers and three medical attendants, or 10 paratroops.

Armament: Usually none. Thai AU-23's armed with one XM-197 cannon and two pod mounted 7.62mm machineguns, plus rockets and bombs.

Operators: Argentina, Austria, Bolivia, Chad, France, Iran, Mexico, Myanmar, Peru, Switzerland, Thailand, UAE, Yugoslavia.

History: Highly regarded for their exceptional STOL performance and low speed handling, the Pilatus Porter and Turbo-Porter STOL utilities are used for a number of utility tasks from paradropping, to liaison, reconnaissance and light transport.

The Porter flew for the first time on May 4 1959. The first production aircraft built, delivered from 1960, were powered by the six cylinder Lycoming GSO-480 piston engine, but it was not long after that a turboprop powered development flew. The first PC-6/A Turbo-Porter flew in May 1961, powered by a 390kW (523shp) Turboméca Astazou II turboprop. The majority of PC-6s built however are PC-6/Bs, powered by the ubiquitous Pratt & Whitney Canada PT6A. PC-6/Cs are powered by a 310kW (575shp) Garrett TPE331 and were first delivered in 1965.

The PC-6/B was first delivered from 1964, and remains in production today. Initial models were powered by the 410kW (550shp) PT6A-6 or -20. The PC-6/B2-H2 was first flown in 1970 and introduced the PT6A-27 and an increased maximum takeoff weight. Current production is of the PC-6/B2-H4 with a further increase in max takeoff weight, larger dorsal fin fillet, revised wingtips, strengthened airframe structure and improved undercarriage.

Fairchild in the USA manufactured the PC-6 under licence as the Heli-Porter. Included in US production was the AU-23 Peacemaker, an armed COIN variant initially ordered by the US Army for evaluation against the Helio Courier. The 15 evaluation AU-23As were subsequently delivered to the Royal Thai Air Force, plus 20 new production aircraft. The survivors still serve.

Photo: A Swiss PC-6 Turbo-Porter. Note the balloon tyres and long span wing. (Swiss MoD)

Pilatus PC-7 Turbo-Trainer

Country of origin: Switzerland

Type: Two seat trainer

Powerplant: One 485kW (650shp) flat rated to 410kW (550shp) Pratt & Whitney Canada PT6A-25A turboprop, driving a three bladed prop.

Performance: Aerobatic category – Max cruising speed 412km/h (222kt), economical cruising speed 317km/h (171kt). Max initial rate of climb 2150ft/min. Service ceiling 33,000ft, max operating altitude 25,000ft. Max range at cruise power and reserves 1200km (647nm). Utility category – Max cruising speed 364km/h (196kt), economical cruising speed 305km/h (165kt). Max initial rate of climb 1290ft/min. Max range at cruise power with reserves 2630km (1420nm).

Weights: Basic empty 1330kg (2932lb), max takeoff aerobatic category 1900kg (4188lb), max takeoff utility category 2700kg (5952lb).

Dimensions: Wing span 10.40m (34ft 1in), length 9.78m (32ft 1in), height 3.21m (10ft 6in). Wing area 16.6m² (179.0sq ft).

Accommodation: Two in tandem.

Armament: Usually none.

Operators: Angola, Austria, Bolivia, Chad, Chile, France, Guatemala, Iran, Malaysia, Mexico, Myanmar, Netherlands, Surinam, South Africa*, Switzerland, UAE, Uruguay.

History: The PC-7 Turbo-Trainer basic trainer is Pilatus' most successful military aircraft program.

The PC-7 is based on the earlier Pilatus P-3, a two seat basic trainer developed for the Swiss Air Force to replace North American T-6s. A total of 78 P-3s was built for Switzerland and Brazil in the mid 1950s. The P-3 was powered by a 195kW (260hp) Lycoming GO-435 flat six piston engine. All have been retired.

The first PC-7s were converted P-3s and the first such prototype flew on April 12 1966. A series of P-3-05 preproduction aircraft were built, however it was not until August 18 1978 that the first production aircraft flew. In that time the PC-7 underwent significant structural redesign (in conjunction with Dornier) to arrive at its current production form. Deliveries of production aircraft (to Myanmar, then Burma) began in December 1978.

Through the early 1980s the PC-7 attracted large orders from a number of air forces. Other than Switzerland, the PC-7 is in service with the air arms of the Netherlands, Abu Dhabi, Bolivia, Iran, Malaysia, Mexico and Myanmar. Optional Martin-Baker ejection seats were offered from 1985.

The basic PC-7 has now been joined by the PC-7 Mk II, which Pilatus developed specifically to meet a South African Air Force requirement to replace T-6 Harvards. The Mk II has been substantially revised and features the PC-9's airframe and a more powerful 520kW (700shp) PT6A-25 engine driving a four bladed prop. South Africa has ordered 60, which it has named Astra, with significant local industrial participation including assembly. The first PC-7 Mk II flew for the first time on September 28 1992. Production of kits for assembly by Atlas began in early 1994. Max cruising speed is 463km/h (250kt) and max takeoff weight is 2700kg (5952lb).

Photo: The Netherlands is one of 17 nations which operate the PC-7. (Paul Merritt)

Pilatus PC-9 & Beech Mk II

Country of origin: Switzerland

Type: Two seat advanced trainer

Powerplant: PC-9 – One 855kW (1150shp) Pratt & Whitney PT6A-62 turboprop (flat rated to 710kW/950shp) driving a four bladed propeller

Performance: PC-9 – Max speed at 20,000ft 555km/h (300kt), max speed at sea level 500km/h (270kt). Max initial rate of climb 4090ft/min. Max operating altitude 25,000ft, service ceiling 35,000ft. Max range at cruise power with reserves 1640km (887nm). Endurance at typical mission power settings, two 1hr sorties plus reserves.

Weights: PC-9 – Basic empty 1685kg (3715lb), max aerobatic category takeoff 2250kg (4960lb), max utility category takeoff 3200kg (7055lb).

Dimensions: PC-9 – Wing span 10.19m (33ft 5in), length 10.18m (33ft 5in), height 3.26m (10ft 8in). Wing area 16.3m² (175.3sq ft).

Accommodation: Two in tandem.

Armament: Usually none.

Operators: PC-9 – Angola, Australia, Cyprus, Iraq, Myanmar, Saudi Arabia, Slovenia, Switzerland, Thailand. PC-9 Mk II – USA*.

History: Pilatus' PC-9 is a more powerful and higher performing turboprop trainer based on the PC-7. Intended for basic and advanced training, the PC-9 was also the successful contender for the USAF/USN's JPATS program.

Design work on the PC-9 began in 1982. Aerodynamic features of the PC-9 were test flown on a modified PC-7 in 1982/3, while the first of two pre production PC-9s had its first flight on May 7 1984. Aerobatic category Swiss civil certification was granted in September 1985.

The PC-9 retains 9% structural commonality with the earlier PC-7. Key differences are the more powerful Pratt & Whitney PT6A-62 turboprop driving a four bladed prop (when the PC-9 was first in development some reports suggested it would be powered by a Garrett TFE331), stepped tandem cockpits with ejection seats and an airbrake under the centre fuselage.

Major PC-9 operators are Australia, Iraq, Saudi Arabia and Thailand. Australia ordered 67 PC-9/As to replace CT-4 Airtrainers and Macchi MB-326s for basic and advanced training. All but the first two were assembled in Australia by Hawker de Havilland and all feature low pressure tyres (as on the PC-7) for grass strip operations and Bendix EFIS displays. Saudi Arabia's 30 PC-9s were sold through British Aerospace as part of a comprehensive arms deal, while Thailand's 20 PC-9s have replaced RFB Fantrainers. In Germany a civil firm operates 10 PC-9Bs equipped for target towing under contract to the Luftwaffe. In all sales of the PC-9 exceed 200.

In June 1995 a slightly modified version of the PC-9 was selected to meet the US Air Force and Navy's Joint Primary Aircraft Training System program, which aimed to find a successor for the USAF's T-37s and the USN's T-34s. The Beech Mk II will be built by Raytheon in Kansas and features a new two piece canopy for increased bird strike protection, an upgraded engine, single point refuelling and zero zero ejection seats. Eventually several hundred will be procured, with an initial operating capability with the USAF planned for 1999.

Photo: One of 30 PC-9s delivered to the Royal Saudi Air Force.

PZL Mielec TS-11 Iskra

Country or origin: Poland

Type: Two seat advanced trainer

Powerplant: One 9.81kN (2205lb) IL SO-1/SO-3 turbojet.

Performance: Max speed at 16,400ft 720km/h (390kt), cruising speed 600km/h (324kt). Max initial rate of climb 2915ft/min. Service ceiling 36,100ft. Range with max fuel 1460km (790nm), standard range 1250km (675nm).

Weights: Empty 2560kg (5645lb), max takeoff 3840kg (8465lb).

Dimensions: Wing span 10.06m (33ft 0in), length 11.17m (36ft 8in), height 3.50m (11ft 6in). Wing area 17.5m² (188.4sq ft).

Accommodation: Two in tandem, or pilot only in Iskra-Bis C.

Armament: One 23mm internal cannon in forward starboard fuselage. Four underwing hardpoints (two on Iskra-Bis A) can carry a max external ordnance of 400kg (82lb), mainly practice weapons.

Operators: India, Poland.

History: The TS-11 Iskra (or Spark) jet trainer was ordered into production for the Polish Air Force despite losing a Warsaw Pact competition to the Czech Aero L-29 Delfin.

The TS-11 and L-29 (and the Yak-30) were designed against the late 1950s requirement for a standardised basic jet trainer to be adopted by Warsaw Pact nations. The XL-29 Delfin prototype flew for the first time on April 5 1959, while the first Iskra first flew some months later on February 5 1960. Subsequent evaluation saw the L-29 selected for production for the USSR and most other Warsaw Pact nations, however, Poland, in the interests of maintaining its aviation industry, elected instead to procure the Iskra. The Iskra entered production in 1963 and the first production aircraft were handed over to the Polish Air Force the following year.

The sleek Iskra features a straight, mid mounted wing, tandem seating with lightweight ejection seats and the rear seat slightly raised, a Polish developed SO-1 or SO-3 turbojet, a 23mm internal gun and four underwing hardpoints (except on early production examples) for practice armament. The tailplane is mounted on a boom to keep the control surfaces clear of the engine's exhaust.

Early production Iskras were powered by the interim 7.65kN (1720lb) H-10 Polish designed turbojet, pending the availability of the more powerful SO-1 (designed by the Instytut Lotnictwa/Aviation Institute and built by PZL Rzeszów). Some Iskras are powered by the improved but similarly rated SO-3.

Initial production was of the Iskra-Bis A with the two underwing hardpoints, while the Iskra-Bis A has four. The Iskra-Bis D weapons trainer is basically similar, and 50 were delivered to India in 1975 and the survivors still serve. The Iskra-Bis C or Iskra 200 was a single seater optimised for light ground attack, although it was only built in small numbers. The Iskra-Bis DF and TS-11R are reconnaissance variants.

Large numbers of TS-11s remain in Polish service although they are due to be replaced by the I-22 Iryda. Likewise India's TS-11s remain in service, although they are also due to be replaced.

Photo: A line up of Iskras from the Polish Air Force's aerobatic display team. (Paul Merritt)

PZL Mielec I-22, M-93 & M-95 Iryda

Country of origin: Poland

Type: Two seat advanced trainer/ground attack aircraft

Powerplants: I-22 – Two 10.8kN (2425lb) PZL-5 turbojets.

Performance: I-22 – Max speed at altitude 835km/h (450kt), max speed at sea level 785km/h (424kt). Max initial rate of climb 4925ft/min. Service ceiling 39,375ft. Time to 16,400ft 4min 24sec. Combat radius with 820kg (1810lb) of external ordnance comprising four 50kg bombs and two rocket pods 200km (108nm). Range clean at 16,400ft and 6650kg (14,660lb) takeoff weight 1150km (620nm). Endurance clean 2hr 33min.

Weights: I-22 – Empty equipped 4560kg (10,053lb), max takeoff 6900kg (15,212lb).

Dimensions: Wing span 9.60m (31ft 6in), length 13.22m (43ft 5in), height 4.30m (14ft 1in). Wing area 19.9m² (214.4sq ft).

Accommodation: Two in tandem, or pilot only in proposed M-97.

Armament: I-22 – Ventral gun pack contains a 23mm GSz-23L twin barrel gun. Four underwing hardpoints can be fitted with total external load of 1100kg (2425lb), including R-60 AAMs, rockets and bombs.

Operators: Poland*

History: The Iryda was developed to replace the TS-11 Iskra and Lim-6 (MiG-17) in Polish Air Force service as an advanced weapons trainer and a light ground attack aircraft.

Poland elected not to adopt the L-39 Albatros as its new advanced trainer and instead launched development of the indigenous Iryda in 1977. Five PZL-5 turbojet powered prototypes were built and the first of these first flew on March 3 1985 (although this aircraft crashed in 1987).

Poland requires about 50 Irydas which will be used for advanced training, ground attack and reconnaissance training. The first of nine pre production Irydas flew in 1992 and was subsequently delivered to the Polish Air Force that October.

The basic I-22 Iryda features stepped tandem cockpits, twin Polish designed and built PZL-5 turbojets mounted either side of the fuselage and a high mounted wing with four underwing hardpoints. The Iryda is designed to accept more powerful engines and greater weapons load in future developments, and to be easy to maintain and repair.

Apart from the basic I-22 PZL Mielec has developed and proposed a number of Iryda variants. The M-93 Iryda has been re-engined to overcome some shortcomings of the PZL-5 turbojet. The M-93K is powered by two 14.7kN (3305lb) Instytut Lotnictwa K-12 turbojets. The M-93R is a proposed two seat reconnaissance variant, the M-93M a proposed maritime attack and naval reconnaissance development. Meanwhile the M-93V is powered by two 14.7kN (3305lb) Rolls-Royce Viper 545 turbojets and is intended primarily for export. The prototype was displayed at the 1995 Paris Airshow.

The proposed M-95 would have mildly swept wings, six underwing hardpoints, a choice of uprated powerplants comprising Vipers, Larzac 04-V3s or K-15s, and an advanced nav attack system.

Finally the M-97 Iryda and M-99 Orkan (Eagle) are single seat attack developments. Both would have wingtip AAM stations, the M-99 could have Adour or Slovak DV-2 turbofans.

Photo: The first production M-93K. (PZL Mielec)

PZL Swidnik (Mil) Mi-2

Countries of origin: Poland & Russia

Type: Light utility helicopter

Powerplants: Two 300kW (400shp) Isotov designed Polish built GTD-350 turboshafts, driving a three bladed main rotor and two bladed tail rotor.

Performance: Max cruising speed 200km/h (108kt), long range cruising speed 190km/h (102kt). Max initial rate of climb 885ft/min. Service ceiling 13,125ft. Hovering ceiling in ground effect 6560ft. Range with max payload and reserves 170km (91nm), range with max fuel 440km (237nm), range with optional fuel 580km (313nm).

Weights: Basic operating 2365kg (5213lb), max takeoff 3550kg (7825lb).

Dimensions: Main rotor diameter 14.50m (47ft 7in), length overall 17.42m (57ft 2in), fuselage length 11.40m (37ft 5in), height to top of rotor head 3.75m (12ft 4in). Main rotor disc area 166.4m² (1791.1sq ft).

Accommodation: Two pilots or one pilot and passenger on flight-deck, and main cabin seating for seven in passenger configuration. Ambulance configurations can accommodate four stretchers and one medical attendant or two stretchers and two attendants. Can carry 700kg (1540lb) of internal freight.

Armament: Mi-2URP – Four 9M14M Malyutka (AT-3 'Sagger') anti armour missiles (with four more in cargo compartment. Mi-2US – One port fuselage side mounted 23mm NS-23m cannon, two 7.62mm gun pods either side of fuselage and two 7.62mm pintle mounted guns in rear cabin. Mi-2URN – As Mi-2US plus two rocket pods.

Operators: Bulgaria, Cuba, Czech Republic, Ghana, Hungary, Latvia, Nicaragua, Poland, Romania, Russia, Slovak Republic, Syria.

History: Poland's most massed produced helicopter was originally developed in Russia by Mil. More than 5200 have been built since the mid 1960s.

Mil originally designed the light utility Mi-2 (NATO reporting name 'Hoplite') in Russia during the early 1960s, resulting in a first flight in September 1961. In January 1964 an agreement between the USSR and Poland transferred development and production to the latter country, which commenced in 1965. The Mi-2 has evolved since that time and it remains in very low rate production today.

Swidnik has developed a diverse number of Mi-2 variants apart from the basic civil Mi-2. The Mi-2T is the basic military transport variant, while the Mi-2RM is a naval version. Three armed Mi-2s are the combat support/reconnaissance Mi-2URN, anti tank Mi-2URP and Mi-2US gunship. Their respective armament fits are described above.

The Kania (or Kitty Hawk) is a substantial upgrade of the basic Mi-2, and features Allison 250-C20B turboshafts, western avionics, composite main and tail rotor blades and US FAR Pt 29 certification. Developed in co-operation with Allison, the Kania first flew on June 3 1979 and US certification was granted in February 1986. The Kania has never entered full scale production but remains on offer, both as a new build aircraft and as an upgrade of existing Mi-2s.

Photo: A Polish Mi-2T transport. (MAP)

PZL Swidnik W-3 Sokol

Countries of origin: Poland

Type: Multirole utility helicopter

Powerplants: Two 670kW (900shp) takeoff rated WSK-PZL Rzeszów PZL-10W (polish built Mars TVD-10) turboshafts, driving a four bladed main rotor and three bladed tail rotor.

Performance: W-3 – Max speed 255km/h (138kt), economical cruising speed 235km/h (127kt), economical cruising speed 220km/h (120kt). Max initial rate of climb 1673ft/min. Hovering ceiling in ground effect 9850ft, out of ground effect 6890ft. Service ceiling 19,680ft. Max range at economical cruising speed 715km (386nm).

Weights: W-3 – Operating empty 3630kg (8002lb), max takeoff 6400kg (14,110lb).

Dimensions: Main rotor diameter 15.70m (51ft 6in), length overall rotors turning 18.85m (61ft 11in), fuselage length 14.21m (46ft 8in), height overall 4.20m (13ft 10in), height to top of rotor mast 3.80m (12ft 6in). Main rotor disc area 193.6m² (2083.8sq ft).

Accommodation: Two pilots or pilot and flight engineer or passenger on flightdeck. Main cabin seating for 12 in passenger configuration, or three medical attendants and eight rescued survivors in SAR Anaconda version, or four stretchers and medical attendants in ambulance configuration, one stretcher and medical attendants in critical care EMS version. Can carry a 2100kg (4630lb) sling load.

Armament: W-3U/W-3W – Undernose GSh-23L 23mm gun. Four hardpoints on outriggers for rockets, Grot anti armour missiles and two 9M32M 'Strela' AAMs

Operators: Myanmar*, Poland*.

History: The multi purpose W-3 Sokol, or Falcon, is the first helicopter to be fully designed and built in Poland.

Developed during the mid 1970s, the Sokol made its first flight on November 16 1979. Following a fairly protracted development program, low rate production of the Sokol commenced during 1985, since when about 70 have been built. The collapse of communism has allowed PZL Swidnik to broaden its sales base and market the Sokol internationally and the production figure may increase significantly in coming years.

The Sokol is of conventional design and construction, with its two PZL-10W turboshafts based on the Russian designed TVD-10B turbo-props. Composites are used in the tail and main rotor blades.

Sokol variants are many and include the improved civil W-3A Sokol which was awarded US civil certification in May 1993. Apart from the basic civil/military W-3 transport, military variants include the W-3RM Anaconda offshore search and rescue development with a watertight cabin, external winch and inflatable flotation bags; the W-3U Salamandra has a roof mounted sight with TV and FLIR and four weapon stations on fuselage outriggers; while the W-3W is similar but without the sight. The W-3WB Huzar flew in demonstrator form and was based on the W-3W but with Denel weapons and systems as developed for the Atlas Rooivalk. Development was suspended when the Polish military failed to support it.

Other W-3 variants to have been proposed include the stretched 14 seat W-3 Sokol-Long and the W-3U-1 Alligator naval ASW variant.

Photo: A W-3RM Anaconda. (Grzegorz Holdanowicz, PZL Swidnik)

PZL Warszawa-Okecie Orlik

Country of origin: Poland

Type: Two seat basic/advanced trainer

Powerplant: PZL-130TC-1 – One 560kW (750shp) Walter M 601 E turboprop driving a five bladed propeller. TC – One 710kW (950shp) Pratt & Whitney Canada PT6A-62.

Performance: PZL-130TC-1 – Max speed at 19,685ft 500km/h (270kt), max speed at sea level 454km/h (245kt). Max initial rate of climb 2620ft/min. Service ceiling 33,000ft. Range with max fuel 970km (523nm), range TC – Max speed at 19,685ft 560km/h (302kt), max speed at sea level 510km/h (274kt). Max initial rate of climb 4055ft/min. Service ceiling 33,000ft. Range with max fuel 930km (500nm), range with two external tanks 2300km (1242nm).

Weights: PZL-130-TC-1 – Empty 1600kg (3527lb), max takeoff 2700kg (5952lb). TC – Empty 1450kg (3197lb), max takeoff same.

Dimensions: Wing span 9.00m (29ft 6in), length 9.00m (29ft 6in), height 3.53m (11ft 7in). Wing area 13.0m² (139.9sq ft).

Accommodation: Two in tandem.

Armament: Six underwing hardpoints (stressed for 160kg/353lb each) for bombs, rockets and 'Strela' air-to-air missiles.

Operators: Poland*

History: The PZL-130 Orlik (Spotted Eagle) was designed as the aircraft centrepiece of the Polish Air Force's System 130 pilot training program.

System 130 called for a new trainer aircraft, aircraft diagnostics equipment and an aircraft simulator. Design work on the aircraft began in 1983 under the leadership of Andrej Frydrychewicz. The Orlik trainer originally began life powered by the Russian radial piston Vedneyev M14. Otherwise though it was similar to contemporary trainers with tandem seating (with the second seat slightly raised) and retractable undercarriage. First flight was on October 12 1984.

The piston powered PZL-130 was hamstrung by supply problems with the Vedneyev engine and instead PZL Warszawa-Okecie was forced to look at alternative powerplants. In 1988 a pre production Orlik made its first flight powered by a Polish Kalisz KS-8A but this aircraft soon proved underpowered and development of a piston powered Orlik was abandoned in 1990.

Development of a turboprop powered Orlik, or Turbo Orlik, dates to 1984 when PZL looked at powering the Orlik with a Pratt & Whitney Canada PT6. A so powered Orlik development aircraft had its first flight on July 13 1986. Subsequent Motorlet M 601 powered and PT6A-25 powered Turbo Orlik development aircraft were designated PZL-130TM and PZL-130T respectively.

The Polish Air Force ordered 48 M 601 powered Turbo Orliks (the Turbo prefix was subsequently dropped) as the PZL-130TB and deliveries against this order are continuing. These aircraft are now being built to improved PZL-130TC-1 standard with Martin-Baker zero zero ejection seats and GPS, while early production TBs were upgraded to TC-1 configuration. The PT6A-62 powered PZL-130TC is aimed primarily at export markets and features Bendix King avionics and a HUD. The PZL-130TC-1 is similar save for its less powerful 560kW (750shp) PT6A-25C.

Photo: Production PZL-130TC-1 Orliks for the Polish Air Force. (PZL Warszawa-Okecie)

Rockwell T-2 Buckeye

Country of origin: United States of America

Type: Two seat carrier capable advanced trainer

Powerplants: T-2C – Two 13.1kN (2950lb) General Electric J85-GE-4 turbojets.

Performance: T-2C – Max speed 840km/h (470kt). Max initial rate of climb 6200ft/min. Service ceiling 40,415ft. Range 1685km (910nm).

Weights: T-2C – Empty 3680kg (8115lb), max takeoff 5977kg (13,179lb).

Dimensions: T-2C – Wing span over wingtip tanks 11.62m (38ft 2in), length 11.67m (38ft 4in), height 4.51m (14ft 10in). Wing area 23.7m² (255.0sq ft).

Accommodation: Two in tandem.

Armament: T-2C – Usually none, but has two underwing hardpoints for practice bombs, rockets and gun pods. T-2D/T-2E – Six underwing hardpoints can carry a total ordnance load of 1588kg (3500lb) for rockets and bombs.

Operators: Greece, Venezuela, USA.

History: The T-2 Buckeye advanced trainer has been responsible for training and carrier qualifying countless thousands of US Navy fast jet pilots since the early 1960s.

In 1956 the US Navy issued its requirement for a new jet powered trainer able to train pilots once they had some basic tuition on the T-34 through to advanced training, weapons and combat training and carrier qualification. Later in 1956 North American Aviation, a company which had already made thousands of SNJ and T-28 Trojan trainers (plus the FJ Fury fighter) for the US Navy was selected to develop its NA-249 design proposal and an initial order for 26 production T2J-1s was placed.

The NA-249/T2J-1 design featured a single 15.1kN (3400lb) Westinghouse J34-WE-36 turbojet fed by two undernose intakes, plus tandem seating, a mid mounted straight wing with tip tanks and an arrester hook for carrier operations/training.

The first T2J-1 had its maiden flight on January 31 1958, there being no prototype. Some 217 T2J-1 (T-2A from 1962) Buckeyes were built, the first entered service in July 1959. In 1960 two T2J-1s were converted to YT2J-2 standard powered by two 13.4kN (3000lb) Pratt & Whitney J60-P-6 turbojets. The first of these flew on August 30 1962 as the YT-2B, while the first production T-2B had its first flight on May 21 1966. The 97 production T-2Bs were delivered to the USN from 1966.

The definitive US Navy Buckeye is the T-2C. The T-2C is powered by two General Electric J85 turbojets (the J85 also powers the F-5), and first flew in 1968. The T-2C was delivered between 1968 and 1976, replacing surviving T-2As and T-2Bs in service. The T-2C itself is now being replaced by the T-45 Goshawk. Small numbers of T-2B and T-2Cs were converted to DT-2 drone controllers.

The Buckeye found export customers in Greece and Venezuela. Venezuela ordered 12 T-2Ds (with some avionics changes and no carrier gear) in 1972. A subsequent batch of 12 T-2Ds featured six underwing hardpoints. Greece's T-2E are essentially similar, with the six underwing hardpoints. Forty were delivered from 1976.

Photo: This T-2C wears the markings of the US Naval Test Pilot School at Patuxent River, Maryland. (MAP)

Rockwell OV-10 Bronco

Rockwell B-1B Lancer

Country of origin: United States of America

Type: Light attack/COIN and FAC aircraft

Powerplants: OV-10A – 535kW (715ehp) Garrett T76-G-416/417 turboprops, driving three bladed propellers.

Performance: OV-10A – Max speed 452km/h (244kt). Max initial rate of climb 2650ft/min. Service ceiling 24,000ft. Takeoff run at normal takeoff weight 225m (740ft). Combat radius with max external ordnance 367km (198nm). Ferry range with external fuel 2300km (1240nm).

Weights: OV-10A – Empty equipped 3160kg (6970lb), max takeoff 6552kg (14,444lb).

Dimensions: OV-10A – Wing span 12.19m (40ft 0in), length 12.67m (41ft 7in), height 4.62m (15ft 2in). Wing area 27.0m² (291.0sq ft).

Accommodation: Two in tandem, plus two stretchers and a medical attendant or five troops in rear fuselage.

Armament: Four 7.62mm machineguns in underfuselage sponsons. Two underwing, one centreline and four under sponson hardpoints for light bombs, rockets and gun pods.

Operators: Bolivia, Indonesia, Morocco, Philippines, Thailand, Venezuela.

History: The OV-10 resulted from the US Marines sponsored Light Armed Reconnaissance Aircraft (LARA) program to find a multirole utility aircraft that could perform recce and light attack missions.

North American's NA-300 design was selected in August 1964. Seven YOV-10A prototypes were ordered for evaluation and the first of these first flew on July 16 1965.

The OV-10 has a unique configuration with two crew in tandem under a large canopy, room in the rear fuselage for five troops or two stretchers, a high wing and twin tailbooms extending from the engine nacelles. Power is from two Garret T76s (one YOV-10 was powered by two T74s/PT6s). Sponsons extending either side of the fuselage house four 7.62mm guns and feature hardpoints for a variety of weaponry.

Production OV-10As were delivered to the USAF, Navy and Marines, and many saw operational service in Vietnam where they were used for forward air control (FAC) and light attack.

The OV-10B designation applies to six Broncos delivered to Germany from 1970 for target towing. A further 18 OV-10B(Z)s for Germany were fitted with an above wing mounted J85 auxiliary turbojet. All have been retired.

The Royal Thai Air Force continues to operate the survivors of 32 OV-10Cs delivered from 1971, while Venezuela took delivery of 16 OV-10Es (and later ex USAF OV-10As). The OV-10C and OV-10E are similar to the OV-10A.

Seventeen OV-10As were converted to OV-10D standard over 1979/80 for the US Marines, the result of the US Navy sponsored OV-10D NOGS (Night Observation/Gunship System) program to give the Bronco an all weather capability. Recently retired, the OV-10Ds featured an undernose turret containing a FLIR, laser designator and automatic video tracker, plus uprated engines and extra underwing hardpoints. The OV-10D saw service during the Gulf War and could be armed with a 20mm M197 three barrel cannon in place of the 7.62mm guns.

Photo: Venezuela operates OV-10Es (pictured) and ex USAF OV-10As.

Country of origin: United States of America

Type: Strategic bomber

Powerplants: Four 64.9kN (14,600lb) dry and 136.9kN (30,780lb) with afterburning General Electric F101-GE-102 turbofans.

Performance: Max speed at altitude Mach 1.25 or 1324km/h (715kt), penetration speed at 200ft over 965km/h (520kt). Service ceiling over 50,000ft. Range with standard fuel approx 12,000km (6475nm).

Weights: Empty equipped 87,090kg (192,000lb), max takeoff 216,365kg (477,000lb).

Dimensions: Wing span fully extended 41.67m (136ft 9in), span wings swept 23.84m (78ft 3in), length 44.81m (147ft 0in), height 10.36m (34ft 10in). Wing area approx 181m² (1950sq ft).

Accommodation: Crew of four comprising pilot, copilot, offensive systems operator (OSO) and defensive systems operator (DSO).

Armament: Max internal payload of 34,020kg (75,000lb) in three internal weapons bays. Weapons include B-61 and B-83 thermonuclear bombs or on SRAM launchers up to 24 AGM-69A short range attack missiles (SRAM-As), 12 B-28, 28 B-61 or 28 B-93 free fall nuclear bombs. When modified for conventional weapons could carry up to 84 500lb/225kg bombs.

Operators: USA

History: The USA's primary strategic nuclear bomber, the B-1 has had to endure criticisms of its high cost, cancellation, a quarter century gestation period and operational serviceability problems.

The B-1 results from the USAF's Advanced Manned Strategic Aircraft (AMSA – or, as it became known, America's Most Studied Airplane) program of 1965 to find a low altitude penetration nuclear bomber to replace the B-52. A North American Rockwell design was eventually selected for further development in 1970 from competing designs from Boeing and General Dynamics.

The first of four B-1A prototypes took to the skies for the first time on December 23 1974. However in 1977 newly elected US President Carter cancelled production of the B-1A (SAC hoped to acquire 250) although test flying was allowed to continue.

The B-1 was resurrected in 1981 when Ronald Reagan was installed as US President and 100 improved production B-1s, designated B-1B, were ordered. Compared with the B-1A the B-1B features improved avionics and systems, incorporation of some low observable features such as RAM coatings, strengthened landing gear, optional weapons bay fuel tanks, external underfuselage hardpoints for fuel and weapons, ejection seats rather than a crew escape capsule, fixed, rather than variable air inlets (limiting top speed to Mach 1.25 rather than the B-1A's Mach 2.3) with ducting masking the engines from radar. The B-1B's offensive systems are based around the Westinghouse APG-164 radar (based on the APG-66) for navigation and terrain following, with a low observable phased array antenna. The core of the defensive systems is the troubled Eaton ALQ-161 continuously upgradable ECM suite.

All 100 production B-1B Lancers had been delivered by April 1988, and despite serviceability troubles and some much publicised attrition losses it is now proving more reliable and capable.

Photo: A B-1B of North Dakota based 28th Bomb Wing. (Bruce Malcolm)

Rockwell/DASA X-31 EFM

Countries of origin: United States of America and Germany

Type: Enhanced manoeuvrability technology demonstrator

Powerplant: One 71.2kN (16,000lb) General Electric F404-GE-400 turbofan.

Performance: Estimated – Max speed approx Mach 1.3. Max initial rate of climb 43,000ft/min. Max operating altitude 40,000ft.

Weights: Empty equipped 5175kg (11,410lb), max takeoff 7228kg (15,935lb).

Dimensions: Wing span 7.26m (23ft 10in), length 14.85m (48ft 9in), height 4.44m (14ft 7in). Wing area 21.0m² (226.3sq ft).

Accommodation: Pilot only.

Armament: None

Operators: Experimental aircraft, not in operational service.

History: The X-31 is a joint American/German research program to evaluate and investigate a number of advanced technologies to improve fighter manoeuvrability.

The X-31A EFM (Enhanced Fighter Manoeuvrability) demonstrators resulted from the merger of previous MBB and Rockwell research programs. Feasibility studies of a joint research/demonstrator were conducted from late 1984. Funding for the two Rockwell assembled prototypes was granted in August 1988 and the first of these flew for the first time on October 11 1990.

Rockwell was responsible for final assembly for the two X-31As, while MBB, now Daimler Benz Aerospace (or DASA), built major sub assemblies such as the wing and designed the flight control and thrust vectoring systems. The second X-31A flew in January 1991.

The X-31A features a cranked delta wing, canard foreplanes, a single General Electric F404 turbofan, thrust vectoring paddles, an airbrake either side of the rear fuselage, fly-by-wire and some composite construction. Various systems have been borrowed from other aircraft, including the F/A-18 Hornet's cockpit canopy, modified F-16 landing gear and electrical systems from the F-16 and failed Northrop F-20. The basic design of the X-31 was based on MBB's work on the TKF (which in part led to the Eurofighter), and Rockwell's HiMAT research drone.

The X-31 program was jointly managed by the US Advanced Research Program Agency through the US Naval Air Systems Command (hence the Bureau of Aeronautics serials) and the German Ministry of Defence. The US Air Force and NASA joined the program in 1992. Funding is 75% from the USA, 25% from Germany.

The X-31's formal test program wound up in 1995 by which time the two demonstrators had successfully completed 530 flights (one of the X-31s crashed in the middle of that year). The X-31 demonstrated so called post stall manoeuvrability, with controllability demonstrated to 70° angle of attack. Other highlights include the 'Herbst Manoeuvre' where the X-31 made a 180° change of direction at 70° angle of attack. Meanwhile at an altitude of 38,000ft and speed of Mach 1.2 the X-31 was able to maintain stability and manoeuvrability using its thrust vectoring paddles while its fin and rudder were used to intentionally destabilise it. The X-31s have also been highly successful in simulated close-in dogfights with F/A-18s and F-14s.

Photo: One of the two X-31 EFM demonstrators built.

Saab 105

Country of origin: Sweden

Type: Two seat basic/advanced trainer and light attack aircraft

Powerplants: Sk 60B – Two 7.3kN (1638lb) Turboméca Aubisique turbofans.

Performance: Sk 60B – Max speed at 20,000ft 765km/h (413kt), max speed at sea level 720km/h (388kt), max cruising speed 685km/h (370kt). Max initial rate of climb 3445ft/min. Time to 29,530ft 15min. Service ceiling 39,370ft. Ferry range 1780km (960nm), standard range 1400km (755nm).

Weights: Sk 60B – Basic empty 2510kg (5535lb), max takeoff 4500kg (9920lb).

Dimensions: Sk 60B – Wing span 9.50m (31ft 2in), length 10.50m (34ft 5in), height 2.70m (8ft 10in). Wing area 16.3m² (175.5sq ft).

Accommodation: Two side by side in all models except Sk 60D, which has seating for four.

Armament: Sk 60B – Six underwing hardpoints can carry a total ordnance load of 700kg (1543lb), including rockets and bombs. Saab 105Ös can carry a 2000kg (4410lb) ordnance load including AIM-9 Sidewinder AAMs.

Operators: Austria, Sweden.

History: The light attack/advanced jet trainer Saab 105 began life as a private venture.

Saab designed the 105 to be capable of a number of different missions as diverse as ground attack, reconnaissance, basic and advanced pilot training, liaison, target towing and even air ambulance. The first of two Saab 105 prototypes made its first flight on June 29 1963, while the following year the Royal Swedish Air Force ordered 130 production aircraft (later 150) as the Sk 60. The first production Sk 60 flew in August 1965.

The Sk 60A trainer entered service in 1966. These aircraft were delivered unarmed but were later retrofitted to carry hardpoints for weapons, allowing a secondary wartime ground attack role. The Sk 60B meanwhile is primarily tasked with weapons training and ground attack. The Sk 60C has a Fairchild KB-18 reconnaissance camera in the nose, but also retains a secondary ground attack capability. The Sk 60D and four seat Sk 60E (with the two ejection seats replaced by four fixed seats) are used for liaison and check rides.

From 1996 to 1998 Sweden's Sk 60 fleet will be progressively re-engined with Williams Rolls FJ44 turbofans. The prototype conversion first flew in October 1995.

The only Saab 105 export customer was Austria, who ordered 40 Saab 105Ös. The 105Ö is based on the General Electric J85 turbojet powered Saab 105XT, which first flew on April 29 1967. The Saab 105XT was intended for export and apart from the more powerful engines has improved avionics, greater internal fuel capacity and a strengthened wing allowing an increased external ordnance load. For many years the 105Ös, armed with AIM-9s, were tasked with air defence and were Austria's only jet fighters until the arrival of the Draken.

Saab has also offered the improved 105G, and more recently a 105 development to meet the USA's JPATS trainer requirement. It was ruled out when the US stipulated tandem seating.

Photo: First flight of the prototype FJ44 powered Saab 105. (Saab)

Saab 32 Lansen

Country of origin: Sweden

Type: EW trainer/aggressor and target tug

Powerplant: J 32B – One 68.1kN (15,190lb) Svenska Flygmotor licence built Rolls-Royce Avon RM6A turbojet.

Performance: J 32B – Max speed Mach 0.91 or 1114km/h (602kt). Max initial rate of climb 19,700ft/min. Service ceiling 52,500ft. Range with external fuel 3220km (1740nm).

Weights: J 32B – Empty 7990kg (17,600lb), max takeoff 13,530kg (29,800lb).

Dimensions: Wing span 13.00m (42ft 8in), length 14.94m (49ft 1in), height 4.65m (15ft 3in). Wing area 37.4m² (402.6sq ft).

Accommodation: Two in tandem.

Armament: J 32 – Four 20mm Aden J 32B cannon in forward lower nose. Four underwing hardpoints now used for EW jammer pods etc, originally designed for Sidewinder AAMs, rockets, bombs and ASMs. A 32 had a max external load of 1360kg (3000lb).

Operators: Sweden

History: Sweden's Lansen (Lance) was a highly capable all weather fighter, reconnaissance and ground attack aircraft. It survives in service today as an electronic warfare trainer and aggressor and as a target tug.

The Lansen was developed to replace the earlier twin piston powered Saab 18. From the outset it was developed in three separate versions to perform all weather fighter (J 32B), all weather ground attack (A 32A) and reconnaissance (S 32C). Development first began in 1948. The Lansen began life first as a twin powered by two de Havilland Ghosts, while a subsequent design, the P1150, would have been powered by a single Swedish developed STAL Dovern turbojet, before development of the Dovern was dropped because of cost and timescale issues. Instead the P1150 gained a Rolls-Royce Avon and became the Saab 32 Lansen. First flight was on November 3 1952. In all 450 production Lansens were built from 1954 through to 1960 and over 30 remain in service.

Aerodynamically the Lansen is straightforward, simple and clean, and it can reach a max speed of Mach 1.12 in a shallow dive, despite a modest thrust to weight ratio. Power is from a Swedish licence built Avon and the rear fuselage is detachable to allow easy access to the engine. In the nose of the A 32 and J 32 were four 20mm cannon, while the A 32 had an Ericsson mapping radar, the J 32 had a S6 fire control radar for lead pursuit interception. The S 32 had various reconnaissance sensors in the nose.

Today Lansens remaining in service are based on the J 32B, which was the most powerful and heavy of the Lansen variants. The J 32E conversions carry various radar and radio/communications jammers in the nose and in underwing pods and chaff dispensers. They are used to provide a realistic electronic warfare environment for military exercises, while three unmodified J 32Bs serve as crew trainers. Finally five converted J 35Ds are used to tow VM-6 aerial targets.

Photo: A J 32E Lansen EW aggressor/trainer. (Paul Merritt)

Saab 35 Draken

Country of origin: Sweden

Type: Multirole fighter

Powerplants: 35X – One 56.9kN (12,790lb) dry and 78.5kN (17,650lb) with afterburning Volvo Flygmotor RM6C turbojet (licence built Rolls-Royce Avon 300).

Performance: 35X – Max speed Mach 2 or approx 2125km/h (1145kt). Max initial rate of climb 34,450ft/min. Time to 36,000ft 2min 36sec, time to 49,200ft 5min 0sec. Radius with internal fuel only, hi-lo-hi 635km (345nm), with two 100lb/455kg bombs and two drop tanks hi-lo-hi 1005km (540nm). Ferry range with max internal and external fuel 3250km (1755nm).

Weights: 35X – Empty 8250kg (18,188lb), max takeoff 15,000kg (33,070lb), max overload takeoff 16,000kg (35,275lb).

Dimensions: Wing span 9.40m (30ft 10in), length 15.35m (50ft 4in), height 3.89m (12ft 9in). Wing area 49.2m² (529.6sq ft).

Accommodation: Pilot only, or two in tandem in Sk 35C and TF-35.

Armament: One or two 30mm Aden cannon (one in each wing). Nine external stores stations can carry 454kg (1000lb) each, weapons include Bofors rockets, 1000lb/455kg and 500lb/225kg bombs, Rb 24 Sidewinder (licence built AIM-9P) and Rb 27 Falcon (licence built AIM-4) AAMs.

Operators: Austria, Finland, Sweden.

History: The remarkable Draken (Dragon) was developed against a demanding 1949 Swedish Air Force requirement to develop an advanced high performance interceptor to replace the Saab J 29 Tunnan.

Among that requirement's specifications was performance 50% greater than any other fighter then entering service. Saab's design team led by Erik Bratt used the unique double delta wing, giving Mach 2 performance and shorter airfield takeoff lengths than contemporaries such as the Mirage III and F-104. The double delta wing configuration was successfully test flown on the Saab 201 research aircraft before the first of three Draken prototypes (powered by an Avon 200) flew for the first time on October 25 1955.

Initial production RM6B powered J 35A fighters were delivered to the Swedish Air Force from 1960. New build and converted J 35Bs featured Saab's S7 fire control radar and a lengthened rear fuselage, while the J35D was powered by an improved and uprated RM6C turbojet. The final Swedish fighter Draken, the J 35F, introduced a Hughes weapon system comprising a pulse doppler radar, automatic fire control system and Falcon AAMs. The J 35F-II has a Hughes infrared sensor. Sixty six J 35Fs have been upgraded to J 35J standard for service through to the end of the 1990s, when they are due to replaced by the JAS 39 Gripen.

Aside from the J 35 fighters the Swedish Air Force acquired reconnaissance S 35Es with a nose containing five cameras and the Sk 35 two seat conversion trainer.

The export 35X was sold to Denmark (as the F-35 fighter, reconnaissance R-35 and two seat TF-35) and Finland which bought 12 J 35XS and later ex Swedish J 35Fs. Finally Austria's J 35ÖEs are rebuilt ex Swedish Air Force J 35Ds (24 were delivered from 1988).

Photo: A Swedish J 35J Draken displays its new grey paint scheme and armament of Sidewinder and Falcon AAMs and rockets. (Paul Merritt)

Saab 37 Viggen

Country of origin: Sweden

Type: Multirole fighter

Powerplant: JA 37 – One 72.1kN (16,203lb) dry and 125kN (28,108lb) with afterburning Volvo Flygmotor RM8B turbofan.

Performance: JA 37 – Max speed above Mach 2, or more than 2125km/h (1145kt), max speed at 330ft Mach 1.2. Time to 32,800ft less than 1min 42sec. Takeoff run approx 400m (1310ft). Tactical radius with external ordnance hi-lo-hi over 1000km (540nm), lo-lo-lo over 500km (270nm).

Weights: Clean takeoff approx 15,000kg (33,070lb), takeoff with normal armament 17,000kg (37,478lb).

Dimensions: Wing span 10.60m (34ft 9in), length overall inc probe 16.40m (53ft 10in), fuselage length 15.58m (51ft 2in), height 5.90m (19ft 4in). Wing area 46.0m^2 (495.1sq ft).

Accommodation: Pilot only, or two in separate cockpits in Sk 37.

Armament: JA 37 – One 30mm Oerlikon KCA cannon in permanent underfuselage pack. Four underwing and three under fuselage hardpoints for Rb 74 Sidewinders, Rb 71 Sky Flashes (licence built BAe Sky Flashes) on each inboard wing pylon, plus rockets. AJ 37 – Weapons include Saab Rb 15F anti ship and Rb 75 Maverick missiles, Rb 27/28 Falcon and Rb 74 Sidewinder AAMs, rockets and bombs.

Operators: Sweden

History: The Viggen (Thunderbolt) currently forms the bulk of Sweden's front line fighter strength and is yet another successful product of a demanding Swedish fighter requirement.

The Viggen was developed as the airborne component of Sweden's System 37 air defence network and to replace the Saab Lansen. Design work of a new single engine fighter began in the early 1960s and considerations included Mach 2 at altitude, supersonic flight at low level and unprecedented STOL performance. To meet these requirements Saab utilised the then unconventional canard delta configuration. The first of seven prototypes flew for the first time on February 8 1967.

The canards or foreplanes are fixed but have trailing edge flaps. The wing arrangement not only gives good agility but also excellent takeoff performance, allowing operations from damaged runways or sections of freeways. Power is from a modified Volvo Flygmotor RM8 licence built Pratt & Whitney JT8D with afterburning. Tandem main undercarriage and thrust reversal allows short, non flare landings.

Initial production was of the AJ 37 Viggen (first delivered in June 1971) optimised for ground attack but with a secondary interception role. 110 were built and they featured an Ericsson PS-37/A radar, Saab digital nav/attack computer and a HUD. The SF 37 (26 built) and SH 37 (26 built) are reconnaissance variants, the SH 37 with radar is optimised for maritime reconnaissance with a secondary maritime strike role. The Sk 37 (18 built) is a two seater.

Final production was of the JA 37 interceptor with an Ericsson PS-46/A multimode, doppler, look down/shoot down radar, Sky Flash and Sidewinder missile armament, an uprated RM8B engine and new avionics. The last of 149 built was delivered in June 1990. Finally 115 AJ, SH and SF 37 Viggens are being modified to multirole AJS 37 standard with expanded weaponry and some new avionics.

Photo: A reconnaissance SF 37 Viggen. (Paul Merritt)

Saab JAS 39 Gripen

Country of origin: Sweden

Type: Lightweight multirole fighter

Powerplant: One 54.0kN (12,140lb) dry and 80.5kN (18,100lb) with afterburning Volvo Flygmotor RM12 turbofan (licence built General Electric F404-GE-400).

Performance: Supersonic at all altitudes. Takeoff and landing strip length approx 800m (2625ft). Range not published.

Weights: Operating empty 6622kg (14,600lb), max takeoff approx 13,000kg (28,660lb).

Dimensions: Wing span 8.40m (27ft 7in), length overall 14.10m (46ft 3in), height 4.50m (14ft 9in).

Accommodation: Pilot only, two in tandem in JAS 39B.

Armament: One 27mm Mauser BK27 cannon. Wingtip stations for Rb 74 (AIM-9) AAMs. One centreline and four underwing hardpoints for rockets, DWS 39 cluster bomb dispensers, Rb 75 (AGM-65) ASMs, RBS 15 anti ship missiles, bombs, AIM-120 or Matra Mica AAMs.

Operators: Sweden*

History: Saab's sixth jet fighter, the Gripen (Griffin) is probably the most advanced and capable single seat fighter currently in air force service.

The Gripen was developed to replace the Royal Swedish Air Force's Viggens and remaining Drakens. Definition studies of the new fighter began in 1980, while government program approval and development funding (including for five prototypes and 30 production aircraft) was approved in 1982. Meanwhile in 1981 the IG JAS (Industry Group JAS) teaming of Saab, Volvo Flygmotor, Ericsson and FFV Aerotech had been formed to develop and build the new aircraft.

From the outset it was recognised that the growing cost of new fighters meant that the new aircraft would be smaller than the Viggen and that it would be powered by a single engine. The General Electric F404 turbofan (as powers the F/A-18 Hornet) was selected for local development and construction, while other design features include the canard delta configuration (for manoeuvrability and to meet the strict short field requirements), lateral instability with fly-by-wire, an Ericsson/GMAv PS-05/A pulse doppler multimode look down/shoot down radar with multiple target track while scan and ground mapping capabilities, and a modern cockpit with three multifunction displays, a wide angle HUD and HOTAS controls. Thirty percent of the Gripen by weight is of composites (including the wing boxes, canards and fin), while the aircraft is designed to be easily maintained in the field.

The first prototype Gripen made its first flight on December 9 1988 but crashed the following February due to fly-by-wire software problems. The second prototype Gripen first flew in May 1990. The first production Gripen delivery was in June 1993 and 130 (out of a total requirement for 280) are on firm order for delivery through to 2002.

Apart from the basic JAS 39A fighter, Gripen variants include the JAS 39B two seater (due to fly in 1996) and the proposed improved JAS 39C/D and export JAS 39X. Unlike the Viggen, Saab is able to aggressively market the Gripen for export and in 1995 signed an international marketing agreement with British Aerospace.

Photo: Unlike earlier Saab fighters, the multirole Gripen is not built in dedicated attack, reconnaissance or interceptor versions. (Saab)

Saab Safari & Supporter & PAC Mushshak

Saab 340

Saab Safari & Supporter & PAC Mushshak

Country of origin: Sweden

Type: Two seat basic trainer

Powerplant: MFI-17 – One 150kW (200hp) Lycoming IO-360-A1B6 flat four piston engine, driving a two bladed propeller.

Performance: MFI-17 – Max speed 236km/h (127kt), cruising speed 208km/h (112kt). Max initial rate of climb 807ft/min. Service ceiling 13,450ft. Endurance 5hr 10min.

Weights: MFI-17 – Empty equipped 646kg (1424lb), max takeoff 1200kg (2646lb).

Dimensions: MFI-17 – Wing span 8.85m (29ft 1in), length 7.00m (23ft 0in), height 2.60m (8ft 7in). Wing area 11.9m² (128.1sq ft).

Accommodation: Standard seating for two side by side, with optional rear facing seat behind them.

Armament: Mushshak – Six underwing hardpoints, inner two stressed for 150kg (330lb) each, outer four for 100kg (220lb), for rocket and gun pods and Bofors Bantam anti tank missiles.

Operators: Safari – Norway. Supporter – Denmark, Zambia. Mushshak – Iran, Oman, Pakistan, Syria.

History: The MFI-15 Safari and MFI-17 Supporter resulted from Saab's adaption of the MFI-9 Junior/Minicom for basic training for civil and military operators.

The original two seat tricycle undercarriage Malmo (of Sweden) MFI-9 flew for the first time on October 10 1958. MBB of Germany acquired production rights to the MFI-9 which it built locally as the Bo 208 Junior (first flight in 1962). In all over 250 75kW (100hp) Rolls-Royce Continental O-200 powered MFI-9s and Bo 208s were built through to the late 1960s, mostly for civil customers.

In 1968 Saab began work on its MFI-15, based on the MFI-9 but with some design changes. Foremost of the changes in the Saab built MFI-15 prototype was the 120kW (160hp) Lycoming IO-320 piston engine. Like the MFI-9/Bo 208 though the MFI-15 retained the unusual braced, mid mounted and forward swept wing and rearward hinging canopy, offering good all round vision. The prototype Saab MFI-15's maiden flight was on July 11 1969. Following testing the MFI-15 gained a more powerful IO-360, while the horizontal tail was relocated to clear it of damage of thrown up debris. First flight in this modified form was in February 1971.

Sold as the MFI-15 Safari, most went to civil customers, however Sierra Leone and Norway took delivery of Safaris for military pilot training. To improve its military market appeal, Saab developed the MFI-17 Supporter, fitted with six underwing hardpoints for light and practice weaponry, giving it weapons training and light COIN capabilities. First flight was on July 6 1972. Important customers were Denmark (designated T-17) and Zambia. Production ended in the late 1970s after about 250 Safaris and Supporters had been built. Most were for civil customers.

Pakistan meanwhile has taken delivery of 18 Saab built Supporters, while 92 have been assembled locally by PAC from knocked down kits and a further 149 were built locally by PAC. It is named Mushshak (Proficient) in Pakistani service.

Photo: A Danish T-17 (MFI-17) Supporter. Thirty two were delivered to the Danish Air Force and Army. (MAP)

Saab 340

Country of origin: Sweden

Type: VIP transport and AEW platform

Powerplants: 340B – Two 1305kW (1750shp) General Electric CT7-9B turboprops driving four bladed propellers.

Performance: 340B – Max cruising speed at 15,000ft 523km/h (282kt), long range cruising speed at 25,000ft 467km/h (252kt). Max initial rate of climb 2000ft/min. Service ceiling 31,000ft. Range with 35 passengers and reserves at max cruising speed 1490km (805nm), at long range cruising speed 1735km (935nm).

Weights: 340B – Operating empty 8140kg (17,945lb), max takeoff 13,155kg (29,000lb).

Dimensions: Wing span 21.44m (70ft 4in), length 19.73m (64ft 9in), height 6.97m (22ft 11in). Wing area 41.8m² (450sq ft).

Accommodation: Flightcrew of two. Main cabin seats up to 37 in passenger configuration. Tp 100 in VIP configuration. AEW Tp 100B has three multifunction workstations in main cabin.

Armament: None

Operators: Sweden*

History: Saab's largest commercial aircraft sales success, the Saab 340 has been adapted for military service as a VIP transport and as an AEW platform.

In 1979 Saab (who wanted to diversify out of military aviation) and Fairchild reached an agreement to conduct joint feasibility and development studies on a 30 to 40 seat commuter. The resulting SF340 design was modern if conventional and powered by two General Electric CT7 turboprops (a commercial development of the T700 which powers Sikorsky's H-60 series of helicopters). Within the 65%/35% Saab-Fairchild partnership Saab was responsible for the fuselage, fin and final assembly, while Fairchild was responsible for the wings, engine nacelles and empennage.

The first of three SF340 prototypes flew for the first time on January 25 1983. Saab assumed total program responsibility on November 1 that year and the SF340 designation was then subsequently changed to 340A.

The first improved development of the Saab 340 is the 340B with more powerful engines improving hot and high performance, while other changes include a higher max takeoff weight and better range. First delivery was in September 1989. The latest development of the 340 is the further improved 340BPlus.

The only 340 military operator is Sweden. A single VIP configured Saab 340B was delivered to the Royal Swedish Air Force's Royal Flight in 1990 as the Tp 100.

Sweden meanwhile has adopted the 340B for airborne early warning and control as the Tp 100B. Six (including the prototype, which first flew in 1994) are on order, fitted with an Ericsson PS-890 Erieye side looking phased array radar in a long canoe fairing mounted above the fuselage. The Erieye has a range of 300km (190nm) against fighter sized targets, including against clutter, and also has a sea surveillance mode. The Tp 100B can be fitted with three multifunction workstations, while commands and information can be transmitted to and from ground stations via datalink. First delivery is due for 1996.

Photo: The prototype Tp 100B/Saab 340AEW&C. (Saab)

Schweizer/Hughes 269, TH-55 Osage & 300

Country of origin: United States of America

Type: Training and light utility helicopter

Powerplant: 300C – One 140kW (190hp) Textron Lycoming HIO-360-D1A fuel injected flat four derated from 170kW (225hp) driving a three bladed main rotor and two bladed tail rotor.

Performance: 300C – Max cruising speed 153km/h (82kt), economical cruising speed 124km/h (67kt). Max initial rate of climb 750ft/min. Hovering ceiling in ground effect 5900ft, out of ground effect 2750ft. Service ceiling 10,200ft. Range with max fuel and no reserves 360km (195nm). Max endurance 3hr 24min.

Weights: 300C – Empty 474kg (1046lb), max takeoff 930kg (2050lb), or 975kg (2150lb) with an external sling load.

Dimensions: Main rotor diameter 8.18m (26ft 10in), length overall 9.40m (30ft 10in), fuselage length 6.80m (22ft 0in), height to top of rotor head 2.66m (8ft 9in). Main rotor disc area 52.5m² (565.5sq ft).

Accommodation: Typical seating for three on a bench seat in 300 or two in 269. Can lift a 475kg (1050lb) payload in an external sling load.

Armament: Usually none.

Operators: Columbia, Greece, Japan, Nigeria, Spain, Sweden, Thailand, Turkey, USA.

History: With over 3000 built by two manufacturers over three decades, the Hughes/Schweizer 260/TH-55/300 series is one of the most successful two/three seat light helicopter families built.

Development of this versatile helicopter dates back to the mid 1950s when Hughes flew the two seat Model 269 for the first time in October 1956. The basic design sparked US Army interest and five were ordered as the YHO-2-HU for evaluation in the scout and observation roles. Deliveries of commercial equivalent Model 269As began in 1961.

The 269A program received a huge boost when Hughes won a US Army contract for a light helicopter primary trainer. Eventually a total of 792 was built as the TH-55A Osage and more than 60,000 US Army helicopter pilots learned to fly in the type. Replacement of the Osage in US Army service is underway with the Bell TH-67 Creek, although TH-55s survive in service with a number of nations including Spain (as the HE.20), Sweden (as the Hkp 5B) and Japan, where Kawasaki built 38 TH-55Js (essentially similar to the TH-55A) under licence.

The three seat, slightly larger 269B, which Hughes marketed as the Hughes 300, first flew in 1964. The 300 was followed from 1969 by the improved 300C, which introduced a more powerful 140kW (190hp) Lycoming HIO-360 engine and increased diameter main rotor, giving an increase in payload of 45%, plus overall performance improvements. The 300C (or 269C) flew in August 1969 and remains in production to this day, basically unchanged.

Since 1983 the 300C has been built by Schweizer in the USA. Schweizer built the 300C initially under licence for Hughes, and then acquired all rights to the helicopter in 1986. Under Schweizer's stewardship more than 250 minor improvements have been made to the 300C, but the basic design has been left unchanged.

Both Schweizer and Hughes have delivered 300s to military customers, while the 300C was also built in small numbers under licence in Italy by Breda Nardi as the NH-300C.

Photo: A US Army TH-55.

SEPECAT Jaguar

Countries of Origin: France and UK

Type: Ground attack aircraft

Powerplants: GR.1A – Two 23.7kN (5320lb) dry and 35.8kN (8040lb) Rolls-Royce/Turboméca Adour Mk 104 turbofans.

Performance: GR.1A – Max speed Mach 1.6 or 1700km/h (917kt), max speed at sea level Mach 1.1 or 1350km/h (730kt). Time to 30,000ft 1min 30sec. Service ceiling 45,930ft. Combat radius hi-lo-hi with internal fuel 850km (460nm), or lo-lo-lo 537km (290nm). Combat radius with external fuel hi-lo-hi 1408km (760nm), lo-lo-lo 917km (495nm). Ferry range with external fuel 3525km (1902nm).

Weights: GR.1A – Empty equipped 7700kg (16,975lb), max takeoff 15,700kg (34,612lb).

Dimensions: GR.1A – Wing span 8.69m (28ft 6in), length inc probe 16.83m (55ft 3in), length exc probe 15.52m (50ft 11in), height 4.89m (16ft 1in). Wing area 24.2m² (260.3sq ft).

Accommodation: Pilot only, or two in tandem in Jaguar/T.2.

Armament: GR.1B – Two 30mm Aden cannon. Two above wing (for AIM-9s only), four underwing and one centreline hardpoint for 4540kg (10,000lb) of ordnance, including bombs and rockets.

Operators: Ecuador, France, India, Nigeria, Oman, UK.

History: The world's first binational military aircraft program began as a trainer but evolved into a highly capable ground attack aircraft.

The Jaguar was the result of a joint British/French requirement for an advanced jet trainer, the British originally requiring a supersonic jet trainer, the French wanting a subsonic, cheap to build trainer/attack aircraft with good field performance. To build such a demanding aircraft the SEPECAT (Société Européenéde Production de l'Avion de Ecole de Combat et Appui Tactique) teaming of Breguet (design leader) and BAC was established in 1966, while Rolls-Royce and Turboméca teamed to develop the Adour engine.

The first of eight prototypes flew for the first time on September 8 1968. Service deliveries began to the French in 1973 and the British in 1974, by which time the Jaguar was viewed solely as a ground attack platform and both the Hawk and Alpha Jet had been launched.

The 200 Jaguars delivered to the RAF comprised 165 GR.1 (Jaguar S) single seaters and 35 two seat T.2s (Jaguar B). The GR.1s (since upgraded to GR.1A with Adour Mk 104s) feature an advanced nav/attack system and laser rangefinder in a chisel shaped nose.

France took delivery of 160 single seaters (Jaguar As) and 40 trainers (Jaguar Es). French Jaguar Es were delivered with a less advanced nav/attack system and twin DEFA cannon. Half were delivered with an undernose laser rangefinder and 30 can carry the ATLIS laser designator pod for the AS.30L laser guided missile. The navalised Jaguar M was passed over for the French Navy in preference to the Dassault Super Etendard.

The Jaguar International was exported with some success (despite Dassault's distinct preference to sell the Mirage and Super Etendard). It was marketed and built by BAe, and was based on the GR.1. India is the largest customer, where, as the Shamsher (Assault Sword), it is built under licence. Some are fitted with an Agave radar and can fire Sea Eagle anti ship missiles.

Photo: An airshow display RAF Jaguar GR.1A. (Bruce Malcolm)

Shenyang J-6/F-6

Countries of origin: Russia and China

Type: Interceptor/ground attack fighter

Powerplants: J-6 – Two 24.5kN (5730lb) dry and 31.9kN (7165lb) with afterburning Liming Wopen-6 (Tumansky R-9BF-811) turbojets.

Performance: J-6 – Max speed Mach 1.45 or 1540km/h (831kt), cruising speed 950km/h (512kt). Max initial rate of climb over 30,000ft/min. Service ceiling 58,725ft. Combat radius with external fuel 685km (370nm). Normal range 1390km (750nm), ferry range with external fuel 2200km (1187nm).

Weights: J-6 – Empty approx 5760kg (12,700lb), max takeoff approx 10,000kg (22,045lb).

Dimensions: J-6 – Wing span 9.20m (30ft 2in), length inc probe 14.90m (48ft 11in), length exc probe 12.60m (41ft 4in), height 3.88m (12ft 9in). Wing area 25.0m² (269.1sq ft).

Accommodation: Pilot only, or two in tandem in JJ-6/FT-6.

Armament: Three 30mm NR-30 cannon (one in each wing root and one in lower forward fuselage). Four underwing hardpoints for 500kg (1100lb) of external ordnance including AAMs (AIM-9 Sidewinders on Pakistani aircraft), rockets and bombs.

Operators: Albania, Bangladesh, China, Egypt, North Korea, Pakistan, Somalia, Tanzania, Zambia.

History: The Shenyang J-6 is a Chinese built development of the 1950s MiG-19 and numerically is the most important combat aircraft in Chinese military service.

The MiG-19 (NATO reporting name 'Farmer') was designed as an interceptor and flew for the first time on January 5 1954. Capable of supersonic speeds in level flight, 2500 were built (including in Czechoslovakia) in several variants including the radar equipped MiG-19P. It was not exported widely and all are believed to have been retired from service (except perhaps Cuba).

China selected the basic MiG-19 for licence manufacture in the late 1950s. Russia supplied production diagrams for the MiG-19P to the Shenyang Aircraft Factory and the first Chinese assembled MiG-19 flew for the first time on December 17 1958, while the first Chinese built MiG-19 flew the following September.

Shenyang and initially Nanchang were assigned to build the MiG-19 (from 1961 the basic MiG-19S 'Farmer-C' dayfighter), however China's political and cultural instability during much of the 1960s meant that production was often sporadic and quality often poor.

From the 1970s stability returned and new Chinese developments appeared, foremost being the JJ-6 trainer (there being no two seat MiG-19). The JZ-6 is a high altitude reconnaissance variant while the J-6III had a variable shock cone in the nose and was often misidentified as the J-6Xin and as having a radar. A J-6 variant that was radar equipped was the J-6A or J-6IV. The J-6C meanwhile is similar to the basic J-6 except for repositioned brake parachute.

As the F-6 (and two seat FT-6) the J-6 was exported widely and production lasted into the 1980s. Total J-6/F-6 production is estimated at 3000.

Photo: A Pakistani F-6. Note the large wing fences.

Shenyang J-8

Country of origin: China

Type: Interceptor

Powerplants: J-8 II – Two 42.7kN (9590lb) dry and 65.9kN (14,815lb) with afterburning Liyang (Guizhou) WP13A II turbojets.

Performance: Max speed at 36,000ft 2338km/h (1262kt). Max initial rate of climb 39,370ft/min. Service ceiling 66,275ft. Ferry range 2200km (1190nm). Combat radius 800km (432nm).

Weights: J-8 II – Empty 9820kg (21,649lb), max takeoff 17,800kg (39,242lb).

Dimensions: J-8 II – Wing span 9.34m (30ft 8in), length 21.59m (70ft 10in), height 5.41m (17ft 9in). Wing area 42.2m² (454.3sq ft).

Accommodation: Pilot only.

Armament: One 23mm Type 23-2 cannon in underfuselage blister fairing. One centreline and six underwing hardpoints for PL-2B infrared guided AAMs, PL-7 medium range semi active radar guided AAMs, unguided air-to-air rockets, air-to-ground rockets and bombs.

Operators: China

History: China's J-8 and J-8 II interceptors have suffered from protracted and fitful development and firmly remain 1960s technology.

The J-8 (NATO reporting name 'Finback') resulted from a 1964 Chinese Air Force requirement for a new interceptor of improved performance compared with the MiG-21. The resulting aircraft was remarkably similar in overall configuration to the MiG-21, being a tailed delta with a nose air intake, ranging radar in the intake centrebody and a single piece forward opening canopy, but much larger and powered by two engines.

The first of two prototypes flew for the first time on July 5 1969, despite China's Cultural Revolution then underway. Because of the Cultural Revolution initial production was not authorised until 1979. Only small numbers of J-8s were built, although around 100 improved J-8 Is were delivered from the mid 1980s. The J-8 I featured a Sichuan SR-4 radar in an enlarged intake centrebody, conferring some all weather capability, plus some aerodynamic changes. First flight was on April 24 1981.

Development of the much improved and revised J-8 II began in 1981 and the first flight took place on June 12 1984. The J-8 II introduced lateral air intakes (similar in configuration to the MiG-23's) and a nose mounted radar and features a ventral folding fin which extends after takeoff and conventional two piece canopy, and has a secondary ground attack role. About 30 have been built and low rate batch production continues. It has been offered for export as the F-8 II.

The Peace Pearl program to fit the J-8 II with US avionics (integrated by Grumman) including the APG-66 radar and US ejection seat, HUD and INS, as well as a bubble canopy with a frameless windscreen was suspended following the 1989 Tienanmen Square massacre. Two J-8 IIs had been delivered to Grumman in the US for conversion but were returned unmodified to China in 1993.

It is unclear if China is pursuing further development of the J-8 II.

Photo: China has offered export versions of the J-8 II as the F-8 II. (Peter Ricketts)

ShinMaywa US-1/SS-2

Country of origin: Japan

Type: Search and rescue amphibian

Powerplants: US-1A – Four 2605kW (3493ehp) Ishikawajima licence built General Electric T46-IHI-10J turboprops, driving three bladed propellers.

Performance: US-1A – Max speed 522km/h (281kt), cruising speed at 10,000ft 426km/h (230kt). Max initial rate of climb, AUW 36,000kg (79,365lb) 2340ft/min. Service ceiling 28,400ft. Max range at 425km/h (230kt) cruising speed 3815km (2060nm).

Weights: US-1A – Empty 23,300kg (51,367lb), empty equipped 25,500kg (56,218lb), max takeoff from water 43,000kg (94,800lb), max takeoff from land 45,000kg (99,200lb).

Dimensions: Wing span 33.15m (108ft 9in), length 33.46m (109ft 9in), height 9.95m (32ft 8in). Wing area 135.8m² (1462.0sq ft).

Accommodation: Flightcrew of two pilots, flight engineer and navigator/radio operator (in main cabin). Main cabin can seat 20 seated survivors or 12 stretcher patients, plus two medical attendants, or alternatively up to 69 passengers.

Armament: None

Operators: Japan

History: An anomaly among modern aircraft, the US-1 is a large four engine amphibian, production of which restarted in the early 1990s.

The search and rescue US-1 is a development of the earlier PS-1 flying boat ASW/maritime patrol aircraft. The first Shin Miewa (ShinMaywa from 1992, Kawanishi up to 1949) PX-S prototype flew for the first time on October 5 1967, while in all, 23 production PS-1s (SS-2s to Shin Meiwa) were delivered to the Japanese Maritime Self Defence Force. Power was from four licence built General Electric T64 turboprops, it was equipped with sonobuoys, a MAD and search radar, and could carry mines, torpedoes and rockets. An auxiliary gas turbine (a GE T58) provided high pressure air for boundary layer control over the flaps, rudder and elevators, allowing the PS-1 to fly at very low speeds and reducing takeoff runs. The last PS-1 was retired from JMSDF service in 1989.

The US-1 (ShinMaywa designation SS-2A) was based closely on the PS-1 and differed mainly in its internal fit and permanent retractable undercarriage. First flight, from water, was on October 16 1974, while the US-1's first flight from land was that December. Initially 13 US-1s were built (for the JMSDF), while in 1992 production restarted against a single order and a second new US-1 was ordered in 1993.

All US-1s have been upgraded to US-1A standard with more powerful T64-IHI-10J engines replacing the original T64-IHI-10s. A further upgrade has been proposed, based around re-engining the US-1s with Allison GMA2100s turboprops (as on the C-130J). In addition a single US-1 was evaluated as a firebomber, fitted with a tank system developed by Comair of Canada.

Photo: The US-1 amphibian provides the Japanese Navy with a unique SAR capability.

Shorts Skyvan

Country of origin: United Kingdom

Type: Light STOL utility transport

Powerplants: Srs 3 – Two 535kW (715shp) Garrett TPE331-2-201A turboprops, driving three bladed propellers.

Performance: 3M – Max cruising speed 324km/h (175kt), normal cruising speed 311km/h (168kt), economical cruising speed 278km/h (150kt). Max initial rate of climb 1530ft/min. Service ceiling 22,500ft. Takeoff run at MTOW 238m (780ft). Range with max fuel 1075km (582nm), range with a 2270kg (5000lb) payload 385km (208nm).

Weights: 3M – Operating empty (in utility configuration) 3355kg (7400lb), max takeoff 6577kg (14,500lb).

Dimensions: 3M – Wing span 19.79m (64ft 11in), length 12.21m (40ft 1in), or 12.60m (41ft 4in) with weather radar, height 4.60m (15ft 1in). Wing area 35.1m² (378sq ft).

Accommodation: Flightcrew of one or two. Seating for up to 22 combat equipped troops, or 16 paratroopers or 12 stretcher patients.

Armament: None

Operators: Austria, Botswana, Ghana, Guyana, Mauritania, Mexico, Nepal, Oman, Singapore, South Africa, Yemen.

History: The box like and rugged Shorts Skyvan STOL utility transport dates back to the civil postwar Miles Aerovan project.

Development of the Skyvan, or SC.7, began in 1959 when Shorts decided to design a small multirole transport with a square sided fuselage to accommodate oversize loads and good STOL performance. The new design incorporated the results of Miles' research into high aspect ratio wings, with Shorts adopting the Aerovan's wing design for the SC.7. The SC.7 first flew in Series 1 prototype form powered by two Continental 290kW (390hp) GTSIO-520 piston engines on January 17 1963.

Unlike the prototype, initial production aircraft were powered by 545kW (730shp) Turboméca Astazou XII turboprops. The original piston powered Series 1 prototype was the first Astazou powered Skyvan to fly (with 390kW/520shp Astazou IIs), in October 1963. The re-engined prototype was designated the Series 1A, while early Astazou powered production aircraft were designated Series 2.

Early on in the SC.7's production run Shorts decided to switch the powerplant choice to 535kW (715shp) Garrett TPE331-201s, resulting in the definitive Series 3 (first flight December 15 1967). Many of the early build Series 2 Skyvans were also converted to Garrett power.

The basic civil Series 3 and the higher takeoff weight Series 3A Skyvans perform a number of utility missions including passenger transport, ambulance, aerial survey and freight work, while the Skyliner was a commuter airliner version.

The definitive military Skyvans are the Series 3M and the higher max takeoff weight 3M-200 with a rear loading freight ramp. The Skyvan proved reasonably popular with third world military customers for operations in undeveloped areas. Almost 60 of the 150 or so Skyvans built were for military customers and many remain in service.

Photo: The Skyvan's roomy fuselage and good STOL performance endear it for military transport missions. (Austrian Armed Forces)

Shorts 330 & C-23 Sherpa

Country of origin: United Kingdom

Type: Utility transport

Powerplants: C-23A – Two 895kW (1120shp) Pratt & Whitney Canada T101-CP-100 (PT6A-45R) turboprops, driving five bladed propellers.

Performance: C-23A – Max cruising speed 352km/h (190kt), economical cruising speed 291km/h (157kt). Max initial rate of climb 1180ft/min. Service ceiling 20,000ft. Takeoff run at MTOW 560m (1840ft). Range with a 2270kg (5000lb) payload 1240km (670nm), range with a 3175kg (7000lb) payload 362km (195nm).

Weights: C-23A – Empty equipped 6680kg (14,727lb), max takeoff 11,565kg (25,500lb).

Dimensions: Wing span 22.76m (74ft 8in), length 17.69m (58ft 1in), height 4.95m (16ft 3in). Wing area 42.1m² (453sq ft).

Accommodation: Flightcrew of two. Typical passenger seating configuration for 30. In combi freight/passenger configuration can house freight in the forward fuselage and 18 passengers in the rear.

Armament: None

Operators: Thailand, USA.

History: The Shorts 330 is a stretched and enlarged development of the modestly successful SC.7 Skyvan.

Beginning life designated the SD3-30, the 330 retained the Skyvan's overall configuration, including the slab sided fuselage cross section, supercritical braced, above fuselage mounted wing design (stretched by 2.97m/9ft 9in) and twin tails. Compared with the Skyvan the fuselage is stretched by 3.78m (12ft 5in), allowing seating for 10 extra passengers. Improved performance over the fairly slow Skyvan is courtesy of the two Pratt & Whitney PT6A turboprops driving five bladed props, a more streamlined nose and retractable undercarriage. More than 60% greater fuel capacity boosts range significantly over the Skyvan.

An engineering prototype of the 330 flew for the first time on August 22 1974, while a production prototype flew on July 8 1975. The first true production aircraft flew that December.

Initial Shorts 330s were powered by PT6A-45As and -45Bs and are known as 330-100s, while definitive 330s feature more powerful PT6A-45s. Known as 330-200s they also feature a number of detail improvements, while equipment previously available as options were made standard. The 330 also forms the basis for the larger 36 seat Shorts 360, which also features more powerful PT6A-65R (or -67R) engines and a conventional single tail.

The 330 has seen only limited military service. Thailand's Army took delivery of two Shorts 330-UTs with rear loading freight ramp. The US Air Force ordered 18 similar C-23A Sherpas (lacking side windows) for transport service between its European bases and they operated between 1984 and 1990. Ten C-23Bs (with cabin windows) were delivered to the US Army National Guard and are used in various support and utility transport roles. In addition 20 ex airline Shorts 360s are being converted to C-23B+ configuration for the US Army National Guard. The conversion involves fitting a rear loading freight ramp and twin tails, plus new avionics. The last conversion was due to be delivered in 1996.

Photo: A Thai Army 330-UT. (Dave Fraser)

SIAI-Marchetti SF.260

Country of origin: Italy

Type: Two seat trainer light COIN aircraft

Powerplant: SF.260W – One 195kW (260hp) Lycoming O-540-E4A5 flat six piston engine driving a two bladed propeller.

Performance: SF.260W – Max speed at sea level 347km/h (187kt), max cruising speed 330km/h (178kt). Max initial rate of climb 1790ft/min. Service ceiling 21,370ft. Ferry range 1715km (925nm). Combat radius with pilot only, 5min combat and reserves 555km (300nm).

Weights: SF.260W – Basic empty 770kg (1697lb), max takeoff 1300kg (2866lb).

Dimensions: SF.260W – Wing span 8.35m (27ft 5in), length 7.10m (23ft 4in), height 2.41m (7ft 11in). Wing area 10.1m² (108.7sq ft)

Accommodation: Seating for two side by side, with optional third seat behind.

Armament: SF.260W – Four underwing hardpoints can carry a max ordnance load of 300kg (660lb) including gun pods, bombs, practice bombs and rockets.

Operators: Belgium, Bolivia, Burkino Faso, Burundi, Chad, Ireland, Italy, Libya, Nicaragua, Philippines, Singapore, Sri Lanka, Thailand, Tunisia, Turkey, UAE, Uganda, Zaire, Zambia, Zimbabwe.

History: The nimble SIAI Marchetti SF.260 is one of the most successful piston enginned military trainers of recent times.

The retractable undercarriage SF.260 was designed by famed Italian aircraft designer Stelio Frati in the early 1960s. It was originally flown in 185kW (250hp) Lycoming O-540 form by the Aviamilano company as the F.250. However SIAI-Marchetti has undertaken all production (initially under licence, it later assumed full responsibility for the program) as the 195kW (260hp) O-540 powered SF.260. The second aircraft to fly was the first built by SIAI-Marchetti and the first powered by the more powerful version of the O-540. This second prototype first flew in 1966.

Initial civil production was of the SF.260A and SF.260B. Improvements launched on the military SF.260M included a stronger undercarriage, a redesigned wing leading edge and a taller fin. It first flew on October 10 1970. The SF.260 has been further developed into E and F form.

The definitive SF.260 military piston powered variant is the SF.260W Warrior, with a further strengthened airframe and two or four underwing hardpoints for up to 300kg (660lb) of rockets and bombs for light ground attack, weapons training and forward air control. The Warrior's first flight was in May 1972.

The 260kW (350shp) Allison 250-B17D turboprop powered SF.260TP meanwhile has been built since the early 1980s. Max speed is increased to 425km/h (236kt). About 60 have been built for the air forces of Dubai, Ethiopia, the Philippines, Sri Lanka and Zimbabwe.

Production of piston powered SF.260s amounts to 860, the vast majority of which are for military customers.

Photo: Belgium is one of a number of nations to use the SF.260 for basic pilot instruction. (Paul Merritt)

SIAI Marchetti S.211

Country of origin: Italy

Type: Two seat jet trainer

Powerplant: S.211 – One 11.1kN (2500lb) Pratt & Whitney JT15D-4C turbofan. S.211A – One 14.2kN (3190lb) JT15D-5C.

Performance: S.211 – Max cruising speed at 25,000ft 667km/h (360kt). Max initial rate of climb 4200ft/min. Service ceiling 40,000ft. Combat radius with four rocket launchers hi-lo-hi 555km (300nm), or lo-lo-lo 230km (125nm). Ferry range with external fuel 2485km (1340nm), range with internal fuel 1665km (900nm). Endurance 3hr 50min. S.211A – Max cruising speed at 25,000ft 767km/h (414kt). Max initial rate of climb 5100ft/min. Service ceiling 42,000ft. Ferry range with external fuel 2685km (1450nm). Endurance 4hr 15min.

Weights: S.211 – Empty equipped 1850kg (4078lb), max takeoff 3150kg (6955lb). S.211A – Empty equipped 2030kg (4475lb), max takeoff 4000kg (8188lb).

Dimensions: Wing span 8.43m (27ft 8in), length 9.50m (31ft 2in), height 3.96m (13ft 0in). Wing area 12.6m² (135.6sq ft).

Accommodation: Two in tandem.

Armament: Four underwing hardpoints can carry a max external ordnance load of 660kg (1455lb) for bombs, practice bombs, rockets and machine gun pods.

Operators: Brunei, Philippines, Singapore.

History: The little S.211 was developed as a private venture to fulfill basic/intermediate and weapons training and light ground attack missions.

Models of SIAI Marchetti's new basic jet trainer were first displayed at the 1977 Paris Airshow, although it was not until almost four years later that the first of two prototypes made the type's first flight on April 10 1981. Production deliveries began in November 1984.

Major customers/operators are Singapore (30) and the Philippines (24), both countries assembling most of their S.211s under licence. The former's aircraft at based near Perth in Australia, where they are free to train without the airspace constraints of Singapore. The Philippines uses its aircraft for both training and ground attack, but the fleet has suffered from high attrition. Haiti took delivery of four but subsequently sold them in the USA.

The S.211 is of conventional design and configuration. The high mounted wing has four hardpoints for light weaponry. Power is from a single Pratt & Whitney JT14D turbofan, which is used in a number of light business jets (including the Beech T-1 Jayhawk), while the crew sit on stepped tandem lightweight Martin Baker ejection seats. The S.211's comparatively low airframe weight results from 61% of external surfaces being made from composite materials.

The uprated S.211A has yet to find a customer and was unsuccessfully offered by Northrop Grumman (originally Grumman) to meet the USAF/USN's JPATS trainer requirement. Other variants which have been mooted but not built include a stretched development and one fitted with a nav/attack suite.

Photo: Singapore's S.211s are based primarily at RAAF Base Pearce in Western Australia. (Keith Anderson)

Sikorsky SH-3 Sea King & S-61R

Country of origin: United States of America

Type: ASW, SAR and utility maritime helicopter

Powerplants: SH-3H – Two 1045kW (1400shp) General Electric T58-GE-10 turboshafts driving five bladed main and tail rotors.

Performance: SH-3H – Max speed 267km/h (144kt), economical cruising speed 219km/h (118kt). Max initial rate of climb 2200ft/min. Service ceiling 14,700ft. Hovering ceiling in ground effect 10,500ft, out of ground effect 8200ft. Range 1005km (542nm).

Weights: SH-3H – Empty 5600kg (12,530lb), max takeoff 9525kg (21,000lb).

Dimensions: Main rotor diameter 18.90m (62ft 0in), length overall rotors turning 22.15m (72ft 8in), fuselage length 16.69m (54ft 9in), height overall 5.13m (16ft 10in). Main rotor disc area 280.5m² (3109sq ft).

Accommodation: Crew of four, optional seating for 15 in main cabin.

Armament: Max external ordnance of 380kg (840lb), typically comprising two torpedoes.

Operators: SH-3 – Argentina, Brazil, Denmark, Italy, Japan, Malaysia, Peru, Spain, Thailand, USA. AS-61R/S-61R/HH-3 – Argentina, Iraq, Italy, USA.

History: For many years the Sea King formed the backbone of the US Navy's ASW helicopter force. While largely replaced by the SH-60 in US service, many other nations rely on the Sea King for ASW, SAR and various maritime utility duties.

The Sikorsky HSS-2 (S-61) Sea King was the end result of a US Navy requirement for a single helicopter that could both detect/track and attack submarines. Sikorsky was awarded the contract to develop such an aircraft in 1957 and the first YHSS-2 prototype made its maiden flight on March 11 1959. At that time the Sea King represented a significant advance on anything before it, featuring as it did twin turboshafts (GE T58s) mounted above the voluminous main cabin which had space to accommodate bulky ASW gear, plus dunking sonar and radar. Other features were a boat hull for amphibious operations and five bladed main and tail rotors.

Initial production was of the SH-3A (HSS-2 pre 1962) and 245 were built, while 73 SH-3Ds had improved sonar and radar and uprated engines. Subsequently over 100 SH-3As were converted to SAR/transport SH-3G form, with ASW gear deleted. The SH-3H (116 converted) was modified for service from aircraft carriers for inner zone ASW, plane guard, and surface surveillance and targeting. Most have been replaced by SH-60Fs. Other US conversions were the UH-3A utility transport, VH-3A/D VIP transport and SAR HH-3A.

Mitsubishi (SH-3A/D/H), Agusta (SH-3D) and Westland (its variants are described separately) all built the Sea King under licence.

The stretched S-61R or CH-3C was developed specifically for the USAF and had a stretched fuselage with a rear loading freight ramp. As the HH-3E 'Jolly Green Giant' it gained fame rescuing downed aircrew in Vietnam. All but six USAF CH/HH-3s have been retired, as have all the US Coast Guard's HH-3F Pelicans. Agusta licence built 35 AS-61Rs for SAR and combat rescue and these remain in use.

Photo: Canada's CH-124 Sea Kings are essentially SH-3As.

Sikorsky CH-53 Sea Stallion

Sikorsky Super Stallion & Sea Dragon

Country of origin: United States of America

Type: Medium/heavylift helicopter

Powerplants: CH-53D – Two 2930kW (3925shp) General Electric T64-GE-413 turboshafts driving a six bladed main rotor and four bladed tail rotor.

Performance: CH-53D – Max speed at sea level 315km/h (170kt), cruising speed 278km/h (150kt). Max initial rate of climb 2180ft/min. Service ceiling 21,000ft. Hovering ceiling in ground effect 13,400ft, out of ground effect 6500ft. Range 415km (225nm).

Weights: CH-53D – Empty 10,653kg (23,485lb), max takeoff 19,050kg (42,000lb).

Dimensions: Main rotor diameter 22.02m (72ft 3in), length overall rotors turning 26.90m (88ft 3in), fuselage length 20.47m (67ft 2in), height overall rotors turning 7.60m (24ft 11in), height to top of rotor head 5.22m (17ft 2in). Main rotor disc area 380.9m² (4099.8sq ft).

Accommodation: Flightcrew of three. Seating in main cabin for 55 equipped troops or 24 stretcher patients and four medical attendants.

Armament: MH-53J – Can be fitted with 12.7mm machine guns and 7.62mm miniguns.

Operators: Germany, Israel, USA.

History: The CH-53 Sea Stallion was the result of a US Marine Corps requirement for a heavylift helicopter for troop transport to replace Sikorsky's CH-37C.

Sikorsky used its CH-54 Tarhe (S-64 Skycrane) as the basis to meet the Marines' 1960 requirement for a new heavylift assault transport. The resulting S-65 used the CH-54's dynamic systems coupled with an all new fuselage, including a watertight hull giving an emergency water landing capability and rear loading freight ramp.

Two prototypes were ordered in August 1962, the first of which flew for the first time on October 14 1964. Production deliveries of CH-53As to the Marine Corps commenced in 1966 and by 1967 it was being used operationally in Vietnam. CH-53A standard Sea Stallions were exported to Austria (two, both sold to Israel in 1980), Germany (112 CH-53Gs, most licence built in Germany) and Israel (45). Israel is upgrading its aircraft with new avionics as the CH-53 2000. The USMC's CH-53D has uprated engines and automatic blade folding.

The US Air Force ordered its first combat rescue variants of the CH-53 in 1966. Eight initial HH-53Bs were followed by 44 HH-53Cs with external fuel tanks and an inflight refuelling probe. Some of these were later converted to HH-53H Pave Low III configuration with terrain following radar, doppler and INS navigation, GPS, nose turret mounted FLIR, and then to MH-53H standard with a night vision goggle compatible cockpit for insertion/extraction missions.

From 1986 39 H-53s have been upgraded to MH-53J Pave Low III Enhanced standard. Equipment fit includes terrain following radar, FLIR, GPS, inflight refuelling probe, secure communications, titanium armour, jammers, flare and chaff dispensers, NVG compatible cockpit, searchlight and external hoist. Due to remain in service until 2010 the survivors have recently undergone a life extension program.

The US Navy's RH-53Ds minesweepers have largely been replaced by MH-53E Sea Dragons. Six were delivered to pre revolutionary Iran.

Photo: A USAF MH-53J Pave Low III Enhanced. (Greg Reeves)

Country of origin: United States of America

Type: CH-53E – Heavylift assault transport. MH-53E – Mine sweeper

Powerplants: CH-53E – Three 3265kW (4380shp) General Electric T64-GE-416 turboshafts, driving a seven bladed main rotor and four bladed tail rotor.

Performance: CH-53E – Max speed at sea level 315km/h (170kt), cruising speed at sea level 278km/h (150kt). Max initial rate of climb (with a 11,340kg/25,000lb payload) 2500ft/min. Service ceiling 18,500ft. Hovering ceiling in ground effect 11,550ft, out of ground effect 9500ft. Operational radius with 9070kg (20,000lb) external payload 925km (500nm), with a 14,515kg (32,000lb) external payload 93km (50nm). Ferry range 2075km (1120nm).

Weights: CH-53E – Empty 15,072kg (33,338lb), max takeoff 31,640kg (69,750lb), max takeoff with external sling load 33,340kg (73,500lb).

Dimensions: CH-53E – Main rotor diameter 24.08m (79ft 0in), length overall rotors turning 30.19m (99ft 1in), fuselage length 22.35m (73ft 4in), height overall rotors turning 8.97m (29ft 5in), height to top of rotor head 5.32m (17ft 6in). Main rotor disc area 455.4m² (4901.4sq ft).

Accommodation: Flightcrew of three. Accommodation in main cabin for 55 equipped troops or light artillery pieces or vehicles.

Armament: Usually none but has been trialled with AIM-9s for self defence.

Operators: CH-53E – USA. MH-53E – Japan, USA.

History: The CH-53E (S-80) Super Stallion is a three engined development of the Sea Stallion, with greatly improved lifting capabilities.

The Super Stallion resulted from a US Marine Corps need for a helicopter with much greater lifting abilities than the already impressive CH-53 that was still able to operate from its amphibious assault ships. Sikorsky met the requirement by adding a third engine and uprated transmission to the CH-53, resulting in the CH-53E (S-80). The third engine (all GE T64-GE-415s) was mounted near the main rotor mast on the aircraft's port side. Other changes to the CH-53E were a lengthened fuselage and enlarged fuselage sponsons housing extra fuel, a removable inflight refuelling probe and a seven blade main rotor.

The first YCH-53E prototype flew for the first time on March 1 1974 (this aircraft was subsequently destroyed during a ground running test). The second YCH-53E was the first to feature the revised tail (the vertical tail is canted 20 degrees to port, while the horizontal tail is braced). Delivered from June 1981, 170 CH-53Es have been funded for the USMC and US Navy. The Marines use them primarily for lifting heavy weapons and equipment (including recovering downed aircraft) alongside CH-53Ds, while the USN's are used for ship supply. Various CH-53E upgrades have been proposed, but these have generally been thwarted by a lack of funding.

The MH-53E Sea Dragon mine countermeasures helicopter was developed for the US Navy to replace RH-53Ds. Identifiable by their extra large composite construction sponsons which house extra fuel, the MH-53Es tow a hydrofoil sledge carrying mechanical, acoustic and magnetic sensors for mine detection. Eleven similar S-80M-1s (without the inflight refuelling probe) were exported to Japan from 1989.

Photo: A USMC CH-53E in flight. (Sikorsky)

Sikorsky UH-60/S-70A Black Hawk

Sikorsky SH-60/S-70B Seahawk

Country of origin: United States

Type: Medium lift helicopter

Powerplants: UH-60A – Two 1150kW (1560shp) General Electric T700-GE-700 turboshafts, driving four bladed main and tail rotors.

Performance: UH-60A – Max speed at sea level 296km/h (160kt), max cruising speed 257km/h (140kt). Max vertical rate of climb from 4000ft 411ft/min. Service ceiling 19,000ft. Hovering ceiling out of ground effect 10,400ft. Range with max internal fuel 592km (319nm), range with four external fuel tanks 2220km (1200nm).

Weights: UH-60A – Empty 5118kg (11,284lb), max takeoff 9185kg (20,500lb).

Dimensions: UH-60A – Main rotor diameter 16.36m (53ft 8in), length overall rotors turning 19.76m (64ft 10in), fuselage length 15.26m (50ft 1in), height overall rotors turning 5.13m (16ft 10in), height to top of rotor head 3.76m (12ft 4in). Main rotor disc area 210.1m² (2262sq ft).

Accommodation: Flightcrew of two with gunner/crew chief behind them. Accommodation in main cabin for 11 equipped troops, or 14 in a high density configuration, or alternatively six stretcher patients.

Armament: Two pintle mounts for machine guns or miniguns, one either side in forward cabin. Four hardpoints on detachable external stores support system (ESSS) usually for fuel but, as on AH-60, can carry Hellfire anti armour missiles and rockets in addition to various stores for special forces operations.

Operators: Argentina, Australia, Bahrain, Brunei, China, Colombia, Egypt, Israel, Japan, Jordan, Morocco, Mexico, Philippines, Saudi Arabia, South Korea*, Taiwan, Turkey*, USA.

History: The UH-60 is the US Army's standard troop transport helicopter, and has been adopted for a number of special mission roles.

The Black Hawk was developed to replace the Bell UH-1 Iroquois, meeting the US Army's 1972 Utility Tactical Transport Aircraft System (UTTAS) requirement. Three YUH-60A prototypes (first flight October 17 1974) were evaluated against prototype Boeing Vertol YUH-61s. Adjudged the better aircraft, the first production UH-60 Black Hawk flew for the first time in October 1978, with first deliveries in 1979.

The basic Black Hawk features twin General Electric T700 turboshafts which bestow excellent speed and hot and high performance and lifting capabilities, the large cabin was designed to accommodate an 11 man squad while the whole aircraft was designed with crash survivability in mind. Basic US Army Black Hawk transport models are the UH-60A and improved UH-60L (with more powerful engines to combat increased weight, first flight 1988). Other US models include the EH-60A ECM jammer; FLIR equipped special missions MH-60A, MH-60L and definitive MH-60K with terrain following radar and in-flight refuelling probe; medevac UH-60Q; Hellfire and rocket armed AH-60L 'Direct Action Penetrator'; and command and control UH-60V, currently under development. The US Air Force operates about 100 MH-60G, now HH-60G combat rescue Black Hawks. The US Marines operates nine VIP VH-60Ns.

Major Black Hawk export customers are Australia (39 S-70A-9s), Japan (28 SAR UH-60Js), Saudi Arabia (21 S-70A-1s/-1Ls) and South Korea (80 UH-60Ps).

Photo: An Australian Black Hawk fitted with external tanks. (Bill Lines)

Country of origin: United States of America

Type: Shipborne ASW helicopter

Powerplants: SH-60B – Two 1415kW (1900shp) General Electric T700-GE-401 turboshafts, driving four bladed main and tail rotors.

Performance: SH-60B – Dash speed at 5000ft 235km/h (126kt). Max vertical rate of climb at sea level 700ft/min. Operational radius with 3hr loiter 93km (50nm), or for a 1hr loiter 278km (150nm).

Weights: SH-60B – Empty for ASW mission 6190kg (13,648lb), max takeoff 9925kg (21,884lb).

Dimensions: SH-60B – Main rotor diameter 16.36m (53ft 8in), length overall rotors turning 19.76m (64ft 10in), fuselage length 15.26m (50ft 1in), height overall rotors turning 5.18m (17ft 10in), height to top of rotor head 3.79m (12ft 6in). Main rotor disc area 210.1m² (2262sq ft).

Accommodation: Pilot and airborne tactical officer on flightdeck, with sensor operator station in main cabin.

Armament: Two Mk 46 or Mk 50 torpedoes or AGM-119 Penguin anti ship missiles, plus pintle mounted machine guns.

Operators: Australia, Greece, Japan, Spain, Taiwan, Thailand*, USA.

History: The Sea Hawk is the US Navy's standard shipborne anti submarine warfare platform and is the most expensive and capable ASW helicopter currently in service.

Sikorsky based its proposal to meet the US Navy's LAMPS (light airborne multipurpose system) Mk III program for a new ASW helicopter on the UH-60 Black Hawk airframe. Sikorsky's bid was selected ahead of a rival proposal from Boeing Vertol, with the result that the prototype YSH-60B first flew on December 12 1979.

The SH-60 features navalised General Electric T700 turboshafts, a repositioned tailwheel with twin wheels, lateral pylons for torpedoes or external fuel, an external winch and a sensor station in the main cabin. The SH-60B Seahawk is based off US Navy frigates, destroyers and cruisers, and is fitted with an undernose mounted APS-124 search radar and a 25 tube sonobuoy launcher on the port side of the fuselage and carries a towed MAD. Primary armament is Mk 46 torpedoes and more latterly Mk 50 torpedoes and AGM-119 Penguin anti ship missiles. Some 260 are required.

The SH-60F Ocean Hawk is the USN's CV Inner Zone ASW helicopter and provides close-in ASW protection for USN aircraft carrier battle groups. It features a dunking sonar, FLIR and ESM, while the search radar is deleted. Eighty one were delivered to replace SH-3H Sea Kings, while Taiwan has 10 similar S-70C(M)-1 Thunderhawks.

Seahawks have been exported to Australia (S-70B-2, fitted with Thomson Thorn Super Searcher radar and different Rockwell Collins avionics suite), Greece (S-70B-6, a hybrid SH-60B/F), Japan (SH-60J) and Spain (HS.23).

Other SH-60 variants include the USN's minigun armed HH-60F Rescue Hawk used for strike rescue (recovery of downed aircrew) and SEAL commando insertion/extraction, the US Coast Guard's HH-60J Jayhawk and the USN's SH-60R. The US Navy plans to remanufacture all its SH-60Bs and SH-60Fs to a common SH-60R standard (with dipping sonar and search radar). The conversion is scheduled to be funded from FY1998.

Photo: One of Australia's 16 S-70B-1 Seahawks. (RAN)

Sikorsky S-76/H-76 Eagle

Country of origin: United States of America

Type: Utility helicopter

Powerplants: H-76 – Two 660kW (885shp) max continuous rated Pratt & Whitney Canada PT6B-36A turboshafts driving four bladed main and tail rotors.

Performance: H-76 – Max speed 287km/h (155kt), cruising speed 270km/h (145kt). Max initial rate of climb 1650ft/min. Max operating altitude 15,000ft. Range at 257km/h (140kt) cruising speed with no reserves 650km (350nm).

Weights: H-76 – Basic empty 2545kg (5610lb), max takeoff 5170kg (11,400lb).

Dimensions: Main rotor diameter 13.41m (44ft 0in), length overall 16.00m (52ft 6in), fuselage length 13.21m (43ft 4in), height overall 4.41m (14ft 6in). Main rotor disc area 141.3m² (1520.5sq ft).

Accommodation: Flightcrew of two. Accommodation for 10 equipped troops. VIP configurations seat six or eight. Medevac configured aircraft can accommodate three stretchers and two medical attendants.

Armament: AUH-76 – Can be fitted with pintle mounted machine gun in main doorways, plus rockets, gun and cannon pods, Hellfire and TOW anti armour missiles and Stinger AAMs. H-76N – Torpedoes and Sea Skua anti ship missiles.

Operators: Chile, Honduras, Philippines, Spain, Thailand*, UAE.

History: Unique among Sikorsky's current helicopter line, the S-76 was designed for civilian use and then adapted for military service, rather than the other way around.

Sikorsky developed the mid sized S-76 to diversify its product lineup away from military work. The S-76 was designed to perform a diverse range of roles including oil rig support and executive transport. Sikorsky began development work on the S-76 (for a time named Spirit) in the mid 1970s and used technologies and knowledge gained from the military H-60/S-70 program. The resulting design featured two Allison 250-C30S turboshafts and a wide cabin with seating for 12. First flight was on March 13 1977.

Civil models comprise the S-76A; the S-76 Mark II (introduced in March 1982) with more powerful Allison engines and numerous detail refinements; the twin Pratt & Whitney Canada PT6T powered S-76B; the S-76C, powered by two Turboméca Arriel 1S1 engines; the S-76A+ – undelivered S-76As subsequently fitted and delivered with Arriel engines and S-76As converted to Arriel power; and the S-76C+ with more powerful Arriel 2S1 engines currently under development.

More than 400 S-76s have been built, but almost all of them have been for civil customers. The Philippines (12 AUH-76s and five S-76 Mk IIs) and Spain (eight S-76Cs designated HE.24 and used for IFR helicopter pilot training) are current operators, while Jordan took delivery of 18 for SAR and VIP transport, but has since sold the survivors. Thailand has ordered six H-76 Eagles, the dedicated military variant developed from the S-76B. The AUH-76 is a cannon, rocket and missile armed gunship, while the navalised H-76N would be fitted with search radar and armed with torpedoes and anti ship missiles, but has not yet been ordered (in 1995 it was on offer to the Australian and New Zealand navies).

Photo: One of eight S-76s delivered to Spain for training.

Sikorsky S-92

Country of origin: United States of America

Type: Medium lift transport helicopter

Powerplants: S-92IU – Two 1415kW (1900shp) takeoff rated General Electric CT7-8 turboshafts, driving four bladed main and tail rotors.

Performance: S-92IU – Max cruising speed 287km/h (155kt), economical cruising speed 260km/h (140kt). Hovering ceiling in ground effect 12,700ft, out of ground effect 8300ft. Range 890km (480nm).

Weights: S-92IU – Max takeoff 10,930kg (24,100lb), max takeoff with sling load 12,020kg (26,500lb). Civil S-92C empty weight 6743kg (14,866lb).

Dimensions: Main rotor diameter 17.71m (56ft 4in), length overall rotors turning 20.85m (68ft 5in), fuselage length 17.32m (56ft 10in), height overall 6.45m (21ft 2in). Main rotor disc area 231.6m² (2492.4sq ft).

Accommodation: Flightcrew of two. Accommodation in main cabin for 22 combat equipped troops.

Armament: None announced.

Operators: Program launched mid 1995, with no military customers announced at the time of writing. Sikorsky estimates a market for 5000 civil and military helicopters in S-92 class between 2000 and 2019.

History: The S-92 is a new medium lift helicopter using dynamic components from the H-60/S-70 series.

Development of the S-92 was first announced in 1992 when Sikorsky unveiled a mockup of the new helicopter. In 1993 however Sikorsky postponed launching the S-92 due to the international helicopter market downturn and instead began searching for international risk sharing partners. By 1995 Sikorsky had formed its Team S-92 partners and formally launched the S-92 at the 1995 Paris Airshow.

Sikorsky will initially build five development S-92s. The first to fly will be a civil S-92C, with first flight scheduled for the second half of 1998. Two S-92Cs (named Helibus) and three military/international utility S-92IU development aircraft are planned.

The S-92 will combine the dynamic systems of the H-60/S-70 series with a larger cabin. Components based on those from the H-60 series include the rotor head, transmission and powerplants. Otherwise the S-92 will be all new with all composite wide chord and drooped tip rotor blades (40% of the aircraft will be of composite construction). The main cabin is wider and longer than the H-60's and features a rear loading freight ramp, while the cockpit will feature four liquid crystal displays, with provision for a fifth.

Team S-92 members include risk sharing partners Mitsubishi Heavy Industries (7.5%, responsible for the main cabin), Gamesa of Spain (7% – cabin interior and transmission housing) and China's Jingdezhen Helicopter Group (2% – tail pylon and tailplane), while Taiwan Aerospace (6.5% – flightdeck) and Embraer (4% – sponsons and fuel system) are fixed price suppliers/partners. Russia's leading helicopter designer Mil is also a program participant.

While at late 1995 the S-92 had no military customers, Sikorsky is offering it to the US Marines as an alternative to the costly MV-22 Osprey to replace CH-46s and to the USAF to replace MH-53Js.

Photo: The S-92 mockup as unveiled in 1992. (Sikorsky)

Singapore Aerospace Super Skyhawk

Countries of origin: USA and Singapore

Type: Light ground attack aircraft

Powerplant: One 48.4kN (10,800lb) General Electric F404-GE-100D non afterburning turbofan.

Performance: Max speed at sea level 1128km/h (609kt), max cruising speed at 30,000ft 825km/h (445kt), economical cruising speed at 35,000ft 785km/h (424kt). Max initial rate of climb 10,913ft/min. Combat ceiling 40,000ft. Range with max payload 1160km (625nm), range with internal and external fuel 3790km (2045nm).

Weights: Operating empty 4450kg (10,250lb), max takeoff 10,205kg (22,5000lb).

Dimensions: Wing span 8.38m (27ft 6in), length 12.72m (41ft 9in), height 4.57m (15ft 0in). Wing area 24.1m² (259.8sq ft).

Accommodation: Pilot only, or two in tandem, separate cockpits in TA-4SU.

Armament: One centreline and four underwing hardpoints for rockets, bombs, AIM-9 Sidewinder AAMs, AGM-65 Maverick ASMs and gun pods.

Operators: Singapore

History: Singapore's program to upgrade the A-4 with a non afterburning F404 turbofan and modern avionics has resulted in perhaps the ultimate Skyhawk variant.

Singapore joined the ranks of McDonnell Douglas A-4 Skyhawk operators in 1970 when the first of 40 refurbished ex USN A-4Bs were delivered (as the A-4S). Lockheed upgraded the first eight aircraft, the remainder were modified in Singapore by Singapore Aerospace. The upgrade to A-4S standard involved installing a more powerful Wright J65-W-20 turbojet, spoilers and new nav attack system. The two seat TA-4S Skyhawk conversion is unique in its installation of separate tandem cockpits. Further ex US Navy Skyhawks were delivered (16 A-4Bs in 1983 and 70 A-4Cs in 1980) and while most of these were broken down for spares, enough were converted to A-4S standard to allow the formation of an additional squadron.

In 1984 Singapore elected to further upgrade its Skyhawks to extend their service lives rather than replace them. Phase one of Singapore Aerospace's two phase Super Skyhawk program involved installing a non afterburning General Electric F404-GE-100D turbofan, plus strengthening to accommodate the new and heavier engine and modification to the air intakes, and was developed with Grumman and General Electric assistance. The 27% more powerful F404 results in a 15% higher dash speed, a 35% greater climb rate, and 40% better level acceleration, plus enhanced takeoff performance and sustained turn rate. The first F404 powered Skyhawk flew for the first time on September 19 1986, while production conversions of 52 A-4S Skyhawks to GE powered A-4SU standard was completed in 1989.

The separate phase two of the Super Skyhawk program was the Ferranti (now part of GEC Marconi) developed avionics upgrade. Features of the avionics upgrade includes a MIL STD 1553B databus, head-up display, a multifunction display, mission computer and ring laser gyro INS.

The first Republic of Singapore Air Force Super Skyhawk squadron became operational in 1992.

Photo: Super Skyhawks are operated by Singapore's 142, 143 and 145 Squadrons. (Paul Merritt)

Slingsby T67/T-3A Firefly

Country of origin: United Kingdom

Type: Two seat basic trainer

Powerplant: T-3A – One 195kW (260hp) Textron Lycoming AEIO-540-D4A5 flat four piston engine driving a three bladed propeller.

Performance: T67C – Max speed at sea level 280km/h (152kt), max cruising speed (75% power) 260km/h (140kt). Max initial rate of climb 1380ft/min. Range with max fuel at 65% power with reserves 755km (410nm).

Weights: T-3A – Empty 807kg (1780lb), max takeoff 1145kg (2525lb).

Dimensions: T-3A – Wing span 10.59m (34ft 9in), length 7.57m (24ft 10in), height 2.36m (7ft 9in). Wing area 12.6m² (136.0sq ft).

Accommodation: Seating for two side by side.

Armament: None

Operators: USA

History: The Firefly two seat basic trainer has been adopted by the USAF as the T-3A for flight screening duties.

The Firefly is a development of the Fournier RF-6B which first flew in March 1974. Forty five were built (powered by a 75kW/100hp Rolls-Royce Continental O-200 flat four) through to the early 1980s. In 1980 Fournier flew a more powerful development of the RF-6B, the 87kW (116hp) Lycoming O-235 powered RF-6B-120. It was this aircraft that formed the basis for Slingsby's T67 Firefly.

Prior to purchasing the manufacturing and development rights for the French Fournier RF-6B two seat aerobatic basic trainer in 1981, Slingsby Aviation specialised in sailplane construction and composite materials. Slingsby initially built nine T67As, which were basically RF-6B-120s, before placing into production is own development of the type, the T67B.

The T67B was the result of a fairly thorough redevelopment of the T67A. The main difference was that the T67B was made almost entirely from glassfibre reinforced plastics (GFRPs), Slingsby drawing on its extensive experience in that field. The benefits of GFRP include better resistance to fatigue, less weight and less drag.

The definitive civil version of the Firefly is the T67C. The T67C is similar to the T67B except for its more powerful 120kW (160hp) Textron Lycoming O-320 engine. Variants of the T67C are the T67C1 with standard fuselage fuel tankage and one piece canopy, the T67C2 with a two piece canopy and the T67C3 with wing tanks and three piece canopy.

The basic military Firefly is the T67M Mk II, which first flew in December 1982. Many are used for initial military pilot training and screening with civil firms under contract (including in the Netherlands, Canada and the UK's Joint Elementary TS). T67Ms have aerobatic engines and two bladed constant speed props, among other changes, compared with the T67C.

In addition 113 T67M260s (powered by a 195kW/260hp AEIO-540) have been ordered by the US Air Force as the T-3A Firefly. The Firefly was selected to meet the USAF's Enhanced Flight Screener contract to replace Cessna T-41 Mescaleros. Northrop Grumman assembled the 113 T-3As in Texas and they were delivered between early 1994 and late 1995.

Photo: USAF training on the T-3A began in early 1994. (Slingsby)

Soko Galeb & Jastreb

Country of origin: Yugoslavia

Type: Two seat trainer (Galeb) and light strike fighter (Jastreb)

Powerplant: G2-A – One 11.1kN (2500lb) Rolls-Royce Viper Mk 22-6 turbojet.

Performance: G2-A – Max speed at 20,350ft 812km/h (438kt), max speed at sea level 755km/h (408kt), max cruising speed at 19,685ft 730km/h (395kt). Max initial rate of climb 4500ft/min. Time to 19,685ft 5min 30sec. Service ceiling 39,375ft. Max range with tip tanks full at 29,520ft (9000ft) 1240km (670nm). Max endurance at 23,000ft 2hr 30min.

Weights: G2-A – Empty equipped 2620kg (5775lb), max takeoff (strike version) 4300kg (9840lb).

Dimensions: G2-A – Wing span over tip tanks 11.62m (38ft 2in), length overall 10.34m (33ft 11in), height overall 3.28m (10ft 9in). Wing area 19.4m² (209.1sq ft).

Accommodation: Two in tandem in Galeb, pilot only in Jastreb.

Armament: G2-A – Two 12.7mm machine guns in nose. Underwing hardpoints for two 50 or 100kg bombs and four rockets. J-1 – Three 12.7mm machine guns in nose. Eight underwing hardpoints, inner most for light bombs, outer hardpoints for single rockets.

Operators: Croatia, Libya, Yugoslavia, Zambia.

History: The Galeb (Seagull) two seat advanced trainer and subsequent Jastreb (Hawk) single seat attack fighter were the first products of Yugoslavia's Soko.

Yugoslavia's VTI (Aeronautical Technical Institute) began design work on the G2-A Galeb began in 1957. The first flight of the first of two prototypes was in May 1961. Production began in 1963, making it the first indigenous jet to be built in that country. Production lasted through to the early 1980s.

The Galeb is similar to the contemporary Aermacchi MB-326 in configuration and indeed both are powered by a single Rolls-Royce Viper turbojet. The Galeb features a straight wing with tip tanks, Folland Type 1-B lightweight ejector seats, sideways hinging canopy transparencies and underwing hardpoints for light bombs and rockets. In all around 270 Galebs were built for the Yugoslav Air Force, Libya, which took delivery of 120, and Zambia (six).

The J-1 Jastreb is a single seat ground attack development of the Galeb. Changes include a more powerful engine, structural strengthening, extra hardpoints for rockets and three, instead of two, 12.7mm guns in the nose. The RJ-1 is a reconnaissance variant, with a fuselage camera and one in each wingtip. Approximately 250 to 300 Jastrebs were built, including 30 or so RJ-1s, plus around 30 two seat JT-1 trainers (basically the Galeb with the Jastreb's strengthening, extra hardpoints and weaponry and more powerful engine). First flight was in 1974, with deliveries from 1975. In addition 20 J-1Es and RJ-1Es were delivered to the Zambian Air Force in 1971, about half of which remain operational.

Both Galebs and Jastrebs have seen service during Yugoslavia's civil war with Serbian forces.

Photo: The Galeb is used for advanced and weapons training with the Yugoslav Air Force.

Soko Super Galeb

Country of origin: Yugoslavia

Type: Advanced trainer and light attack aircraft

Powerplants: G-4 – One 17.8kN (4000lb) Rolls-Royce Viper Mk 632-46 turbojet.

Performance: G-4 – Max speed at 32,800ft Mach 0.81, max speed at 13,120ft 910km/h (490kt), max cruising speed at 19,700ft 845km/h (455kt), economical cruising speed at 19,700ft 550km/h (297kt). Max initial rate of climb 6100ft/min. Service ceiling 42,160ft. Range with max internal fuel at 36,090ft 1900km (1025nm), range with max external and internal fuel 2500km (1350nm). Range with cannon and four BL-755 cluster bombs 1300km (700nm).

Weights: G-4 – Empty equipped 3172kg (6993lb), max takeoff 6300kg (13,890lb).

Dimensions: G-4 – Wing span 9.88m (32ft 5in), length overall 12.25m (40ft 2in), fuselage length 11.02m (36ft 2in), height 4.30m (14ft 0in). Wing area 19.5m² (209.9sq ft).

Accommodation: Two in tandem.

Armament: Removable ventral gun pod contains a GSh-23L twin barrel cannon. Four underwing hardpoints can carry 1280kg (2820lb) of bombs, cluster bombs and rockets. G-4M has wingtip rails for R-60 (AA-8 'Aphid') AAMs and can also carry AGM-65 Mavericks on outboard hardpoints.

Operators: Croatia, Myanmar, Yugoslavia.

History: The Super Galeb advanced trainer was developed to replace the Galeb and Lockheed T-33 in Yugoslav service, and has a secondary ground attack mission.

Design of the new trainer began in 1973 and was undertaken by VTI, Yugoslavia's Aeronautical Technical Institude (which also designed the Novi Avion MiG-21 replacement light fighter which was cancelled in 1992). Prototype construction began in 1975 while first flight was on July 17 1978. The prototype and six pre series Super Galebs were designated G-4 PPP.

The Super Galeb is of conventional design and configuration for an advanced trainer. Features include its swept wing with four underwing hardpoints, stepped cockpits, a Rolls-Royce Viper turbojet and anhedral on the all moving tailplane. The basic Yugoslav version is designated G-4. The improved G-4M would have featured advanced avionics including a HUD and multifunction displays, a greater payload and wingtip rails for AAMs. The G-4M was designed to take over some of the weapons training syllabus of front line combat aircraft. First flight was planned for 1992 but was abandoned due to the Yugoslav civil war.

About 135 Super Galebs were built for the Yugoslav Air Force (production aircraft entered service in 1985), while Myanmar took delivery of 12 in the early 1990s. In 1992 during the Yugoslav civil war the Soko plant at Mostar, within Bosnia, was abandoned (including several incomplete aircraft). The Super Galeb jigs were transferred to UTVA within the new Yugoslav state (Serbia and Montenegro), however Super Galeb production is not thought to have resumed.

Photo: Super Galebs were used for light ground attack during Yugoslavia's civil war. (Les Bushell)

Soko Orao & Avioane IAR-93

Countries of origin: Yugoslavia and Romania

Type: Ground attack aircraft

Powerplants: IAR-93B – Two 17.8kN (4000lb) dry and 22.2kN (5000lb) with afterburning Turbomecanica/Orao licence built Rolls-Royce Viper Mk 633-47 turbojets.

Performance: IAR-93B – Max speed at sea level 1085km/h (585kt), max cruising speed at 15,240ft 1090km/h (587kt). Max initial rate of climb 12,800ft. Service ceiling 44,625ft. Radius with four rocket launchers and 5min over target lo-lo-lo 260km (140nm), radius with two rocket launchers, six 100kg (220lb) bombs and one drop tank, with 10min over target, hi-lo-hi 450km (243nm), radius with four 250kg (550lb) bombs and one drop tank with 5min over target hi-hi-hi 530km (285nm).

Weights: IAR-93B – Empty equipped 5750kg (12,675lb), max takeoff 10,900kg (24,030lb).

Dimensions: Wing span 9.30m (30ft 6in), length overall inc probe 14.90m (48ft 11in), two seater length overall inc probe 15.38m (50ft 6in), height 4.52m (14ft 10in). Wing area 26.0m² (279.9sq ft).

Accommodation: Pilot only, or two in tandem in two seaters.

Armament: IAR-93 – Two GSh-23L 23mm twin barrel cannon in lower forward fuselage. One centreline and four underwing hardpoints can carry a max external stores load of 1500kg (3305lb), for rockets, bombs and AAMs (up to eight on twin launchers on each underwing hardpoint).

Operators: Croatia, Romania, Yugoslavia.

History: The J-22 Orao (Eagle) and IAR-93 were the results of a joint collaboration between the aircraft industries of Yugoslavia and Romania to meet similar requirements for a ground attack fighter.

A joint team of Romanian and Yugoslav designers began work on the J-22/IAR-93 in 1970 under the project name Yurom. Planning called for the new aircraft to be built in single seat ground attack and two seat advanced trainer/conversion trainer versions, with service entry around 1977. Both countries built single seat prototypes which both made their first flights on October 31 1974, similarly two two seaters, one built in each country, had their maiden flights on January 29 1977. After 30 pre series prototypes were built (15 in each country), series production began in Romania (with IAv Craiova, now Avioane) in 1979 and with Soko in Yugoslavia in 1980.

Romanian IAR-93s and Yugoslav Oraos are generally similar. Romanian production models comprise the initial non afterburning single and two seat IAR-93A (26 single seat and 10 two seaters built), and the single and two seater IAR-93B with afterburning engines (first flight 1985, 165 built).

Yugoslav Orao variants are the non afterburning Orao 1 (17 built), which was considered underpowered and was relegated to reconnaissance duties as the IJ-22 (two two seaters were designated INJ-22), the NJ-22 production two seat reconnaissance variant (35 built, some with afterburning) and the J-22 Orao production single seater (most with afterburning). Soko built 75 J-22s at Mostar in Bosnia until 1992 when the factory was abandoned and the J-22 jigs were transferred to UTVA within the new Yugoslav state.

Photo: Note deployed airbrakes on this Yugoslav Orao. (MAP)

Sukhoi Su-17/-20/-22

Country of origin: Russia

Type: Ground attack/strike fighter

Powerplant: Su-22M-4 – One 76.5kN (17,200lb) dry and 110.3kN (24,800lb) Lyulka AL-21F-3 turbojet.

Performance: Su-22M-4 – Max speed Mach 1.74 or 1850km/h (1000kt). Max speed at sea level Mach 1.1 or 1350km/h (730kt), or with external stores Mach 1.02 or 1250km/h (675kt). Max initial rate of climb 45,275ft/min. Service ceiling 49,865ft. Range with external fuel at altitude 2550km (1375nm), at low level 1400km (755nm).

Weights: Su-22M-4 – Empty equipped 10,767kg (23,737lb), max takeoff 19,400kg (42,770lb).

Dimensions: Wing span extended 13.68m (44ft 11in), wing span fully swept 10.03m (32ft 11in), length inc probes 19.03m (62ft 5in), fuselage length 15.87m (52ft 1in), height 5.13m (16ft 10in). Wing area wings extended 38.5m² (414.3sq ft), wings swept 34.9m² (375.1sq ft).

Accommodation: Pilot only, or two in tandem in Su-17U/Su-22U.

Armament: Two 30mm NR-30 guns, one in each wing root. Nine hardpoints for 4000kg (8820lb) of armament including bombs, gun pods, rockets, two R-13M, R-60 or R-73A AAMs, Kh-25ML, Kh-27, Kh-29 and Kh-58 ASMs.

Operators: Afghanistan, Algeria, Czech Republic, Hungary, Iraq, Libya, Peru, Poland, Russia, Slovakia, Syria, Ukraine, Yemen.

History: For many years Sukhoi's Su-17/20/22 (NATO name 'Fitter') formed the backbone of Warsaw Pact nations' ground attack forces.

The swing wing Su-17 was the end result of Sukhoi's efforts to improve the swept wing Su-7 'Fitter-A's payload range and takeoff performance. The prototype for the Su-17, designated S-22I or Su-7IG (Izmenyaemaya Geometriya – variable geometry) and designated by NATO 'Fitter-B', flew for the first time on August 2 1966 (unlike other variable geometry aircraft, each wing pivots midway along its length, outboard of a large wing fence). Two squadrons of similar Lyulka AL-7 powered 'improved Fitter-B' pre series Su-17s were noted in service in the early 1970s.

Initial production was of the Su-17M 'Fitter-C' with ranging radar, a 110.3kN (24,802lb) AL-21F-3 turbojet and a new nav/attack system. It was exported as the Su-20. In addition small numbers of reconnaissance pod carrying Su-17Rs and Su-20Rs were built.

The improved Su-17M-2 and shorter fuselage Su-17M-2D (both 'Fitter-D') were built from 1974 and introduced a slightly cut down nose for better pilot visibility, a fixed intake centrebody carrying a laser rangefinder and a doppler radar in an undernose pod. The 'Fitter-D' was exported as the Tumansky powered Su-22 'Fitter-F'.

A two seat development of the Su-17M-2 is the Tumansky R-29 powered Su-22U 'Fitter-E'.

Lyulka powered two seater Su-17UM-3 'Fitter-G' conversion trainers and single seat Su-17M-3 'Fitter-Hs' have a deeper spine and modified tail, the Su-17M-3 also has an internal doppler radar. Respective export variants are the Tumansky or Lyulka powered Su-22UM-3K 'Fitter-G' and Tumansky or Lyulka powered Su-22M-3 'Fitter-J'.

The Lyulka powered Su-17M-4 and export Su-22M-4 (both 'Fitter-K') have a dorsal air inlet for cooling and were delivered from 1980.

Photo: A Czech Su-22M-4 'Fitter-K'. (Paul Merritt)

Sukhoi Su-24

Country of origin: Russia

Type: Long range strike fighter

Powerplants: Su-24M – Two 75.0kN (16,864lb) dry and 109.8kN (24,690lb) with afterburning Saturn/Lyulka AL-21F-3A turbojets.

Performance: Su-24M – Max speed Mach 1.35, max speed at low level with six FAB-500 bombs 1200km/h (648kt). Service ceiling 36,090ft. Ferry range with external fuel 2500km (1350nm). Combat radius with six FAB-500 bombs 410km (220nm).

Weights: Su-24M – Empty equipped 22,300kg (49,163lb), max take-off 39,570kg (87,235lb).

Dimensions: Su-24M – Wing span extended 17.64m (57ft 11in), span wings swept 10.37m (34ft 0in), length inc probe 24.60m (80ft 8in), height 6.19m (20ft 4in). Wing area wings extended 55.2m² (593.8sq ft), wing area wings swept 51.0m² (549.2sq ft).

Accommodation: Pilot and weapon systems operator side by side.

Armament: Nine external stores stations for TN-1000 and TN-1200 nuclear weapons, or four TV or laser guided bombs, or Kh-23 (AS-7 'Kerry'), Kh-25ML (AS-10 'Karen'), Kh-58 (AS-11 'Kilter'), Kh-25MP (AS-12 'Kegler'), Kh-59 (AS-13 'Kingbolt'), Kh-29 (AS-14 'Kedge') and Kh-31 (AS-17 'Krypton') ASMs, two R-60 (AA-8 'Aphid') AAMs for self defence, rockets and conventional bombs.

Operators: Algeria, Iran, Iraq, Libya, Russia, Syria, Ukraine.

History: The formidable Su-24 (NATO reporting name 'Fencer') strike fighter was developed to replace Il-28 and Yak-28 medium bombers.

Sukhoi originally planned to meet the new bomber requirement with its delta wing T-6 with four RD-36-35 auxiliary lift jets to improve takeoff performance. A T-6-1 prototype first flew in July 2 1967, but the jet lift configuration was abandoned in favour of using swing wings to reach the desired field performance. Thus a variable geometry T-6-2IG prototype (without lift jets) flew for the first time on January 17 1970. The T-6-2IG was adopted for production as the Su-24 and more than 900 have been built.

The basic Su-24 was built in three variants, which NATO designated 'Fencer-A', 'Fencer-B' and 'Fencer-C'. The 'Fencer-A' first flew in late 1971 but served only in small numbers with a trials unit. The 'Fencer-B' was the first major production variant while the 'Fencer-C' had improved avionics.

The improved Su-24M 'Fencer-D' is the major production strike/bomber development. It is believed to have a terrain following radar (rather than terrain avoiding radar), a retractable inflight refuelling probe, a longer nose for new avionics including a Kaira laser/TV weapons guidance system, wing root fences (on Russian aircraft only) and a single nose probe. The export version is the Su-24MK.

The Su-24MR 'Fencer-E' reconnaissance variant has a Shtik side looking radar in a shortened nose (with dielectric panels), infrared and TV sensors, a panoramic camera in the nose and an oblique camera in the lower fuselage (and no wing root fences). The Su-24MR can also carry various reconnaissance and Elint pods.

The final Su-24 variant is the EW, jammer and Sigint Su-24MR 'Fencer-F', developed to replace the Yak-28PPP. Only 12 are thought to have been built.

Photo: An Su-24 demonstrator. (Jim Thorn)

Sukhoi Su-27, Su-30 & Su-33

Country of origin: Russia

Type: Air superiority/multirole/carrier based fighter

Powerplants: Su-27P – Two 79.4kN (17,857lb) dry and 122.6kN (27,557lb) with afterburning Saturn/Lyulka AL-31F turbofans.

Performance: Su-27P – Max speed at altitude Mach 2.35 or 2500km/h (1350kt), max speed at sea level Mach 1.1 or 1345km/h (725kt). Max initial rate of climb 60,040ft/min. Service ceiling 59,055ft. Range with max fuel 3680km (1985nm). Intercept radius with four AAMs 1500km (810nm).

Weights: Su-27P – Empty approx 17,700kg (39,020lb), max takeoff 33,000kg (72,750lb).

Dimensions: Su-27P – Span 14.70m (48ft 3in), length exc probe 21.94m (72ft 0in), height 5.93m (19ft 6in). Wing area 62.0m² (667.4sq ft).

Accommodation: Pilot only, or two in tandem in Su-27UB and Su-30.

Armament: Su-27P – One GSh-301 30mm cannon. Ten external hardpoints for up to 10 AAMs comprising semi active radar guided R-27Rs (AA-10A 'Alamo-A'), IR guided R-27Ts (AA-10B 'Alamo-B'), semi active radar guided R-27ERs (AA-10C 'Alamo-C'), IR guided R-27ETs (AA-10D 'Alamo-D'), R-73s (AA-11 'Archer') and R-60s (AA-8 'Aphid').

Operators: China, Russia, Ukraine, Vietnam.

History: The Su-27 'Flanker' is a formidable fighter, boasting long range without external tanks, a large missile armament, modern radar and sensors and unmatched manoeuvrability.

The Su-27 was designed as a manoeuvrable all weather interceptor and bomber escort with a secondary ground attack capability. Development work began in 1969 under the leadership of Pavel Sukhoi, resulting in the first flight of a prototype designated T-10-1 (and powered by two AL-21F-3 turbojets) on May 20 1977. Designated 'Flanker-A' by NATO, the T-10-1 and subsequent T-10 prototypes exhibited serious control problems and so the aircraft was considerably redesigned, resulting in the T-10S-1. The T-10S-1 first flew on April 20 1981 and closely resembled production Su-27s.

Su-27 design features include the blended wing/fuselage design, widely separated AL-31 turbofans, all moving tailplanes, a large F-15 style airbrake, leading edge slats, an IRST and laser rangefinder set which allows passive target detection and engagement, fly-by-wire, HUD and Zhuk look down/shoot down and track while scan radar.

The Su-27P 'Flanker-B' is a single seat air defence fighter; the Su-27S has wingtip EW pods and multirole tasking and can carry a 4000kg (8820lb) bomb load (available for export as the Su-27SK); while the Su-27UB 'Flanker-C' is the two seat operational trainer. A modified Su-27, designated P-42, set a series of time to height world records.

The two seat Su-30 air defence fighter is designed for up to 10 hour missions and can provide targeting information for other Su-27s by datalink. The Su-30MK is a multirole variant offered for export.

The Russian Navy has over 20 carrier capable Su-33 'Flanker-D' air defence fighters for its conventional carrier *Kuznetsov*. First flown in Su-27K prototype form, features include folding wings, canards, strengthened undercarriage, refuelling probe and arrester hook.

Photo: About 400 basic Su-27s (P, S & UBs) have been built, plus 20 or so Su-33s and a small number of Su-30s. (Jim Thorn)

Sukhoi Su-35

Country of origin: Russia

Type: Multirole fighter

Powerplants: Two 137.3kN (30,865lb) with afterburning Saturn/Lyulka AL-35F turbofans.

Performance: Max speed at altitude Mach 2.35 or 2500km/h (1350kt), max speed at sea level Mach 1.14 or 1400km/h (755kt). Service ceiling 59,055ft. Range with max internal fuel over 4000km (2160nm), range with inflight refuelling over 6500km (3510nm).

Weights: Empty approx 18,415kg (40,565lb), max takeoff approx 34,000kg (74,956lb).

Dimensions: Wing span over wingtip ECM pods 15.00m (49ft 3in), length 22.20m (72ft 10in), height 6.36m (20ft 10in).

Accommodation: Pilot only.

Armament: One GSh-30 30mm cannon. Twelve external hardpoints can carry 8000kg (17,655lb) of weapons, including R-27 (AA-10 'Alamo'), R-40 (AA-6 'Acrid'), R-60 (AA-8 'Aphid'), R-73A (AA-11 'Archer') and R-77 (AA-12 'Adder') AAMs, Kh-25ML (AS-10 'Karen'), Kh-25MP (AS-12 'Kegler'), Kh-29 (AS-14 'Kedge') and Kh-31 (AS-17 'Krypton') ASMs, KAB-500 bombs and rocket pods.

Operators: Russia*

History: The Su-35 is an advanced multirole development of the basic Su-27 which has perhaps resulted in the most capable fighter currently flying, bar the F-22.

Development of advanced Su-27s variants is understood to have first begun in the early 1980s. A development Su-27 fitted with canards flew for the first time in May 1985, while the first prototype for what would become the Su-35, the T-10S-70, first flew on June 28 1988. For a time the improved Su-27 was designated Su-27M, it has since been redesignated Su-35.

Changes over the basic Su-27 are numerous. Canard foreplanes were added further enhancing the Su-27's already impressive agility, while power is from two upgraded Saturn AL-35F (or AL-31MF) turbofans. Flight control is provided by a digital fly-by-wire system with quadruplex redundancy (the Su-27's fly-by-wire system is analog). The reprofiled nose houses a multimode Phazotron N011 Zhuk 27 radar (with a larger diameter, flat plate antenna) which has a search range of 100km (55nm), can track 24 targets simultaneously and has terrain following/avoidance. The tailcone meanwhile houses a N014 radar thought to be designed for use in conjunction with rearwards facing and firing IR guided AAMs. A new IRST set has been repositioned on the nose. The EFIS cockpit features three colour CRTs and a HUD and the Su-35 is compatible with the full range of Russian precision guided missiles and bombs. Other features are a retractable inflight refuelling probe, taller squared off fins each containing an auxiliary fuel tank and twin nosewheels.

Further features under development for production Su-35s include a Zhuk-PH phased array radar and thrust vectoring. At least one Su-35 development aircraft has flown with three dimensional thrust vectoring. Others have been noted with large ECM wingtip pods.

The Russian Air Force hopes to introduce the Su-35 into service in the late 1990s, although a lack of funding may thwart these plans.

Photo: The Su-35 is available for export. (Paul Merritt)

Sukhoi Su-32FN/Su-34

Country of origin: Russia

Type: Long range strike aircraft

Powerplants: Su-34 – Two 137.3kN (30,865lb) with afterburning Saturn/Lyulka AL-35F turbofans.

Performance: Su-34 – Max speed approx Mach 1.8, max speed at sea level Mach 1.15 or 1400km/h (755kt). Range with max internal fuel approx 4000km (2160nm).

Weights: Su-34 – Max takeoff 44,360kg (97,800lb).

Dimensions: Wing span 14.70m (48ft 3in), length 25.20m (82ft 8in), height 6.20m (20ft 4in). Wing area 62.0m^2 (667.4sq ft).

Accommodation: Pilot and weapon systems operator side by side.

Armament: One 30mm GSh-301 cannon in forward starboard fuselage. Two wingtip stations for self defence AAMs. Six underwing, plus centreline and under intake hardpoints for full range of Russian precision guided bombs and missiles such as TV or laser guided bombs, or Kh-23 (AS-7 'Kerry'), Kh-25ML (AS-10 'Karen'), Kh-25MP (AS-12 'Kegler'), Kh-59 (AS-13 'Kingbolt'), and Kh-29 (AS-14 'Kedge') ASMs, Kh-58 (AS-11 'Kilter') anti radiation missiles, and Kh-31 (AS-17 'Krypton') anti ship missiles, plus rockets and conventional bombs.

Operators: Russia*

History: The Su-32FN is a two seat (side by side, rather than tandem) development of the Su-27 fighter intended for long range strike, replacing older types such as the Su-17, MiG-27 and Su-24.

When the Su-32FN first appeared in 1991 confusion surrounded its intended role, with the first prototype, '42', variously identified as an aircraft carrier trainer designated Su-27KU (Korabelnii Uchebno or shipborne trainer) and a strike fighter as the Su-27IB (Istrebitel Bombardirovschik or fighter bomber). An August 1991 TASS news photo showed '42' on approach as if to land on the carrier *Tbilsi* (but without an arrester hook) and it may well be that the two seat side by side 'Flanker' was originally designed for carrier training for Su-27K/Su-33 pilots, but instead was adopted for strike, a logical step given the Su-27's massive range and good payload lifting abilities.

Sukhoi designated another pre series strike 'Flanker', '43', the Su-34 and it appeared this appellation would be adopted for production aircraft, however, a third pre series aircraft, '45', was displayed at the 1995 Paris Airshow and was designated Su-32FN and it now seems likely that this final designation will be adopted.

Features of the Su-32FN (aside from side by side seating) include twin nosewheels and tandem main undercarriage units, canards, AL-35F turbofans, a multimode radar with terrain following/avoidance (the Su-34 had a rearwards facing radar in the tailcone, as on the Su-35), a retractable inflight refuelling probe, broader chord tailfins, multifunction displays in the cockpit and modern avionics with a high level of automization. Access to the cockpit is via an integral ladder aft of the nosewheel, while behind the two crew seats in the humped fuselage is a small galley and toilet. The crew sit on Z-36 zero/zero ejection seats and the cockpit is protected by titanium armour.

The Su-32FN may enter Russian Air Force service as early as 1996, and, if funding permits, will replace Su-17s, MiG-27s and early Su-24s.

Photo: The Su-32FN at Paris. The type's all new nose section has earned the aircraft the nickname Platypus. (Paul Merritt)

Sukhoi Su-25

Country of origin: Russia

Type: Close support/ground attack aircraft

Powerplants: Two 44.2kN (9920lb) Soyuz/Tumansky R-195 turbojets.

Performance: Su-25T – Max speed at sea level 950km/h (512kt), max cruising speed at 650ft 700km/h (378kt), economical cruising speed 650km/h (350kt). Max initial rate of climb 11,415ft/min. Service ceiling 32,800ft. Combat radius with a 2000kg (4410lb) weapon load at altitude 700km (278nm), at low level 400km (215nm). Ferry range 2500km (1350nm).

Weights: Su-25T – Max takeoff 19,500kg (42,990lb).

Dimensions: Su-25T – Wing span 14.52m (47ft 8in), length overall 15.35m (50ft 5in), height 5.20m (17ft 1in). Wing area 31.1m² (324.0sq ft).

Accommodation: Pilot only, or two in tandem in Su-25UB.

Armament: Su-25T – One NNPU-8M 30mm gun. Ten underwing hardpoints for two self defence R-60 (AA-8 'Aphid') AAMs, laser guided rockets, bombs, Vikhr (AT-9) anti armour tube launched missiles, laser guided Kh-25ML (AS-10 'Karen') and Kh-29L (AS-14 'Kedge') ASMs, KAB-500 laser guided bombs and Kh-58 (AS-11 'Kilter') anti radiation missiles.

Operators: Angola, Bulgaria, Czech Republic, Iraq, North Korea, Slovakia, Russia, Ukraine.

History: The Su-25 ('Frogfoot' to NATO) was designed specifically for close air support missions in support of ground forces.

Su-25 development began in 1968, although it wasn't until February 22 1975 that a prototype, designated T-8-1, first flew. This prototype was powered by twin Tumansky RD-9Bs, (non afterburning developments of the MiG-19's engine). Between then and 1984 when the first Soviet Su-25 units were declared operational, the Su-25 underwent a number of detail modifications and engine changes.

A unit of Su-25s, initially pre production aircraft, saw combat in Afghanistan where experience resulted in a number of modifications including bolt on chaff/flare dispensers, engine exhaust IR signature suppressors and titanium shielding between the engines.

The Su-25 features titanium cockpit armouring and wingtip pod airbrakes. The Su-25's engines can run on kerosene, diesel or petrol if necessary while the aircraft can self deploy its own ground support and maintenance equipment in four underwing pods.

The basic Su-25 and export Su-25K (both 'Frogfoot-A') account for most Su-25 production. The Su-25UB and export Su-25UBK (both 'Frogfoot-B') are two seat conversion trainers with a ground attack capability. The Su-25UT, later Su-28 (both also 'Frogfoot-B'), was offered as a dedicated advanced trainer. Ten carrier capable two seat Su-25UTGs (with arrester hook and strengthened undercarriage) were built for carrier trials while 10 similar Su-25UBPs were ordered, but may have been cancelled. Su-25BMs are single seater target tugs.

The Su-25T is a dedicated anti tank variant based on the two seaters but with the rear cockpit faired over for additional fuel and avionics including a new nav system, plus chaff/flare dispenser in the base of the tail and a laser rangefinder and TV camera in the nose for target tracking. Deliveries of production aircraft began in 1991.

Photo: An Su-25T prototype. About 30 Su-25Ts have been built for the Russian Air Force, while it is available for export as the Su-25TK.

Transall C-160

Countries of origin: France and Germany

Type: Tactical transport

Powerplants: Two 4550kW (6100ehp) Rolls-Royce Tyne RTy.20 Mk 22 turboprops driving four bladed propellers.

Performance: Max speed 513km/h (277kt). Max initial rate of climb 1300ft/min. Service ceiling at 45,000kg (99,210lb) AUW 27,000ft. Takeoff run 715m (2345ft). Range with 8 tonne (17,640lb) payload and reserves 5095km (2750nm), range with a 16 tonne (35,275lb) payload and reserves 1853km (1000nm). Max ferry range with centre section wing fuel tank 8850km (4780nm).

Weights: Min operating empty 28,000kg (61,730lb), typical operating empty 29,000kg (63,935lb), max takeoff 51,000kg (112,435lb).

Dimensions: Wing span 40.00m (13ft 3in), length exc probe 32.40m (106ft 4in), height 11.65m (38ft 3in). Wing area 160.1m² (1722sq ft).

Accommodation: Flightcrew of three. Main cabin can seat up to 93 equipped troops, or 61 to 68 paratroops, or 62 stretcher patients and four medical attendants, or armoured vehicles, artillery and 4WD vehicles and trucks. Can airdrop an 8 tonne load.

Armament: None

Operators: France, Germany, South Africa, Turkey.

History: The Transall C-160 tactical transport forms the backbone of the transport fleets of the German and French air forces.

Germany and France formed Transall Allianz in January 1959 to design and build a tactical transport for each countries' air force, plus for export. Germany and France participated in the program on a 50/50 basis, with program partners comprising Germany's MBB and VFW and France's Aerospatiale. Design features settled upon included a high wing, voluminous fuselage, rear loading freight door and two Rolls-Royce Tyne turboprops.

First flight occurred on February 25 1963. Production lines were established in France (at Toulouse) and Germany and aircraft were delivered from 1967 for the air forces of Germany (110 C-160Ds), France (50 C-160Fs) and South Africa (9 C-160Zs, retired in 1993 but then returned to service in 1995). Turkey took delivery of 20 C-160Ts, all ex German aircraft.

Transall production initially ceased in 1972, but a French requirement saw a further 33 C-160s (including four for an Indonesian civil operator) built between 1981 and 1985. These new aircraft are designated C-160NG (Nouvelle Generation) and feature a fixed inflight refuelling probe. Ten C-160NGs have a secondary tanker role and are fitted with a hose drum unit in the port undercarriage sponson. Five more C-160NGs are plumbed to be converted to tankers.

Two C-160NGs were converted as Sigint platforms before delivery as the C-160 GABRIEL or C-160G. Features include wingtip pods, a blister fairing on the rear port fuselage, a large retractable dome under the forward fuselage and various antennae around the fuselage. Four other French C-160s, designated the C-160H ASTARTE, carry a Rockwell Collins TACAMO VLF radio for communications with France's nuclear submarines.

The C-160 was offered for export in C-160S maritime patrol (with search radar) and C-160SE elint forms, but these were not ordered.

Photo: A Luftwaffe Transall C-160D.

Tupolev Tu-16 & Xian H-6

Country of origin: Russia

Type: Multirole bomber & reconnaissance aircraft

Powerplants: Tu-16K-11-16 – Two 93.2kN (20,945lb) Mikulin AM-3M-500 turbojets.

Performance: Tu-16K-11-16 – Max speed at 19,685ft 1050km/h (565kt), cruising speed 850km/h (460kt). Service ceiling 49,200ft. Range with a 3000kg (6615lb) weapon load 7200km (4475nm).

Weights: Tu-16K-11-16 – Empty equipped 37,200kg (82,012lb), max takeoff 75,800kg (167,110lb).

Dimensions: Tu-16K-11-16 – Wing span 32.99m (108ft 3in), length 34.80m (114ft 2in), height 10.36m (34ft 0in). Wing area 164.7m² (1772.3sq ft).

Accommodation: Normal crew of four, comprising two pilots side by side on flightdeck, navigator/bombardier in nose, and tail gunner, plus two observation stations (blisters either side of rear fuselage).

Armament: Defensive armament comprises six 23mm cannon, two in tail, two in forward dorsal turret and two in rear ventral turret. Normal conventional bomb load of 3000kg (6600lb). Standoff missiles include a Kh-26 (AS-6 'Kingfish') anti ship missile (with conventional or nuclear warhead) carried on port underwing hardpoint, or the Kh-10 (AS-2 'Kipper') anti ship missile semi recessed in bomb bay.

Operators: H-6 – China. Tu-16 – Egypt, Iraq, Russia, Ukraine.

History: One of Russia's first effective jet bombers, the Tupolev Tu-16 has enjoyed a frontline service career matched by few other types.

The Tu-16 was made possible by the development of the Mikulin AM-3 turbojet, which also powered the four engined Myasishchyev M-4 'Bison'. A prototype designated Tu-88 and powered by AM-3A turbojets flew for the first time on April 27 1952. A second, considerably lightened prototype flew later that year and the type was subsequently selected for production ahead of the rival Ilyushin Il-46.

Early production Tu-16s covered by NATO's 'Badger-A' designation include the Tu-16A nuclear bomber, torpedo armed naval Tu-16T and the Tu-16N tanker for other Tu-16s (using the unique wingtip to wingtip method). Of the 'Badger-A's, only Tu-16Ms survive in service, although over 100 Chinese built Xian H-6s remain in service.

The first anti ship missile launching Tu-16 was the Kh-1 (AS-1 'Kennel') firing Tu-16KS-1 'Badger-B' with retractable radome (now retired). The Tu-16K-10 'Badger-C' is identifiable by its large, flat nose radome housing the I-band 'Puff Ball' radar and carried a single Kh-10S (AS-2 'Kipper') missile semi recessed under the fuselage (modified to Tu-16K-10-26 'Badger-C Mod' standard it could carry a single Kh-26/AS-6 'Kingfish'). The similar Tu-16K-11-16 'Badger-G' was developed to carry the 320km (170nm) range Mach 1.2 Kh-11/Kh-15 (AS-5 'Kelt'). 'Badger-G's modified to fire the Kh-26 are designated Tu-16K-26 'Badger-G Mod'.

Many of the 1800 plus Tu-16s built were converted to Elint/reconnaissance platforms. The Tu-16Ye is an elint conversion of 'Badger-C's, as is the Tu-16P 'Badger-K' and Tupolev Tu-16P 'Badger-L', while the Tu-16R 'Badger-E' and Tu-16P 'Badger-F' are optical reconnaissance variants.

Finally the Tu-16PP 'Badger-H' and Tu-16RM and Tu-16KRM, both 'Badger-J', are EW jammers.

Photo: A late 1970s photo of a Tu-16R intercepted by a US Navy F-4.

Tupolev Tu-95 & Tu-142

Country of origin: Russia

Type: Strategic bomber (Tu-95) and maritime patrol platform (Tu-142).

Powerplants: Tu-95MS – Four 11,035kW (14,795ehp) KKBM Kuznetsov NK-12MV turboprops, driving eight bladed counter rotating propellers.

Performance: Tu-95MS – Max speed at 25,000ft 925km/h (500kt), at sea level 650km/h (350kt), cruising speed 710km/h (385kt). Ceiling 39,370ft. Radius with a 11,340kg (25,000lb) payload 6400km (3455nm).

Weights: Tu-95MS – Empty 120,000kg (264,550lb), max takeoff 187,000kg (412,258lb).

Dimensions: Tu-95MS – Wing span 50.04m (164ft 2in), length 49.13m (161ft 2in), height 13.30m (43ft 8in). Wing area 289.9m² (3120sq ft).

Accommodation: Seven crew – two pilots, comms operator, nav/defensive systems operator, flight engineer, navigator and tail gunner.

Armament: Tu-95MS – Up to six Kh-55 (AS-15A 'Kent') cruise missiles on a rotary launcher in the bomb bay.

Operators: Tu-95 – Russia, Ukraine. Tu-142 – India, Russia.

History: The massive Tu-95 was first developed in the early 1950s when the turboprop offered the best compromise between speed and range.

The Tu-95 (NATO reporting name 'Bear') was developed around the 8950kW (12,000shp) Kuznetsov NK-12 turboprop and the fuselage cross section originally introduced on the Tu-4 'Bull', the USSR's unlicenced copy of the B-29 Superfortress. The engines delivered their power through eight bladed counter rotating propellers, while the wings, unique for a propeller driven aircraft, are swept. The Tu-95's unique powerplant/airframe combination gives it a top speed over Mach 0.8, while its massive internal fuel capacity and the relative efficiency of the turboprops gives intercontinental range.

The prototype Tu-95 flew for the first time on November 12 1952. Initial production was of the Tu-95M 'Bear-A' high altitude freefall nuclear bomber (now withdrawn from use). Some were converted as Tu-95U crew trainers. Tu-95Ms were converted to Kh-20 (AS-3 'Kangaroo') cruise missile launching Tu-95K-20 'Badger-B' standard with a nose mounted radar. The Tu-95KD was similar but had an inflight refuelling probe. The similar Tu-95KM 'Bear-C' (thought to be new build aircraft) had an inflight refuelling probe, Elint antennae and some reconnaissance sensors. The Tu-95K-22 'Bear-G' had a revised radome profile and carried two Kh-22 (AS-4 'Kitchen') missiles, one under each wing root. The final bomber variant was the Tu-95MS 'Bear-H', developed specifically to carry the Kh-55 (AS-15A 'Kent') and was built from 1983.

Surplus Tu-95M bombers were converted to maritime reconnaissance Tu-95RT 'Bear-D' and Tu-95MR 'Bear-E' configurations. The Tu-95RT has an undernose radome and was used for missile mid course guidance and reconnaissance duties, while the Tu-95MR has various cameras in the bomb bay.

The Tu-142 is a dedicated ASW platform developed from the Tu-95. The Tu-142 'Bear-F' features a slight fuselage stretch and a maritime search radar in a ventral radome. It carries sonobuoys, torpedoes and mines. The later Tu-142M 'Bear-F Mod 2' introduced a Magnetic Anomoly Detector (MAD) on top of the tail. The Tu-142MR 'Bear-J' is used as a submarine communications relay.

Photo: A Tu-95MS 'Bear-H'. (Paul Merritt)

Tupolev Tu-22

Country of origin: Russia

Type: Strategic bomber/electronic warfare aircraft

Powerplants: Tu-22K – Two 123.5kN (27,560lb) dry and 163.0kN (36,375lb) with afterburning Dobrynin RD-7M-2 turbojets.

Performance: Tu-22K – Max speed at 39,350ft Mach 1.52 or 1610km/h (970kt), max speed at sea level 890km/h (480kt). Service ceiling 43,635ft. Combat radius hi-lo-hi with a 400km (215nm) full throttle dash 2200km (1190nm). Ferry range with internal fuel 4900km (2645nm).

Weights: Tu-22K – Empty 38,100kg (83,995lb), normal loaded 85,000kg (187,390lb), max rocket assisted takeoff 94,000kg (207,230lb).

Dimensions: Tu-22K – Wing span 23.50m (77ft 0in), length 42.60m (139ft 9in), height 10.67m (35ft 0in). Wing area 162.0m² (1744sq ft).

Accommodation: Crew of three in tandem, with navigator/systems operator system forward of pilot in lower forward nose.

Armament: One NR-23 23mm gun in tail for self defence. Weapons bay can hold 8 tonnes (17,600lb) of bombs. Tu-22K can alternatively carry a single Kh-22 (AS-4 'Kitchen') supersonic cruise missile semi recessed in the weapons bay.

Operators: Libya, Iraq, Russia.

History: The Tu-22 was Russia's first successful attempt at fielding a supersonic bomber.

The Tu-22 ('Blinder' in NATO parlance) dates from a 1955 study to build a supersonic bomber capable of penetrating then modern air defences and carrying a payload similar to the subsonic Tu-16. The new aircraft (Tupolev's own designation was Tu-105) flew for the first time in September 1959 (piloted by Yu I Alasheyev). The Tu-22 remained unknown in the west until two years later at the Tushino Aviation Day flypast when 10 Tu-22s (one with an Kh-22/AS-4 'Kitchen' cruise missile) made a flypast.

The Tu-22's most unusual feature is the position of the engines at the base of the fin, which had the dual benefits of leaving the fuselage free for fuel (and without the need for long inlet ducts) and gave the two engines (mounted side by side) largely undisturbed airflow. The lips of the intakes move forward for takeoff creating a gap through which extra air is drawn. The slender, area ruled fuselage houses a bombing/navigation radar in the nose, a crew of three with the navigator in the lower forward fuselage with the pilot and radio operator/gunner in tandem behind him, an internal weapons bay, 45,000 litres internal fuel capacity and a 23mm defensive cannon in the tail. The large swept wing features pods into which the main undercarriage units retract into.

Approximately 250 Tu-22s were built. Initial production was of the Tu-22 'Blinder-A' conventional and nuclear bomber. About 150 Tu-22s were Kh-22 cruise missile firing Tu-22K 'Blinder-C's with an enlarged radome for the 2.8m diameter multimode radar. The Tu-22U 'Blinder-D' trainer had a raised second cockpit aft of the normal cockpit, while about 60 of the Tu-22R 'Blinder-E's were built, fitted with a range of reconnaissance sensors. Most surviving Tu-22s in Russian service have been converted as EW jammers, while survivors of 17 Tu-22s supplied to Libya and nine to Iraq still remain in use.

Photo: Two Tu-22s soon after takeoff.

Tupolev Tu-22M

Country of origin: Russia

Type: Strategic and maritime strike/reconnaissance bomber

Powerplants: Tu-22M-3 – Two 245.2kN (55,115lb) with afterburning Kuznetsov/KKBM NK-25 turbofans.

Performance: Tu-22M-3 – Max speed at high altitude Mach 1.88 or 2000km/h (1080kt), max speed at low level Mach 0.86 or 1050km/h (567kt), normal cruising speed at altitude 900km/h (485kt). Service ceiling 43,635ft. Supersonic combat radius with a 12,000kg (26,455lb) weapons load 1500 to 1850nm (810 to 1000nm). Subsonic combat radius with max weapons load hi-hi-hi 2200km (1190nm). Subsonic combat radius with 12,000kg (26,455lb) bomb load lo-lo-lo 1500 to 1665km (810 to 900nm), or hi-lo-hi 2410km (1300nm).

Weights: Tu-22M-3 – Empty 54,000kg (119,050lb), max takeoff 124,000kg (273,370lb), rocket assisted takeoff 126,400kg (278,660lb).

Dimensions: Tu-22M-3 – Wing span wings extended 34.28m (112ft 6in), span wings swept 23.30m (76ft 6in), length overall 42.46m (139ft 4in), height 11.05m (36ft 3in). Wing area wings extended 183.6m² (1976.1sq ft), wing area wings swept 175.8m² (1892.4sq ft).

Accommodation: Crew of four with pilot and copilot side by side, with navigator and weapons systems operator behind them.

Armament: One GSh-23 twin barrel 23mm cannon in the tail. Can carry 24,000kg (52,910lb) of conventional bombs or mines in bomb bay, or six Kh-15P (AS-16 'Kickback') ASMs on a rotary launcher in bomb bay and four underwing, or three Kh-22 (AS-4 'Kitchen') ASMs, one semi recessed under fuselage and one on each underwing hardpoint.

Operators: Russia, Ukraine.

History: The Tu-22M was conceived as a swing wing conversion of the Tu-22 but evolved into essentially an all new aircraft and one with impressive payload/range capabilities.

Tupolev first looked at fitting the Tu-22 with swing wings in 1961. Wind tunnel tests revealed that fitting the Tu-22 with swing wings and a minimum of other changes would almost double combat radius while halving field length. Design work on this aircraft, designated Tu-22M, began in 1962, however Tupolev took the opportunity to substantially redesign the basic Tu-22 to even further improve performance. Apart from the swing wings the other key change was the powerplants, two Kuznetsov NK-20 afterburning turbofans mounted in the rear of the fuselage. The engines were fed by two F-4 style intakes with variable splitter plates. The nose was redesigned, while new six wheel main undercarriage units retracted into the fuselage.

The first Tu-22M-0 prototype, a much converted Tu-22, first flew on August 30 1964, although the west did not identify the new bomber until September 1969. The NATO reporting name 'Backfire-A' was subsequently adopted. Production was of the further redesigned Tu-22M-2 (with a new nav/attack radar) and did not begin until 1972.

About 200 Tu-22M-2 'Backfire-Bs' were built before production switched to the Tu-22M-3, which first flew in 1980. The Tu-22M-3 is powered by two increased thrust NK-25 turbofans fed by new wedge shaped air inlets, and introduced a new multimode radar in a reprofiled nose and has an increased max takeoff weight. About 150 have been built.

Photo: A Tu-22M-3. Note the bomb racks. (Paul Merritt)

Tupolev Tu-160

Country of origin: Russia

Type: Strategic bomber

Powerplants: Four 137.3kN (30,865lb) dry and 245.2kN (55,115lb) with afterburning Samara/Trud NK-231 turbofans

Performance: Max speed at 40,000ft Mach 2.05 or 2220km/h (1200kt), cruising speed at 45,000ft 960km/h (518kt). Max initial rate of climb 13,780ft/min. Service ceiling 49,200ft. Radius of action at Mach 1.3 2000km (1080nm). Max unrefuelled range 12,300km (6640nm).

Weights: Empty 118,000kg (260,140lb), max takeoff 275,000kg (606,260lb).

Dimensions: Wing span wings extended 55.70m (182ft 9in), wing span wings swept 35.60m (116ft 9in), length 54.10m (177ft 6in), height 13.10m (43ft 0in). Wing area wings extended 360.0m² (3875sq ft).

Accommodation: Crew of four, with two pilots side by side and with navigator/bombardier and electronic systems operator behind them.

Armament: Max weapon load 40,000kg (88,185lb), comprising freefall bombs or ASMs in two internal bomb bays. One rotary launcher can be carried in each bay to carry six Kh-55MS (AS-15 'Kent') ALCMs or 12 Kh-15P (AS-16 'Kickback') SRAMs. No defensive armament.

Operators: Russia, Ukraine.

History: The massive Tu-160 ('Backfire' to NATO) is the heaviest and most powerful bomber ever built and was developed as a direct counter to the Rockwell B-1A.

Tupolev began design work under the leadership of V I Bliznuk of its all new 'Aircraft 70', a direct response to the B-1, in 1973. Although the B-1A was cancelled in 1977, design and development work on the new bomber continued, resulting in a first flight on December 19 1981, about a month after it was first spotted by a US spy satellite. Production of 100 Tu-160s was authorised in 1985 although only about 40 were built before the line closed in 1992.

The Tu-160 is similar in overall configuration to the B-1, but is much larger overall and has a number of different features. The four NK-231 afterburning turbofans are the most powerful engines fitted to a combat aircraft and are mounted in pairs under the inner fixed wings. The variable geometry air inlets are designed for speed (Mach 1 at low level, over Mach 2 at altitude). The Tu-160 has a retractable inflight refuelling probe although it is rarely used due to the aircraft's massive 130 tonne internal fuel capacity.

The variable geometry wings have full span leading edge slats and double slotted trailing edge flaps, while the airframe is free of any protuberances (except for a small video camera window for the pilots) and is covered in a light RAM coating. The nav/attack radar is believed to have a terrain following function, while the Tu-160 has a comprehensive ECM jamming system. The four crew sit on their own ejection seats and the pilots have fighter style sticks. The Tu-160 has a fly-by-wire flight control system.

In late 1995 about a dozen Tu-160s where in Russia and 20 were in the Ukraine, although these may be transferred to Russian control.

The Tu-160SK is a commercial variant being offered as a launch vehicle for the Burlak-Diana satellite launching rocket.

Photo: The Tu-160 is designed for high and low level penetration.

Tupolev Tu-134

Country of origin: Russia

Type: VIP transport

Powerplants: Tu-134 – Two 64.9kN (14,490lb) Soloviev D-30 turbofans. Tu-134A – Two 66.7kN (14,990lb) Soloviev D-30 Srs II turbofans.

Performance: Tu-134 – Max cruising speed 900km/h (485kt), economical cruising speed 750km/h (405kt). Normal operating ceiling 39,730ft. Range with 7000kg (15,420lb) payload and reserves 2400km (1295nm), with 3000kg (6600lb) payload 3500km (1890nm). Tu-134A – Max cruising speed 900km/h (485kt), long range cruising speed 750km/h (405kt). Range with 5000kg (11,025lb) payload and reserves 3020km (1630nm).

Weights: Tu-134 – Operating empty 27,500kg (60,627lb), max takeoff 44,500kg (98,105lb). Tu-134A – Operating empty 29,050kg (64,045lb), max takeoff 47,000kg (103,600lb).

Dimensions: Tu-134 – Wing span 29.00m (95ft 2in), length 34.35m (112ft 8in), height 9.02m (29ft 7in). Wing area 127.3m² (1370.3sq ft). Tu-134A – Same except length 37.05m (121ft 7in), height 9.14m (30ft 0in).

Accommodation: Two pilots and a navigator. Tu-134 seats 72, Tu-134A seats up to 84. Most military Tu-134s are fitted with a VIP interior.

Armament: None

Operators: Angola, Bulgaria, Czech Republic, Poland, Russia.

History: For many years the Tupolev Tu-134 (700 built) was the standard short haul jet airliner in the USSR and eastern Europe. Today small numbers are in military service as VIP transports.

The Tupolev design bureau was responsible for the Soviet Union's first jet powered airliner, the Tu-104 (which was in fact based on the Tu-16 'Badger' bomber), and the Tu-104's smaller brother the Tu-124. Both of these short range jetliners had a number of performance and technology shortfalls however, and the Tu-134 was developed to address these problems. Initially the Tu-134 was based fairly closely on the Tu-124, and for a time was designated the Tu-124A. However the decision was instead taken to change the aircraft's overall configuration to feature rear fuselage mounted engines and T tail.

Flight testing of the Tu-134 began during 1962, with six development aircraft being built. Production began in 1964 although it was not until September 1967 that Aeroflot launched full commercial services.

Initial production was of the standard fuselage length Tu-134. The stretched Tu-134A entered Aeroflot service in the second half of 1970 and could seat up to 76 passengers in a single class. Tu-134A features include a 2.10m (6ft 11in) fuselage stretch, a reprofiled nose, more powerful D-30 engines and an APU. Other versions are the Tu-134B with a forward facing position for the third crew member between and behind the pilots, the Tu-134B-1 which has a revised interior to seat up to 90 passengers without a galley, and the Tu-134B-3 which can seat 96 with full galley and toilet facilities.

Apart from converted Tu-134s serving in a VIP role, Russia operates a small number converted as bomber trainers. The Tu-134BSh is a bombardier trainer and features the Tu-22M's radar in the nose. The Tu-134UBL meanwhile is a Tu-160 crew trainer with the 'Blackjack's avionics and radar in a Tu-160 shaped nose.

Photo: A Bulgarian Air Force VIP Tu-134A. (Keith Gaskell)

Tupolev Tu-154

Country of origin: Russia

Type: Medium range airliner

Powerplants: Tu-154 – Three 93.9kN (20,950lb) Kuznetsov NK-8-2 turbofans. Tu-154M – Three 104kN (23,380lb) Aviadvigatel (Soloviev) D-30KU-154-II turbofans.

Performance: Tu-154 – Max cruising speed 975km/h (527kt), economical cruising speed 900km/h (486kt), long range cruising speed 850km/h (460kt). Range with max payload and reserves 3460km (1870nm), range with max fuel and 13,650kg (31,100lb) payload 5280km (2850nm). Tu-154M – Max cruising speed 950km/h (513kt). Range with max payload 3900km (2105nm), range with max fuel and 5450kg (12,015lb) payload 6600km (3563nm).

Weights: Tu-154 – Operating empty 43,500kg (95,900lb), max takeoff 90,000kg (198,415lb). Tu-154M – Basic operating empty 55,300kg (121,915lb), max takeoff 100,000kg (220,460lb).

Dimensions: Wing span 37.55m (123ft 3in), length 47.90m (157ft 2in), height 11.40m (37ft 5in). Wing area 201.5m² (2169sq ft).

Accommodation: Flightcrew of three or four. Typical single class seating for 158 to 164 at six abreast, or 167 in a high density layout for Tu-154; Tu-154M seats a maximum of 180. Most military Tu-154s have been converted with a VIP interior

Armament: None

Operators: Czech Republic, Germany, North Korea, Poland, Russia.

History: The Tu-154 is Tupolev's sixth commercial airliner design and is currently Russia's standard medium range airliner. Small numbers of the 900 built are in military service.

The Tu-154 was developed to replace the turbojet powered Tupolev Tu-104, plus the An-10 and Il-18 turboprops. Design criteria in replacing these three relatively diverse aircraft included the ability to operate from gravel or packed earth airfields, the need to fly at high altitudes above most Soviet Union air traffic, and good field performance. In meeting these aims the initial Tu-154 design featured three Kuznetsov (now KKBM) NK-8 turbofans, triple bogey main undercarriage units which retract into wing pods and a rear engine T tail configuration.

The Tu-154's first flight occurred on October 4 1968. Regular commercial service began in February 1972. Three Kuznetsov powered variants of the Tu-154 were built, the initial Tu-154, the improved Tu-154A with more powerful engines and a higher max takeoff weight and the Tu-154B with a further increased max takeoff weight. Tu-154S is a freighter version of the Tu-154B.

Current production is of the Tu-154M, which first flew in 1982. The major change introduced on the M was the far economical, quieter and reliable Soloviev (now Aviadvigatel) turbofans. The Tu-154M2 is a proposed twin variant powered by two Perm PS90A turbofans.

Most Tu-154s in military service are used for VIP transport, while Germany has converted one with various sensors for Open Skies treaty verification flights.

Photo: A German Tu-154M. (Paul Merritt)

Valmet Miltrainer/Vinka & Redigo

Country of origin: Finland

Type: Two seat basic trainer

Powerplant: L-70 – One 150kW (200hp) Lycoming AEIO-360-A1B6 flat four piston engine, driving a two bladed propeller. L-90TP – One 375kW (500shp) Allison 250-B17F turboprop driving a three bladed prop.

Performance: L-70 – Max speed at sea level 235km/h (127kt), cruising speed at 5000ft 2220km/h (120kt). Max initial rate of climb 1120ft/min. Service ceiling 16,405ft. Range 950km (512nm). L-90TP – Max speed 415km/h (224kt), max cruising speed 352km/h (190kt), economical cruising speed 312km/h (168kt). Max initial rate of climb 1170ft/min. Service ceiling 25,000ft. Range 1400km (755nm). Endurance 6hr 20min.

Weights: L-70 – Operating empty 767kg (1690lb), max takeoff 1250kg (2755lb). L-90TP – Empty equipped 950kg (2095lb), max takeoff 1900kg (4190lb).

Dimensions: L-70 – Wing span 9.63m (31ft 7in), length 7.50m (24ft 8in), height 3.31m (10ft 11in). Wing area 14.0m² (150.7sq ft). L-90TP – Wing span 10.60m (34ft 9in), length 8.53m (28ft 0in), height 3.20m (10ft 6in). Wing area 14.7m² (158.8sq ft).

Accommodation: Two side by side. Two extra seats can be installed in rear of cabin.

Armament: L-70 – Up to 300kg (660lb) on underwing hardpoints, including rockets, gun pods and light bombs. L-90TP – Up to 800kg (1765lb) of armament on six underwing hardpoints. Weapon options similar to L-70.

Operators: L-70 – Finland. L-90TP – Finland

History: Valmet's L-70 is currently Finland's basic military trainer. The turboprop powered L-90TP Redigo development is the last locally designed production aircraft to be built in Finland.

The L-70 Miltrainer flew for the first time on July 1 1975. The L-70 is of standard configuration for a basic trainer, with seating for the student and instructor side by side, fixed tricycle undercarriage and a Lycoming AEIO-360 flat four piston engine driving a two bladed prop. Hardpoints under the wing are designed for practice bombs or light armament including gun pods or rockets.

In 1978 the Finnish Air Force ordered 30 L-70 Miltrainers, which it named Vinka (Blast), to replace its Saab Safir basic trainers. They were delivered between 1980 and 1982. Apart from their basic training role one Vinka serves with each fighter squadron as a liaison aircraft.

The L-90TP Redigo is a turboprop powered development of the Miltrainer. Powered by an Allison 250 driving a three bladed prop, other changes to the Redigo include retractable undercarriage, a slight fuselage stretch, lengthened wings and greater external weapons load. First flight was on July 1 1986. Ten were built for the Finnish Air Force and others went to Mexico. A second prototype was flown in 1987 powered by a Turboméca TP 319, although no production aircraft were built to this standard.

Photo: Vinkas (pictured) and Redigos serve side by side at the Finnish Air Force's Air Academy. Finnish Air Force pilots learn to fly on the Vinka before transiting to the Redigo and then the BAe Hawk.

Vickers VC10

Country of origin: United Kingdom

Type: Strategic transport & tanker

Powerplants: C.1 – Four 97.0kN (21,800lb) Rolls-Royce Conway RCo.43 Mk 301 turbofans.

Performance: C.1 – Max cruising speed 935km/h (505kt) at 31,000ft, economical cruising speed 885km/h (478kt). Max initial rate of climb 3050ft/min. Service ceiling 42,000ft. Range with max payload 6275km (3385nm).

Weights: C.1 – Empty 66,225kg (146,000lb), max takeoff 146,510kg (323,000lb). K.2 – Max takeoff 142,000kg (313,056lb). K.3 – Max takeoff 151,900kg (334,882lb).

Dimensions: C.1 & K.2 – Wing span 44.55m (146ft 2in), length excluding probe 48.38m (158ft 8in), height 12.04m (39ft 6in). Wing area 272.4m² (2932sq ft). K.3 – Same except length excl probe 52.32m (171ft 8in).

Accommodation: C.1 – Flightcrew of two pilots and flight engineer. Seating for up to 150 in main cabin, or alternatively 76 stretchers and six medical attendants. K.2 – Practical max fuel weight 74,000kg (163,142lb). K.3 – Practical max fuel weight 80,000kg (176,370lb).

Armament: None

Operators: UK

History: The VC10 forms the backbone of the Royal Air Force's tanker/transport fleet.

Work on the VC10 dates back to 1956. Design of the VC10 was mainly against a BOAC (the British long haul international airline) requirement for a jet airliner capable of serving its routes to Africa, the Far East and Australasia, and thus dictated the requirement for good airfield and hot and high performance. BOAC officially selected the VC10 in May 1957, and ordered 35 of the type on January 14 1958.

The VC10 had its first flight on June 29 1962. Features of the basic design included four rear mounted Rolls-Royce Conway turbofans, T tail and an advanced wing with complex high lift features. Awarded civil certification in April 1964, the VC10 at the time was the largest aircraft to enter production in western Europe.

The VC10 was also selected by the Royal Air Force to meet its 1960 requirement for a strategic transport for the then Transport Command and 14 were ordered as VC10 C.1s. These aircraft differed from standard airliner VC10s in having uprated Conways, a refuelling probe, a large freight door, extra fuel in the fin and rear facing passenger seats. The first flight of an RAF C.1 was in November 1965 and deliveries began early the following year. VC10 C.1s remain in RAF service, eight were fitted with two underwing refuelling pods from 1992 as C.1(K)s, giving them a secondary tanker role.

The first VC10 tankers though were delivered from 1984. Five VC10s and four stretched Super VC10s, all ex airliners, were converted to dedicated tankers, involving fitting fuel tanks on the main deck, closed circuit TV to monitor tanking operations, two underwing refuelling pods and a rear fuselage mounted refuelling unit. The VC10 tankers are designated K.2, the Super VC10s K.3. The K.4 designation applies to five additional Super VC10s converted to tankers in the late 1980s. The K.4s do not feature main deck fuel tanks.

Photo: A VC10 K.4. (Paul Merritt)

Vought F-8 Crusader

Country of origin: United States of America

Type: Carrier borne fighter

Powerplant: F-8E(FN) – One 47.6kN (10,700lb) dry and 80.1kN (18,000lb) with afterburning Pratt & Whitney J57-P-20A turbojet.

Performance: F-8E(FN) – Max speed at 36,000ft 1827km/h (986kt), cruising speed at 40,000ft 900km/h (485kt). Max initial rate of climb 21,000ft/min. Service ceiling approx 58,000ft. Ferry range 2250km (1215nm). Combat radius 965km (520nm).

Weights: F-8E(FN) – Empty 9038kg (19,925lb), max takeoff 15,420kg (34,000lb).

Dimensions: F-8E(FN) – Wing span 10.87m (35ft 8in), length 16.61m (54ft 6in), height 4.80m (15ft 9in). Wing area 32.5m² (350.0sq ft).

Accommodation: Pilot only.

Armament: F-8E(FN) – Four Colt Mk 12 20mm cannon. Two underwing and four fuselage side hardpoints for AIM-9 Sidewinder or Matra Magic or R 530 AAMs.

Operators: France

History: The F-8 Crusader was the US Navy's first supersonic day interceptor and its last single engine, single crew fighter.

The Crusader resulted from Vought's proposal to meet a 1952 US Navy requirement for a supersonic fighter but with a landing speed below 185km/h (100kt) and powered by a Pratt & Whitney J57 turbojet. Vought's design was selected for development ahead of the North American Super Fury, a navalised F-100. The prototype of the new fighter, designated XF8U-1, flew for the first time on March 25 1955.

The F8U Crusader's most unusual feature was its high mounted variable incidence wing, which rotated to a high angle of attack for takeoff to increase lift and for landing to increase drag and to give the pilot better forward vision. The F8U also featured folding wings, all moving horizontal tails, four 20mm cannon, a fire control radar and supersonic performance in level flight.

In all, 1259 Crusaders were built through to 1965. Initial production was of the F8U-1 (F-8A from 1962), followed by the more powerful F8U-1E (F-8B), the reconnaissance F8U-1P (RF-8A), the F8U-2 (F-8C) with four fuselage side missile rails and a more powerful engine and the all weather F8U-2N (F-8D). The final production model was the multirole F8U-2NE or F-8E, with an APQ-94 fire control radar and a weapons load of 2265kg (5000lb), including Bullpup ASMs. Rebuilds to extend many F-8s' service lives saw F-8Ds become F-8Hs, F-8Es become F-8Js, F-8Cs become F-8Ks, and F-8Bs upgraded as F-8Ls.

Apart from the Philippines, France has been the only country outside the US to operate the Crusader. The French Navy ordered 42 F-8E(FN)s for its carriers *Foch* and *Clemenceau*. The F-8E(FN) differs from the basic F-8E in having blown flaps and other high lift devices to allow it to operate off the smaller French carriers. The surviving F-8E(FN)s (the only Crusaders remaining in service) are due to be replaced by Rafale Ms from 1998.

Photo: The F-8E(FN) is an agile dogfighter but lacks a long range missile capability, thus limiting its effectiveness in the naval air defence role. Note the raised wing and deployed flaps and slats of this French Crusader on its landing run. (Paul Merritt)

Westland Wasp

Country of origin: United Kingdom

Type: Naval utility helicopter

Powerplant: One 785kW (1050shp) derated to 530kW (710shp) Rolls-Royce (Bristol Siddeley) Nimbus Mk 503 turboshaft driving a four bladed main rotor and two bladed tail rotor.

Performance: Max speed at sea level 193km/h (104kt), max and economical cruising speed 180km/h (96kt). Max initial rate of climb 1440ft/min. Hovering ceiling in ground effect 12,500ft, out of ground effect 8800ft. Max range with standard fuel 488km (263nm), range with four passengers 435km (235nm).

Weights: Empty 1565kg (3452lb), max takeoff 2495kg (5500lb).

Dimensions: Main rotor diameter 9.83m (32ft 3in), length overall rotors turning 12.29m (30ft 4in), fuselage length 9.24m (30ft 4in), height overall tail rotor turning 3.56m (11ft 8in), height to top of rotor head 2.72m (8ft 11in). Main rotor disc area 75.9m² (816.9sq ft).

Accommodation: Operational crew of three, or up to four passengers.

Armament: Two Mk 44 torpedoes or a single Mk 46 torpedo, or depth charges, or two Aerospatiale AS 12 wire guided anti ship missiles if fitted with a roof mounted sight.

Operators: Indonesia, Malaysia, New Zealand.

History: The Westland Wasp is a specialised maritime development of the Scout utility and anti tank helicopter operated by the British Army for many years.

The helicopter that eventually evolved into the Wasp started life as a Saunders Roe design before that company merged with Westland. That original design was the P.531 which Saunders Roe began design work on in 1956. The first of two prototype P.531s flew for the first time on July 20 1958.

The new turboshaft powered helicopter attracted the interest of the British Army Air Corp and a pre production batch of P.531-2 Mk 2s was ordered for evaluation, which occurred from October 1960. The British Army's initial order for what would become 150 Scout AH.1s was placed in October 1960. The AH.1 could be armed with up to four SS 11 anti tank missiles and a number saw operational service in the Falklands War.

The last Scouts were retired from British Army service in 1994, leaving a single example with the Empire Test Pilot School the only Scout in military service. Two Scouts were exported to the Royal Australian Navy and three to Jordan but these no longer serve.

Soon after its merger with Saunders Roe, Westland began work on a naval P.531 development. The Royal Navy ordered two such naval P.531s, which it designated Sea Scout HAS.1, for trials. The Sea Scout name was subsequently changed to Wasp before the first Wasp/Sea Scout flew for the first time on October 28 1962. The Wasp differs from the Scout primarily in that it has wheels for undercarriage rather than skids. It lacks any sensors of its own but can carry up to two torpedoes.

In all, 133 Wasps were built, comprising 98 for the Royal Navy and 35 for export to Brazil, the Netherlands, New Zealand and South Africa. Current operators are Indonesia (with ex Netherlands aircraft), Malaysia (ex RN aircraft) and New Zealand (new build and ex RN aircraft).

Photo: One of New Zealand's five surviving Wasps.

Westland Wessex

Countries of origin: USA and UK

Type: Utility transport/SAR helicopter

Powerplants: HC.2 – Two 1005kW (1350shp) Rolls-Royce (Bristol Siddeley) Gnome Mk 110/111 turboshafts, driving a four bladed main rotor and four bladed tail rotor.

Performance: HC.2 – Max speed at sea level 212km/h (115kt), max cruising speed 195km/h (105kt). Max initial rate of climb 1650ft/min. Hovering ceiling out of ground effect 4000ft. Ferry range with auxiliary fuel 1040km (560nm). Range with standard fuel 770km (415nm).

Weights: HC.2 – Operating empty 3767kg (8304lb), max takeoff 6123kg (13,500lb).

Dimensions: HC.2 – Main rotor diameter 17.07m (56ft 0in), length overall rotors turning 20.04m (65ft 9in), fuselage length 14.74m (48ft 5in), height overall 4.93m (16ft 2in), height to top of rotor head 4.39m (14ft 5in). Main rotor disc area 228.1m² (2643.0sq ft).

Accommodation: Two pilots on flightdeck with up to 16 equipped troops in main cabin. In medevac configuration can be fitted for eight stretcher patients, two seated patients and a medical attendant.

Armament: None usually.

Operators: UK, Uruguay.

History: The Wessex is a re engined and re engineered development of Sikorsky's S-58, developed initially for the Royal Navy as an ASW platform.

The Sikorsky S-58 arose from a 1951 US Navy requirement for an ASW helicopter. The Wright R-1820 radial piston engine powered S-58 flew for the first time on March 8 1952 and was adopted by the US Navy as the HSS-1 Seabat (or SH-34G from 1962). Other S-58 variants include the US Army's CH-34 Choctaw and the US Marine Corp's UH-34 Seahorse. All piston powered S-58s have now been retired from military service, although small numbers of twin Pratt & Whitney Canada PT6T turboshaft S-58T conversions serve in Thailand and Indonesia.

UK interest in the S-58 came about when the Royal Navy cancelled development of the twin Napier Gazelle turboshaft powered Bristol 191 in 1956. The 191 was being developed to meet an ASW helicopter requirement but instead the RN opted for the development of a single Napier powered development of the S-58 to meet its requirement. A Westland re engined Napier powered S-58 flew for the first time on May 17 1957, and the type was ordered into production as the Wessex HAS.1 (with dunking sonar and armed with torpedoes).

Now retired Wessex variants include the HAS.1, more powerful HAS.3 with a new automatic flight control system, the Royal Marines' HU.1 troop transport and the RAF's HC.5, a transport conversion of RN HAS.1/HAS.3s.

The RAF's major Wessex variant is the HC.2, which differs significantly from the Royal Navy's Wessexes in that it is powered by two Bristol Sideley Gnome turboshafts joined through a combining gearbox. About 60 HC.2s still serve with the RAF for search and rescue and utility transport, while HC.2s exported to Brunei (as the Mk 54), Iran (Mk 52) and Ghana (Mk 53) have all been retired.

Photo: A search and rescue configured Wessex HC.2. (Paul Merritt)

Westland Lynx AH.1, AH.7 & AH.9

Country of origin: United Kingdom

Type: Battlefield transport & anti tank helicopter

Powerplants: AH.9 – Two 845kW (1135shp) Rolls-Royce Gem 42-1 turboshafts, driving four bladed main and tail rotors.

Performance: AH.9 – Max continuous cruising speed 255km/h (138kt), max endurance cruising speed 130km/h (70kt). Max initial rate of climb approx 2480ft/min. Hovering ceiling out of ground effect 10,600ft. Range 685km (370nm).

Weights: AH.9 – Operating empty in troop transport configuration 3495kg (7707lb), max takeoff 5125kg (11,300lb).

Dimensions: AH.9 – Main rotor disc diameter 12.80m (42ft 0in), length overall rotors turning 15.24m (50ft 0in), length rotors folded 13.24m (53ft 5in), height overall rotors turning 3.73m (12ft 3in). Main rotor disc area 128.7m² (1385.4sq ft).

Accommodation: Max seating for pilot and 12 equipped troops, or six stretcher patients and a medical attendant in medevac layout.

Armament: Eight TOW anti tank missiles in two fuselage side launchers in anti tank configuration. Can also be fitted with pintle mounted machine guns and 20mm cannon on fuselage sides.

Operators: UK

History: Westland's Lynx is well regarded for its exceptional agility and good speed. Land based versions serve widely with the British Army for troop transport and anti armour missions.

The origins of the Lynx lie in the Westland WG.13, one of three helicopter designs covered by the February 1967 British/French helicopter coproduction agreement which also included the Gazelle and Puma. Unlike the Gazelle and Puma, which are of French design with some Westland production content, the Lynx is entirely of Westland design with Aerospatiale (now Eurocopter) responsible for 30% of production (including the forged titanium rotor hub for the four bladed semi rigid main rotor, which is the key to the Lynx's agility). Other Lynx features are its digital flight control system and all weather avionics.

The first of 13 Lynx prototypes flew for the first time on March 21 1971. The Lynx was originally intended as a ship borne ASW/anti surface warfare helicopter for the British and French navies, but its large cabin and excellent performance attracted British Army interest for troop transport and anti tank missions to replace Scouts.

The British Army's first Lynx model was the AH.1, which first flew in 1977. Most of the 113 AH.1s built have now been upgraded to AH.7 standard with improved systems and an IR suppressor on the exhaust, while the tail rotor is made from composites and rotates in the opposite direction to reduce noise. The latest British Army Lynx model is the AH.9, which is equivalent to the export Battlefield Lynx (none ordered). The AH.9 features wheeled undercarriage rather than skids, no TOW capability, composite construction main rotor blades with swept tips and an increased max takeoff. Sixteen new build AH.9s were ordered plus seven conversions. Five have been outfitted as command posts.

Photo: The Lynx AH.9 has wheeled undercarriage. (Westland)

Westland Lynx – Naval Models

Country of origin: United Kingdom

Type: Ship borne ASW, ASuW, SAR and utility helicopter

Powerplants: HAS.8 – Two 845kW (1135shp) Rolls-Royce Gem 42-1 turboshafts, driving four bladed main and tail rotors.

Performance: HAS.8 – Max continuous cruising speed 232km/h (125kt), max endurance cruising speed 130km/h (70kt). Max initial rate of climb approx 2170ft/min. Hovering ceiling out of ground effect 8450ft. Max range approx 595km (320nm). Combat radius with four Sea Skua anti ship missiles 275km (148nm). Radius of action for a 140min ASW patrol with one torpedo 37km (20nm). Surveillance mission endurance 140km (75nm) from ship 245min.

Weights: HAS.8 – Basic empty 3290kg (7255lb), max takeoff 5125kg (11,300lb).

Dimensions: HAS.8 – Main rotor disc diameter 12.80m (42ft 0in), length overall rotors turning 15.24m (50ft 0in), length with main rotor blades and tail folded 10.85m (35ft 7in), height overall rotors turning 3.67m (12ft 1in). Main rotor disc area 128.7m² (1385.4sq ft).

Accommodation: Crew of two or three.

Armament: Two Mk 44, Mk 46, A244S or Stingray torpedoes, or two Mk 11 depth charges in ASW configuration. For anti ship missions up to four Sea Skua anti ship missiles. French Lynx can fire up to four AS 12 wire guided missiles.

Operators: Brazil, Denmark, France, Germany, Netherlands, Nigeria, Norway, Portugal, South Korea, UK.

History: Naval Lynx variants form an important part of the inventories of several NATO navies, performing ASW, ASuW, SAR, vertrep and various utility missions.

When the 1967 Anglo/French helicopter production deal was signed covering the Lynx (originally WG.13), Gazelle and Puma, the Lynx had been planned from the outset as a ship based ASW/ASuW helicopter and it was not until later that land based variants for the British Army (described separately) were developed. The first Lynx prototype flew for the first time on March 21 1971, while the first production Lynx HAS.2 for the Royal Navy had its maiden flight in February 1976. All naval Lynx feature wheeled undercarriage, an advanced automatic flight control system and a folding tail and main rotor.

Features of the RN's Lynx HAS.2 include a Ferranti Seaspray search radar and dunking sonar. France's HAS.2(FN) is similar but has a OMERA-Segid search radar. The RN's HAS.3 has uprated RR Gem 42-1 turboshafts and a modified GEC-Marconi Seaspray radar. Most export Lynx are of similar standard to the HAS.2/HAS.3.

The most advanced naval Lynx variant is the HAS.8, which features composite main rotor blades with swept tips, uprated engines, a nose mounted GEC Sea Owl thermal imager and improved ESM and processing equipment. A rear mounted MAD and 360° coverage Sea Spray radar were planned, but dropped due to a lack of funding. Forty five RN Lynx HAS.3s are being upgraded to HAS.8 standard.

The export Super Lynx is similar to the HAS.8 and so far has sold to Portugal and South Korea (both these countries' Lynx lack the Sea Owl thermal imager).

Photo: A Royal Navy Lynx HAS.8. Conversion of 45 Lynx HAS.3s to HAS.8 standard is due to be completed in 2001. (Westland)

Westland Sea King & Commando

Countries of origin: USA and UK

Type: ASW, SAR and utility transport helicopter.

Powerplants: HC.4 – Two 1240kW (1660shp) Rolls-Royce Gnome H.1400-1T turboshafts, driving a five bladed main rotor and six bladed tail rotor.

Performance: HC.4 – Cruising speed at sea level 245km/h (132kt). Max initial rate of climb 2030ft/min. Max vertical rate of climb 808ft/min. Hovering ceiling in ground effect 6500ft, out of ground effect 4700ft. Ferry range with auxiliary fuel 1740km (940nm). Range with max payload (28 troops) 395km (215nm).

Weights: HC.4 – Typical operating empty 5620kg (12,390lb), max takeoff 9752kg (21,500lb).

Dimensions: Main rotor diameter 18.90m (62ft 0in), length overall rotors turning 22.15m (72ft 8in), fuselage length 17.02m (55ft 10in), height overall rotors turning 5.13m (16ft 10in), height to top of rotor head 4.72m (15ft 6in). Main rotor disc area 280.6m^2 (3020.3sq ft).

Accommodation: Two pilots with normal seating in main cabin for up to 28 in Commando. Normal Sea King crew of four (two pilots, radar operator and sonar operator).

Armament: Commando – Door mounted machine guns, can be fitted with sponsons for rockets. Sea King – Up to four torpedoes.

Operators: Sea King – Australia, Belgium, Germany, India, Norway, Pakistan, UK. Commando – Egypt, Qatar.

History: Despite appearances, Westland's Sea King and Commando are very different aircraft from Sikorsky's SH-3 Sea King.

Westland developed its own Sea King development in response to a Royal Navy requirement for an advanced long endurance ASW helicopter to replace the Wessex. Changes over the SH-3 were numerous and included Rolls-Royce Gnome turboshafts and British avionics and ASW systems, including the search radar, dunking sonar and processing equipment. First flight was on May 7 1969.

Initial Westland production was of the Sea King HAS.1 – 56 were delivered to the Royal Navy followed by 21 improved HAS.2s (plus 37 conversions) with uprated engines, six blade tail rotors and air intake deflectors/filters. From 1980 30 improved Sea King HAS.5s with a Sea Searcher radar and ESM were delivered, while the final RN ASW Sea King is the HAS.6 (six new build and 69 conversions delivered from 1990). They feature improved processing and ESM. ASW Sea Kings have also been delivered to Australia, India and Pakistan. Current export standard is the Advanced Sea King with uprated engines.

The Royal Navy also operates Sea King AEW.2s with a EMI Searchwater radar mounted in a swivel radome on the starboard side of the fuselage. Development was spurred by the Falklands War.

Search and rescue Sea Kings include the RN's HAR.5 and the RAF's HAR.3 and HAR.3A. Germany, Belguim and Norway also operate SAR Westland Sea Kings.

Finally the Westland Commando is a troop transport/assault development with seating for 28 troops and no ASW gear or floats. It was sold to Egypt, Qatar (three with full Sea King systems), while the Royal Navy operates the similar Sea King HC.4 for the Royal Marines.

Photo: Three RN Sea King HC.4 (Commando) squadrons served in the Gulf War. (Westland)

Yakovlev Yak-38

Country of origin: Russia

Type: Carrier based V/STOL fighter

Powerplants: One 66.7kN (14,990lb) Tumansky R-27V-300 turbojet, plus two 31.9kN (7175lb) RKBM RD-36-35FVR lift jets.

Performance: Yak-38 – Max speed at 36,000ft 1010km/h (545kt), max speed at sea level 978km/h (528kt). Max initial rate of climb 14,765ft/min. Service ceiling 39,370ft. Combat radius with max weapons load hi-lo-hi 370km (200nm), or lo-lo-lo 240km (130nm). Time on station on combat air patrol with AAMs and external fuel 185km (100nm) from ship 75min.

Weights: Yak-38 – Operating empty (inc pilot) 7485kg (16,500lb), max takeoff (for a short takeoff) 13,000kg (28,660lb).

Dimensions: Yak-38 – Wing span 7.32m (24ft 0in), length 15.50m (50ft 10in), height 4.37m (14ft 4in). Wing area 18.5m^2 (199.1sq ft).

Accommodation: Pilot only in Yak-38/Yak-38M, two in tandem in Yak-38U.

Armament: Four underwing hardpoints for up to 2000kg (4410lb) of armament such as 23mm cannon pods, rockets, 250 and 500kg bombs, Kh-23 (AS-7 'Kerry') ASMs and R-60 (AA-8 'Aphid') AAMs.

Operators: Russia (status unclear).

History: The unique Yak-38 (NATO reporting name 'Forger') was Russia's first and only operational V/STOL aircraft, although its operational effectiveness is limited.

The forebear to the operational Yak-38 fighter was the Yak-36 'Freehand', a fighter like research platform developed to explore VTOL flight. The Yak-36 was powered by a pair of turbojets mounted in the centre fuselage whose exhaust exited through vectoring nozzles. First flight was in 1966.

Experience with the Yak-36 led to the all new Yak-38 'Forger', which, unlike the Yak-36, features two vertically mounted lift jet engines (used only for takeoff and landing) in addition to the main Tumansky turbojet. The two lift jets are mounted just behind the cockpit. The main turbojet exhausts through two vectoring nozzles, one either side of the rear fuselage.

The prototype Yak-38 (reportedly designated Yak-36MP) flew for the first time in 1971, while sea trials aboard the STOL carrier *Kiev* were observed in 1975. Yak-38 production is estimated at 75 aircraft, including single seat Yak-38 'Forger-A's and a small number of two seat Yak-38U 'Forger-B' trainers. The Yak-38U has a longer and drooped nose with two cockpits in tandem, while the rear fuselage is stretched to compensate for the lengthened nose.

Yak-38 design features aside from the lift jet arrangement include a small ranging radar in the nose and four underwing hardpoints for light AAMs and ASMs, rockets and bombs. The wings fold to reduce carrier stowage space. Small numbers of late build Yak-38Ms feature modernised systems and can carry auxiliary fuel tanks.

In late 1995 the operational status of the Yak-38 was unclear. Some reports suggest the fleet has been retired, although small numbers may have remained in use aboard the carrier *Kiev*, which remained in Russian Navy service.

Photo: A Yak-38 demonstrates its VTOL abilities. Note open air inlet and exhausts for the auxiliary lift jets.

Yakovlev Yak-41/Yak-141

Country of origin: Russia

Type: V/STOL multirole fighter

Powerplants: One 107.7kN (24,205lb) dry and 152.0kN (34,170lb) with afterburning MNPK Soyuz R-79V-300 turbofan and two 41.8kN (9392lb) RKBM RD-41 turbojet lift jets.

Performance: Max speed at 36,000ft Mach 1.7 or 1800km/h (970kt). Service ceiling over 49,215ft. Range with external fuel and a short takeoff 2100km (1133nm), range with internal fuel after a vertical takeoff 1400km (755nm).

Weights: Max weight for a short takeoff 19,500kg (42,990lb).

Dimensions: Wing span 10.10m (33ft 2in), wing span wings folded 5.90m (19ft 4in), length overall 18.30m (60ft 0in), height 5.00m (16ft 5in).

Accommodation: Pilot only.

Armament: Provision for a GSh-310 30mm cannon in lower port forward fuselage. Four underwing hardpoints for a variety of weaponry, likely to include R-60 (AA-8 'Aphid'), R-27 (AA-10 'Alamo'), R-73 (AA-11 'Archer') and R-77 (AA-12 'Adder') AAMs, laser guided Kh-25ML (AS-10 'Karen'), Kh-29L (AS-14 'Kedge') ASMs, radar homing Kh-31P/A (AS-17 'Krypton') ASMs, TV guided Kh-29T (AS-14 'Kedge') ASMs, TV guided bombs, cluster bombs and rockets pods.

Operators: None

History: The Yakovlev Yak-141 'Freestyle' was to have been Russia's second generation V/STOL fighter to replace Yak-38s on 'Kiev' class carriers, but official development was cancelled due to a lack of funding.

The operational limitations of the Yak-38 – it is subsonic, has poor payload range performance and only rudimentary avionics – meant that the development of a replacement was both logical and inevitable. Development of the improved V/STOL fighter began in 1975, just four years after the first Yak-38 had flown. A western spy satellite spotted a Yak-141 prototype at Russia's Zhukhovsky test centre in the mid 1980s, although it was not until March 1989 that the first of two Yak-141 prototypes made its first flight.

The Yak-141's powerplant configuration is similar to that of the Yak-38, with two RKBM lift turbojets located in tandem immediately behind the cockpit. Unlike the Yak-38 however the Yak-141's main engine's exhaust exits through a single vectoring nozzle which is located just aft of the wing between the tail booms.

Other design features include supersonic flight courtesy of the powerful Soyuz turbofan and clean aerodynamic design, a relatively short span wing with four underwing hardpoints and fly-by-wire flight controls (with mechanical backup). The radar is said to be the same as on the MiG-29, giving compatibility with a range of modern Russian AAMs and ASMs. Like the MiG-29 the Yak-141 has a helmet mounted sight for off boresight IR AAM targeting.

The Russian Navy was forced to cancel the Yak-141 (it would have been designated Yak-41 in service) in 1992 due to a lack of funding. However Yakovlev continues to market the aircraft and has been looking for an international marketing/production partner.

Photo: A Yak-141 demonstrates its hovering abilities. Note open air intake for lift jets and downward vectored main engine nozzle. (Jim Thorn)

Yakovlev/Aermacchi Yak-130

Country of origin: Russia

Type: Two seat advanced trainer and ground attack aircraft

Powerplants: Two 21.6kN (4850lb) Povazske Stojàrne/Klimov RD-35M turbofans.

Performance: Max speed at altitude 950 to 1000km/h (512 to 540kt). Max initial rate of climb approx 12,000ft/min. Service ceiling over 39,400ft. Max ferry range with conformal fuel tank 2200km (1185nm). Combat radius hi-lo-hi over 600km (325nm), lo-lo-lo approx 380km (205nm).

Weights: Normal takeoff 6000kg (13,230lb), max takeoff 8500kg (18,740lb).

Dimensions: Wing span 10.64m (34ft 11in), length 11.90m (39ft 1in), height 4.70m (15ft 5in). Wing area 23.5m² (253.0sq ft).

Accommodation: Two in tandem.

Armament: Seven hardpoints can carry up to 3000kg (6605lb) of weapons of both Russian and western origin, such as R-27 AAMs, GSh-23, GSh-30, DEFA or Aden cannon pods, rockets, bombs, laser guided bombs and ASMs such as AGM-65 Mavericks or Kh-25s.

Operators: None

History: The Yak-130 is one of two contenders for the Russian Air Force's advanced trainer requirement and is being offered for export in conjunction with Aermacchi.

The Yak-130 is in competition with the Mikoyan MiG-AT to meet the Russian Air Force's requirement to replace approximately 1000 Aero L-29 and L-39 jet trainers. The Russian Air Force will acquire 200 of the winning design for basic, advanced, weapons and combat training.

Design work on the Yak-130 began in 1987. In 1993 Yakovlev signed a collaborative agreement covering design and marketing with Aermacchi. Aermacchi has had considerable input into refining the basic Yak-130 including 5000 hours of windtunnel testing of various configurations and 3000 hours of rig testing of the Yak-130's fly-by-wire system. The first prototype Yak-130 publicly rolled out in May 1995 although first flight had not occurred by late of that year.

Features of the basic Yak-130 include twin RD-35 turbofans (originally designed in the Ukraine, now built in Slovakia but with some Russian design input) which gives the trainer a 0.8 thrust to weight ratio and a healthy climb rate. Aerodynamic features include wingtips, leading edge slats and LEXs, permitting flight up to 35° angle of attack to be flown.

The baseline aircraft features modern Russian avionics built around a western standard Mil Std 1553 databus (which allows easy integration of western avionics and weapons), a HUD in the front cockpit and two colour LCD displays in each cockpit. The Yak-130's fly-by-wire system may later be programmed so that the aircraft's flight envelope can be gradually increased as the student pilot becomes more proficient.

Aside from the basic Yak-130 as offered to the Russian Air Force, other variants have been proposed including a single seat light fighter and a carrier capable trainer.

All production Yak-130's will be built in Russia. Yakovlev is responsible for marketing within the CIS, Aermacchi for the rest of the world.

Photo: The first Yak-130 at the 1995 Paris Airshow. (Alex Radetski)

HAVE YOU ENJOYED THIS, OUR INAUGURAL

DIRECTORY OF MILITARY AIRCRAFT?

If so, then don't forget that this edition will be replaced by a new updated version in early 1998.

In the meantime, the second edition of our **International Directory of Civil Aircraft** will be available from early 1997 with this being superseded by a new and revised edition two years later.

Every year we will release a new Directory – even years are for military and odd years are for civil aircraft.

Ensure you don't miss one of these affordable high quality unique reference works – place an advance order with your newsagency or bookshop today.

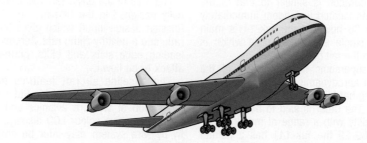

THE 1996/97 WORLD AIRPOWER GUIDE

A list of the inventories of the world's air arms.

AFGHANISTAN
Air Force
25+ MiG-23. 60+ MiG-21. 25+ MiG-17. 50+ Su-17/20/22. 13 MiG-15UTI. 24 L-39C. 22 L-29. 15+ Yak-11/Yak-18. 6 An-32. 21 An-26. 1 An-24. 12 An-12. 6 Il-14. 1 Il-18. 12+ An-2. 55 Mi-24. 45 Mi-8/17. 14 Mi-4. Operational status of some of these aircraft unknown.

ALBANIA
Air Force
13 Shenyang F-7. 62 Shenyang F-6. 36 Shenyang F-5/FT-5. 6 Shenyang F-2. 14 Shenyang FT-2. 13 Nanchang CJ-5. 6 Yak-11. 3 Il-14M. 7 Li-2. 10 Y-5. 17 Harbin Z-5. Operational status of some of these aircraft unknown.

ALGERIA
Air Force
20 MiG-25/R/U. 63 MiG-23B/E/BN/U. 95 MiG-21MF/bis/U. 10 Su-24. 30 Su-20. 12 Su-7BM/U. 10 L-39ZA. 21 CM 170. 3 MiG-15UTI. 19 Zlin 142. 6 T-34C. 6 An-12. 3 Il-76. 16 C-130H/H-30. 3 F27 400/600. 3 Gulfstream III. 2 Falcon 900. 2 Super King Air 200T. 36 Mi-24. 48 Mi-8/17. 12 Mi-4. 3 SA 330. 3 Alouette III.

ANGOLA
Air Force
19 MiG-23. 15 MiG-21MF/bis. 14 Su-22. 9 Su-25. 4 PC-7/9. 1 Fokker F27MPA. 2 Embraer EMB-111A. 6 MiG-21U. 3 MiG-15UTI. 5 Yak-11. 3 Cessna 172. 2 L-100-20. 10 An-26. 6 CASA 212. 6 BN-2A. 4 An-2. 5 Dornier Do 27. 1 Boeing 707. 29 Mi-25/Mi-35. 25 Mi-8/-17. 5 SA 365M. 6 SA 342M. 5 SA 341. 14 SA 316. 30 IAR 316. Operational status of some of these aircraft unknown.

ARGENTINA
Air Force
19 Mirage IIIC/B. 19 Mirage IIIE/D. 9 Mirage 5. 21 Dagger A/B. 6 Canberra B.62/T.64. 28 A-4P. 36 A-4M/OA-4M. 40+ IA-58A. 19 T-34A. 27 EMB-312. 98 IA-63. 27 MS-760B. 3 PA-34. 3 PA-28R. 2 KC-130H. 6 C-130E/H. 1 L-100-30. 5 Boeing 707-320B/C. 13 F27 400/600. 5 F28-1000/1000C. 9 C-47. 7 DHC-6-200. 15 IA-50. 2 Merlin IVA. 1 Sabreliner 75A. 5 Learjet 35A. 1 PA-31. 10 Commander 560. 1 Cessna 310. 37 Cessna A182J. 2 CH-47C. 2 Sikorsky S-61R. 2 AS 332B. 7 Bell 212. 4 UH-1D/H. 22 Hughes 369/500D. 4 SA 315B. 2 Sikorsky S-58T. 6 Bell 47G/OH-13/TH-13.

Naval Aviation
12 Super Etendard. 5 A-4Q. 5 MB-339A. 3 MB-326GB. 12 EMB-326. 10 T-34C. 9 S-2E/A. 6 L-188. 3 F28-3000. 9 Super King Air 200. 5 Queenair B80. 2 PC-6B. 9 SH-3D/H. 6 SH-2F. 4 Agusta A 109A. 6 Alouette III.

Coastguard
5 C-212. 1 AS 332B. 1 SA 330H. 6 HB 350B. 2 Hughes 500.

Army Aviation
23 OV-1. 6 Cessna T-41. 5 Cessna T-207. 2 Cessna U-17. 1 CASA 212. 3 Aeritalia G222. 2 DHC-6. 1 Sabreliner 75A. 1 Citation II. 3 Merlin III. 3 Merlin IV. 1 Queenair B-80. 3 AS 332B. 2 SA 330L. 1 Bell 212. 4 Bell 205A1. 22 Bell UH-1H. 5 Agusta A 109A. 5 SA 315B. 2 UH-12ET.

ARMENIA
Small number of Mi-8s and Mi-24s believed operational.

AUSTRALIA
Air Force
32 F-111C/G. 4 RF-111C. 71 F/A-18A/B. 3 P-3A*. 19 P-3C. 31 MB-326H. 65 PC-9. 24 C-130E/H. 5 Boeing 707-320C. 14 DHC-4. 5 Falcon 900. 10 HS.748. 4 C-47.

Naval Fleet Air Arm
16 Sikorsky S-70B-2. 6 Westland Sea King 50/50A. 6 AS 350BA. 3 Bell 206B-1. 2 HS.748EW.

Army Aviation Corps
38 S-70A-9. 25 UH-1H. 24 Bell 206B-1. 18 AS 350BA.

AUSTRIA
Air Force
24 J35ÖE. 28 Saab 105ÖE. 16 PC-7. 5 O-1E. 11 Cessna L-19. 2 Skyvan 3M. 12 PC-6. 23 AB 212. 21 AB 204B. 11 AB 206A. 10 OH-58B. 24 Alouette III.

AZERBAIJAN
Some MiG-21s and Mi-24s thought to be operational.

BAHAMAS
Air Force
1 Cessna 421C. 1 Cessna 404.

A RAAF F-111G down in the weeds and on full 'burner. Australia will end up being the sole operator of this impressive strike aircraft following the decision to retire most USAF examples before the end of 1996. Australia operates 37 F-111s, four of which have been modified to RF-111C reconnaissance configuration. (Mal Lancaster RAAF)

The air defence of Austria lies in the hands of 24 J35ÖE Drakens. This remarkable aircraft is also in service with Finland and Sweden. (Austrian Armed Forces)

The Brazilian Army took delivery of 36 Eurocopter AS 565UA Panthers which it operates for troop transport.

BAHRAIN
Air Force
12 F-16C/D. 11 F-5E/F. 14 AH-1E. 3 BO 105. 2 BO 105ASW. 1 S-70A. 4 Bell 412/205A-1. 2 Hughes 369D.

BANGLADESH
Air Force
25 Shenyang F-6/FT-6. 15 Xian F-7M. 9 MiG-21MF. 8 L-39ZA. 12 T-37B. 2 MiG-15UTI. 14 CM 170. 34 Nanchang CJ-6. 6 Cessna 152/337F. 3 An-32. 6 An-26/An-24. 12 Mi-17. 11 Bell 212. 2 Bell 206L.

BELGUIM
Air Force
98 F-16A/B. 30 Alpha Jet E. 11 CM 170. 36 SF.260M. 12 C-130H. 3 HS.748. 2 Boeing 727QC. 5 Merlin III. 2 Falcon 20. 1 Falcon 900. 5 Sea King.
Naval Aviation
3 Alouette III.
Army Aviation
10 BN-2. 46 Agusta A-109HA/HO. 32 Alouette II.

BENIN
Air Force
2 An-26. 2 C-47. 2 Dornier 128-2. 2 Antonov An-2. 1 Commander 500B. 2 AS 350B. 1 Kamov Ka-26.

BOLIVIA
Air Force
3 F-86F Sabre. 31 AT-33A/N. 22 PC-7. 4 AT-6G. 3 SF.260C. 14 T-23 Uirapuru/Tangara. 12 Cessna 152. 9 Cessna 172K/T-41D. 8 C-130A/H/L-100-30. 5 F27-400. 3 CV-440. 1 C-54. 2 C-47. 1 IAI-201. 1 C-212. 15 PC-6B. 1 L-188C. 2 Sabreliner 60/65A. 2 Learjet 25/35A. 4 King Air F90/200/200C. 1 Commander 690. 4 Cessna 402B/404/421B. 29 Cessna 185/206/210/310. 2 Bell 212. 19 UH-1H. 10 Hughes 500M. 15 SA 3158/HB 315.
Army/Naval Aviation
2 C-212. 1 King Air 200. 1 Cessna U206G. 1 Cessna 402C. 1 OV-10.

BOTSWANA
Air Force
7 BAC 167 Strikemaster. 6 PC-7. 7 BN-2A. 2 CN-235. 2 Skyvan 3M. 1 BAe 125-800. 2 Cessna 152. 5 Bell 412. 1 AS 350.

BRAZIL
Air Force
20 Mirage IIIEBR/DBR. 47 F-5. 8 F-5B/F. 78 AMX/AMX-T*. 177 EMB-326. 121 EMB-312. 99 EMB-312 ALX*. 122 T-25 Universal. 65 T-23 Uirapuru. 12 S-2A/E. 21 EMB-111A. 4 Boeing 707-320C. 2 KC-130H. 8 C-130E/H. 3 RC-130E. 20 DHC-5A. 11 HS.748. 127 EMB-110. 2 Boeing 737-200. 12 HS.125. 12 Learjet 36A. 10 EMB-120. 7 EMB-121. 33 EMB-810C. 9 Caravan 1. 94 U-27A/L-42/U-42. 7 AS 332M. 57 UH-1D/H. 6 Bell 206A/B. 4 Hughes OH-6A. 27 HB 350B Esquilo. 10 AS 355F.
Naval Aviation
10 Agusta/Sikorsky SH-3D. 7 Lynx 21/23. 8 Super Lynx. 5 AS 332F. 15 Bell 206B. 20 HB 350B/AS 355F-2 Esquilo.
Army Aviation
20 AS 550 Fennec*. 16 HB 350-1 Esquilo. 36 SA 365K*.

BRUNEI
Air Force
16 Hawk 100/200. 2 SF.260W. 10 C-212. 6 BO 105CB/CBS. 2 Bell 206B. 2 Sikorsky S-70C. 1 Bell 214ST.

BULGARIA
Air Force
20 MiG-29A/UB. 3 MiG-25R. 46 MiG-23BN/MF. 9 MiG-23UM. 17 MiG-21M. 6 MiG-21RF. 17 MiG-21U/UM. 20 Su-22M/U. 39 Su-25K/U. 37 L-39. 83 L-29. 8 An-24/An-26. 1 An-30. 5 L 410UVP-E. 2 Tu-134. 1 Yak-40. 44 Mi-24. 26 Mi-8/17. 14 Mi-2.
Naval Aviation
6 Mi-14PL. 2 Ka-25BSH.

BURKINA FASO
Air Force
9 SF.260W/WP. 2 HS.748-2A. 2 C-47. 2 N-262C. 2 MH-1521M Broussard. 1 Commander 500B. 2 SA 365N. 1 SA 316B.

BURUNDI
Army Aviation
5 SF.260W. 5 SF.260TP. 3 SF.260C. 3 Cessna 150. 1 Dornier Do 27Q. 4 SA 342L. 3 SA 316B.

CAMBODIA
Air Force
22 MiG-21PF. 5 Shenyang F-6. 3 Mi-24. 3 An-24RV. 2 Yak-40. 8 Mi-8/17. Operational status of some of these aircraft unknown.

CAMEROON
Air Force
4 Alpha Jet. 9 CM 170. 3 C-130H. 4 DHC-5D. 3 DHC-4A. 1 IAI-201. 2 Dornier 128D-6. 1 PA-23. 1 Boeing 707. 2 AS 332L. 1 SA 365N. 1 SA 319B. 1 SA 318C. 3 Bell 206L-3. 4 SA 342L.

CANADA
Air Command
125 CF-18A/B Hornet. 18 CP-140 Aurora. 3 CP-140A Arcturus. 139 CT-114 Tutor. 60 CT-133. 5 CC-137 (707). 5 CC-150 (A310). 30 CC-130E/H Hercules. 13 CC-115 Buffalo. 6 CC/CT-142 Dash 8. 7 CC-138 Twin Otter. 23 CC-144 Challenger. 13 CH-113A Labrador (CH-46). 17 CH-118 Iroquois. 29 CH-124A/B Sea King. 46 CH-135 Twin Huey (UH-1N). 108 CH-146 Griffon (Bell 412)*. 61 CH-136 Kiowa.

CAPE VERDE
Air Force
1 Dornier 228

CENTRAL AFRICAN REPUBLIC
Air Force
1 C-337. 5 Aermacchi AL-60. 5 Broussard MH 1521. 1 Mystére Falcon 20C. 1 AS 350 Ecureuil. 1 SE 3130.

CHAD
Air Force
2 PC-7. 2 SF.260W. 4 C-130A/B/H. 1 CASA 212. 3 C-47. 2 DC-4. 2 PC-6B. 5 Reims-Cessna FTB-337.

The venerable C-130 Hercules first flew in 1954 and over 2000 have been built. The first generation C-130 is now being superseded by the far more capable and cheaper to operate C-130J Hercules II. Britain's RAF and the US are launch customers, while many existing C-130 operators are likely to upgrade to the J in time. (Canadian Forces)

CHILE

Air Force
14 Mirage 50C/50CN. 2 Mirage 50DC/IIIB. 15 F-5E/F. 2 Canberra PR.9. 28 A-37B. 20 A-36. 16 T-36. 21 T-37B/C. 78 T-35A/B Pillan. 8 Cessna T-41D. 5 T-25 Universal. 18 Piper PA-28-236 Dakota. 3 707-320B/C. 2 IAI Phalcon. 3 UP-3A Orion. 4 C-130H. 2 Y-7 (An-24). 4 C-47. 14 DHC-6 100/200. 9 Beech 99A. 1 King Air 100. 1 Super King Air 200CT. 2 Learjet 35A. 7 Twin Bonanza. 6 Extra 300. 3 O-1 Bird Dog. 1 AS 332. 11 UH-1D/H. 1 Bell 212. 6 SA 315B. 6+ BO 105CB.

Naval Aviation
6 EMB-111. 1 Falcon 20. 10 PC-7. 3 EMB-110CN. 3 CASA 212. 5 AS 332F. 6 BO 105. 6 Bell 206. 5 AS 532C. 8 P-3A.

Army Aviation
16 R172K. 2 CN-235M. 6 C 212A. 1 PA-31. 2 Cessna 337G. 1 Citation III. 1 Falcon 200. 2 AS 332B. 10 SA 330F/L. 2 UH-1H. 2 Bell 206B. 12 SA 315B. 15 Enstrom 280FX. 5 MD 530F.

CHINA

Air Force
128 Xian H-6 (Tu-16). 108 Harbin H-5 (Il-28). 550 Nanchang Q-5. 26 Su-27. 411 Shenyang J-8/J-8II. 600 Xian J-7. 2500 Shenyang J-6. 525 Shenyang J-5. 355 Shenyang J-4. 8 SA 342L-1. 1500 CJ-6. 22 Y-7/An-24. 12 Y-14/An-26. 8 An-30. 7 Il-18. 25 Hanzhang Y-8 (An-12). 15 Harbin Y-11/Y-12. 33 Li-2. 58 Il-12. 300 Y-5. 14 SA 321. 22 S-70C-II. 56 Mi-8/17. 350 Harbin Z-5/Z-6 (Mi-4). 20 Harbin Z-9 (Dauphin). 18 Trident 1E/2E. 2 CL-601. 6 AS 332.

Naval Aviation
150 Harbin H-5 (Il-28). 5 Harbin SH-5. 12 Beriev Be-6 'Madge'. 325 Shenyang J-6. 118 Shenyang J-5. 103 Nanchang Q-5. 2 Y-7. 9 Li-2. 23 Y-5. 4 Harbin Z-5. 3 Harbin Z-9. Operational status of some of these aircraft unknown.

COLOMBIA

Air Force
13 Kflr C7/TC7. 11 Mirage VCOA/VCOR. 2 Mirage VCOD. 25 A-37B/OA-37B. 8 T-37C. 3 IA 58A. 13 EMB-312. 20 T-34A/B. 31 T-41D. 5 C-130B/H-30. 1 707-320C. 4 DC-6. 11 C-47/AC-47. 2 IAI-201. 2 EMB-110P. 1 F28-1000. 1 Citation II. 2 King Air C90. 1 Queenair. 2 Commander 680/695. 2 PA-31 Navago. 1 PA-31 Cheyenne. 1 PA-44 Seminole. 1 Mitsubishi MU-2. 4 Cessna 404/401/340. 2 Cessna 310. 9 DHC-2. 1 H-550 Courier. 1 PA-32 Cherokke Six. 1 Cessna 185. 1 Bell 412. 4 Bell 212. 16 UH-60A*. 39 UH-1B/H. 21 OH-6A/Hughes 500MD. 7 Hughes 530MG/500E. 10 Bell 206B. 4 UH-12E. 13 TH-55/Hughes 300C. 11 Bell 47D/G.

Naval Aviation
1 PA-31 Navago. 3 Commander 500. 4 PA-28 Cherokee. 4 BO 105CB.

CONGO

Air Force
10 MiG-21. 11 MiG-17F. 1 MiG-15UTI. 6 An-24/An-26. 1 N.2501F Noratlas. 1 727. 2 SA 318. 2 SA 316. Operational status of some of these aircraft unknown.

The Czech Republic operates around 35 Su-22M swing wing fighter bombers. (Paul Merritt)

COSTA RICA

Civil Guard
7 Cessna 337/Soloy 206. 2 Aztec/Seneca. 1 Commander 680. 1 Cherokee Six. 3 Hughes 269C/500E.

COTE D'IVOIRE

Air Force
5 Alpha Jet. 5 Beech F33C. 2 Reims Cessna F150H. 1 F28. 2 Fokker 100. 1 Gulfstream IV. 1 Beech Super King Air 200. 1 Cessna 421. 2 SA 330H. 3 SA 365C. 1 SA 319. 1 SA 318.

CROATIA

Air Force
18 MiG-21bis/MF. 2 Orao. 5 Super Galeb. 3 An-26. 3 An-2. 2 CL-601. 1 Dornier Do 28. 5 Cessna 172/188. 5 Mi-24. 16 Mi-8. 11 SA 342. 6 Bell UH-1/212. 1 Bell 205. 2 Hughes 500. Operational status of some of these aircraft unknown.

CUBA

Air Force
36 MiG-29. 18 MiG-23M. 33 MiG-23BN. 2 MiG-23U. 100 MiG-21F/MF/PFMA. 77 MiG-21bis. 18 MiG-21U. 29 MiG-19SF. 18+ MiG-17. 10+ MiG-15bis. 15 MiG-15UTI. 20 L-39C. 20 Zlin Z 326. 4 An-24. 21 An-26. 2 An-32. 12+ Il-14. 3 Yak-40. 30 An-2. 19 Mi-24. 10 Mi-14. 48 Mi-8/Mi-17. 20 Mi-4. 5 Mi-2.

CYPRUS

National Guard
2 PC-9. 1 BN-2B. 3 SA 342L-1. 2 Hughes 500. 2 Bell B206B.

CZECH REPUBLIC

Air Force
53 MiG-23BM/MF/UM. 87 MiG-21. 25 Su-25BK/UBK. 33 Su-22M-4/U. 70 L-159*. 84 L-39C/MS/V/ZA. 13 L-29. 33 Zlin Z 42/Z 326. 1 An-12. 20 An-24/An-26. 20 L-410M/T/UVP. 1 Tu-154. 1 Tu-134A. 10 An-2. 30 Mi-24. 31 Mi-8/17. 25 Mi-2. 40 Mi-1.

DENMARK

Air Force
81 F-16A/B. 3 C-130H. 3 Gulfstream III. 8 Sikorsky S-61A. 27 T-17 Supporter.

DJIBOUTI

Air Force
2 C-212. 1 Cessna U206G. 1 Socata 235GT. 2 AS 355F. 1 AS 350.

DOMINICAN REPUBLIC

Air Force
6 A-37B. 5 O-2A. 8 T-34B. 3 C-47. 2 Aero Commander 680. 2 Queenair 80. 2 PA-31. 1 Cessna 210. 5 T-41D. 9 Bell 205A/UH-1H. 3 Alouette II/III. 2 Hughes 369. 1 SA 365C.

ECUADOR

Air Force
13 Mirage F1JE/JB. 10 IAI Kfir C2/TC2. 8 Jaguar International S/B. 15 Strikemaster. 7 A-37B. 22 AT-33A. 15 T-34C. 11 SF-260ME. 11 T-41D/Cessna 172F. 13 Cessna 150L. 2 C-130H/L-100-30. 2 DHC-5D. 4 HS.748-2A. 5 DHC-6 300. 3 Sabreliner 40R/60/75. 1 King Air E90. 4 AS 332. 1 SA 330. 4 UH-1H. 1 Bell 212. 3 SA 315B. 6 SA 316B.

Naval Aviation
3 T-34C. 1 CN-235M. 1 Citation I. 1 Super King Air 200. 5 Cessna 320E/337. 4 Bell 206B.

Army Aviation
2 DHC-5D. 1 CN-235M. 3 IAI-201. 3 PC-6B. 1 Sabreliner 40R. 1 Learjet 24D. 2 King Air 100/200. 5 Cessna 172/185/206. 13 SA 342K/L. 5 AS 332B. 5 SA 330. 1 Bell 214B. 1 UH-1. 4 AS 350B. 3 SA 315B.

EGYPT

Air Force
24 F-4E. 130 F-16A/B/C/D. 19 Mirage 2000C/B. 68 Mirage 5D/E/E2. 11 Mirage 5SDR/SDD. 168 Xian F-7/MiG-21. 40 Shenyang F-6/FT-6. 40 Alpha Jet. 6 Beech 1900/C. 3 707. 21 C-130H. 8 DHC-5D. 4 Gulfstream III/IV. 1 Super King Air. 3 Falcon 20. 40 L-29. 45 L-39. 23 L-59E. 36 Al-Gumhuria. 53 EMB-312. 74 SA 342K/L/M. 15 CH-47C. 27 Westland Commando. 39 Mi-8. 2 UH-60A. 17 Hiller UH-12E. 24 AH-64A. 5 Westland Sea King. 5 E-2C Hawkeye.

EL SALVADOR

Air Force
8 Ouragan. 9 A-37B. 5 CM 170. 13 O-2A. 6 AC-47. 1 T-41A. 3 IAI-201. 1 DC-6. 2 C-123K. 8 C-47/Turbo-67. 3 Cessna 180/185. 2 Dornier Do 28. 2 Rallye 235GS. 1 Hughes 300C. 60 UH-1H/M. 6 Hughes 500/500M.

ETHIOPIA

Air Force
16 MiG-23BN. 15 MiG-21MF. 15 L-390ZO. 4 An-12. 1 Yak-40. 16 Mi-24. 21 Mi-8. 2 Mi-14.

Army Aviation
2 DHC-6. 2 UH-1H.

FINLAND

Air Force
64 F/A-18C/D*. 36 Saab 35S/FS. 9 Saab 35BS/CS. 15 MiG-21bis. 4 MiG-21UM. 54 Hawk 51/51A. 28 L-70. 3 Fokker F27. 3 Learjet 35. 6 PA-31-350 Cheiftain. 10 L-90. 8 PA-28 Arrow II/IV. 7 Mi-8. 2 Hughes 500D.

A Dassault Super Etendard returns to its carrier. Armed with the Exocet anti shipping missile, Argentine Super Etendards gained brief notoriety following their successful use against the Royal Navy in the 1982 Falklands War. France is the only other country to operate the type.

FRANCE
Air Force
140 Rafale B*. 95 Rafale C*. 18 Mirage IV-P. 34 Mirage F1C/C-200. 45 Mirage F1CR-200. 40 Mirage F1CT. 15 Mirage F1B. 145 Mirage 2000C/B. 50 Mirage 2000D. 68 Mirage 2000N. 108 Jaguar A/E. 4 E-3F. 130 Alpha Jet E. 70 CM 170. 139 Epsilon. 30 EMB-312. 46 CAP 10/230. 11 C-135FR. 2 A310-300. 4 DC-8-55/62CF/72. 48 Transall C-160/C-160NG. 6 Transall C-160NG (command post/ECM). 12 C-130H/H-30. 8 CN-235M. 3 Caravelle 11R. 25 Nord 262 Fregate. 10 DHC-6. 15 Falcon 20. 6 Falcon 50/900. 24 EMB-121. 30 MS-760 Paris. 10 Jodel D 140E. 5 PC-7. 5 AS 332C/L. 30 SA 330B/H. 3 SA 365N. 40 AS 355F-1/N Ecureuil/Fennec. 20 Alouette II/III.
Naval Aviation
19 F-8E(N). 78 Rafale*. 71 Super Etendard. 19 Etendard IVP/MP. 27 Alizé. 31 Atlantic I. 42 Atlantique ATL2. 5 Falcon 20H. 22 Nord 262. 16 CM 175. 8 MS-760. 10 CAP 10B. 15 Rallye 100S/100ST. 8 Falcon 10/10MER. 16 EMB-121. 12 PA-31. 2 Robin HR 100. 16 SA 321. 37 Lynx HAS.2(FN)/HAS.4 (FN). 4 SA 365F. 21 AS 350B. 33 Alouette III/III ASW. 8 Alouette II.
Army Aviation
133 SA 330B/H. 24 AS 332M. 157 SA 341M/F. 30 SA 342L1. 155 SA 342M. 10 AS 555. 56 SE 3160. 125 SE 3130/SA 318C. 2 Cessna F406. 2 Socata TBM 700. 5 Pilatus PC-6.

GABON
Air Force
9 Mirage V. 1 C-130H. 2 L-100-30. 1 EMB-110P. 1 EMB-111A. 2 NAMC YS-11A. 3 SA 330C/H. 5 SA 342L. 1 SA 316/319.
Presidential Guard
6 CM 170. 4 T-34C-1. 1 ATR 42F. 1 EMB-110P. 1 Falcon 900. 1 Gulfstream III. 1 SA 332L.

GERMANY
Air Force
151 F-4F. 237 Tornado IDS. 35 Tornado ECR. 24 MiG-29A/UB. 35 Alpha Jet. 85 C-160. 1 An-26. 3 A310. 4 Boeing 707-320. 2 Tu-154M. 7 CL-601. 3 VFW 614. 4 L 410UVP. 41 T-38A. 33 T-37B. 103 UH-1D. 6 Mi-8T/S. US based training units operate 7 F-4E, 41 T-38 and 33 T-37B.
Naval Aviation
64 Tornado IDS. 18 Atlantic 1. 2 Do 28. 1 228. 22 Sea King 41. 23 Sea Lynx 88.
Army Aviation
107 CH-53G. 175 UH-1D. 205 Bo 105P. 97 Bo 105M. 42 Alouette II.

GHANA
Air Force
4 MB-326K. 2 MB-339A. 11 L-29. 10 Bulldog 122/122A. 5 Fokker F27. 1 F28-3000. 1 C-212. 6 Skyvan 3M. 2 Bell 212. 4 SA 319. 2 Mi-2.

GREECE
Air Force
75 F-4E. 24 RF-4E. 40 Mirage 2000EG/BG. 80 F-16C/D*. 49 A-7H/TA-7H. 35 A-7E/TA-7C*. 92 F-104G/TF-104G. 90 F-5A/RF-5A/F-5B/NF-5A/NF-5B. 33 Mirage F1CG. 8 HU-16B Albatross. 1 C-130H. 6 NAMC YS-11A. 10 C-47. 14 CL-215. 47 T-33A. 19 Cessna T-41A. 31 T-37B/C. 35 T-2E. 23 G-164 Ag-cat. 27 PZL Dromader. 13 AB 205A. 2 AB 206A. 4 Bell 47G. 20 Nardi-Hughes 500. 3 Bell 212.
Army Aviation
12 UH-60*. 12 AH-64A. 10 CH-47C. 99 UH-1/AB-205A. 15 AB 206A. 1 Agusta A 109A. 26 Nardi-Hughes 300C. 4 Bell 47G. 20 Cessna U-17A (185). 1 King Air 200. 2 Commander 680.
Naval Aviation
12 AB 212ASW. 4 Alouette III.

GUATEMALA
Air Force
9 A-37B. 2 T-33A. 10 PC-7. 5 IAI-201. 6 C-47. 1 DC-6B. 3 F27. 8 Cessna 172/180/182. 5 Cessna 185/206. 1 Super King Air 200. 9 Bell 412/212. 9 UH-1D/H. 3 Bell 206L.

GUINEA REPUBLIC
Air Force
7 MiG-21. 3 MiG-17F. 2 MiG-15UTI. 3 L-29. 5 Yak-18. 2 An-12. 3 An-14. 1 SA 342K. 1 SA 330. 1 IAR 330. 1 SA 316B. 4 Mi-4.

GUINEA-BISSAU
Air Force
2 MiG-17F. 1 MiG-15UTI. 1 SA 318. 2 SA 319.

GUYANA
Air Corps
1 Skyvan 3M. 1 BN-2A. 1 Bell 412. 1 Bell 206B.

HAITI
Air Corps
6 0-2/337. 5 SF.260TP. 1 F33. 4 172/150. 3 C-47. 1 DHC-6 200. 1 BN-2A. 2 DHC-2. 2 Baron. 1 Cessna 402. Operational status of some of these aircraft unknown.

HONDURAS
Air Force
12 F-5E/F. 9 A-37B. 4 C-101B. 10 EMB-312. 6 T-41D. 2 C-130A. 6 C-47. 1 L-188A. 1 PA-31. 4 Cessna 180. 9 UH-1B/H. 9 412SP. 1 S-76.

HUNGARY
Air Force
27 MiG-29A/UB. 9/2 MiG-23MF/UB. 48 MiG-21. 13 Su-22M. 20 L-39Z. 7 An-26. 12 Yak-52. 3 L-410. 6+ Zlin 43. 32 Mi-24D/V. 6+ Mi-17/P. 20 Mi-8. 19 Mi-8S/T. 8 Mi-17/PP. 1 Mi-9. 28 Mi-2.

ICELAND
Coast Guard
1 F27-200. 1 AS 332L1. 1 SA-365N. 1 AS-350B.

INDIA
Air Force
10 MiG-33*. 56 MiG-29. 65 MiG-27M. 8 MiG-25R/U. 128 MiG-23MF/BN. 244 MiG-21PFMA/bis. 158 MiG-21FL/MF. 36 MiG-21U/UM. 46 Mirage 2000H/TH. 98 Jaguar IS/IB. 16 Jaguar IM. 66 Hunter F.56/T.66. 46 Canberra B(I).58/PR.57/T.54. 110 HPT-32. 19 HT-2. 222 Kiran 1/2. 38 TS-11. 3 Gulfstream III. 2 Learjet 29. 3 707-320C. 20 Il-76MD. 111 An-32. 60 HS.748. 2 737-200. 20 DHC-3. 42 Dornier 228. 98 Mi-8/Mi-17. 32 Mi-24/Mi-35. 10 Mi-26. 177 Alouette III. 156 Lama. 6 SA 365N.

Germany will retain its now elderly though updated F-4F Phantoms till well after the Eurofighter 2000 becomes operational in the 2002-2005 period. Most Luftwaffe Phantom interceptors are now equipped with a Hughes APG-65 radar (as on the F/A-18) and enhanced avionics, and can fire the AIM-120 Amraan AAM. The Phantom II first flew in 1958 and soldiers on in service with a number Japan, Israel, USA, Turkey, Greece, South Korea and Spain. (Luftwaffe)

Naval Aviation

23 Sea Harrier FRS.51. 4 Harrier T.60. 12 Kiran 1/2. 8 HPT-32. 14 BN-2A. 10 Tu-142M. 7 Alizé. 24 Dornier 228. 11 Sea King 42/42A. 19 Sea King 42B. 6 Sea King 42C. 8 Ka-27 Helix. 5 Ka-25. 22 Alouette III. 4 Hughes 269B.

Coast Guard

2 F27. 36 Dornier 228. 6 Alouette III.

INDONESIA
Air Force

12 F-16A/B. 14 F-5E/F. 27 A-4E/TA-4H. 12 OV-10F. 16 Hawk 53. 24 Hawk 100/200*. 24 T-34C. 39 AS 202. 3 737-2X9. 2 C-130H-MP. 2 KC-130B. 19 C-130B/H/H-30. 1 L-100-30. 7 F27-400M. 1 F28-1000. 1 Skyvan 3M. 7 C-47. 10 NC 212. 1 707-320C. 2 Jetstar 6. 32 CN-235. 6 DHC-3. 6 401/402. 7 T207/F33A. 11 T-41D. 6 Wilga 32. 7 AS 332. 13 SA 330. 2 204B. 12 BO 105C/CB. 1 S-61A. 12 S-58T. 2 206. 3 Alouette III. 12 Hughes 500C.

Naval Aviation

18 Nomad Searchmaster B/L. 6 PA-38. 6 CN-235. 8 NC-212. 4 HU-16B. 3 Commander 100. 25 AS 332L. 4 BO 105C. 9 Wasp HAS.1.

Army Aviation

4 NC-212. 2 C-47. 1 BN-2A. 1 310P. 2 Commander 680. 17 PZL Wilga 32. 4 O-1/185. 28 NB-412*. 16 205A-1. 21 BO 105C/CB. 9 Hughes 300C. 8 Soloy Bell 47G.

IRAN
Air Force

35 F-4D/E/RF-4E. 30 F-14A. 35 MiG-29. 24 Su-24. 44 F-5E/F. 9 T-33A. 25 EMB-312. 33 PC-7. 18 Beech F-33A/C. 25 Mushshak. 9 Boeing 747F. 48 C-130E/H. 18 F27. 4 Dornier 228. 2 Jetstar 2. 13 Mystère Falcon 20. 2 Aero Commander 690. 14 PC-6B. 44 Cessna 185/180/150. 30 CH-47. 60 AH-1J. 53 AB 214A. 40 AB 205. 10 AB 212.

Naval Aviation

4 F27-400M/600. 4 Falcon 20E. 7 Commander 500/690. 2 RG-53D. 7 AB 212AS. 15 AB 205. 10 AB 206.

Army Aviation

4 F27 400M/600. 2 Falcon 20E. 5 Commander 690. 10 Cessna O-2A. 6 Cessna 310. 23 Cessna 185. 11 AH-1J. 62 CH-47. 230 AB 214A. 12 AB 212. 21 AB 205A-1. 88 AB 206A/B. Operational status of some of these aircraft unknown.

IRAQ
Air Force

4 Tu-22. 1 Tu-16. 16 MiG-25. 14 MiG-29. 33 MiG-23MF/ML. 38 MiG-23/MiG-27. 140 MiG-21MF/bis/U/F-7. 50 Su-20/22. 8 Su-24. 28 Su-25. 33 Mirage F1EQ/BQ. 20 L-29. 26 L-39. 5 An-12. 10 SA 321. 16 SA 330. 40 SA 342L. 22 Alouette III. 33 Bell 214ST. 5 AS-61TS. 19 BK 117A/B. 55 MBB BO 105C. 28 Mi-24/Mi-25. 90 Mi-8/Mi-17. 15 Mi-6. 1 Adnan AEW. Operational status of some of these aircraft unknown.

IRELAND
Air Corps

6 CM 170. 7 SF.260. 6 FR172/K. 2 CASA CN-235N. 1 Beech SKA200. 1 Gulfstream IV. 5 SA 365N. 8 SA 316B. 2 SA 342L.

ISRAEL
Air Force

140 F-4E/2000. 38 F-15A/B. 28 F-15C/D. 11 F-16A/B. 148 F-16C/D. 150 Kfir C2/C7. 160 A-4M. 80 CM 170. 35 Piper PA-18 Super Cub. 4 E-2C. 13 707-320. 10 IAI-201. 3 KC-130H.

One of the most successful fighters of the modern era is the Lockheed Martin F-16 Fighting Falcon. With over 4000 sales to date the multirole fighter is operated by more than a dozen air arms and is likely to remain in production well into the next century. Pictured are F-16Cs of the Hellenic Air Force. (Greek MoD)

25 C-130E/H. 19 C-47. 4 Super King Air 200. 10 RU-21A/RC-12D King Air. 16 Queenair B80. 6 Dornier Do 28. 3 Seascan. 21 Cessna U206C. 42 AH-64A. 40 AH-1G/1S. 33 500MG. 36 CH-53. 55 Bell 212. 40 AB 206/206L. 2 HH-65A Dauphin.

ITALY
Air Force

24 Tornado ADV. 93 Tornado IDS. 138 F-104S. 24 RF-104. 20 TF-104G. 136 AMX. 93 MB-339A. 13 MB-339CD*. 60 MB-326. 38 SF.260AM. 18 Atlantic. 4 707-320. 12 C-130H. 31 G222. 6 G222VS/RM. 2 DC-9-32. 2 Gulfstream III. 4 Falcon 50. 20 PD-808RM/ECM. 10 P-166M. 6 P-166DL-3. 37 S.208M. 32 AS-61R (HH-3F). 2 SH-3D-TS. 38 AB 212/412. 10 NH-500E.

Naval Aviation

10 AV-8D. 2 TAV-8D. 10 EH 101*. 30 SH-3D/H. 64 AB 212ASW.

Army Aviation

60 A 129. 26 CH-47C. 16 AB 412. 24 AB 212. 93 AB 205A. 9 AB 204B. 23 A 109EOA. 4 A 109A. 134 AB 206A. 21 AB 47G/OH-13H Sioux. 8 Dornier 228-200. 40 SM 1019.

JAMAICA
Air Force

2 BN-2A. 1 King Air 100. 2 Cessna 210M. 4 Bell 205. 2 Bell 212. 4 Bell 206B.

JAPAN
Air Self Defence Force

111 F-4EJ. 20 RF-4E/EJ. 180 F-15J/DJ. 68 Mitsubishi F-1. 10 E-2C. 84 Mitsubishi T-2. 130 Kawasaki T-4. 40 T-33. 58 Fuji T-1A/B. 48 Fuji T-3. 28 Kawasaki C-1. 20 C-130H. 10 NAMC YS-11. 2 Boeing 747-400. 5 BAe 125-800. 9 Queenair A65. 29 MU-2J/S. 20 CH-47J. 30 KV-107. 10 UH-60J. 10 T-400.

Naval Aviation

98 P-3C. 9 P-2J. 4 EP-2J/UP-2J. 5 EP-3C/NP-3C. 10 US-1/1A. 10 NAMC YS-11T/M. 26 King Air TC-90/UC-90. 6 Queenair 65. 23 Fuji T-5 (KM-2D). 33 Fuji KM-2. 4 Learjet 36A. 9 MH-53E. 13 S-61A. 101 SH-3A/B. 42 SH-60J. 3 UH-60J. 2 KV-107-IIA. 10 OH-6D/J.

Army Aviation

16 MU-2. 2 Fuji TL-1. 77 AH-IF*. 31 CH-47J*. 55 KV-107-II. 3 AS 332L. 179 UH-1B/H*. 230 OH-6D/J*. 33 Hughes TH-55J.

The Sea King, in original Sikorsky SH-3 plus Westland and Agusta built forms, is one of the most widely used medium sized helicopters used today. This Agusta built example is operated by the Italian Navy.

JORDAN
Air Force
24 F-16A/B. 31 Mirage F1B/C/E. 68 F-5E/F. 15 C-101CC. 11 Bulldog 125/125A. 4 C-130H. 2 C 212. 2 CN-235. 1 TriStar 500. 23 AH-1G/1S. 3 UH-60A. 10 AS 332M-1. 8 MD 500MG. 1 Alouette III.

KENYA
Air Force
10 F-5E/F. 8 Hawk 52. 1 Strikemaster 87. 11 Shorts Tucano 51. 7 Bulldog 103/127. 6 DHC-5D. 3 DHC-8-100. 6 Dornier Do 28D. 1 PA-31-350 Chieftain. 20 SA 330/IAR-330. 18 Hughes 500MD/ME. 15 Hughes 500MD/M. 1 BO 105S. 1 SA 342K.

KUWAIT
Air Force
40 F/A-18C/D. 18 Mirage F1CK/BK. 18 A-4KU/TA-4KU. 6 Hawk 64. 15 Shorts Tucano. 2 L-100-30. 4 AS 332AF. 6 SA 330H. 20 SA 342K.

LAOS
Air Force
30 MiG-21PF. 7 C-47/AC-47. 3 C-123K. 7 An-24/An-26. 11 An-2. 2 Yak-40. 1 Mi-6. 9 Mi-8. 3 Sikorsky UH-34D Choctaw. Operational status of some of these aircraft unknown.

LATVIA
Air Force
12 An-2. 6 Mi-2. 2 L 410.

LEBANON
Air Force
3 Hunter F.70/T.66C. 5 CM 170. 4 Bulldog 126. 7 SA 330L. 5 SA 342L. 32 UH-1.

LESOTHO
Air Wing
2 C-212. 1 Cessna 182Q. 2 Bell 412SP/EP. 2 MBB BO 105CBS.

LIBERIA
Army Aviation
2 DHC-4. 4 IAI-101B. 1 Cessna Caravan 1. 3 Cessna 337G. 4 Cessna 185/172.

LIBYA
Air Force
61 MiG-25/U. 120 MiG-23/BN/U. 66 MiG-21bis. 50 Su-20/-22BM. 5 Su-24MK. 6 Tu-22. 28 Mirage F1A/E/B. 70 Mirage 5. 6 Mirage F1BD. 70 G-2A Galeb. 150 L-39. 20 SF.260W. 18 Il-76. 11 C-130H/L-100-30/L-100-20. 14 An-26. 16 G-222. 15 L 410UVP. 18 Mi-2. 60 Mi-24/Mi-35. 33 Mi-8/-17.
Army Aviation
10 O-1E. 11 CH-47C. 5 AB 206A. 30 SA 342. 10 Alouette III. 7 AB 47G.
Naval Aviation
5 SA 321. 24 Mi-14PL.

LITHUANIA
Air Force
3 Mi-8. 4 L-39. 2 L 410. 22 An-2. 1 An-24. 3 An-26.
National Defence Force
2 An-2. 1 Yak-18T. 18 Yak-52. 1 Yak-55. 1 PA-38A. 4 W-35A. 14 L-13. 3 Yak-16M. 2 Yak-12. 1 Jantar-Standart.

MACEDONIA (FYROM)
Defence Force
4 Mi-17.

MADAGASCAR
Air Force
7 MiG-21FL. 4 MiG-17F. 3 An-26. 2 C-212. 3 BN-2A. 1 PA-23. 1 Cessna 310R. 1 Cessna F337. 4 Cessna 172. 5 Mi-8.

MALAWI
Army Air Force
2 C-47. 2 Dornier 228. 1 Dornier Do 28D. 1 HS.125-800. 1 Beech King Air C90. 3 SA 330F. 1 SA 365N. 2 AS 350L-1. 1 SA 319.

MALAYSIA
Air Force
18 MiG-29SE. 8 F/A-18D*. 15 F-5E/F. 2 RF-5E. 27 Hawk 100/200. 11 MB-339A. 39 PC-7. 10 Bulldog 102. 3 C-130H-MP. 11 C-130H. 13 DHC-4A. 4 Beech King Air 200. 1 F28-1000. 1 Falcon 900. 9 Cessna 402B. 34 S-61A Nuri/AS 61N. 1 Agusta A 109C. 24 Alouette III. 7 Bell 47G.
Naval Aviation
6 Wasp HAS.1.

MALI REPUBLIC
Air Force
9 MiG-21. 4 MiG-17F. 1 MiG-15UTI. 6 L-29. 2 Yak-18. 4 Yak-11. 1 An-26. 2 An-24. 2 An-2. 1 Mi-8. 2 Mi-4.

MALTA
Armed Forces
3 AB 47G. 1 Bell 47G. 1 AB 206. 2 NH.500M. 5 Cessna L-19.

MAURITANIA
Air Force
6 BN-2A. 4 Cessna 337G. 2 PA-31 Cheyenne II. 2 DHC-5D. 1 Skyvan 3M. 1 Caravelle. 1 Gulfstream II. 1 Broussard. 1 AL-60. 4 Hughes 500M.

MAURITIUS
Air Arm
1 Dornier 228-101. 1 BN-2T. 3 SA 316B.

MEXICO
Air Force
9 F-5E/F. 39 AT-33A. 75 PC-7. 32 F33C/F-33F. 10 Musketeer. 15 CAP 10B. 10 C-130A. 8 C-47. 3 C-118 (DC-6). 12 IAI-201. 2 Skyvan. 3 727-100. 2 737-200. 1 757. 1 Jetstar 8. 2 Gulfstream III. 1 Citation I. 2 Sabreliner 60/75A. 5 King Air 90. 2 Merlin IV. 16 Commander 500S. 25 Bell 212. 1 Bell 205A-1. 10 MD 530F. 9 Bell 206. 5 AS 332L. 3 SA 350F. 4 Sikorsky Black Hawk. 4 PC-6. 14 Stearman PT-17. 10 Maule MXT-7-180. 6 Maule M-T-235
Naval Aviation
8 C-212-200. 10 F-33C Bonanza. 5 Cessna 152. 1 DHC-5D. 1 FH-227. 1 Learjet 24D. 1 King Air 90. 1 Commander 695. 2 Cessna 402. 9 B55 Baron. 1 Cessna 337G. 6 Cessna 152. 11 BO 105C/CB. 3 Alouette III. 2 MD 500E.

MOLDOLVA
Armed Forces
30 MiG-29. 8 Mi-8.

MONGOLIA
Air Force
11 MiG-21MF. 11 MiG-17F. 3 MiG-15UT1. 13 Yak-18. 7 An-24/An-26. 38 An-2. 3 PZL-104. 11 Mi-8.

MOROCCO
Air Force
20 F-16A/B. 27 Mirage F1CH/EH. 19 F-5E/F. 12 F-5A/B. 1 RF-5A. 4 OV-10A. 22 Alpha Jet. 23 CM 170. 12 T-34C. 10 AS-202A. 8 CAP 10B/230/231. 17 KC/C-130H. 1 Boeing 707. 7 CN-235M. 3 Dornier Do 28D. 3 Falcon 20. 1 Falcon 50. 2 Gulfstream II/III. 2 Citation V. 9 King Air A100/200C. 6 Broussard. 7 CH-47. 27 SA 330C. 44 AB 205A/212. 18 AB 206A/B. 24 SA 342L. 4 SA 319.

MOZAMBIQUE
Air Force
40 MiG-21. 5 An-26. 2 C-212. 1 Cessna 172. 2 Cessna 152. 3 PA-32. 4 Mi-24. 5 Mi-8.

MYANMAR (BURMA)
Armed Forces
33 F-7M/F-6*. 12 Super Galeb G-4. 22 PC-7/PC-9. 4 F27/FH-227. 1 C-212. 7 PC-6B. 1 Citation II. 5 Cessna 180. 11 Bell 205A-1. 7 HH-43B Huskie. 12 W-3 Sokol*. 10 SE 3160. Operational status of some of these aircraft unknown.

As aircraft become more complex and expensive to operate, air arms around the world are turning more and more to simulators to help maintain and improve aircrew currency. Ever more powerful computers, vastly improved software and greater affordability are all making military simulation an increasingly important aspect of modern day training regimes. (Paul Merritt)

NATO
E-3 Component
18 E-3A. 3 707-320.

NEPAL
Air Force
1 HS.748-2A. 2 Skyvan 3M. 1 DHC-6-300. 1 AS 332L. 2 SA 330C/G. 4 SA 316B.

NETHERLANDS
Air Force
183 F-16A/B. 10 PC-7. 2 KDC-10-30*. 2 C-130H-30. 4 Fokker 60*. 14 F27-100/-300M. 27 BO 105C. 48 Alouette III. 3 AB 412SP. 13 CH-47D*. 17 Cougar Mk2*.
Naval Aviation
13 P-3C. 1 Super King Air 200. 21 SH-14D Lynx.

NEW ZEALAND
Air Force
20 A-4K/TA-4K. 17 MB-339CB. 15 CT-4B Airtrainer. 6 P-3K. 5 C-130H. 2 727-100C. 9 Andover C.1. 13 UH-1H. 5 Wasp HAS 1. 5 Bell 47GB-2.

NICARAGUA
Air Force
4 L-39Z. 5 SF.260W. 3 Cessna 337. 4 An-26. 2 C-212A. 4 C-47. 6 An-2. 2 Commander 500/680. 10 Cessna 180/U-17/T-41. 19 Mi-8/Mi-17. 4 Mi-2. 2 Alouette III.

NIGER
Defence Force
2 C-130H. 1 Boeing 737-200. 2 Cessna F337. 1 Dornier Do 28D. 1 Dornier 228.

NIGERIA
Air Force
15 Jaguar SN/BN. 16 MiG-21. 4 MiG-21UTI. 19 Alpha Jet. 22 L-39MS. 12 MB-339AN. 8 C-130H/H-30. 5 G222. 3 Dornier 228. 17 Dornier 128-6. 2 SA 330. 4 AS 332. 15 BO 105C. 14 Hughes 300C.
Naval Aviation
2 Lynx Mk 89.

NORTH KOREA
Air Force
30 MiG-29. 50 MiG-23. 157 MiG-21PF/PFMA. 40 A-5. 128 Shenyang F-6. 176 Shenyang F-4. 30 Su-7BMK. 18 Su-25. 80 Harbin H-5 (Il-28). 10 MiG-21U. 38 Shenyang FT-2. 15 L-39. 114 CJ-5/CJ-6. 12 Yak-11. 207 Y-5. 12 An-24. 5 Il-14. 4 Il-18D. 3 Tu-154B. 1 Il-62M. 80 Hughes 300/500. 40 Mi-8/Mi-4. Operational status of some of these aircraft unknown.

NORWAY
Air Force
58 F-16A/B. 15 F-5A/B. 6 P-3C/N. 3 Falcon 20. 6 C-130H. 3 DHC-6 100/200. 17 Saab MFI-15 Safari. 10 Sea King Mk 43. 18 Bell 412SP. 5 Lynx 86.

OMAN
Air Force
22 Jaguar S/B. 18 Hunter FGA.73/T 67. 16 Hawk 200/100*. 11 Strikemaster 82/82A. 6 BN-2A. 3 C-130H. 1 CN-235. 1 Dornier 228. 15 Skyvan 3M. 3 BAC One-Eleven 475. 3 Mushshak. 10 Bell 214B/214ST. 19 AB 205A. 3 AB 212.

One of the most vital aspects of modern air combat is real time intelligence. An air arm without an airborne warning and control system (AWACS) simply won't be able to defend its airspace for long against a well trained foe who has this capability. Our photo depicts the radar plotting control centre aboard a Boeing E-3 Sentry, the most sophisticated AWACS platform in service and presently in the inventories of USAF, NATO, Saudi Arabia, France and Britain. (Boeing)

PAKISTAN
Air Force
38 F-16A/B. 94 F-7M/P. 53 Shenyang A-5 Fantan. 99 Shenyang F-6/FT-6. 16 Mirage IIIEP. 15 Mirage IIIRP/DP. 50 Mirage IIIO. 60 Mirage 5. 23 Shenyang FT-5. 6 Shenyang FT-2. 14 T-33A/RT-33A. 57 T-37B. 88 Mushshak. 16 K-8 Karakorum*. 3 P-3C. 4 Atlantic 1. 4 707-320. 12 C-130B/E/L-100-20. 1 F27. 1 Falcon 20E. 2 Travelair. 1 Commander 680. 1 Twin Bonanza. 2 PA-34. 4 Cessna 172N. 1 SA 330J. 4 HH-43B Huskie. 11 Alouette III. 7 SA 315B.
Naval Aviation
2 F27. 6 Sea King 45. 1 Maritime Defender. 4 Alouette III.
Army Aviation Corps
108 Mushshak. 40 O-1E. 2 Commander 840/SMA. 1 Cessna 421. 18 AH-1S. 35 SA 330J. 9 Mi-8. 14 Bell-205/UH-1H. 10 Bell-206. 22 Alouette III. 12 Bell 47G.

PANAMA
National Air Service
9 A-37B. 6 T-35D Pillan. 2 C-212. 1 CN-235. 1 BN-2A. 1 Piper Seneca I. 9 UH-1B/H. 6 Bell 212/UH-1N.

PAPUA NEW GUINEA
Defence Force
4 N22 Nomad. 2 CN-235. 4 UH-1H.

PARAGUAY
Air Force
9 EMB-326. 11 AT-6G Texan. 5 EMB-312. 13 T-35D Pillan. 5 T-25 Universal. 8 T-23 Uirapuru. 4 C-212. 1 Convair C-131D. 7 C-47. 1 DHC-6. 3 Cessna 421. 1 DHC-3. 3 UH-1B. 3 HB 350B. 1 Hiller UH-12. 4 Bell 47G.

PERU
Air Force
12 Mirage 2000P/DP. 16 Mirage V. 50 Su-20/22M/U. 19 Canberra B(I).68/B.52/B.56. 2 Canberra T.54. 25 A-37B. 13 MB-339AP. 28 EMB-312. 14 T-41D. 4 Cessna 150F. 1 707-320C. 8 L-100-20/30. 5 C-130A/D. 19 An-32. 13 DHC-5A. 18 DHC-6. 2 DC-8-62CF. 1 FH-227. 6 Y-12. 1 EMB-120. 1 F28-1000. 1 Falcon 20F. 4 Learjet 25B/36A. 3 King Air 90. 11 Queenair. 1 PA-31T. 1 Cessna 421. 12 PC-6B. 5 Cessna U206/185. 22 Mi-24. 6 Mi-6. 33 Mi-8/17. 2 Bell 412HP. 11 Bell 212. 5 Bell 214ST. 12 UH-1H. 23 BO 105C/L. 11 Bell 206B. 12 Bell 47G. 3 AS 350B. 2 Alouette III.
Naval Aviation
11 S-2E/G. 3 EMB-110. 6 T-34C. 2 C-130A. 4 C-47. 6 Super King Air 200/200C. 4 SH-3H. 6 AB 212ASW. 6 UH-1D. 2 Alouette III. 8 Bell 206B.
Army Aviation
1 Queenair. 1 Cessna 337. 5 U-10A Courier. 8 Cessna U-17A/150/206. 2 Mi-6. 27 Mi-8. 6 Alouette III. 8 SA 315B/Alouette II. 6 Bell 47G.

PHILIPPINES
Air Force
3 F-5A/B. 21 OV-10. 6 T-33A. 13 S.211. 37 SF.260M/W. 12 Cessna T-41D. 1 F27 MPA. 9 C-130H/L-100-20. 7 F27. 12 GAF N22. 6 BN-2A. 15 Cessna U-17B. 1 Cessna 210. 1 S-70A. 1 Bell 214. 2 Bell 412SP. 61 UH-1H. 5 Bell 205A-1. 15 Sikorsky S-76/AUH-76. 23 MD 520 Defender.
Naval Aviation
9 BN-2A. 2 BO 105C.
Operational status of some of these aircraft unknown.

POLAND
Air Force
11 MiG-29A/UB. 31 MiG-23MF/UM. 154 MiG-21PFM/M/MF. 68 MiG-21bis. 30 MiG-21R/RF. 20 MiG-21UM/US. 86 Su-20MK/22M. 14 Su-22U-3M. 50 I-22*. 97 TS-11. 47 PZL-130. 1 An-12B. 26 An-26. 4 An-28. 26 An-2. 6 Il-14. 2 Tu-154M. 3 Tu-134. 12 Yak-40. 17 PZL 104. 40 Mi-24D/W. 30 Mi-8/17. 2 Mi-6A. 100 Mi-2. 15 W-3*.

A Russian Air Force Sukhoi Su-24 Fencer waits in front of its hardened shelter. The breakup of the USSR has left the various CIS Republics with a large array of sophisticated equipment, however their operational readiness is debatable. In many instances the level of decline in aircraft availability and aircrew capability has rendered the majority of the region's air arms largely ineffective in practical terms. (Ivan Miliski)

Naval Aviation
3 TS-11. 3 An-28. 10 An-2. 15 Mi-14PL/PS. 5 Mi-2. 3 W-3.
Army Aviation
14 Mi-8/17. 8 Mi-2.

PORTUGAL
Air Force
20 F-16A/B. 29 A-7P/TA-7P. 40 Alpha Jet. 16 Epsilon. 11 Cessna FTB337G. 24 C-212. 6 C-130H-30. 6 P-3P. 4 Falcon 20/50. 18 SA 316 Alouette III. 10 SA 330C.
Naval Aviation
5 Lynx Mk 95.

QATAR
Air Force
12 Mirage 2000-5*. 6 Alpha Jet. 5 AS 332F. 12 Commando 2A/2C/3. 6 AS 332F. 13 SA 342L. 2 SA 341G.

ROMANIA
Air Force
12 MiG-29A/UB. 33 MiG-23MF/UM. 115 MiG-21. 190 IAR-93A/B. 14 H-5R (II-28). 33 L-39. 6 MiG-17F. 13 MiG-15bis/UTI. 30 L-29. 50 IAR-99. 40 IAR-823. 28 Yak-18. 10 IAR-28M. 16 An-24/An-26. 3 An-30. 2 II-18. 1 Tu-154. 2 Boeing 707-320. 4 C-130B*. 3 BN-2A. 10 An-2. 90 IAR-330. 7 Mi-8. 6 Mi-2. 99 IAR 316. 12 IAR 317.

RUSSIA
Air Force
12 Tu-160. 100 Tu-22M. 90 Tu-95. 150+ Su-27. 430 MiG-29. 85 MiG-25. 400 MiG-23. 30 MiG-31. ? MiG-33*. ? Su-30*. ? Su-35*. 12 Su-32FN/Su-34*. 560 Su-24. 170 Su-17. 210 Su-25. 400 MiG-27. ? L-20. 1000+ L-39. 300 II-76. 10 II-78M. ? An-12. ? An-26. 50 An-32. ? An-70*. 20 An-72. 7+ An-124. Tu-134, Tu-154 and II-62 used in small numbers for VIP transport.
Air Defence Force
200+ Su-27. 200+ MiG-31. 200+ MiG-25PD.

600+ MiG-23P/MiG-23PLD. 15 A-50. 10 Tu-126. Unknown number of An-12 and An-24 transports.
Naval Aviation
160 Tu-22M. 70 Tu-95/142. 400 Tu-16. 20 Tu-22R. 20 Su-33. 55 Su-25. 120 Su-24. 35 Su-17. 45 MiG-29. 40 MiG-27. 50 II-38. 25 Be-12. 20 A-40 Albatross*. Approx 500 helicopters including 65 Mi-14, Ka-25, Ka-27, 30+ Ka-29.
Army Aviation
10 Ka-50. 2000+ Mi-8/Mi-17. 1200+ Mi-24. ? Mi-6. 60 Mi-26. ? Mi-28FN. ? Mi-2. ? Mi-40*. ? An-2.
Border Guards
? Mi-24. 6 An-72P. 15* SM-92 Finist.

RWANDA
Air Force
2 Rallye 235. 1 N-2501 Noratlas. 2 BN-2. 5 SA 342L. 5 SA 316. Operational status of these aircraft unknown.

SAUDI ARABIA
Air Force
72 F-15S*. 92 F-15C/D. 24 Tornado ADV. 48 Tornado IDS*. 80 F-5E/F. 10 RF-5E. 13 F-5B. 5 E-3A. 8 KE-3A. 29 Hawk. 30 PC-9. 35 BAC Strikemaster 80/80A. 13 Cessna 172G/H/M. 1 Jetstream 31. 8 KC-130H. 28 C-130E/H. 2 VC-130H. 2 C-130H. 4 CN-235. 3 Boeing 747SP. 1 Boeing 737-200. 1 Lockheed TriStar. 4 BAe 146. 1 Gulfstream III. 4 HS 125-800. 3 Learjet 25/35A. 1 Super King Air 200. 1 Cessna 310. 17 KV-107-II. 3 AS 61A. 47 AB 205A/212. 26 AB 206A.
Army Aviation
12 AH-64A. 21 S-70A/UH-60L. 6 SA 365N. 15 Bell 406CS.

SENEGAMBIA
Air Force
4 CM 170. 3 Rallye 235. 4 Rallye 160ST/235A. 5 F27-400M. 1 Boeing 727-200. 1 EMB-111P. 2 MH-1512 Broussard. 1 PA-23 Aztec. 2 SA 330F. 1 SA 341H. 1 SA 318C.

SEYCHELLES
Coast Guard – Air Wing
1 BN-2A. 1 Caravan II. 1 Cessna 152.

SINGAPORE
Air Force
6 F-16A/B. 42 F-5E/F. 6 RF-5E. 70 A-4S/S-U. 4 Fokker 50 Enforcer 2. 4 E-2C. 6 CH-47D*. 10 C-130B/H/H-30. 6 Skyvan 3M. 20 AS 332B/M. 40 UH-1B/H. 4 AB 205A/A-1. 20 AS 550C-2/U-2. 15 TA-4S/S-1. 29 S.211. 26 SF.260M/W. 6 AS 350E.

SLOVAK REPUBLIC
Air Force
24 MiG-29A/UB. 39 MiG-21MF. 8 MiG-21R. 13 MiG-21US/UM. 22 Su-25K/UBK. 20 Su-22M-4/U. 17 Mi-24. 24 Mi-8/17. 17 Mi-2. 9 L 410M/T/UVP. 20 L-39. 16 L-29. 4 An-24. 1 An-12. 1 Tu-154B.

SLOVENIA
Air Force
3 Bell 412ER. 1 A 109A 3 Zlin 242L. 3 UTVA 75. 1 Let L 410VP-E.

The British Aerospace Hawk is one of the most successful trainers on the international market and should remain in production for many years to come. Pictured are Saudi Hawk 60s. (BAe)

SOMALIA
Aeronautical Corps
8 MiG-21. 20 Shenyang F-6. 7 Hunter FGA.76. 1 Hunter FR.76A. 1 Hunter T.77. 8 MiG-17F. 2 MiG-15UTI. 4 SF.260W. 11 Yak-11. 2 Cessna FRA150L. 3 An-24/An-26. 1 G222. 3 BN-2A. 4 Piaggio P.166DL. 2 Cessna 150M/185A. 4 AB 204B/AB 212. Nominal strength only. Most of these aircraft are not operational.

SOUTH AFRICA
Air Force
22 Mirage F1AZ. 2 Mirage F1CZ. 1 Mirage IIICZ. 16 Atlas Cheetah. 19 Atlas Impala II. 30 Atlas Impala I. 5 Boeing 707-320. 7 C-130B/E. 8 C-160. 38 C-47/Turbo Dak. 3 Falcon 900. 4 HS.125-400B. 3 BN-2A. 5 Beech Super King Air 200. 29 Cessna 185A/D/E. 12 Cessna 208. 3 Cessna Citation II. 3 C-212-200. 1 CN-235. 1 Shorts Skyvan SC-7. 63 PC-7 Mk II Astra. 1 Dauphin. 49 Atlas Oryx. 3 Atlas Gemsbok/AS 532. 15 Atlas CSH-2. 9 MBB BK 117A-1/3. 20 SA 330H/L. 49 SE 3160B Alouette III.

SOUTH KOREA
Air Force
64 F-4D. 58 F-4E. 120 F-16C/D*. 39 F-16A/B. 20 Hawk Mk 60. 17 RF-4C. 197 F-5E/F. 47 F-5A/B. 27 A-37B. 38 T-33A. 42 T-37C. 20 T-28D. 20 T-41B. 11 Cessna O-2A. 12 CN-235. 10 C-130H-30. 13 C-123J/K. 9 C-46F. 10 C-54D. 1 C-118A. 2 HS.748. 1 Boeing 737. 2 Commander 520/560F. 5 DHC-2 Beaver. 26 O-1A/E. 3 AS 332L. 3 Bell 412. 7 Bell 212/UH-1N. 5 UH-1D/H.
Army Aviation
49 AH-1J/S/F. 17 CH-47D. 80 UH-60P. 60 UH-1B/H. 249 MD 500MD/TOW. 5 Kawasaki KH-4 (Bell 47G). 11 DHC-2 Beaver. 13 O-1A.
Naval Aviation
8 P-3C. 24 S-2A/E. 12 Lynx 99. 29 MD 500M/ASW. 11 Alouette III. 2 Bell 206B.

SPAIN
Air Force
71 EF-18A/B. 24 F/A-18A*. 8 RF-4C. 53 Mirage F-1C/E/B. 33 F-5A/B/RF. 7 P-3A/B. 3 F27-400 Maritime. 80 C-101B. 36 T-35C. 24 F-33A/Bonanza. 5 B55 Baron. 3 Boeing 707-320. 5 KC-130H. 7 C-130H/H-30. 18 CN-235. 74 C-212. 21 CL-215T. 5 Falcon 20. 3 Falcon 50. 17 Hughes 269 C/TH-55. 7 Sikorsky S-76. 5 SA 330. 16 AS 332. 2 Cessna Citation IV.
Naval Aviation
10 EAV-8B. 9 AV-8S/TAV-8S. 3 Cessna Citation II. 11 SH-3H. 6 SH-60B. 10 AB 212. 10 Hughes 500M.
Army Aviation
58 UH-1H. 68 BO 105. 6 AB 212. 17 AS 332. 18 CH-47. 17 OH-58A.

SRI LANKA
Air Force
4 FT-7. 1 FT-5. 9 SF.260. 3 Cessna 337. 5 Cessna 150. 3 HS.748. 1 An-32. 7 Y-12. 2 Y-8. 1 Beech Super King Air 200. 1 Cessna 421C. 14 Bell 212/412. 6 Bell 206B. 6 IA 58. 3 Mi-17. Numbers may have been affected by ongoing guerilla activity.

One of Russia's best chances of selling its formidable military technology abroad lies with the formidable MiG-29 'Fulcrum'. This example is operated by the Slovak Air Force. (Paul Merritt)

SUDAN
Air Force
9 F-5E/F. 3 MiG-23. 7 MiG-21PF. 16 Shenyang F-6. 7 Shenyang F-5/FT-5. 3 Jet Provost Mk 55. 3 Strikemaster. 3 MiG-15UTI. 4 MiG-21UTI. 5 C-130H. 5 An-24. 3 DHC-5D. 5 C-212. 1 F27-100. 6 EMB-110P. 2 Falcon 20. 8 IAR 330 Puma. 10 AB 412. 2 Mi-24. 5 Mi-8. 4 Mi-4.

SURINAM
Air Force
1 PC-7. 2 BN-2B 1 Cessna TU206G. 1 Bell 205. 1 Alouette III.

SWEDEN
Air Force
126 JAS 39*. 14 JAS 39B*. 136 JA 37. 82 AJS/AJ 37. 47 SF/SH 37. 62 J 35J. 11 Sk 35C. 22 J 32B/D/E. 133 Sk 60. 60 Sk 61 (Bulldog). 8 C-130E/H. 2 Tp 86 Sabreliner. 1 Tp 100 (Saab 340). 3 Tp 101 (King Air). 11 AS 332M-1. 3 Gulfstream 4. 12 Saab 340/FSR 890.
Naval Aviation
1 C-212. 3 PA-31 Cheiftain. 14 BV 107/KV-107. 10 AB 206B.
Army Air Corps
16 AB 204B. 20 BO 105CB. 18 AB 206A. 25 Hughes 300C.

SWITZERLAND
Air Force
34 F/A-18C/D*. 100 F-5E/F. 47 Mirage III/S/RS. 4 Mirage III/BS. 18 Hawk 100. 38 PC-7. 12 PC-9. 2 Learjet 36. 18 PC-6B. 2 Dornier Do 27. 15 AS 332M-1. 69 Alouette III.

SYRIA
Air Force
37 MiG-29A/UB. 33 MiG-25/25R/25U. 94 MiG-23ML/MS. 60 MiG-23BN/UM. 235 MiG-21. 20 Su-24MK. 68 Su-20/22BKL. 35 MiG-17F. 35 MiG-15UTI. 97 L-39. 60 L-29. 46 Flamingo. 6 Mushshak. 2 Il-76T. 4 An-26. 1 An-24. 5 Il-14. 4 Il-18B. 2 Yak-40. 2 Falcon 20. 2 PA-31 Navajo. 35 Mi-24. 110 Mi-8/17. 10 Mi-6. 8 Mi-2. 56 SA 342.
Naval Aviation
2 Mi-14. 5 Ka-25.

TAIWAN
Air Force
120 A-1 Ching-Kuo*. 150 F-16A/B*. 60 Mirage 2000-5*. 290 F-5E/G. 35 F-5A/B. 94 F-104G/RF-104G. 39 F-104D/TF-104G. 21 T-38A. 59 AT-3/3B. 43 T-34C. 44 T-CH-1B. 4 E-2B. 12 C-130H. 40 C-119G Packet. 9 C-123. 1 DC-6B. 9 C-47. 11 Beech 1900C-1. 5 720B/727-100. 14 S-70C. 57 UH-1H. 6 OH-6A. 10 Bell 47G/OH-13.
Army Aviation
3 BV-234. 59 UH-1H. 8 AH-1W. 7 CH-34 Choctaw. 13 O-1.
Naval Aviation
32 S-2E/F. 20 S-70B. 11 MD 500MD/ASW.

TANZANIA
Defence Force
11 J-7. 10 J-6. 2 J-5. 2 MiG-15UTI. 5 PA-28 Cherokke. 4 DHC-5D. 3 HS.748. 1 Y-7. 9 Cessna 404/310. 1 Cessna 206. 2 F28. 1 BAe 125-700B. 4 AB 205B. 6 Bell 206. Operational status of some of these aircraft unknown.

THAILAND
Air Force
36 F-16A/B. 43 F-5E/F. 10 F-5A/B. 4 Northrop RF-5A. 11 A-37B. 27 OV-10C. 6 AC-47. 25 AU-23. 35 T-33A/RT-33A. 15 T-37B/C. 47 Fantrainer 400/600. 20 PC-9. 12 SF.260MT. 24 CT-4A. 10 DHC-1. 12+ H-36. 8 C-130H/H-30. 6 G222. 10 C-123B/K. 8 HS.748. 15 C-47. 3 CASA C-212. 22 N22B. 3 IAI-201. 1 A310-300. 1 Boeing 737-300. 3 Learjet 35A. 3 Merlin IVA. 2 Beech King Air 200. 1 Commander 690. 6 Cessna T-41D. 30 Cessna O-1. 6 Grob G 109. 16 Sikorsky S-58T. 25 Bell UH-1H. 4 Bell 212/412. 3 AS 332L2*.
Naval Aviation
18 A-7E/TA-7E*. 8 AV-8S/TAV-8S*. 2 P-3T. 1 UP-3T. 6 S-2F/US-2C. 3 F27. 2 F27 400M. 3 Dornier 228. 2 CL-215. 9 Summit Sentry O-2-337. 5 N24A Searchmaster. 3+ U-17A/B. 3+ O-1A/E. 4 214ST. 8 212ASW. 4 UH-1H.
Army Aviation
4 Shorts 330UTT. 1 King Air 200. 1 PA-31T Cheyenne. 1 Beech 99. 23 T-41A. 65+ O-1. 4 AH-1F. 3 BV-234 Chinook. 4 Bell 214B. 2 Bell 214ST. 34 212. 5+ UH-1B/D/H. 14 Bell 206A/B. 68+ Hughes 269/300C. 10+ 47G/OH-13. 1 C-47. 2 DHC-4. 3 Skyvan 3M. 4 PC-6B. 5 AU-23. 3 Dornier 28D. 2 Cessna 310. 1 CT-4A. 2 Bell 214. 26 Bell 205/212/412. 8 Bell 206B.

TOGO
Air Force
5 Alpha Jet. 4 EMB-326G. 3 Epsilon. 4 CM 170. 2 DHC-5D. 1 Boeing 707-320B. 1 F28 3000. 2 Beech 58 Baron. 2 Reims-Cessna F337. 1 Dornier Do 27A-4. 1 AS 332L. 1 SA 330. 2 SA 315B. 1 SA 319. Operational status of some of these aircraft unknown.

Spain's CASA has had considerable success in placing its CN-235 turboprop with a large number of operators (such as Turkey, pictured) looking for a rugged STOL airlifter in the C-123 class. The aircraft is also available in a specialised maritime patrol/surveillance version in addition to being a regional airliner of note. (CASA)

TUNISIA
Air Force
15 F-5E/F. 10 MB-326B/K/L. 18 SF.260C/W. 2 C-130H. 12 L-59T*. 2 SIAI Marchetti S.208A. 15 AB-205A. 4 UH-1N/H. 5 SA 341. 6 SA 313. 6 AS 350B. 1 AS 365. 3 SA 316.

TURKEY
Air Force
165 F-4E. 8 RF-4E. 240 F-16C/D. 21 F-104S. 150+ F-104G/CF-104. 23+ TF-104G/CF-104D. 6 RF-104G. 135+ F-5A/B. 20 RF-5A. 33 S-2A/E. 20 T-38A. 75+ T-33A. 12 T-37B/C. 40 SF.260D. 20+ T-41D. 2 KC-135A*. 7 KC-135R*. 9 C-130B/E. 20 C-160. 40+ C-47. 52 CN-235M. 3 Viscount 700. 4 Citation II. 2 BN-2A. 50+ UH-1H. 5 UH-19.
Army Aviation
40 Citabria 150S. 15 T-42A Baron. 19 Do 28D Skyservant. 1 DHC-2 Beaver. 5 Do 27A. 1 PA-32 Cherokee Six. 28+ Bell 206. 50+ O-1. 10+ PA-18 Super Cub. 12 AH-1W. 185+ AB 205A/UH-1H. 23 AB 204B/212. 20 AS 532UL. 24 AB 206A. 30 Hughes 300C. 15+ AB 47G. 92 S-70A Black Hawk*. 28 AB 212/205A/204B1. 15+ AB 206A.
Naval Aviation
16 AB 212ASW. 3 AB 204AS.

UGANDA
Army Air Force & Police Air Wing
4 MiG-17F. 1 AS-202 Bravo. 1 L-100. 2 Mi-8. 1 Gulfstream II. 3 Aero L-39. 5 SF.260. 4 AB 412. 3 Bell 212/412. 3 Bell 206. 1 DHC-6. 1 DHC-4. 1 DHC-2 Beaver. 4 Bell 212. 2 Bell 206B. Operational status of some of these aircraft unknown.

UKRAINE
Air Force
19 Tu-160. 30 Tu-22M. 28 Tu-95. 90 Su-27. 120 MiG-29. 250 Su-24. 120 Su-17. 30 Il-78M. Plus Il-76 and An-26 and other transport types as well as helicopters (300 combat helicopters allowed under CFE treaty).

UNITED ARAB EMIRATES
Abu Dhabi
35 Mirage 2000E/R/D. 29 Mirage VAD/RAD/DAD. 34 Hawk 63A/100. 23 PC-7. 4 C-130H. 5 DHC-5D. 4 C-212. 1 BN-2A. 10 AS 332F/L. 11 SA 330. 1 AS 350. 20 AH-64. 11 SA 342. 7 Alouette III. 1 AB-206B.

Dubai
5 MB-326KD/LD. 5 MB-339A. 8 Hawk 61. 5 SF.260TP. 2 L-100-30. 1 G222. 1 BN-2T. 2 PC-6B. 1 182. 8 Bell 212/214B. 6 Bell 205A. 5 206B/AB-206A. 1 206L. 6 BO 105S.

UNITED KINGDOM
Air Force
227 Tornado GR.1/GR.1A/GR.1B. 3 Tornado F.2/F.2T. 173 Tornado F.3. 54 Jaguar GR.1/T.2. 13 Harrier T.4. 106 Harrier GR.7/T.10. 26 Nimrod MR.2. 2 Nimrod MR.1P. 7 Sentry AEW.1. 9 Canberra PR.9/T.4/E.15. 9 TriStar K.1/KC.1/K.2. 14 VC10 K.2/K.3/K.4. 13 VC10 C.1/C.1K. 5 Hercules C.1K. 24 Hercules C.1/C.1P. 30 Hercules C.3. 3 BAe 146 C.2. 8 HS.125 CC.2/CC.3. 2 Islander CC.2. 47 Chinook HC.1/2. 41 Puma HC.1. 25 Sea King HAR.3/3A. 62 Wessex HC.2. 2 Wessex HCC.4. 30 Gazelle HT.3/HCC 4. 116 Bulldog T.1. 73 Chipmunk T.10. 164 Hawk T.1/T.1A. 20 Dominie T.1. 11 Jetstream T.1. 130 Tucano T.1.
Naval Fleet Air Arm
20 Sea Harrier FRS.1/2. 4 Harrier T.4/T.8. 51 Sea King HAS 5/6. 8 Sea King AEW.2. 29 Sea King HC.4. 9 Lynx HAS.3/8. 17 Gazelle HT.2/3. 15 Jetstream T.2/3. 5 Canberra TT.18. 6 Hawk. 9 Hunter T.7/8.
Army Air Corps
108 Lynx AH.1/7. 24 Lynx AH.9. 164 Gazelle AH.1. 7 Islander AL.1. 21 Chipmunk T.10. 4 A 109A.

USA
Air Force
230 A-10/OA-10. 84 B-1B. 20 B-2A*. 85 B-52H. 82 C-5A/B. C-9 23. 72 C-12. 40 C-17*. 78 C-21. 3 C-23. 9 C-27. 330 C-130E/H/AC-130/EC-130/HC-130/N/P. 320 C-135/EC-135/KC-135/NKC-135/RC-135. 8 C-137/EC-137. 194 C-141/NC-141. 34 E-3. 2 E-4. 2 E-8. 2 E-9. 9 EC-18/E-18. 650 F-15/F-15E. 790 F-16. 144 F-111/EF-111A. 57 F-117/YF-117. 85 HH-1/UH-1. 6 HH-3. 49 H-53/MH-53. 54 HH-60/M/HH-60G/UH-60. 87 T-1A. 24 T-3. 1 T-33. 490 T-37. 500 T-38/AT-38. 6 T-39. 50 T-41. 12 T-43/CT-43. 1 U-26. 2 UV-18.
Air Force Reserve
44 A/OA-10. 10 AC-130A. 9 B-52H. 110 C-130E/H. 36 C-141B. 33 C-5A. 120 F-16A/B/C/D. 10 HC-130N/P. 25 HH-60G. 60 KC-135E/R. 10 WC-130H.
Air National Guard
60 RF-4/F-4G. 105 A-10. 11 B-1B. 12 C-5. 6 C-12. 215 C-130. 16 C-141. 4 C-21. 4 C-22. 34 C-26. 140 F-15. 740 F-16. 21 HH-60. 225 KC-135. 2 T-43.
Navy
136 A-6E. 17 C-130F/T. 7 C-20D/G. 2 C-28A. 38 C-2A. 27 C-9. 28 CH-46D. 17 CH-46E. 39 CH-53E. 7 CT-39E/G. 3 DC-130A. 94 E-2C. 16 E-6A. 2 EA-3B. 128 EA-6B. 2 EA-7L. 1 EC-24A. 10 EP-3E/J. 3 ERA-3B. 15 ES-3A. 380 F-14A/B/D. 11 F-16N. 3 TF-16N. 23 F-5E/F. 524 F/A-18A/B/C/D. 43 HH-1N. 43 HH-46D. 24 HH-60H. 11 KC-130. 7 LC-130F/R. 45 MH-53E. 4 OH-58A. 6 OH-6B. 3 OV-10A. 290 P-3A/B/C. 4 RC-12F/M. 19 RH-53D. 1 RP-3A. 130 S-3A/B. 26 SH-2F/G. 50 SH-3D/G/H. 230 SH-60B/F. 130 T-2C. 320 T-34C. 8 T-38A. 1 T-39D. 56 T-44A. 30 T-45A. 2 TA-3B. 125 TA-4J. 5 TA-7C. 20 TAV-8B. 2 TC-130G/Q. TC-4C. 1 TE-2C. 90 TH-57B/C. 11 TP-3A. 3 U-21A. 2 U-6A. 62 UC-12B/F/M. 50 UH-3A/H. 13 UH-46D. 3 UH-60A. 10 UP-3A/B. 5 US-3A. 4 VH-3A. 5 VP-3A. This listing does not include stored, experimental, evaluation or test aircraft.
Marine Corps
185 AH-1W. 140 AV-8B. 26 AV-8B/TAV-8B. C-9B. 56 CH-53D. 96 CH-53E. 22 CH-53D/E. 220 CH-46E. 3 CT-39A/D/G. 168 F/A-18A/C. 72 F/A-18D Night Attack. 30 F/A-18A/C/D. 13 F-5E/F. 60 KC-130F/R/T. 8 KC-130F/R/T. 18 UC-12B/F. 100 UH-1N. 11 VH-3D. 8 VH-60N.

The Harrier GR.7 forms an important part of Britain's ground attack force. (BAe)

Army Aviation

590 AH-64A. 430 AH-1E/F/G/P/S. 2 EH-1. 881 OH-58A/C. 290 OH-58D. 1 OH-6A. 60+ AH-6C/G/MH-6B/E/H. 930 UH-60A/L. 60 EH-60A. 46 MH-60K. 1200 UH-1B/H/V. 331 CH-47C/D. 56 OV-1D. 3 RV-1D. 2 F27-400. 108 C-12*. 30 RC-12D/H/K. 50 U-21A/F/G/H. 20 RU-21B/C/D/H. 157 TH-67A*.

Army National Guard

27 C-12. 8 RU-21. 14 T-42A. 6 UV-18A Twin Otter. 48 U-8F Seminole. 60 U-21. 490 AH-1E/F/G/P/S. 160 AH-64A. 45 CH-54 Tarhe. 220 OH-6A. 630 OH-58A. 170 UH-60.

URAGUAY
Air Force

11 A-37B. 7 T-33A. 4 IA-58B. 4 EMB-110. 3 CASA C-212. 1 F27. 3 C-130B. 2 Cessna 182. 8 Queenair. 5 U-17. 11 T-34A/B. 5 T-41D. 5 PC-7U. 2 Bell 212. 3 UH-1H.

Naval Aviation

1 PA-34-200T. 1 Cessna 182 Skylane. 6 S-2A/G. 1 Beech Super King Air 200T. 2 PA-18. 2 T-28S Fennec (Trojan). 2 T-34B. 2 T-34C. 1 Wessex 60. 1 Bell 47G. 1 Bell 222. 2 CH-34.

VENEZUELA
Air Force

24 F-16A/B. 16 CF-5A/D. 6 NF-5A. 15 Mirage 50EV/DV. 22 OV-10E. 19 T-2D. 30 EMB-312. 13 T-34A. 5 C-130H. 8 G222. 1 707-320C. 1 737-200. 1 DC-9-15. 3 Gulfstream II/III/IV. 3 Falcon 20D. 2 Learjet 24D. 4 Citation I/II. 4 Super King Air 200. 7 Queenair. 1 PA-31 Navajo. 2 Beech TravelAir. 11 Cessna 182N. 8 AS 332M-1. 4 412/214ST. 1 212. 15 UH-1D. 15 Alouette III.

Naval Aviation

1 Dash 7. 4 C-212-200AS. 1 King Air 90. 1 402C. 2 310R. 1 PA-23 Aztec. 2 Bell 412. 12 AB 212ASW.

Army Aviation

4 IAI-201. 1 Super King Air 200. 1 Queenair. 1 BN-2A. 7 U206G/182. 4 AS-61A. 11 UH-1H/205A. 2 206B/L. 6 A 109A.

VIETNAM
Army Air Force

8 MiG-23ML/UM. 160 MiG-21PF/bis. 77 MiG-17F. 73 Su-22BKL. 30 Su-17. 18 F-5A/B/E/RF-5A. 5 A-37B. 12 Be-12. 14 MiG-15UTI. 25 L-39. 33 Yak-11/18. 40 An-26. 8 An-24. 12 Il-14. 2 Il-18. 24 Li-2/C-47. 20 An-2. 11 Yak-40. 5 C-130A/B. 30 Mi-24. 16 Ka-25. 66 Mi-8. 10 Mi-6. 36 Mi-4. Operational status of some of these aircraft unknown.

YEMEN
Air Force

22 MiG-23BN. 29 MiG-21. 14 F-5E/B. 44 MiG-17F. 57 Su-22BKL/M-2/U. 4 MiG-15UTI. 18 Yak-11. 2 C-130H. 1 An-12B. 13 An-24/26. 8 Il-14. 14 Mi-24. 56 Mi-8. 6 AB 212. 2 AB 204B. 5 Mi-4. 5 AB 206B. Operational status of some of these aircraft unknown.

FEDERAL REPUBLIC OF YUGOSLAVIA
Air Force

15 MiG-29A/B. 55 MiG-21. 24 J-1. 44 G-4M. 65 J-22. 40 Mi-8/-17. 65 SA 342. 5 Ka-25. 3 Ka-27. 13 Mi-14. 12 An-12. 6 An-26. 4 Il-18. 6 Yak-40. 35 UTVA-75. 2 Boeing 707-320C. 2 Falcon 50. 14 Pilatus PC-6. Operational status of some of these aircraft unknown.

ZAIRE
Air Force

14 MB-326GB/K. 19 Reims F337. 9 SF.260MZ. 11 Cessna 150. 4 C-130H. 3 DHC-5D. 7 C-47. 1 BN-2A. 1 MU-2J. 11 Cessna 310R. 1 AS 332. 8 SA 330. 7 Alouette III. 6 47G. Operational status of some of these aircraft unknown.

ZAMBIA
Air Force

11 MiG-21MF. 11 Shenyang F-6. 16 MB-326GB. 12 Galeb G-2. SF.260MZ. 2 MiG-21U. 2 FT-5. 5 C-47. 4 An-26. 2 DC-6B. 3 DHC-4. 4 DHC-5D. 6 Dornier Do 28. 1 HS.748. 3 Yak-40. 11 Mi-8. 9 AB 205A/AB 212. 12 AB 47G. Operational status of some of these aircraft unknown.

ZIMBABWE
Air Force

12 F-7. 1 FT-7. 12 Hunter FGA.9. 12 Hawk 60/60A. 15 Reims-Cessna C337G. 29 SF.260M/W/TP. 10 C-47. 11 C-212. 6 PBN-2A. 2 AS 532UL. 10 AB 412. 2 AB 205. 24 SA 319.

The incredibly expensive Northrop Grumman B-2 Spirit 'stealth bomber'. At around a billion US dollars a copy it is not surprising that the USAF has been able to only afford 20 of these awesome long range strike aircraft. (Northrop Grumman)

GLOSSARY OF TERMS AND ACRONYMS

AAA – Anti aircraft artillery.

AAC – Army Air Corps (UK).

AAM – Air-to-air missile.

ABM – Anti ballistic missile. A missile capable of destroying hostile ballistic missiles or their payloads before they impact on their target.

ACC – Air Combat Command (USAF).

ACM – Air combat manoeuvring.

ACMI – Air combat manoeuvring instrumentation.

ACMR – Air combat manoeuvring range.

ADF – Australian Defence Force.

ADIZ – Air defence identification zone.

AEW – Airborne early warning.

AEW&C – Airborne early warning and control.

AF – Air force.

AFB – Air force base (US).

AFMC – Air Force Materiel Command (USAF).

ALBM – Air launched ballistic missile.

ALCM – Air launched cruise missile.

AMC – Air Mobility Command (USAF).

Amraam – Advanced medium range air-to-air missile, the Hughes AIM-120.

ANG – Air National Guard (USA).

APU – Auxiliary power unit.

ARM – Anti Radiation missile.

ASM – Air-to-surface missile.

ASPJ – Airborne self protection jammer.

Asraam – Advanced short range air-to-air missile. An IR guided missile under development by BAe.

AST – Air staff target.

ASTOVL – Advanced short takeoff and vertical landing

ASV – Anti surface vessel.

ASW – Anti submarine warfare. All measures designed to reduce or nullify the effectiveness of hostile submarines.

ASuW – Anti surface warfare.

ATBM – Anti tactical ballistic missile.

AUW – All up weight.

AWACS – Airborne Warning and Control System. In particular refers to Boeing E-3 Sentry.

BAe – British Aerospace.

BVR – Beyond visual range.

C2 – Command and control.

C3 – Command, control and communications.

C3I – Command, control, communications and intelligence.

CAF – Canadian Armed Forces, now Canadian Forces

CAP – Combat air patrol.

CAS – Close air support.

CDU – Control display unit.

CEA – Circular error average.

CEP – Circular Error Probable. A measure of the accuracy of missiles or bombs, the CEP is the radius of a circle in which half the shots are statistically likely to fall.

CF – Canadian Forces.

CFE – Conventional Forces Europe.

CIWS – Close-In Weapon System (US).

COIN – Counter insurgency.

CRT – Cathode ray tube.

CV – Attack aircraft carrier, conventionally powered (US).

CVN – Attack aircraft carrier, nuclear powered (US).

DA – Dalnyaya Aviatsiya, Long Range Aviation, Russian AF command in charge of strategic bombers.

DEW – Distant early warning (US).

DFC – Distinguished Flying Cross: Air Force decoration.

DGPS – Differential GPS.

DoD – Department of Defence.

ECCM – Electronic counter countermeasures. A form of electronic warfare designed to overcome enemy use of ECM and thus continue to make effective use of the electromagnetic spectrum.

ECM – Electronic countermeasures. A form of electronic warfare designed totally or partially to prevent effective use by the enemy of part of the electromagnetic spectrum.

ECR – Electronic combat reconnaissance, German Panavia Tornado variant.

EFIS – Electronic flight instrument system.

ELINT – Electronic intelligence. Intelligence derived from enemy electronic transmissions other than telecommunications (ie radar).

Endurance – The length of time an aircraft's fuel load will permit it to remain airborne.

ESM – Electronic support measures.

EW – Electronic warfare • Early warning.

FA – Frontal Aviation, Russian AF command in charge of tactical fighters.

FAA – Fleet Air Arm (UK, Aus) • Fuerza Aerea Argentina, Argentine AF.

FAB – Forca Aera Brasileira, Brazilian AF.

FAC – Forward air control/forward air controller • Fuerza Aerea de Chile, Chilean AF • Fuerza Aerea Colombiana, Colombian AF.

FAE – Fuel air explosives • Fuerza Aerea Ecuatoriana, Ecuadorian AF.

FBW – Fly-by-wire (electronic signalling of flight controls).

fire-and forget missile – AAM or ASM with self guiding capability.

FLIR – Forward looking infrared.

fly-by-wire – Flight-control system with electric signalling.

FMS – Foreign military sale (US).

g – Force of gravity.

GCA – Ground controlled approach. An instrument approach procedure provided by a ground controller on the basis of radar displays. The aircraft is 'talked down' to within sight of the runway when weather conditions would otherwise preclude a safe landing. This predates ILS.

GCI – Ground-controlled intercept.

GE – General Electric.

GPS – Global positioning system. A worldwide system by which the user can derive his position by receiving signals from Navstar Satellites.

HF – High frequency: 3 to 30 MHz.

HOTAS – Hands on throttle and stick.

hp – horsepower

hr – Hour/s

HUD – Head-up display.

HUDWAC – HUD weapon aiming computer.

HUDWASS – HUD weapon aiming subsystem.

IADS – Integrated air defence system.

IAS – Indicated airspeed shown on the airspeed indicator, when corrected for instrument error.

ICBM – Intercontinental ballistic missile. Land based missile with range in excess of 5600km (3000nm).

IFF – Identification friend or foe.

IGE – In ground effect.

ILS – Instrument landing system.

Imp – Imperial (UK).

INS – Inertial navigation system. A navigation system in which displacement from the point of departure is determined by measuring the acceleration exerted upon a gyroscopically stabilised platform by vehicle movement.

IOC – Initial operational capability. Date when a weapon system can be considered capable of being used by troops even though not fully developed and troops not fully trained (US).

IR – Infrared.

IRAN – Inspect and Repair As Necessary.

IRBM – Intermediate range ballistic missile. Land based missile with range of 2780km (1500nm) to 5600km (3000nm).

IRCM – Infrared countermeasure.

ISA – International Standard Atmosphere.

IRS – Inertial reference system.

IRST – Infrared search and track.

JASDF – Japan Air Self Defence Force.

JAST – Joint Advanced Strike Technology.

JGSDF – Japan Ground Self Defence Force.

JMSDF – Japan Maritime Self Defence Force.

J-STAR – Joint Surveillance Target Attack Radar System, as in Northrop Grumman E-8.

JSF – Joint Strike Fighter (USA), replaces JAST. A current program to find a multirole fighter for the USAF, USN and USMC.

JTIDS – Joint Tactical Information Distribution System.

KCAS – Calibrated airspeed in knots.

kg – Kilogram/s.

KIAS – Knots indicated airspeed.

km – Kilometre.

km/h – Kilometres per hour.

kN – KiloNewton (1000 Newtons, 1 Newton = 0.2248lb of force).

Knot – Aviation and maritime unit of velocity. 1 knot = 1 nautical mile per hour.

KT – Kiloton. Explosive yield equivalent in effect to 1000 tons of TNT.

Kt/kt – Knot/s

KTAS – True airspeed in knots.

kW – KiloWatt. SI measure of power.

LAMPS – Light airborne multi purpose system (US).

LANTIRN – Low altitude targeting infrared for night.

LABS – Low Altitude Bombing System.

LAPES – Low Altitude Parachute Extraction System.

lb – Pounds, either of mass or thrust.

LCD – Liquid crystal display.

LF – Low frequency: 30 to 300 kHz.

LGB – Laser guided bomb.

LO – Low observables, ie stealth.

LRMP – Long range maritime patrol aircraft.

LZ – Landing zone.

Mach number, M – Ratio of true airspeed to speed of sound in surrounding air (which varies as square root of absolute temperature). In standard conditions, the speed of sound (Mach 1) is 1223km/h (661kt) at sea level and 1063km/h (575kt) at 36,000ft.

MAC – Military Airlift Command, now AMC (USAF).

MAD – Magnetic Anomaly Detector. ASW equipment designed to detect disturbances in the Earth's magnetic field.

MAP – Military Assistance Program (USA).

MAW – Marine Air Wing (USMC).

MCM – Mine countermeasures.

MFD – Multi Function Display.

min – Minute/s.

MLU – Mid life update.

MoD – Ministry of Defence.

MPA – Maritime patrol aircraft.

MR – Maritime reconnaissance.

MRBM – Medium range ballistic missile. Land based missile with range of 1100km (600nm) to 2780km (1500nm).

MSIP – Multi Stage Improvement Program (US).

MTOW – Maximum takeoff weight.

NAS – Naval air station.

NASA – National Aeronautics & Space Administration (US).

NATO – North Atlantic Treaty Organisation. Current members are Belgium, Canada, Denmark, France, Germany, Greece, Iceland, Luxembourg, Netherlands, Norway, Portugal, Spain, Turkey, UK, USA.

Nautical mile – Unit of measurement of distance. 1nm is one minute of great circle of the earth, standardised at 6080ft (1853m) but actually varying with latitude from 6046ft to 6108ft (1842 to 1861m).

nav/attack system – One offering either pilot guidance or direct command of aircraft to ensure accurate navigation and weapon delivery against surface target.

nm – Nautical mile.

OCU – Operational Conversion Unit.

OGE – Out of ground effect; supported by lifting rotor(s) in free air with no land surface in proximity.

OTH-B – Over-the Horizon Backscatter Radar. This transmits signals that extend beyond the line-of-sight along the ground. Range is of the order of 2900km (1570nm).

OTHR – Over-the-horizon radar.

OTHT – Over the horizon targeting.

PACAF – Pacific Air Force (USAF).

Passive – Not itself emitting. Usually used when describing detection devices which do not use electro-magnetic emissions to operate. They cannot be detected in the way that 'active' devices can.

Payload – Weapon and/or cargo capacity of an aircraft or missile.

PGM – Precision guided munition.

PID – Passive identification device.

PNGDF – Papua New Guinea Defence Force.

PVO – Protivo-Vozdushnoy Oborony, Air Defence Force, the independent Russian military service equipped with interceptors and SAMs.

R&D – Research and development.

RAAF – Royal Australian Air Force.

RAAWS – Radar altimeter and altitude warning system.

RAF – Royal Air Force (UK).

RAM – Radar absorbing material.

RAN – Royal Australian Navy.

RAST – Recovery assist, secure and (deck) traverse system.

RATO – Rocket assisted takeoff.

RCS – Radar cross section.

Recce – Reconnaissance.

RMAF – Royal Malaysian Air Force.

RN – Royal Navy (UK).

RNeAF – Royal Netherlands Air Force.

RNZAF – Royal New Zealand Air Force.

ROE – Rules of Engagement.

RoKAF – Republic of Korea Air Force (Sth Korea).

RPV – Remotely piloted vehicle.

RR – Rolls-Royce.

RSAF – Republic of Singapore Air Force • Royal Saudi AF.

RWR – Radar warning receiver.

SAAF – South African Air Force.

SAC – Strategic Air Command (USAF, merged into ACC).

SAM – Surface-to-air missile.

SAR – Search and rescue.

SEAD – Suppression of enemy air defences.

SENSO – Sensor operator.

SLAR – Side looking airborne radar.

Sigint – Signals intelligence.

Smart – Device possessing precision guidance. Normally used to describe ASMs and bombs with terminal guidance to differentiate them from iron or gravity bombs.

Sonobuoy – A small sonar device dropped by aircraft into the sea. The device floats for several hours and transmits information to the aircraft above. It then sinks automatically to prevent retrieval by a hostile agency.

SSM – Surface-to-surface missile.

Stealth – Stealth (or low observables) technology is used to render aircraft or satellites invisible or near invisible to visual, radar or infrared detection. The Northrop Grumman B-2 Spirit and the Lockheed F-117 Night Hawk are stealth aircraft.

STO – Short takeoff

STOL – Short takeoff and landing.

STOVL – Short Takeoff Vertical Landing.

TAC – Tactical Air Command (USAF, now merged into ACC).

TACAMO – Take Charge And Move Out.

TACAN – Tactical Aid to Navigation. Military UHF navaid.

TACCO – Tactical coordinator.

TANS – Tactical Air Navigation System.

TBO – Time Between Overhauls.

TFR – Terrain following radar.

TIALD – Target Identification Airborne Laser Designation.

TNI-AU – Tentara Nasional Indonesia-Angkatan Udara, Indonesian AF.

TOW – Tube launched, Optically tracked, Wire guided. Anti armour missile.

UAV – Unmanned aerial vehicle.

UHF – Ultra-high frequency: 300MHz to 3GHz.

UN – United Nations.

USAF – United States Air Force.

USAFE – US Air Forces in Europe.

USMC – United States Marine Corps.

USN – United States Navy.

VHF – Very high frequency: 3 to 300MHz.

V/STOL – Vertical or short takeoff and landing.

VTOL – Vertical takeoff and landing.

VVS RF – Voenno-Vozdushniye Sily Rossiskoi Federatsii, the Russian Federation Air Force.

WSO – Weapon system operator (occasionally weapon systems officer).

zero-zero seat – Ejection seat qualified for operation at zero height, zero airspeed; ie pilot can safely eject from parked aircraft.

INDEX